MOON HANDBOOKS

COASTAL MAINE

HILARY NANGLE

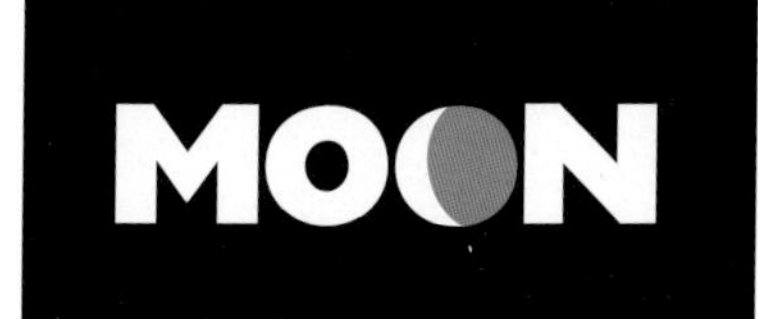

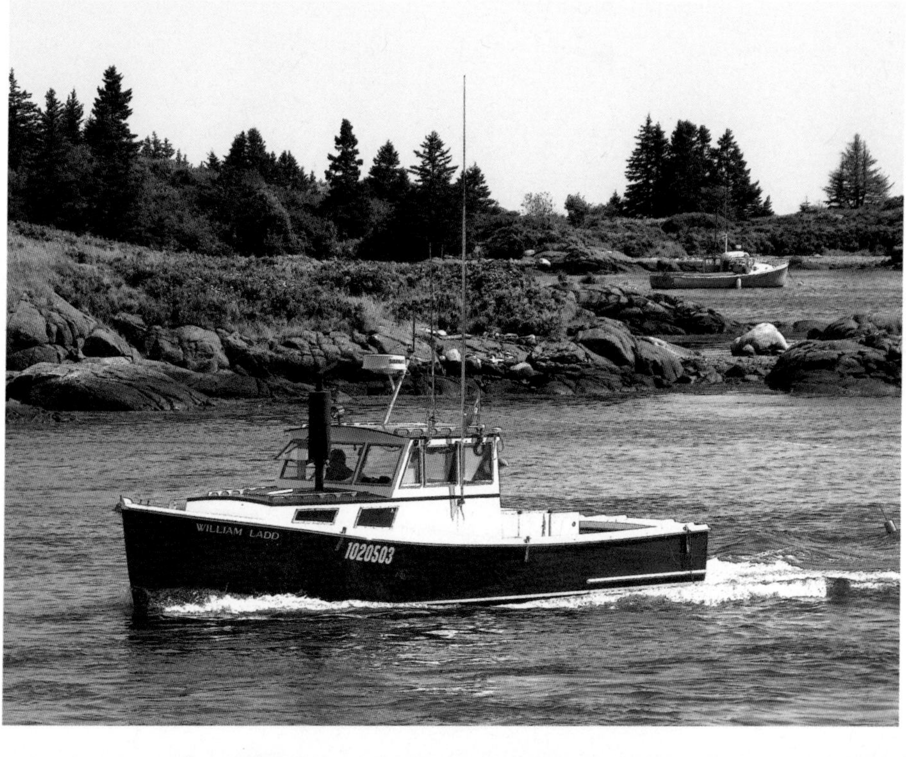

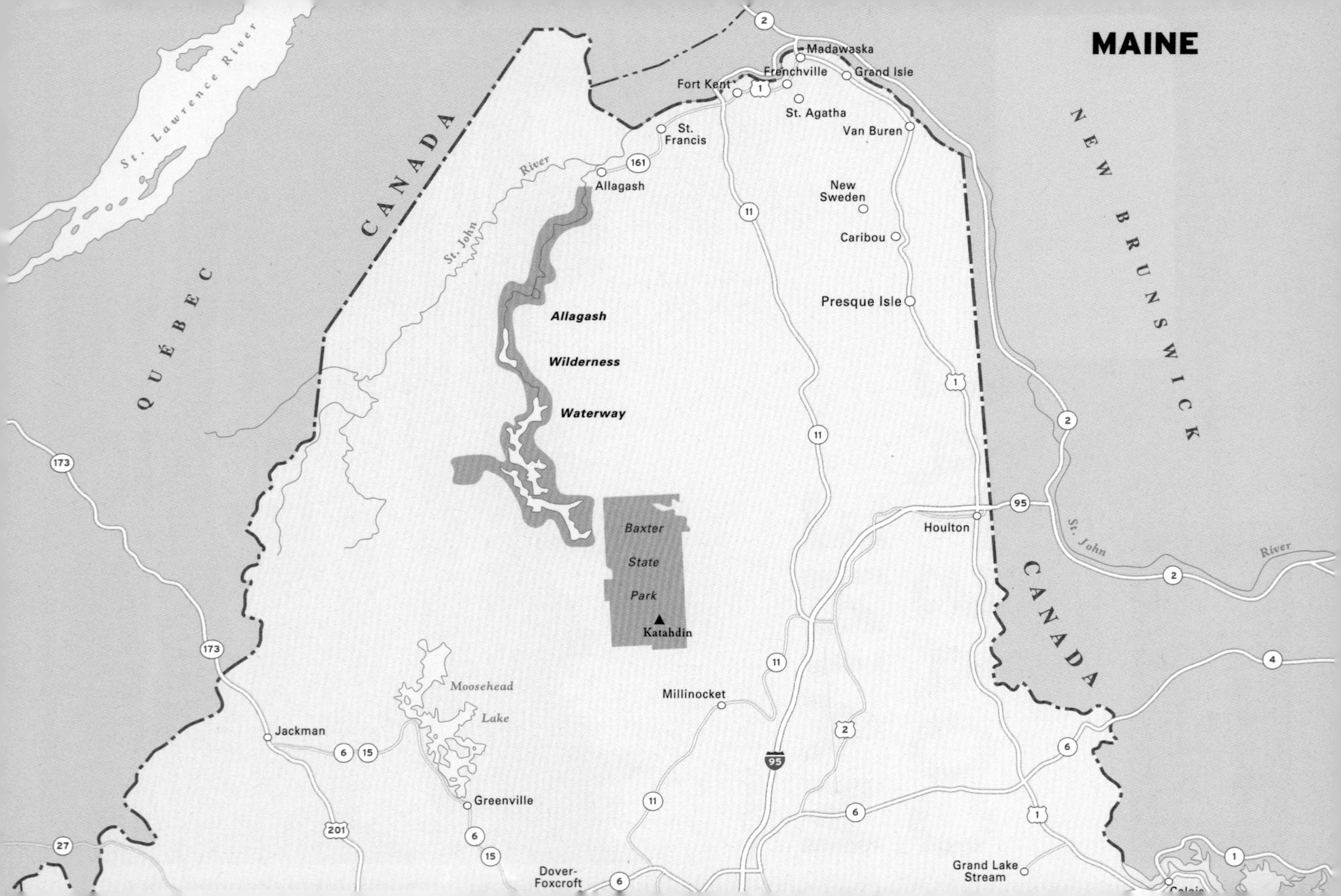
MAINE
NEW BRUNSWICK
CANADA
QUÉBEC
CANADA
St. Lawrence River
St. John River
St. John River
Madawaska
Frenchville
Grand Isle
Fort Kent
St. Agatha
Van Buren
St. Francis
Allagash
New Sweden
Caribou
Presque Isle
Houlton
Allagash Wilderness Waterway
Baxter State Park
Katahdin
Millinocket
Moosehead Lake
Jackman
Greenville
Dover-Foxcroft
Grand Lake Stream
2
1
161
11
95
4
6
15
173
201
27

Eastport
Campobello Island
Lubec
Grand Manan
Machias
Jonesport
Beals
Great Wass Island
Milbridge
Winter Harbor
Acadia National Park
Bar Harbor
Cadillac Mtn
Mount Desert Island
Swans Island
Isle au Haut
Ellsworth
Bucksport
Blue Hill
Sedgwick
Deer Isle
Penobscot Bay
Vinalhaven Island
Islesboro Island
Orono
Bangor
Searsport
Belfast
Lincolnville
Camden
Rockport
Rockland
Thomaston
St. George
Waldoboro
Cushing
Damariscotta
Newcastle
Wiscasset
Boothbay Harbor
Monhegan Island
Waterville
AUGUSTA
Belgrade Lakes
Skowhegan
Bingham
Kingfield
Sugarloaf Mtn
Rangeley
Farmington
Bethel
White Mountain National Forest
Oxford
Lewiston
Auburn
Long Lake
Fryeburg
Sebago
Cornish
Brunswick
Bath
Freeport
Yarmouth
PORTLAND
Casco Bay
Old Orchard Beach
Saco
Biddeford
The Kennebunks
Alfred
Wells
Ogunquit
Berwick
Dover
Eliot
The Yorks
Kittery
NEW HAMPSHIRE
ATLANTIC OCEAN
0
25 mi
0
25 km
© AVALON TRAVEL

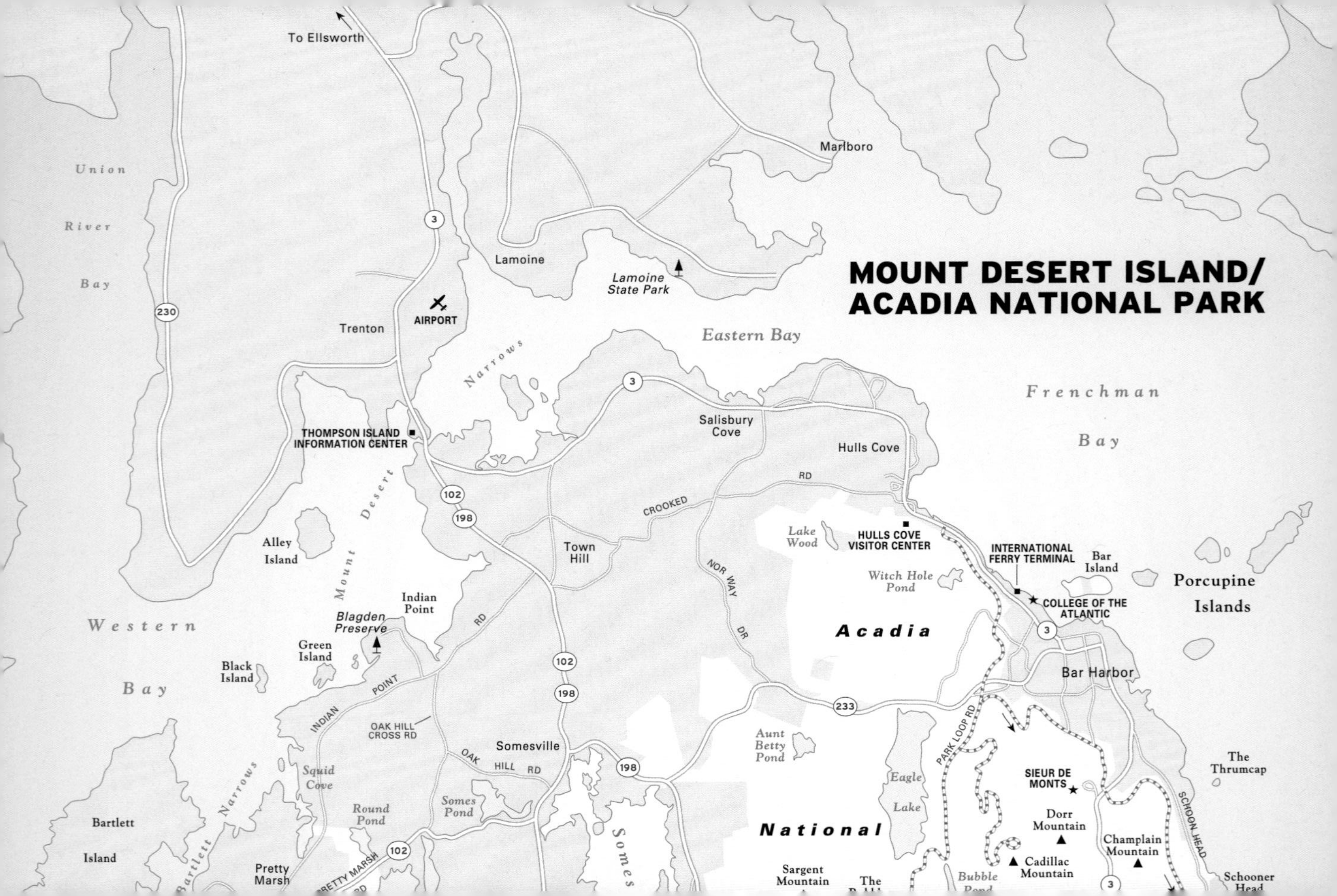
MOUNT DESERT ISLAND/
ACADIA NATIONAL PARK
To Ellsworth
Marlboro
Union
River
Bay
Lamoine
Lamoine
State Park
Trenton
AIRPORT
Eastern Bay
Narrows
Frenchman
Bay
Salisbury
Cove
Hulls Cove
THOMPSON ISLAND
INFORMATION CENTER
Mount
Desert
CROOKED
RD
Alley
Island
Town
Hill
Lake
Wood
HULLS COVE
VISITOR CENTER
INTERNATIONAL
FERRY TERMINAL
Bar
Island
Porcupine
Islands
Witch Hole
Pond
NOR WAY
DR
COLLEGE OF THE
ATLANTIC
Indian
Point
Blagden
Preserve
Acadia
Western
Bay
Green
Island
Black
Island
Bar Harbor
INDIAN
POINT
RD
OAK HILL
CROSS RD
Somesville
OAK
HILL
RD
Aunt
Betty
Pond
PARK LOOP RD
Eagle
Lake
SIEUR DE
MONTS
The
Thrumcap
Dorr
Mountain
Champlain
Mountain
SCHOON HEAD
Squid
Cove
Round
Pond
Somes
Pond
Somes
National
Cadillac
Mountain
Bartlett
Island
Narrows
Bartlett
Pretty
Marsh
PRETTY MARSH
Sargent
Mountain
The
Bubble
Pond
Schooner
Head
230
3
102
198
233

Acadia National Park
Park
Acadia National Park
Pretty Marsh Harbor
Folly Island
Moose Island
Long Pond
Hodgdon Pond
Seal Cove Pond
Echo Lake
Hall Quarry
Sound
SARGENT DR
Parkman Mountain
Penobscot Mountain
Pemetic Mountain
The Beehive
Great Head
Gorham Mountain
Jordan Pond
Hadlock Ponds
Norumbega Mountain
JORDAN POND HOUSE
WILDWOOD STABLES
Otter Creek
Sand Beach
THUNDER HOLE OVERLOOK
Otter Cliffs
RD
Acadia Mountain
Beech Mountain
Mansell Mountain
Bernard Mountain
WESTERN MOUNTAIN RD
LONG POND RD
FERNALD POINT RD
Northeast Harbor
ASTICOU AZALEA GARDEN
THUYA GARDEN
Day Mountain
BLACKWOODS
Little Long Pond
INFORMATION CENTER
Seal Harbor
SOUTHWEST HARBOR/ TREMONT CHAMBER OF COMMERCE
Seal Cove
SEAL COVE RD
WENDELL GILLEY MUSEUM
Southwest Harbor
Greening Island
Bear Island
Eastern Way
Sutton Island
CLARK POINT RD
Manset
West Tremont
Little Cranberry Island
Islesford
Tremont
Great Cranberry Island
Green Nubble
Crow Island
Baker Island
Bernard
SEAWALL
Bass Harbor
SWANS ISLAND FERRY TERMINAL
BASS HARBOR HEAD LIGHT
Western Way
Blue Hill Bay
ATLANTIC OCEAN
Great Gott Island
0
2 mi
0
2 km
102
102A
198
3
PARK LOOP ROAD
TWO-WAY
ONE-WAY
© AVALON TRAVEL

Contents

- **Discover Coastal Maine** 8
  - Planning Your Trip 10
  - Explore Coastal Maine 13
    - Icons of the Maine Coast 13
    - Mount Desert Island with Kids 15
    - Lighthouses, Lobster, and L. L. Bean 16
    - 14-Day Best of the Real Maine 18
    - Destination Dining Tour 20
    - Antiques and Junktiques: A Shopper's Tour 23
- **Southern Coast** 25
  - Kittery 28
  - The Yorks 33
  - Ogunquit and Wells 42
  - The Kennebunks 53
  - Old Orchard Beach Area 68
- **Greater Portland** 75
  - Portland 79
  - Freeport 107
- **Mid-Coast Region** 116
  - Brunswick Area 119
  - Bath Area 130
  - Wiscasset Area 144
  - Boothbay Peninsula 151
  - Pemaquid Region 164
- **Penobscot Bay** 180
  - Thomaston Area 183
  - Cushing Peninsula 185
  - St. George Peninsula 187
  - Monhegan Island 192
  - Rockland 198
  - Vinalhaven and North Haven Islands 209
  - Greater Camden 218
  - Belfast 235
  - Searsport Area 242
  - Bucksport Area 248
- **Blue Hill Peninsula and Deer Isle** 252
  - Blue Hill 255

Brooklin/Brooksville/ Sedgwick 262
Castine 269
Deer Isle 276
Isle au Haut 293

▸ **Acadia Region** **297**
Ellsworth 301
Acadia National Park on Mount Desert Island 307
Bar Harbor and Vicinity 314
Northeast Harbor 331
The Quiet Side 337
Islands near Mount Desert 346
Schoodic Peninsula 350

▸ **The Down East Coast** **366**
Milbridge 369
Jonesport/Beals Area 373
Machias Bay Area 380
Lubec and Vicinity 387
Campobello Island 394
Eastport and Vicinity 398
Calais and Vicinity 406

▸ **Background** **413**
The Land 413
History 419
Government and Economy 426
The People 427
Culture 429

▸ **Essentials** **436**
Getting There 436
Getting Around 438
Tips for Travelers 441
Health and Safety 444
Information and Services 446

▸ **Resources** **449**
Glossary 449
Suggested Reading 451
Internet Resources 454

▸ **Index** **457**

▸ **List of Maps** **469**

Discover Coastal Maine

From the glacier-scoured beaches of the Southern Coast to the craggy cliffs Down East, Maine's coastline follows a zigzagging route that would measure about 5,500 miles if you stretched it taut. But taut it isn't. Eons ago, glaciers came crushing down from the north, inch by massive inch, and squeezed Maine's coastline into a wrinkled landscape with countless bony fingers reaching seaward.

Thanks to its geography, most Maine coast vistas are intimate, full of spruce-clad islands and gray granite and sometimes-forbidding headlands. Now add 64 lighthouses, 90 percent of the *nation's* lobsters, and the eastern seaboard's highest peak. Each peninsula has its own character, as does each island offshore and each harbor village.

When it comes to character, no individuals are more rugged than the umpteenth-generation fishermen who make their living from these bone-chilling waters. Even the summerfolk tend to be different here – many return year after year, generation after generation, to the same place and the same neighbors and the same pursuits.

Shore breezes mingle the aromas of pine, balsam, or rugosa rose with the briny scent of the sea. Sometimes you can almost taste the salt in the air.

Then there's Maine's coastal symphony: waves lapping and crashing,

birds crying or singing, fog horns calling and bell buoys ringing, and in the quiet of a preserve, streams gurgling and leaves rustling.

Lobster, of course, is king, and Maine's seafood is ultra fresh, but don't overlook luscious wild blueberries, sweet Maine maple syrup, delicious farmstead cheeses, and homemade pies sold at roadside stands. Access to this bounty is one reason why talented chefs are drawn to the state.

Even if you don't dine at one of the hot restaurants with nationally known chefs, you can visit cheesemakers, fish smokers, artisan bakers, microbrewers, and organic farmers. But balance that with classic Maine fare: a bean-hole or chowder *suppah*, where you can share a table with locals and, if you're lucky, hear a genuine Maine accent (here's a hint: "Ayuh" isn't so much a word as a sharp two-part intake of breath).

Yes, there's a reason why more than eight million people visit Maine every year, why longtime summerfolk finally just pick up stakes and *settle* here. Maine boldly promotes itself as "The Way Life Should Be" – spend a little time in this extraordinarily special place and you'll see why.

Planning Your Trip

▸ WHERE TO GO

Southern Coast

Sand beaches, occasionally punctuated by rocky headlands, are the jewels of Maine's Southern Coast, but this region also oozes history. Colonial roots are preserved in historical buildings; fishing traditions echo in fish shacks turned trendy boutiques; its arts legacy is preserved in museums and galleries. Complementing (or detracting) from these are Route 1's endless shopping opportunities: antiques, boutiques, and factory outlets.

Greater Portland

In this compact region are rocky coastline and sand beaches, lighthouses and lobster shacks, coastal islands and L. L. Bean. Brine-scented air, cackling gulls, lobster boats, and fishing trawlers give notice this is a seafaring town, but it's also Maine's cultural center, rich in museums and performing-arts centers, and the state's shopping hub. Increasingly, Portland's earning national repute as a destination for culinary travelers.

Mid-Coast Region

No region of Maine has more lobster shacks or as rich a maritime history as this peninsula-rich stretch of coastline. Shaped by powerful freshwater rivers, the Mid-Coast is dotted with traditional fishing villages as well as towns that were once thriving ports, mill towns, or shipbuilding centers. The Maine Maritime Museum preserves that heritage; Bath Iron Works continues it; and the grand homes, brick townscapes, renovated mills, and plentiful shops brimming with maritime treasures and worldly antiques keep it alive.

IF YOU HAVE . . .

- **A LONG WEEKEND:** Explore Greater Portland, with an excursion to Kennebunkport.
- **ONE WEEK:** Add Mount Desert Island and Acadia National Park.
- **10 DAYS:** Add Bath, a mosey down the Pemaquid Peninsula or St. George Peninsula, Rockland or Camden, and Monhegan Island.
- **TWO WEEKS:** Add Belfast, Blue Hill Peninsula and Deer Isle, the Schoodic Peninsula, and the Down East Coast.

Monhegan Island encourages relaxation.

Penobscot Bay

With the Camden hills as backdrop, island-studded Penobscot Bay delivers the Maine coast in microcosm. Boat-filled harbors, sandy pocket beaches, soaring spruce trees, and lighthouses illuminating treacherous ledges pepper the shoreline. Gentrifying fishing villages neighbor cosmopolitan towns; traditional seafarers share driveways with summer rusticators. Antiques shops, art galleries, artisans' studios, and museums are as plentiful as lobster boats.

Blue Hill Peninsula and Deer Isle

Water, water everywhere. Around nearly every bend is a river or stream, a cove, a boat-filled harbor, or a serene pond. It's an inspired and inspiring landscape, one dotted with historic homes and forts and classic fishing villages. Locals, a blend of summer rusticators, genteel retirees, artists, boatbuilders, and back-to-the-landers, have worked diligently to preserve not only the landscape but also the heritage. It's a fine place to kick back, relax, and savor the good life.

Acadia Region

Mountains tumbling to the sea, ocean waves crashing upon granite ledges, serene lakes and soaring cliffs—Acadia has it all, in spades. Watch the sun rise out of the Atlantic from Cadillac Mountain's summit, mosey along Acadia National Park's icon-rich Park Loop Roads, hike through forests and up coastal peaks, pedal the famed carriage roads, paddle coastal nooks and crannies. Intimate yet expansive, wild yet civilized, Acadia is as accessible or as remote as you desire.

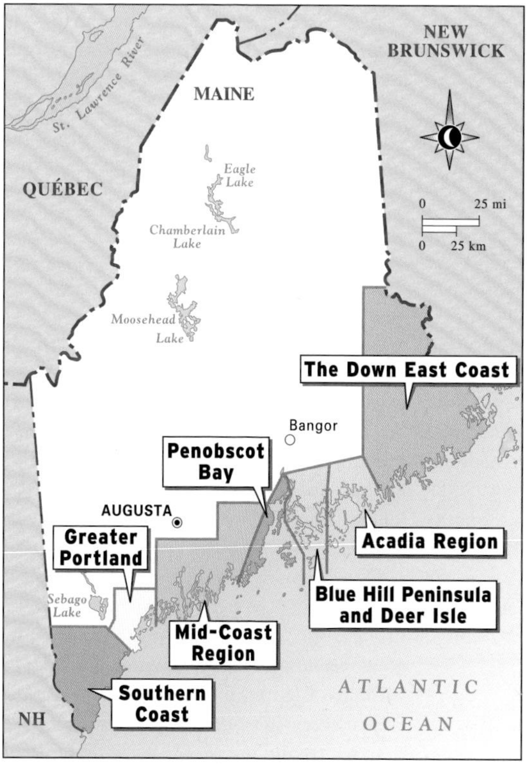

The Down East Coast

Remote, rural, and scarcely populated, this is what many folks picture when they envision Maine. Here the pace slows. Traffic subsides. Fast-food joints and traffic lights all but disappear. Blueberry barrens color the landscape; huge tides rule daily life. Two national wildlife reserves and numerous preserves lure hikers and bird-watchers, but the main attraction is the rugged and wild expanse of coastline.

WHEN TO GO

Late May through mid-October is prime season, with July and August, the warmest months, being the busiest. Recreation options seem unlimited, and festivals and special events crowd the calendar. Of course, that means peak-season rates, congested roads, and difficulty getting reservations at the best restaurants and accommodations. Late June and late August tend to be a bit quieter, yet everything's still in full swing.

September through mid-October is arguably the best season to travel. Days are warm and mostly dry, nights are cool, fog is rare, bugs are gone, and crowds are few. Foliage is turning by early October, usually reaching its peak by mid-month. While the prevailing wisdom sends people inland, seeing those brilliant reds, oranges, and yellows mixed with evergreens against a deep blue sea is without compare. And at many accommodations, rates are lower in autumn.

Rockland's lobster-trap Christmas tree is draped with buoys.

For the most part, the Maine Coast slumbers in winter, often blanketed in white. Skiing, snowshoeing, and ice skating replace hiking, biking, and boating. Choices in lodging, dining, and activities are fewer, but rates are generally far lower. In areas with solid year-round populations, life goes on full tilt.

BEFORE YOU GO

Transportation

Getting to Maine is easy; getting around isn't. Two major **airports** service the state: Portland (convenient for the Southern Coast through Penobscot Bay regions) and Bangor (convenient for Penobscot Bay through the Down East regions). **Buses** and **Amtrak trains** connect Boston to Portland, stopping at various locations en route, with buses continuing to Bangor. Once here, unless you're visiting a destination with bus service, such as Portland or Bar Harbor, you'll want a **car**.

What to Take

Weather can be unpredictable along Coastal Maine, with fog, rain, and temperatures ranging from the low 30s on a cold spring day to the 90s on a hot summer one. But even summer sees days when a **fleece pullover** or jacket and a **lightweight, weatherproof jacket** are quite welcome. A hat and mittens are a plus when venturing far off shore on a windjammer or whale-watching boat. Other handy items are **binoculars** for sighting boats, offshore lighthouses, birds, and wildlife; a small **backpack** for day trips or light hiking; and a small or collapsible **cooler** for picnics or storing food.

Unless you're dining at the White Barn Inn or Arrows, you won't need fancy clothing. Resort casual is the dress code in most good restaurants and in downtown Portland, with nice T-shirts and shorts being acceptable almost everywhere in beach communities.

In winter and spring, add warm waterproof boots, gloves, hat, and winter-weight clothing to your list.

Explore Coastal Maine

▸ ICONS OF THE MAINE COAST

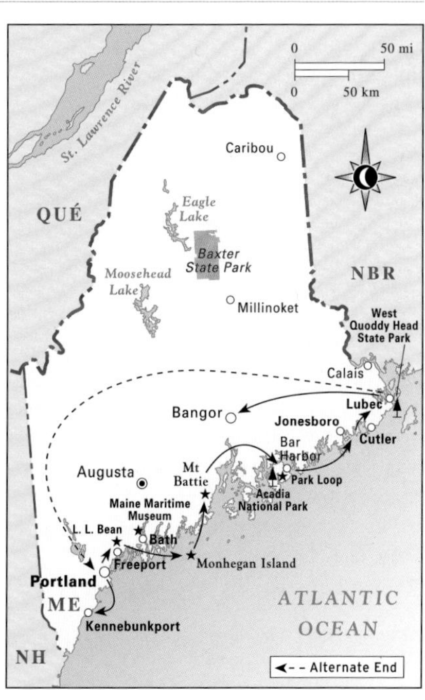

This itinerary exposes you to a good chunk of Maine while taking in most of the state's icons in 10 days. Be forewarned: You'll be doing a fair bit of driving on Route 1, the major thoroughfare that strings these sights together. It's primarily a two-lane road, where speeds through towns are often 25 mph or below; not ideal for a speed trip through Maine. While this itinerary is planned as 10 days, you'll be rewarded if you spend longer in any of the locations, but especially on Mount Desert.

If you're arriving by airplane, your best bet is to arrive at Portland International Jetport and depart from Bangor International. If you can't swing that, use Portland only (but add a tenth night in Portland). Book your first two nights' lodging in Portland, nights three and four in Rockland or vicinity, nights five and six on Mount Desert Island, and nights seven and eight in either the Jonesport or Lubec area, to coincide with taking a puffin-sighting trip from either location (make reservations). Book your ninth night in Eastport.

Day 1

Stretch your legs after your journey to Maine with a refreshing walk on Ogunquit Beach, one of Maine's prettiest and proof that there's plenty of sand along Maine's fabled rockbound coast. Afterward, head to Kennebunkport and indulge your passions: shopping in the boutiques and galleries that crowd Dock Square, taking a walking tour to view the historic homes, or enjoying a leisurely drive along the waterfront.

Day 2

Begin with a visit to Portland Head Light, a Cape Elizabeth landmark and Maine's oldest lighthouse (1791), at the edge of 94-acre Fort Williams Park. Spend the afternoon in the Portland Museum of Art, Maine's premier art museum, smack in the heart of the state's largest city. End the day with a sunset cruise on Casco Bay.

Day 3

Make a pilgrimage to gigantic sports retailer and outfitter L. L. Bean, hub of the hubbub in Freeport. Either spend the morning shopping or taking a Walk-on Adventure class. In the afternoon, visit the Maine Maritime Museum in Bath, 10 acres of indoor and outdoor exhibits celebrating the state's nautical heritage.

Day 4

Take a day trip to Monhegan Island from Port Clyde. This car-free, carefree gem, about a dozen miles off the coast, is laced with hiking trails and has earned a place in art history books as the Artists' Island.

Day 5

Drive or hike to the top of Mt. Battie, in Camden Hills State Park, for panoramic vistas over Penobscot Bay. Continue up the coast to Mount Desert Island and begin your explorations of Acadia National Park. If you've arrived on the island before noon, pick up a picnic lunch and then drive the Park Loop, a perfect introduction to Acadia that covers many of the highlights. Otherwise, take a whale-watching trip from Bar Harbor (reservations are wise).

Day 6

Welcome the day by watching the sunrise from the summit of Cadillac Mountain. Afterward, if you haven't either driven or bicycled the Park Loop, do so. If you have, then explore the park in more depth: Go hiking, bicycling, or sea kayaking, take a carriage ride, or book an excursion boat to Islesford or a whale-watching excursion.

Day 7

Depart Mount Desert Island and continue north on Route 1, dipping down the Gouldsboro Peninsula and looping through the Schoodic section of Acadia National Park. Continue to either the Jonesport or Cutler areas (wherever your lodging reservations are for that night).

Days 8 and 9

These two days are interchangeable. Book a puffin-sighting trip on day eight, with day nine as a weather backup (reservations required). Afterward, drive to Lubec and visit West Quoddy Head State Park. On day nine, drive north to Eastport, home of the highest tides in the country.

The Maine Maritime Museum's 20-acre campus in Bath is on the site of the former Percy and Small Shipyard. A sculpture gives visitors an idea of the size of ships once constructed on the grounds.

Day 10

A travel day. Return to Bangor via Route 1 north to Route 9 west (allow three hours); connect to I-95 if you're heading to Portland (allow three hours) or points south or west.

MOUNT DESERT ISLAND WITH KIDS

Acadia National Park is a great place to introduce kids to the great outdoors. Begin at park headquarters, where you can sign them up as **junior rangers.** Then pick and choose from the programs offered, including **ranger-led hikes** that appeal to your family's interests and abilities. Good choices for **easy family hikes** include the Ocean Trail, Jordan Pond Nature Trail, Ship Harbor Nature Trail, and Wonderland. If you're into **geocaching,** ask about the park's EarthCache program. In between park visits, you'll find plenty of other activities with real kid appeal. Here are a few sure bets.

SLIMY SEA CREATURES

You can't beat the wow appeal of **Diver Ed's Dive-In Theater Boat Cruise.** Ed dives to the depths with an underwater camera, while you wait onboard and watch the action. When he resurfaces, he brings along with him a variety of creatures from the depths for passengers to see, touch, and learn about.

OLYMPICS OF THE FOREST

Expert lumberjack Tina Scheer and her crew perform the most amazing skills at **The Great Maine Lumberjack Show.** During the 75-minute performance, two teams compete in 14 events, including ax throwing and log rolling. You can participate in some and even arrange for your youngster to learn how to log roll. Talk about a great story for that "What I did on my summer vacation" assignment.

I SCREAM, YOU SCREAM

Enjoy the ultimate kid-in-a-candy-store experience at **Ben & Bill's** in Bar Harbor, where you can buy not only chocolates made on-site but also to-die-for ice cream in both adult- and kid-pleasing flavors.

CRAFT CRAZY

Need a new teddy bear? Want to make a mug or create a mosaic piece? It's easy for your kids (and you) to express creativity at **All Fired Up!** in Bar Harbor. This rainy-day godsend is worth visiting anytime, especially if your kids are craft oriented. There are no specific class times – just walk in and start making your own souvenir.

HANDS-ON NATURE

"Please touch" is the philosophy at the **George B. Dorr Natural History Museum,** a small museum on the College of the Atlantic campus in Bar Harbor. Kids have the opportunity to touch fur, skulls, and even whale baleen.

A WHALE OF A TIME

Skeletons, a model of a prehistoric walking whale, and a video of whales in their natural habitat all enthrall kids at the **Bar Harbor Whale Museum.** If the kids can't get enough (and if they're good on boats and able to handle a three-hour trip), consider pairing the museum visit with a **whale-watching** tour.

FERRY HOPPING

Spend the better part of a day on the **Cranberry Isles,** visiting both Big and Little Cranberry and either walking or biking around, or take the passenger ferry to **Winter Harbor,** and hop on the Island Explorer bus to visit the Schoodic section of Acadia National Park. En route, watch for seals, seabirds, and lobster boats hauling traps.

NATIVE AMERICAN CULTURE

Check with the **Abbe Museum** in Bar Harbor about special kids' programs scheduled, and time your visit to take advantage of them. There's a resource room for children downstairs and a few other kid-friendly exhibits at this Native American history museum, but the events bring it all to life.

LAUGH FEST

Improv Acadia in Bar Harbor stages a family-friendly show every evening.

▸ LIGHTHOUSES, LOBSTER, AND L. L. BEAN

Portland Head Light

Maine's biggest draws are the three Ls: lighthouses, lobster, and L. L. Bean. Maine's 64 lighthouses stretch from York's Nubble to candy-striped West Quoddy Head, in Lubec. Lobster, of course, can be found practically everywhere along the coast, but the best way to enjoy it is at a no-fuss lobster shack. Bean's ever-expanding campus in Freeport is the massive outdoor retailer's mothership, but it also has an outlet in Ellsworth.

the boot that built L. L. Bean's retail empire

This six-day tour concentrates on the Greater Portland, Mid-Coast, and Penobscot Bay regions. Book your first nights' lodging in Portland, the second two in Damariscotta/Newcastle, and the last two in the Thomaston/Rockland area. If you're arriving by airplane, use Portland International Jetport.

Day 1

Try to arrive in Portland in time to enjoy an afternoon cruise with Lucky Catch Lobster Tours; perhaps you'll catch your dinner. If not, you can still enjoy a lobster on the waterfront.

Day 2

Loop out to South Portland and Cape Elizabeth to visit Portland Harbor Museum, Spring Point Ledge Light, and Portland Head Light, a Maine icon. You won't find a better setting for lunch than the Lobster Shack, with views of crashing surf and Cape Elizabeth Light. In the afternoon, consider visiting the Portland Museum of Art to view masterworks by Maine-related artists or book a sail amid the islands of Casco Bay. Still craving lobster? Try an inspired version by one of Maine's nationally recognized chefs (advance reservations required).

Day 3

Get an early start and begin at famed outlet store L. L. Bean in Freeport. You might even take a Walk-on Adventure with Bean's Discovery School. In the afternoon, visit the Maine Maritime Museum in Bath, and, if time permits, take a lighthouse cruise on

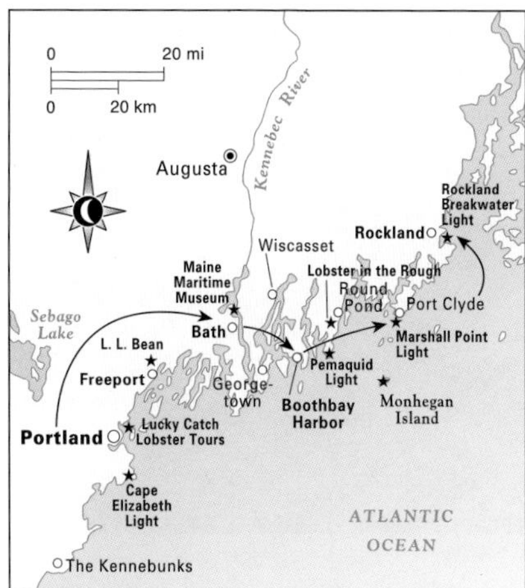

the Kennebec River. Perhaps mosey down to Georgetown for dinner at Five Islands or stop in Wiscasset for a lobster roll.

Day 4

Spend the morning in Boothbay Harbor, stepping back in time for a visit with light keeper Joseph Muise and his family on a Burnt Island Tour. In the afternoon, drive down to Pemaquid Point to view Pemaquid Point Lighthouse, perhaps climbing to the top. Be sure to also visit the Fisherman's Museum in the keeper's house. End the day with lobster in the rough in Round Pond.

Day 5

Begin the day with a visit to Marshall Point Light, in Port Clyde, and then board the mail boat to Monhegan Island. Be sure to visit the museum in the lighthouse keeper's house. Lunch? Lobster at Fish House Fish, of course.

Day 6

Greet the day with a sunrise walk out the breakwater to Rockland Breakwater Light. Afterwards, tour the Maine Lighthouse Museum and Farnsworth Art Museum. In the afternoon, take a lighthouse-themed cruise or sea kayak tour out of Rockport or Rockland. End the day and your lobster-infused vacation at the James Beard Award–winning lobster shack Waterman's Beach Lobster in South Thomaston. En route, take the short side jaunt out to Owls Head Light, in Owls Head.

Hiking trails lead to Monhegan Island's back shore and its soaring rocky headlands.

Postcard-perfect harbors await those who mosey down coastal peninsulas.

14-DAY BEST OF THE REAL MAINE

For many folks, the Down East, Acadia, and Blue Hill–Deer Isle regions represent the *real* Maine. With the notable exception of Ellsworth through Bar Harbor, life's pace really is slower here.

Spend two weeks poking around, and you can visit Acadia National Park, browse the studios of mega-talented artisans, go whale-watching or puffin-sighting, hike magnificent trails, kayak along undeveloped coastline, experience working lobstering villages, and view lighthouses. This tour circles you clockwise through the region, beginning in Calais and ending with the Blue Hill Peninsula, but you can reverse it.

The best air access is via Bangor International Airport. Book your first two nights' lodging in Eastport, the third in Lubec, nights four and five in or around Jonesport (Addison, Jonesboro, Columbia Falls), nights six and seven on the Schoodic Peninsula, nights 8–10 on Mount Desert Island, and your last three nights on the Blue Hill Peninsula.

Day 1

A travel day. From Bangor, drive Route 9 (The Airline) to Calais and then head south on Route 1 to Eastport (allow about three hours).

Day 2

Awaken early to catch sunrise; Eastport is the first U.S. city to see the sun's rays each morning. It's also home to some of the largest tides on the East Coast, so check the height of the tide at the waterfront and then revisit it six hours later. In between, take a whale-watching cruise, tour Raye's Mustard Mill, browse downtown shops, take an easy hike out to Shackford Head, and just soak up the small-town Down East life.

Day 3

Drive south to Lubec and visit West Quoddy Head State Park, allowing time to visit the museum at the base of the candy-striped lighthouse and to walk the trail edging the seaside cliffs. If time permits, head over the bridge (passport required) to Campobello Island for a look-see at the Roosevelt estate.

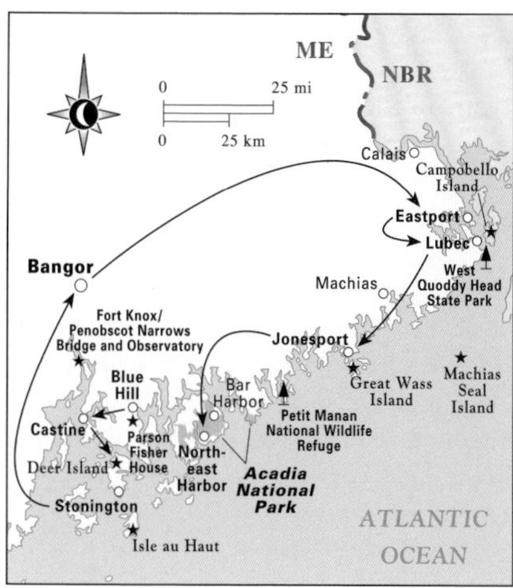

Day 4

Spend the morning on an excursion with Tours of Lubec and Cobscook, getting an insider's view, and then work your way down to the Jonesport area, noticing the blueberry barrens and perhaps touring some of Machias's historical sites en route.

candy-striped West Quoddy Head Light, in Lubec

Days 5 and 6

You'll need two days in the Jonesport area to maximize your odds of taking a puffin-watching trip to Machias Seal Island. While here, go hiking and bird-watching on Great Wass Island and/or Petit Manan National Wildlife Refuge; poke around Jonesport, the real deal when it comes to lobstering; and visit the Sardine History Museum and Maine Central Model Railroad, in Jonesport, and the Ruggles House, in Columbia Falls. For local color, don't miss a meal at Tall Barney's; sit at the Liars' Table, if you dare, and jaw with the lobstermen.

Day 7

Drive or bicycle the loop around the Schoodic section of Acadia National Park. Depending on your interests, spend the rest of the day hiking, sea kayaking, or browsing the numerous artisans' galleries tucked in all corners of the region.

Day 8

Head for Mount Desert Island. Begin on the outskirts, visiting Northeast Harbor and Southwest Harbor, with stops to see the Asticou and Thuya Gardens, Somes Sound, and the Wendell Gilley Museum. Enjoy a lobster dinner at Thurston's Lobster Pound.

Day 9

Spend the day in Acadia National Park. Begin by driving or bicycling the Park Loop to take in the park's highlights and then indulge your passions: hiking, sea kayaking, bicycling, a carriage tour. Be sure to stop for tea and popovers at the Jordan Pond House.

Day 10

Visit the Abbe Museum and go whale-watching, and in between poke around Bar Harbor.

Day 11

Depart Mount Desert for the Blue Hill Peninsula. In Blue Hill, tour the Parson Fisher House and visit some of the many galleries in town. Do ask locally to see if the Flash! In the Pans Community Steel Band is performing during your days on the peninsula, and make it a point to see them.

Day 12

Noodle over to Castine and pick up a brochure for a self-guided walking tour. Spend the afternoon on a guided sea-kayaking tour.

Day 13

Explore Deer Isle and Stonington, allowing plenty of time to browse the galleries along the way or hike on one of the island's preserves. If time permits, hop a cruise to Isle au Haut.

Day 14

Visit Fort Knox and the Penobscot Narrows Bridge and Observatory in the morning before heading home. If you're flying out of Bangor, you can either mosey up Route 15 or connect via Route 174 to Route 1A North.

▸ DESTINATION DINING TOUR

In recent years, Maine's restaurant scene has gained increasing national attention, with top awards and mentions in foodie magazines such as *Bon Appétit, Food and Wine, Gourmet,* and *Saveur.* If you want to dine your way through Maine, here's where to go to hit the biggies. You definitely want to plan well in advance for a summer visit; even then, you might have to be flexible in your seating time.

Camden's Francine Bistro won't be a secret for long.

Southern Coast

ARROWS

A quiet country farmhouse is the understated setting for this restaurant, named by *Gourmet* as one of America's Top 50 Restaurants. Chefs Clark Frasier and Mark Gaier are frequently nominated for a James Beard Award and have received accolades from, besides *Gourmet,* magazines such as *Bon Appétit* and even *Time.* They're renowned for their fresh, flavorful cuisine, with many ingredients sourced from the restaurant's gardens. Jacket preferred for men.

WHITE BARN INN

Maine's only five-diamond and *Relais Gourmand* restaurant regularly earns kudos from publications such as *Food and Wine, Travel + Leisure,* and *Condé Nast Traveler.* The dining room is an elegantly restored barn, where chef Jonathan Cartwright's fixed-price four-course menu, offering contemporary New England cuisine with European accents, is served by formally dressed waiters. Jackets are required for gentlemen.

The White Barn Inn is the only five-star, five-diamond experience north of New York City.

AND WHILE YOU'RE HERE . . .

Don't miss Provence, a lovely country French Ogunquit restaurant, owned by chef Pierre Gignac, that always wins top marks from local critics, and consider Blue Sky on York Beach, Boston celebrity chef Lydia Shire's restaurant.

LOCAL COLOR

Slather on the secret sauce at Flo's Steamed Dogs, in Cape Neddick; pick up taffy kisses at The Goldenrod in York Beach; grab a lobster roll or fried clams at Kennebunkport's Clam Shack.

Greater Portland

For any of these three, you'll feel most comfortable in resort casual wear. There's no need for jackets, although you wouldn't feel out of place in one, either.

FORE STREET

Ask any Maine foodie who the dean of Maine foods is, and likely the answer will be Sam Hayward. Here, Hayward has teamed with another highly regarded restaurateur, Dana Street of Street and Company. The result won Hayward the Best Chef in the Northeast award from the James Beard Foundation and must-dine status from any publications advising travelers visiting Portland.

HUGO'S

Chef-owner Rob Evans has won two coveted titles: Best Chef in the Northeast, from the Beard Foundation, and one of America's 10 Best New Chefs by *Food and Wine.* Evans prepares New American cuisine, in small and large plates.

FIVE FIFTY-FIVE

Food and Wine dubbed chef-owner Steve Corry one of America's 10 Best New Chefs, and he's been a nominee for the Beard Foundation's Best Chef in the Northeast award. Corry's ever-changing menu takes advantage of whatever's fresh and local.

AND WHILE YOU'RE HERE . . .

At tiny Bresca, chef Krista Kerns prepares Mediterranean-accented dishes that have earned her fame among area foodies. Newer

Natalie's at the Camden Harbour Inn offers a French-accented menu.

on the scene is Evangeline, where Kerns's husband, chef Eric Desjarlais, serves classic French cuisine. And for elegant fine dining, don't miss Back Bay Grill, where chef Larry Matthews adds his touch to classic cuisine.

LOCAL COLOR

Watch boats come and go while chowing down all you can eat at The Porthole's Friday-night fish fry; savor the Belgian-style fries or *poutine* at Duckfat; head to the Lobster Shack, in Cape Elizabeth, for lobster in the rough.

Penobscot Bay

PRIMO

James Beard Award–winning chef Melissa Kelly and her partner Price Kushner keep earning kudos for their farmhouse restaurant on the Rockland/Owls Head border. Resort casual is the preferred dress.

WATERMAN'S BEACH LOBSTER

What's a lobster-in-the-rough spot doing on this list? Well, the folks at the James Beard house thought it deserved an award, and we think you deserve a night where you can dress down and drink in the view (if you want anything more potent to drink, be sure to bring it with you). You'll be eating lobster at a picnic table; jeans or shorts and a T-shirt is the dress code.

AND WHILE YOU'RE HERE . . .

Don't miss Francine Bistro, chef-owner Brian Hill's lovely little bistro in a residential section of downtown Camden, or Natalie's at the Camden Harbour Inn, where chef Lawrence Klang turns out fabulous French fare with a Maine accent (or maybe that's Maine fare with a French accent) and other worldly inspirations.

LOCAL COLOR

Fried seafood is served with a dose of local color and a slab of pie at both Anglers Restaurant and Just Barb's. Aim for a Sunday morning and order the fishcakes at Surfside, on Vinalhaven island.

Acadia Region

LE DOMAINE

It doesn't look like much from the road, but step inside. Former chef-owner Nicole Purslow created a touch of France on the coast of Maine, right down to the wine list, and her successors are keeping up the tradition. When you make dining reservations, book a room for the night, too. Then all you'll have to do after wining and dining is head upstairs. Any local folks celebrating a special occasion likely will be dressed to the nines, but resort casual is fine.

AND WHILE YOU'RE HERE . . .

Have dinner at Burning Tree, long considered one of Mount Desert Island's best restaurants. Chef-owners Allison Martin and Elmer Beal Jr. create imaginative entrées that honor the best of what's fresh, local, and, when possible, organic. Or book a table at up-and-coming chef-owner Kyle Yarborough's Mache Bistro for rustic French fare.

LOCAL COLOR

Gossip's served along with mighty-fine home cooking at Chester Pike's Galley, in Sullivan, but go early if you want to snag one of the homemade doughnuts or a seat for the Friday-night fish fry. The locals don't order it, but it's doubtful you'll find lobster ice cream anywhere else but Ben and Bill's Chocolate Emporium in Bar Harbor.

ANTIQUES AND JUNKTIQUES: A SHOPPER'S TOUR

Searching for treasures? Whether you have a practiced eye or just enjoy the thrill of the hunt, you'll find these the best places to seek genuine antiques and collectibles or can't-resist treasures. This seven-day tour stretches from Wells, in the Southern Coast region, to Searsport, in the Penobscot Bay region. Book your first two nights in Wells or a nearby town, your third and fourth nights in Bath or Wiscasset, and your last two nights in Belfast or Searsport. If you're arriving by air, fly in and out of Portland.

Days 1 and 2

Wells and Vicinity: Flea market–style shops, antiquarian bookstores, huge barns, and old houses filled with genuine antiques or overflowing with "good stuff" line both sides of Route 1 in Wells and overflow into nearby towns. Don't miss R. Jorgensen Antiques, with 11 rooms filled with fine European and American antiques, or Douglas N. Harding Rare Books for antiquarian volumes and ephemera. Continue up to Kennebunk to Antiques on Nine for more finds.

Day 3

Brunswick and Bath: Spend a morning in Brunswick. A choice selection fills five rooms at Day's Antiques. For more variety, explore Cabot Mill Antiques, where more than 140 dealers show and sell their wares in

Bath's Lower Front Street is lined with antiques and junktiques shops.

the renovated Fort Andross mill complex next to the Androscoggin River. Then continue to Bath. The lower end of Bath's Front Street has side-by-side antiques shops, some with good-size collections of antiquarian books. While here, take a gander at the lovely historical homes lining Washington Street, and don't miss the Maine Maritime Museum, with its emphasis on nautical and boat-building antiquities.

Day 4

Woolwich and Wiscasset: Get an early start for the best pickings at famous Montsweag Flea Market. Afterward, continue north on Route 1, stopping at Avalon Antiques Market, a large multidealer shop along the way. Spend the afternoon in downtown Wiscasset, prowling though your choice of about two dozen antiques shops. If time permits, visit two antiques-filled treasure houses in Wiscasset, Castle Tucker and the Nickels-Sortwell House, and the Musical Wonder House, brimming with antique music boxes.

Day 5

Dozens of antiques dealers have set up shops in the Pemaquid Region. Mosey down Route 130, where numerous barns have been converted into shops. Return to Route 1 and continue north, stopping at the many antiques shops and auction houses along the way. You'll find clusters in Nobleboro, Thomaston, and Lincolnville. Do stop at Nobleboro Antique Exchange, a multidealer antiques mall that's much, much larger than it first appears.

Day 6

Searsport: Hard to believe there could be a town that rivals Wiscasset for the title Antiques Capital, but Searsport does. Sea captains' homes and big barns now house individual and group shops, such as Pumpkin Patch, which emphasizes Maine antiques, and the Searsport Antique Mall, with more than 70 dealers. You'll also find a few roadside flea markets worth poking around. Learn more about how all these treasures arrived here by visiting the Penobscot Marine Museum.

Serious shoppers are in line when the doors open on Saturday morning at Liberty Tool Company.

Day 7

Return to Belfast and then take Route 17 West, stopping in Liberty to visit the three floors of antiques at Liberty Tool Company, with most of the wares being tools. Then continue west to I-95, and head south to Portland for an afternoon flight home.

SOUTHERN COAST

Drive over the I-95 bridge from New Hampshire into Maine's Southern Coast region on a bright summer day, and you'll swear the air is cleaner, the sky bluer, the trees greener, the roadside signs more upbeat: Welcome to Maine: The Way Life Should Be. (*Is* it? Or maybe the way life *used* to be?)

Most visitors come to this region for the spectacular attractions of the justly world-famous Maine coast—the inlets, islands, and especially the beaches—but it's rich in history, too.

Southernmost York County, part of the Province of Maine, was incorporated in 1636 (only 16 years after the *Mayflower* pilgrims reached Plymouth, Massachusetts) and reeks of history: ancient cemeteries, musty archives, and architecturally stunning homes and public buildings. Probably the best places to dive into that history are in the sites of the Old York Historical Society in York Harbor.

Geological fortune smiled on this 50-mile ribbon, endowing it with a string of sandy beaches—nirvana for sun worshippers, less enchanting to swimmers, who need to steel themselves to be able to spend much time in the ocean (especially in early summer, before the water temperature has reached a tolerable level).

Complementing those beaches are amusement parks and arcades, fishing shacks turned chic boutiques, a surprising number of good restaurants (given the region's seasonality), and some of the state's prettiest parks and preserves.

Spend some time poking around the small

HIGHLIGHTS

Old York Historical Society: York dates from the 1640s, and on this campus of historic buildings you can peek into early life in the area (page 33).

Nubble Light/Sohier Park: You'll likely recognize this often-photographed Maine Coast icon, which is the easiest lighthouse to see in the region (page 35).

Ogunquit Museum of American Art (OMAA): It's hard to say which is more jaw dropping, the art or the view (page 42).

Marginal Way: Escape the hustle and bustle of Ogunquit with a stroll on this paved shorefront path (page 43).

Wells Reserve at Laudholm Farm: Orient yourself at the visitors center, where you can learn about the history, flora, and fauna, and then take a leisurely walk to the seashore, passing through a variety of habitats (page 44).

Seashore Trolley Museum: Ring-ring-ring goes the bell...and zing-zing-zing go your heartstrings, especially if you're a trolley fan (page 53).

Dock Square: Brave the shopping crowds and browse the dozens of fish shacks-turned-boutiques in Kennebunkport's heart (page 56).

St. Anthony's Monastery: It's hard to believe this oasis of calm is just a short stroll from busy-busy-busy Dock Square (page 56).

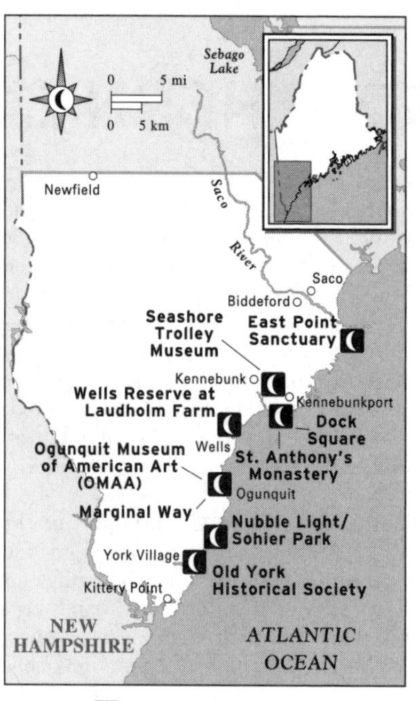

LOOK FOR ☾ TO FIND RECOMMENDED SIGHTS, ACTIVITIES, DINING, AND LODGING.

East Point Sanctuary: A must for bird-watchers, this coastal preserve provides dramatic views (page 70).

villages that give the region so much character. Many have been gussied up and gentrified quite a bit yet retain their seafaring or farming bones.

Some Mainers refer to the Southern Coast as northern Massachusetts. Sometimes it can seem that way, not only for the numbers of commonwealth plates in evidence but also because many former Massachusetts residents have moved here for the quality of life but continue to commute to jobs in the Boston area. The resulting downside is escalating real-estate prices that have forced families off land that's been in their families for generations and pushed those in traditional seafaring occupations inland. Still, if you nose around and get off the beaten path, you'll find that Real Maine is still here.

PLANNING YOUR TIME

The good news is that Maine's Southern Coast is a rather compact region. The bad news is

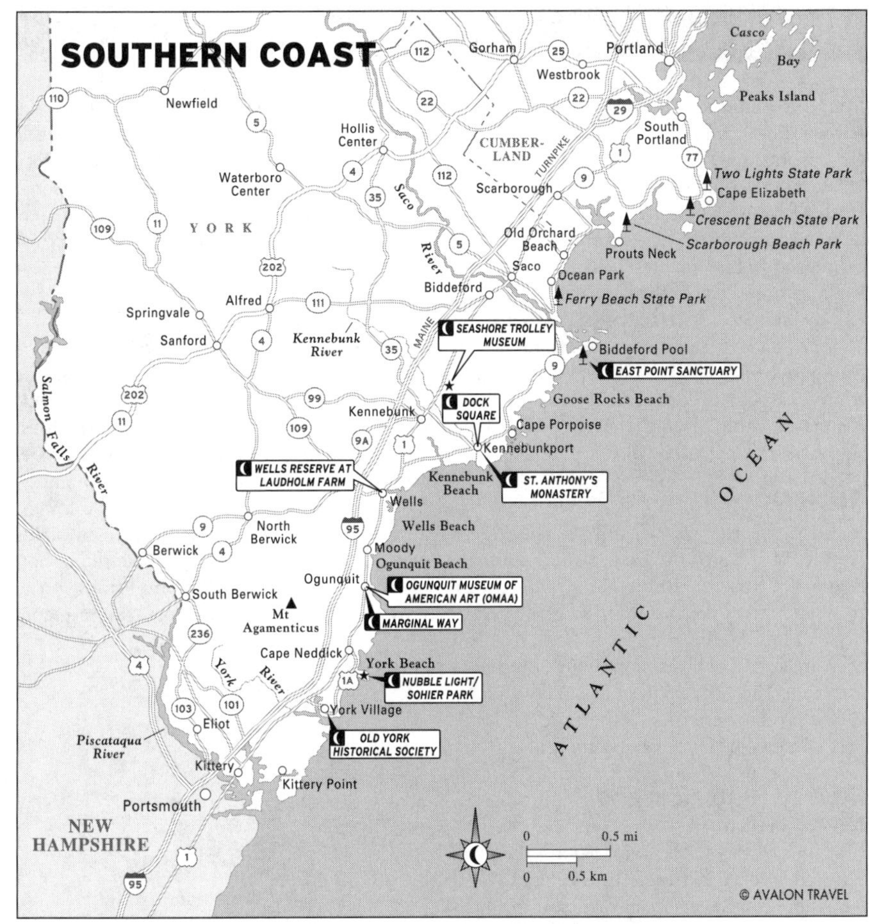

that it's heavily congested, especially in summer. Still, with a minimum of four days, you should be able to take in most of the key sights, from beaches to museums, as long as you don't spend too many hours basking in the sun.

Route 1, the region's primary artery, is often bumper-to-bumper traffic. If you're hopscotching towns, consider using I-95, which has exits for York, Kennebunk, and Saco/Biddeford/Old Orchard Beach. Parking, too, can be a challenge and expensive, but a trolley system operates in summer and connects most towns, making it easy to avoid the hassles and help the environment.

July and August are the busiest months. If you can avoid them, do. Spring and fall are lovely times to visit, and most attractions are open. In winter, you can walk the beaches without running into another soul, it's easy to get dinner reservations, and lodging prices plummet; the trade-off is that fewer businesses are open.

Kittery

Maine is home to a lot of well-kept secrets, Kittery being one of them. Shoppers rarely get beyond the 120-plus outlets along Route 1, but there's equal value in exploring the back roads of Maine's oldest town, settled in 1623 and chartered in 1647. Parks, a small nautical museum, historic architecture, and foodie finds are only a few of the attractions in Kittery and its "suburb," Kittery Point. It was also on Kittery's Badger Island where the sloop *Ranger* was launched in 1777. The shipbuilding continues at Portsmouth Naval Shipyard, on Kittery's Dennet's Island, the first government shipyard in America.

SIGHTS

Avoid the outlet sprawl and see the prettiest part of the area by driving along squiggly Route 103 from the Route 1 rotary in Kittery through Kittery Point (administratively part of Kittery) and on to Route 1A in York. You can even make a day of it, stopping at the sights mentioned here. Be very careful and watch for cyclists and pedestrians, as there are no shoulders and lots of blind corners and hills.

Kittery Historical and Naval Museum

Maritime history buffs shouldn't miss the small but well-stocked Kittery Historical and Naval Museum (200 Rogers Road Ext., near the junction of Rtes. 1 and 236, Kittery, 207/439-3080, www.kitterymuseum.com, 10 A.M.–4 P.M. Tues.–Sat. June–mid-Oct., $3 adults, $1.50 children 7–15, family max. $6). A large exhibit hall and a small back room contain ship models, fishing gear, old photos and paintings, and an astonishing collection of scrimshaw (carved whale ivory).

Lady Pepperrell House

The 1760 Georgian Lady Pepperrell House (Pepperrell Rd., Rte. 103, shortly before the Fort McClary turnoff) is now privately owned and no longer open to the public, but it's worth admiring from afar. Nearby, across from the First Congregational Church, is the area's most-visited burying ground. Old-cemetery buffs should bring rubbing gear here for some interesting grave markers. The tomb of Levi Thaxter (husband of poet Celia Thaxter) bears an epitaph written for him by Robert Browning.

Fort McClary Historic Site

Since the early 18th century, fortifications have stood on this 27-acre headland, protecting Portsmouth Harbor from seaborne foes. Contemporary remnants at Fort McClary (Rte. 103, Kittery Point, 207/439-2845, $3 adults, $1 children 5–11) include several outbuildings, an 1846 blockhouse, granite walls, and earthworks—all with a view of Portsmouth Harbor. Opposite are the sprawling buildings of the Portsmouth Naval Shipyard. Bring a picnic

© TOM NANGLE

Fort McClary has guarded Portsmouth Harbor since the early 18th century.

(covered tables and a lily pond are across the street) and turn the kids loose to run and play. It's officially open May 30–October 1, but the site is accessible in off-season. The fort is 2.5 miles east of Route 1.

Fort Foster

The only problem with Fort Foster (Pocahontas Rd., off Rte. 103, Gerrish Island, Kittery Point, 207/439-3800, 10 A.M.–8 P.M. daily late May–early Sept. and weekends May and Sept., $10 vehicle pass, $5 adult walk-in, $1 child walk-in) is that it's no secret, so parking can be scarce at this 90-acre municipal park at the entrance to Portsmouth Harbor. On a hot day, arrive early. Then you can swim, hike the nature trails, fish off the pier (no license needed), picnic, and investigate the tide pools. Bring your sailboard and a kite; there's almost always a breeze. From nearby **Seapoint Beach** (park in the small roadside lot and walk down to the beach; the lower lot is for residents only, no facilities), on a clear day there's a wide-open view of the offshore Isles of Shoals, owned jointly by Maine and New Hampshire.

ENTERTAINMENT

Concerts in the Park

Kittery Recreation (207/439-3800, www.kittery.org) presents a free summer concert series on Memorial Field (Old Post Rd., 6:30–8 P.M.); call for schedule, which varies year to year.

SHOPPING

No question, you'll find bargains at Kittery's 120-plus factory outlets (www.thekitteryoutlets.com), actually a bunch of mini-malls clustered along Route 1. All the household names are here: Bass, Calvin Klein, Eddie Bauer, J. Crew, Mikasa, Esprit, Lenox, Timberland, Tommy Hilfiger, GAP, Villeroy and Boch, and plenty more (all open daily). Anchoring it all is the **Kittery Trading Post** (301 Rte. 1, 207/439-2700 or 888/587-6246, www.kitterytradingpost.com), a humongous sporting-goods and clothing emporium. Try to avoid the outlets on weekends, when you might need to take a number for the fitting rooms.

RECREATION

Brave Boat Harbor

One of the Rachel Carson National Wildlife Refuge's 10 Maine coastal segments is Brave Boat Harbor (207/646-9226), a beautifully unspoiled 560-acre wetlands preserve in Kittery Point with a four-mile (round-trip) trail. The habitat is particularly sensitive here, so be kind to the environment. Take Route 103 to Chauncey Creek Road, and continue past the Gerrish Island bridge to Cutts Island Lane. Just beyond it and across a small bridge is a pullout on the left. You have a couple of options for hikes: a 1.8-mile loop trail, including a spur, or a half-mile loop. Bring binoculars to spot waterfowl in the marshlands.

Captain and Patty's Piscataqua River Tours

Take a spin around the Piscataqua River Basin with Captain and Patty's Piscataqua River Tours (Town Dock, Pepperrell Rd., Kittery Point, 207/451-8156 or 877/439-8976, www.capandpatty.com, $12 adults, $8 kids under 10). The 80-minute historical tour aboard an open launch departs six times daily. En route, Captain Neil Odams points out historic forts, lighthouses, and the Naval shipyard.

ACCOMMODATIONS

Rates reflect peak season.

Put a little ooh and aah into your touring with a visit to the **Portsmouth Harbor Inn and Spa** (6 Water St., Kittery, 207/439-4040, www.innatportsmouth.com, $160–190). The handsome brick inn, built in 1889, looks out over the Piscataqua River, Portsmouth, and the Portsmouth Naval Shipyard. Five attractive Victorian-style rooms (most with water views) are furnished with antiques and have air-conditioning, TV, and phones. There's an outdoor hot tub, and beach chairs are available. Breakfasts are multicourse feasts. Request a back room if you're noise sensitive, although air-conditioning camouflages traffic noise in summer. Rooms on the 3rd floor have the best views, but these also have hand-held showers.

RAMBLE THROUGH THE BERWICKS

Probably the best known of the area's present-day inland communities is the riverside town of South Berwick, thanks to a historical and literary tradition dating to the 17th century, and antique cemeteries to prove it. The 19th- and 20th-century novels of Sarah Orne Jewett and Gladys Hasty Carroll have lured many a contemporary visitor to explore their rural settings, an area aptly described by Carroll as "a small patch of earth continually occupied but never crowded for more than three hundred years."

A ramble through the Berwicks, South Berwick and its siblings, makes a nice diversion from the coast, and because it's off most tourists' radar screens, it's a good alternative for lodging and dining, too. For an easy day trip, loop northwest on Route 236 from Kittery or Route 91 from York to South Berwick, on the New Hampshire border, continue northeast on Route 236 to Berwick, then head northeast on Route 9 to North Berwick. Continue on Route 9 to return to Wells and the coast.

Don't blink or you might miss the tiny sign outside the 1774 **Sarah Orne Jewett House** (5 Portland St., Rtes. 4 and 236, South Berwick, 207/384-2454, www.historicnewengland.org, 11 A.M.-5 P.M. Fri.-Sun. June 1-Oct. 15, $5) smack in the center of town. Park on the street and join one of the tours to learn details of the Jewett family and its star, Sarah (1849-1909), author of *The Country of the Pointed Firs,* a New England classic. Books by and about Sarah are available in the gift shop. House tours are at 11 A.M. and 1, 2, 3, and 4 P.M. The house is one of two local Historic New England properties.

The other property is the 18th-century **Hamilton House** (40 Vaughan's La., South Berwick, 207/384-2454, www.historicnewengland.org, 11 A.M.-5 P.M. Wed.-Sun. June 1-Oct. 15, $8), which crowns a bluff overlooking the Salmon Falls River and is flanked by handsome colonial revival gardens. Knowledgeable guides relate the house's fascinating history. Tours begin only on the hour, last one at 4 P.M. In July, the **Sunday in the Garden** concert series takes place on the lawn ($8 admission, including a free pass to come back and see the house). Pray for sun; the concert is moved indoors on rainy days. From Route 236 at the southern edge of South Berwick (watch for a signpost), turn left onto Brattle Street and take the second right onto Vaughan's Lane.

Also here is the 150-acre hilltop campus of **Berwick Academy,** Maine's oldest prep school, chartered in 1791 with John Hancock's signature. The coed school's handsome gray-stone William H. Fogg Memorial Library ("The Fogg") is named for the same family connected with Harvard's Fogg Art Museum. The highlight of the library is an incredible collection of dozens of 19th-century stained-glass windows, most designed by Victorian artist Sarah Wyman Whitman, who also designed jackets for Sarah Orne Jewett's books. Thanks to a diligent fund-raising effort, the windows were restored to their former glory.

When you're ready to stretch your legs, head to **Vaughan Woods State Park** (28 Oldfields Rd., South Berwick, 207/384-5160, 9 A.M.-8 P.M. daily late May-early Sept., but accessible all year, $3 adults, $1 children 5-11, free over 65 or under 5) and wander along the three miles of trails in the 250-acre riverside preserve. It adjoins Hamilton House and is connected via a path, but there's far more parking at the park itself.

Another reason to venture inland is to catch a production at the **Hackmatack Playhouse** (538 School St./Rte. 9, Berwick, 207/698-1807, www.hackmatack.org), midway between North Berwick and Berwick. The popular summer theater, operating since 1972, is based in a renovated barn reminiscent of a past era and has 8 P.M. performances Wednesday-Saturday, a 2 P.M. matinee Thursday, and children's shows. Tickets are $22 adults, $20 seniors, $10 students under 20; matinees are $2 less.

FOOD

A local institution since 1960, **Fogarty's** (471 Main St., South Berwick, 207/384-8361, 11 A.M.-8:30 P.M. daily) has expanded through the years from a simple takeout place to a local

© HILARY NANGLE

The 18th-century Hamilton House, in South Berwick, is open for guided tours during the summer.

favorite for inexpensive family-friendly dining. Ask for a river-view table in the back room.

Far jazzier is **Pepperland Café** (279 Main St., South Berwick, 207/384-5535, 11 A.M.–11:30 P.M. Tues.–Sat., 9 A.M.–3 P.M. Sun.), a family-friendly pub-meets-bistro serving comfort food with pizzazz. Make a meal from smaller plates and salads ($5–10) or go big with the entrées ($17–24).

Relish (404 Main St., South Berwick, 207/384-8249, 5:30–9 P.M. Tues.–Sat.), previously known as Margaux, is an intimate, low-key neighborhood bistro where Linda Robinson and Christine Prunier serve well-crafted dinners, with most entrées less than $20.

ACCOMMODATIONS

These two inns are sleepers! (Sorry, couldn't resist.) Both are within easy striking distance of the coast, yet provide far more value than similar properties in the name communities.

Once the headmaster's residence for nearby Berwick Academy, the elegant turn-of-the-20th-century **Academy Street Inn Bed and Breakfast** (15 Academy St., South Berwick, 207/384-5633) has crystal chandeliers, leaded-glass windows, working fireplaces, and high-ceilinged rooms full of antiques. Paul and Lee Fopeano's handsome home has five rooms with private baths ($99–109 d). Full breakfast or afternoon lemonade on the 60-foot screened porch is a real treat. It's open all year.

Innkeepers Ben Gumm and Sally McLaren have turned the outstanding 25-room Queen Anne–style Hurd mansion into the **Angel of the Berwicks** (2 Elm St., North Berwick, 207/676-2133, www.angeloftheberwicks.com, $99–179), an elegant antiques-filled inn. The Historic Register–listed property has 11-foot ceilings, stained-glass windows, hand-carved friezes, and ornate mantelpieces. There's even a baby grand in the music room. Rates include a full breakfast and afternoon refreshments.

Now for the aah part: The inn also has a full-service spa.

After a day of power shopping, retreat to **Ocean's Edge Bed & Breakfast** (11 Trafton La., Kittery, 207/439-3350, www.oceansedgebnb.com, $150–275), which fronts on tidal Spruce Creek. Three guestrooms, one with shared bath, vary in size and amenities, but all have air-conditioning, Wi-Fi, and CD/DVD players. Guests have access to a home theater and an exercise room. Rates include a full breakfast prepared from organic ingredients. Guests can rent canoes and kayaks, a motorboat, and bicycles for explorations.

FOOD

Local Flavors

Kittery has an abundance of excellent specialty food stores that are perfect for stocking up for a picnic lunch or dinner. Most are along the section of Route 1 between the Portsmouth bridge and the traffic circle.

Three are within steps of each other. At **Beach Pea Baking Co.** (53 Rte. 1, 207/439-3555, 7:30 A.M.–6 P.M. Mon.–Sat.) you can buy fabulous breads and pastries. Sandwiches and salads are made to order 11 A.M.–3 P.M. daily. There's pleasant seating indoors and on a patio. Next door is **Golden Harvest** (7 A.M.–6:30 P.M. Mon.–Sat., 9 A.M.–6 P.M. Sun.), where you can load up on luscious produce. Across the street is **Terracotta Pasta Co.** (52 Rte. 1, 207/475-3025, www.terracottapastacompany.com, 10 A.M.–6 P.M. Mon., 9 A.M.–6:30 P.M. Tues.–Sat., noon–4 P.M. Sun.), where in addition to handmade pastas you'll find salads, soups, sandwiches, prepared foods, and lots of other goodies.

Just off Route 1 is **Enoteca Italiana** (20 Walker St., 207/439-7216, 10 A.M.–7 P.M. Mon. and Wed.–Sat., noon–4 P.M. Sun.), which carries wine, an extensive selection of cured meats, fine cheeses, and other gourmet items.

What's a meal without chocolate? At **Cacao** (64 Government St., just off the town green, 207/438-9001, noon–6 P.M. Tues.–Fri., 10 A.M.–4 P.M. Sat.), Susan Tuveson handcrafts outrageously decadent chocolate truffles and caramels. Flavors vary from the familiar to the exotic: Some are made with chilies (habanero lime!), some with cheeses (gorgonzola). The strawberry balsamic vinegar with black pepper truffle and the fleur de sel caramel are particularly sublime.

Old World artisan breads made from organic ingredients are available at the company store for **When Pigs Fly** (447 Rte. 1, 207/439-3114, www.sendbread.com).

Craving a down-home breakfast or lunch? The **Sunrise Grill** (182 State Rd./Rte. 1, Kittery traffic circle, Kittery, 207/439-5748, www.sunrisegrillinc.com, 6:30 A.M.–2 P.M. daily) delivers with waffles, granola, omelets, Diana's Benedict, salads, sandwiches, and burgers.

Casual Dining

Executive Chef Charlie Cicero's commitment to using fresh and local foods and his flair for bringing big flavors out of simple ingredients have earned **Anneke Jans** (60 Wallingford Sq., Kittery, 207/439-0001, www.annekejans.net, 5–10 P.M. daily) kudos far beyond Kittery. Signature dishes include the fried olives, an appetizer, and Bangs Island mussels prepared with bacon, shallots, and blue cheese, available as an appetizer or entrée. Charcoal walls, white tablecloths and moss centerpieces, a wine bar, and windows that open to the street create an especially hip and stylin' atmosphere. The French/American bistro menu has prices ranging $17–33. The extensive wine list has more than 30 available by the glass. This is a local hot spot with a lively crowd; reservations are recommended.

Ethnic Fare

Craving Cal-Mex? Some of the recipes in Luis Valdez's **Loco Coco's Tacos** (36 Walker St., Kittery, 207/438-9322, www.lococococos.com, 11 A.M.–9 P.M. daily) have been passed down for generations, and the homemade salsas have flavor and kick. If you're feeling really decadent, go for the artery-busting California fries. There's a kids' menu, too. Most choices are less than $10. Choose from self-serve, dining room, or bar seating.

After years of operating a prepared-foods operation, chefs Janet Howe and Rajesh Mandekar opened **Tulsi** (2 Government St., Kittery, 207/451-9511, www.tulsiindianrestaurant.com, 5–10 P.M. Tues.–Sat., 5–9 P.M. Sun., $9–20). Mandekar, from Mumbai, has cooked at venues ranging from five-star restaurants to a cruise line, and blends techniques drawn from Indian, French, and Italian cuisines to create rave-worthy Indian fare. It's a tiny spot; reservations are recommended.

Lobster and Clams

If you came to Maine to eat lobster, **Chauncey Creek Lobster Pier** (16 Chauncey Creek Rd., off Rte. 103, Kittery Point, 207/439-1030, www.chaunceycreek.com, 11 A.M.–8 P.M. daily, to 7 P.M. after early Sept., mid-May–Columbus Day) is the real deal. Step up to the window, place your order, take a number, and grab a table (you may need to share) overlooking tidal Chauncey Creek and the woods on the close-in opposite shore. It's a particularly picturesque—and extremely popular—place. Parking is a nightmare. BYOB and anything else that's not on the menu.

If clams are high on your must-have list, pay a visit to **Bob's Clam Hut** (315 Rte. 1, Kittery, 207/439-4233, www.bobsclamhut.com, 11 A.M.–9 P.M. Mon.–Thurs., to 9:30 P.M. Fri. and Sat., to 8:30 P.M. Sun.), next to the Kittery Trading Post. Using vegetable oil for frying, Bob's turns out everything from scallops to shrimp to calamari to, of course, clams; the tartar sauce is the secret weapon. Expect to pay market rates, but nothing is too pricey. Bob's is open all year.

The Yorks

Four villages with distinct personalities—upscale **York Harbor,** historic **York Village,** casual **York Beach,** and semirural **Cape Neddick**—make up the Town of York. First inhabited by Native Americans, who named it Agamenticus, the area was settled as early as 1624, so history is serious business here. Town high points were its founding, by Sir Ferdinando Gorges, and the arrival of well-to-do vacationers in the 19th century. In between were Indian massacres, economic woes, and population shuffles. The town's population explodes in summer (pretty obvious in July and August, when you're searching for a free patch of York Beach sand or a parking place). York Beach, with its seasonal surf and souvenir shops and amusements, has long been the counterpoint to genteel York Village, but that's changing with the restoration and rebirth of York Beach's downtown buildings and the arrival of tony restaurants, shops, and condos.

History and genealogy buffs can study the headstones in the Old Burying Ground or comb the archives of the Old York Historical Society. For lighthouse fans, there are Cape Neddick Light Station ("Nubble Light") and, six miles offshore, Boon Island. You can rent horses or mountain bikes on Mt. Agamenticus, board a deep-sea fishing boat in York Harbor, or spend an hour hiking the Cliff Path in York Harbor. For the kids, there's a zoo, a lobsterboat cruise, a taffy maker, or, of course, the beach.

SIGHTS

Old York Historical Society

Based in York Village, the Old York Historical Society (207 York St., York Village, 207/363-4974, www.oldyork.org, museum buildings open 10 A.M.–5 P.M. Mon.–Sat. early June–mid-Oct., $10 adults or $5 one building, $9 seniors or $4 one building, $5 children 6–16 or $3 one building, $20 family or $15 one building) is the driving force behind a collection of eight colonial and postcolonial buildings (plus a research library) open throughout the summer. Start at the Jefferds' Tavern Visitor Center (5 Lindsay Rd., York Village), where you'll need

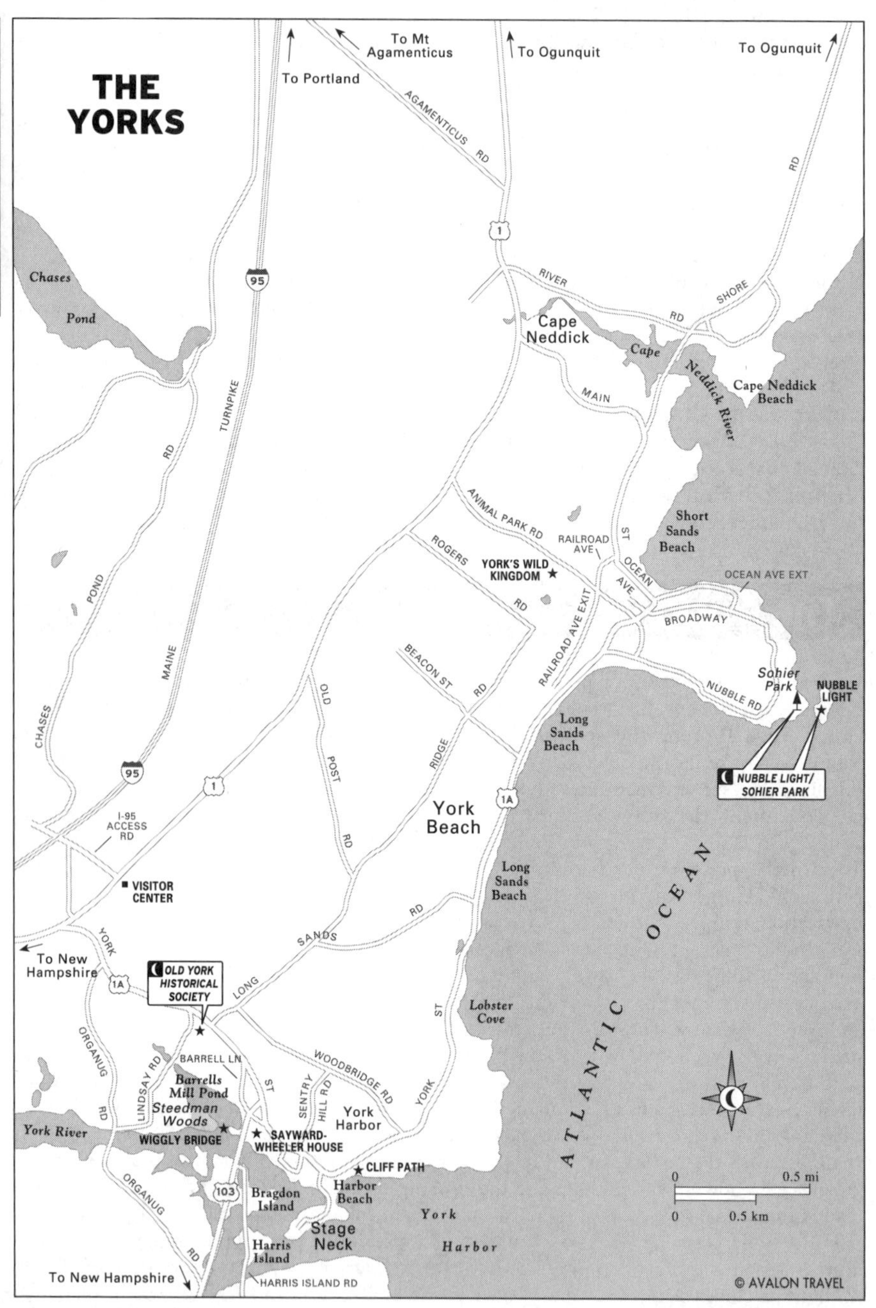

THE YORKS
To Portland
To Mt Agamenticus
To Ogunquit
To Ogunquit
AGAMENTICUS RD
SHORE RD
RIVER RD
Chases Pond
Cape Neddick
Cape Neddick River
Cape Neddick Beach
MAIN
TURNPIKE
RD
MAINE
POND
CHASES
ANIMAL PARK RD
RAILROAD AVE
ST
OCEAN AVE
Short Sands Beach
OCEAN AVE EXT
ROGERS RD
YORK'S WILD KINGDOM
BROADWAY
RAILROAD AVE EXIT
BEACON ST
RD
OLD POST RD
RIDGE
Sohier Park
NUBBLE RD
NUBBLE LIGHT
Long Sands Beach
NUBBLE LIGHT/ SOHIER PARK
York Beach
I-95 ACCESS RD
VISITOR CENTER
Long Sands Beach
ATLANTIC OCEAN
RD
SANDS
LONG
To New Hampshire
YORK
OLD YORK HISTORICAL SOCIETY
ST
Lobster Cove
ORGANUG RD
LINDSAY RD
BARRELL LN
ST
SENTRY HILL RD
WOODBRIDGE RD
YORK
Barrells Mill Pond
Steedman Woods
York Harbor
York River
WIGGLY BRIDGE
SAYWARD-WHEELER HOUSE
CLIFF PATH
ORGANUG RD
Bragdon Island
Harbor Beach
0 0.5 mi
0 0.5 km
York Harbor
Stage Neck
Harris Island
HARRIS ISLAND RD
To New Hampshire
© AVALON TRAVEL

© HILARY NANGLE

Historic New England owns the 1718 Sayward-Wheeler House, one of York's architectural treasures.

to pick up tickets for visiting. Don't miss the Old Burying Ground, dating from 1735, across the street (rubbings are a no-no). Nearby are the Old Gaol and the School House (both fun for kids), Ramsdell House, and the Emerson-Wilcox House. About a half mile down Lindsay Road, on the York River, are the John Hancock Warehouse and the George Marshall Store Gallery (140 Lindsay Rd., operated in the summer as a respected contemporary-art gallery); across the river is the Elizabeth Perkins House. Antiques buffs shouldn't miss the Wilcox and Perkins Houses. These two and the Ramsdell House are open by guided tour; other buildings are self guided. Visit some or all of the buildings, at your own pace; no one leads you from one to another. Note: Some sites you can walk to from the tavern; others you'll need a car to reach and parking may be limited.

Nubble Light/Sohier Park

The best-known photo op in York is the distinctive 1879 lighthouse known formally as Cape Neddick Light Station and familiarly as "The Nubble." Although there's no access to the lighthouse's island, Sohier Park Welcome Center (Nubble Rd., off Rte. 1A, between Long and Short Sands Beaches, York Beach, 207/363-7608, 9 A.M.–7 P.M. daily mid-May–mid-Oct.) provides the perfect viewpoint (and has restrooms). Parking is limited, but the turnover is fairly good. It's not a bad idea, however, to walk from the Long Sands parking area or come by bike, even though the road has inadequate shoulders. Weekdays this is also a popular spot for scuba divers.

Sayward-Wheeler House

Owned by the Boston-based Historic New England, the 1718 Sayward-Wheeler House (9 Barrell Lane Ext., York Harbor, 207/384-2454, www.historicnewengland.org, $5) occupies a prime site at the edge of York Harbor. It's open with tours on the hour 11 A.M.–4 P.M. the second and fourth Saturday of the month, from June through mid-October. In the house are original period furnishings, all in excellent condition. Take Route 1A to Lilac Lane (Rte.

103) to Barrell Lane and then to Barrell Lane Extension.

York's Wild Kingdom

More than 250 creatures—including tigers, zebras, llamas, deer, lions, elephants, and monkeys—find a home at York's Wild Kingdom (102 Railroad Ave., off Rte. 1, York Beach, 207/363-4911 or 800/456-4911, www.yorkzoo.com). It's not what you'd call a state-of-the-art zoo, but it keeps the kids entertained. Elephant shows and other animal "events" occur three times daily in July and August. Between the zoo and the amusement-park rides, it's easy to spend a day here. Admission (covering the zoo and some of the rides) is in the neighborhood of $20 adults, $15 children 4–10, $5 age 3 and younger; an unlimited-rides day pass is $10. Zoo-only admission is $15 adults, $9 children 4–10, $1 age 3 and younger. The zoo's open 10 A.M.–5 P.M. daily, to 6 P.M. weekends and July and August, from late May to late September; amusement park hours are noon–9:30 P.M. daily late June through early September.

© TOM NANGLE

York's Wild Kingdom is a kid magnet, with more than 250 creatures in residence.

ENTERTAINMENT

Live Music

Inn on the Blues (7 Ocean Ave., York Beach, 207/351-3221, www.innontheblues.com) has live music (acoustic, blues, reggae) every night but Monday during the summer. If you want to be close to both the music and the beach, consider booking one of the suites upstairs ($125–375).

The **Ship's Cellar Pub** in the York Harbor Inn frequently has live entertainment, too.

Free concerts are often held at the **Ellis Park Gazebo,** usually 7–9 P.M. from early July to early September. Check local papers for schedule.

Make Your Own Pottery

Rainy day? Paint a design on white clay bisque plates, mugs, or bowls at **Naked Plates** (470 Rte. 1, York, 207/351-1002, www.nakedplates-pottery.com), which will glaze and fire it for you. Studio time is $4 for the first hour, $2 for each additional, and pottery pieces begin at $5.

EVENTS

Each year, the Old York Historical Society invites decorators to transform a local house for the **Decorator Show House,** culminating in an open house from mid-July to mid-August.

From late July into early August, the **York Days** festivities enliven the town for 10 days with concerts, dances, walking tours, a road race, sandcastle contests, antiques and art shows, a dog show, fireworks, a parade, and public suppers.

York Village's **Annual Harvestfest** takes place 10 A.M.–4 P.M. the weekend after Columbus Day in October and combines colonial crafts and cooking demonstrations, hayrides, museum tours, entertainment for adults and kids, and an ox roast with beanhole beans. This is one of the town's most popular events; most activities are free.

The annual **Lighting of the Nubble,** in

late November, includes cookies, hot chocolate, music, and an appearance by Santa Claus. The best part, though, is seeing the lighthouse glowing for the holidays.

SHOPPING

Expect to wash your hands before examining any of the 400-plus museum-quality antique quilts at Betsy Telford's **Rocky Mountain Quilts** (130 York St., York Village, 207/363-6800 or 800/762-5940, www.rockymountainquilts.com). This isn't a place for browsers.

Fans of fine craft shouldn't miss **Panache** (1949 Rte. 1, Cape Neddick, 207/646-4878). It boasts of having New England's largest selection of fine contemporary art glass, but there's so much more here. It's a visual treat. Find it just south of the Ogunquit Playhouse, on the York-Ogunquit town line.

RECREATION

Walk the Walks

Next to Harbor Beach, near the Stage Neck Inn, a sign marks the beginning of the **Cliff Path,** a walkway worth taking for its dramatic harbor views in the shadow of elegant summer cottages. On the one-hour round-trip, you'll pass the York Harbor Reading Room (an exclusive club). The path is on private property, traditionally open to the public courtesy of the owners, but controversy surfaces periodically about property rights, vandalism, and the condition of some sections of the walk. Note: It's called the Cliff Path for a reason. It's not a good choice for little ones.

A less strenuous route is known variously as the **Shore Path, Harbor Walk,** or **Fisherman's Walk,** running west along the harbor and river from Stage Neck Road (next to Edwards' Harborside Inn) and passing the Sayward-Wheeler House before crossing the tiny green-painted Wiggly Bridge leading into the **Steedman Woods** preserve. Carry binoculars for good boat watching and birding in the 16-acre preserve, owned by the Old York Historical Society. A one-mile double-loop trail takes less than an hour of easy strolling.

Mt. Agamenticus

Drive to the summit of Mt. Agamenticus ("The Big A") and you're at York County's highest point. It's only 692 feet, but on a clear day you'll have panoramic views of ocean, lakes, woods, and sometimes the White Mountains. The 10,000-acre preserve (www.agamenticus.org), one of the largest remaining expanses of undeveloped forests in coastal New England, is considered among the most biologically diverse wildernesses in Maine. It includes vernal pools and ponds and is home to rare and endangered species. At the summit are a billboard map of the 40-mile trail network and a curious memorial to St. Aspinquid, a 17th-century Algonquian Indian leader. Also here are riding stables, offering trail rides Memorial Day to mid-September. Mountain biking is also hugely popular on Agamenticus. Take a picnic, a kite, and binoculars. In the fall, if the wind's from the northwest, watch for migrating hawks; in winter, bring a sled for the best downhill run in southern Maine. From Route 1 in Cape Neddick, take Mountain Road (also called Agamenticus Rd.) 4.2 miles west to the access road.

Golf

The **Ledges Golf Club** (1 Ledges Dr., off Rte. 91, York, 207/351-9999, www.ledgesgolf.com) is an 18-hole course with daily public tee times.

Swimming

Sunbathing and swimming are big draws in York, with four beaches of varying sizes and accessibility. Bear in mind that traffic can be gridlocked along the beachfront (Rte. 1A) in midsummer, so it may take longer than you expect to get anywhere. **Lifeguards** are usually on duty 9:30 A.M.–4 P.M. mid-June–Labor Day at Short Sands Beach, Long Beach, and Harbor Beach. Bathhouses at Long Sands and Short Sands are open 9 A.M.–7 P.M. daily in midsummer. The biggest parking area (metered) is at Long Sands, but that 1.5-mile beach also draws the most customers. Scarcest parking is at Harbor Beach, near the Stage Neck Inn, and at Cape Neddick (Passaconaway) Beach, near the Ogunquit town line.

Sea Kayaking

Kayak rentals begin at $40 a day single, $50 double, from **Excursions: Coastal Maine Outfitting Company** (1740 Rte. 1, Cape Neddick, 207/363-0181, www.excursionsinmaine.com), owned by Mike Sullivan. Or sign up for one of their half-day tours: $60 ages 15 and older, $50 children. A four-hour basics clinic for ages 16 and older is $85. Excursions is based at Dixon's Campground on Route 1, four miles north of the I-95 York exit.

Harbor Adventures (Harris Island Rd., York Harbor, 207/363-8466, www.harboradventures.com) offers instruction and guided sea-kayaking trips from Kittery through Kennebunkport. Prices begin around $45 for a two-hour harbor tour.

Surfing

Want to catch a wave? For surfing information, lessons, or rentals, call **Liquid Dreams Surf Shop** (171 Long Beach Ave., York, 207/351-2545, www.liquiddreamssurf.com, 10 A.M.–5 P.M. Fri.–Sun.). It's right across from the beach.

Bicycling

The **Daily Spin** (Rte. 1A, York Beach, 207/363-5040) rents bicycles for $10 per hour to $20 full day. It's located at the Daily Grind coffee shop near the zoo.

Fishing

Local expert on fly-fishing, spin fishing, and conventional tackle is **Eldredge Bros. Guide Service** (1480 Rte. 1, Cape Neddick, 207/373-9269, www.eldredgeflyshop.com). Four-hour guided trips for one or two anglers begin at $250 freshwater, $300 saltwater. Kayak and rod and reel rentals are available.

ACCOMMODATIONS

York Harbor

BED-AND-BREAKFASTS

Hosts Donna and Paul Archibald have turned Fannie Chapman's 1889 summer cottage into the elegant and romantic **Chapman Cottage** (370 York St., York Harbor, 207/363-2059 or 877/363-2059, www.chapmancottagebandb.com, $170–250), a truly special retreat. Rooms are huge and plush, with air-conditioning, Wi-Fi, TV, and spacious baths; most have whirlpool baths and fireplaces (some in the bathrooms), and a few have private decks and river views. The pampering includes a welcome fruit basket, fresh flowers, bathrobes, and fine linens. Dinner may be available off season.

Inviting Adirondack-style chairs accent the green lawn rolling down to the harbor at **Edwards' Harborside Inn** (7 Stage Neck Rd., York Harbor, 207/363-3037 or 800/273-2686, www.edwardsharborside.com, $200–240 rooms, $270–350 suites). Many of the 10 rooms can be combined into suites, and most have water views. All have TV, phone, and air-conditioning. One suite has a party-size whirlpool tub facing the harbor, another a grand piano. Watch the sunset from the inn's 210-foot pier, stroll the adjacent shorefront paths, wander over to the beach, or just settle into one of those shorefront chairs and watch the world go by. A lovely full buffet breakfast is served in the water-view sunporch.

Bill and Bonnie Alstrom, former innkeepers at Tanglewood Hall, weren't looking to downsize, but on a lark they stumbled upon this woodland cottage, and they were smitten. After more than a year of renovations, they opened **Morning Glory Inn** (120 Seabury Rd., York Harbor, 207/363-2062, www.morninggloryinnmaine.com, $155–225). A boutique bed-and-breakfast catering to romantics, the Morning Glory has just three rooms, all very spacious and private, and all with doors to private patios or yards, air-conditioning, TV with DVD, fridge, Wi-Fi, and plentiful other little amenities. The living room, in the original section of the house, was a 17th-century cottage, barged over from the Isles of Shoals; the newer post-and-beam great room doubles as a dining area, where a hot breakfast buffet is served. The property is ultra quiet—listen to the birds singing in the gardens; it's truly a magical setting, far removed yet convenient to everything York offers.

FULL-SERVICE INNS

York Harbor Inn (Rte. 1A, York Harbor, 207/363-5119 or 800/343-3869, www.yorkharborinn.com, $99–349 d) is an accommodating spot with a country-inn flavor and a wide variety of room and package-plan options throughout the year. The oldest section of the inn is a 17th-century cabin from the Isles of Shoals. Accommodations are spread out in the inn, adjacent Yorkshire building, and two elegantly restored houses, both with resident innkeepers: neighboring Harbor Hill, and 1730 Harbor Crest, about a half mile away. All have TV, phones, free Wi-Fi, and air-conditioning; some have four-poster beds, fireplaces, and whirlpools; many have water views. Rates include a generous continental breakfast.

You can't miss the **Stage Neck Inn** (100 Stage Neck Rd., York Harbor, 207/363-3850 or 800/340-9901, www.stageneck.com, $285–405), occupying its own private peninsula overlooking York Harbor. Modern, resort-style facilities include two pools (one indoors), tennis courts, golf privileges, spa, fitness center, and spectacular views from balconies and terraces. The formal Harbor Porches restaurant (no jeans; entrées $21–30) and the casual Sandpiper Bar and Grille are open to the public. Open all year.

York Beach

HOTEL AND MOTEL

For more than 150 years, **The Union Bluff** (8 Beach St., York Beach, 207/363-1333 or 800/833-0721, www.unionbluff.com, $179–379) has stood sentry, like a fortress, overlooking Short Sands Beach. Many of the rooms have ocean views. All have TV, air-conditioning, and phone; some have fireplace, whirlpool bath, or ocean-view deck. Furnishings are modern motel-style. Also on the premises are the Beach Street Grill dining room and a pub serving lighter fare. Best deals are the packages, which include breakfast and dinner. The hotel and pub are open year-round; the restaurant is seasonal. It's probably best to avoid dates when there's a wedding in-house.

Art deco fans take note: The **Nevada Motel** (Rte. 1A, York Beach, 207/363-4504, $135–190) is a classic. Built in 1951 (with few, if any, updates since), the white two-story motel with aqua trim faces Long Sands Beach. It's well maintained but the rooms are small, the bathrooms tiny. No frills, period.

BED-AND-BREAKFASTS

Everything's casual and flowers are everywhere at the brightly painted **Katahdin Inn** (11 Ocean Ave., York Beach, 207/363-1824, www.thekatahdininn.com, $95–145), overlooking the breakers of Short Sands Beach. Longtime owners Rae and Paul LeBlanc appropriately refer to it as a "bed and beach." It was built in 1863 and has always been a guesthouse. Nine smallish 1st-, 2nd-, and 3rd-floor rooms (eight with water views) have four-poster beds and mostly shared baths. Breakfast is not included, but coffee is always available, the rooms have refrigerators, and several eateries are nearby. It's open year-round.

Not oceanfront, but offering ocean views from many rooms and just a short walk from Short Sands Beach, is Barbara and Michael Sheff's **Candleshop Inn** (44 Freeman St., York Beach, 207/363-4087 or 888/363-4087, www.candleshopinn.com, $120–185). The 10 guest rooms (private and shared baths) are decorated in a country cottage style, with area rugs, painted furniture, and florals; many are set up for families. The day begins with a vegetarian breakfast and a yoga class. Spa services, including massage and Reiki, are available on-site by appointment.

CONDOMINIUM SUITES

Fabulously sited on the oceanfront and overlooking the Nubble Light, the high-end **ViewPoint** (229 Nubble Rd., York Beach, 207/363-2661, www.viewpointhotel.com, $375 one-bedroom–$625 three-bedroom per night, $2,700–4,200 per week) comprises luxuriously appointed one-, two-, and three-bedroom suites. All have gas fireplace; fully equipped kitchen; washer-dryer; TV-VCR; phone; private patio, porch, or deck; Wi-Fi; and daily maid service. On the premises are an outdoor heated pool, grilling area, gardens, and playground.

CAMPING

Dixon's Coastal Maine Campground (1740 Rte. 1, Cape Neddick, 207/363-3626, www.dixonscampground.com, $30–36) has more than 100 well-spaced sites on 26 wooded and open acres. It can accommodate tents and small RVs. Electric and water hookups are available. Facilities include a playground and a good-size outdoor heated pool. It's also the base for Excursions sea kayaking.

FOOD

Local Flavors

Both *Gourmet* and *Saveur* know where to get dogs here. Sometimes the line runs right out the door of the low-ceilinged, reddish-brown roadside shack that houses local institution **Flo's Steamed Dogs** (Rte. 1, opposite the Mountain Rd. turnoff, Cape Neddick). Founder Flo Stacy died at age 92 in June 2000, but her legend and her family live on. No menu here—just steamed Schultz wieners, buns, chips, beverages, and an attitude. The secret? The spicy, sweet-sour hot-dog sauce (allegedly once sought by the H. J. Heinz corporation, but the proprietary Stacy family isn't telling or selling). The cognoscenti know to order their dogs only with mayonnaise and the special sauce—nothing heretical such as ketchup or mustard. It's open 11 A.M.–3 P.M., and not a minute later, Thursday–Tuesday year-round.

See those people with their faces pressed to the glass? They're all watching the taffy makers inside **The Goldenrod** (2 Railroad Ave., York Beach, 207/363-2621, www.thegoldenrod.com), where machines spew out 180 Goldenrod Kisses a minute, 65 tons a year—and have been at it since 1896. The Goldenrod is an old-fashioned place, with a tearoom, gift shop, old-fashioned soda fountain (135 ice cream flavors), and rustic dining room, with equally old-fashioned prices. It's open for breakfast (8 A.M.), lunch, and dinner daily late May–Columbus Day.

The *best* pies and other goodies come from **Pie in the Sky Bakery** (corner of Rte. 1 and River Rd., Cape Neddick, 207/363-2656, www.pieintheskymaine.com, 9 A.M.–6 P.M. Fri.–Mon.). You can pick up a slice for $4.50; whole pies begin around $30. Possibilities are numerous: apple crumb, blueberry, bumbleberry, jumbleberry, peach raspberry, and so on; all are handcrafted and made without preservatives or trans fats.

After viewing The Nubble, head across the road to **Brown's Ice Cream** (232 Nubble Rd., York Beach, 207/363-1277), where unusual flavors complement the standards.

Prepared foods by the pound are sold at **Lucia's Kitchen** (1151A Rte. 1, Cape Neddick, 207/363-5557, www.luciaskitchen.net, 11:30 A.M.–7 P.M. Mon.–Fri., to 6 P.M. Sat.), but sandwiches, cookies, and burritos are always available, too.

Craving jerk chicken or curried goat? Stop by **Jamaican Jerk Center** (1400 Rte. 1, Cape Neddick, 207/351-3033), a take-out stand.

Stop in at the **Gateway Farmers Market** (York Chamber of Commerce Visitor Center, Rte. 1, York, 9 A.M.–1 P.M. Sat. mid-June–mid-Oct., 2–5:30 P.M. Tues. July–Aug.) and stock up for a picnic. If you still need more, head next door to Stonewall Kitchen.

Family Favorites

The York Harbor Inn's **Ship's Cellar Pub** (11:30 A.M.–11:30 P.M. Mon.–Thurs., to midnight Fri. and Sat., 3:30–11:30 P.M. Sun.) attracts even the locals. On the menu are soups, sandwiches, and salads as well as heftier entrées ($16–31). The pub doubles as a favorite local watering hole, with live music Wednesday–Sunday. Happy hour, with free munchies, is 4–6 P.M. weekdays and sometimes draws a raucous crowd.

Wood-fired pizza and finger-licking ribs are the best sellers at **Ruby's Genuine Wood Grill** (433 Rte. 1, a mile south of the I-95 exit, York, 207/363-7980, www.rubyswoodgrill.com, 11:30 A.M.–10 P.M., to 11 P.M. Fri. and Sat.), but there's plenty more on the menu. Some of the pizzas are downright intriguing—pulled pork and barbecue sauce, for instance. Entrées vary from St. Louis ribs to fajitas to mahimahi, most priced in the low teens. Pastas, sandwiches, salads, and burgers fill out the menu. There's lots of variety and flair here. In nice weather, opt for the enclosed deck, where there's often live music Saturday nights.

Wild Willy's (765 Rte. 1, York, 207/363-9924, www.wildwillysburgers.com, 11 A.M.–8 P.M. Mon.–Sat.) has turned burgers into an art form. More than a dozen hefty mouthwatering burgers, all made from certified Angus beef, are available, from the classic Willy burger to the Rio Grande, with roasted green chiles from New Mexico and cheddar cheese. Don't miss the hand-cut fries. Chicken sandwiches, steak chili, and frappes are also served, as are beer and wine. Order at the counter before grabbing a seat in the dining area or out on the back deck; the servers will find you when it's ready. Cash only; burgers run about $6.

Locals swear by **Rick's All Seasons Café** (240 York St., York, 207/363-5584), where the food is good, and the gossip is even better. Go for breakfast or lunch; the fried clams earn raves. Have patience: Almost everything is cooked to order. Rick's also serves dinner on Wednesdays and Thursdays.

Casual to Fine Dining

It's hard to know whether Food or Shopping is the right category for **Stonewall Kitchen** (Stonewall La., York, 207/351-2712 or 800/207-5267, www.stonewallkitchen.com), a phenomenally successful company that concocts imaginative condiments and other food products, many of which have received national awards. The headquarters building, home to a handsome shop with tasting areas and a "viewing gallery" where you can watch it all happen, is next to the York Chamber of Commerce building, on Route 1. Go hungry: There are an espresso bar and an excellent café on the premises, open daily for breakfast and lunch and light fare in the late afternoon. Dinner may be served during peak season; call.

Don't let the forlorn and faded exterior deter you. Serving "food that loves you back," **Frankie and Johnny's Natural Foods** (1594 Rte. 1 N., Cape Neddick, 207/363-1909, www.frankie-johnnys.com, from 5 P.M. Wed.–Sun., $18–30) is vibrant inside. Chef-owner John Shaw's eclectic menu includes vegan and vegetarian choices in addition to creative treatments of steak, chicken, and fish; the house-made pastas are excellent. Reservations are recommended for summer weekends. Be forewarned: Portions are more than generous. No credit cards ("plastic is not natural"). BYOB.

Renowned Boston chef Lydia Shire's restaurant **Blue Sky on York Beach** (Rte. 1A, York Beach, 207/363-0050) added a new tone to downtown York Beach. The 2nd-floor restaurant in The Atlantic House is elegant yet welcoming, with gleaming wood floors and a wood-burning fireplace. In summer, dinner also is served on the porch. The dining room opens nightly at 5:30 P.M. The menu ranges from pizza to lobster. Entrées range $20–40, and sides are additional; a lounge menu is less pricey. Be forewarned, food quality is uneven and service can be abysmal.

Lobster

Before heading for the **Cape Neddick Lobster Pound/Harborside Restaurant** (Shore Rd., Cape Neddick, 207/363-5471, www.capeneddick.com, noon–9 P.M. daily), check the tide calendar. The rustic shingled building dripping with lobster-pot buoys has a spectacular harbor view (especially from the deck) at high tide, and a rather drab one at low tide, so plan accordingly.

INFORMATION AND SERVICES

The Maine Tourism Association operates a **Maine State Visitor Information Center** (207/439-1319) in Kittery, between Route 1 and I-95, with access from either road. It's chock-full of brochures and has restrooms and a picnic area.

For York area information, head for the shingle-style palace of the **York Chamber of Commerce** (1 Stonewall La., off Rte. 1, York, 207/363-4422, www.gatewaytomaine.org), at I-95's York exit. Inside are restrooms. It's open daily in summer.

GETTING AROUND

The Maine Turnpike, a toll road, is generally the fastest route if you're trying to get between two towns. Route 1 parallels the turnpike, on the ocean side. It's mostly two lanes and is lined with shops, restaurants, motels, and other tourist-oriented sites, which means stop-and-go traffic that often slows to a crawl. If you're traveling locally, it's best to walk or use the local trolley systems, which have the bonus of saving you the agony of finding a parking spot.

The **York Trolley** (207/748-3030, www.yorktrolley.com) operates a **York Beach Shuttle** from late June to early September. The service between Long and Short Sands Beaches runs every 30 minutes 10 A.M.–10:15 P.M. ($1.50 one-way, $3 complete loop).

The **Shore Road Shuttle** (207/324-5762, www.shorelineexplorer.com) operates hourly between York's Short Sands Beach and Ogunquit's Perkins Cove from late June through Labor Day; check for exact schedule. Fare is $1 each way; a 12-ride pass is $10; 18 and younger ride free.

The Route 103 bridge over the York River is being replaced and is expected to remain closed until May 2011.

Ogunquit and Wells

Ogunquit has been a holiday destination since the indigenous residents named it "beautiful place by the sea." What's the appeal? An unparalleled, unspoiled beach, several top-flight (albeit pricey) restaurants, a dozen art galleries, and a respected art museum with a view second to none. The town has been home to an art colony attracting the glitterati of the painting world starting with Charles Woodbury in the late 1880s. The summertime crowds continue, multiplying the minuscule year-round population of just under 1,400. These days, it's an especially gay-friendly community, too. Besides the beach, the most powerful magnet is Perkins Cove, a working fishing enclave that looks more like a movie set. The best way to approach the cove is via trolley-bus or on foot, along the shoreline Marginal Way from downtown Ogunquit; midsummer parking in the cove ($3 per hour) is madness.

Wells, once the parent of Ogunquit and since 1980 its immediate neighbor to the north, was settled in 1640. Nowadays, it's best known as a long, skinny, family-oriented community with about 10,300 year-round residents, seven miles of splendid beachfront, and heavy-duty commercial activity: lots of antiques and used-book shops. It also claims two spectacular nature preserves worth a drive from anywhere. At the southern end of Wells, abutting Ogunquit, is **Moody,** an enclave named after 18th-century settler Samuel Moody.

SIGHTS

Ogunquit Museum of American Art (OMAA)

Not many museums can boast a view as stunning as the one at the Ogunquit Museum of American Art (543 Shore Rd., Ogunquit, 207/646-4909, www.ogunquitmuseum.org,

© HILARY NANGLE

A wall of windows frames sculpture gardens and waves crashing on distant ledges at the Ogunquit Museum of American Art.

10 A.M.–5 P.M. Mon.–Sat., 1–5 P.M. Sun. July–Oct., $7 adults, $5 seniors, $4 students, free for children under 12), nor can many communities boast such renown as a summer art colony. Overlooking Narrow Cove, 1.4 miles south of downtown Ogunquit, the museum prides itself on its distinguished permanent 1,600-piece American art collection. Works of Marsden Hartley, Rockwell Kent, Walt Kuhn, Henry Strater, and Thomas Hart Benton, among others, are displayed in five galleries. Special exhibits are mounted each summer, when there is an extensive series of lectures, concerts, and other programs, including the annual "Almost Labor Day Auction," a social season must. OMAA has a well-stocked gift shop, wheelchair access, and landscaped grounds with sculptures, a pond, and manicured lawns.

Marginal Way

No visit to Ogunquit is complete without a leisurely stroll along Marginal Way, the mile-long foot path edging the ocean from Shore Road (by the Sparhawk Resort) to Perkins Cove. It's been a must-walk since Josiah Chase gave the right-of-way to the town in the 1920s. The best times to appreciate this shrub-lined, shorefront walkway in Ogunquit are early morning or when everyone's at the beach. En route are tide pools, intriguing rock formations, crashing surf, pocket beaches, benches (though the walk's a cinch, even partially wheelchair-accessible), and a marker listing the day's high and low tides. When the surf's up, keep a close eye on the kids—the sea has no mercy. A midpoint access is at Israel's Head (behind a sewage plant masquerading as a tiny lighthouse), but getting a parking space is pure luck.

Perkins Cove

Turn-of-the-20th-century photos show Ogunquit's Perkins Cove lined with gray-shingled shacks used by a hardy colony of local fishermen, fellows who headed offshore to make a tough living in little boats. They'd hardly recognize it today. Though the cove remains a working lobster-fishing harbor, several old shacks have been reincarnated as boutiques and restaurants, and photographers go crazy shooting the quaint inlet spanned by a little pedestrian drawbridge. In the cove are galleries, gift shops, a range of eateries (fast food to lobster to high-end dining), boat excursions, and public restrooms.

Wells Reserve at Laudholm Farm

Known locally as Laudholm Farm (the name of the restored 19th-century visitors center), Wells National Estuarine Research Reserve (342 Laudholm Farm Rd., Wells, 207/646-1555, www.wellsreserve.org) occupies 1,690 acres of woods, beach, and coastal salt marsh on the southern boundary of the Rachel Carson National Wildlife Refuge, just one-half mile east of Route 1. Seven miles of trails wind through the property. The best trail is the Salt Marsh Loop, with a boardwalk section leading to an overlook with panoramic views of the marsh and Little River inlet. Another winner is the Barrier Beach Walk, a 1.3-mile round-trip that goes through multiple habitats all the way to beautiful Laudholm Beach. Allow 1.5 hours for either; you can combine the two. Ticks carrying Lyme disease have been found here, so tuck pant legs into socks and stick to the trails (some of which are wheelchair-accessible). The informative exhibits in the visitors center (10 A.M.–4 P.M. Mon.–Sat., noon–4 P.M. Sun. late May–mid-Oct., Mon.–Fri. Oct.–Mar., closed mid-Dec.–mid-Jan.) make a valuable prelude for enjoying the reserve. An extensive program schedule, April–November, includes lectures, nature walks, and children's programs. Reservations are required for some programs. Trails are accessible 7 A.M.–dusk. From late May to mid-October, admission is charged, $3 adults, $1 children 6–16.

Rachel Carson National Wildlife Refuge

Ten chunks of coastal Maine real estate—now more than 4,700 acres, eventually 7,600 acres, between Kittery Point and Cape Elizabeth—make up this refuge (Rte. 9, 321 Port Rd., Wells, 207/646-9226, http://rachelcarson.fws.gov) headquartered at the northern edge of Wells, near the Kennebunkport town line. Pick up a *Carson Trail Guide* at the refuge office (parking is very limited) and follow the mile-long walkway (wheelchair-accessible) past tidal creeks, salt pans, and salt marshes. It's a bird-watcher's paradise during migration seasons. As with the Laudholm Farm reserve, the Lyme disease tick has been found here, so tuck pant legs into socks and stick to the trail. Office hours are 8 A.M.–4:30 P.M. Monday–Friday year-round; trail access is sunrise to sunset year-round. Leashed pets are allowed.

Ogunquit Arts Collaborative Gallery

Closer to downtown Ogunquit is the Ogunquit Arts Collaborative Gallery (also known as the Barn Gallery, Shore Rd. and Bourne La., Ogunquit, 207/646-8400, www.barngallery.org, 11 A.M.–5 P.M. Mon.–Sat., 1–5 P.M. Sun. late May–early Oct., free), featuring the works of member artists, an impressive group. The OAC is the showcase for the Ogunquit Art Association, established by Charles Woodbury, who was inspired to open an art school in Perkins Cove in the late 19th century. Special programs throughout the season include concerts, workshops, gallery talks, and an art auction.

Wells Auto Museum

The late Glenn Gould's collection of more than 85 vintage vehicles, some restored, others not, plus a collection of old-fashioned nickelodeons (bring nickels and dimes, they work), are jam-packed into the Wells Auto Museum (Rte. 1, Wells, 207/646-9064, 10 A.M.–5 P.M. daily late June–late Sept., $7 adults, $4 children 6–12). From the outside it looks like a big warehouse; inside it's a treasure, with gems including an original 1918 Stutz Bearcat, four Pierce Arrows, a Stanley Steamer, and an emphasis on Brass Era vehicles.

Local History Museum

Ogunquit's history is preserved in the **Ogunquit Heritage Museum** (86 Obeds La., Dorothea Jacobs Grant Common, Ogunquit, 207/646-0296, www.ogunquitheritagemuseum.org, 1–5 P.M. Tues.–Sat. June–Sept., donation appreciated). The museum opened in 2001 in the restored Captain James Winn House, a 1785 cape listed on the National Register. Exhibits here and in a new ell focus on Ogunquit's role as an art colony, its maritime heritage, town history, and local architecture.

ENTERTAINMENT

Theater

Having showcased top-notch professional theater since the 1930s, the 750-seat **Ogunquit Playhouse** (Rte. 1, Ogunquit, 207/646-5511, www.ogunquitplayhouse.org), a summer classic, knows how to do it right: presenting comedies and musicals daily in summer, with big-name stars. The air-conditioned building is wheelchair-accessible. The box office is open daily in season, beginning in early May. Prices range $41–60. The playhouse also presents a children's series. Parking can be a hassle; consider walking the short distance from the Bourne Lane trolley-bus stop.

Live Music

Ogunquit has several nightspots with good reputations for food and live entertainment. Best known is **Jonathan's** (2 Bourne La., Ogunquit, 207/646-4777, 800/464-9934 in Maine), where national headliners often are on the schedule upstairs. Advance tickets are cheaper than at the door, and dinner guests (entrées $19–32) get preference for seats; all show seats are reserved.

Ogunquit Performing Arts (207/646-6170) presents a full slate of programs, including classical concerts, ballet, and theater.

The **Wells Summer Concert Series** runs from early July through early September, most Saturday evenings, at the Hope Hobbs Gazebo in Wells Harbor Park. A wide variety of music is represented, from sing-alongs to swing.

FESTIVALS AND EVENTS

Harbor Fest, a concert, craft fair, parade, chicken barbecue, and children's activities, takes place the second weekend of July in Harbor Park in Wells.

In mid-August Ogunquit Beach hosts a **Sandcastle-Building Contest,** and in late August is the annual **Sidewalk Art Show and Sale.**

Capriccio is a performing arts festival, with daytime and evening events as well as a kite festival, held during the first week of September. The second weekend that month, Wells National Estuarine Research Reserve (Laudholm Farm) hosts the **Laudholm Nature Crafts Festival,** a two-day juried crafts fair with children's activities and guided nature walks. This is an especially fine event. The third weekend of September, the **Annual Ogunquit Antiques Show** benefits the Historical Society of Wells and Ogunquit.

SHOPPING

Antiques and Antiquarian Books

Antiques are a Wells specialty. You'll find more than 50 shops, with a huge range of prices. The majority are on Route 1. **R. Jorgensen Antiques** (502 Post Rd./Rte. 1, Wells, 207/646-9444), is a phenomenon in itself, filling 11 showrooms in two buildings with European and American 18th- and 19th-century furniture and accessories. **MacDougall-Gionet Antiques and Associates** (2104 Post Rd./Rte. 1, Wells, 207/646-3531) has been in business since 1959, and its reputation is stellar. The 65-dealer shop, in an 18th-century barn, carries American and European country and formal furniture and accessories.

If you've been scouring antiquarian bookshops for a long-wanted title, chances are you'll find it at **Douglas N. Harding Rare Books** (2152 Post Rd./Rte. 1, Wells, 207/646-8785 or 800/228-1398). Well cataloged and organized, the sprawling bookshop at any given time stocks upward of 100,000 books, prints, and maps, plus a hefty selection of Maine and New England histories.

Lighthouse Extravaganza

Several mini-lighthouses stand watch over the **Lighthouse Depot** (Post Rd./Rte. 1, Wells, 207/646-0608 or 800/758-1444, www.lighthousedepot.com), a must-stop for lighthouse aficionados. Imagine this: two floors of lighthouse books, sculptures, videos, banners, Christmas ornaments, lawn ornaments, paintings, and replicas running the gamut from pure kitsch to attractive collectibles. Depot owners Tim Harrison and Kathy Finnegan also publish the *Lighthouse Digest,* a monthly magazine focusing on North American lighthouses (annual subscription $28), and produce a large mail-order catalog.

RECREATION

Beaches

One of Maine's most scenic and unspoiled sandy beachfronts, Ogunquit's 3.5-mile stretch of sand fringed with seagrass is a magnet for hordes of sunbathers, spectators, swimmers, surfers, and sandcastle builders. Getting there means crossing the Ogunquit River via one of three access points. For Ogunquit's **Main Beach**—with a spanking new bathhouse and big crowds—take Beach Street. To reach **Footbridge Beach,** marginally less crowded, either take Ocean Street and the footbridge or take Bourne Avenue to Ocean Avenue in adjacent Wells and walk back toward Ogunquit. **Moody Beach,** at Wells's southern end, is technically private property, a subject of considerable legal dispute. Lifeguards are on duty all summer at the public beaches, and there are restrooms in all three areas. The beach is free, but parking is not. Main Beach is $4 per hour; the others are $15–20 per day and fill up early on warm midsummer days. After 3:30 P.M., some are free. It's far more sensible to opt for the frequent trolley-buses.

Wells beaches continue where Ogunquit's leave off. **Crescent Beach,** Webhannet Drive between Eldredge and Mile Roads, is the tiniest, with tide pools, no facilities, and limited parking. **Wells Beach,** Mile Road to Atlantic Avenue, is the major (and most crowded) beach, with lifeguards, restrooms, and parking. Around the other side of Wells Harbor is **Drakes Island Beach** (take Drakes Island Road, at the blinking light), a less crowded spot with restrooms and lifeguards. Walk northeast from Drakes Island Beach and you'll eventually reach Laudholm Beach, with great birding along the way. Summer beach-parking fees are $15 a day for nonresidents ($5 for a motorcycle, $25 for an RV); if you're staying longer, a $50 10-visit pass is a better bargain.

Bike, Kayak, and Surfboard Rentals

At **Wheels and Waves** (579 Post Rd./Rte. 1, Wells, 207/646-5774, www.wheelsnwaves.com), mountain-bike rentals begin at $20 a day; tandems are $40. Surfboards are $25.

Put in right at the harbor and explore the estuary from **Webhannet River Kayak and Canoe Rentals** (345 Harbor Rd., Wells, 207/646-9649, www.webhannetriver.com). Rates begin at $25 solo, $40 tandem, for two hours.

Boating Excursions

Depending on your interest, you can go deep-sea fishing or whale-watching or just gawking out of Perkins Cove, Ogunquit.

Between April and early November, Captain Tim Tower runs half-day (departing 4 P.M.; $45 pp) and full-day (departing 7 A.M.; $75 pp) **deep-sea-fishing trips** aboard the 40-foot *Bunny Clark* (207/646-2214, www.bunnyclark.com), moored in Perkins Cove. Reservations are necessary. Tim has a science degree, so he's a wealth of marine biology information. All gear is provided, and the crew will fillet your catch for you; dress warmly and wear sunblock.

Perkins Cove (Barnacle Billy's Dock) is also home port for the Hubbard family's

Finestkind Cruises (207/646-5227, www.finestkindcruises.com). Motorboat options include: 1.5-hour 14-mile Nubble Lighthouse cruises; one-hour cocktail cruises; a 75-minute breakfast cruise, complete with coffee, juice, and muffin; and 50-minute lobster-boat trips. Rates run $15–22 adults, $8–12 children. Also available are 1.75-hour sails aboard *The Cricket,* a locally built wooden sailboat ($30 pp). Reservations are advisable but usually unnecessary midweek. No credit cards.

Golf

The 18-hole Donald Ross–designed **Cape Neddick Country Club** (650 Shore Rd., 207/361-2011, www.capeneddickgolf.com) is a semiprivate 18-hole course with restaurant and driving range.

Sea Kayaking

World Within Sea Kayaking (746 Ocean Ave., Wells, 207/646-0455, www.worldwithin.com) has both tours and rentals. Rentals are available on the tidal Ogunquit River to experienced kayakers for $15/hour single, $25/hour double. Guided tours begin with one hour of land instruction followed by two hours on the water for $70 pp.

ACCOMMODATIONS

Rates are for peak season; most charge less in spring and fall. Most properties are open only seasonally.

Ogunquit

MOTELS

You're almost within spitting distance of Perkins Cove at the 37-room **Riverside Motel** (159 Shore Rd., 207/646-2741, www.riverside-motel.com, $189–199), where you can perch on your balcony and watch the action or, for that matter, join it. Rooms have phone, air-conditioning, refrigerator, Wi-Fi, cable TV, and fabulous views. Rates include continental breakfast. The entire 3.5-acre property is smoke free.

Juniper Hill Inn (336 Main St., 207/646-4501 or 800/646-4544, www.ogunquit.com, $149–234) is a particularly well-run motel-style lodging on five acres close to downtown Ogunquit, with a footpath to the beach. Amenities include refrigerators, cable TV, coin-operated laundry, fitness center, indoor and outdoor pools and hot tubs, and golf privileges. Rooms have all the amenities, including free Wi-Fi. Open all year.

You can't get much closer to the water than the **Above Tide Inn** (66 Beach St., 207/646-7454, www.abovetideinn.com, $190–250), which is built on a wharf over the tidal Ogunquit River and has views to the open Atlantic. It's steps from the beach and downtown Ogunquit. Each of the nine rooms has air-conditioning, TV, and minifridge but no phone; a light breakfast is provided.

COTTAGE COLONIES

It's nearly impossible to land a peak-season cottage at **The Dunes** (518 Main St., 207/646-2612, www.dunesonthewaterfront.com), but it's worth trying. The property is under its third generation of ownership and guests practically will their weeks to their descendants. Nineteen tidy, well-equipped one- or two-bedroom housekeeping cottages, with screened porches and wood-burning fireplaces, and 17 guest rooms are generously spaced on shady, grassy lawns that roll down to the river, with the dunes just beyond. Facilities include a dock with rowboats, pool, and lawn games. Amenities include Wi-Fi, TV, phones, and refrigerators. It's all meticulously maintained. In peak season, one- and two-bedroom cottages require a one- or two-week minimum stay; guest rooms require three nights. Rooms begin at $130, cottages at $220 per night; weekly cottage rentals begin at $1,540.

ECLECTIC PROPERTIES

It's not easy to describe the **Sparhawk Oceanfront Resort** (41 Shore Rd., 207/646-5562, www.thesparhawk.com, $190–310), a sprawling, one-of-a-kind place popular with honeymooners, sedate families, and seniors. There's lots of tradition in this thriving six-acre complex—it's had various incarnations since the turn of the 20th century—and the Happily Filled sign regularly hangs out front. Out back is the Atlantic, with forever views, and the Marginal Way starts right here. It offers tennis court, gardens, and heated pool; breakfast is included. The 87 rooms, in four buildings, vary from motel-type (best views) rooms and suites to inn-type suites. There's a seven-night minimum during July and August.

The Beachmere Inn (62 Beachmere Pl., 207/646-2021 or 800/336-3983, www.beachmereinn.com, $155–360) is another unique property. The private family-owned and -operated oceanfront property comprises an updated Victorian inn, a new seaside motel, and other buildings, all meticulously maintained and often updated, as well as its own beaches. All rooms have air-conditioning, TV, and phone; many rooms have kitchenettes; most have balconies, decks, or terraces; some have fireplaces. There's also a small spa, with hot tub, steam sauna, and fitness room. Morning coffee and pastries are provided. Open year-round.

BED-AND-BREAKFASTS

Built in 1899 for a prominent Maine lumbering family, **Rockmere Lodge** (40 Stearns Rd., 207/646-2985, www.rockmere.com, $175–225) underwent a meticulous six-month restoration in the early 1990s, thanks to preservationists Andy Antoniuk and Bob Brown, and in 2006 the duo, along with Doug Flint, gave the inn and grounds a complete rejuvenation, lightening the decor a bit. Near the Marginal Way on a peaceful street, the handsome home has eight very comfortable Victorian guest rooms, all with CD players and cable TV (a 1,000-title library of DVDs and VCR tapes and CDs is available) and most with ocean views. Rates include a generous breakfast. A wraparound veranda, a gazebo, and "The Lookout," a 3rd-floor windowed nook with comfy chairs, make it easy to settle in and just watch the passersby on the Marginal Way. The woodwork throughout is gorgeous, and the grounds double as a public garden. Beach towels, chairs, and umbrellas are provided for guests. No pets; four dogs in residence. Open year-round.

Jacqui Grant's warm welcome, gracious hospitality, and stellar breakfasts combined with a quiet residential location within walking distance of both the village and Footbridge Beach have earned **Almost Home** (27 King's Lane, 207/641-1754, www.almosthomeinnogunquit.com, $149–179) a stellar reputation. She often serves afternoon cheese with wine from her son's California winery. Rooms are spacious and have nice seating areas, and the backyard makes a quiet retreat.

RESORTS

Founded in 1872, **The Cliff House Resort and Spa** (Shore Rd., 207/361-1000, www.cliffhousemaine.com, $285–360), a self-contained complex, sprawls over 70 acres topping the edge of Bald Head Cliff, midway between the centers of York and Ogunquit. Third-generation innkeeper Kathryn Weare keeps updating and modernizing the facilities. Among the most recent additions is a spa building with oversize rooms with king-size beds, gas fireplaces, and balconies, as well as a full-service spa, indoor pool, outdoor infinity pool, and glass-walled fitness center overlooking the Atlantic. A central check-in building with indoor amphitheater connects the main building to the spa building. The 150 rooms and suites vary widely in decor, from old-fashioned to contemporary; all have cable TV and phones, some have gas fireplaces, most have a spectacular ocean view. Other facilities include a dining room, lounge, family indoor and outdoor pools, games room, and tennis courts. Eight pet-friendly rooms ($25 per night) have bowl, bed, and treats, and there's a fenced-in exercise area. Packages offer the best bang for the buck. Open late March–early December.

Wells

Once part of a giant 19th-century dairy farm, the **Beach Farm Inn** (97 Eldredge Rd., 207/646-8493, www.beachfarminn.com, $100–155) is a 2.5-acre oasis in a rather congested area 0.2 mile off Route 1. Guests can swim in the pool, relax in the library, or walk one-quarter mile down the road to the beach. Five of the eight rooms have private baths (two are detached); 3rd-floor rooms have air-conditioning. Rates include a full breakfast; two cottages go for $695 and $975 a week. Open all year.

Even closer to the beach is **Haven by the Sea** (59 Church St., Wells Beach, 207/646-4194, www.havenbythesea.com, $219–269), a heavenly bed-and-breakfast in a former church. Innkeepers John and Susan Jarvis have kept the original floor plan, which allows some surprises. Inside are hardwood floors, cathedral ceilings, and stained-glass windows. The confessional is now a full bar, and the altar has been converted to a dining area that opens to a marsh-view terrace—the bird-watching is superb. Guest rooms have sitting areas, and the suite has a whirlpool tub and fireplace. Guests have plenty of room to relax, including a living area with fireplace. Rates include a full breakfast and afternoon hors d'oeuvres.

FOOD

Ogunquit

LOCAL FLAVORS

The Egg and I (501 Maine St./Rte. 1, 207/646-8777, www.eggandibreakfast.com, 6 A.M.–2 P.M. daily, to 8 P.M. Fri. and Sat. in July and Aug.) has more than 200 menu choices and earns high marks for its omelets and waffles. You can't miss it; there's always a crowd. Open for breakfast, with lunch choices also served after 11 A.M. No credit cards.

Equally popular is **Amore Breakfast** (309 Shore Rd., 207/646-6661, www.amorebreakfast.com, 7 A.M.–1 P.M. daily). Choose from 14 omelets, eight versions of eggs Benedict (including lobster and a spirited rancheros version topped with salsa and served with guacamole), as well as French toast, waffles, and all the regulars and irregulars.

Eat in or take out from **Village Food Market** (Main St., Ogunquit Center, 207/646-2122, www.villagefoodmarket.com). A breakfast sandwich is less than $3, subs and sandwiches are available in three sizes, and there's even a children's menu. The Pick Three prepared dinner special includes an entrée and two veggies or starches for $9.95.

Scrumptious baked goods, tantalizing salads, and vegetarian lunch items are available to go at Mary Breen's fabulous **Bread and Roses** (246 Main St., 207/646-4227, www.breadandrosesbakery.com, 7 A.M.–11 P.M. daily), a small bakery right downtown with a few tables outside.

Harbor Candy Shop (26 Main St., 207/646-8078 or 800/331-5856) is packed with the most outrageous chocolate imaginable. Fudge, truffles, and turtles are all made here in the shop.

ETHNIC FARE

The closest thing to an upscale-rustic French country inn is the dining room at **Provence,** also referred to as 98 Provence (262 Shore Rd., 207/646-9898, www.98provence.com, 5:30 P.M.–close Wed.–Mon.). Chef-owner Pierre Gignac produces cuisine to match, turning out appetizers and superb entrées in the $22–32 range, but there are also three fixed menus (around $29–45). Possibilities may include foie gras, escargot, rabbit, cassoulet, and always a fish of the day. Service is attentive and well paced. Don't miss it, and be sure to make reservations.

The best and most authentic Italian dining is at **Angelina's Ristorante** (655 Main St./Rte. 1, 207/646-0445, www.angelinasogunquit.com, 4:30–10 P.M. daily). Chef-owner David Giarusso uses recipes handed down from his great grandmother, Angelina Peluso. Dine in the dining room, wine room, lounge, or out on the terrace, choosing from pastas, risottos (the house specialty), and other classics ($15–27). Open year-round.

CASUAL DINING

Gypsy Sweethearts (10 Shore Rd., 207/646-7021, www.gypsysweethearts.com, 5:30–9 P.M. Tues.–Sun.) serves in four rooms on the ground floor of a restored house and a garden. It's one of the region's most reliable restaurants, and the creative menu is infused with ethnic accents and includes vegetarian choices (entrées $20–30). Seating is both inside and out. Reservations advised midsummer.

Equally reliable and just to the south is **Five-O** (50 Shore Rd., 207/646-6365, www.five-oshoreroad.com, 5–10 P.M. daily), which turns out classics with flair complemented by well-conceived inspirations. The menus changes frequently, but entrées usually run $25–33; a three-course prix fixe menu is offered nightly ($35–45). Lighter fare ($15–18) is available until 11 P.M. in the lounge, where martinis are a specialty. Service is excellent. In the off-season, multicourse regional dinners are held about once a month ($70). There's even valet parking.

THE VIEW'S THE THING

There's not much between you and Spain when you get a window seat at **MC** (Oarweed La., Perkins Cove, Ogunquit, 207/646-6263, www.mcperkinscove.com, 11:30 A.M.–2:30 P.M. and 5:30–11 P.M. daily late May–mid-Oct., Wed.–Sun. off season, closed Jan., dinner entrées $24–34), sister restaurant of the mega-high-end Arrows Restaurant. Actually, almost every table on both floors has a view. Service is attentive, and the food is fab, creative, and, in keeping with chefs Mark Gaier and Clark Frasier, ultra fresh. If you can't justify the splurge for Arrows, get a taste of their cuisine here. The bar menu, also served in the dining room by request, is served until 11 P.M. Keep it light with a burger or fish tacos, or opt for the dinner menu, where choices might include sesame-crusted deep-fried rainbow trout or lobster "mac and cheese." There's often live music on Thursday nights. A jazz brunch is served beginning at 11 A.M. Sunday from September until June. Open year-round. Reservations are essential for dinner.

Equally if not more impressive are the views from the dining room at **The Cliff House** (Shore Rd., 207/361-1000). Go for the Sunday breakfast buffet, 7:30 A.M.–1 P.M. Sunday. Service can be so-so. Before or after dining, wander the grounds.

DESTINATION DINING

Restrain yourself for a couple of days and then splurge on an elegant dinner at **Arrows** (Berwick Rd., about 1.5 miles west of Rte. 1, 207/361-1100, www.arrowsrestaurant.com), one of Maine's finest—and priciest—restaurants. In a beautifully restored 18th-century farmhouse overlooking well-tended gardens (including a one-acre kitchen garden that supplies about 90 percent of the produce), co-owners and chefs Mark Gaier and Clark Frasier do everything right here, starting with the artistic presentation. "Innovative" is too tame to describe the menu, which presents each dish in detail. One might begin with roasted quail in the nest (comprising fried noodles, smoked baby pearl onions, poached quail egg, and a stinging nettle sauce), then proceed to Arrows surf and turf (wood-roasted eye of the ribeye au poivre and chilled lobster cocktail with Meyer lemon–tomato cocktail sauce). Entrées cost close to $50, or consider the six-course tasting menu ($95); serious foodies might splurge on the indulgence tasting menu (10 courses for $135). A credit card is required for reservations—essential in midsummer and on weekends. Jackets are preferred for men; no shorts. It's open for dinner at 6 P.M. mid-April–early December: Tuesday–Sunday in July and August, Wednesday–Sunday in June and September–mid-October; Thursday–Sunday in late April, May, late October, and December; and Friday–Sunday in November. Off-season, ask about winemaker, regional, and bistro nights, and specialty dinners and cooking classes.

LOBSTER

Creative marketing, a knockout view, and efficient service help explain why more than 1,000 pounds of lobster bite the dust every summer day at **Barnacle Billy's** (Perkins Cove, 207/646-5575 or 800/866-5575, 11 A.M.–9 P.M. daily seasonally). For ambience, stick with the original operation; Barnacle Billy's Etc. next door (formerly the Whistling

© HILARY NANGLE

You can't get much closer to crashing surf than Ogunquit's Cliff House.

Oyster) is an upmarket version of the same thing with a broader menu. Full liquor license. Try for the deck, with a front-row seat on Perkins Cove.

Less flashy and less pricey is **The Lobster Shack** (Perkins Cove, 207/646-2941, www.lobster-shack.com, 11 A.M.–9 P.M. daily, until 11 P.M. Fri.), serving lobsters, stews, chowders, and some landlubber choices, too.

Wells

LOCAL FLAVORS

Bean suppers are held 5–7 P.M. on the first Saturday of the month, May–October, at the Masonic Hall on Sanford Road.

For scrumptious baked goods and made-to-order sandwiches, head to **Borealis Bread** (Rte. 1, 8 A.M.–5:30 P.M. Mon.–Sat., 9 A.M.–4 P.M. Sun.), in the Aubuchon Hardware plaza adjacent to the Wells Auto Museum.

Pick up all sorts of fresh goodies at the **Wells Farmers Market** in the Town Hall parking lot, 2–5:30 P.M. Wednesdays.

FAMILY FAVORITES

No eatery in this category qualifies as heart healthy; don't say you weren't forewarned.

For fresh lobster, lobster rolls, fish-and-chips, chowders, and homemade desserts, you can't go wrong at the Cardinali family's **Fisherman's Catch** (Harbor Rd./Rte. 1, 207/646-8780, www.fishermanscatchwells.com, 11:30 A.M.–8 P.M. daily early May–mid-Oct., $7–21). Big windows in the rustic dining room frame the marsh; some even have binoculars for wildlife spotting. It might seem out of the way, but trust me, the locals all know this little gem.

Surf and Turf: A good steak in the land of lobster? You betcha. **The Steakhouse** (1205 Post Rd./Rte. 1, 207/646-4200, www.thesteakhouse.com, 4–9:30 P.M. Tues.–Sun.) is a great big barn of a place where steaks are hand cut from USDA prime and choice corn-fed Western beef that's never been frozen. Chicken, seafood, lobster (great stew), and even a vegetarian stir-fry are also on the menu (entrées $14–26); children's menu available. Service is efficient. No reservations, so be prepared for a wait. This place is *very* popular.

Locals rave about the seafood chowder and the lobster stew at **Lord's Harborside Restaurant** (Harbor Rd., Wells Harbor, 207/646-2651, www.lordsharborside.com, noon–9 P.M. Wed.–Mon., to 8 P.M. spring and fall). They should also rave about the view, a front-row seat on the Wells working harbor. Sure, it's touristy, but with these views, who cares? The menu has a bit of everything, but the emphasis is on fish and seafood, with most prices in the teens; lobster higher. Kids' menu available.

FINE DINING

Chef Joshua W. Mather of **Joshua's** (1637 Rte. 1, 207/646-3355, www.joshuas.biz, 5–10 P.M. Mon.–Sat.) grew up on his family's nearby organic farm, and produce from that farm highlights the menu. In a true family operation, his parents not only still work the farm, but they also work in the restaurant, a converted 1774 home with many of its original architectural elements. Everything is made on the premises, from the fabulous bread to the hand-churned ice cream. Entrées range $20–30. The Atlantic haddock, with carmelized onion crust, chive oil, and wild mushroom risotto, is a signature dish and it alone is worth coming for. A vegetarian pasta entrée is offered nightly. Do save room for the maple walnut pie with maple ice cream. Yes, it's gilding the lily, but you can always walk the beach afterward. Reservations are essential for the dining rooms, but the full menu is also served in the bar.

INFORMATION AND SERVICES

At the southern edge of Ogunquit, right next to the Ogunquit Playhouse, the **Ogunquit Chamber of Commerce's Welcome Center** (Rte. 1, Ogunquit, 207/646-2939, www.ogunquit.org) provides all the usual visitor information and has public restrooms. Ask for the Touring and Trolley Route Map, showing the Marginal Way, beach locations, and public restrooms. The chamber of commerce's annual visitor booklet thoughtfully carries a high-tide calendar for the summer.

Just over the Ogunquit border in Wells (actually in Moody) is the **Wells Information Center** (Rte. 1 at Bourne Ave., 207/646-2451, www.wellschamber.org).

The handsome fieldstone **Ogunquit Memorial Library** (74 Shore Rd., Ogunquit, 207/646-9024) is downtown's only National Historic Register building. Or visit the **Wells Public Library** (1434 Post Rd./Rte. 1, 207/646-8181, www.wells.lib.me.us).

GETTING THERE

Amtrak's **Downeaster** (800/872-7245, www.thedowneaster.com), which connects Boston's North Station with Portland, Maine, stops in Wells. The Shoreline Explorer trolley connects in season.

GETTING AROUND

The Maine Turnpike, a toll road, is generally the fastest route if you're trying to get between two towns. Route 1 parallels the turnpike, on the ocean side. It's mostly two lanes and is lined with shops, restaurants, motels, and other tourist-oriented sites, which means stop-and-go traffic that often slows to a crawl. If you're traveling locally, it's best to walk or use the local trolley systems, which have the bonus of saving you the agony of finding a parking spot.

Trolleys

The **Shoreline Explorer** (207/324-5762, www.shorelineexplorer.com) trolley system makes it possible to connect from York to Kennebunkport without your car. Each town's system is operated separately and has its own fees.

Ogunquit Trolley Co. (207/646-1411, www.ogunquittrolley.com) operates seasonal service in Ogunquit, with 39 stops (signposted) weaving through Ogunquit. Each time you board, it'll cost you $1.50 (kids 10 and younger $1), exact fare, but for the same price you can go the whole route—a great way to get your bearings—in about 40 minutes. Hours are 9 A.M.–8 P.M. weekends in June, 8 A.M.–11 P.M.

late June–early September, with reduced service until mid-October.

Wells's seasonal **Shoreline Trolley System** on Route 1 runs every 20–30 minutes, 9 A.M.–11 P.M. late June–Labor Day. Fare is $1 per trip or $3 for a day pass; kids 18 and younger are free. It operates between Wells and Kennebunk's Lower Village.

The Kennebunks

The world may have first learned of Kennebunkport when George Herbert Walker Bush was president, but Walkers and Bushes have owned their summer estate here for three generations. Visitors continue to come to the Kennebunks (the collective name for **Kennebunk, Kennebunkport, Cape Porpoise,** and **Goose Rocks Beach**—combined population about 15,200) hoping to catch a glimpse of the former first family, but they also come for the terrific ambience, the bed-and-breakfasts, boutiques, boats, biking, and beaches.

The Kennebunks' earliest European settlers arrived in the mid-1600s. By the mid-1700s, shipbuilding had become big business in the area. Two ancient local cemeteries—North Street and Evergreen—provide glimpses of the area's heritage. Its Historic District reveals Kennebunk's moneyed past—the homes where wealthy shipowners and shipbuilders once lived, sending their vessels to the Caribbean and around the globe. Today, unusual shrubs and a dozen varieties of rare maples still line Summer Street—the legacy of ship captains in the global trade. Another legacy is the shiplap construction in many houses—throwbacks to a time when labor was cheap and lumber plentiful. Closer to the beach, in Lower Village, stood the workshops of sailmakers, carpenters, and mastmakers whose output drove the booming trade to success.

While Kennebunkport draws most of the sightseers and summer traffic, Kennebunk feels more like a year-round community. Its old-fashioned downtown has a mix of shops, restaurants, and attractions. Yes, its beaches, too, are well known, but many visitors drive right through the middle of Kennebunk without stopping to enjoy its assets.

SIGHTS

Seashore Trolley Museum

There's nothing quite like an antique electric trolley to dredge up nostalgia for bygone days. With a collection of more than 250 transit vehicles (more than two dozen trolleys on display), the Seashore Trolley Museum (195 Log Cabin Rd., Kennebunkport, 207/967-2800, www.trolleymuseum.org, $8 adults, $6 seniors, $5.50 children 6–16) verges on trolleymania. Whistles blowing and bells clanging, restored streetcars do frequent trips (between 10:05 A.M. and 4:15 P.M.) on a 3.5-mile loop through the nearby woods. Ride as often as you wish, then check out the activity in the streetcar workshop and go wild in the trolley-oriented gift shop. Bring a picnic lunch and enjoy it here. Special events are held throughout the summer, including Ice Cream and Sunset Trolley Rides at 7 P.M. every Wednesday and Thursday in July and August ($4, includes ice cream). And here's an interesting wrinkle: Make a reservation, plunk down $50, and you can have a one-hour "Motorman" experience driving your own trolley (with help, of course). The museum is 1.7 miles southeast of Route 1. It's open 10 A.M.–5 P.M. daily late May–mid-October, and weekends in May, late October, and Christmas Prelude.

Walker's Point: The Bush Estate

There's no public access to Walker's Point, but you can join the sidewalk gawkers on Ocean Avenue overlooking George and Barbara Bush's summer compound. The 41st president and his wife lead a low-key, laid-back life when they're here, so if you don't spot them through binoculars, you may well run into them at a shop or restaurant

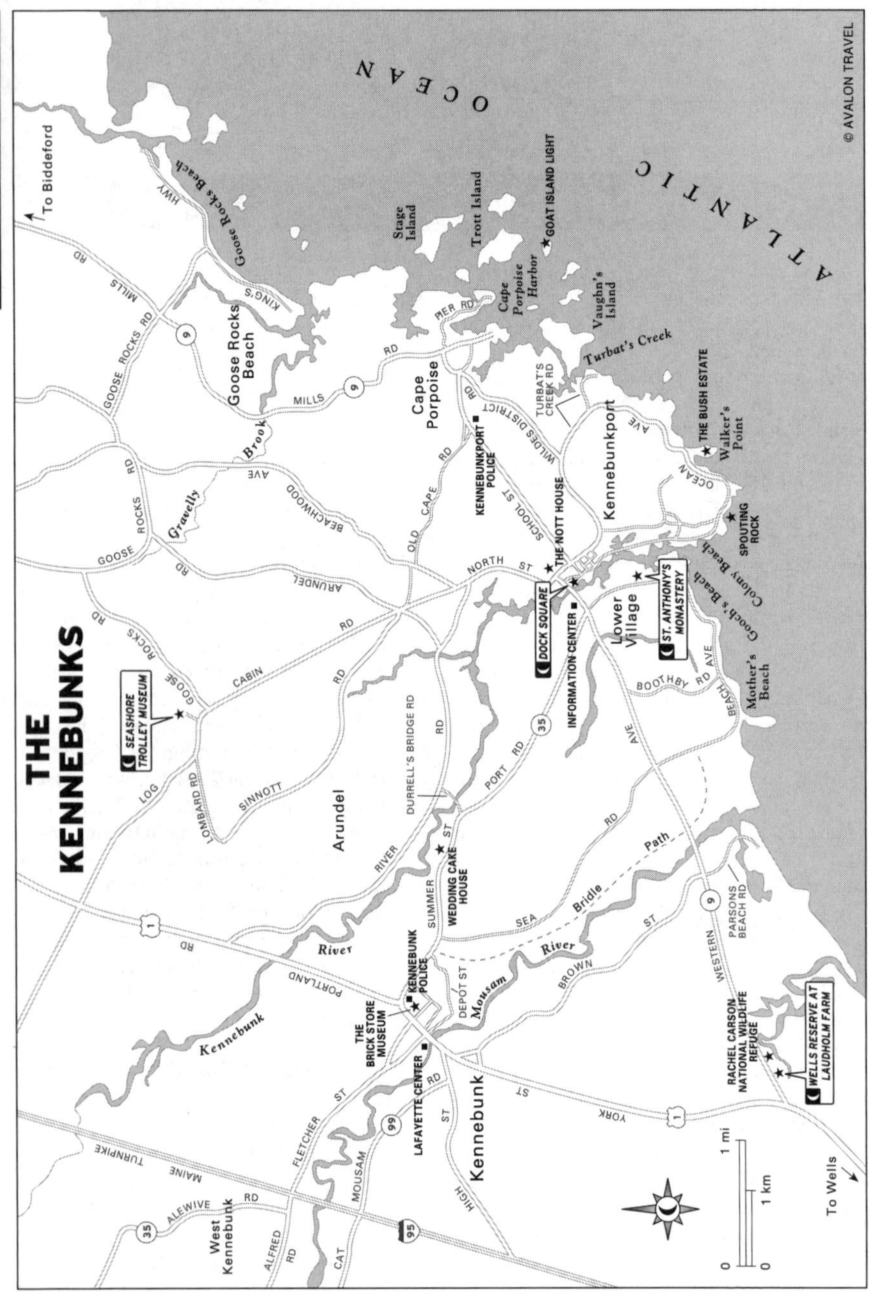

THE KENNEBUNKS
ATLANTIC OCEAN
© AVALON TRAVEL
To Biddeford
To Wells
Goose Rocks Beach
Stage Island
Trott Island
GOAT ISLAND LIGHT
Cape Porpoise Harbor
Vaughn's Island
Turbat's Creek
THE BUSH ESTATE
Walker's Point
SPOUTING ROCK
Colony Beach
Gooch's Beach
Mother's Beach
Kennebunkport
Cape Porpoise
KENNEBUNKPORT POLICE
THE NOTT HOUSE
DOCK SQUARE
INFORMATION CENTER
ST. ANTHONY'S MONASTERY
Lower Village
SEASHORE TROLLEY MUSEUM
Arundel
WEDDING CAKE HOUSE
KENNEBUNK POLICE
THE BRICK STORE MUSEUM
LAFAYETTE CENTER
Kennebunk
West Kennebunk
RACHEL CARSON NATIONAL WILDLIFE REFUGE
WELLS RESERVE AT LAUDHOLM FARM
Kennebunk River
Mousam River
Gravelly Brook
Sea Bridle Path
KING'S HWY
MILLS RD
GOOSE ROCKS RD
PIER RD
TURBAT'S CREEK RD
WILDES DISTRICT RD
OCEAN AVE
SCHOOL ST
NORTH ST
OLD CAPE RD
BEACHWOOD AVE
ARUNDEL RD
CABIN RD
LOG CABIN RD
LOMBARD RD
SINNOTT RD
DURRELL'S BRIDGE RD
RIVER RD
PORT RD
SUMMER ST
BOOTHBY RD
BEACH AVE
SEA RD
PARSONS BEACH RD
WESTERN AVE
BROWN ST
DEPOT ST
PORTLAND RD
YORK ST
FLETCHER ST
HIGH ST
MOUSAM
CAT
ALFRED RD
ALEWIVE RD
MAINE TURNPIKE
9
35
1
99
95
0
1 mi
1 km

in town. Intown Trolley's regular narrated tours go right past the house—or it's an easy, scenic family walk from Kennebunkport's Dock Square. On the way, you'll pass **St. Ann's Church,** whose stones came from the ocean floor, and the paths to **Spouting Rock** and **Blowing Cave,** two natural phenomena that create spectacular water fountains if you manage to be there midway between high and low tides.

Wedding Cake House

The Wedding Cake House (104 Summer St., Kennebunk) is a private residence, so you can't go inside, but it's one of Maine's most-photographed buildings. Driving down Summer Street (Rte. 35), midway between the downtowns of Kennebunk and Kennebunkport, it's hard to miss the yellow and white Federal mansion with gobs of gingerbread and Gothic Revival spires and arches. Built in 1826 by shipbuilder George Bourne as a wedding gift for his wife, the Kennebunk landmark remained in the family until 1983.

Cape Porpoise

When your mind's eye conjures an idyllic lobster-fishing village, it probably looks a lot like Cape Porpoise, only 2.5 miles from busy Dock Square. Follow Route 9 eastward from Kennebunkport; when Route 9 turns north, continue straight, and take Pier Road to its end. From the small parking area, you'll see lobster boats at anchor, a slew of working wharves, and 19th-century **Goat Island Light,** now automated, directly offshore.

Local History Museums

Occupying four restored 19th-century buildings (including the 1825 William Lord store) in downtown Kennebunk, **The Brick Store Museum** (117 Main St., Kennebunk, 207/985-4802, www.brickstoremuseum.org, 10 A.M.–4:30 P.M. Tues.–Fri., 10 A.M.–1 P.M. Sat.) has garnered a reputation for unusual exhibits: a century of wedding dresses, a two-century history of volunteer firefighting, life in southern Maine during the Civil War. Admission is by donation ($5 suggested). The museum

© HILARY NANGLE

Dock Square is the heart of Kennebunkport's shopping district.

encourages appreciation for the surrounding Kennebunk Historic District with hour-long **architectural walking tours,** usually from May to mid-October ($5, call for current schedule). If the schedule doesn't suit, the museum sells a walk-it-yourself booklet for $5.

Owned and maintained by the Kennebunkport Historical Society, **The Nott House** (8 Maine St., Kennebunkport, 207/967-2751, www.kporthistory.org) is a mid-19th-century Greek Revival mansion filled with Victorian furnishings. Be sure to visit the restored gardens. It's open for guided tours 10 A.M.–4 P.M. and 7–9 P.M. Thursday, 1–4 P.M. Friday, and 10 A.M.–1 P.M. Saturday early July–late August; reduced hours spring and fall. Tour tickets are $7 adults, free under 18. Hour-long architectural walking tours of the Kennebunkport Historic District depart from the Nott House at 11 A.M. Thursday in July and August and Saturday July–mid-October. Cost is $7 per adult, free for children under 18. At the house, you can buy a guidebook for a do-it-yourself tour for $4.

Dock Square

Even if you're not a shopper, make it a point to meander through the heart of Kennebunkport's shopping district, where one-time fishing shacks have been restored and renovated into upscale shops, boutiques, galleries, and dining spots. Some shops, especially those on upper floors, offer fine harbor views. If you're willing to poke around a bit, you'll find some unusual items that make distinctive souvenirs or gifts—pottery, vintage clothing, books, specialty foods, and, yes, T-shirts.

St. Anthony's Monastery

Long ago, 35,000 Native Americans used this part of town for a summer camp. They knew a good thing. So did a group of Lithuanian Franciscan monks who in 1947 fled war-ravaged Europe and acquired the 200-acre St. Anthony's Franciscan Monastery (Beach St., Kennebunk, 207/967-2011). From 1956 to 1969, they ran a high school here. The monks still occupy the handsome Tudor great house, but the well-tended grounds (sprinkled with

© HILARY NANGLE

The walking trails at St. Anthony's Monastery provide nice views of Kennebunkport.

shrines and a recently restored sculpture created by Vytautas Jonynas for the 1964 World's Fair) are open to the public sunrise–sunset. A short path leads from the monastery area to a peaceful gazebo overlooking the Kennebunk River. No pets or bikes. Public restrooms are available. The grounds are open 6 A.M.–8:30 P.M. in summer, until 6 P.M. in winter.

RECREATION

Parks and Preserves

Thanks to a dedicated coterie of year-round and summer residents, the foresighted **Kennebunkport Conservation Trust** (KCT, www.thekennebunkportconservationtrust.org), founded in 1974, has become a nationwide model for land-trust organizations. The KCT has managed to preserve from development several hundred acres of land (including 11 small islands off Cape Porpoise Harbor), and most of this acreage is accessible to the public, especially with a sea kayak. The trust has even assumed ownership of 7.7-acre Goat Island, with its distinctive lighthouse visible from Cape Porpoise and other coastal vantage points.

VAUGHN'S ISLAND PRESERVE

To visit Vaughn's Island you'll need to do a little planning, tidewise, since the 96-acre island is about 600 feet offshore. Consult a tide calendar and aim for low tide close to the new moon or full moon (when the most water drains away). Allow yourself an hour or so before and after low tide, but no longer, or you may need a boat rescue. Wear treaded rubber boots, since the crossing is muddy and slippery with rockweed. Keep an eye on your watch and explore the ocean (east) side of the island, along the beach. It's all worth the effort, and there's a great view of Goat Island Light off to the east. From downtown Kennebunkport, take Maine Street to Wildes District Road. Continue to Shore Road (also called Turbat's Creek Road), go 0.6 mile, jog left 0.2 mile more, and park in the tiny lot at the end.

EMMONS PRESERVE

Also under Kennebunkport Conservation Trust's stewardship, the Emmons Preserve has three trails (blazed blue, yellow, and pink) meandering through 146 acres of woods and fields on the edge of Batson's River (also called Gravelly Brook). The yellow trail gives best access to the water. Fall colors here are brilliant, birdlife is abundant, and you can do a loop in half an hour. But why rush? This is a wonderful oasis in the heart of Kennebunkport. From Dock Square, take North Street to Beachwood Avenue (right turn) to Gravelly Brook Road (left turn). The trailhead is on the left.

PICNIC ROCK

About 1.5 miles up the Kennebunk River from the ocean, Picnic Rock is the centerpiece of the **Butler Preserve,** a 14-acre enclave managed by the Nature Conservancy. Well named, the rock is a great place for a picnic and a swim, but don't count on being alone. A short trail loops through the preserve. Consider bringing a canoe or kayak (or renting one) and paddle with the tide past beautiful homes and the Cape Arundel Golf Club. From Lower Village Kennebunk, take Route 35 west and hang a right onto Old Port Road. When the road gets close to the Kennebunk River, watch for a Nature Conservancy oak-leaf sign on the right. Parking is along Old Port Road; walk down through the preserve to Picnic Rock, right on the river.

Beaches

Ah, the beaches. The Kennebunks are well endowed with sand but not with parking spaces. Parking permits are required, and you need a separate pass for each town. Many lodgings provide free permits for their guests—be sure to ask when making room reservations. Or you can avoid the parking nightmare altogether by hopping aboard the Intown Trolley, which goes right by the major beaches.

The main beaches in **Kennebunk** (east to west, stretching about two miles) are 3,346-foot-long Gooch's (most popular), Kennebunk (locally called Middle or Rocks Beach), and Mother's (a smallish beach next to Lords Point, where there's also a playground).

Lifeguards are on duty at Gooch's and Mother's Beaches July–Labor Day. Ask locally about a couple of other beach options. Between mid-June and mid-September, you'll need to buy a parking permit ($15 a day, $25 a week, $50 a season) from the Kennebunk Town Hall (4 Summer St., 207/985-3675).

Kennebunkport's claim to beach fame is three-mile-long Goose Rocks Beach, one of the loveliest in the area. Parking spaces are scarce, and a permit is required. Permits ($6 per day, $25 per week, $50 per season) are available from the Kennebunkport Police Station (101 Main St., 207/967-4243), Kennebunkport Town Hall, or the chamber of commerce. (The police station is open 24 hours; other locations are not.)To reach the beach, take Route 9 from Dock Square east and north to Dyke Road (Clock Farm Corner). Turn right and continue to the end (King's Highway).

The prize for tiniest beach goes to Colony (officially Arundel) Beach, near The Colony resort complex. It's close to many Kennebunkport lodgings and an easy walk from Dock Square; no permit necessary.

Bicycling

Cape-Able Bike Shop (83 Arundel Rd., Town House Corners, Kennebunkport, 207/967-4382, www.capeablebikes.com), a local institution since 1974, has all kinds of rentals and accessories, repairs your wounded gear, sponsors Saturday-morning group rides, and provides a free area bike map and the best insider information. (The bike map is also available at the chamber of commerce.) Rentals begin around $23 per day. Delivery service is available, but the shop operates a seasonal outpost in Lower Village, next to the chamber of commerce. Also available are guided tours. The 10–15 mile Comfort Beach Tour lasts about 2.5–3 hours and costs $59 adults, $29 children 15 and younger, including a snack. A Singletrack Adventure two-hour mountain bike ride for experienced cyclists covers about 8 miles and costs $59 adults with rental, $40 without, and includes a snack.

Golf

Three 18-hole golf courses make the sport a big deal in the area. **Cape Arundel Golf Club** (19 River Rd., Kennebunkport, 207/967-3494), established in 1897, and **Webhannet Golf Club** (8 Central Ave., Kennebunk, 207/967-2061), established in 1902, are semiprivate and open to nonmembers; call for tee times at least 24 hours ahead. At Cape Arundel, where George Bush plays, no jeans or sweatpants are allowed. In nearby Arundel, **Dutch Elm Golf Course** (5 Brimstone Rd., Arundel, 207/282-9850) is a public course with rentals, pro shop, and putting greens.

Whale Watches and Lobster-Boat Cruises

Join Capt. Gary aboard the 87-foot ***Nick's Chance*** (4 Western Ave., Lower Village, Kennebunk, 207/967-5507 or 800/767-2628, www.firstchancewhalewatch.com, $48 adults, $28 children ages 3–12, $10 up to age 3) for 4.5-hour whale watches to Jeffrey's Ledge, weather permitting. The destination is the summer feeding grounds for finbacks, humpbacks, minkes, the rare blue whale, and the endangered right whale. The boat departs once or twice daily from late June to early September, weekends only spring and fall, from Performance Marine in Kennebunk Lower Village (behind Bartley's Restaurant).

Under the same ownership and departing from the same location is the 65-foot open lobster boat ***Kylie's Chance,*** which departs four times daily in July and August for 1.5-hour scenic lobster cruses; reduced schedule spring and fall. A lobstering demonstration is given on most trips, but never on the evening one. Cost is $20 adults, $15 children 3–12.

Sailing Excursions

For day sailing, the 37-foot one-ton former racing yacht ***Bellatrix*** (95 Ocean Ave., Kennebunkport, 207/590-1125, www.sailingtrips.com) charges $50 per person for a three-hour sail. The handsome 55-foot gaff-rigged schooner ***Eleanor*** (Arundel Wharf, 43 Ocean

© TOM NANGLE

Rent a canoe or kayak and paddle the Kennebunk River, but be wary of the tide.

Ave., Kennebunkport, 207/967-8809, www.gwi.net/schoonersails) heads out for two-hour sails, weather and tides willing, 1–3 times daily during the summer. Cost is $40 per person.

Canoe and Kayak Rentals and Tours

Explore the Kennebunk River by canoe or kayak. **Kennebunkport Marina** (67 Ocean Ave., Kennebunkport, 207/967-3411) rents canoes and single kayaks for $25/two hours or $45 half day; double kayaks are $45/two hours or $60 half day. Hint: Check the tide before you depart, and plan your trip to paddle with it, rather than against it.

Coastal Maine Kayak (8 Western Ave., Lower Village, Kennnebunk, 207/967-6065, www.coastalmainekayak.com) offers guided kayak tours to Cape Porpoise and on the Kennebunk and Mousam Rivers for $75 per day, including instruction and equipment but not lunch. Rental kayaks are $30 half day, $55 full day, and $300 per week.

Sportfishing

Saltwater, light tackle, and fly sportfishing are the specialties of **Lady J Sportfishing Charters** (207/985-7304, www.ladyjcharters.com). Two-hour Discover Fishing trips for families ($200) include hauling lobster traps. Inshore trips for stripers and bluefish begin at $200 for two hours. Eight-hour specialty trips for shark or groundfish are $600. Trips leave from behind Performance Marine, Route 9, Lower Village, Kennebunk.

Surfing

If you want to catch a wave, stop by **Aquaholics Surf Shop** (166 Port Rd., Kennebunk, 207/967-8650, www.aquaholicsurf.com). The shop has boards, wetsuits, and related gear for both sale and rental, and it offers lessons and surf camps.

ENTERTAINMENT

Kennebunk Parks and Recreation sponsors **Concerts in the Park,** a weekly series of free concerts 6:30–7:30 P.M. Wednesdays late June to mid-August, in Rotary Park on Water Street.

The Breakwater Inn screens free **Movies on the Lawn** Thursday evenings at 8 P.M.

Live, professional summer theater is on tap at the **Arundel Barn Playhouse** (53 Old Post Rd., Arundel, 207/985-5552, www.arundelbarnplayhouse.com), with productions staged in a renovated 1888 barn, June–September; tickets $28–39.

River Tree Arts (RTA)

The area's cultural spearhead is River Tree Arts (35 Western Ave., Kennebunk, 207/967-9120, www.rivertreearts.org), an incredibly energetic volunteer-driven organization that sponsors concerts; classes, workshops, exhibits, and educational programs throughout the year.

Events

The **Fine Living Festival** in early June celebrates art and food with exhibits, social events, food and wine tastings, celebrity chef dinners, and live music.

The first two weekends of December mark the festive **Christmas Prelude,** during which spectacular decorations adorn historic homes, candle-toting carolers stroll through the Kennebunks, stores have special sales, and Santa Claus shows up in a lobster boat.

SHOPPING

Lots of small, attractive boutiques surround **Dock Square,** the hub of Kennebunkport, so gridlock often develops in midsummer. Avoid driving through here at the height of the season. Take your time and walk, bike, or ride the local trolley-bus. This is just a sampling of the shopping opportunities.

Antiques and Art

English, European, and American furniture and architectural elements and garden accessories are just a sampling of what you'll find at **Antiques on Nine** (Rte. 9, Lower Village, Kennebunk, 207/967-0626). Another good place for browsing high-end antiques as well as home accents is **Hurlburt Designs** (Rte. 9, Lower Village, Kennebunk, 207/967-4110). More than 30 artists are represented at **Wright Gallery** (Pier Rd., Cape Porpoise, 207/967-5053).

Jean Briggs represents nearly 100 artists at her topflight **Mast Cove Galleries** (Maine St. and Mast Cove La., Kennebunkport, 207/967-3453, www.mastcove.com), in a handsome Greek Revival house near the Graves Memorial Library. Prices vary widely, so don't be surprised if you spot something affordable. The gallery often sponsors 2.5-hour evening jazz concerts in July and August ($15 donation includes light refreshments). Call for schedule.

The Gallery on Chase Hill (10 Chase Hill Rd., Kennebunkport, 207/967-0049), in the stunningly restored Captain Chase House, mounts rotating exhibits and represents a wide variety of Maine and New England artists. It's a sibling of the **Maine Art Gallery** (14 Western Ave, Kennebunkport, 207/967-0049, www.maine-art.com), which is right down the street. **Compliments** (Dock Sq., 207/967-2269) has a truly unique and fun collection of contemporary fine American crafts, with an emphasis on glass and ceramic wear.

Clothing and Gifts

Since 1968, **Port Canvas** (9 Ocean Ave., Kennebunkport, 207/985-9765 or 800/333-6788) has been turning out the best in durable cotton-canvas products. Need a new double-bottomed tote bag? It's here. Also here are golf-bag covers, belts, computer cases, day packs, and of course duffel bags.

Quilt fans should make time to visit **Mainely Quilts** (108 Summer St., Rte. 35, Kennebunk, 207/985-4250), behind the Waldo Emerson Inn. The shop has a nice selection of contemporary and antique quilts.

Most of the clothing shops clustered around Dock Square are rather pricey. Not so **Arbitrage** (28 Dock Sq., 207/967-9989), which combines designer consignment clothing with new fashions, vintage designer costume jewelry, shoes, and handbags.

All-natural beeswax bowls can be filled with sand, rocks, plants, and other natural objects at **Presence of Nature** (10 Ocean Ave., Kennebunkport, 207/604-4779).

Irresistible eye-dazzling costume jewelry, hair ornaments, handbags, lotions, cards, and other delightful finds fill every possible space at **Dannah** (123 Ocean Ave., Kennebunkport, 207/967-8640), in the Breakwater Spa building, with free customer-only parking in the rear.

Earth-Friendly Toiletries

Tom's of Maine Natural Living Store (Storer St., just off Main St., Kennebunk, 207/985-3874) is an eco-sensitive local-turned-global firm that makes soaps, toothpaste, oils, and other products. The "factory seconds" are real bargains.

ACCOMMODATIONS

Rates listed are for peak season; most stay open through Christmas Prelude.

Inns and Hotels

Graciously dominating its 11-acre spread at the mouth of the Kennebunk River, **The Colony Hotel** (140 Ocean Ave. at King's Hwy., Kennebunkport, 207/967-3331 or 800/552-2363, www.thecolonyhotel.com/maine) springs right out of a bygone era, and its distinctive cupola is an area landmark. It's had a longtime commitment to the environment, with recycling, waste-reduction, and educational programs. There's a special feeling here, with cozy corners for reading, lawns and gardens for strolling, an ocean-view swimming pool, room service, tennis privileges at the exclusive River Club, bike rentals, massage therapy, and lawn games. Doubles begin at $183, including breakfast, plus a $5 per person daily service charge. Pets are $25 per night.

The White Barn Inn and its siblings have cornered the ultra-high-end boutique inn market, with four in this category. Most renowned is the **White Barn Inn** (37 Beach Ave., Kennebunk, 207/967-2321, www.whitebarninn.com, $440–925). Also part of the empire

The Colony Hotel is a Kennebunkport landmark.

are **The Beach House Inn** (211 Beach Ave., Kennebunk, 207/967-3850, www.beachhseinn.com, $315–565), **The Breakwater Inn, Hotel, and Spa** (127 Ocean Ave., Kennebunkport, 207/967-3118, www.thebreakwaterinn.com, $269–419), **The Yachtsman Lodge and Marina** (Ocean Ave., Kennebunkport, 207/967-2511, www.yachtsmanlodge.com, $339–389), and three restaurants. Rooms in all properties have air-conditioning, phones, satellite TV, and VCR and CD players; bikes and canoes are available for guests. Rates include bountiful continental breakfasts and afternoon tea, but check out the off-season packages, especially if you wish to dine at one of the restaurants. All but the Beach House are within walking distance of Dock Square.

The White Barn Inn is the most exclusive, with five-diamond and Relais & Châteaux status. It's home to one of the best restaurants in the *country.* Many rooms have fireplaces and marble baths with separate steam showers and whirlpool tubs (you can even arrange for a butler-drawn bath). Service is impeccable, and nothing has been overlooked in terms of amenities. There's an outdoor heated European-style disappearing edge pool, where lunch is available weather permitting, and a full-service spa. For a truly away-from-it-all feeling, consider staying at one the inn's ultra-private riverfront Wharf Cottages ($700–1,500), which face Dock Square from across the river. The inn also has a Hinckley Talaria-44 available for charter.

The Beach House Inn faces Middle Beach and is a bit less formal than the White Barn, but the service is on par. It also has a two-bedroom cottage ($650). The Breakwater, at the mouth of the Kennebunk River, comprises a beautifully renovated historical inn with wrap-around porches and an adjacent more modern newly renovated building with rooms and a full-service spa; a riverside studio cottage is $599. The complex also is home to Stripers Restaurant. Finally, there's the Yachtsman, an innovative blend of a motel and bed-and-breakfast, with all rooms opening onto patios facing the river and the marina where George H. W. Bush keeps his boat.

All but two rooms at the **Cape Arundel Inn** (208 Ocean Ave., Kennebunkport, 207/967-2125, www.capearundelinn.com, $320–395) overlook crashing surf and the Bush estate. The compound comprises the shingle-style main inn building, the Rockbound motel-style building, and the Carriage House Loft, a large suite on the upper floor of the carriage house; an expanded continental breakfast buffet is included. Most rooms have fireplaces; Rockbound and Carriage House have TV. Open March–January 1. The inn's restaurant, where every table has an ocean view, earns raves for its intriguingly creative cuisine; entrées are $27–38.

The sprawling riverfront **Nonantum Resort** (95 Ocean Ave., Kennebunkport, 207/967-4050 or 800/552-5651, www.nonantumresort.com, $249–449) complex, which dates from 1884, includes a bit of everything, from simple rooms with old-fashioned Victorian decor to modern family suites with kitchenettes. Facilities include a dining room, outdoor heated pool, and docking facilities; lobster boat and sailing tours, fishing charters, and kayak rentals are available. A slew of activities are offered daily. All 115 rooms have air-conditioning, Wi-Fi, and TV; some have refrigerators. Rates include a full breakfast. The dining room is also open for dinner and, in July and August, lunch. Packages, many of which include dinner, are a good choice. Do note: Weddings take place here almost every weekend.

Bed-and-Breakfasts

Three of Kennebunkport's loveliest inns are rumored to have been owned by brothers-in-law, all of whom were sea captains. Rivaling the White Barn Inn for service, decor, amenities, and overall luxury is the three-story **Captain Lord Mansion** (Pleasant St., Kennebunkport, 207/967-3141 or 800/522-3141, www.captainlord.com, $259–499), which is one of the finest bed-and-breakfasts anywhere. And no wonder: Innkeepers Rick and Bev Litchfield have been at it since 1978, and they're never content to rest on their laurels. Each year the inn improves upon seeming perfection. If you want to be pampered and stay in a meticulously decorated and historical bed-and-breakfast with marble bathrooms (heated floors, many with double whirlpool tubs), fireplaces, original artwork, phones, TV, Wi-Fi, and air-conditioning in all rooms and even a few cedar closets, then look no further. Even breakfast is a special affair, with fresh-squeezed orange juice made from oranges flown in daily. Bicycles and beach towels and chairs are available. Afternoon treats are provided.

The elegant Federal-style **Captain Jefferds Inn** (5 Pearl St., Kennebunkport, 207/967-2311 or 800/839-6844, www.captainjefferdsinn.com, $160–366), in the historic district, provides the ambience of a real captain's house. Each of the 15 rooms and suites (11 in the main house and four more in the carriage house) have plush linens, fresh flowers, down comforters, CD players, Wi-Fi, and air-conditioning; some have fireplaces, whirlpool tubs, and other luxuries. A three-course breakfast and afternoon tea are included.

The Captain Fairfield Inn (8 Pleasant St., Kennebunkport, www.captainfairfield.com, $275–385) is perhaps the most modest architecturally of the three, but it doesn't scrimp on amenities. Rooms are divided between traditional and contemporary decor, but all have flat-screen TVs, air-conditioning, and Wi-Fi; some have gas fireplaces, double whirlpools, and rainfall showers. The lovely grounds are a fine place to retreat for a snooze in the hammock or a game of croquet. Rates include a four-course breakfast and afternoon cookies.

Hidden in a woodsy, private residential neighborhood, the lovely **Old Fort Inn** (Old Fort Ave., Kennebunkport, 207/828-3678, www.oldfortinn.com, $180–395) is the kind of place that you might not want to leave, even for touring or shopping. Once part of a Colony-style grand hotel, the stable has been renovated into elegant, spacious guest rooms, many with fireplaces and/or jetted tubs, all with fancy linens and wet bars equipped with fridge and microwave. The main building houses a huge common room and a screened porch. On the 15-acre grounds are a heated pool, tennis court, and antiques shop. Breakfast is a lavish hot-and-cold buffet. Spa services are available.

The inspiration for the **English Meadows Inn** (141 Port Rd., Lower Village, Kennebunk, 207/967-5766, www.englishmeadowsinn.com, $146–286) came from those lovely English manor homes, elegant yet comfortable. The 1860s original Greek Revival architecture was married to the Victorian Queen Anne style later in the century. Inside, the woodwork gleams; the floors, scattered with Asian-style rugs, shine; and the country comfort pieces mix with an unusual collection of Asian and English antiques, collected by the owner when living abroad. Books fill the inn's many nooks and crannies. Rooms are split between the main house, carriage house, where children are welcome, and a pet-friendly two-bedroom cottage ($146–286), a good choice for young families. Breakfast is elaborate; a cream tea is served Thursday–Saturday afternoons for $14.95.

The low-key turn-of-the-20th-century **Green Heron Inn** (126 Ocean Ave., Kennebunkport, 207/967-3315, www.greenheroninn.com, $190–215) sees many repeat guests thanks to a primo cove-side location, welcoming hosts, and to-die-for breakfasts. Ten rooms and a two-story cottage ($345) have TV, phones, and air-conditioning; some have fireplace, microwave, or refrigerator; and most have cove views. Children are welcome; some pets are accepted ($15 per night).

Neighboring the Wedding Cake House, **The Waldo Emerson Inn** (108 Summer St., Rte. 35, Kennebunk, 207/985-4250, www.waldoemersoninn.com, $145–160) has a charming colonial feel, as it should, since the main section was built in 1784. Poet Ralph Waldo Emerson spent many a summer here; it was his great-uncle's home. Three of the six attractive rooms have working fireplaces. Rates include a full breakfast. In-room massages are available. Quilters, take note: In the barn is Mainely Quilts, a well-stocked quilt shop; ask about retreats and workshops.

Motels

Patricia Mason is the 9th-generation innkeeper at **The Seaside Motor Inn** (80 Beach Ave., Kennebunk, 207/967-4461 or 800/967-4461, www.kennebunkbeach.com, $229–259), a property that has been in her family since the mid-1600s. What a location! The 22-room motel is the only truly beachfront property in the area, with a private beach for guests. Rooms are spacious, with TV, air-conditioning, and refrigerators. A continental breakfast is included in the rates.

With indoor and outdoor heated pools and whirlpools and a good-size fitness center, the **Rhumb Line Motor Lodge** (Ocean Ave., Kennebunkport, 207/967-5457 or 800/337-4862, www.rhumblinemaine.com, $149–189) is a magnet for families. It's located in a quiet residential area three miles from Dock Square and has easy access to the trolley-bus service. Fifty-nine large rooms have private balcony or patio, phones, air-conditioning, Wi-Fi, cable TV, and small refrigerators. Free continental breakfast. From late May to mid-September, weather permitting, there are nightly poolside lobster bakes. Kids 12 and under stay free. Closed in January.

Second-generation innkeepers David and Paula Reid keep the **Fontenay Terrace Motel** (128 Ocean Ave., Kennebunkport, 207/967-3556, www.fontenaymotel.com, $140–175) spotless. It borders a tidal inlet and has a private grassy and shaded lawn, perfect for retreating from the hubbub of busy Kennebunkport. Each of the eight rooms has air-conditioning, mini-fridge, microwave, Wi-Fi, cable TV, and phone; some have water views. A small beach is 300 yards away, and it's a pleasant one-mile walk to Dock Square.

The clean and simple **Cape Porpoise Motel** (12 Mills Rd., Rte. 9, Cape Porpoise, 207/967-3370, www.capeporpoisemotel.com, $129–150) is a short walk from the harbor. All rooms have TV and air-conditioning, some have kitchenettes; rates include a continental breakfast, with homemade baked goods, fresh fruit, cereals, and bagels. Also available by the week or month are efficiencies with full kitchens, phones, and one or more bedrooms.

Here's a bargain: The nonprofit **Franciscan Guest House** (28 Beach Ave., Kennebunk, 207/967-4865, www.franciscanguesthouse.com), on the grounds of the monastery, has accommodations spread among two buildings, as well as three other Tudor-style cottages. Decor is vintage 1970s and frills are few, but there are some nice amenities, including TV, air-conditioning, saltwater pool, Wi-Fi, and beach passes. Location is walking distance to the beach and Dock Square. A buffet breakfast is included in the rates, and a buffet dinner often is available. There is no daily maid service, but fresh towels are provided daily. Rooms are $89–154, and one- to three-bedroom suites are $129–279. No credit cards.

FOOD

Hours are for peak season, when reservations are advised. Call ahead September–June.

Local Flavors

All Day Breakfast (55 Western Ave., Rte. 9, Lower Village, Kennebunk, 207/967-5132, 7 A.M.–1:30 P.M. Mon.–Fri., to 2 P.M. Sat.–Sun.) is a favorite meeting spot, offering such specialties as invent-your-own omelets and crepes, Texas French toast, and the ADB sandwich. Closed mid-December–mid-January.

It's hard to choose the perfect pastry from the large selection at **Port Bakery and Café** (181 Port Rd., Kennebunk, 207/967-2263, 6 A.M.–6 P.M. daily). Hot breakfasts are also available, as are soups and sandwiches and other goodies. Eat in or outside on the deck or take it all to go.

Conveniently near the Kennebunk and Kennebunkport Chamber of Commerce, **H. B. Provisions** (15 Western Ave., Lower Village, Kennebunk, 207/967-5762, 6 A.M.–10 P.M. daily) has an excellent wine selection, along with plenty of picnic supplies, newspapers,

© HILARY NANGLE

The oceanfront Seaside Motor Inn has a private beach for guests.

and all the typical general-store inventory. It also serves breakfast and prepares hot and cold sandwiches, salads, and wraps. Open year-round.

Equal parts fancy food and wine store and gourmet café, **Cape Porpoise Kitchen** (Rte. 9, Cape Porpoise, 207/967-1150, 7 A.M.–6 P.M. daily) sells sandwiches, salads, prepared foods, desserts, and everything to go with.

While away an afternoon with a traditional English tea at the **English Meadows Inn** (141 Port Rd., Lower Village, Kennebunk, 207/967-5766, 2–4 P.M. Thurs.–Sat.). The cream tea ($14.95), including tea, scones, and sweets, is beautifully presented, served in a lovely room or perhaps the garden. Reservations required.

The **Kennebunk Farmers Market** sets up shop mid-May–mid-October in the Grove Street municipal parking lot off Route 1 (adjacent to Village Pharmacy). Hours are 8 A.M.–noon Saturday.

Family Favorites

A bit off the beaten track is **Lucas on 9** (62 Mills Rd./Rte. 9, Cape Porpoise, 207/967-0039, www.lucason9.com, noon–9 P.M. Wed.–Mon.), a family-friendly family-operated restaurant. The Lane family knows food. Chef Jonathan Lane makes everything from scratch and delivers on his mother Deborah's mission of "Good American food at affordable prices." Jonathan's travels have infused his preparations with more than a bow toward his work on Southern riverboats (Louisiana spicy crab soup, bread pudding with whiskey). There are at least six specials nightly in addition to plenty of other choices ($8–30).

Grab a stool at the counter, slip into a booth, or wait for a table at the **Wayfarer** (Pier Rd., Cape Porpoise, 207/967-8961), a casual restaurant that serves breakfast, lunch, and dinner to locals and in-the-know tourists (dinner entrées $10–19). It's open 7 A.M.–12:30 P.M. and 5–8 P.M. Tuesday–Saturday and 7 A.M.–noon Sunday. Good lobster stew; nightly dinner specials. Most choices are in the $14–19 range. No credit cards.

Burgers, pizza, sandwiches, even a turkey dinner with the trimmings—almost everything on the menu is less than $10 at **Duffy's Tavern**

& Grill (4 Main St., Kennebunk, 207/985-0050, www.duffyskennebunk.com). Extremely popular with locals, Duffy's is located inside a renovated mill in Lafayette Center. It's an inviting space with exposed beams, gleaming woodwork, brick walls, and big windows framing the Mousam River. And if you want to catch the game while you eat, big-screen high-def TVs make it easy. Open for lunch and dinner beginning at 11 A.M. daily, and serving breakfast on weekends from 7 A.M.

Casual Dining

Just west of the junction of Routes 9 and 35 is **Grissini** (27 Western Ave., Kennebunk, 207/967-2211, www.restaurantgrissini.com, 5:30–8:30 P.M. daily, to 9 P.M. Fri.–Sat.), a sibling of the White Barn Inn. Attentive service, a wood-burning oven, an inspired Tuscan menu (entrées $15–36), and a bright open-beamed space anchored by a walk-in fireplace make it an appealing spot. Pizzas are a specialty, but don't miss the capesante (pan-seared scallops). In nice weather, try for the sunken patio. Downstairs, **Grotta** serves lighter fare ($7–13). Open year-round.

The views complement the food at **Hurricane Restaurant** (29 Dock Sq., Kennebunkport, 207/967-9111, www.hurricanerestaurant.com, 11:30 A.M.–9 P.M. daily). Thanks to a Dock Square location and a dining room that literally hangs over the river, it reels in the crowds for both lunch and dinner (entrées $19–45).

Eat well and feel good about it at **Bandaloop** (2 Dock Sq., Kennebunkport, 207/967-4994, www.bandaloop.biz, 5:30–9:30 P.M. daily), a hip, vibrant restaurant where chef-owner W. Scott Lee likes to push boundaries. Lee named the restaurant for author Tom Robbins's fictional tribe that knew the secret to eternal life. Lee believes the secret is fresh, local, organic, and cruelty free. Selections vary from meats and fish to vegetarian and vegan ($17–29) prepared with creativity.

Floor-to-ceiling windows frame the Kennebunk River breakwater, providing perfect views for those indulging at **Stripers** (at the Breakwater Inn, 127 Ocean Ave., Kennebunkport, 207/967-5333), another White Barn Inn sibling, where fish and seafood are the specialties. The emphasis on fish is also accented by a saltwater tank with coral reef and exotic fish. Most entrées are in the $18–30 range. A lighter menu is served in the bar. Dress is casual. Valet parking is available. It's open noon–2 P.M. and 5–9 P.M. daily; 11 A.M.–2 P.M. for Sunday brunch.

Fancy to Fine Dining

Every table at the **Cape Arundel Inn** (208 Ocean Ave., Kennebunkport, 207/967-2125, www.capearundelinn.com) has a knockout view of crashing surf, and the food matches the view. White-clothed tables topped with cobalt blue glassware add to the inn's casual yet elegant feel. Local artwork covers the walls. Chef Rich Lemoine's menu emphasizes fish and seafood in classic preparations, all prepared and served with care. Prices range $27–39. Open for dinner daily (closed Mon. off season).

Fusion cuisine reigns at **On the Marsh** (46 Western Ave./Rte. 9, Lower Village, Kennebunk, 207/967-2299, www.onthemarsh.com), a restored barn overlooking marshlands leading to Kennebunk Beach. Entrées range $18–28. The space is infused with arts and antiques and European touches, courtesy of owner Denise Rubin, an interior designer with a passion for the continent. Dining locations include the two-level dining area and an "owner's table" in the kitchen; there's also a bar menu. Quiet piano music adds to the elegant but unstuffy ambience on weekends; service is attentive. Reservations are essential in midsummer. It's open for dinner 5:30–9:30 P.M. daily in season. Closed January.

Both the view and the food are outstanding at **Pier 77** (77 Pier Rd., Cape Porpoise, 207/967-8500, www.pier77restaurant.com, 11:30 A.M.–2:30 P.M. and 5–9 P.M. daily). Chef Peter and his wife, Kate, have created an especially welcoming restaurant, where the menu varies from paella to seafood mixed grill (entrées $17–32). Frequent live entertainment provides nice background and complements the views over Cape Porpoise Harbor, with lobster boats hustling to and fro. Reservations are advisable. Practically hidden downstairs is **The Ramp Bar and Grille** (11:30 A.M.–9 P.M. daily), with lighter fare as well as the full menu and a sports-pub decor.

Destination Dining

One of Maine's biggest splurges and worth every penny is **The White Barn Inn** (37 Beach Ave., Kennebunkport, 207/967-2321, www.whitebarninn.com, 6–9 P.M. Mon.–Thurs., 5:30–9:15 P.M. Fri.–Sun.), with haute cuisine and haute prices, in a haute-rustic barn. In summer, don't be surprised to run into members of the senior George Bush clan (probably at the back window table). Soft piano music accompanies impeccable service and chef Jonathan Cartwright's outstanding four-course (plus extras) fixed-price menu ($95 pp). Reservations are essential—well ahead during July and August—and you'll need a credit card (cancel 24 hours ahead or you'll have a charge). No jeans or sneakers; jackets required. It's New England's only five-star, five-diamond, Relais Gourmand restaurant. Closed most of January.

Lobster and Clams

Nunan's Lobster Hut (9 Mills Rd., Cape Porpoise, 207/967-4362, 5 P.M.–close daily) is an institution. Sure, other places might have better views, but this casual dockside eatery with indoor and outdoor seating has been serving lobsters since 1953.

Adjacent to the bridge connecting Kennebunkport's Dock Square to Kennebunk's Lower Village is another time-tested classic, **The Clam Shack** (Rte. 9, Kennebunkport, 207/967-2560, www.theclamshack.net). The tiny take-out stand serves perhaps the state's best lobster rolls, jam-packed with meat and available with either butter or mayo, and dee-lish fried clams. It opens at 11 A.M. daily May–October for lunch and dinner.

Lobster and crab rolls are the specialties at

© HILARY NANGLE

The best fried clams come from this take-out stand just off Dock Square.

Port Lobster (122 Ocean Ave., Kennebunkport, 207/967-2081, www.portlobster.com), a fresh fish store located just northeast of Dock Square.

INFORMATION AND SERVICES

Information

The **Kennebunk and Kennebunkport Chamber of Commerce** (17 Western Ave., Rte. 9, Lower Village, Kennebunk, 207/967-0857, www.visitthekennebunks.com) produces an excellent area guide to accommodations, restaurants, area maps, bike maps, tide calendars, recreation, and beach parking permits.

Check out **Louis T. Graves Memorial Public Library** (18 Maine St., Kennebunkport, 207/967-2778, www.graves.lib.me.us) or **Kennebunk Free Library** (112 Main St., 207/985-2173, www.kennebunklibrary.org), which has a café serving light fare.

Public Restrooms

Public toilets are at Gooch's and Mother's Beaches and at St. Anthony's Monastery, the chamber of commerce building (17 Western Ave.), and at the chamber's Dock Square Hospitality Center.

GETTING THERE AND AROUND

Amtrak's **Downeaster** (800/872-7245, www.thedowneaster.com) connects Boston's North Station with Portland, Maine, with stops in Wells, Saco, and Old Orchard Beach (seasonal).

From Memorial Day to mid-October, the **Intown Trolley** (207/967-3686, www.intowntrolley.com) operates a narrated sightseeing tour throughout Kennebunk and Kennebunkport, originating in Dock Square and making regular stops at beaches and other attractions. The entire route takes about 45 minutes, with the driver providing a hefty dose of local history and gossip. Seats are park bench–style. An all-day ticket is $15 adults, $5 children 3–17. You can get on or off at any stop. The trolley operates hourly 10 A.M.–5 P.M. in July and August, to 4 P.M. in spring and fall.

The **Shoreline Explorer Kennebunk Shuttle** (www.shorelineexplorer.com) circulates hourly between Grove Street parking lot, Stop and Shop, Landing Store, Lower Village, and the beaches 10 A.M.–10:30 P.M. late June–Labor Day. It connects with the Shoreline and Intown trolleys. Fee is $1 one way, $3 per day, or $10 for a 12-ride pass; children 18 and younger ride free.

Old Orchard Beach Area

Seven continuous miles of white sand beach have been drawing vacation-oriented folks for generations to the area stretching from Camp Ellis in Saco to Pine Point in Scarborough. Cottage colonies and condo complexes dominate at the extremities, but the center of activity has always been and remains **Old Orchard Beach.**

In its heyday, Old Orchard Beach's pier reached far out into the sea, huge resort hotels lined the sands, and wealthy Victorian folk (including Rose Fitzgerald and Joe Kennedy, who met on these sands in the days when men strolled around in dress suits and women toted parasols) came each summer to see and be seen.

Storms and fires have taken their toll through the years, and the grand resorts have been replaced by endless motels, many of which display *Nous parlons Français* signs to welcome the masses of French Canadians who arrive each summer. They're joined by young families, who come for the sand and surf, and T-shirted and body-pierced young pleasure seekers, who come for the nightlife. (You'd better like people if you stop here, because the population expands from about 8,000 in winter to about 100,000 in midsummer.)

Although some residents are pushing gentrification, and a few projects are moving things in that direction, Old Orchard Beach remains somewhat honky-tonk, and most of its visitors would have it no other way. French fries, cotton candy, and beach-accessories shops line the downtown, and as you get closer to the pier, you pass arcades and amusement parks. There's not a kid on earth who wouldn't have fun in Old Orchard—even if some parents might find it all a bit much.

Much more sedate are the villages on the fringes. The **Ocean Park** section of Old Orchard, at the southwestern end of town, was established in 1881 as a religious summer-cottage community. It still offers interdenominational services and vacation Bible school, but it also has an active cultural association that sponsors concerts, Chautauqua-type lectures, films, and other events throughout the summer. All are open to the public.

South of that is **Camp Ellis.** Begun as a small

© HILARY NANGLE

Old Orchard Beach's pier, although not as long as it once was, still stretches over the beach toward the sea.

fishing village named after early settler Thomas Ellis, Camp Ellis is crowded with longtime summer homes that are in a constant battle with the sea. A nearly mile-long granite jetty—designed to keep silt from clogging the Saco River—has taken the blame for massive beach erosion since constructed. But the jetty is a favorite spot for wetting a line (no fishing license needed) and for panoramic views off toward Wood Island Light (built in 1808) and Biddeford Pool. Camp Ellis Beach is open to the public, with lifeguards on duty in midsummer. Parking—scarce on hot days—is $10 a day.

As you head north from Old Orchard you'll pass **Pine Point,** another longtime community of vacation homes. Services are few and parking is $10 a day.

Most folks get to Old Orchard by passing through **Saco** and **Biddeford,** which have long been upstairs/downstairs sister cities, with wealthy mill owners living in Saco and their workers (and workplaces) in Biddeford. But even those personalities have always been split—congested, commercial Route 1 is part of Saco, and the exclusive enclave of Biddeford Pool is, of course, in below-stairs Biddeford. Saco still has an attractive downtown, with boutiques and stunning homes on Main Street and beyond.

Blue-collar Biddeford is working hard to change its mill-town image. It's home to the magnificent Biddeford City Theater and the University of New England, and as a Main Street community it's getting a much-needed sprucing up. New shops and restaurants are balancing the numerous thrift shops downtown, and artisans and woodworkers are filling vacant mills. Another Biddeford hallmark is its Franco-American tradition, thanks to the French-speaking workers who sustained the textile and shoemaking industries in the 19th century.

SIGHTS

Saco Museum

Founded in 1866, the Saco Museum (371 Main St., Saco, 207/283-3861, www.dyerlibrarysacomuseum.org, noon–4 P.M. Tues.–Thurs. and Sun. June–Dec., to 8 P.M. Fri., 10 A.M.–4 P.M. Sat., $4 adults, $3 seniors, $2 students/children 6 and older) rotates selections from its outstanding collection, including 18th- and 19th-century paintings, furniture, and other household treasures. Lectures, workshops, and concerts are also part of the annual schedule. Admission is free after 4 P.M. Friday.

Wood Island Lighthouse

The all-volunteer Friends of Wood Island Light (207/286-3229, www.woodislandlighthouse.org) are restoring Maine's second-oldest lighthouse, which was commissioned by president Thomas Jefferson, built in 1808 (reconstructed in 1858) on 35-acre Wood Island, and abandoned in 1986. The Friends offer guided tours of the two-story keeper's house and 42-foot-tall stone tower, relating tales of former keepers and their families to bring the site to life. You can even climb the 60 stairs to the tower's lantern room for splendid views. The roughly two-hour tour departs from Vine's Landing, in Biddeford Pool. Once on-island, it's about a half-mile walk to the site. Reservations are accepted within one week of tour date; see the website or call for current schedule. Tours are by donation, with a minimum of $10 per person recommended.

ENTERTAINMENT

Every Thursday late June–Labor Day **free concerts** are staged in Old Orchard's Memorial Park at 6 P.M., followed by **fireworks** set off by the pier at 9:45 P.M.

Family concerts and other performances are staged at the outdoor **Seaside Pavilion** (Union Ave. and 6th St., 207/934-2024, www.oobpavilion.org).

Live music, concerts by nationally recognized performers, dance parties, and comedy nights are all staged at **The Landing at Pine Point** (353 Point Point Rd., Scarborough, 207/774-4527, www.thelandingatpinepoint.com).

Ocean Park's **Temple,** a 19th-century octagon that seats 800-plus, is the venue for Sunday-night concerts (7:30 P.M., $10 adults) and many other programs throughout the summer.

Designed by noted architect John Calvin Stevens in 1896, the 500-seat National Historic Register **City Theater** (205 Main St., Biddeford, 207/282-0849, www.citytheater.org) in Biddeford has been superbly restored, and acoustics are excellent even when Eva Gray, the resident ghost, mixes it up backstage. A respected community theater group mounts a winter drama season and showcases other talent throughout the year.

A rainy day godsend, Saco's new in 2009 **IMAX Theater** (779 Portland Rd./Rte. 1, Saco, 207/282-6234, www.cinemagicmovies.com) has digital sound, stadium seating, a restaurant, and online ticketing.

EVENTS

La Kermesse (meaning the fair or the festival) is Biddeford's summer highlight, when nearly 50,000 visitors pour into town on the last full weekend in June (Thurs.–Sun.) to celebrate the town's Franco-American heritage. Local volunteers go all out to plan block parties, a parade, games, carnival, live entertainment, and traditional dancing. Then there's *la cuisine franco-américaine;* you can fill up on *boudin, creton, poutine, tourtière, tarte au saumon,* and crepes (although your arteries may rebel).

The **Biddeford Art Walk** (www.biddefordartwalk.com) takes place the last Friday of the month March–December.

In July, the parishioners of St. Demetrios Greek Orthodox Church (186 Bradley St., Saco, 207/284-5651) go all out to mount the annual **Greek Heritage Festival,** a three-day extravaganza of homemade Greek food, traditional Greek music and dancing, and a craft fair. Be sure to tour the impressive $1.5 million domed church building.

The beaches come to life in July with the annual **parade and Sandcastle Contest** in Ocean Park.

One weekend in mid-August, Old Orchard Beach's **Beach Olympics** is a family festival of games, exhibitions, and music benefiting Maine's Special Olympics program.

RECREATION

Parks and Preserves

Saco Bay Trails (www.sacobaytrails.org), a local land trust, has produced a very helpful trail guide that includes the Saco Heath, the East Point Sanctuary, and more than a dozen other local trails. The Cascade Falls trail, for example, is a half-mile stroll ending at a waterfall. Copies are available for $10 at a number of Biddeford and Saco locations (including the Dyer Library) or from Saco Bay Trails. Trail information is also on the organization's website.

EAST POINT SANCTUARY

Owned by Maine Audubon (207/781-2330, www.maineaudubon.org), the 30-acre East Point Sanctuary is a splendid preserve at the eastern end of Biddeford Pool. Crashing surf, beach roses, bayberry bushes, and offshore Wood Island Light are all features of the two-part perimeter trail here, which skirts the exclusive Abenakee Club's golf course. Allow at

AMUSEMENT PARKS AND AMUSING PLACES

If you've got kids or just love amusement parks, you'll find Maine's best in the Old Orchard area, where sand and sun just seem to complement arcades and rides perfectly.

The biggie is **Funtown/Splashtown USA** (774 Portland Rd./Rte. 1, Saco, 207/284-5139 or 800/878-2900, www.funtownsplashtownusa.com). Ride Maine's only wooden roller coaster; fly down New England's longest and tallest log flume ride; free fall 200 feet on Dragon's Descent; get wet and go wild riding speed slides, tunnel slides, raft slides, and river slides or splashing in the pool. Add a huge kiddie ride section, games, food, and other activities for a full day of family fun. Funtown opens weekends in early May, Splashtown in mid-June; everything's up and running daily late June–Labor Day, when Funtown is open 10 A.M.–9 P.M., to 10 P.M. Saturday, and Splashtown 10 A.M.–6 P.M. Ticketing options vary by activities included and height, ranging $22–35 Big (48 inches and taller), $18–26 Little (38–48 inches tall) and Senior (age 60+), and free for kids less than 38 inches tall.

Three miles north of Funtown/Splashtown USA, **Aquaboggan Water Park** (980 Portland Rd./Rte. 1, Saco, 207/282-3112, www.aquabogganwaterpark.com, 10 A.M.–6 P.M. daily late June–Labor Day) is wet and wild, with such stomach turners as the Yankee Ripper, the Suislide, and the Stealth, with an almost-vertical drop of 45 feet – enough to accelerate to 30 mph on the descent. Wear a bathing suit that won't abandon you in the rough-and-tumble. Also, if you wear glasses, safety straps and plastic lenses are required. Besides all the water stuff, there are mini-golf, an arcade, go-karts, and bumper boats. A day pass for all pools, slides, and mini-golf is $20 (4 feet and taller), $16 (under 4 feet tall), $5 (under 38 inches tall). Mondays are $12 general admission days. A $30 superpass also includes two go-kart rides and unlimited bumper-boat rides.

The biggest beachfront amusement park, **Palace Playland** (1 Old Orchard St., Old Orchard, 207/934-2001, www.palaceplayland.com) has more than 25 rides and attractions packed into four acres, including a giant water slide, fun house, bumper cars, Ferris wheel, roller coaster, and a 24,000-square-foot arcade with more than 200 games. For a bird's-eye view of the area, ride the 75-foot-high gondola Sunwheel. Rev up the action on two roller coasters, one with a five-story drop, both with high-speed twisting turns. Kiddie Land has more than a dozen rides, including a fun house and a splashing whale. An unlimited pass is $28.95 per day; a kiddie pass good for all two-ticket rides is $21.95; two-day, season, and single tickets are available. Open Memorial Day–Labor Day.

Palace Playland has been keeping kids happy for generations.

The Old Orchard Pier, jutting 475 feet into the ocean from downtown, is a mini-mall of shops, arcades, and fast-food outlets. Far longer when it was built in 1898, it's been lopped off gradually by fires and storms. The current incarnation has been here since the late 1970s.

least an hour; even in fog, the setting is dramatic. During spring and fall migrations, it's one of southern Maine's prime birding locales, so you'll have plenty of company if you show up then, and the usual streetside parking may be scarce. It's poorly signposted (perhaps deliberately?), so here are the directions: From Route 9 (Main St.) in downtown Biddeford, take Route 9/208 (Pool Rd.) southeast about five miles to the Route 208 turnoff to Biddeford Pool. Go 0.6 mile on Route 208 (Bridge Rd.), and then left onto Mile Stretch Road. Continue to Lester B. Orcutt Boulevard, turn left, and go to the end.

THE HEATH

Owned by the Nature Conservancy, 870-acre Saco Heath Preserve is the nation's southernmost "raised coalesced bog," where peat accumulated through eons into two above-water dome shapes that eventually merged into a single natural feature. A bit of esoterica: It's the home of the rare Hessel's hairstreak butterfly. Pick up a map at the parking area and follow the mile-long self-guided trail through the woods and then into the heath via a boardwalk. Best time to come is early–mid-October, when the heath and woodland colors are positively brilliant and insects are on the wane. You're likely to see deer and perhaps even spot a moose. The preserve entrance is on Route 112, Buxton Road, two miles west of I-95.

FERRY BEACH STATE PARK

When the weather's hot, arrive early at Ferry Beach State Park (Bay View Rd., off Rte. 9, Saco, 207/283-0067, $6 adults, $2 seniors, $1 children 5–11), a pristine beach backed by dune grass on Saco Bay. In the 117-acre park are changing rooms, restrooms, lifeguard, picnic tables, and five easy interconnected nature trails winding through woodlands, marshlands, and dunes. (Later in the day, keep the insect repellent handy.) It's open daily late May–late September, but accessible all year. (Trail markers are removed in winter.)

Golf

Opened in 1922 as a nine-hole course, the **Biddeford-Saco Country Club** (101 Old Orchard Rd., Saco, 207/282-5883) added a back nine in 1987 (toughest hole on the par-71 course is the 11th). Tee times not usually needed. Fees are moderate.

Covering more than 300 acres is the challenging 18-hole, par-71 **Dunegrass Golf Club** (200 Wild Dunes Way, Old Orchard Beach, 207/934-4513 or 800/521-1029). Tee times are essential. Greens fees are a bit steep. The sprawling modern clubhouse has a restaurant and pro shop.

Sea Kayaking

Gone with the Wind (Yates St., Biddeford Pool, 207/283-8446, www.gwtwonline.com) offers two tours, afternoon and sunset, with prices varying with the number of people on the tour (for two people it's about $85 pp). Wetsuits are supplied. The most popular trip is to Beach Island. Also available are rentals ($40 half day, $60 full day).

Surfing

A seasonal branch of **Aquaholics Surf Shop** (www.aquaholicsurf.com) rents surfboards, bodyboards, wetsuits, and related gear from a kiosk next to the pier and Palace Playland.

ACCOMMODATIONS

The area has hundreds of beds—mostly in motel-style lodgings. The chamber of commerce is the best resource for motels, cottages, and the area's more than 3,000 campsites.

The Old Orchard Beach Inn (6 Portland Ave., Old Orchard Beach, 207/934-5834 or 877/700-6624, www.oldorchardbeachinn.com, $135–200) was rescued from ruin by owner Steve Cecchetti and opened in summer 2000. Built in 1730, and most recently known as the Staples Inn, the National Historic Register building has 18 antiques-filled rooms with air-conditioning, phones, and TV. Continental breakfast is included in the rates; a two-bedroom suite is $425–450. Open all year.

Practically next door is **The Atlantic Birches Inn** (20 Portland Ave., Rte. 98, Old Orchard Beach, 207/934-5295 or 888/934-5295, www.atlanticbirches.com, $121–141), with 10 air-conditioned guest rooms in a Victorian house and separate cottage. Breakfast is hearty continental, and there's a swimming pool. The beach is an easy walk. It's open all year, but call ahead off-season.

FOOD

Old Orchard Beach

Dining is not Old Orchard's strong point. Nicest (although service and quality are inconsistent) is **Joseph's by the Sea** (55 W. Grand Ave., Old Orchard Beach, 207/934-5044, www.josephsbythesea.com, 7–11 A.M. and 5–9 P.M. daily), a quiet shorefront restaurant amid all the hoopla. Request a table on the screened patio. The menu—French with a dash of Maine—has entrées in the $18–30 range. Reservations advisable in midsummer.

Camp Ellis

Two well-seasoned family restaurants service Camp Ellis. At **Huot's Seafood Restaurant** (Camp Ellis Beach, Saco, 207/282-1642, www.huotsseafoodrestaurant.com, 11:30 A.M.–9 P.M. Tues.–Sun.), under third-generation management, the menu is huge, portions are large, and prices are reasonable. It's a good value for fresh seafood.

Wormwood's Restaurant (16 Bay Ave., Camp Ellis Beach, Saco, 207/282-9679, 11:30 A.M.–9 P.M. daily), next to the stone jetty, still draws the crowds and keeps its loyal clientele happy with ample portions and $6–16 entrées. Cajun-style seafood is a specialty.

Saco

Craving fast-ish food? The Camire family operates Maine's best home-grown option, **Rapid Ray's** (189 Main St., 207/283-4222, www.rapidrays.biz, 11 A.M.–12:30 A.M. Mon.–Thurs., to 1 A.M. Fri.–Sat., noon–10 P.M. Sun.). Burgers, dogs, and fried foods are the specialty at the standing-room-only joint.

For more leisurely dining, book a reservation at **Mia's** (17 Pepperell Square, Saco, 207/284-6427, www.miasatpepperellsquare.com, 5–9 P.M. daily), where chef-owner Steve Rogers excels at creating classic fare without fuss. Dinner entrées, such as shrimp and sausage fettuccini and seared duck breast, run $17–25.

Biddeford/Biddeford Pool

For a town grounded in Franco-American culture, Biddeford has an expanding array of inexpensive ethnic choices, including a few that garner praise far beyond city limits: For well-prepared Indian cuisine, seek out **Jewel of India** (26 Alfred St., 207/282-5600, 11 A.M.–10 P.M. Mon.–Sat., 4–10 P.M. Sun.). If you're craving pho and Vietnamese coffee, head into **Que Huong** (49 Main St., 207/571-8050, 11 A.M.–8 P.M. Mon.–Sat.), a tiny and very inexpensive Vietnamese restaurant.

Buffleheads (122 Hills Beach Rd., 207/284-6000, www.buffleheadsrestaurant.com, 11:30 A.M.–2 P.M. and 5–8:30 P.M. daily) is a family dining find with spectacular ocean views. Ray and Karen Wieczoreck opened the restaurant in 1994 and have built a strong local following through the years. The kids can munch on pizza, burgers, spaghetti, and other favorites while adults savor well-prepared seafood with a homestyle spin or landlubber classics. Lobster pie and a turkey dinner with all the trimmings are both perennial favorites. Prices range $7–26. It's closed Monday off-season. Hills Beach Road branches off Route 9 at the University of New England campus.

Take your lobster or fried seafood dinner to an oceanfront picnic table on the grassy lawn behind **F. O. Goldthwaite's** (3 Lester B. Orcott Blvd., Biddeford Pool, 207/284-8872, 11 A.M.–7:30 P.M. daily), an old-fashioned general store. Salads, fried seafood, sandwiches, and kid-friendly fare round out the menu.

INFORMATION AND SERVICES

Sources of tourist information are **Biddeford-Saco Chamber of Commerce and Industry**

(110 Main St., Saco, 207/282-1567, www.biddefordsacochamber.org), **Old Orchard Beach Chamber of Commerce** (1st St., Old Orchard Beach, 207/934-2500 or 800/365-9386, www.oldorchardbeachmaine.com), and **Ocean Park Association** (207/934-9068, www.oceanpark.org).

The **Dyer Library** (371 Main St., Saco, 207/282-3031, www.sacomuseum.org), next door to the Saco Museum, attracts scads of genealogists to its vast Maine history collection. Also check out **Libby Memorial Library** (Staples St., Old Orchard Beach, 207/934-4351, www.ooblibrary.org).

GETTING THERE

Amtrak's **Downeaster** (800/872-7245, www.thedowneaster.com) connects Boston's North Station with Portland, Maine, with stops in Wells, Saco, and Old Orchard Beach (seasonal).

GETTING AROUND

Bus and Trolley

The **Biddeford-Saco-Old Orchard Beach Transit Committee** (207/282-5408, www.shuttlebus-zoom.com) operates three systems that make getting around simple. Between late June and Labor Day, the **Old Orchard Beach Trolley** operates two routes on a regular schedule, connecting restaurants and campgrounds. You can flag it down anywhere en route. Service begins at 10 A.M. and ends at midnight. Cost is $1 per ride; children under five ride free. **ShuttleBus Local Service** provides frequent weekday and less-frequent weekend service (except national holidays) between Biddeford, Saco, and Old Orchard Beach. One-way fare is $1.25 ages five and older, exact change required. **ShuttleBus InterCity Service** connects Biddeford, Saco, and Old Orchard with Portland, South Portland, and Scarborough. Fares vary by zones, topping at $5 for anyone over five.

GREATER PORTLAND

Whenever national magazines highlight the 10 best places to live, Greater Portland often makes the list. The very things that make the area so popular with residents make it equally attractive to visitors. Small in size, but big in heart, Greater Portland entices visitors with the staples—lighthouses, lobster, and L. L. Bean—but wows them with everything else it offers. It's the state's cultural hub, with performing-arts centers, numerous festivals, and varied museums; it's also a dining destination, with nationally recognized chefs as well as an amazing assortment and variety of everyday restaurants; and despite its urban environment, it has a mind-boggling amount of recreational opportunities. No wonder the National Heritage Trust named it a Distinctive Destination.

Portland's population hovers around 65,000, but when the suburbs are included, it climbs to nearly a quarter of a million souls, making it Maine's largest city, by far. Take a swing through the bedroom communities of Scarborough, Cape Elizabeth, and South Portland, and you'll better understand the area's popularity: easily accessible parks, beaches, rocky ledges, and lighthouses, all minutes from downtown, and a slew of ferry-connected islands dotting Casco Bay. Head north through suburban Falmouth and Yarmouth and you'll arrive in Freeport, home of mega-retailer L. L. Bean. En route, you'll still see the vestiges of the region's heritage: sailboats and lobster boats, traps and buoys piled on lawns or along driveways, and, tucked here and there, farms with farmstands brimming with fresh produce.

HIGHLIGHTS

The Old Port: Plan to spend at least a couple of hours browsing the shops, dining, and enjoying the energy of this restored historic district (page 79).

Portland Museum of Art (PMA): This museum houses works by masters such as Winslow Homer, John Marin, Andrew Wyeth, Edward Hopper, and Marsden Hartley, as well as works by Monet, Picasso, and Renoir (page 82).

Victoria Mansion: Visit one of the most richly decorated dwellings of its period remaining in the country (page 82).

Portland Observatory: Climb the 103 steps to the orb deck of the only remaining maritime signal tower on the eastern seaboard, and you'll be rewarded with views from the White Mountains to Casco Bay's islands (page 83).

Portland Head Light: Commissioned by president George Washington, this lighthouse is fabulously sited on the rocky ledges of Cape Elizabeth (page 85).

Casco Bay Tour: Take a three-hour tour on the mail boat, which stops briefly at five islands en route (page 87).

Lobstering Cruise: Go out on a working lobster boat in Portland Harbor, see the sights, and perhaps return with a lobster for dinner (page 96).

L. L. Bean: The empire's flagship store is in Freeport, and no trip to this shopping mecca is complete without a visit (page 107).

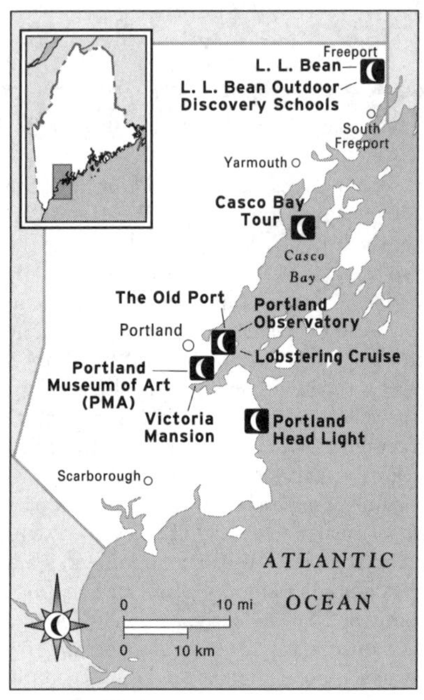

LOOK FOR [symbol] TO FIND RECOMMENDED SIGHTS, ACTIVITIES, DINING, AND LODGING.

L. L. Bean Outdoor Discovery Schools: Don't miss the opportunity for an inexpensive introduction to a new sport (page 111).

Greater Portland also marks a transitional point on Maine's coastline. The long sand beaches of the Southern Coast begin to give way to a different coastline, one dotted with islands and edged with a jumble of rocks and ledges interrupted by rivers and coves.

While it's tempting to dismiss Portland in favor of seeking the Real Maine elsewhere along the coast, the truth is, the Real Maine is here. And while Portland alone provides plenty to keep a visitor busy, it's also an excellent base for day trips to places such as the Kennebunks, Freeport, Brunswick, and Bath, where more of that Real Maine flavor awaits.

PLANNING YOUR TIME

July and August are the most popular times to visit, but Greater Portland is a year-round destination. Spring truly arrives by mid-May, when most summer outfitters begin operations at least on weekends. September is perhaps the loveliest month of the year weatherwise, and by mid-October those fabled New England maples are turning crimson.

To do the region justice, you'll want to spend at least three or four days here, more if your plans call for using Greater Portland as a base for day trips to more distant points. You can easily kill two days in downtown Portland alone, what with all the shops, museums, historical sites, waterfront, and neighborhoods to explore. If you're staying in town and are an avid walker, you won't need a car to get to the intown must-see sights.

You will need a car to reach beyond the city. Allow a full day for a leisurely tour through South Portland and Cape Elizabeth and on to Prouts Neck in Scarborough.

Rabid shoppers should either stay in Freeport or allow at least a day for L. L. Bean and the 100 or so outlets in its shadow. If you're traveling with a supershopper, don't despair. Freeport has parks and preserves that are light years removed from the frenzy of its downtown, and the fishing village of South Freeport offers seaworthy pleasures.

HISTORY

Portland's downtown, a crooked-finger peninsula projecting into Casco Bay and today defined vaguely by I-295 at its "knuckle," was named Machigonne (Great Neck) by the Wabanaki, the Native Americans who held sway when English settlers first arrived in 1632. Characteristically, the Brits renamed the region Falmouth (it included present-day Falmouth, Portland, South Portland, Westbrook, and Cape Elizabeth) and the peninsula Falmouth Neck, but it was 130 years before they secured real control of the area. Anglo-French squabbles, spurred by the governments' conflicts in Europe, drew in the Wabanaki from Massachusetts to Nova Scotia. Falmouth was only one of the battlegrounds, and it was a fairly minor one. Relative calm resumed in the 1760s, only to be broken by the stirrings of rebellion centered on Boston. When Falmouth's citizens expressed support for the incipient revolution, the punishment was a 1775 naval onslaught that wiped out 75 percent of the houses—a debacle that created a decade-long setback. In 1786, Falmouth Neck became Portland, a thriving trading community where shipping flourished until the 1807 imposition of the Embargo Act. Severing trade and effectively shutting down Portland Harbor for a year and a half, the legislation did more harm to America's fledgling colonies than to the French and British it was designed to punish.

In 1820, when Maine became a state, Portland was named its capital. The city became a crucial transportation hub with the arrival of the railroad. The Civil War was barely a blip in Portland's history, but the year after it ended, the city suffered a devastating blow: exuberant Fourth of July festivities in 1866 sparked a conflagration that virtually leveled the city. The Great Fire spared only the Portland Observatory and a chunk of the West End. Evidence of the city's Victorian rebirth remains today in many downtown neighborhoods.

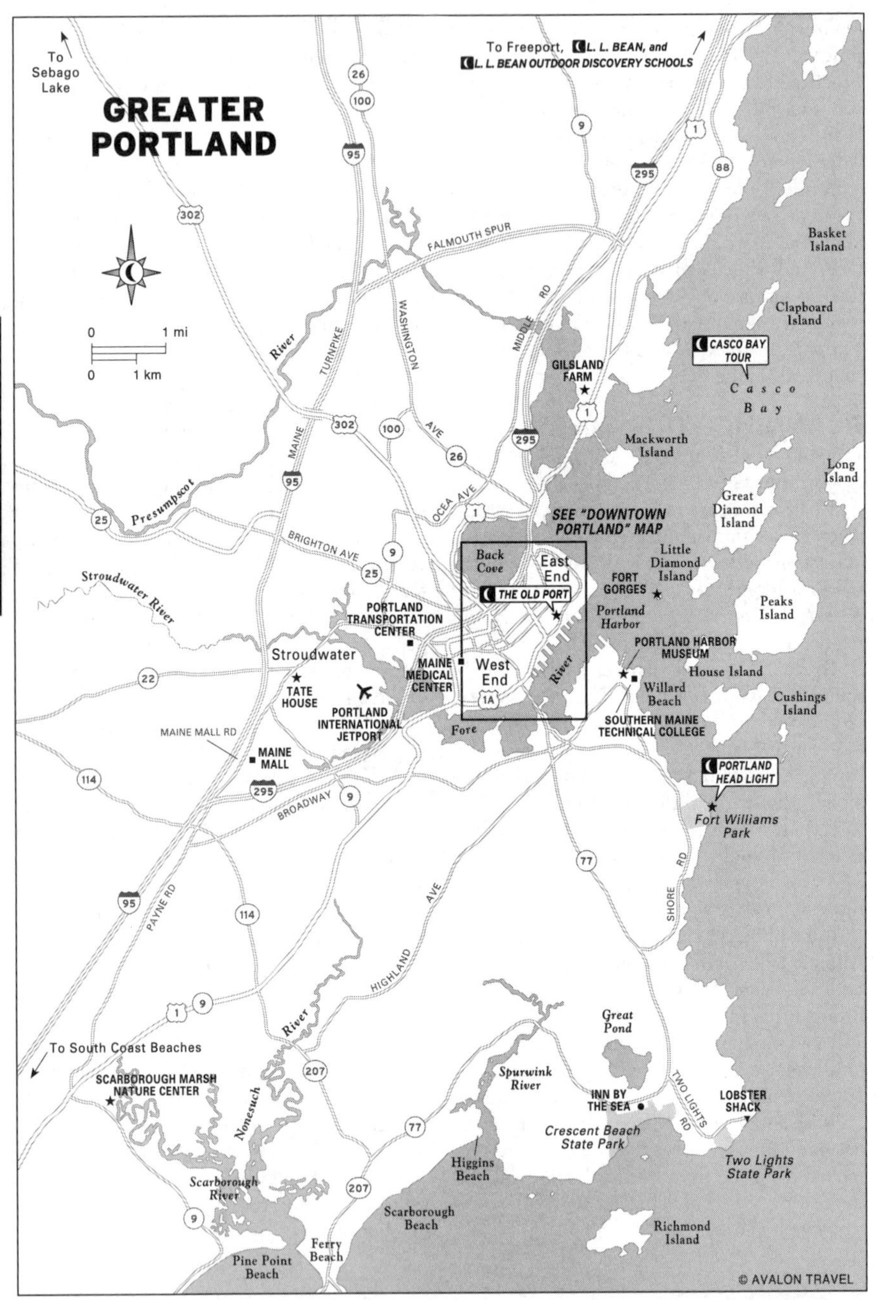
GREATER PORTLAND
To Sebago Lake
To Freeport, L. L. BEAN, and L. L. BEAN OUTDOOR DISCOVERY SCHOOLS
0 1 mi
0 1 km
FALMOUTH SPUR
WASHINGTON AVE
MAINE TURNPIKE
MIDDLE RD
Presumpscot River
BRIGHTON AVE
OCEAN AVE
Stroudwater River
Stroudwater
GILSLAND FARM
CASCO BAY TOUR
Casco Bay
Basket Island
Clapboard Island
Mackworth Island
Long Island
Great Diamond Island
Little Diamond Island
Peaks Island
House Island
Cushings Island
SEE "DOWNTOWN PORTLAND" MAP
Back Cove
East End
THE OLD PORT
FORT GORGES
Portland Harbor
PORTLAND HARBOR MUSEUM
Willard Beach
SOUTHERN MAINE TECHNICAL COLLEGE
PORTLAND TRANSPORTATION CENTER
MAINE MEDICAL CENTER
West End
Fore River
TATE HOUSE
PORTLAND INTERNATIONAL JETPORT
MAINE MALL RD
MAINE MALL
BROADWAY
PORTLAND HEAD LIGHT
Fort Williams Park
SHORE RD
PAYNE RD
HIGHLAND AVE
To South Coast Beaches
SCARBOROUGH MARSH NATURE CENTER
Nonesuch River
Scarborough River
Spurwink River
Great Pond
INN BY THE SEA
TWO LIGHTS RD
LOBSTER SHACK
Crescent Beach State Park
Two Lights State Park
Higgins Beach
Scarborough Beach
Richmond Island
Ferry Beach
Pine Point Beach
© AVALON TRAVEL

After World War II, Portland slipped into decline for several years, but that is over. The city's waterfront revival began in the 1970s and continues today, despite commercial competition from South Portland's Maine Mall; Congress Street has blossomed as an arts and retail district; public green space is increasing; and an influx of immigrants is changing the city's cultural makeup. With the new century, Portland is on a roll.

Portland

Often compared to San Francisco (an oft-cited, unchallenged, but never verified statistic boasts that it vies with San Francisco for the title of most restaurants per capita), Portland is small, friendly, and easily explored on foot—although at times it may seem that no matter which direction you head, it's uphill. The heart of Portland is the peninsula jutting into Casco Bay. It's bordered by the Eastern and Western Promenades, Back Cove, and the working waterfront. Salty sea breezes cool summer days and make winter ones seem even chillier. Unlike that other city by the bay, snow frequently blankets Portland from December into March.

Portland is Maine's most ethnically diverse city, with active refugee resettlement programs and dozens of languages spoken in the schools. Although salty sailors can still be found along the waterfront, Portland is increasingly a professional community, with young, upwardly mobile residents spiffing up Victorian houses and infusing new energy and money into the city's neighborhoods.

The region's cultural hub, Portland has world-class museums, performing-arts centers, active historical and preservation groups, an art school and a university, a symphony orchestra, numerous galleries, coffeehouses, and enough activities to keep culture vultures busy well into the night, especially in the thriving, handsomely restored Old Port and the up-and-coming Arts District.

Portland's also a sports- and outdoor-lovers' playground, with trails for running, biking, skating, and cross-country skiing, water sports aplenty, and a beloved minor league baseball team, the Sea Dogs. When city folks desire to escape, they often hop a ferry for one of the islands of Casco Bay or head to one of the parks, preserves, or beaches in the suburbs.

Still, Portland remains a major seaport. Lobster boats, commercial fishing vessels, long-distance passenger boats, cruise ships, and local ferries dominate the working waterfront, and the briny scent of the sea—or bait—seasons the air.

PORTLAND NEIGHBORHOODS

The best way to appreciate the character of Portland's neighborhoods is on foot. So much of Portland can (and should) be covered on foot that it would take a whole book to list all the possibilities, but several dedicated volunteer groups have produced guides to facilitate the process.

Greater Portland Landmarks (207/774-5561, www.portlandlandmarks.org) is the doyenne, founded in 1964 to preserve Portland's historic architecture and promote responsible construction. The organization has published more than a dozen books and booklets, including *Discover Historic Portland on Foot,* a packet of four well-researched walking-tour guides to architecturally historic sections of Portland's peninsula: Old Port, Western Promenade, State Street, and Congress Street. It's available online or for $5.95 at local bookstores, some gift shops, and the Visitor Information Center (14 Ocean Gateway Pier, 207/772-5800).

The Old Port

Tony shops, cobblestone sidewalks, replica streetlights, and a casual upmarket crowd (most of the time) set the scene for a district once filled with derelict buildings. Scores of

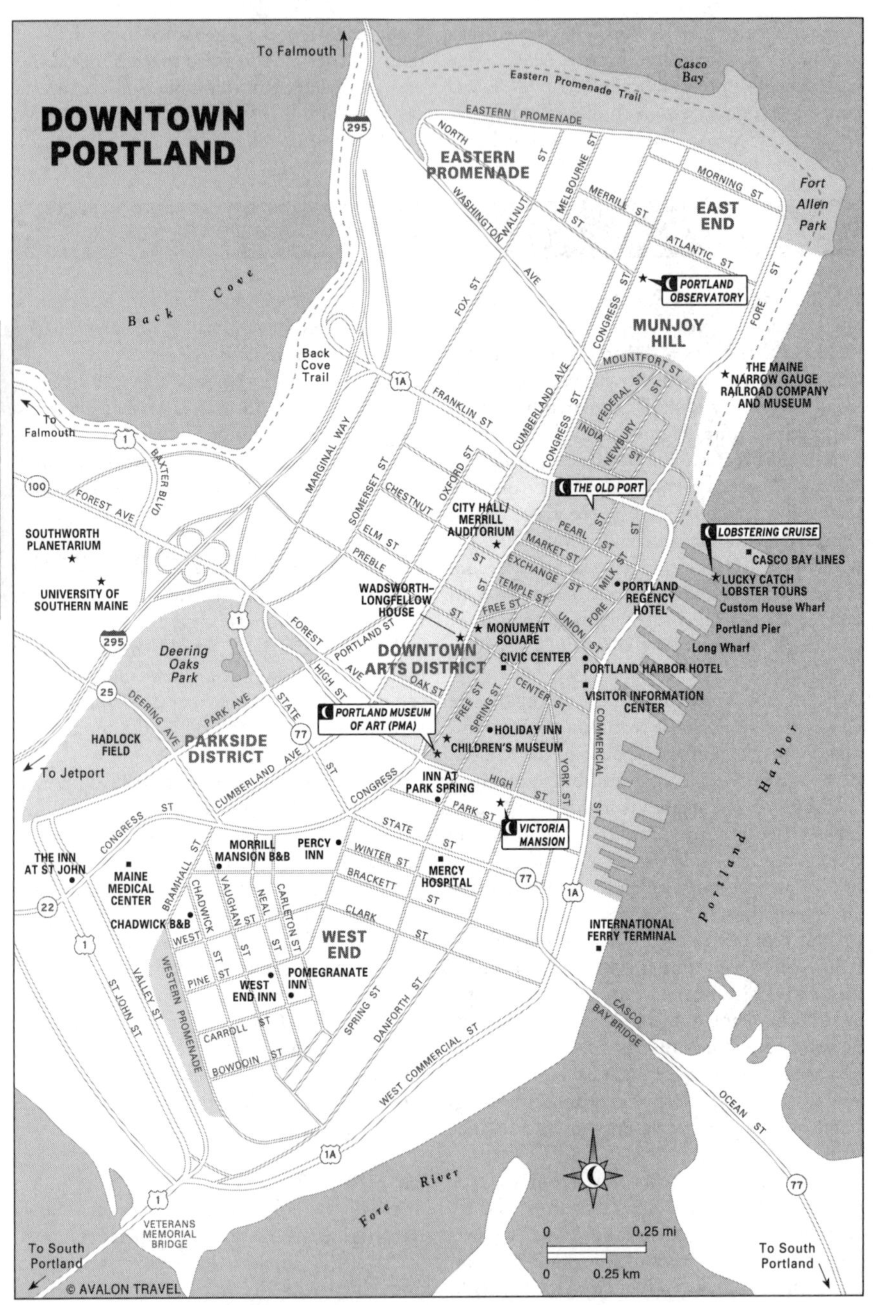
DOWNTOWN PORTLAND
To Falmouth
Casco Bay
Eastern Promenade Trail
EASTERN PROMENADE
EASTERN PROMENADE
EAST END
Fort Allen Park
MORNING ST
MERRILL ST
ATLANTIC ST
PORTLAND OBSERVATORY
MUNJOY HILL
Back Cove
Back Cove Trail
THE MAINE NARROW GAUGE RAILROAD COMPANY AND MUSEUM
To Falmouth
THE OLD PORT
LOBSTERING CRUISE
CASCO BAY LINES
LUCKY CATCH LOBSTER TOURS
Custom House Wharf
Portland Pier
Long Wharf
SOUTHWORTH PLANETARIUM
UNIVERSITY OF SOUTHERN MAINE
CITY HALL/ MERRILL AUDITORIUM
WADSWORTH-LONGFELLOW HOUSE
MONUMENT SQUARE
PORTLAND REGENCY HOTEL
Deering Oaks Park
DOWNTOWN ARTS DISTRICT
CIVIC CENTER
PORTLAND HARBOR HOTEL
VISITOR INFORMATION CENTER
HADLOCK FIELD
PARKSIDE DISTRICT
PORTLAND MUSEUM OF ART (PMA)
HOLIDAY INN
CHILDREN'S MUSEUM
To Jetport
INN AT PARK SPRING
VICTORIA MANSION
THE INN AT ST JOHN
MORRILL MANSION B&B
PERCY INN
MERCY HOSPITAL
MAINE MEDICAL CENTER
CHADWICK B&B
WEST END
INTERNATIONAL FERRY TERMINAL
POMEGRANATE INN
WEST END INN
Portland Harbor
CASCO BAY BRIDGE
OCEAN ST
Fore River
VETERANS MEMORIAL BRIDGE
To South Portland
To South Portland
0 0.25 mi
0 0.25 km
© AVALON TRAVEL

© HILARY NANGLE

Cruise ships and freighters dock side by side in Portland's busy harbor.

boutiques, enticing restaurants, and spontaneous street-corner music make it a fun area to visit year-round. Nightlife centers on the Old Port, and a couple of dozen bars keep everyone hopping until after midnight. Police keep a close eye on the district, but it can get a bit dicey after 11 P.M. on weekends. Caveat emptor—or maybe caveat peregrinator!

At 10:30 A.M. daily July–early October, knowledgeable guides from Greater Portland Landmarks (207/774-5561, www.portlandlandmarks.org) lead fascinating 90-minute **Old Port walking tours** in downtown Portland. No reservations needed; first-come, first served. Purchase tickets ($10; kids under 16 with an adult are free) at the walk meeting place; locations vary so check online or call first.

Congress Street/ Downtown Arts District

Bit by bit, once-declining Congress Street is becoming revitalized, showcasing the best of the city's culture. Artists, starving and otherwise, spend much of their time here, thanks largely to encouragement from the energetic grassroots Downtown Arts District Association (DADA). Galleries, artists' studios, coffeehouses, cafés and bistros, as well as libraries, museums, and performing-arts centers are all part of the ongoing renaissance.

West End

Probably the most diverse of the city's downtown neighborhoods, and one that largely escaped the Great Fire of 1866, the West End includes the historically and architecturally splendid Western Promenade, Maine Medical Center (the state's largest hospital), the city's best bed-and-breakfasts, a gay-friendly community with a laissez-faire attitude, and a host of cafés and restaurants, as well as a few niches harboring the homeless and forlorn.

Munjoy Hill/East End

A once slightly down-at-the-heels neighborhood enclave with a pull-'em-up-by-the-bootstraps attitude, Portland's East End is rapidly gentrifying. Munjoy Hill is probably best known for the distinctive wooden tower that adorns its summit.

Named for George Munjoy, a wealthy 17th-century resident, this district has a host of architectural and historic landmarks—well worth a walking tour. Fortunately, Greater Portland Landmarks (207/774-5561, www.portlandlandmarks.org) has produced a 24-page booklet, *Munjoy Hill Historic Guide* ($3), which documents more than 60 notable sites, including the National Historic Register Eastern Cemetery and, with spectacular harbor views, the Eastern Promenade and Fort Allen Park. From early June to early October, Landmarks also offers guided walking tours of the East End/Munjoy Hill and the historic **Eastern Cemetery,** the oldest burial ground on the peninsula; call for current schedules and fees.

Bayside and Parkside

A babel of languages reverberates in these districts just below Portland City Hall. Bayside experienced the arrival of refugees—Cambodian, Laotian, Vietnamese, Central European, and Afghan families—from war-torn lands during the 1980s and 1990s. Nowadays, you'll hear references to Somali Town, an area named for all the resettled refugees from that shattered country. Others have come from Sudan and Ethiopia. Portland's active Refugee Resettlement Program has assisted all. Many newcomers have become entrepreneurs, opening restaurants and small markets catering to their compatriots but increasingly gaining customers among local residents.

Stroudwater

Off the downtown peninsula at the western edge of Portland, close to the Portland Jetport, is the historic area known as Stroudwater, once an essential link in Maine water transport. The 20-mile-long **Cumberland and Oxford Canal,** hand-dug in 1828, ran through here as part of the timber-shipping route linking Portland Harbor, the Fore and Presumpscot Rivers, and Sebago Lake. Twenty-eight wooden locks allowed vessels to rise the 265 feet between sea level and the lake. By 1870, trains took over the route, condemning the canal to oblivion. The centerpiece of the Stroudwater area today is the historic 18th-century Tate House.

SIGHTS

Portland Museum of Art (PMA)

Three centuries of art and architecture: That's what you'll discover at Maine's oldest (since 1882) and finest art museum, the Portland Museum of Art (7 Congress Sq., 207/775-6148, recorded info 207/773-2787 or 800/639-4067, www.portlandmuseum.org, 10 A.M.–5 P.M. daily, to 9 P.M. Fri., closed Mon. mid-Oct.–late May, $10 adults, $8 seniors and students, $4 ages 6–17, free admission 5–9 P.M. every Fri.). The museum's topflight collection of American and impressionist masters and fine and decorative arts is displayed in three architecturally stunning connected buildings: the award-winning Charles Shipman Payson building, designed by I. M. Pei and opened in 1983; the newly restored Federal-era McLellan House; and the Beaux-Arts L. D. M. Sweat Memorial Galleries, designed by noted Maine architect John Calvin Stevens. The museum also has a well-stocked gift shop and a pleasant café that's open for lunch daily (11 A.M.–4 P.M.) and for dinner Friday (to 7:30 P.M.). Check the website for current family activities, lectures, and other events, including **Movies at the Museum,** showcasing foreign, classical, and art films ($7).

Victoria Mansion

The jaws of first-time visitors literally drop when they enter the Italianate Victoria Mansion, also called the Morse-Libby Mansion (109 Danforth St., 207/772-4841, www.victoriamansion.org, 10 A.M.–4 P.M. Mon.–Sat. and 1–5 P.M. Sun. May–Oct., special hours in Dec., $15 adults, $13.50 seniors, $5 children 6–17, $35 family; holiday season no senior discount). It's widely considered the most magnificently ornamented dwelling of its period remaining in the country. The National Historic Landmark is rife with Victoriana—carved marble fireplaces, elaborate porcelain and paneling, a freestanding mahogany staircase, gilded glass chandeliers, a restored 6-by-25-foot stained-glass ceiling window, and unbelievable trompe l'oeil touches. It's even more

© TOM NANGLE

The Victoria Mansion is a nationally renowned gem, although you wouldn't know it from the exterior.

spectacular at Christmas, with yards of roping, festooned trees, and carolers. (This is the best time to bring kids, as the house itself may not particularly intrigue them.) The mansion was built in the late 1850s by Ruggles Sylvester Morse, a Maine-born entrepreneur whose New Orleans–based fortune enabled him to hire 93 craftsmen to complete the house. The interior, designed by Gustave Herter, still boasts 90 percent of the original furnishings. Guided 45-minute tours begin every half hour (on the quarter hour) in season; tours are self-guided during the holidays.

Portland Observatory

Providing a head-swiveling view of Portland (and the White Mountains on a clear day), the octagonal red-painted Portland Observatory (138 Congress St., 207/774-5561, www.portlandlandmarks.org, 10 A.M.–5 P.M. daily late May–Columbus Day, last tour at 4:30 P.M., sunset tours 5–8 P.M. Thurs. in July and Aug., $7 adults, $4 children 6–16 with paid adult) is the only remaining marine signal tower on the eastern seaboard. Built in 1807 at a cost of $5,000 by Captain Lemuel Moody to keep track of the port's shipping activity, the tower has 122 tons of rock ballast in its base. Admission in those days (only men were allowed to climb the 103 interior steps) was 12.5 cents. Today, admission includes the small museum at the tower's base and a guided tour to the top.

The Longfellow Connection

A few blocks down Congress Street from the PMA, you'll step back in time to the era of Portland-born poet Henry Wadsworth Longfellow, who lived in the accurately restored **Wadsworth-Longfellow House** (485 Congress St., 207/774-1822, www.mainehistory.org, 10:30 A.M.–4 P.M. Mon.–Sat., noon–4 P.M. Sun. May 1–Oct. 31, special holiday hours Nov.–Dec., $8 adults, $7 seniors and students, $3 children 5–17) as a child in the early 1800s—long before the brick mansion was dwarfed by surrounding high-rises. Wadsworth and Longfellow family furnishings fill the three-story house (owned by the Maine Historical Society), and savvy guides provide insight into Portland's 19th-century life. Don't miss the urban oasis—a wonderfully peaceful garden—behind the house (same hours, free admission). Buy tickets at the adjacent Center for Maine History, which also houses the **Maine History Gallery** (489 Congress St., 207/774-1822, www.mainehistory.org, 10 A.M.–5 P.M. Mon.–Sat., noon–5 P.M. Sun., $5 adults, $4 seniors, $2 children), where you can take in the Maine Historical Society's current exhibits and find an extensive collection of Maine history books in the gift shop.

Maine Narrow Gauge Railroad and Museum

A three-mile ride along Portland's waterfront is the highlight of a visit to the Maine Narrow Gauge Railroad Company and Museum (58 Fore St., 207/828-0814, www.mngrr.org). The museum (10 A.M.–4 P.M. daily late May–late Oct., Mon.–Fri. only off-season, $2 adults, $1 seniors and children 3–12 or free with train ticket) owns more than three dozen train cars and has others on long-term loan—most from Maine's five historic narrow-gauge railroads (the last one closed in 1943). You can board a number of the cars and see others undergoing restoration. For a fee, you can ride the two-foot rails aboard a multicar train. The schedule roughly follows museum hours, with rides on the hour ($10 adults, $9 seniors, $6 children 3–12). The track edges Casco Bay along the Eastern Promenade—a short but enjoyable excursion that's a real kid pleaser.

Museum of African Culture

Here's a little treasure. Founded in 1998, the Museum of African Culture (13 Brown St., 207/871-7188, www.museumafricanculture.org, 10:30 A.M.–4 P.M. Tues.–Fri., noon–4 P.M. Sat., $5 donation) is the brainchild of Nigerian-born Oscar Mokeme (the director) and Arthur Aleshire. It's devoted to sub-Saharan African arts and culture. Among the museum's 2,500 or so treasures—not all on display at once—are Nigerian tribal masks and Benin lost-wax bronzes.

Children's Museum of Maine

Here's the answer to parents' prayers—a whole museum in downtown Portland catering to kids. At the Children's Museum of Maine (142 Free St., 207/828-1234, www.kitetails.com, 10 A.M.–5 P.M. Mon.–Sat., noon–5 P.M. Sun., closed Mon. early Sept.–late May, $8 adults, free children 1 and younger, $1 admission 5–8 P.M. first Fri. of each month) lots of hands-on displays encourage interaction and guarantee involvement for a couple of hours.

Breweries

Look for the keg topping the flagpole at **Shipyard Brewery** (86 Newbury St., 207/761-0807, www.shipyard.com). Video tours of the award-winning microbrewery are offered on the hour 11 A.M.–4 P.M. Monday–Saturday, noon–4 P.M. Sunday. Tours begin with a short promotional video explaining the brewing process, then visit the bottling line, and end with a tasting. Even if you're not a beer/ale drinker, go and enjoy the soda that is also brewed on the premises.

Other Portland breweries offering tours are **Allagash Brewing Company** (50 Industrial Way, 207/878-5385, www.allagash.com), three times daily on weekdays, and **Geary's Brewing Company** (38 Evergreen Dr., 207/878-2337, www.gearybrewing.com), by appointment.

BEYOND THE DOWNTOWN PENINSULA

Seeing Stars

Under a 30-foot dome with comfy theater seats and a state-of-the-art laser system, the **Southworth Planetarium** (96 Falmouth St., Science Building, lower level, University of Southern Maine, 207/780-4249, www.usm.maine.edu/~planet, 7 and 8:30 P.M. Fri.–Sat., $6–9 adults, $5–8 seniors and children) presents astronomy shows. Computer-savvy kids will head for the interactive computers in the exhibit area; the gift shop stocks astronaut ice cream and other science stuff. For recorded information on moon and planet positions, eclipses, and other astronomical happenings, call the **Skywatch Hotline** (207/780-4719). Take exit 6B off I-295 and go west on Forest Avenue to Falmouth Street (left turn). The Science Building is on the left, after the parking lot.

Tate House

Just down the street from the Portland International Jetport, in the Stroudwater district, is the 1755 Tate House (1270 Westbrook St., 207/774-6177, www.tatehouse.org, 10 A.M.–4 P.M. Wed.–Sat., 1–4 P.M. Sun., mid-June–mid-Oct., $7 adults, $5 seniors, $2 children 6–12), a National Historic Landmark owned by the Colonial Dames of America. Built by Captain George Tate, who was prominent in shipbuilding, the house has superb period furnishings and a lovely 18th-century herb garden (more than 70 varieties) overlooking the Stroudwater River. Tours last 40 minutes. Wednesdays mid-June–mid-September are "summer garden days," when tea and goodies follow tours of the garden (for an extra charge).

Portland Harbor Museum

The maritime history of Casco Bay and Maine is the focus of the small Portland Harbor Museum (510 Congress St., 207/773-3800, www.portlandharbormuseum.org, 10 A.M.–4 P.M. daily late May–mid-Oct., $3 adults, $2 seniors).

Portland Head Light

Just four miles from downtown Portland, Fort Williams, in Cape Elizabeth, feels a world away. This oceanfront town park, a former military base, is home to Portland Head Light (1000 Shore Rd., Fort Williams Park, Cape Elizabeth, 207/799-2661, www.portlandheadlight.com, dawn–dusk daily). Commissioned by president George Washington and first lit in 1791, it has been immortalized in poetry, photography, and philately. The surf here is awesome—perhaps too awesome. The *Annie C. Maguire* was shipwrecked below the lighthouse on Christmas Eve, 1886. There's no access to the 58-foot automated light tower, but the superbly restored keeper's house has become **The Museum at Portland Head Light** (10 A.M.–4 P.M. daily late May–mid-Oct. and weekends late spring and late fall, but call first to confirm, $2 adults, $1 children 6–18). It's filled with local history and lighthouse memorabilia. The 90-acre oceanfront park offers much else to explore, including ruins of the fort and the Goddard mansion. Walk the trails, play a game of tennis, dip your toes in the surf at the rocky beach—but be careful, as there's a strong undertow here. You might even catch the Portland Symphony Orchestra, which occasionally performs here in summer. The grassy headlands are great places to watch the boat traffic going in and out of Portland Harbor. Bring a picnic lunch, and don't forget a kite. From downtown Portland, take Route 77 and then Broadway, Cottage Road, and Shore Road; the route is marked.

© HILARY NANGLE

Portland Head Light guards the ledgy shores of Cape Elizabeth.

GREATER PORTLAND

TOURS AND TRAILS

Walking Tours

PORTLAND FREEDOM TRAIL

Pick up a copy of this free map and brochure (also available online) detailing a self-guided walking tour of a baker's dozen marked sights related to Portland's role in Maine's Underground Railway (www.portlandfreedomtrail.org). Among the highlights are the Abyssinian Meeting House, the third-oldest African American Meeting House still standing in the United States (undergoing restoration); First Parish Unitarian Universalist Church, where abolitionist William Lloyd Garrison spoke in 1832; and Mariners' Church, location of an antislavery bookstore and print shop that printed the first Afrocentric history of the world.

PORTLAND WOMEN'S HISTORY TRAIL

Another self-guided walking tour, this one details four loops—Congress Street, Munjoy

LIGHTHOUSES AND PARKS TOUR

Whether in a car or on a bike, it's easy to loop through South Portland and Cape Elizabeth on a route that takes in lighthouses, forts, beaches, and parks.

Begin just over the Casco Bay Bridge from downtown Portland (Rte. 77), take Broadway and continue to the end at **Southern Maine Community College (SMCC),** overlooking the bay. (Best time to come here is evenings and weekends, when there's ample parking.) Unless it's foggy (when the signal is deafening) or thundering (when you'll expose yourself to lightning), walk out along the 1,000-foot granite breakwater to the **Spring Point Ledge Light** (207/699-2676, www.springpointlight.org) with fabulous views in every direction; call or check the website for current hours. Also here are picnic benches, the remains of Fort Preble, and the **Spring Point Shoreline Walkway,** a scenic three-mile pathway with views off to House, Peaks, and Cushings Islands. At the end of the shoreway, you'll reach crescent-shaped **Willard Beach,** a neighborhoody sort of place with lifeguards, a changing building, a snack bar, and those same marvelous views.

From the SMCC campus, return on Broadway to the major intersection with Cottage Road and bear left. Cottage Road becomes Shore Road at the Cape Elizabeth town line. Loop into Fort Williams Park and make a pilgrimage to **Portland Head Light** before continuing on Shore Road to its intersection with Route 77. Bear left and follow to Two Lights Road and follow signs to 40-acre **Two Lights State Park.** Almost a vest-pocket park, it has picnicking and restroom facilities, but its biggest asset is the panoramic ocean view from atop a onetime gun battery. Summer admission is $4.50 adult nonresidents, $3 adult residents, $1.50 senior nonresidents, $1 children 5-11.

Before or after visiting the park, take a left just before the park entrance (it's a continuation of Two Lights Road; the sign says Lighthouses). Continue to the parking lot at the end, where you'll see the signal towers for which Two Lights is named. (There's no access to either one; only one still works.) If you haven't brought a picnic for the state park, there are few places finer to enjoy the view and a lobster than at **The Lobster Shack.**

To eke out some beach time, return to Route 77 and continue to **Crescent Beach State Park,** a 243-acre park with changing rooms, lifeguard, restrooms, picnic tables, and a snack bar. Admission is $6.50 adult nonresidents, $4.50 adult residents, $1.50 senior nonresidents, $1 children 5-11. Directly offshore is Saco Bay's **Richmond Island,** a 200-acre private preserve with a checkered past dating to the 17th century.

Hill, State Street, and the West End—with about 20 stops on each. Among the sites: a long-gone chewing-gum factory where teenage girls worked 10-hour shifts. The trail guide is available online (www.usm.maine.edu/~history/newtrail.html) or for $8.50 in selected bookstores and at the Maine History Gallery gift shop (489 Congress St., 207/879-0427).

GREATER PORTLAND LANDMARKS

Greater Portland Landmarks (207/774-5561, www.portlandlandmarks.org) sponsors neighborhood walking tours as well as an annual **summer tour program,** featuring four or five walking trips and excursions to offshore islands, historic churches, revamped buildings, and gardens. Many of the destinations are private or otherwise inaccessible, so these are special opportunities. Registration is limited, and there's only one trip to each site. Tours run mid-July–mid-October, primarily on weekends.

MAINE FOODIE TOURS

Just as the name promises, Maine Foodie Tours (10 Moulton St., 207/233-7485, www.mainefoodietours.com) delivers a taste of

© HILARY NANGLE

Kids of all ages find plenty to quack about on Downeast Duck tours.

Maine. The Old Port Culinary Tour ($39) visits seven vendors selling everything from cheese to lobster to chocolate; Just Desserts makes four stops.

Casco Bay Tour

Casco Bay Lines (Commercial and Franklin Sts., Old Port, 207/774-7871, www.cascobaylines.com), the nation's oldest continuously operating ferry system (since the 1920s), is the lifeline between Portland and six inhabited Casco Bay islands. What better way to sample the islands than to take the three-hour ride along with mail, groceries, and island residents? The Casco Bay Lines mail boat stops—briefly—at **Long Island, Chebeague, Cliff,** and **Little** and **Great Diamond Islands.** Departures are 10 A.M. and 2:15 P.M. daily mid-June–Labor Day (plus 7:45 A.M. weekdays), 10 A.M. and 2:45 P.M. other months. Fares are $14.50 adults, $12.50 seniors, and $7.25 children 5–9. The longest cruise on the Casco Bay Lines schedule is the five-hour, 45-minute narrated summertime trip (late June–early Sept.) to **Bailey Island,** with a two-hour stopover, departing from Portland at 10 A.M. daily ($24 adults, $21.25 seniors, $11 children 5–9). Dogs (on leashes) and bicycles need separate tickets—$6 for bikes, $3.75 for animals.

Land and Sea Tours

Various commercial operators offer area land-and-sea tours, but frankly, none is first rate. On each, guides often present incorrect information. Still, such tours are a good way to get the city's general layout.

The best of the lot is the 1.5-hour narrated sightseeing tour of Portland in a trolley-bus, by **Portland Discovery Land and Sea Tours** (3 Moulton St., Old Port, 207/774-0808, www.portlanddiscovery.com). Cost is $18 adults, $12 children. You can combine this tour with a 90-minute Lighthouse Lover's cruise on Casco Bay. The combined price is $33 adults, $21 children.

An alternative, especially if you're traveling with kids, is the 60-to-70-minute **Downeast Duck Adventures** (tours depart from DiMillo's Long Wharf, Commercial St., 207/774-3825, www.downeastducktours.com, early May–early Oct., $24 adults, $20 seniors, $17 children 6–12, $5 5 and younger). Purchase tickets aboard. Prepare to do a lot of quacking on the tour and to hear a lot of quackery regarding local history.

CASCO BAY ISLANDS

Casco Bay is dotted with so many islands that an early explorer thought there must be at least one for every day of the year and so dubbed them the Calendar Islands. Truthfully, there aren't quite that many, even if you count all the ledges that appear at low tide. No matter, the islands are as much a part of Portland life as the Old Port.

Casco Bay Lines (207/774-7871, www.cascobaylines.com) is the islands' lifeline, providing car and passenger service daily in summer. For an island taster, take the daily mail-boat run. Indeed, on hot days, it may seem as if half the city's population is hopping a ferry to enjoy the cool breezes and calming views.

PEAKS ISLAND

Peaks Island is a mere 20-minute ferry ride from downtown Portland, so it's no surprise that it has the largest year-round population. Historically a popular vacation spot – two lodges were built for Civil War veterans – it's now an increasingly popular suburb.

Although you can walk the island's perimeter in 3-4 hours, the best way to see it is via bike. If you bring your own, the ferry fee is $6.50 adults, $3.25 children. Rental bikes are available on the island from Brad Burkholder at **Brad and Wyatt's Bike Shop** (115 Island Ave., 207/766-5631, $15/day, hourly rentals available, usually 10 A.M.-6 P.M. daily but call to be sure). Pedal around clockwise. It can take less than an hour to do the five-mile island circuit, but plan on relaxing on the beach, savoring the views, and visiting the museums.

Another way to see the island is on a golf-cart tour with **Island Tours** (207/653-2549, islandtours@att.net, $15 adults, $12 seniors, $8 children), which offers a variety of 90-minute island tours.

Civil War buffs have two museums worth a visit. The **Fifth Maine Regiment Center** (45 Seashore Ave., 207/766-3330, www.fifthmainemuseum.org, 11 A.M.-4 P.M. Sat.-Sun. late May-mid-Oct., noon-4 P.M. Mon.-Thurs. July 1-early Sept., $5 donation requested), a Queen Anne-style cottage built by Civil War veterans in 1888, now houses exhibits on the war and island history. Just a few steps away is the **Eighth Maine Regimental Memorial** (13 Eighth Maine Ave., 207/766-5086, noon-3 P.M. Tues.-Sat. July 1-early Sept., $5 donation requested). Tours detail the building's fascinating history and its collection of artifacts pertaining to the Eighth Maine as well as material on the island, World War II, and more. Rustic lodging is available.

Another museum perhaps worthy of a visit just for its quirkiness is the **Umbrella Cover Museum** (207/766-4496, call for hours, donation), where owner Nancy 3. Hoffman (yes, 3) displays her collection.

Food

Both **The Cockeyed Gull** (78 Island Ave., 207/766-2880, www.cockeyedgull.com, 11:30 A.M.-9 P.M. daily) and the **Shipyard Brewhaus** (33 Island Ave., www.innonpeaks.com) have inside dining as well as outdoor tables with water views.

Accommodations

The **Inn on Peaks Island** (33 Island Ave., www.innonpeaks.com, $250-300) overlooks the ferry dock and has jaw-dropping sunset views over the Portland skyline. No island roughing it here. The spacious cottage-style suites have fireplaces, sitting areas, whirlpool baths, TV and VCR, and refrigerators; rates include a continental breakfast.

On the other end of the Peaks Island luxury scale is the extremely informal and communal **Eighth Maine Living Museum and Lodge** (13 Eighth Maine Ave., 207/766-5086, mid-May-mid-Sept., 914/237-3165 off-season, www.eighthmaine.com, $90-120 d), a shorefront rustic living-history lodge overlooking White Head Passage. Shared baths and a huge shared kitchen allow you to rusticate in much the same manner as did the Civil War vets who built this place, in 1891, with a gift from a veteran who had won the Louisiana Lottery. It has no housekeeping – you're responsible for stripping the linens and cleaning the room and your kitchen space before departing.

© HILARY NANGLE

Casco Bay Lines ferry docks in the heart of the action on Peaks Island.

GREAT CHEBEAGUE

Everyone calls Great Chebeague just "Chebeague" (shuh-BIG). Yes, there's a Little Chebeague, but it's a state-owned park, and no one lives there. Chebeague is the largest of the bay's islands – 4.5 miles long, 1.5 miles wide – and the relatively level terrain makes it easy to get around. Don't plan to bring a car; it's too complicated to arrange. You can bike the leisurely 10-mile circuit of the island in a couple of hours, but unless you're in a hurry, allow time to relax and enjoy your visit.

If the tide is right, cross the sandspit from The Hook and explore **Little Chebeague.** Start out about two hours before low tide (preferably around new moon or full moon, when the most water drains away) and plan to be back on Chebeague no later than two hours after low tide.

Back on Great Chebeague, when you're ready for a swim head for **Hamilton Beach,** a beautiful small stretch of sand lined with dune grass not far from the Chebeague Island Inn. Also on this part of the island is **East End Point,** with a spectacular panoramic view of Halfway Rock and the bay.

Chebeague Transportation Company, from Cousins Island, Yarmouth, also services the island.

Food

Visitors to Chebeague Island have two food choices. For simple home-cooked fare, head to **Calder's Clam Shack** (108 North Rd., 207/846-5046, www.caldersclamshack.com, 11:30 A.M.-8 P.M. Tues.-Sun.), a take-out place serving burgers, pizza, chowders, salad, sandwiches, and of course, fried seafood. On the fancier side is **Chebeague Island Inn** (61 South Rd., 207/846-5155, www.chebeagueislandinn.com, 7 A.M.-9 P.M. daily). Dinner entrées, such as seafood linguini, New York strip, or baked stuffed haddock, run $18-35.

(continued on next page)

CASCO BAY ISLANDS (continued)

Accommodations

The comfortable **Chebeague Orchard Inn** (453 North Rd., 207/846-9488, $135-165) has five rooms (two sharing one bath); some have water views. A full breakfast – if you're lucky, perhaps lobster quiche – is served overlooking the backyard's bird feeders and apple orchard. Get that old-timey island experience at the **Chebeague Island Inn** (61 South Rd., 207/846-5155, www.chebeagueislandinn.com, $145-295), a nicely updated historical inn that charms guests with an artsy spirit and comforts them with down duvets and fancy sheets. The inn's dining room serves all meals.

EAGLE ISLAND

Seventeen-acre Eagle Island (207/624-6080, www.pearyeagleisland.org, 10 A.M.-5 P.M. daily mid-June-early Sept.) juts out of Casco Bay, rising to a rocky promontory 40 feet above the crashing surf. On the bluff's crest, Robert Edwin Peary, the first man to lead a party of fellow men to the North Pole without the use of mechanical or electrical devices, built his dream home. It's now a state historic site that's accessible via excursion boats from Portland or Freeport. The half-day trip usually includes a narrated cruise to the island and time to tour the house, filled with Peary family artifacts, and wander the nature trails. (Note: Trails are usually closed until approximately mid-July to protect nesting eider ducks.)

Peary envisioned the island's rocky bluff as a ship's prow and built his house to resemble a pilot house. Wherever possible, he used indigenous materials from the island in the construction, including timber drift, fallen trees, beach rocks, and cement mixed with screened beach sand and small pebbles. From the library, Peary corresponded with world leaders, adventurers, and explorers, such as Teddy Roosevelt, the Wright Brothers, Roald Amundson, and Ernest Shackleton, and planned his expeditions. Peary reached the North Pole on April 6, 1909, and his wife, Josephine, was on Eagle when she received word via telegraph of her husband's accomplishment. After Peary's death in 1920, the family continued to spend summers on Eagle until Josephine's death in 1955. It was a unanimous family decision to donate the island to the State of Maine.

ENTERTAINMENT AND NIGHTLIFE

The best places to find out what's playing at area theaters, cinemas, concert halls, and nightclubs are the *Portland Phoenix* (www.portlandphoenix.com) and the *Go* supplement in the Thursday edition of the *Portland Press Herald* (www.mainetoday.com). Both have online listings; hard copies are available at bookstores and supermarkets; the *Phoenix* is free.

Merrill Auditorium

The magnificently restored Merrill Auditorium (20 Myrtle St., box office 207/874-8200, www.portlandevents.com) is a 1,900-seat theater inside Portland City Hall (on Congress Street) with two balconies and one of the country's only municipally owned pipe organs, the **Kotzschmar Organ** (207/553-4363, www.foko.org). A summer classical organ concert series with guest artists is held at 7:30 P.M. most Tuesdays mid-June–August ($10 donation).

Special events and concerts are common at Merrill, and the auditorium is also home to a number of the city's arts organizations. The **Portland Symphony Orchestra** (207/842-0800, www.portlandsymphony.org) and **PCA Great Performances** (207/773-3150, www.pcagreatperformances.org) have extensive, well-patronized fall and winter schedules; the PSO presents three summer Independence Pops concerts as well. The **Portland Opera Repertory Theatre** (437 Congress St., 207/879-7678, www.portopera.org) performs a major opera each summer. In addition, there are films, lectures, and other related events throughout July. Tickets for the PSO, PCA, and PORT are available through PortTix (207/942-0800, www.porttix.com).

1 Longfellow Square

Diverse programming is the hallmark of 1 Longfellow Square (207/761-1757, www.onelongfellowsquare.com), an intimate venue for performances and lectures at the corner of Congress and State Streets.

Drama

Innovative staging and controversial contemporary dramas are typical of the **Portland Stage Company** (Portland Performing Arts Center, 25A Forest Ave., 207/774-0465, www.portlandstage.com), established in 1974 and going strong ever since. Equity pros present a half dozen plays each winter season in a 290-seat performance space.

Live Music

The Portland Conservatory of Music presents free weekly **Noonday Concerts** at First Parish Church (425 Congress St., 207/773-5747) at 12:15 P.M. Thursdays October–early April (excluding late November). The music varies widely, from saxophone to Scottish fiddle and dance, a string quartet to Irish baroque.

Portland Parks and Recreation sponsors **Summer in the Parks** (207/756-8275, www.portlandmaine.gov/rec/summer.htm, July and Aug., free), a number of evening concert series and a midday kids' performance series in downtown parks.

In summer, take the ferry to Peaks Island for Reggae Sundays on the deck at **Jones Landing** (at the ferry landing, Peaks Island, 207/766-4400); doors open at 11:30 A.M.

Brewpubs and Bars

Portland is a beer town, with an ever-increasing number of microbreweries and brewpubs. It's also vigilant about enforcing alcohol laws, so even if you're well older than 21, be sure to bring identification proving so.

Not only is **Gritty McDuff's** (396 Fore St., Old Port, 207/772-2739, 11:30 A.M.–1 A.M. daily) one of Maine's most popular breweries, its brewpub was the state's first—opened in 1988. The menu includes pub classics such as fish-and-chips and shepherd's pie, as well as burgers, salads, and sandwiches. Among the Gritty's beers and ales on tap are Sebago Light and Black Fly Stout. Gritty's also books live entertainment fairly regularly. Tours by appointment. Gritty's also has a branch in Freeport.

A longtime favorite pub, **$3 Dewey's** (241 Commercial St., Old Port, 207/772-3310, www.threedollardeweys.com) is so authentic that visiting Brits, Kiwis, and Aussies often head here to assuage their homesickness. Inexpensive fare, 36 brews on tap, free popcorn, and frequent live music make it a very popular spot.

Especially popular in the late afternoon and early evening is **J's Oyster** (5 Portland Pier, 207/772-4828, 11:30 A.M.–1 A.M. daily), a longtime fixture (some might call it a dive) on the waterfront known for its raw bar and for pouring a good drink.

Of all Portland's neighborhood hangouts, **Ruski's** (212 Danforth St., 207/774-7604, 7 A.M.–12:45 A.M. Mon.–Sat., 9 A.M.–12:45 A.M. Sun.) is the most authentic—a small, usually crowded onetime speakeasy that rates just as high for breakfast as for nighttime schmoozing. Expect basic homemade fare for well under $10, plus darts and a big-screen TV. Dress down or you'll feel out of place. No credit cards.

That said, it's **Rosie's** (330 Fore St., 207/772-5656) that *Esquire* named as one of America's best bars. **Blackstones** (6 Pine St., 207/775-2885, www.blackstones.com) claims to be Portland's oldest neighborhood gay bar.

Novare Res Bier Cafe (4 Canal Plaza, 207/761-2437, www.novareresbiercafe.com, 4 P.M.–1 A.M. Mon.–Thurs., 3 P.M.–1 A.M. Fri., noon–1 A.M. Sat.–Sun.) carries more than 300 bottled beers from around the world. Pair them with selections from the meat and cheese bar, sandwiches, or small plates.

West of I-295, **The Great Lost Bear** (540 Forest Ave., 207/772-0300, www.greatlostbear.com, 11:30 A.M.–11:30 P.M. Mon.–Sat., noon–11 P.M. Sun.) has 65 brews on tap, representing 15 Maine microbreweries and others from New England. The bear motif and the punny menus are a bit much, but the 15 or so varieties of burgers are not bad. It's a kid pleaser.

For more upscale tippling, head for **Top of the East** (157 High St., near Congress Sq., 207/775-5411), the lounge at the top of the Eastland Park Hotel, where all of Portland's at your feet. **Una** (505 Fore St., 207/828-0300) is a hip cocktail and wine bar serving a tapas-style menu.

Bars with Entertainment

There are so many possibilities in this category that the best advice is to scope out the scene when you arrive; the *Portland Phoenix* has the best listings. Most clubs have cover charges. **Asylum** (121 Center St., 207/772-8274, www.portlandasylum.com) caters to a young crowd with dance jams, CD release parties, DJ nights, and live bands. **Geno's** (13 Brown St., 207/772-7891) has been at it for years—an old reliable for rock, with an emphasis on local bands. Ever popular for Wednesday hip-hop and weekend bands is **The Big Easy** (55 Market St., 207/871-8817, www.bigeasyportland.com). **Blue** (650A Congress St., 207/774-4111, www.portcityblue.com) presents local artists and musicians in a small space and serves beer, wine, tea, and light fare; traditional Irish music is always featured on Wednesday evenings, jazz on Saturdays. Wanna rock? See what's on the calendar at **Empire Dine and Dance** (575 Congress St., 207/879-8988, www.portlandempire.ning.com), where the entertainment includes live music and CD release parties upstairs, and daily entertainment ranging from bluegrass to jazz downstairs.

Comedy

Portland's forum for stand-up comedy is the **Comedy Connection** (16 Custom House Wharf, 207/774-5554, www.mainecomedy.com, Thurs.–Sun. evenings), a crowded space that draws nationally known pros. Avoid the front tables unless you enjoy being the fall guy/guinea pig, and don't bring anyone squeamish about the F-word.

EVENTS

Pick up a free copy of the Portland Area Arts and Events Calendar at Portland shops and cafés, the Visitor Information Center, or City Hall (389 Congress St.).

June brings a host of events. The **Old Port Festival** (one of Portland's largest festivals), usually the first weekend, has entertainment, food and craft booths, and impromptu fun in Portland's Old Port. The **Greek Heritage Festival,** usually the last weekend, features Greek food, dancing, and crafts at Holy Trinity Church (133 Pleasant St.).

Some of the world's top runners join upward of 500 racers in the **Beach to Beacon Race,** held in late July/early August. The 10K course goes from Crescent Beach State Park to Portland Head Light in Cape Elizabeth.

In mid-August, the **Italian Street Festival** showcases music, Italian food, and games at St. Peter's Catholic Church (72 Federal St.).

Artists from all over the country set up in 350 booths along Congress Street for the annual **Sidewalk Arts Festival** in late August.

The **Maine Brewers' Festival,** the first weekend in November at the Portland Exposition Building, is a big event that expands every year, thanks to the explosion of Maine microbreweries, and has samples galore. From Thanksgiving weekend to Christmas Eve, **Victorian Holiday** in downtown Portland harks back with caroling, special sales, concerts, tree lighting, horse-drawn wagons, and Victoria Mansion tours and festivities.

SHOPPING

The Portland peninsula—primarily Congress Street and the Old Port waterfront district—is thick with non-cookie-cutter shops and galleries. These listings offer just a taste to spur your explorations.

Bookstores

Carlson-Turner Books (241 Congress St., 207/773-4200 or 800/540-7323), based on Munjoy Hill, seems to have Portland's largest used-book inventory. Look for unusual titles and travel narratives. For good reads, contemporary fiction, and a big selection of cookbooks, visit **Cunningham Books** (199 State St., Longfellow Sq., 207/775-2246). Antique maps and atlases are the specialty at the Old Port's **Emerson Booksellers** (18 Exchange St., 207/874-2665), but it also has an excellent used-book selection.

Cookbook mavens will drool over the collection at **Rabelais Books** (86 Market St., 207/774-1044, www.rabelaisbooks.com), ideally situated in Portland's foodie neighborhood. Don and Samantha Hoyt Lindgren specialize in food and wine, carrying a delicious blend of thousands of current, rare, and out-of-print books covering culinary history, food lit, cookbooks, wine, and related topics.

Art Galleries

Intown Portland's galleries host a **First Friday Artwalk** (www.firstfridayartwalk.com) on the first Friday evening of each month, with exhibition openings, open houses, meet-the-artist gatherings, and other such artsy activities.

Galleries specializing in contemporary art are clustered in the Arts District. These include **June Fitzpatrick Gallery** (112 High St., 207/879-5742, www.junefitzpatrickgallery.com) and **Institute for Contemporary Art** (Maine College of Art, 522 Congress St., 207/879-5742, www.meca.edu), with walk-in tours at 12:15 P.M. every Wednesday. Another gallery hotbed is the Old Port, where you can visit **Aucocisco** (89 Exchange St., 207/553-2222, www.aucocisco.com), specializing in contemporary fine art, and **Greenhut Galleries** (146 Middle St., 207/772-2693, www.greenhutgalleries.com), specializing in contemporary Maine art and sculpture. More than 15 Maine potters—with a wide variety of styles and items—market their wares at the **Maine Potters Market** (376 Fore St., 207/774-1633, www.mainepottersmarket.com).

Offbeat Shopping

Bring home a nautical treasure from **Shipwreck and Cargo** (207 Commercial St., Old Port, 207/775-3057, www.shipwreckandcargo.com), which stocks a wide assortment of marine-related items—boat models, barometers, navy surplus stuff, and more.

Woof. The company outlet **Planet Dog** (211 Marginal Way, 207/347-8606, www.planetdog.com) is a howling good time for dogs and their owners. You'll find all sorts of wonderful products, and Planet Dog, committed to "think globally and act doggedly," has established a foundation to promote and serve causes such as therapy, service, search and rescue, bomb sniffing, and police dogs.

RECREATION

Parks, Preserves, and Beaches

Greater Portland is blessed with green space, thanks largely to the efforts of 19th-century mayor James Phinney Baxter, who had the foresight to hire the famed Olmsted Brothers firm to develop an ambitious plan to ring the city with public parks and promenades. Not all the elements fell into place, but the result is what makes Portland such a livable city.

ON THE DOWNTOWN PENINSULA

Probably the most visible of the city's parks, 51-acre **Deering Oaks** (Park and Forest Aves. and Deering St.) may be best known for the quaint little duck condo in the middle of the pond. Other facilities and highlights here are tennis courts, playground, horseshoes, rental paddleboats, a snack bar, the award-winning Rose Circle, a Saturday farmers market (7 A.M.–noon), and, in winter, ice skating. After dark, steer clear of the park.

At one end of the Eastern Promenade, where it meets Fore Street, **Fort Allen Park** overlooks offshore Fort Gorges (coin-operated telescopes bring it closer). A central gazebo is flanked by an assortment of military souvenirs dating as far back as the War of 1812. All along the Eastern Prom are walking paths, benches, play areas, even an ill-maintained fitness trail—all with that terrific view. Down by the water is **East End Beach,** with parking, token sand, and the area's best launching ramp for sea kayaks or powerboats.

WEST OF THE DOWNTOWN PENINSULA

Just beyond I-295, along Baxter Boulevard (Rte. 1) and tidal **Back Cove,** is a skinny green strip with a 3.5-mile trail for walking, jogging,

WINSLOW HOMER

Discovering Maine in his early 40s, Winslow Homer (1836-1910) was smitten – enough to spend the last 27 years of his life in Prouts Neck (Scarborough, south of Portland), a small fishing village gradually morphing into an exclusive summer enclave. Here, in a cluttered, rustic studio converted from a onetime stable (recently acquired by the Portland Museum of Art, which plans to open it to the public on a limited basis), he produced his finest works, the seascapes that have become so familiar to us all. He painted the sea in every mood, the rocks in every light, the snow in all its bleakness, the hardy trees bent to the wind. Occasional forays to the Bahamas, the Adirondacks, and the Canadian wilderness inspired other themes, but Prouts Neck always lured him back. Homer's last work, an oil titled *Driftwood* painted in 1909 when his health was in major decline, depicts once again the struggle of man against the roiling surf that Homer knew so intimately from his life on the coast of Maine.

or just watching the sailboards and the skyline. Along the way, you can cross Baxter Boulevard and spend time picnicking, playing tennis, or flying a kite in 48-acre **Payson Park.**

Talk about an urban oasis. The 85-acre **Fore River Sanctuary,** owned by Maine Audubon, has two miles of blue-blazed trails that wind through a salt marsh, link with the historic Cumberland and Oxford Canal towpath, and pass near **Jewell Falls,** Portland's only waterfall, protected by Portland Trails. From downtown Portland, take Congress Street West (Rte. 22), past I-295. From here there are two access routes: Either turn right onto Stevens Avenue (Rte. 9), continue to Brighton Avenue (Rte. 25), turn left and go about 1.25 miles to Rowe Avenue, and then turn left and park at the end of the road; or continue past Stevens Avenue, about one-half mile to Frost Avenue, take a hard right, and then left into the Maine Orthopedic Center parking lot. Portland Trails raised the funds for the handsome 90-foot pedestrian bridge at this entrance to the sanctuary. Open sunrise to sunset daily. No pets.

Bird-watchers flock to 239-acre **Evergreen Cemetery** (Stevens Ave.) in May to see warblers, thrushes, and other migratory birds that gather in the ponds and meadows. During peak periods, it's possible to see as many as 20 warbler species in a morning, including the Cape May, bay breasted, mourning, and Tennessee. Naturalists from Maine Audubon often are on-site helping to identify birds. For more info, check the events calendar at www.mainebirding.net.

SCARBOROUGH

Scarborough Beach Park (Black Point Rd., Rte. 207, 207/883-2416, www.scarboroughbeachstatepark.com, $4 adults, $2 children), a long stretch of sand, is the best beach for big waves. Between the parking area and the lovely stretch of beach you'll pass Massacre Pond, named for a 1703 skirmish between resident Indians and resident wannabes. (Score: Indians 19, wannabes 0.) The park is open all year for swimming, surfing (permit required), beachcombing, and ice skating, but on weekends in summer the parking lot fills early.

At 3,100 acres, **Scarborough Marsh** (Pine Point Rd., Rte. 9, 207/883-5100, www.maineaudubon.org, 9:30 A.M.–5:30 P.M. daily mid-June–early Sept., weekends in late May and Sept.), Maine's largest salt marsh, is prime territory for bird-watching and canoeing. Rent a canoe ($16 one hour, $23 for 1.5 hours, $30 for two hours) at the small nature center operated by Maine Audubon, and explore on your own. Or join one of the daily 90-minute guided tours (call for the schedule, $11 adults, $9 children, subtract $1.50 pp if you have your own canoe). Guided full-moon tours ($12 adults, $10 children) June–September are particularly exciting; dress warmly and bring a flashlight. Other special programs, some geared primarily for children, include wildflower walks, art classes, and dawn bird-watching trips; all require reservations and very reasonable fees. Also here is a walking-tour trail of less than one mile. Pick up a map at the center.

Overlooking the marsh is 52-acre **Scarborough River Wildlife Sanctuary** (Pine Point Rd./Rte. 9), with 1.5 miles of walking trails that loop to the Scarborough River and by two ponds.

FALMOUTH (NORTH OF PORTLAND)

Nearly a dozen of Falmouth's parks, trails, and preserves, official and unofficial, are described and mapped in the *Falmouth Trail Guide,* a handy little booklet published by the Falmouth Conservation Commission. Copies are available at Gilsland Farm, Falmouth Town Hall, and local bookstores. Two of the best options are described below.

A 65-acre wildlife sanctuary and environmental center on the banks of the Presumpscot River, **Gilsland Farm** (20 Gilsland Farm Rd., 207/781-2330, www.maineaudubon.org, dawn–dusk daily) is state headquarters for Maine Audubon. More than two miles of easy, well-marked trails wind through the grounds, taking in salt marshes, rolling meadows, woodlands, and views of the estuary. Observation blinds allow inconspicuous spying during bird-migration season. In the education center (9 A.M.–5 P.M. Mon.–Sat., noon–4 P.M. Sun.) are hands-on exhibits, a nature store, and classrooms and offices. Fees are charged for special events, but otherwise it's all free. The visitors center is one-quarter mile off Route 1.

Once the summer compound of the prominent Baxter family, Falmouth's 100-acre **Mackworth Island,** reached via a causeway, is now the site of the Governor Baxter School for the Deaf. Limited parking is just beyond the security booth on the island. On the 1.5-mile vehicle-free perimeter path (great Portland Harbor views), you'll meet bikers, hikers, and dog walkers. Just off the trail on the north side of the island is the late governor Percival Baxter's stone-circled pet cemetery, maintained by the state at the behest of Baxter, who donated this island as well as Baxter State Park to the people of Maine. From downtown Portland, take Route 1 across the Presumpscot River to Falmouth Foreside. Andrews Avenue (third street on the right) leads to the island. Open sunrise–sunset year-round.

Trail Network

Portland Trails (305 Commercial St., 207/775-2411, www.trails.org), a dynamic membership conservation organization incorporated in 1991, is dedicated to creating and maintaining a 50-mile network of hiking and biking trails in Greater Portland. It already has 30 mapped trails to its credit, including the 2.1-mile Eastern Promenade Trail, a landscaped bayfront dual pathway circling the base of Munjoy Hill and linking East End Beach to the Old Port, and a continuing trail connecting the Eastern Prom with the 3.5-mile Back Cove Trail, on the other side of I-295. Trail maps are available online. The group also holds organized walks ($5 nonmembers)—a great way to meet some locals. Better still, join Portland Trails ($35 a year) and support its ambitious efforts.

Bicycling

The **Bicycle Coalition of Maine** (207/623-4511, www.bikemaine.org) has an excellent website that lists nearly two dozen trails in Greater Portland. You'll also find info on events, organized rides, bike shops, and more. Another good resource is **Casco Bay Bicycle Club** (www.cascobaybicycleclub.org), a recreational cycling club with rides several times weekly. Check its website for details.

For rentals (hybrids $25/day) and repairs visit **Cycle Mania** (59 Federal St., 207/774-2933, www.cyclemania1.com).

The best locales for island bicycling—fun for families and beginners but not especially challenging for diehards—are Peaks and Great Chebeague Islands, but do remember to follow the rules of the road.

Golf

You'll have no problem finding a place to tee off in Greater Portland. Some of the best courses are private, so if you have an "in," so much the better—but there are still plenty of public and semiprivate courses for every skill level. Free advice on helping you choose a course is offered by Maine's Golf Concierge (info@golfme.com).

Let's just consider Greater Portland's 18-hole courses. **Sable Oaks Golf Club** (505 Country Club Dr., South Portland, 207/775-6257, www.sableoaks.com) is considered one of the toughest and best of Maine's public courses. Since 1998, **Nonesuch River Golf Club** (304 Gorham Rd., Rte. 114, Scarborough, 207/883-0007 or 888/256-2717, www.nonesuchgolf.com) has been drawing raves for the challenges of its par-70 championship course and praise from environmentalists for preserving wildlife habitat; there's a full-size practice range and green, too. The City of Portland's **Riverside Municipal Golf Course** (1158 Riverside St., 207/797-3524, www.playriverside.com) has an 18-hole par-72 course (Riverside North) and a nine-hole par-35 course (Riverside South). Opt for the 18-hole course.

Sea Kayaking

With all the islands scattered through Casco Bay, Greater Portland has become a hotbed of sea-kayaking activity. The best place to start is out on Peaks Island, 15 minutes offshore via Casco Bay Lines ferry. **Maine Island Kayak Company** (MIKCO, 70 Luther St., Peaks Island, 207/766-2373 or 800/796-2373, www.maineislandkayak.com) is a successful tour operation that organizes half-day, all-day, and multiday local kayaking trips as well as national and international adventures. An introductory half-day tour in Casco Bay is $65 per person; a full day is $110, including lunch. Reservations are essential. MIKCO also does private lessons and group courses and clinics (some require previous experience). MIKCO's owner, Tom Bergh, has a flawless reputation for safety and skill.

Lobstering Cruise

Learn all kinds of lobster lore and maybe even catch your own dinner with **Lucky Catch Lobster Tours** (170 Commercial St., 207/233-2026 or 888/624-6321, www.luckycatch.com, $25 adults, $25 seniors and children 13–18, $15 2–12). Captain Tom Martin offers three different 80-to-90-minute cruises on his 37-foot lobster boat. On each (except late Saturdays and all-day Sundays, when state law prohibits it), usually 10 traps are hauled and the process and gear explained. You can even help if you want. Any lobsters caught are available for purchase after the cruise for wholesale boat price (and you can have them cooked nearby for a reasonable rate). Wouldn't that make a nice story to tell the folks back home?

Boating Excursions

Down on the Old Port wharves are several excursion-boat businesses. Each has carved out a niche, so choose according to your interest and your schedule. Dress warmly and wear rubber-soled shoes. Remember that all cruises are weather-dependent.

Portland Discover – Land & Sea Tours (Long Wharf, 207/774-0808, www.portlanddiscovery.com) comprises **Mainely Tours, Eagle Island Tours** and **Bay View Cruises.** Options include a Lighthouse Lover's Cruise, departing two to three times daily, for $18 adults, $12 children; a 90-minute Sunset Lighthouse Cruise, $20 adults, $14 children; and a four-hour cruise to Eagle Island, departing five days weekly late June through August, weekends only in September, for $30 adults, $20 children. The Eagle Island cruise visits the island where Arctic explorer Admiral Robert Peary built his summer home, allowing time on the island to visit the house and wander the grounds. Pack a picnic.

Cruise up to 20 miles offshore seeking whales with **Odyssey Whale Watch** (Long Wharf, 170 Commercial St., 207/775-0727, www.odysseywhalewatch.com, $45 adults, $40 seniors and children 13–17, $35 under 12). Four- to five-hour whale watches aboard the *Odyssey* depart daily at 10 A.M. late June–early September, plus spring and fall weekends. (Don't overload on breakfast that day, and take preventive measures if you're motion-sensitive.)

Sail quietly across the waters of Casco Bay

© HILARY NANGLE

Portland Schooner Company's historic sailing vessels dock near the city's whaling wall.

aboard a windjammer with **Portland Schooner Company** (Maine State Pier, 56 Commercial St., 207/766-2500, www.portlandschooner.com, late May–Oct., $35 adults, $10 children 3–12). Three or four two-hour sails are offered daily on two schooners, the 72-foot *Bagheera* and the 88-foot *Wendameen,* both historical vessels designed by John G. Alden and built in East Boothbay. Overnight windjammer trips also are available for $240 per person, including dinner and breakfast.

Spectator Sports

A pseudo-fierce mascot named Slugger stirs up the crowds at baseball games played by the **Portland Sea Dogs** (Hadlock Field, 271 Park Ave., 207/879-9500 or 800/936-3647, www.portlandseadogs.com), a AA Boston Red Sox farm team. Ever since the team arrived in 1994, loyal local fans have made tickets scarce, so it's wise to reserve well ahead (you'll pay a minimal reservation surcharge). The season schedule (early Apr.–Aug.) is available after January 1. Tickets are less than $10.

For ice hockey action, the **Portland Pirates** (207/775-3458, www.portlandpirates.com, $12–17), a farm team for the American Hockey League's Buffalo Sabres, plays winter and spring home games at the 8,700-seat Cumberland County Civic Center.

The newest entry into Portland's professional teams is the **Red Claws** (207/210-6655, www.maineredclaws.com), an NBA development team for the Boston Celtics. Home court is the Portland Expo.

ACCOMMODATIONS

Downtown Portland

Portland's peninsula doesn't have an overwhelming amount of sleeping space, but it does have good variety in all price ranges. Rates reflect peak season.

INNS AND BED-AND-BREAKFASTS

All of these are in older buildings without elevators. Stairs may be steep.

Railroad tycoon John Deering built **The Inn at St. John** (939 Congress St., 207/773-6481 or 800/636-9127, www.innatstjohn.com, $89–259) in 1897. The comfortable (if somewhat tired) moderately priced 37-room hostelry welcomes children and pets and even has bicycle storage. Cable TV, air-conditioning, free local calls, free parking, free airport pickup, and a meager continental breakfast are provided. Most rooms have private baths (some are detached); some have fridge and microwave. The downside is the lackluster neighborhood—in the evening you'll want drive or take a taxi when going out. It's about a half-hour walk to the Old Port or an $8 taxi fare.

Staying at **The Pomegranate Inn** (49 Neal St. at Carroll St., 207/772-1006 or 800/356-0408, www.pomegranateinn.com, $185–295) is an adventure in itself, with faux painting, classical statuary, art, antiques, and whimsical touches everywhere—you'll either love it or find it a bit much. The elegant 1884 Italianate mansion has seven guest rooms and a suite, all with air-conditioning, TV, and phones, some with fireplaces. Afternoon refreshments are served.

Take a carefully renovated 1830s town house, add contemporary amenities and a service-oriented innkeeper, and the result is the **Morrill Mansion Bed and Breakfast** (249 Vaughan St., 207/774-6900 or 888/566-7745, www.morrillmansion.com, $149–239), on the West End. Six rooms and one suite are spread out on the 2nd and 3rd floors. No frilly Victorian accents here—rather, the decor is understated yet tasteful, taking advantage of hardwood floors and high ceilings. You'll find free Wi-Fi and local calls and TV with DVD player in each room. A continental breakfast is included; off-street parking is free. It's near the hospital, so you might hear a siren or two.

In the same neighborhood is **The Chadwick Bed & Breakfast** (140 Chadwick St., 207/774-5141 or 800/774-2137, www.thechadwick.com, $150–175), where innkeeper Buddy Marcum welcomes guests warmly and treats them like royalty with plush linens, cozy robes, and memorable breakfasts. All rooms have flat-screen TVs with DVD players and Wi-Fi; a movie library is available.

Former travel writer Dale Northrup put his experience to work in opening the **Percy Inn** (15 Pine St., 207/871-7638 or 888/417-3729, www.percyinn.com, $129–209), just off Longfellow Square. You can easily hole up in the air-conditioned guest rooms, which are furnished with phones, fax machines, CD players, TVs with VCRs, wet bars, and stocked refrigerators. It's best suited for independent-minded travelers who don't desire much contact with the host or other guests, as public rooms are few and the innkeeper is rarely on-site. Breakfast is a continental buffet.

Built in 1835, **The Inn at Park Spring** (135 Spring St., 207/774-1059 or 800/427-8511, www.innatparkspring.com, $139–185) is one of Portland's longest-running bed-and-breakfasts. Current innkeepers Nancy and John Gonsalves are adding their own touches to make guests feel right at home. The location is fab; just steps from most Arts District attractions. Six somewhat quirky guest rooms are spread out on three floors. All have air-conditioning and phones, some have Internet access; one has a private patio and entrance. There's a guest fridge on each floor. Rates include a full breakfast served around a common table.

Built in 1877, the handsome Georgian-style **West End Inn** (146 Pine St. at Neal St., 207/772-1377 or 800/338-1377, www.westendbb.com, $175–225) has six nicely decorated 2nd- and 3rd-floor guest rooms. A full breakfast and afternoon refreshments are served. Pack light if you're on the 3rd floor.

FULL-SERVICE HOTELS

You might have trouble finding the **Portland Regency** (20 Milk St., 207/774-4200 or 800/727-3436, www.theregency.com, $250–300): This lovely hotel is secreted in a renovated armory in the heart of the Old Port. Local calls, Wi-Fi, and shuttles to all major Portland transportation facilities are free. Be forewarned: Room configurations vary widely—some provide little natural window light or are strangely shaped. All have 27-inch TVs, mini-bars, and air-conditioning. A restaurant, spa, and fitness center are on-site.

Newest and most luxurious is the **Portland Harbor Hotel** (468 Fore St., 207/775-9090 or 888/798-9090, www.portlandharborhotel.com, $249–379), an upscale boutique hotel in the Old Port built around a garden courtyard. Rooms are plush, with chic linens, duvets, down pillows on the beds, Wi-Fi and digital cable TV, and bathrooms with separate soaking tubs and showers. Bike rentals are available for $15 per day, and the hotel offers a free local car service. The restaurant is excellent. The downside is that the neighborhood can be noisy at night, so request a room facing the interior courtyard, preferably on the upper floors. Best splurge are the suites, added in 2009.

Yes, it's a chain, and yes, it's downright ugly, but the service-oriented **Holiday Inn by the Bay** (88 Spring St., 207/775-2311 or 800/345-5050, www.innbythebay.com, $160–200) provides a lot of bang for the buck. It's conveniently situated between the waterfront and the Arts District; rooms on upper floors have views either over Back Cove or Portland Harbor; Wi-Fi and parking are free as is a shuttle service. It also has an indoor pool, sauna, fitness room, on-site laundry facilities, restaurant, and lounge.

The 'Burbs

South of Portland are two upscale beachfront inns.

In 2007, the **Black Point Inn Resort** (510 Black Point Rd., Prouts Neck, Scarborough, 207/883-2500 or 800/258-0003, www.blackpointinn.com, $240–300 pp, including breakfast, afternoon tea, and dinner) reopened after being dramatically downsized and upscaled. The historic shingle-style hotel opened in 1878 at the tip of Prouts Neck. It overlooks Casco Bay from one side and down to Old Orchard from the other, and it has beaches out the front and back doors. Now owned by a local partnership, the inn has returned to its roots, catering to wealthy rusticators. The Point Restaurant is open to the public by reservation (6–9 P.M. daily, $24–38), and the less-fussy Chart Room (11:30 A.M.–9 P.M. daily) serves lighter fare ($10–18)—but first, have cocktails on the porch at sunset. Staying here is splurge worthy. Guests have access to a private 18-hole golf course and tennis courts.

Equally splurge worthy and especially suited for families is the oceanfront **Inn by the Sea** (40 Bowery Beach Rd., Rte. 77, Cape Elizabeth, 207/799-3134 or 800/888-4287, www.innbythesea.com), just seven miles south of downtown Portland. Guests stay in handsome suites and cottages, most with kitchens or expanded wet bars, comfy living rooms, and big views (peak rates begin around $400). A major renovation and expansion in 2008 added a cozy lounge, full-service spa, and small cardio room. Big windows frame ocean views at **Sea Glass** (207/299-3134), where chef Mitchell Kaldrovich favors Maine ingredients in his creative breakfasts, lunches, and dinners. Other facilities include an outdoor pool, *boules* court, wildlife habitats, and a private boardwalk winding through a salt marsh to the southern end of Crescent Beach State Park. By reservation, pets are honored guests here (they even have their own room-service menu).

FOOD

Downtown Portland alone has more than 100 restaurants, so it's impossible to list even all the great ones—and there are many. The city's proximity to fresh foods, from both farms and the sea, makes it popular with chefs, and its Italian roots and growing immigrant population mean a good choice of ethnic dining, too. Here is a choice selection, by neighborhood, with open days and hours provided for peak season. You'll note that some restaurants don't list a closing time; that's because they shut the doors when the crowd thins, so to be safe call ahead if you're heading out much after 8 P.M. Do make reservations, whenever possible, and as far in advance as you can, especially in July and August. If you're especially into the food scene, check www.portlandfoodmap.com for a breakdown by cuisine of Portland restaurants, with links to recent reviews.

In addition to the many restaurant options listed here, check the Community News listings in each Wednesday's *Portland Press Herald.* Under "Potluck," you'll find listings of **public meals,** usually benefiting nonprofit organizations. Prices are always quite low (under $10 for adults, $2–4 for children), mealtimes quite early (5 or 6 P.M.), and the flavor quite local.

When you need a java fix, **Coffee by Design** (locations at 620 Congress St.; 67 India St.; 43 Washington Ave.) is the local choice, not only for its fine brews but also for its support of local artists and community causes.

The Portland Farmers Market sets up on Wednesdays on Monument Square and on Saturdays in Deering Oaks Park.

The Old Port and the Waterfront

LOCAL FLAVORS

All of these are east of the Franklin Street Arterial, between Congress and Commercial Streets.

Best known for the earliest and most filling breakfast, **Becky's Diner** (Hobson's Wharf, 390 Commercial St., Old Port, 207/773-7070, www.beckysdiner.com, 4 A.M.–9 P.M. daily) has more than a dozen omelet choices, just for a start. It also serves lunch and dinner, all at downright cheap prices.

The color's a lot more local just down the street at **The Porthole** (20 Custom House Wharf, Commercial St., Old Port, 207/774-6652, www.portholemaine.com, 7 A.M.–2 A.M. daily), a onetime dive that's been gussied up a bit. The $5.95 all-you-can-eat Friday fish fry pulls in *real* fishermen, in-the-know locals, and fearless tourists. Eat inside or on the wharf. I like it for breakfast or the Friday fish fry.

Enjoy pizza with a view at **Flatbread Company** (72 Commercial St., 207/772-8777, www.flatbreadcompany.com, 11:30 A.M.–10 P.M. daily), part of a small New England chain. The all-natural pizza is baked in a primitive wood-fired clay oven and served in a dining room with a wall of windows overlooking the ferry terminal and Portland Harbor. Vegan option available.

For gourmet goodies don't miss **Browne Trading Market** (Merrill's Wharf, 262 Commercial St., 207/775-7560, www.brownetrading.com). Owner Rod Mitchell became the Caviar King of Portland by wholesaling Caspian caviar, and he's now letting the rest of us in on it. Fresh fish and shellfish fill the cases next to the caviar and cheeses. The mezzanine is wall-to-wall (literally) wine, specializing in French.

When you're craving carbs, want pastries for breakfast, or need to boost your energy with a sweet, follow your nose to **Standard Baking Company** (75 Commercial St., 207/773-2112), deservedly famous for its handcrafted breads and pastries.

CASUAL DINING

Walter's (2 Portland Sq., 207/871-9258, www.walterscafe.com, 11 A.M.–2:30 P.M. and 5–9 P.M. daily, no lunch Sun., $16–26) has been serving creative fusion fare since the 1990s (although in a new location as of late 2009). Despite the longevity, it's never tiresome.

Chef-entrepreneur Harding Lee Smith's **The Grill Room** (84 Exchange St., 207/774-2333, www.thefrontroomrestaurant.com, 11:30 A.M.–2:30 P.M. Mon.–Sat. and 5:30–9 P.M. daily, to 10 P.M. Thurs.–Sat., $8–37) turns out excellent steaks, seafood, and pizzas from its wood-fired grill and oven.

FISH AND SEAFOOD

Ask around, and everyone will tell you the best seafood in town is at **Street and Company** (33 Wharf St., Old Port, 207/775-0887, 5–9:30 P.M., to 10 P.M. Fri.–Sat.). Fresh, beautifully prepared fish (entrées begin about $18) is what you get, often with a Mediterranean flair. Tables are tight, and it's often noisy in the informal brick-walled rooms.

For a broader seafood menu and more landlubber options, consider **Old Port Sea Grille and Raw Bar** (93 Commercial St., 207/879-6100, www.theoldportseagrill.com, opens 11:30 A.M. daily), a sleek modern spot near the waterfront with a fabulous raw bar and 500-gallon aquarium inside. Entrées run $20–33.

For lobster in the rough, head to **Portland Lobster Company** (180 Commercial St.,

207/775-2112, www.portlandlobstercompany.com, 11 A.M.–10 P.M. daily). There's a small inside seating area, but it's much more pleasant to sit out on the wharf and watch the excursion boats come and go. Expect to pay in the low $20 range for a one-pound lobster with fries and slaw. Other choices ($8–23) and a kids' menu are available.

ETHNIC FARE

Be forewarned: Your first foray into **Bresca** (111 Middle St., 207/772-1004, opens 5:30 P.M. Tues.–Sat., $18–28) won't be your last. Chef Krista Kerns delivers big flavor in this tiny, Mediterranean-flavored space next to Portland's police station. She shops each morning, buying just enough for that night's meal (yes, items do sell out). You'll need a reservation to land one of the 20 seats. Service is personal, the meal is leisurely, the food divine. Do save room for dessert: Krista initially made her name as a pastry chef.

Top-notch for northern Italian is **Cinque Terre Ristorante** (36 Wharf St., 207/347-6154, www.cinqueterremaine.com, 5–9 P.M. Sun.–Thurs., to 10 P.M. Fri.–Sat.). Chef Lee Skawinski is committed to sustainable farming, and much of the seasonal and organic produce used comes from the restaurant owners' Laughing Stock Farm and other Maine farms. Choose from half- or full-size portions ranging $12–28. Service can be iffy.

The Corner Room Kitchen and Bar (110 Exchange St., 207/879-4747, www.thefrontroomrestaurant.com, 11:30 A.M.–10 P.M. Mon.–Fri., 5–10 P.M. Sat., 4–9 P.M. Sun., $8–15), another of popular local chef Harding Lee Smith's restaurants, takes its cue from rustic Italian fare, with hearty and delicious pizzas, pastas, and paninis.

Pasta doesn't get much more authentic than that served at **Paciarino** (468 Fore St., www.paciarino.com, 11:30 A.M.–2:30 P.M. and 6–9 P.M. daily, $16–26). Owners Fabiana De Savino and Enrico Barbiero moved here from Milan in 2008, and they make their pastas and sauces fresh daily using recipes from De Savino's *nonna*.

Vegan and vegetarian cuisine comes with an Asian accent at **Green Elephant** (608 Congress St., 207/347-3111, www.greenelephantmaine.com, 11:30 A.M.–2:30 P.M. and 5–9:30 P.M. Tues.–Sat., $9–14). There's not one shred of *real* meat on the creative menu, but you won't miss it.

Irish fare with a Maine accent fills the menu at **Ri-Ra** (72 Commercial St., Old Port, 207/761-4446, www.rira.com, 11:30 A.M.–10 P.M. daily). Entrées in the glass-walled 2nd-floor dining room (overlooking the Casco Bay Lines ferry terminal) are $12–25. The ground-floor pub, elegantly woody with an enormous bar, is inevitably stuffed to the gills on weekends—a great spot for such traditional fare as corned beef and cabbage (pub entrées $8–16) as long as you can stand the din. No reservations, so be prepared to wait, especially on weekends.

DESTINATION DINING

Plan well in advance to land a reservation at **Fore Street** (288 Fore St., Old Port, 207/775-2717, www.forestreet.biz, 5:30–10 P.M. Sun.–Thurs., to 10:30 P.M. Fri.–Sat.). Chef Sam Hayward, renowned for his passionate and creative use of Maine-sourced ingredients, won the James Beard Award for Best Chef in the Northeast in 2004 and has been featured in most of the foodie publications. The renovated former warehouse has copper-topped tables, an open kitchen, and industrial decor chic—quiet it's not. Entrées begin around $20. The restaurant is a joint project with Street and Company owner Dana Street.

Arts District

These restaurants are clustered from Danforth Street up to and around and along Congress Street.

LOCAL FLAVORS

Can't make up your mind? Peruse the choices available at **Public Market House** (28 Monument Sq., 207/228-2056, www.publicmarkethouse.com, 8 A.M.–6 P.M. Mon.–Sat., 10 A.M.–5 P.M. Sun.), a growing space with vendors selling meats, cheeses, breads, Greek food, sandwiches, baked goods, soups, and other fresh fare.

Be sure to have a reservation if you're going, pre-theater, to **BiBo's Madd Apple Café** (23 Forest Ave., 207/774-9698, www.bibosportland.com, 11:30 A.M.–2 P.M. Wed.–Fri., 5:30–9 P.M. Wed.–Sat., plus 11 A.M.–2 P.M. Sat.–Sun.)—it's right next to the Portland Performing Arts Center. On the other hand, it's popular anytime, thanks to chef Bill Boutwell (BiBo). There's no way of predicting what will be on the bistro-fusion menu. Dinner entrées begin around $17.

Well off most tourists' radar screens is **Artemisia Café** (61 Pleasant St., 207/761-0135, 9 A.M.–3 P.M. Mon.–Fri., 9 A.M.–2 P.M. Sat.–Sun.), a cheery neighborhood café with a creative menu drawing upon international influences.

ETHNIC FARE

Portland has a number of good Japanese restaurants, with **Yosaku** (1 Danforth St., 207/780-0880, 11:30 A.M.–2 P.M. and 5–9:30 P.M. Mon.–Thurs., to 10:30 P.M. Fri.–Sat., noon–3 P.M. and 5–9:30 P.M. Sun.) being one of the better choices.

Miyake (129 Spring St., 207/871-9170, 5–9 P.M. Mon.–Thurs., to 9:30 P.M. Fri.–Sat.) is another. Chef Masa Miyake's tiny, ultra-informal neighborhood joint is considered a must-go among discerning sushi lovers, who think nothing of $35 for dinner; BYOB. The decor is Pepsi and plastic, but don't let that dissuade you—you can always get it to go.

Ever-popular **Local 188** (685 Congress St., 207/761-7909, www.local188.com, 5:30–10 P.M. Mon.–Fri., 9 A.M.–2 P.M. and 5:30–10 P.M. Sat.–Sun.) serves fabulous Mediterranean-inspired food with a tapas-heavy menu. It doubles as an art gallery, with rotating exhibits. Most tapas selections are under $10, most heartier choices and entrées run $16–20. Free parking behind the building.

Just outside the Arts District, **El Rayo Taqueria** (101 York St., 207/780-8226, www.elrayotaqueria.com, 11 A.M.–10 P.M. Tues.–Sat.), in a former gas station, delivers Cal-Mex flavors, with almost everything costing less (often far less) than $10.

DESTINATION DINING

Fun, whimsical, and artsy best describes most restaurants in the Arts District, but not **Five Fifty-Five** (555 Congress St., 207/761-0555, www.fivefifty-five.com, 5–9:30 P.M. Mon.–Thurs., to 10:30 P.M. Fri.–Sat., 9:30 A.M.–2 P.M. and 5–9:30 P.M. Sun.), where chef Steve Corry was named by *Food and Wine* as one of the top 10 Best New Chefs in the country. Fresh, local, and seasonal are blended in creative ways on his ever-changing menu, which is divided into small plates, green plates, savory plates, cheese plates, and sweet plates, with prices ranging about $8–32. A five-course tasting menu is around $60. If you can't afford to splurge in the main restaurant, Corry serves lighter fare in the lounge.

Another up-and-comer is Erik Desjarlais, whose classical French techniques and fare are earning national attention for **Evangeline** (190 State St., 207/791-2800, www.restaurantevangeline.com, 5:30–10 P.M. Mon.–Sat.) on Longfellow Square. The menu changes frequently, with entrées usually beginning around $21. On Monday nights, Desjarlais offers a three-course prix fixe menu, often prepared with his wife, chef Krista Kerns of Bresca. Lighter, but no less classic, fare is served in the bar.

West End

Chef Abby Harmon's **Caiola's Restaurant** (58 Pine St., 207/772-1111, www.caiolas.com, 5:30–9:30 P.M. Tues.–Thurs., to 10 P.M. Fri.–Sat., 9 A.M.–2 P.M. Sun.) delivers comfort food with pizzazz in a cozy neighborhood bistro. This little gem is off most visitors' radar screens, but locals fill it nightly. Entrées begin around $14.

Superb thin-crust pizzas in usual and unusual flavor combos emerge from the wood-fired oven at chef Oliver Outerbridge's **Bonobo** (46 Pine St., 207/347-8267, lunch 11:30 A.M.–2:30 P.M. Wed.–Fri., noon–4 P.M. Sat., dinner

4–10 P.M. Sun.–Thurs., to 11 P.M. Fri.–Sat.). After the pizza, head to the ice cream window, serving Maple's Organics gelato.

Have breakfast or lunch or pick up prepared foods at **Aurora Provisions** (64 Pine St., 207/871-9061, www.auroraprovisions.com, 8 A.M.–6:30 P.M. Mon.–Sat.), a combination market and café with irresistible goodies, most made on the premises.

Tiny **Dogfish Cafe** (953 Congress St., 207/253-5400, www.thedogfishcafe.com, 11:30 A.M.–9:30 P.M. Mon.–Wed., to 10 P.M. Thurs.–Sat., 10 A.M.–2 P.M. Sun., $8–12) packs 'em in for salads and sandwiches and grilled goodies. It's just a couple of doors down from the Inn on St. John.

Bayside

Portlanders have long favored **Bintliff's American Café** (98 Portland St., 207/774-0005, www.bintliffscafe.com, 7 A.M.–2 P.M. daily) for its breakfasts and brunches ($7–12); the menu is humongous. No reservations, so expect to wait in line on weekends.

For an elegant meal in a true fine-dining setting, reserve a table at the **Back Bay Grill** (65 Portland St., near the main post office, 207/772-8833, 5:30–9:30 P.M. Mon.–Thurs., to 10 P.M. Fri.–Sat.). The serene dining room is accented by a colorful mural, and arts-and-crafts wall sconces cast a soft glow on the white linen-draped tables. The menu, which highlights fresh, seasonal ingredients, ranks among the best in the city, and the wine list is long and well chosen. Service is professional. Entréees are $19–35 and worth every penny.

East End

These dining spots are all east of the Franklin Street Arterial. Poke around this end of the city and you'll find quite a few ethnic hole-in-the-wall places on and around Washington Avenue. It's an ever-changing array, but if you're adventurous (or budget confined), give one a try.

LOCAL FLAVORS

Chocoholics take note: When a craving strikes, head to **Dean's Sweets** (82 Middle St., 207/899-3664) for adult-flavored dark-chocolate truffles made without nuts.

If you're a tea fan, don't miss **Homegrown Herb & Tea** (195 Congress St., 207/774-3484, www.homegrownherbandtea.com), an Ayurvedic shop that blends black, green, and herbal teas and serves light fare, including a delightful lavender shortbread.

The most incredible fries come from **Duckfat** (43 Middle St., 207/774-8080, www.duckfat.com, 11 A.M.–9 P.M. Mon.–Sat., to 5 P.M. Sun., $5–13), an ultra-casual order-at-the-counter joint owned by chef Rob Evans (of Hugo's fame)—so you know it's not only good, but it has that spark, too. Fries—fried in duck fat, of course—are served in a paper cone and accompanied by your choice of six sauces; the truffle ketchup is heavenly. Want to really harden those arteries? Order the *poutine,* Belgian fries topped with Maine cheese curd and homemade duck gravy. In addition, Duckfat serves paninis, soups, salads, and really good milk shakes; wine and beer are available, too.

Mainers love their Italian sandwiches, and **Amato's** (71 India St., 207/773-1682, www.amatos.com, 6:30 A.M.–11 P.M. daily) is credited with creating this drool-worthy sub, usually made with ham, cheese, tomatoes, green peppers, black olives, and onions wrapped in a doughy roll and drizzled with olive oil. Also available are calzones, salads, and other Italian-inspired foods. Amato's has outlets throughout southern Maine. This one has outdoor patio seating.

Micucci's Grocery Store (45 India St., 207/775-1854) has been servicing Portland's Italian community since 1949. It's a great stop for picnic fixings and a nice selection of inexpensive wines. It's also home to baker Stephen Lanzalotta's to-die-for breads, pastries, and pizzas.

Huge portions at rock-bottom prices make **Silly's** (40 Washington Ave., 207/772-0360, www.sillys.com, 11:30 A.M.–9 P.M. Tues.–Sun.) an ever-popular choice among the young and budget minded; it has a huge menu, too, with lots of international flair and milk shakes in dozens of wacko flavors. And the decor? Vintage 1950s Formica and chrome.

Traditional Salvadorian foods (think Mexican with attitude) have turned hole-in-the-wall **Tu Casa** (70 Washington Ave., 207/828-4971, www.tucasaportland.com, 11 A.M.–9 P.M. Sun.–Fri.) into a must-visit for in-the-know foodies. It's also a budget find, with almost everything on the menu going for less than $10.

It's hard not to like **North Star Cafe** (225 Congress St., 207/699-2994, www.northstarmusiccafe.com, 7 A.M.–10 P.M. Mon.–Wed., to 11 P.M. Thurs.–Sat., 8 A.M.–4 P.M. Sun.), a low-key and comfy coffeehouse serving excellent soups, sandwiches, and salads, most made from locally sourced and organic ingredients. Live music or readings occur almost every evening.

Just try *not* to walk out with something from **Two Fat Cats Bakery** (47 India St., 207/347-5144)—oh, the cookies! The breads! The pies!

CASUAL DINING

Blue Spoon (89 Congress St., 207/773-1119, 11 A.M.–3 P.M. and 5–9 P.M. Tues.–Sat.) was one of the first upscale eateries on Portland's gentrifying East End. Chef-owner David Iovino, who studied at the French Culinary Institute, has created a warm, welcoming, and inexpensive neighborhood bistro (entrées $9–15), where one of the best sellers is roast chicken that's pan seared and then roasted beneath a hot brick. Vegetarian and vegan selections are available.

Big flavors come out of the small plates served at **Bar Lola** (100 Congress St., 207/775-5652, www.barlola.net, 5–10 P.M. Wed.–Sat.), an intimate and cozy neighborhood bistro serving a tapas-oriented menu.

Primo rustic Italian fare is the rule at **Ribollita** (41 Middle St., 207/774-2972, www.ribollitamaine.com, 5–9 P.M. Tues.–Thurs., to 10 P.M. Fri.–Sat.). You'll want reservations at this small, casual trattoria that's justly popular for delivering fabulous food at fair prices ($13–20); just be in the mood for a leisurely meal.

You never know what'll be on the menu (Indonesian chicken, North African stuffed peppers, maybe Caribbean shrimp cakes?) at funky **Pepperclub** (78 Middle St., 207/772-0531, www.pepperclubrestaurant.com, 5–9 P.M. Sun.–Thurs., to 10 P.M. Fri.–Sat.), but take the risk. Vegetarian and vegan specials are always available, as are local and organic meats and seafood. If your kids are even vaguely adventuresome, they'll find food to like here—and the prices are reasonable (entrées $12–18). In the mornings, it morphs into **The Good Egg** (7–11 A.M. Tues.–Fri., 8 A.M.–1 P.M. Sat.–Sun.), serving breakfast, including gluten-free foods.

DESTINATION DINING

Accolades and honors keep accruing for Rob Evans, chef-owner of **Hugo's** (88 Middle St., corner of Franklin St., 207/774-8538, www.hugos.net, 5:30–9 P.M. Tues.–Thurs., to 9:30 P.M. Sat.–Sun.). In 2009, he won the James Beard award for Best Chef in the Northeast; in 2004, *Food and Wine* named him one of America's 10 Best New Chefs, making Hugo's a destination unto itself. (Not that savvy Portlanders hadn't already been beating a path to his door for his outstanding New American cuisine.) Evans and partner Nancy Pugh offer a menu of small plates ($9–28), making it easy and fun to taste the inspired cuisine. Bar seating is available; for the dining room, reservations are essential.

Beyond the Downtown Peninsula

Craving pho? **Thanh Thanh** (782 Forest Ave., 207/828-1114, 10 A.M.–9:30 P.M. daily) is the go-to for Vietnamese cuisine.

The 'Burbs

Gorgeous presentation, rare cheeses, a ripening room, and a knowledgeable staff all add up to making **The Cheese Iron** (200 Rte. 1, 207/883-4057, www.thecheeseiron.com) a major destination for cheeseheads. Add wine, sandwiches, and a handful of other gourmet goodies, and you've got a first-class picnic or party.

Great sunset views over Portland's skyline,

The Lobster Shack at Two Lights in Cape Elizabeth is the ideal setting for a lobster dinner.

a casual atmosphere, and excellent fare have earned **Saltwater Grille** (231 Front St., South Portland, 207/799-5400, www.saltwatergrille.com, 11 A.M.–3 P.M. and 5–9 P.M. daily) an excellent reputation. Dine inside or on the waterfront deck. Dinner entrées run $18–25.

If you're venturing out to Cape Elizabeth, detour into **The Good Table** (527 Ocean House Rd./Rte. 77, Cape Elizabeth, 207/799-4663, 8 A.M.–9 P.M. Tues.–Sun. in summer, opens 11 A.M. weekdays rest of year). Lisa Kostopoulos's popular local restaurant serves homestyle favorites as well as Greek specialties; entrées $11–16.

Every Mainer has a favorite lobster eatery (besides home), but **The Lobster Shack** (222 Two Lights Rd., Cape Elizabeth, 207/799-1677, www.lobstershack-twolights.com, 11 A.M.–8 P.M. daily late Mar.–mid-Oct.) tops an awful lot of lists. Seniority helps—it's been here since the 1920s. Scenery, too—a panoramic vista in the shadow of Cape Elizabeth Light. Plus the menu—seafood galore (and burgers and hot dogs for those who'd rather not have lobster). Opt for a sunny day; the lighthouse's foghorn can kill your conversation when the fog rolls in.

INFORMATION AND SERVICES

Information

The **Visitor Information Center of the Convention and Visitors Bureau of Greater Portland** (14 Ocean Gateway Pier, 207/772-5800, www.visitportland.com) has tons of brochures, plenty of restaurant menus, and public restrooms. The **Portland Downtown District** (94 Free St., 207/772-6828, www.portlandmaine.com) has a useful website.

Check out the **Portland Public Library** (5 Monument Sq., 207/871-1700, www.portlandlibrary.com).

Public Restrooms

In the Old Port area, you'll find restrooms at the Visitor Information Center (14 Ocean Gateway Pier), Spring Street parking garage (45 Spring St.), Fore Street Parking Garage (419 Fore St.), and Casco Bay Lines ferry terminal (Commercial and Franklin Sts.).

© HILARY NANGLE

Ferries are the lifeline between Portland and the islands of Casco Bay. They're also a convenient and reasonably priced way to get afloat.

On Congress Street, find restrooms at Portland City Hall (389 Congress St.) and the Portland Public Library (5 Monument Sq.). In Midtown, head for the Cumberland County Civic Center (1 Civic Center Sq.). In the West End, use Maine Medical Center.

GETTING THERE AND AROUND

The best overall resource for transportation planning is the website www.transportme.org. It lists schedules, fares, and other information for airlines, buses, ferries, and trains.

The ultra-clean and comfortable **Portland Transportation Center** (100 Thompson Point Rd., 207/828-3939) is the base for **Concord Coachlines** (800/639-3317, www.concordtcoachlines.com) and **Amtrak's Downeaster** (800/872-7245, www.thedowneaster.com). Parking is $3 per day, and the terminal has free coffee, free newspapers (while they last), and vending machines. The **Metro** (114 Valley St., 207/774-0351, $1.25, exact change) and the Zoom buses, with service from Biddeford/Saco, stop here and connect with **Portland International Jetport** (207/774-7301, www.portland-jetport.org), **Vermont Transit Lines** (950 Congress St., 207/772-6587 or 800/552-8737), and **Casco Bay Lines ferry service** (www.cascobaylines.com). If you show your Trailways or Amtrak ticket stub to the Metro bus driver, you'll get a free ride downtown. Taxis charge $1.90 for the first one-tenth mile plus $0.30 for each additional one-tenth mile; minimum fare from the airport is $5.

Parking

Metered street parking is $1 per hour. Parking garages and lots are strategically situated all over downtown Portland, particularly in the Old Port and near the civic center. Some lots accept Park and Shop stickers, each valid for one free hour, from participating merchants. A day of parking generally runs $8–16. The Casco Bay Lines website (www.cascobaylines.com) has a very useful parking map, listing parking lots and garages and their fees.

For winter parking-ban information, call 207/879-0300.

Freeport

Freeport has a special claim to historic fame—it's the place where Maine parted company from Massachusetts in 1820. The documents were signed on March 15, making Maine its own separate state.

At the height of the local mackerel-packing industry here, countless tons of the bony fish were shipped out of South Freeport, often in ships built on the shores of the Harraseeket River. Splendid relics of the shipbuilders' era still line the streets of South Freeport, and no architecture buff should miss a walk, cycle, or drive through the village. Even downtown Freeport still reflects the shipbuilder's craft, with contemporary shops tucked in and around handsome historic houses. Some have been converted to bed-and-breakfasts, others are boutiques, and one even disguises the local McDonald's franchise.

Today, Freeport is best known as the mecca for the shop-till-you-drop set. The hub, of course, is sporting giant L. L. Bean, which has been here since 1912, when founder Leon Leonwood Bean began making his trademark hunting boots (and also unselfishly handed out hot tips on where the fish were biting). More than 120 retail operations now fan out from that epicenter, and you can find almost anything in Freeport (pop. about 7,700)—except maybe a convenient parking spot in midsummer.

When (or if) you tire of shopping, you can always find quiet refuge in the town's preserves and parks and plenty of local color at the Town Wharf in the still honest-to-goodness fishing village of South Freeport.

An orientation note: Don't be surprised to receive directions (particularly for South Freeport) relative to "the Big Indian"—a 40-foot-tall landmark at the junction of Route 1 and South Freeport Road. If you stop at the Maine Visitor Information Center in Yarmouth and continue on Route 1 toward Freeport, you can't miss it.

SHOPPING

Logically, this category must come first in any discussion of Freeport, since shopping's the biggest game in town. It's pretty much a given that anyone who visits Freeport intends to darken the door of at least one shop.

L. L. Bean

If you visit only one store in Freeport, it's likely to be "Bean's." The whole world beats a path to L. L. Bean (95 Main St./Rte. 1, 207/865-4761 or 800/341-4341, www.llbean.com)—or so it seems in July, August, and December. Established as a hunting/fishing supply shop, this giant sports outfitter now sells everything from kids' clothing to cookware on its ever-expanding downtown campus. In 2007, it moved the hunting and fishing store into the expanded main store, and in 2009, the outlet

© HILARY NANGLE

Giant outdoor retailer and outfitter L. L. Bean put Freeport on America's shopping map.

store—a great source for deals on equipment and clothing—moved into the Village Square Shops across Main Street.

Until the 1970s, Bean's remained a rustic store with a creaky staircase and a closet-size women's department. Then a few other merchants began arriving, Bean's expanded, and a feeding frenzy followed. The Bean reputation rests on a savvy staff, high quality, an admirable environmental consciousness, and a no-questions-asked return policy. Bring the kids—for the indoor trout pond, the clean restrooms, and the "real deal" outlet store. The store's open-round-the-clock policy has become its signature; if you show up at 2 A.M. you'll have much of the store to yourself, and you may even spy vacationing celebrities or the rock stars who often visit after Portland shows.

Outlets and Specialty Stores

After Bean's, it's up to your whims and your wallet. The stores stretch for several miles up and down Main Street and along many side streets. Pick up a copy of the *Official Map and Visitor Guide* at any of the shops or restaurants, at one of the visitor kiosks, or at the Hose Tower Information Center (23 Depot St., two blocks east of L. L. Bean). All the big names are here, as are plenty of little ones. Don't overlook the small shops tucked on the side streets, such as **Earrings and Company, Wilbur's of Maine Chocolate Confections,** and **Edgecomb Potters.**

SIGHTS

Desert of Maine

Okay, so maybe it's a bit hokey, but talk about sands of time: More than 10,000 years ago, glaciers covered the region surrounding the Desert of Maine (95 Desert Rd., 207/865-6962, www.desertofmaine.com, early May–mid-Oct., $8.75 adults, $6.75 children 13–16, $5.75 ages 5–12). When they receded, they scoured the landscape, pulverizing rocks and leaving behind a sandy residue that was covered by a thin layer of topsoil. Jump forward to 1797, when William Tuttle bought 300 acres and moved his family here, as well as his house and barn, and cleared the land. Now jump forward again to the present and tour where a once-promising farmland has become a desert wasteland. The 30-minute guided safari-style tram tours combine history, geology, and environmental science and an opportunity for children to hunt for "gems" in the sand. Decide for yourself: Is the desert a natural phenomenon? A man-made disaster? Or does the truth lie somewhere in the middle?

Harrington House and Pettengill Farm

A block south of L. L. Bean is the Harrington House (45 Main St./Rte. 1, 207/865-3170, www.freeporthistoricalsociety.org, free), home base of the Freeport Historical Society. You can pick up walking maps detailing Freeport's architecture for a small fee and tour the house (call for current hours). Exhibits pertaining to Freeport's history and occasionally ones by local artists are presented in two rooms in the restored 1830 Enoch Harrington House, a National Historic Register property.

Also listed on the register is the society's Pettengill Farm, a 19th-century saltwater farm comprising a circa 1810 saltbox-style house, woods, orchards, salt marsh, and lovely perennial gardens. The farmhouse is open only during the annual Pettengill Farm Days in the fall, but the grounds are open at all times. From Main Street, take Bow Street and go 1.5 miles. Turn right onto Pettengill Road. Park at the gate, and then walk along the dirt road for about 15 minutes to the farmhouse.

Maine Potato Vodka

Find out how many Maine-grown potatoes it takes to make Cold River Vodka (Rte. 1, 207/865-4828, www.coldrivervodka.com). Free tours of the distillery cover the process from farm to vodka: cooking, distilling, blending, and bottling. Tours are offered Tuesday through Saturday afternoons, but call in advance to be sure a guide is available.

Eartha

She's a worldly woman, that Eartha. The

DeLorme Mapping Co. (Rte. 1, Yarmouth, 207/846-7000, www.delorme.com/about/eartha.aspx) is home to the world's largest rotating and revolving globe, a three-story tall spherical scale model of Earth. Eartha, as she's known, is quite robust. She measures 41 feet in diameter (with a 130-foot waist) and weighs nearly three tons. Eartha spins in DeLorme's glass-walled lobby, making her visible to passersby, but she's best appreciated up close and, well, as personal as you can get with a monstrous globe. Each continent is detailed with mountains and landforms, vegetation and civilization. Better yet, she spins! Eartha actually resides in Yarmouth. She can be viewed 9:30 A.M.–5 P.M. Monday–Friday. Take Route 1 south from downtown Freeport to the I-295 exit 17 interchange; DeLorme is on the left.

ENTERTAINMENT

Shopping seems to be more than enough entertainment for most of Freeport's visitors, but don't miss the **L. L. Bean Summer Concert Series** (800/341-4341, ext. 37222). At 7:30 P.M. each Saturday early July–Labor Day weekend, Bean's hosts free big-name family-oriented events in Discovery Park, in the Bean's complex. Arrive early (these concerts are *very* popular) and bring a blanket or a folding chair. Call for more info.

Almost every night's a party at **Venue** (5 Depot St., 207/865-1780, www.venuemusicbar.com), with live music varying from open mic to jazz nights. Light menu available.

RECREATION

Parks, Preserves, and Other Attractions

MAST LANDING SANCTUARY

Just one mile from downtown Freeport, Mast Landing Audubon Sanctuary (Upper Mast Landing Rd., 207/781-2330, www.maineaudubon.org, free) is a reprieve from the crowds. Situated at the head of the tide on

GREATER PORTLAND

MAINE WILDLIFE PARK

If you want to see where Maine's wild things are, venture a bit inland to visit the Maine Wildlife Park (56 Game Farm Rd., Gray, 207/657-4977, www.mainewildlifepark.com, 9:30 A.M.–6 P.M. daily, gate closes 4:30 P.M. mid-Apr.–early Nov., $7 ages 13–60, $5 ages 4–12 and 61+). Nearly 25 native species of wildlife can be seen at this state-operated wildlife refuge, including such ever-popular species as moose, black bear, white-tailed deer, and bald eagle. The park began in 1931 as a state-run game farm. For more than 50 years, the Department of Inland Fish and Game reared pheasants here for release during bird-hunting season. At the same time, wildlife biologists and game wardens with the state's Department of Inland Fisheries and Wildlife needed a place to care for orphaned or injured animals.

In 1982, the farm's mission was changed to that of a wildlife and conservation education facility. Today the park is a temporary haven for wildlife, although those who cannot survive in the wild live here permanently.

Among the wildlife that have been in residence at the park are lynx, deer, opossum, black bear, bobcat, porcupine, raccoon, red-tailed hawk, barred and great horned owl, mountain lion, bald eagle, raven, skunk, woodchuck, and coyote. Other frequent guests include wild turkey, fisher, gray fox, kestrel, turkey vulture, wood turtle, and box turtle. Most are here for protection and healing, and visitors are able to view them at close range.

In addition to the wildlife, there are numerous interactive exhibits and displays to view, nature trails to explore, a nature store, snack shack, and even picnic facilities. Special programs and exhibits are often offered on weekends mid-May–mid-September.

The park is 3.5 miles north of Maine Turnpike exit 63. From the coast, take Route 115 from Main Street in downtown Yarmouth to Gray, and then head north on Route 26 for 3.5 miles.

the Harraseeket River estuary, the 140-acre preserve has 3.5 miles of signed trails weaving through an apple orchard, across fields, and through pines and hemlocks. And the name? Ages ago it was the source of masts for the Royal Navy. To find it, take Bow Street (across from L. L. Bean) one mile to Upper Mast Landing Road and turn left. The sanctuary is 0.25 mile on the left.

© HILARY NANGLE

It's possible to sight ospreys nesting on adjacent Googins Island from Wolfe's Neck Woods State Park.

WOLFE'S NECK WOODS STATE PARK

Five miles of easy to moderate trails meander through 233-acre Wolfe's Neck Woods State Park (Wolfe's Neck Rd., 207/865-4465, $3 ages 11–64, $1 children 5–11), just a few minutes' cycle or drive from downtown Freeport. You'll need a trail map, available near the parking area. The easiest route (partly wheelchair-accessible) is the Shoreline Walk, about three-quarters of a mile, starting near the salt marsh and skirting Casco Bay. Sprinkled along the trails are helpful interpretive panels explaining various points of natural history—bog life, osprey nesting, glaciation, erosion, and tree decay. Guided tours are offered at 2 P.M. daily mid-July–late August, weather permitting. Leashed pets are allowed. Adjacent **Googins Island,** an osprey sanctuary, is off-limits. From downtown Freeport, follow Bow Street (across from L. L. Bean) for 2.25 miles; turn right onto Wolfe's Neck Road (also called Wolf Neck Rd.) and go another 2.25 miles.

WOLFE'S NECK FARM

Kids love Wolfe's Neck Farm (10 Burnett Rd., 207/865-4469, www.wolfesneckfarm.org), a 626-acre saltwater farm dedicated to sustainable agriculture and environmental education. Visit with farm animals and enjoy the farm's trails and varied habitats—fields, forests, seashore, and gardens—at no charge.

WINSLOW MEMORIAL PARK

Bring a kite. Bring a beach blanket. Bring a picnic. Bring a boat. Bring binoculars. Heck, bring a tent. Freeport's 90-acre oceanfront town-owned playground, Winslow Memorial Park (207/865-4198, www.freeportmaine.com, $2 nonresidents) has a spectacular setting on a peninsula extending into island-studded Casco Bay. Facilities include a boat launch ($3–5), campground ($20–27, no hookups), fishing pier, volleyball court, scenic trails, playground, restrooms, picnic facilities, and a sand beach—best swimming is at high tide; no lifeguard. On Thursday evenings in July and August, local bands play. The park is 5.5 miles from downtown. Head south on Route 1 to the Big Indian (you'll know it when you see it), go left on the South Freeport Road for one mile to Staples Point Road and follow it to the end.

BRADBURY MOUNTAIN STATE PARK

Six miles from the hubbub of Freeport you're in tranquil, wooded 590-acre Bradbury Mountain State Park (Rte. 9, Pownal, 207/688-4712, $3 adults, $1 children 5–11), with facilities for picnicking, hiking, mountain biking, and rustic camping, but no swimming. Pick up a trail map at the gate and take the easy 0.4-mile (round-trip) Mountain Trail to the 485-foot summit, with superb views east to the ocean and southeast to Portland. In fall, it's gorgeous. Or take the Tote Road Trail, on the western side of the park, where the ghost of Samuel Bradbury occasionally brings a chill to hikers in a hemlock grove. A playground keeps the littlest tykes happy. The nonresident camping fee is $14 per site per night ($11 for residents). The park season is May 15–October 15, but there's winter access for cross-country skiing. From Route 1, cross over I-95 at exit 20 and continue west on Pownal Road to Route 9 and head south.

PINELAND FARMS

Once a home for Maine's mentally disabled citizens, the 1,600-acre Pineland (15 Farm View Dr., New Gloucester, 207/688-4539, www.pinelandfarms.org) campus was closed in 1996. In 2000, the Libra Foundation bought it; now the property comprises 19 buildings and 5,000 acres of farmland, and much of it is open for recreation. Walk or ski the trails, sight birds in the fields and woods, watch cheese being made, stroll through the garden, fish the pond or skate on it in winter, play tennis, go mountain biking or orienteering, or even take a horseback-riding lesson. It's a vast outdoor playground, but your first stop should be the market and visitors center (8 A.M.–7 P.M. daily) to see a list of any events (frequent ones include guided farm tours and family experiences), pick up maps, pay any necessary fees, shop for farm-fresh products, or even grab lunch or snacks. Some activities, such as cross-country and mountain-biking trail access and horseback-riding lessons, require fees. No dogs.

L. L. Bean Outdoor Discovery Schools

Since the early 1980s, the sports outfitter's Outdoor Discovery Schools (888/552-3261, www.llbean.com) have trained thousands of outdoors enthusiasts to improve their skills in fly-fishing, archery, hiking, canoeing, sea kayaking, winter camping, cross-country skiing, orienteering, and even outdoor photography. Here's a deal that requires no planning. **Walk-On Adventures** provides 1.5-to-2.5-hour lessons in sports such as kayak touring, fly casting, archery, clay shooting, snowshoeing, and cross-country skiing for $15, including equipment. All of the longer fee programs, plus canoeing and camping trips, require preregistration well in advance because of their popularity. Some of the lectures, seminars, and demonstrations held in Freeport are free, and a regular catalog lists the schedule. Bean's waterfront **Flying Point Paddling Center** hosts many of the kayaking, saltwater fly-fishing, and guiding programs and is home to the annual **PaddleSports Festival** in June, with free demonstrations, seminars, vendors, lessons, and more.

Excursion Boats

Atlantic Seal Cruises (Town Wharf, South Freeport, 207/865-6112 or 877/285-7325), owned and operated by Captain Tom Ring, makes two or three 2.5-hour cruises daily to 17-acre **Eagle Island** (www.pearyeagleisland.org), a State Historic Site once owned by Admiral Robert Peary of North Pole fame. The trip includes a lobstering demonstration (except Sunday, when lobstering is banned). Fee is $30 adults, $22 children 5–12, $17 ages 1–4. Also ask about daylong excursions to **Seguin Island,** off the Phippsburg Peninsula, where you can climb the light tower and see Maine's only first-order Fresnel lens, the largest on the coast.

Sail the waters of Casco Bay from South Freeport Harbor aboard ***Nimbus*** (207/232-1751, www.sailfreeport.com), a 37-foot classic wooden sloop designed by John G. Alden and built in 1938. Capt. Troy Scott offers two- or three-hour sails from Stout's Point Wharf Co. Rates begin at $40 per person.

Kayak and Canoe Rentals

Ring's Marine Service (Smelt Brook Rd., South Freeport, 207/865-6143 or 866/865-6143, www.ringsmarineservice.com) rents single kayaks for $38, tandems for $60, and canoes for $28 per day, with longer-term rentals and delivery available.

© HILARY NANGLE

Admiral Peary's Eagle Island home is open to visitors who arrive via the *Atlantic Seal.*

ACCOMMODATIONS

If you'd prefer to drop where you shop, Freeport has plentiful accommodations. Rates listed are for peak season.

Downtown

One of Freeport's pioneering bed-and-breakfasts is on the main drag yet away from much of the traffic, in a restored house where Arctic explorer Admiral Donald MacMillan once lived. The 19th-century **White Cedar Inn** (178 Main St., 207/865-9099 or 800/853-1269, www.whitecedarinn.com, $145–290) has seven attractive guest rooms and a two-bedroom suite with antiques, air-conditioning, and Wi-Fi; some have gas fireplaces; one has a TV and accepts dogs ($25). The full breakfast will power you through a day of shopping.

Two blocks north of L. L. Bean, the **Harraseeket Inn** (162 Main St., 207/865-9377 or 800/342-6423, www.harraseeket-inn.com, $199–315) is a splendid 84-room country inn with an indoor pool, cable TV, air-conditioning, phones, and Wi-Fi; many rooms have fireplaces and hot tubs. One room is decorated with Thomas Moser furnishings, otherwise decor is colonial reproduction in the two antique buildings and a modern addition. Rates include a hot-and-cold buffet breakfast and afternoon tea with finger sandwiches and sweets—a refreshing break. Pets are permitted in some rooms. The $25/night fee includes a dog bed, small can of food, treat, and dishes. Ask about packages, which offer excellent value. Children 12 and younger stay free. If you're traveling solo, the nightly Innkeeper's Table (reservation required by 5:30 P.M. for 6:30 P.M. seating, 207/865-1085) is a communal table hosted by an innkeeper and a great way to meet other guests.

Three blocks south of L. L. Bean, on a quiet side street shared with a couple of other bed-and-breakfasts, is **The James Place Inn** (11 Holbrook St., 207/865-4486 or 800/964-9086, www.jamesplaceinn.com, $155–185). Innkeepers Robin and Tori Baron welcome guests to seven comfortable rooms, all with air-conditioning, Wi-Fi, and TV, a few with double whirlpool tubs, and one with a fireplace and private deck. If the weather's fine, enjoy breakfast on the deck. After shopping, collapse on the hammock for two.

Beyond Downtown

Here's a throwback. Three miles north of downtown is the **Maine Idyll** (1411 Rte. 1, 207/865-4201, www.maineidyll.com, $63–103), a tidy cottage colony operated by the Marstaller family for three generations. Twenty studio to three-bedroom pine-paneled cottages are tucked under the trees. All have refrigerators, fireplaces, and TV, and most have limited cooking facilities. Wi-Fi is available near the office. A light breakfast is included. Well-behaved pets are $4.

The family-run **Casco Bay Inn** (107 Rte. 1, 207/865-4925 or 800/570-4970, www.cascobayinn.com, $99–129) is a bit fancier than most motels. It has a pine-paneled lounge with fieldstone fireplace and guest Internet station, plus Wi-Fi throughout. The spacious rooms have double sinks in the bath area, and some have a refrigerator and microwave. A continental breakfast with newspaper is included.

Here's a find, if you're lucky enough to snag it, given there's only one guest room. **Wolf Neck Bed and Breakfast** (93 Birch Point Rd., 207/865-1725, www.wolfneckbb.com, $175) is Dianne Gaudet and Steve Norton's waterfront shingle-style home, built in 2002, where the one guest suite comes complete with sitting room and private deck. Longtime area residents, Dianne and Steve are a great resource on the region. They also provide a full breakfast. Bring your own boat and launch it right here or rent a canoe or kayaks from the hosts.

Camping

For anyone seeking peace, quiet, and low-tech camping in a spectacular setting, **Recompence Shore Campsites** (134 Burnett Rd., 207/865-9307, www.freeportcamping.com, $26–44) is it. Part of Wolfe's Neck Farm, the eco-sensitive campground has 175 wooded tent sites (a few hookups are available), many on the farm's three-mile-long Casco Bay shorefront. Swimming depends on the tides; check the tide calendar in a local newspaper. Take Bow Street (across from L. L. Bean) to Wolfe's Neck Road, turn right, go 1.6 miles, then left on Burnett Road.

FOOD

Freeport has an ever-increasing number of places to eat, but nowhere near enough to satisfy hungry crowds at peak dining hours on busy days. Go early or late for lunch, and make reservations for dinner. Days and hours are for peak season, but it's always wise to verify.

Local Flavors

South of downtown, **Royal River Natural Foods** (443 Rte. 1, 207/865-0046, www.rrnf.com) has a small selection of prepared foods, including soups, salads, and sandwiches, and a seating area.

Craving a proper British tea? **Jacqueline's Tea Room** (201 Main St., 207/865-2123, www.jacquelinestearoom.com) serves a four-course tea by reservation for about $25 per person in an elegant setting. Seatings for the two-hour indulgence are between 11 A.M. and 1 P.M. Tuesday–Friday and every other weekend.

At the Big Indian **Old World Gourmet Deli and Wine Shop** (117 Rte. 1, 207/865-4477, www.oldworldgourmet.com), the offerings are just as advertised, with sandwiches, soups, salads, and prepared foods. There are a few tables inside, but it's mostly a to-go place.

Casual Dining

The Harraseeket Inn's woodsy-themed **Broad Arrow Tavern** (162 Main St., 207/865-9377 or 800/342-6423, 11:30 A.M.–10 P.M. daily, to 11 P.M. Fri.–Sat.), just two blocks north of L. L. Bean but seemingly a world away, is a perfect place to escape shopping crowds and madness. The food is terrific, with everything made from organic and naturally raised foods; prices run $10–23. Can't decide? Opt for the extensive all-you-can-eat lunch buffet ($17) that highlights a bit of everything.

Good wine and fine martinis are what reels them into **Conundrum** (117 Rte. 1, 207/865-0303, 4:30–10 P.M. Tues.–Sat.), near Freeport's

Big Indian, but the food is worth noting, too. Dozens of wines by the glass, more than 20 martinis, and 20 champagnes will keep most oenophiles happy. The food, varying from pâtés and cheese platters to cheeseburgers and maple-barbecued chicken, helps keep patrons sober.

Ethnic Fare

Dine indoors or out on the tree-shaded patio at **Azure Italian Café** (123 Main St., 207/865-123, www.azurecafe.com, 11:30 A.M.–9 P.M. daily, to 10 P.M. Fri.–Sat.). Go light, mixing selections from antipasto, *insalate,* and *zuppa* choices, or savor the heartier entrées ($18–32). The service is pleasant and the indoor dining areas are accented by well-chosen contemporary Maine artwork. Live jazz is a highlight some evenings.

Down the side street across from Azure is **Mediterranean Grill** (10 School St., 207/865-1688, www.mediterraneangrill.biz, 11 A.M.–10 P.M. daily). Because it's off Main Street, the Cigri family's excellent Turkish-Mediterranean restaurant rarely gets the crowds. House specialties such as moussaka, lamb chops, and *tiropetes* augment a full range of kebab and vegetarian choices. Or simply make a meal of the appetizers—the platters are meals in themselves. Sandwiches and wraps are available at lunch. Entrées go for $16–25.

Two surprisingly good, easy-on-the-budget Asian restaurants share a building on the south end of town. **China Rose** (23 Main St., 207/865-6886, 11 A.M.–9:30 P.M. daily, to 10 P.M. Fri.–Sat.) serves Szechuan, Mandarin, and Hunan specialties in a pleasant 1st-floor dining area. Upstairs is **Miyako** (207/865-6888, same hours), with an extensive sushi bar menu, and it also serves other Japanese specialties, including tempura, teriyaki, *nabemono,* and noodle dishes. Luncheon specials are available at both.

Good food and attentive service has made **Thai Garden** (491 Rte. 1, 207/865-6005, 11 A.M.–9 P.M. daily) an ever popular choice.

Fine Dining

The Harraseeket Inn's **Maine Dining Room** (207/865-1085, 6–9 P.M. daily, to 9:30 P.M. Fri.–Sat.) is the finest in town, but it's not

© HILARY NANGLE

Harraseeket Lunch and Lobster hangs over the South Freeport harbor.

GREATER PORTLAND

overly fancy or fussy. The service is excellent, and chef Theda Lyden's menu favors natural and organic foods. Tableside preparations (for 2–7), such as Caesar salad, chateaubriand, and flaming desserts, add an understated note of theater. Dinner entrées are $24–38. Brunch (11:45 A.M.–2 P.M. Sun., $24.95) is a seemingly endless buffet, with whole poached salmon and Belgian waffles among the highlights.

Lobster

In South Freeport, order lobster in the rough at **Harraseeket Lunch and Lobster Company** (36 Main St., Town Wharf, South Freeport, lunch counter 207/865-4888, lobster pound 207/865-3535, 11 A.M.–8:45 P.M. daily in summer, closes at 7:45 P.M. spring and fall). Grab a picnic table, place your order, and go at it. Be prepared for a wait in midsummer. Fried clams are particularly good here, and they're prepared either breaded or battered. Order both and decide for yourself which is better. BYOB; no credit cards.

Craving a crab or lobster roll? Pick up one to go at **Day's Seafood Takeout** (1269 Rte. 1, Yarmouth, 207/836-3436, 11 A.M.–8 P.M. daily), just south of the Freeport line. The fried clams are mighty tasty, too. There are a few picnic tables out back on a tidal estuary.

INFORMATION AND SERVICES

Freeport Merchants Association (Hose Tower, 23 Depot St., 207/865-1212 or 800/865-1994, www.freeportusa.com) produces an invaluable foldout map-guide showing locations of all the shops, plus sites of lodgings, restaurants, visitor kiosks, pay phones, restrooms, and car and bike parking.

Just south of Freeport is the **Maine Visitor Information Center** (Rte. 1, at I-95 exit 17, Yarmouth, 207/846-0833), part of the statewide tourism-information network. Also here are restrooms, phones, picnic tables, vending machines, and a dog-walking area.

MID-COAST REGION

In contrast to the Southern Coast's gorgeous sandy beaches, the Mid-Coast Region is characterized by a deeply indented shoreline with snug harbors and long, gnarled fingers of land. Even though these fingers are inconvenient for driving and bicycling, this is where you'll find picturebook Maine in a panorama format. Mosey to the tips of the peninsulas and come upon lighthouses, fishing villages, country inns, and lobster wharves. The Mid-Coast, as defined in this chapter, stretches from Brunswick through Waldoboro.

The Bath-Brunswick area is one of the least touristy areas of the coast. Not that visitors don't come, but this area has a strong and varied economic base other than tourism, which means that no matter when you visit, you'll find shops, restaurants, and lodgings open and activities scheduled. Bowdoin College, Bath Iron Works, and the Brunswick Naval Air Station (slated for closure by 2011) also contribute to a population more ethnically diverse than in most of Maine and there's an active retiree population. Still, as you drive down the peninsulas that reach seaward from Bath and Brunswick, the vibrancy gives way to traditional fishing villages pressed by the hard realities of maintaining such lifestyles in a modern world and hanging on to waterfront properties in the face of escalating real-estate values.

Wiscasset still clings to the nickname of prettiest village in Maine, but for many travelers heading through it on Route 1, Wiscasset is nothing but a headache. Traffic often backs up for miles, inching forward through the bottleneck village. Although many are just glad to

HIGHLIGHTS

Bowdoin College: This beautiful shady campus is home to the Bowdoin College Museum of Art, the Peary-MacMillan Arctic Museum, and the Maine State Music Theater (page 119).

Maine Maritime Museum: It's easy to while away a half day touring the exhibits in this museum's main and outer buildings and just enjoying the riverfront setting (page 131).

Burnt Island Tour: Step back in history and visit with a lighthouse keeper's family circa 1952 on a living-history tour (page 152).

Coastal Maine Botanical Gardens: This seaside garden comprises more than 240 acres of well-planned exhibits, trails, and art (page 155).

Pemaquid Point Lighthouse: It's hard to say which is Maine's prettiest lighthouse, but Pemaquid's is right up there. It's also depicted on the Maine state quarter (page 166).

Colonial Pemaquid/Fort William Henry: A beautiful setting overlooking John's Bay, a partially reconstructed fort, and remnants from archaeological digs researching one of the first English settlements in America make this site well worth a visit (page 166).

Lobster in the Rough: Lobster wharves abound in Maine, but the Pemaquid Peninsula has a concentration of scenic spots for lobster lovers (page 179).

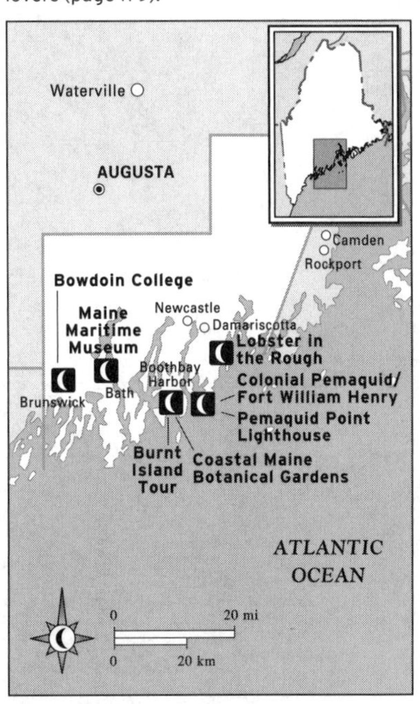

LOOK FOR TO FIND RECOMMENDED SIGHTS, ACTIVITIES, DINING, AND LODGING.

get through it, those who take time to explore Wiscasset are rewarded with multitudes of antiques shops and lovely architecture.

The tempo changes northeast of Wiscasset. Traffic eases and there's less roadside development. Detour down the Boothbay and Pemaquid Peninsulas, and you'll be rewarded with the Maine of postcards. These two peninsulas appear unchallenged as home to more lobster-in-the-rough spots than elsewhere on the coast, and Maine's creative economy is blossoming here, as evidenced by the artists' and artisans' studios that pepper these peninsulas.

PLANNING YOUR TIME

Route 1 is the primary artery connecting all the points in the Mid-Coast Region, and Wiscasset, a major bottleneck, is smack-dab in the middle. For this reason, it's best to split your lodging and explorations into two parts: south of Wiscasset and north of Wiscasset. Even then, driving down the long fingers of land requires patience. The towns south of Wiscasset are less touristy than those on the Boothbay or Pemaquid Peninsulas, with Orr's and Bailey's Islands and the Phippsburg Peninsula being the best places to sprout roots for old-time summer flavor.

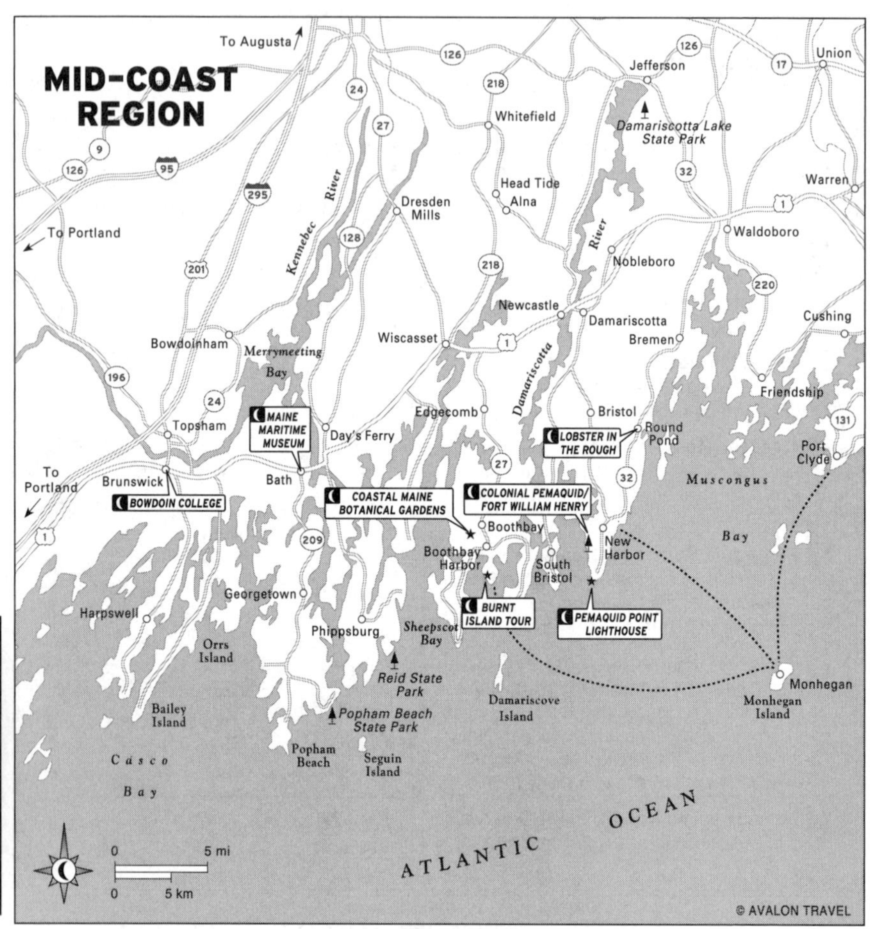

To cover the region, you'll need 4–5 days. Antiques mavens should concentrate their efforts in Bath, Wiscasset, and Damariscotta. Allow at least two days to appreciate the fine museums in Brunswick and Bath, and another day to tour Wiscasset's historical house museums and nearby fort. If you're an avid or even aspiring kayaker, you'll want time to puzzle through the nooks and crannies of the coastline in a boat, and if you value parks and preserves, this region offers plenty worth your time.

Brunswick Area

Brunswick (pop. 20,520), straddling Route 1, relies partly on modern defense dollars, but it was incorporated in 1738 and is steeped in history. The town is home to both prestigious Bowdoin College and the sprawling Brunswick Naval Air Station—an unusual and sometimes conflicting juxtaposition that makes this a college town with a difference. You'll find lots of classic homes and churches, several respected museums, and year-round cultural attractions.

Brunswick and **Topsham** face each other across roiling waterfalls on the Androscoggin River. The falls, which Native Americans knew by the tongue-twisting name of Ahmelahcogneturcook ("place abundant with fish, birds, and other animals"), were a source of hydropower for 18th-century sawmills and 19th- and 20th-century textile mills. Franco-Americans arrived in droves to beef up the textile industry in the late 19th century (but eventually lost their jobs in the Depression). Those once-derelict mills now house shops, restaurants, and offices.

Brunswick is also the gateway to the **Harpswells,** a peninsula-archipelago complex linked by causeways, several bridges, and a unique granite cribstone bridge. Scenic back roads on Harpswell Neck inspire detours to the fishing hamlets of **Cundy's Harbor, Orr's Island,** and **Bailey Island,** and once you're here, it's easy to want to linger.

SIGHTS

Bowdoin College

Bowdoin College (Brunswick, 207/725-3000, www.bowdoin.edu) got its start here nearly 150 years before the Naval Air Station landed on the nearby Brunswick Plains. Founded in 1794 as a boys' college with a handful of students, Bowdoin (coed since 1969) now has 1,550 students. The college has turned out such noted

Hubbard Hall, which faces Bowdoin's campus quad, is home to the Peary-MacMillan Arctic Museum.

graduates as authors Nathaniel Hawthorne and Henry Wadsworth Longfellow, sex pioneer Alfred Kinsey, U.S. president Franklin Pierce, Arctic explorers Robert Peary and Donald MacMillan, U.S. senators George Mitchell and William Cohen, and a dozen Maine governors. Massachusetts Hall, the oldest building on the 110-acre campus, dates from 1802. The stately Bowdoin pines, on the northeast boundary, are even older. The striking **David Saul Smith Union,** occupying 40,000 square feet in a former athletic building on the east side of the campus, has a café, pub, lounge, and bookstore open to the public. Call for information on admissions and campus tours (207/725-3100) and on campus concerts, lectures, and performances open to the public (207/725-3375).

Photos and artifacts bring Arctic expeditions to life at the small but fascinating **Peary-MacMillan Arctic Museum** (Hubbard Hall, 207/725-3416, www.bowdoin.edu/arctic-museum, 10 A.M.–5 P.M. Tues.–Sat., 2–5 P.M. Sun., free). Among the specimens are animal mounts, a skin kayak, fur clothing, snow goggles, and Inuit carvings—most collected by Arctic pioneers Robert E. Peary and Donald B. MacMillan, both Bowdoin grads. Permanent exhibits highlight the natural and cultural diversity of the Arctic. The small gift shop specializes in Inuit books and artifacts.

An astonishing array of Greek and Roman artifacts is only one of the high points at the **Bowdoin College Museum of Art** (Walker Art Building, 207/725-3275, www.bowdoin.edu/art-museum, 10 A.M.–5 P.M. Tues.–Sat., 2–5 P.M. Sun., free). Designed in the 1890s by Charles McKim of the famed McKim, Mead, and White firm, it's a stunning neoclassical edifice with an interior rotunda and stone lions flanking the entry. In 2007, the museum was expanded and modernized for the 21st century, adding a striking bronze-and-glass entry pavilion to preserve the facade while also achieving accessibility. The college's prized Assyrian reliefs, previously in the magnificent rotunda, were moved to a glass-walled addition facing Brunswick's Park Row. The renovated museum is far more user friendly and a fitting setting for the impressive

© HILARY NANGLE

A stunning glass pavilion provides access to the neoclassical Bowdoin College Museum of Art.

permanent collection of 19th- and 20th-century American art and other works.

Pejepscot Historical Society Museums

Side by side in an unusual cupola-topped duplex facing Brunswick's Mall (village green) are two museums operated by the Pejepscot Historical Society (159 and 160 Park Row, Brunswick, 207/729-6606, www.community.curtislibrary.com/pejepscot.htm), the **Pejepscot Museum** (159 Park Row, 10 A.M.–5 P.M. Mon.–Fri., free) and the **Skolfield-Whittier House** (161 Park Row, tours at 11 A.M. and 3 P.M. Thurs.–Sat. late May–late Oct., $5 adults, $2.50 children). Focusing on local history, the museum has a collection of more than 50,000 artifacts and mounts an always interesting special exhibit each year. The 17-room Skolfield-Whittier House, on the right-hand side of the building, looks as though the owners just stepped out for the afternoon. Unoccupied 1925–1982, the onetime sea captain's house has elegant Victorian furnishings and lots of exotic artifacts collected on global seafaring stints.

Also operated by the Pejepscot Historical Society, the **Joshua L. Chamberlain Museum** (226 Maine St., Brunswick, 207/729-6606, tours on the hour 10 A.M.–3 P.M. Tues.–Sat., $5 adults, $2.50 children), across from First Parish Church, commemorates the Union Army hero of the Civil War's Battle of Gettysburg, who's now gaining long-overdue respect. The partly restored house where Chamberlain lived in the late 19th century (and Henry Wadsworth Longfellow lived 30 years earlier) is a peculiar architectural hodgepodge with six rooms of exhibits of Chamberlain memorabilia, much of it Civil War–related. A gift shop stocks lots of Civil War publications, especially ones covering the Twentieth Maine Volunteers. A combination ticket for both historical houses is $8 adults, $4 children.

Uncle Tom's Church

Across the street from the Chamberlain museum is the historic 1846 **First Parish Church** (9 Cleaveland St. at Bath Rd., Brunswick, 207/729-7331), a Gothic Revival (or carpenter Gothic) board-and-batten structure crowning the rise at the head of Maine Street. Scores of celebrity preachers have ascended this pulpit, and Harriet Beecher Stowe was inspired to write *Uncle Tom's Cabin* while listening to her husband deliver an antislavery sermon here. Arrive here before noon any Tuesday early July–early August (or call ahead for details), when guest organists present 40-minute lunchtime concerts (12:10–12:50 P.M.) on the 1883 Hutchings-Plaisted tracker organ. A $5 donation is requested. At other times, the church is open by appointment.

© TOM NANGLE

Civil War hero Joshua L. Chamberlain served as president of Bowdoin College and governor of Maine.

Brunswick's Noted Women

With more than 20 points of interest, the **Brunswick Women's History Trail** covers such national notables as authors Harriet Beecher Stowe and Kate Douglas Wiggin and lesser-known lights, including naturalist Kate Furbish, pioneering Maine pediatrician Dr. Alice Whittier, and the Franco-American

JOSHUA L. CHAMBERLAIN, CIVIL WAR HERO

When the American Civil War began in 1861, Joshua Chamberlain was a 33-year-old logic instructor at Bowdoin College in Brunswick; when it ended, in 1865, Chamberlain earned the Congressional Medal of Honor for his "daring heroism and great tenacity in holding his position on the Little Round Top." He was designated by Ulysses S. Grant to formally accept the official surrender of Confederate General John Gordon (both men represented the infantry). He later became governor of Maine (1867–1871) and president of Bowdoin College, but Chamberlain's greatest renown, ironically, came more than a century later – when 1990s PBS filmmakers focused on the Civil War and highlighted his strategic military role.

Joshua Lawrence Chamberlain was born in 1828 in Brewer, Maine, the son and grandson of soldiers. After graduating from Bowdoin in 1852, he studied for the ministry at Bangor Theological Seminary and then returned to his alma mater as an instructor.

With the nation in turmoil in the early 1860s, Chamberlain signed on to help, receiving a commission as a lieutenant colonel in the Twentieth Maine Volunteers in 1862. After surviving 24 encounters and six battle wounds and having been promoted to general (brigadier, then major), Chamberlain was elected Republican governor of Maine in 1866 – by the largest margin in the state's history – only to suffer through four one-year terms of partisan politics. In 1871, Chamberlain became president of Bowdoin College, where he remained until 1883. He then dove into speechmaking and writing, his best-known work being *The Passing of the Armies*, a memoir of the Civil War's final campaigns. From 1900 to 1914, Chamberlain was surveyor of the Port of Portland, a presidential appointment that ended only when complications from a wartime abdominal wound finally did him in. He died at the grand old age of 86.

Brunswick's Joshua L. Chamberlain Museum, in his onetime home at 226 Maine Street, commemorates this illustrious Mainer, and thousands of Civil War buffs annually stream through the door in search of Chamberlain "stuff." To make it easier, the Pejepscot Historical Society has produced a helpful map titled Joshua Chamberlain's Brunswick, highlighting town and college ties to the man – his dorm rooms, his presidential office, his portraits, even his church pew (number 64 at First Parish Church). Chamberlain's gravesite, marked by a reddish granite stone, is in Brunswick's Pine Grove Cemetery, just east of the Bowdoin campus.

Biennially, the museum celebrates **Chamberlain Days** with a symposium that concentrates on his roles in the war and in Maine. Typically, events include lectures by authors and scholars; field trips to places of interest connected with Chamberlain's life; tours of his home, concentrating on the most recent restoration work; musical or dramatic performances; and group discussions.

women who slaved away in the textile mills at the turn of the 20th century. Buy the walking-tour booklet at the Pejepscot Museum gift shop ($2). The museum offers guided tours lasting about one hour once a month in June, July, and August (donation requested).

Brunswick Literary Art Walk

Cast your eyes downward while walking along Maine Street. Four bronze plaques recognize Brunswick's most famous writers: Henry Wadsworth Longfellow, Nathaniel Hawthorne, Harriet Beecher Stowe, and Robert P. T. Coffin. Each plaque bears a quote from the author commemorated.

Go, Fish!

If you're in town between mid-May and late June, plan to visit Central Maine Power's **Brunswick Hydro** generating station, straddling the falls on the Androscoggin River, Lower Maine Street, next to Fort Andross, Brunswick-Topsham town line (207/729-7644 or 207/623-3521, ext. 2116, weekdays, or 800/872-9937). A glass-walled viewing room lets you play voyeur during the annual ritual of anadromous fish heading upstream to spawn. Amazingly undaunted by the obstacles, such species as alewives (herring), salmon, and smallmouth bass make their way from salt water to fresh via a 40-foot-high, 570-foot-long man-made fish ladder. The viewing room, which maxes out at about 20 people, is open 1–5 P.M. Wednesday–Sunday during the brief spring spawning season.

ENTERTAINMENT

The region's extremely active arts organization, **Five Rivers Arts Alliance** (108 Main St., Brunswick, 207/798-6964, www.fiveriversartsalliance.org), maintains a calendar of area concerts, gallery openings, art shows, lectures, exhibits, and other arts-related events and also sponsors a few key events. Listings also appear on www.midcoastmaine.com/events.

The **Maine State Music Theatre** (Pickard Theater, Bowdoin College, box office 22 Elm St., Brunswick, 207/725-8769, www.msmt.org) has been a summer tradition since 1959. The renovated state-of-the-art air-conditioned theater brings real pros to its stage for four musicals (mid-June–late Aug., $30–52). Nonsubscription tickets go on sale in early May. Performances are at 8 P.M. Tuesday–Saturday; matinees are staged at 2 P.M. on an alternating schedule—each week has matinees on different days. (No children under four are admitted, but special family shows are performed during the season, $7–11.)

The **Bowdoin International Music Festival** (box office 12 Cleveland St., Brunswick, 207/725-3895, www.summermusic.org) is a showcase for an international array of classical talent of all kinds late June–early August. The six-week festival, part of an international music school, presents a variety of concert opportunities—enough so that there's music almost every night of the week. Venues vary and tickets range free–$30. Call or check the website for the current schedule.

Second Friday Art Walks (207/725-4366) take place in downtown Brunswick 5–7:30 P.M.

MID-COAST REGION

© TOM NANGLE

Pickard Theater, on the Bowdoin College campus, is home to the Maine State Music Theatre in summer.

on the second Friday of the month May–November. Gallery openings, wine tastings, light refreshments, and other activities are usually part of the mix.

Music on the Mall presents family band concerts at 7 P.M. Wednesdays (Thursday if it rains) in July and August on the Brunswick Mall (the lovely park in the center of town).

FESTIVALS AND EVENTS

The first full week of August, the **Topsham Fair** is a weeklong agricultural festival with exhibits, demonstrations, live music, ox pulls, contests, harness racing, and fireworks at the Topsham Fairgrounds.

The third Saturday of August, the **Maine Highland Games,** sponsored by the St. Andrew's Society of Maine, mark the annual wearing of the plaids—but you needn't be Scottish to join in the games or watch the Highland dancing or browse the arts and crafts booths. (Only a Scot, however, can appreciate that unique concoction called haggis.)

September's **Annual Bluegrass Festival** is a four-day event with nonstop bluegrass, including big-name artists. Kickoff is Thursday at noon.

SHOPPING

Downtown Brunswick invites leisurely browsing, with most of the shops concentrated on Maine Street. Do take special care when crossing the four-lane-wide street, and do so only at marked crosswalks.

Art, Craft, and Antiques Galleries

The **Bayview Gallery** (58 Maine St., Brunswick, 800/244-3007), mounts half a dozen superb shows annually, specializing in contemporary New England artists.

Facing the Mall, **Day's Antiques** (153 Park Row, Brunswick, 207/725-6959) occupies five rooms and the basement of the handsome historic building known as the Pumpkin House. Quality is high at David Day's shop; prices are fair.

More than 140 dealers show and sell their wares at **Cabot Mill Antiques** (14 Maine St., 207/725-2855), in the renovated Fort Andross mill complex next to the Androscoggin River.

Part gallery, part resource center, **Maine Fiberarts** (13 Maine St., Topsham, 207/721-0678, www.mainefiberarts.org) is a must-stop for anyone interested in fiber-related artwork: knitting, quilting, spinning, basketry. If you're really interested in finding artists and resources statewide, buy a copy of its resource book.

Nearly two dozen local artists exhibit their works in varied media at **Sebascodegan Artists Gallery** (Rte. 24, Great Island, Harpswell, 207/833-6260).

Bookstore

With an eclectic new-book inventory that includes lots of esoterica, **Gulf of Maine Books** (134 Maine St., Brunswick, 207/729-5083) has held the competition at bay since the early 1980s. The fiction selection is particularly good, as are the religion, health, and poetry sections. Poet-publisher–renaissance man Gary Lawless oversees everything.

RECREATION

Excursion Train

Ride in restored vintage railcars on the scenic **Maine Eastern Railroad** (207/596-6725 or 800/637-2457, www.maineeasternrailroad.com), operating between Rockland and Brunswick with stops in Wiscasset and Bath. The train operates late May–early November, with special holiday trains in December. Adult fares are $40 round-trip, $25 one-way; ages 5–15 pay $20/$15; seniors are $35/$25; family rate is $100/$75 covering two adults and two kids. Packages with lodging, meals, and theater are available. Crated pets can travel for $20.

Hiking

In the village of Bailey Island, a well-maintained path edges the cliffs and passes the **Giant Stairs,** a waterfront stone stairway of mammoth proportions. To get there, take Route 24 from Cooks Corner toward Bailey Island and Land's End, keeping an eye out for Washington Avenue, on the left about 1.5 miles after the cribstone bridge. (Or drive to Land's

End, park the car with the rest of the crowds, survey the panorama, and walk 0.8 mile back along Route 24 to Washington Avenue from there.) Turn onto Washington Avenue, go 0.1 mile, and park at the Episcopal Church (corner of Ocean St.). Walk along Ocean Street to the shorefront path. Watch for a tiny sign just before Spindrift Lane. Don't let small kids get close to the slippery rocks on the surf-tossed shoreline. (The same advice, by the way, holds for Land's End, where the rocks can be treacherous.)

Thank the **Brunswick-Topsham Land Trust** (108 Maine St., Brunswick, 207/729-7694, www.btlt.org), founded in 1985, for access to the 11-acre **Captain Alfred Skolfield Nature Preserve.** One of the two blue-blazed nature-trail loops skirts a salt marsh, where you're apt to see egrets, herons, and osprey in summer. Adjacent to the preserve is an ancient Indian portage site that linked Middle Bay and Harpswell Coves when Native Americans spent their vacations here. (No dopes, they!) Take Route 123 (Harpswell Rd.) south from Brunswick about three miles; when you reach the Middle Bay Road intersection (on the right), continue on Route 123 for 1.1 miles. Watch for a small sign, and a small parking area, on your right.

The 103-acre **Cox Pinnacle,** owned by the town of Brunswick, comprises wooded hills, rocky ledges, and wetlands laced with about 1.5 miles of old logging and farming roads. The trails lead to Cox Pinnacle, the highest point of land in Brunswick (350 feet). Take the Durham Road, then turn right at the blinking light onto Hacker Road and drive 0.3 mile to the parking lot on the left.

Swimming

Thomas Point Beach (29 Meadow Rd., Brunswick, 207/725-6009 or 877/872-4321, www.thomaspointbeach.com, 9 A.M.–sunset mid-May–September, $3.50 adults, $2 children under 12) is actually 85 acres of privately owned parkland with facilities for swimming (lifeguard on duty, bathhouses), fishing, field sports, picnicking (500 tables), and camping (75 tent and RV sites at $22; no water or sewer hookups, but electricity and dump station available). No pets, skateboards, or motorcycles are allowed. The sandy beach is tidal, so the swimming "window" is about two hours before high tide until two hours afterward; otherwise, you're wallowing in mudflats. (The same timing applies to kayakers and canoeists.) Toddlers head for the big playground; teenagers gravitate to the arcade and the ice cream parlor. The park is also the site of several annual events, including the Maine Highland Games and the Bluegrass Festival. At Cooks Corner, where Bath Road meets Route 24 South, go 1.5 miles on Route 24, then turn left, and follow signs for less than two miles to the park.

For freshwater swimming, head to town-owned **Coffin Pond** (River Rd., Brunswick, 207/725-6656, 10 A.M.–7 P.M. daily, $5.50 adults, $3.25 children 12 and younger), a man-made swimming hole with a sandy beach, lifeguards, water slide, picnic tables, playground, changing rooms, and snack bar. Heading west on Route 1 (Pleasant St.), turn right onto River Road and go about a half mile to the parking area (on the right).

Another terrific but non-secret spot for freshwater swimming is **White's Beach** (White's Beach and Campground, Durham Rd., Brunswick, 207/729-0415, www.whitesbeachandcampground.com, $3.50 adults, $2.50 seniors and children 12 and younger). The sandy-bottomed pond maxes out at nine feet. In mid-July, the campground hosts a popular family bluegrass festival. Park facilities include a snack bar, playground, hot showers, and campsites. Campsites are $20–30. From Route 1 just south of the I-95 exit into Brunswick, take Durham Road 2.2 miles northwest.

Golf

Established in 1901 primarily for Bowdoin College students, the **Brunswick Golf Club** (River Rd., Brunswick, 207/725-8224) is now an especially popular 18-hole public course. Another possibility is the nine-hole **Brunswick Naval Air Station Golf Club** (Bath Rd., Brunswick, 207/921-2155).

Boating Excursions

Departing at noon from the Cook's Lobster House wharf (Cook's Landing) in Bailey Island (off Rte. 24), a large, sturdy **Casco Bay Lines ferry** (207/774-7871, www.cascobaylines.com, $15.50 adults, $7.25 children 5–9) does a 1.75-hour nature-watch circuit of nearby islands, including Eagle Island, the onetime home of Admiral Robert Peary (there are no stopovers on these circuits). Reservations aren't needed.

For a more intimate excursion in a smaller boat, Captain Les McNelly, owner of **Sea Escape Charters** (Bailey Island, 207/833-5531, www.seaescapecottages.com), operates two-hour on-demand sightseeing cruises throughout the summer (weather permitting) for $85 per person (two people) or $55 per person (four people). Or he'll take you out to Eagle Island for $160 a couple (lower rate if there are more passengers). He also offers fishing trips: $225 for four hours, including bait and tackle ($110 each additional person); no fishing license required; bring your own lunch. Call to schedule a trip. Trips operate out of Sea Escape Cottages, one- and two-bedroom well-equipped cottages with full kitchens and oceanside decks that rent for $150–160 per night or $920–1,030 per week, including linens and one change of towels.

Sea Kayaking

H2Outfitters (Orr's Island, 207/833-5257 or 800/205-2925, www.h2outfitters.com) has been a thriving operation since 1978. Based in a wooden building on the Orr's Island side of the famed cribstone bridge, this experienced company organizes guided trips, including island camping; all gear is included. A half-day tour is $65.

Seaspray Kayaking (207/443-3646 or 888/349-7772, www.seaspraykayaking.com) has bases on the New Meadows River in Brunswick and Sebasco Harbor Resort in Phippsburg, and rental centers in Bay Point, Georgetown, and Hermit Island Campground, Small Point. The New Meadows base is particularly good for those nervous about trying the sport. Rentals are $15–25 for the first hour, $5–10 for additional hours, $25–50 per day. Equipment options include solo and tandem kayaks, recreational kayaks, surf kayaks, and canoes. Tours, led by Registered Maine Guides, vary from sunset paddles to three-day expeditions and include moonlight paddles ($40), island-to-island tours, and inn-to-inn tours. Rates begin at $50 adults, $25 children for shorter tours. A striper-fishing kayak tour, including tackle and instruction, is $85.

If you're an experienced sea kayaker, consider exploring Harpswell Sound from the boat launch on the west side of the cribstone bridge; kayaks can also put in at Mackerel Cove, near Cook's Lobster House. A launch with plentiful parking is at Sawyer Park on the New Meadows River, on Route 1, just before you cross the river heading north.

ACCOMMODATIONS

Motels and Inns

A dozen miles down Route 24 from Cooks Corner is the turnoff for Jo Atlass's **Little Island Motel** (44 Little Island Rd., Orr's Island, 207/833-2392, www.littleislandmotel.com, $125–145), a nine-unit complex on its own spit of land with deck views you won't believe. Basic rooms have cable TV and small fridge. Rates include buffet breakfast and use of bikes, boats, and a little beach. No credit cards.

Continue another mile down Route 24, cross the cribstone bridge, and you'll come to Chip Black's **Bailey Island Motel** (Rte. 24, Bailey Island, 207/833-2886, www.baileyislandmotel.com, $135), a congenial, clean, no-frills waterfront spot with 11 rooms and wowser views. Kids under 10 are free; 10 and older are $15. Continental breakfast is included, and rooms have cable TV. A dock is available for boat launching. Open mid-May–late October.

Looking rather like an old-fashioned tear-jerker film set, the family-run **Driftwood Inn** (81 Washington Ave., Bailey Island, 207/833-5461, www.thedriftwoodinnmaine.com) has 25 simple pine-paneled rooms in four buildings (some with private toilet and sink; all with shared showers), six housekeeping cottages, a saltwater pool, a stunning view, a dining room (open to the public), and a determinedly rustic ambience. No frills, period, but it has oceanfront porches, games, and an old-fashioned simplicity that you rarely find anymore, and you'll sleep at night listening to the waves crash on the rocky shore. It's all on three oceanfront acres near the Giant Stairs. The dining room, open to the public by reservation, serves a set home-cooked meal nightly (usually with a fish-of-the-day alternative), late June–early September, for $16–19. Breakfast is $7. Rooms are $85–130; a weekly rate including breakfast and dinner is $668 per person. Cottages rent by the week in season, $665–700; off-season $115–125 per night. Dogs are allowed in the cottages. No credit cards. Open mid-May–October.

Bed-and-Breakfasts

Right downtown, facing the tree-shaded Mall, is the **Brunswick Inn on Park Row** (165 Park Row, Brunswick, 207/729-4914 or 800/299-4914, www.brunswickbnb.com, $135–200), a handsome 30-room Greek Revival mansion built in 1849 and decorated with contemporary flair. Original works by Maine artists are displayed throughout the inn, including in the wine bar. Fifteen guest rooms are split between the main house and the renovated Carriage House (with two fully accessible rooms); all have Wi-Fi and phones, and Carriage House suites have TV. Open all year.

Within walking distance of downtown Brunswick, but across the bridge spanning the Androscoggin River, is the **Black Lantern B&B** (57 Elm St., Topsham, 207/725-4165 or 888/306-4165, www.blacklanternbandb.com, $110), Tom and Judy Connelie's lovely 1860s riverfront home. All rooms are decorated with an emphasis on comfort, and two have water views. Judy's quilts will warm you on a cool night.

On the outskirts of town, in a rural location smack-dab on Middle Bay, is **Middle Bay Farm Bed and Breakfast** (287 Pennellville Rd., Brunswick, 207/373-1375, www.middlebayfarm.com, $170–190), lovingly and beautifully restored by Phyllis Truesdell, who bought the property after it sat all but abandoned for a decade. Once the site of the Pennell Brothers Shipyard, the farmhouse and sail loft now house guests seeking an away-from-it-all yet convenient location. Four water-view guest rooms in the 1834 farmhouse are decorated with antiques and have TV-VCRs. Also in the main house is a living room with fireplace and grand piano. Two suites in the sail loft each have a living room with kitchenette and two tiny bedrooms and share an open porch. All guests receive a full breakfast in the water-view dining room. Bring a sea kayak to launch from the dock. Open all year.

At the 1761 **Harpswell Inn** (108 Lookout Point Rd., South Harpswell, 207/833-5509 or 800/843-5509, www.harpswellinn.com), innkeepers Anne and Richard Moseley operate a comfortable, welcoming antiques-filled oasis on 2.5 secluded water-view acres. It's tough to break away from the glass-walled great room, but Middle Bay sunsets from the porch can do it. And just down the hill is Allen's Seafood, where you can watch lobstermen unload their catches in a gorgeous cove, and grab a lobster roll. In fall, the foliage on two little islets in the cove turns brilliant red. The bed-and-breakfast has nine lovely rooms (most with private baths; $115–165), three suites ($245–259), and four cottages ($975–1,450 per week). Prices are slightly higher for one-night stays. Open all year.

After many years as an extremely popular dining destination 13 miles south of Cooks Corner, **The Log Cabin** (Rte. 24, Bailey Island, 207/833-5546, www.logcabin-maine.com, $169–329) in 1996 added lodging to its repertoire, and now it serves meals only to guests. Nine nicely decorated rooms have phones, TV-VCRs, private decks facing the bay, and, weather permitting, splendid sunset views to the White Mountains. Four rooms have kitchen facilities; some have gas fireplaces or whirlpool tubs. There's also an outdoor heated pool. Full breakfast is included; dinner ($18–33) is available.

FOOD

Brunswick and the Harpswells have an overabundance of dining options, from inexpensive cafés, delis, and coffeehouses to ethnic spots and seafood joints. Hours noted are for peak season, but are subject to change. It's wise to call ahead, especially when traveling off season.

Local Flavors

Wild O.A.T.S. Bakery and Café (149 Maine St., Tontine Mall, Brunswick, 207/725-6287, www.wildoatsbakery.com, 7:30 A.M.–5 P.M. Mon.–Sat., 8 A.M.–3 P.M. Sun.) turns out terrific made-from-scratch breads and pastries, especially the breakfast kind, in its cafeteria-style place. (Just so you know, the name stands for Original and Tasty Stuff.) It has inside and outside tables, moderate prices, good-for-you salads, and great sandwiches.

For food on the run—no-frills hot dogs straight from the cart—head for Brunswick's Mall, the village green where **Danny's on the Mall** (no phone) has been cooking dirt-cheap tube steaks since the early 1980s.

Fat Boy Drive-In (Bath Rd., Old Rte. 1, Brunswick, 207/729-9431, 11 A.M.–8:30 P.M. daily) is a genuine throwback—a landmark since 1955, boasting carhops, window trays, and a menu guaranteed to clog your arteries. Fries, frappes, and BLTs are specialties. No credit cards.

Choose from up to 32 flavors of gelato and *sorbetto* at **The Gelato Fiasco** (74 Maine St., Brunswick, 207/607-4002).

A favorite for chowder is **Salt Cod Cafe** (1894 Harpswell Islands Rd., Orr's Island, 207/833-6210, 8 A.M.–5 P.M. daily), with a primo location overlooking the cribstone bridge. Sandwiches, wraps, rolls, and baked goods also are available.

The **Brunswick Farmers Market** sets up rain or shine on the Mall (village green) 8:30 A.M.–2 P.M. Tuesday and Friday May–November (Friday is the bigger day). On Saturday the market moves to Crystal Spring Farm, Pleasant Hill Road (8:30 A.M.–12:30 P.M.). You'll find produce, cheeses, crafts, condiments, live lobsters, and serendipitous surprises—depending on the season.

The chocolates and truffles and bark made by Melinda Harris Richter are divine at **Island Candy Company** (Harpswell Islands Rd., Orr's Island, 207/833-6639, 11 A.M.–8 P.M. daily in season), and there are baked goods and ice cream, too.

Family Favorites

Just over the bridge from Brunswick, in the renovated Bowdoin Mill complex overlooking the Androscoggin River, is the **Sea Dog Brewery** (1 Main St., Topsham, 207/725-0162, www.seadogbrewing.com, 11:30 A.M.–1 A.M. daily), with seating inside and on a deck overhanging the river. The menu ranges from burgers and sandwiches to full plate entrées ($11–18). It offers frequent acoustic entertainment. There are also games for kids and a games room with video arcade and pool tables.

A bit out of the way is **Blackbird Cafe** (506 Harpswell Neck Rd./Rte. 123, Harpswell, 207/721-1157, 7 A.M.–8:30 P.M. Thurs.–Sat., to 3 P.M. Sun.–Mon.), a family-friendly local favorite with a comfy down-home attitude.

Casual Dining

Scarlet Begonias (16 Station Ave., Brunswick, 207/721-0403, www.scarletbegoniasmaine.com, 11 A.M.–8 P.M. Mon.–Thurs., to 9 P.M. Fri., noon–9 P.M. Sat.) is an especially cheerful place with a Mediterranean-influenced bistro-type pizza-and-pasta menu. In late 2009, it moved to larger digs in the new Maine Street Station project, adding table service and a bar.

Sharing the same building is **Bacari** (212 Maine St., Brunswick, 207/725-2600, 5–10 P.M. Tues.–Sat.), which specializes in small plates ($8–16).

A local fave just enough off Maine Street to befuddle visitors, **Back Street Bistro & Wine Bar** (11 Town Hall Plaza, Brunswick, 207/725-4060, 5–8 P.M. Mon., to 9 P.M. Tues.–Sat., 10 A.M.–2 P.M. and 5–8 P.M. Sun.) is worth finding for well-prepared dishes, such as pistachio-crusted Atlantic salmon, crispy pan-seared porcini mushroom risotto cakes, and braised lamb shanks ($17–28).

Still casual, but a bit fancier (tablecloths!), is **Clementine** (44 Maine St., Brunswick, 207/721-9800, 5–9 P.M. Tues.–Sun.). The menu changes seasonally, but usually includes fish, poultry, and meat prepared with a dash of creativity and artful presentation; entrées $17–29. A four-course tasting menus is $45 per person or $55 paired with wines.

Ethnic and Eclectic Fare

Eclectic doesn't begin to describe **Frontier Cafe** (Mill 3, Fort Andross, 14 Maine St. at Rte. 1 overpass, Brunswick, 207/725-5222, www.explorefrontier.com, 9 A.M.–9 P.M. Mon.–Thurs., to 10 P.M. Fri., 11 A.M.–10 P.M. Sat.; kitchen closes one hour earlier), a combination café, gallery, and cinema inspired by founder Michael Gilroy's world travels. The menu of soups, sandwiches, and salads changes weekly but usually includes wonderful market plates emphasizing the cuisine of a country or region—Maine, France, the Middle East, Italy. Desserts are homemade, and there's a kids' menu, too. Wine and beer are served. Films are screened ($7 adults), and there are frequent events such as the monthly Knit and Fiddle, concerts, and other entertainment.

Generous portions, moderate prices, efficient service, and narrow aisles are the story at **The Great Impasta** (42 Maine St., Brunswick, 207/729-5858, www.thegreatimpasta.com, 11 A.M.–9 P.M. Mon.–Thurs., to 10 P.M. Fri.–Sat., $13–22), a cheerful, informal eatery where the garlic meets you at the door. There are gluten-free choices and a "bambino menu" for the kids.

Hip, funky, and full of personality are words often used to describe **El Camino** (15 Cushing St., Brunswick, 207/725-8228, 5–9 P.M. Tues.–Sat.), which uses fresh, local, and often organic ingredients to create innovative Cal-Mex fare. Prices top out around $15.

Lobster and Seafood

In late 2006, the Holbrook Community

© HILARY NANGLE

The Dolphin Chowder House, in South Harpswell, tops many a Mainer's list for the best chowder and views.

Foundation took ownership of Holbrook's Wharf, site of **Holbrook's Wharf and Grille** (984 Cundy's Harbor Rd., 207/729-0848), along with Holbrook's General Store and the Trufant mansion, preserving this slice of Maine-fishing-village life for future generations. The wharf lobster shack is a leased operation, and quality varies year to year. Ask locally. When it's on, this is the real thing for authentic lobster in the rough, and the view's superb. Call for current hours.

You want fresh? Fish doesn't get any fresher than that served at **Allen's Seafood** (119 Lookout Point Rd., Harpswell, 207/833-2828, 11 A.M.–7 P.M. daily), a seasonal take-out trailer overlooking Middle Bay. Chowders, fried fish, lobster, and similar fare are prepared fresh from the bounty of the daily catch. Order and then grab a picnic table. Moorings and a dock are available if you arrive by boat.

Arguments rage endlessly about who makes the best chowder in Maine, but **The Dolphin Chowder House** (Dolphin Marina, 515 Basin Point Rd., South Harpswell, 207/833-6000, www.dolphinmarinaandrestaurant.com, 11 A.M.–8 P.M. daily May–Nov., $5–25) heads lots of lists for its fish chowder, accompanied by a blueberry muffin. Equally famed is its lobster stew. Plus you can't beat the scenic 13-mile drive south from Brunswick and the spectacular water views through two walls of windows at the tip of Harpswell Neck.

INFORMATION AND SERVICES

The **Southern Midcoast Chamber of Commerce** (2 Main St., Topsham, 877/725-8797, www.midcoastmaine.com) publishes the *Guide to Southern Midcoast Maine.*

For information on Harpswell, visit Harpswell Business Association's website (www.harpswellmaine.org).

Check the website of **Curtis Memorial Library** (23 Pleasant St., Brunswick, 207/725-5242, www.curtislibrary.com) for excellent local resources and guides.

Bath Area

One of the smallest in area of Maine's cities, Bath—with a population of about 9,920—packs a wallop in only nine square miles. Like Brunswick, it straddles Route 1, edges a river, and relies on modern military funding, but Bath's centuries of historical and architectural tradition and well-preserved Victorian downtown have earned it a prized designation: The National Trust for Historic Preservation named it a Distinctive Destination.

The defense part is impossible to ignore, since giant cranes dominate the riverfront cityscape at the huge Bath Iron Works complex, source of state-of-the-art warships—your tax dollars at work. Less evident (but not far away) is the link to the past: Just south of Bath, in Popham on the Phippsburg Peninsula, is the poorly marked site where a trouble-plagued English settlement, a sister colony to Jamestown, predated the Plymouth Colony by 13 years. (Of course, Champlain arrived before that, and Norsemen allegedly left calling cards even earlier.) In 1607 and 1608, settlers in the Popham Colony managed to build a 30-ton pinnace, *Virginia of Sagadahoc,* designed for transatlantic trade, but they lost heart during a bitter winter and abandoned the site. (A replica is planned. For details, visit www.mainesfirstship.org.)

Bath is the jumping-off point for two peninsulas to the south—**Phippsburg** (of Popham Colony fame) and **Georgetown.** Both are dramatically scenic, with glacier-carved farms and fishing villages. Drive (bicycling is best left to experienced pedalers) a dozen miles down any of these fingers and you're in different worlds, ones where artists and photographers, hikers and historians go crazy with all the possibilities.

Across the soaring Sagadahoc Bridge from

Bath is Woolwich, from which you can continue northeastward along the coast or detour northward on Route 128 to the hamlet of Day's Ferry. Named after 18th-century resident Joseph Day, who shuttled back and forth in a gondola-type boat across the Kennebec here, the picturesque village has a cluster of 18th- and 19th-century homes and churches—all part of the Day's Ferry Historic District. And the village's Old Stage Road saw many a stagecoach in its day; passengers would ferry from Bath and pick up the stage here to travel onward.

SIGHTS

Bath Iron Works

Known locally as BIW or The Yard, Bath Iron Works has been building ships on this 50-acre riverfront site since 1890. Currently, its roughly 5,600 employees build destroyers for the U.S. Navy. BIW is open to the public for launchings, when it's a mob scene with hordes of politicos, townsfolk, and military pooh-bahs in their scrambled eggs and brass. The best way to get a peek at the workaday world behind the gates is on a **Bath Iron Works Trolley Tour** with the Maine Maritime Museum.

Maine Maritime Museum

Spread over 25 acres on the Kennebec River is the state's premier marine museum, the Maine Maritime Museum (243 Washington St., Bath, 207/443-1316, www.mainemaritimemuseum.org, 9:30 A.M.–5 P.M. daily, $12 adults, $11 over 65, $9 children 4–16). On the grounds are five original 19th-century buildings from the Percy and Small Shipyard (1897–1920), a late-Victorian home, and hands-on exhibits, but the first thing you see is the architecturally dramatic Maritime History Building, locale for permanent and temporary displays of marine art and artifacts and a shop stocked with nautical books and gifts. Bring a picnic (or purchase lunch at the seasonal Even Keel Snack Bar) and let the toddlers loose in the children's pirate's play area. Then either wander the campus on your own or join one of the guided tours. Don't miss the boatshop,

Watch volunteers build and restore boats at the Maine Maritime Museum in Bath.

where volunteers build and restore small vessels. Shipyard demonstrations are held on a rotating schedule, and brown-bag lectures are often given. In summer, weather permitting, the museum sponsors a variety of special river cruises; call for information. From May–mid-October, the museum offers fascinating one-hour **Bath Iron Works Trolley Tours** ($28 adults, $15 children 16 and younger, includes two-day museum admission) conducted by former BIW employees. You'll need to reserve a week or longer in advance; it's well worth the effort. Pair it with a one-hour cruise to view the yard from the river. The museum is open year-round; the Percy and Small Shipyard is open winter as conditions permit (with reduced-price admissions).

Bath History Preserved

Sagadahoc Preservation (www.sagadahocpreservation.org), founded in 1971 to rescue the city's architectural heritage, has produced podcasts of three different self-guided walking and driving architectural tours that accompany a foldout brochure (with maps). The podcasts can be downloaded from www.cityofbath.com: Click on Visiting, then Walking Tours links. The free map and guide *The Historic Architecture of Downtown Bath, Maine* is available from Main Street Bath (4 Centre St., Bath, 207/442-7291, www.mainstbath.com). Sagadahoc Preservation also offers an annual house tour, usually in June; check the website for details.

FORT POPHAM HISTORIC SITE

A mile down the road, at the end of Route 209, is the seven-acre Fort Popham Historic Site, where kids of all ages can explore the waterfront tower and bunkers of a 19th-century granite fort. No swimming here—the current is dangerous—but there's fun fishing from the rocks (no license needed), plus picnic tables and restrooms.

Phippsburg Peninsula

Thanks to a map-brochure produced by the Phippsburg Historical Society (download from www.phippsburghistorical.com) and

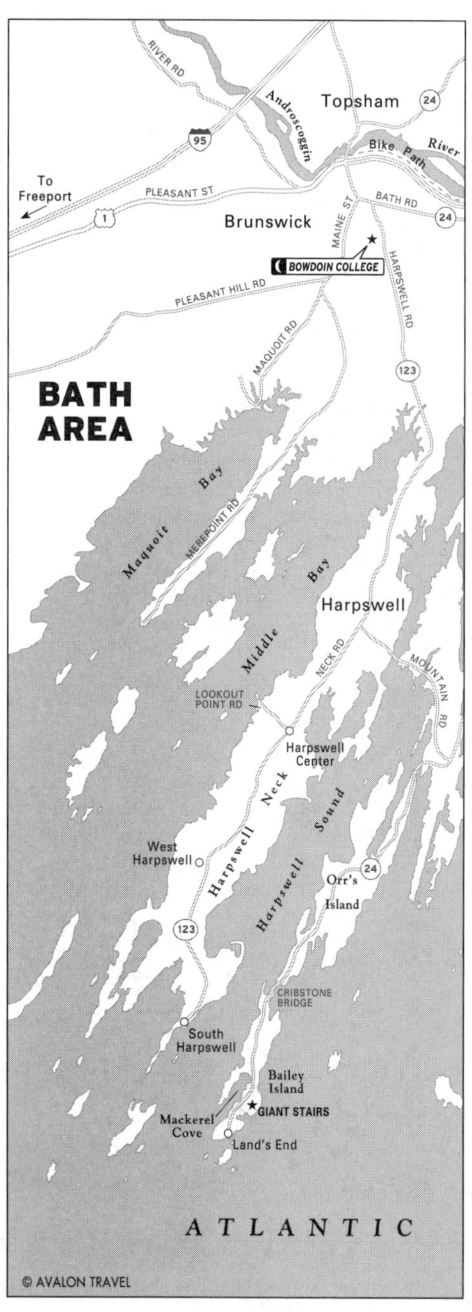

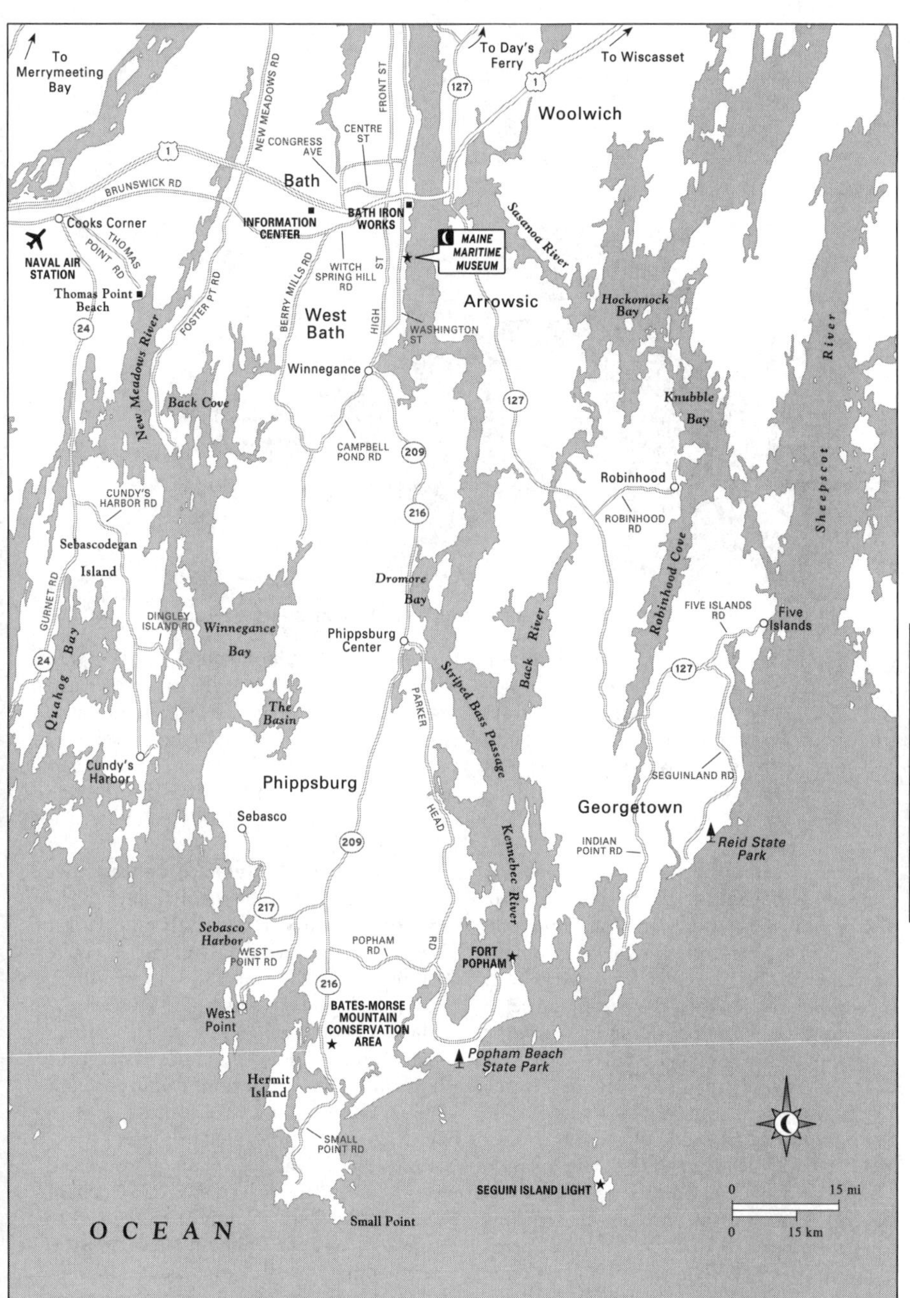

To Merrymeeting Bay
To Day's Ferry
To Wiscasset
Woolwich
Bath
West Bath
Arrowsic
Cooks Corner
NAVAL AIR STATION
Thomas Point Beach
INFORMATION CENTER
BATH IRON WORKS
MAINE MARITIME MUSEUM
Sasanoa River
Hockomock Bay
Knubble Bay
Sheepscot River
New Meadows River
Back Cove
Winnegance
Robinhood
Sebascodegan Island
Quahog Bay
Winnegance Bay
Dromore Bay
Phippsburg Center
The Basin
Cundy's Harbor
Phippsburg
Striped Bass Passage
Back River
Robinhood Cove
Five Islands
Georgetown
Sebasco
Kennebec River
Reid State Park
Sebasco Harbor
FORT POPHAM
West Point
BATES-MORSE MOUNTAIN CONSERVATION AREA
Popham Beach State Park
Hermit Island
SEGUIN ISLAND LIGHT
Small Point
OCEAN
0 15 mi
0 15 km
MID-COAST REGION

© HILARY NANGLE

Kids can sail off on an adventure at the Maine Maritime Museum's Pirates Paradise.

the Phippsburg Business Association, you can spend a whole day—or, better still, several days—exploring the peninsula that drops from Bath. Along the way are campgrounds, bed-and-breakfasts, an updated traditional resort, restaurants, a unique state park, hiking trails, secluded coves, spectacular scenery, and tons of history.

About two miles south of Bath is a causeway known as **Winnegance,** a Wabanaki name usually translated as "short carry" or "little portage." Native Americans crossed here from the Kennebec to the New Meadows River. Early settlers erected nearly a dozen tide-powered mills to serve the shipbuilding industry, but they're long gone. About 1.5 miles beyond the causeway is a left turn onto Fiddler's Reach Road, leading to the **Morse Cove Public Launching Facility,** one of the state's most scenic boat-launch sites. If you have a kayak, plan to go downriver on the ebb tide and return on the flow (otherwise you'll be battling the strong Kennebec River current). There's plenty of paved parking here, plus a restroom.

Back on Route 209, it's another 1.3 miles to the **Dromore Burying Ground** (on the right), with great old headstones; the earliest is dated 1743. The next mile opens up with terrific easterly views of Dromore Bay. Right in the line of sight is 117-acre Lee Island (which the owners sold to the state in 1995). From May through mid-July, the island is off-limits to protect nesting eagles and waterfowl.

Next you're in **Phippsburg Center,** alive with shipbuilding from colonial days to the early 20th century. Hang a left onto Parker Head Road (but avoid this detour if you're on a bicycle; it's too narrow and winding). After the Phippsburg Historical Museum (in an 1859 schoolhouse) and the Alfred Totman Library, turn left onto Church Lane to see the **Phippsburg Congregational Church,** built in 1802. Out front is a "Constitution Tree," a huge English linden planted in 1774.

Parker Head Road continues southward and meets Route 209, which takes you to **Popham Beach State Park.** Continue to the end of Route 209 for **Fort Popham Historic Site,** where parking is woefully inadequate in summer (and costs an exorbitant $7 at nearby

Percy's Store). The fort is accessible Memorial Day–September. Youngsters love this place—they can fish from the rocks, climb to the third level of the 1865 stone fortress, picnic on the seven-acre grounds, and create sand castles on the tiny beach next to the fort. Resist the urge to swim, though; the current is dangerous, and there's no lifeguard. Across the river is Bay Point, a lobstering village at the tip of the Georgetown Peninsula. **Percy's Store** (207/389-2010), by the way, with a handful of tables, is the best place down here for pizza, picnic fare, fried dough, and fishing tackle.

Across the cove from the fort is Fort Baldwin Road, a one-lane-wide winding road leading to the shorefront site of the 1607 Popham Colony. Climb the path up Sabino Hill to what's left of World War I–era **Fort Baldwin,** the best vantage point for panoramic photos.

Backtrack about four miles on Route 209, turn left onto Route 216, and head toward **Small Point.** Go about 0.9 mile to Morse Mountain Road, on the left, which leads to the parking area and trailhead for **Bates-Morse Mountain Preserve.** Farther south are Head Beach and Hermit Island.

Returning northward on Route 216, you'll hook up with Route 209 and then see a left turn (Rte. 217) to Sebasco Harbor Resort. Take the time to go beyond the resort area. When the paved road goes left (to the Water's Edge Restaurant), turn right at a tiny cemetery and continue northward on the Old Meadowbrook Road, which meanders for about four miles along the west side of the peninsula. About midway along is **The Basin,** regarded by sailors as one of the Maine coast's best "hurricane holes" (refuges in high winds). As you skirt the Basin and come to a fork, bear right to return to Route 209; turn left and return northward to Bath.

ENTERTAINMENT AND EVENTS

Bath's most diversified entertainment setting is the **Center for the Arts at the Chocolate Church** (804 Washington St., Bath, 207/442-8455, www.chocolatechurch.com), a chocolate-brown board-and-batten structure built in 1846 as the Central Congregational Church. Year-round activities at the arts center include music and dance concerts, dramas, exhibits, and children's programs.

At 7 P.M. every Tuesday and Friday mid-June–August, the **Gazebo Concert Series** brings live entertainment to Bath's Library Park.

Five Rivers Arts Alliances holds **Third Friday Art Walks** (various locations, Bath, 207/798-6964, 5–8 P.M.) on the third Friday of the month June–October.

Throughout the summer, the **Maine Maritime Museum** (207/443-1316) schedules special events, often hinging on visits by tall ships and other vessels. Some of the visiting boats are open to the public for an extra fee. Call the museum to check.

From November through April, 60 dealers show their wares at the monthly **Bath Antiques Shows** (207/443-8983, www.bathantiquesshows.com, $4) at the Bath Middle School.

SHOPPING

Front and Center Streets are lined with fun, independent shops, including a number of shops selling antiques and antiquarian books clustered on lower Front Street.

Bath's home to a good independent bookstore successfully bucking the megastore trend, the **Bath Book Shop** (96 Front St., Bath, 207/443-9338). For cheap beach reads and eclectic finds, visit **The Library Bookstore** (194 Front St., Bath, 207/443-1161).

Right in the shadow of the Route 1 overpass is an incredible resource for knitters and weavers. **Halcyon Yarn** (12 School St., Bath, 207/442-7909 or 800/341-0282, www.halcyonyarn.com), a huge warehouse of a place, carries domestic and imported yarns, looms, spinning wheels, how-to videos, kits, and pattern books.

About nine miles down Route 127, you'll come to **Georgetown Pottery** (Rte. 127, Georgetown, 207/371-2801), a top-quality ceramics studio and shop.

Anyone who appreciates fine woodworking tools *has* to visit the Shelter Institute's **Woodbutcher Tools** (873 Rte. 1, Woolwich, 207/442-7938) retail shop and bookstore, five miles north of Bath.

Flea Market

One of Maine's biggest and most enduring flea markets is right on Route 1 north of Bath, often creating near-accidents as rubbernecking motorists slam to a halt. **Montsweag Flea Market** (Rte. 1 at Mountain Rd., Woolwich, 207/443-2809, www.montsweagfleamarket.com) is a genuine treasure trove about seven miles northeast of Bath's Sagadahoc bridge. It's open weekends, from 6:30 A.M., May–mid-October, plus on Wednesday in summer (antiques and collectibles only, from 5:30 A.M.).

RECREATION

Golf

The 18-hole **Bath Country Club** (Whiskeag Rd., Bath, 207/442-8411) has moderate greens fees, a pro shop, and a restaurant serving lunch and dinner.

The **Sebasco Harbor Resort** has a nine-hole course (expanding to 18 holes) open to nonguests on a space-available basis; call the resort's pro shop (207/389-9060) to inquire. Watch out for the infamous second hole, which gives new meaning to the term water hole, and be sure to say good morning to Sarah on the sixth tee. If you look nearby, you'll find a gravestone inscribed "Sarah Wallace—1862." A local rhyme goes:

Show respect to Sarah
You golfers passing by;
She's the only person on this course,
Who can't improve her lie.

Bicycling

Bath-area headquarters for anything to do with bikes is **Bath Cycle and Ski** (Rte. 1, Woolwich, 207/442-7002 or 800/245-3626, www.bikeman.com). Rentals are $80/week, route maps are available, and the shop sponsors weekly rides on Tuesday nights and Saturday and Sunday mornings.

Hiking

The Kennebec Estuary Land Trust (www.kennebecestuary.org) maintains two preserves worth a visit. In Bath at the end of High Street, at the tip of land where Whiskeag Creek meets the Kennebec River, is the **Thorn Head Preserve.** Allow a half hour for the easy walk to the headland and its stone "picnic" table with views toward Merrymeeting Bay. Allow longer if you wish to explore any of the side trails. For terrific views of this section of coast, hike the loop trail to the bedrock summit of Georgetown's **Higgins Mountain.** The Route 127 trailhead is on the right, 7.6 miles south of Route 1.

BATES-MORSE MOUNTAIN CONSERVATION AREA

Consider visiting Phippsburg's lovely 600-acre Bates-Morse Mountain Conservation Area *only* if you are willing to be extra-conscientious about the rules for this private preserve. A relatively easy four-mile round-trip hike takes you through marshland (you'll need insect repellent) and to the top of 210-foot Morse Mountain, with panoramic views, and then down to privately owned Seawall Beach. On a clear day, you can see New Hampshire's Mt. Washington from the summit. No pets or vehicles; no recreational facilities; stay on the preserve road and the beach path at all times (side roads are private). Least terns and piping plovers—both endangered species—nest in the dunes, so avoid this area, especially mid-May–mid-August. Bird-watching hint: Morse Mountain is a great locale for spotting hawks during their annual September migration southward. Pick up a map (and the rules) from the box in the parking area, Morse Mountain Road, off Route 216 (just under a mile south of the Rte. 209 intersection).

PHIPPSBURG HIKING TRAILS

The town of Phippsburg and the Phippsburg Land Trust (207/443-6309, www.

phippsburglandtrust.org) have prepared a handy free brochure with map that describes nine preserves with trails. Three—Center Pond, Spirit Pond, and Ridgewell Preserve—have detailed maps and field guides available at trailhead boxes. The Land Trust also hosts guided walks mid-June–mid-September.

Preserves

HAMILTON SANCTUARY

Owned by Maine Audubon (207/781-2330, www.maineaudubon.org), Hamilton Sanctuary in West Bath is a peaceful site for walking and nature study on the New Meadows River, with 1.5 miles of trails winding through meadows and forests and along the Back Cove shoreline. From Route 1 between Bath and Brunswick, take the New Meadows Road exit. Head south on New Meadows. When it becomes Foster Point Road, go four miles to the sanctuary entrance.

JOSEPHINE NEWMAN SANCTUARY

A must-see for any nature lover, the 119-acre Josephine Newman Sanctuary (Rte. 127, Georgetown, no phone) has 2.5 miles of blazed loop trails winding through 110 wooded acres and along Robinhood Cove's tidal shoreline. Josephine Oliver Newman (1878–1968), a respected naturalist, bequeathed her family's splendid property to Maine Audubon (207/781-2330, www.maineaudubon.org), which maintains it today. The 0.6-mile self-guided trail is moderately difficult, but the rewards are 20 informative markers highlighting special features: glacial erratics, reversing falls, mosses, and marshes. The easiest route is the 0.75-mile Horseshoe Trail, which you can extend for another mile or so by linking into the Rocky End Trail. No pets or bikes. To find this hidden gem, take Route 127 from Route 1 in Woolwich (the road to Reid State Park) for 9.1 miles. Turn right at the sanctuary sign and continue up the narrow, rutted dirt road (pray no one's coming the other way) to the small parking lot. A map of the trail system is posted at the marsh's edge and available in the box.

ROBERT P. TRISTRAM COFFIN WILDFLOWER SANCTUARY

The New England Wildflower Society (www.newfs.org) owns this 177-acre trail-laced preserve bordering Merrymeeting Bay, with more than 100 species of wildflowers. To find it, take Route 127 north for 2.2 miles, then Route 128 for 4.5 miles, and look for a small parking area on the left.

Swimming

POPHAM BEACH

On hot July and August weekends, the parking lot at Popham Beach State Park (Rte. 209, Phippsburg, 207/389-1335, $6 nonresident adults, $4 resident adults, $2 nonresident seniors, free resident seniors, $1 children 5–11), 14 miles south of Bath, fills up by 10 A.M., so plan to arrive early at this huge crescent of sand backed by sea grass, beach roses, and dunes. Facilities include changing rooms, outside showers, restrooms, and seasonal lifeguards. It's officially open April 15–October 30, but the beach is accessible all year.

HEAD BEACH

Just off Route 216, about two miles south of the Route 209 turnoff to Popham Beach, is Head Beach, a sandy crescent that's open daily until 10 P.M. A day-use parking fee ($5) is payable at the small gatehouse; there's a restroom on the path to the beach and a store within walking distance.

Reid State Park

Reid State Park, on the Georgetown Peninsula (Seguinland Rd., Georgetown, 207/371-2303, $6.50 nonresident adults, $4.50 Maine resident adults, $2 nonresident seniors, free resident seniors, $1 children 5–11), is no secret, so plan to arrive early on summer weekends, when parking is woefully inadequate. Highlights of the 765-acre park are 1.5 miles of splendid beach (in three distinct sections), marshlands, sand dunes, and tide pools. Kids love the tide pools, treasure troves left by the receding tide. Facilities include changing rooms (with showers), picnic tables, restrooms, and snack bars.

Test the water before racing in; even in midsummer, it's breathtakingly cold. In winter, bring cross-country skis and glide along the shoreline. The park—14 miles south of Route 1 (Woolwich) and two miles off Route 127—is open daily all year.

Just half a mile beyond the Reid State Park entrance is **Charles Pond,** where the setting is unsurpassed for freshwater swimming in the long, skinny pond. You'll wish this were a secret, too, but it isn't. No facilities.

Excursion Boats

The 50-foot ***Yankee*** operates out of Small Point's Hermit Island Campground Monday–Saturday throughout the summer. You can go on nature cruises, enjoy the sunset, or visit Eagle Island; the schedule is different each day and rates vary widely by trip. Call for information and reservations (207/389-1788).

The M/V ***Ruth,*** a 38-foot excursion boat, runs cruises out of Sebasco Harbor Resort late June–Labor Day. You don't need to be a Sebasco guest to take the trips, but reservations are essential. The schedule changes weekly, but possible options are a nature cruise, Cundy's Harbor lunch cruise, lobstering demos, sunset cruise, and Pirate Island, at lengths varying from one to two hours. Call the resort (207/389-1161) for the current week's schedule and rates.

Long Reach Cruises (207/442-0092 or 888/538-6785, www.longreachcruises.com) offers a variety of one- to three-plus-hour cruises, departing from the Maine Maritime Museum. Options include narrated history, lighthouses, seal-watching, eagle-watching, and sunset cruises. Prices range $24–45 adults, $10–25 children, including two-day museum admission.

If you prefer a custom tour, call **River Run Tours** (207/504-2628, www.riverruntours.com). Whether you want to view lighthouses or wildlife or cruise up river to Swans Island, Captain Ed Rice will design an itinerary, based on per-hour charges of $30 per adult, $15 child age 12 and younger. His comfortable pontoon boat accommodates six. Plan on at least two hours.

Canoeing and Kayaking

Close to civilization, yet amazingly undeveloped, 392-acre **Nequasset Lake** is a great place to canoe. You'll see a few anglers, a handful of houses, and near-wilderness along the shoreline. Personal watercraft and motors over 10 hp are banned. Take Route 1 from Bath across the bridge to Woolwich. Continue to the flashing caution light at Nequasset Road; turn right and go 0.1 mile. Turn left, and left again, into the parking area for the Nequasset Stream Waterfront Park, a popular swimming hole. Launch your canoe and head upstream, under Route 1, to the lake.

Paddle the relatively calm and safe waters of Winnegance Creek with a rental canoe or kayak from **Paddle Up the Creak** (Rte. 209, Phippsburg, 207/443-4845, www.rentkayaks.com). Fee is $10 per person for three hours.

Seaspray Kayaking (888/349-7774, www.seaspraykayaking.com) operates from bases at the Sebasco Harbor Resort, in Sebasco Estates; Hermit Island Campground, on Small Point; and Bay Point Kayaking Center, in Georgetown. Hourly rentals begin at $15–25 the first hour plus $5–10 for each additional hour, up to $25–50 daily, with longer-term rates and delivery available. A variety of guided tours also are offered, with half-day options for $50 adults, $25 children, and specialty paddles, such as sunset or moonlight, for $40 per person.

Fishing Charters

Cast a line for stripers, bluefish, pike trout, and smallmouth bass with **Kennebec Tidewater Charters** (207/737-4695, www.kennebectidewater.com). Captain Robin Thayer, a Master Maine Guide, offers freshwater and saltwater cruises, beginning at $300 for four hours. Tackle is provided and instruction is available. Catch-and-release is encouraged.

ACCOMMODATIONS

Bath

Most of Bath's intown bed-and-breakfasts and inns are in historic residences built by shipping magnates and their families, giving you a chance to appreciate the quality of craftsmanship they demanded in their ships and their homes alike. All are open year-round.

The flamboyant pink and plum Italianate **Galen Moses House** (1009 Washington St., Bath, 207/442-8771 or 888/442-8771, www.galenmoses.com, $119–259) is a standout in the city's Historic District. Original architectural features—soaring ceilings, friezes, chandeliers, elaborate woodwork, stained-glass windows—and period antiques make it equally appealing inside, as do hosts Jim Haught and Larry Kieft. All rooms have air-conditioning and Wi-Fi. It has plenty of common rooms for relaxing, including one with TV and VCR. A fancy full breakfast (communal table) and afternoon refreshments are included. Pets are allowed in one room for $15 per night.

Innkeeper Elizabeth Knowlton blends elegance and comfort at the **Inn at Bath** (969 Washington St., Bath, 207/443-4294 or 800/423-0964, www.innatbath.com, $170–200). Her culinary skills, honed as chef and co-owner of a Montana fly-fishing lodge, have garnered national attention. Guest rooms in the 1810 Greek Revival–style inn are decorated with antiques and each has air-conditioning, TV-VCR, Wi-Fi, and phone. Two have wood-burning fireplaces, and two have two-person whirlpool tubs. Kids over four and dogs are welcome. One room is ADA compliant.

Just a few miles from downtown Bath, yet feeling a world away, is the **Fairhaven Inn** (118 North Bath Rd., Bath, 207/443-4391 or 888/443-4391, www.mainecoast.com/fairhaveninn, $115–150). Antiques and country pieces furnish Dawn and Andrew Omo's truly rambling 1790 colonial, built on 16 country acres with views over the Kennebec River. Six rooms have Wi-Fi and air-conditioning. The Omos grew up in Bath, so they know the area well. A pet is $15 per night.

Phippsburg Peninsula

The trouble with staying at the **Sebasco Harbor Resort** (Rte. 217, Sebasco Estates, 207/389-1161 or 800/225-3819, www.sebasco.com), a self-contained resort on 575 waterfront acres, is that between the beautiful setting and the bountiful offerings, you might not set foot off the premises during your entire vacation. Situated at the mouth of the saltwater New Meadows River, 12 miles south of Bath, Sebasco has attracted families who return year after year—since 1930, when it opened. Sebasco changed hands in 1997, and owner Bob Smith has brought the resort up to 21st-century standards while keeping its old-style rusticity. You'll have to look far and wide to find a better family resort. Scattered around the well-tended property are the main lodge and a variety of cottages (from 1–6 bedrooms; the two-bedroom units with shared living room are a great choice for families), a main lodge, a four-story cupola-topped lighthouse building edging the harbor, and two new suites buildings, Harbor Village and the waterfront Fairwinds Spa, with more contemporary amenities. All have private baths, phones, and cable TV; many have water views; some have refrigerators or kitchenettes. Rates begin around $200; kids 10 and under are free. MAP rate, including breakfast and dinner, is an additional $48 per person (10 and younger no charge when dining with an adult and off the kids' menu). Weekly summer events include a Sunday-evening reception and grand buffet, lobster bakes, family barbecues, bingo, live entertainment, and the Camp Merrit children's program ($12 per day, including lunch). Recreational facilities include two all-weather tennis courts, nine-hole championship golf course and a three-hole regulation course for beginners and families, the state's largest outdoor saltwater pool, boat tours aboard the *Ruth,* sailing trips, sea kayak excursions, mountain-bike tours, candlepin bowling, horseshoes, a playground, a well-equipped fitness center, and as much or as little organized activity as you want.

Right on the beach between Popham Beach State Park and Fort Popham is the **Popham Beach Bed and Breakfast** (4 Ocean View La., Popham Beach, Phippsburg, 207/389-2409, www.pophambeachbandb.com, $185–235 d), a unique hostelry in a restored 1883 Coast Guard station. Innkeeper Peggy Johannessen

© HILARY NANGLE

Once a lifesaving station, the Popham Beach Bed and Breakfast is ideal for those who want to work off hearty breakfasts with a stroll on the sand.

takes guests to the rooftop lookout tower and shares the building's history as a maritime lifesaving center. Inside are three rooms and a suite, two with gas fireplaces. A full breakfast is served in the dining room each morning, and guests can hang out in the large oceanfront living room. Open all year.

Magnificent gardens surround **Edgewater Farm Bed and Breakfast** (71 Small Point Rd./Rte. 216, Sebasco Estates, 207/389-1322 or 877/389-1322, www.ewfbb.com, $130–225), Carol and Bill Emerson's comfy, unfussy 19th-century farmhouse, just south of the turnoff to Popham Beach and close to the access for Morse Mountain. Families usually choose the carriage house, where kids can play in the huge recreation room. A brunch-size breakfast served in the many-windowed solarium benefits from lots of organic produce grown on the four-acre grounds. (The Emersons always plant extra to donate to the Bath food pantry each summer.) And then there's the four-foot-deep indoor lap pool, a hot tub outside on the deck, and the Benedictine labyrinth Bill created in a wooded grove. English, Spanish, a bit of French, and German are all spoken. Pets are possible.

Rock Gardens Inn (Rte. 218, Sebasco Estates, Phippsburg, 207/389-1339, www.rockgardensinn.com) hosts numerous artists' workshops, and no wonder. It sits on its own peninsula, and the pretty grounds are landscaped with wild and cultivated flowers. Guests stay in one of three inn rooms ($140–160 d, $185–205 s) or 10 cottages and have use of an outdoor heated pool and sea kayaks. Cottage rates begin at $150 d per person and include breakfast and dinner—and the weekly lobster cookout. After the minimum rate is reached per cottage, kids pay $55–115, depending upon age. Sebasco Harbor Resort is just steps away, and guests have access to its facilities, too. Ask about all-inclusive art retreats.

The 1774 Inn (44 Parker Head Rd., Phippsburg Center, 207/389-1774, www.1774inn.com, $125–185) is a gorgeous four-square Georgian colonial National Historic Register property with an 1870 ell and barn. Many colonial details have been preserved, including shutters with peep-holes and strong bars to defend against attack, paneled wainscoting, ceiling moldings, fluted columns, and wide pine floors. Most of the eight rooms (all but two with private bath) have views of the Kennebec River.

Georgetown Peninsula

It'll be hard to tear yourself away from the scenery and sanctuary at **The Mooring Bed and Breakfast** (132 Seguinland Rd., Georgetown, 207/371-2790 or 866/828-7348, www.themooringb-b.com, $150–200), the original home of Walter Reid, who donated Reid State Park to the state. His great-grandaughter Penny Barabe and her husband, Paul, have beautifully restored the house, situated on lovely oceanfront grounds with island-studded views. Each room has a water view and air-conditioning. There's plenty of room to spread out, including the appropriately named Spanish room. A full breakfast is served.

Even more secluded is **Coveside Bed & Breakfast** (6 Gott's Cove La., Georgetown, 207/371-2807 or 800/232-5490, www.covesidebandb.com, $135–200), a dreamy spot on five oceanfront acres near Five Islands. Tom and Carolyn Church have four guest rooms and a cottage. Some rooms have fireplaces; one has a whirlpool tub. Carolyn's pastry-chef skills are evident at breakfast. Wi-Fi is available, and a separate building has a TV and exercise room. Guests have use of bicycles and a canoe.

Campgrounds

Plan to book a site in January if you want a waterfront campsite in midsummer at the Phippsburg Peninsula's **Hermit Island Campground** (6 Hermit Island Rd., Phippsburg, 207/443-2101, www.hermitisland.com). With 275 campsites (no vehicles larger than pickup campers; no hookups) spread over a 255-acre causeway-linked island, this is oceanfront camping at its best. The well-managed operation has a store, snack bar, seasonal post office, boat rentals, boat excursions, trails, and seven private beaches. The hub of activity (and registration) is the Kelp Shed, next to the campsite entrance. Open and wooded sites run $35–57 (two adults and two kids) mid-June–Labor Day, $33 early and late in the season. Reservations for a week's stay or longer and Memorial and Labor Day weekends can be made by mail beginning in early January and by phone in early February (call for exact date). Reservations for stays of less than one week are accepted after March 1. It's open mid-May–Columbus Day, but full operation is really June–Labor Day. The campground is at the tip of the Phippsburg Peninsula. No pets, no credit cards.

FOOD

Hours noted are for peak season, but are subject to change. It's wise to call ahead, especially when traveling off season.

Local Flavors

In Waterfront Park on Commercial Street, the **Bath Farmers Market** operates 8:30 A.M.–noon every Saturday May–October, featuring crafts, plants, condiments, baked goods, and cheeses in addition to seasonal produce.

For breakfast, lunch, or sweets, drop into the **Starlight Café** (15 Lambard St., 207/443-3005, 7 A.M.–2 P.M. Mon.–Fri.), a too-cute and too-tiny daylight-basement space across a side street from the Customs House. It's bright and cheerful, and the food is fab.

A wonderful, multifaceted find is Susan Verrier's **North Creek Farm** (24 Sebasco Rd., Phippsburg, 207/389-1341, 9 A.M.–6:30 P.M. daily, lunch 11:30 A.M.–3:30 P.M.), an 1850s saltwater farm with fabulous organic gardens, including ornamental display gardens and lots of rugosa roses (a specialty—Susan's written two books). Visitors can meander down by a waterfall, creek, and salt marsh. Inside the barn is a small store stocked with garden and gourmet goodies and a small café, where Susan makes delicious soups and sandwiches to order ($5–7). There are tables indoors, but there also are chairs and tables scattered in the gardens.

On the Georgetown Peninsula, **Five Islands Farm** (1375 Rte. 127, Five Islands,

297/371-9383, www.fiveislandsfarm.com) is a fine stop for picnic fixings, with an excellent assortment of Maine cheeses, along with breads, meats, chips, salsa, and even wine.

Patty Mains retired early from Bath Iron Works to pursue her passion, chocolate. Her handcrafted chocolates are made from the best ingredients and from traditional recipes—try the needhams, made with mashed potatoes. While chocolates are the centerpiece at **MainSweets** (Rte. 127, Georgetown, 207/371-2806), she also sells home-baked breads, cookies, brownies, fudge, and other sweet treats.

Some argue the state's best thin-crust pizza (and praise-worthy garlic knots) comes from the ovens at **The Cabin** (552 Washington St., Bath, 207/443-6224, 10 A.M.–10 P.M., to 11 P.M. Thurs.–Sat.), a somewhat rough-and-tumble working-class joint that's been a local fave since 1973. It's across from Bath Iron Works. Avoid it during BIW shift changes (3–5 P.M. Mon.–Fri.); no credit cards.

Barbecue

Finger-licking Memphis-style barbecue, along with other Southern specialties, is served in big quantities at **Beale Street Barbeque and Grill** (215 Water St., Bath, 207/442-9514, 11 A.M.–9 P.M. daily, to 10 P.M. Fri.–Sat.). Everything's made on the premises. Find it next to the municipal parking lot.

Casual Dining

Kate and Andy Winglass operate **Mae's Café and Bakery** (160 Centre St. at High St., Bath, 207/442-8577, www.maescafeandbakery.com), a longtime local favorite bakery and café with seating indoors and on a front deck. It's *the* place to go for brunch (reservations essential on weekends). Breakfast and lunch are served 8 A.M.–4 P.M. daily; dinner is served until 8 P.M. Friday and Saturday in summer. Most choices are in the $7–12 range, dinner entrées run $15–20. Rotating art shows enliven the open and airy dining rooms.

The cool and contemporary Danish decor matches the food at **Solo Bistro** (128 Front St., Bath, 207/443-3373, www.solobistro.com, from 5 P.M. daily), a sophisticated storefront restaurant downtown where the choices might range from a bistro burger to pan-seared wild salmon ($13–28). A nightly three-course fixed-price menu is usually around $23. The wine bar features jazz on Friday nights. Note: Both the food and the service suffered from a 2009 expansion, so you might want to ask locally if it's back in the groove.

The View's the Thing

All places listed here are seasonal.

Even if you're not staying at **Sebasco Harbor Resort** (Rte. 217, Sebasco Estates, 207/389-1161 or 800/225-3819, www.sebasco.com), you can dine in either of its two waterfront restaurants, both with gasp-producing sunset views. Binoculars hang by windows in the **Pilot House** (5:30–9 P.M. Mon.–Sat.), the more formal of the two, so diners can get a better view of the boats or birds happening by. Dinner entrées range $17–27. Below it is the casual Ledges Pub (11:30 A.M.–2 P.M. and 5–10 P.M. daily), with indoor and outdoor seating and a menu varying from kid-friendly burgers and fried foods to salmon salad ($6–18).

Gaze at seals playing in the Kennebec River, Fort Popham, and out to open ocean from **Spinney's Restaurant** (987 Rte. 209, Popham Beach, 207/389-2052, 8 A.M.–8:30 P.M. daily). Food varies in quality from year to year. (Best advice: Keep it simple). Entrées run $10–30; sandwiches and hot dogs are less than $5, but you can't beat the view. Keep it budget friendly by coming for breakfast.

Lobster in the Rough

PHIPPSBURG PENINSULA

The rustic buoy-draped **Lobster House** (395 Small Point Rd./Rte. 216, Small Point, 207/389-1596 or 207/389-2178, www.thelobsterhouse.net, 11:30 A.M.–9 P.M. Tues.–Sun. late May–early Sept.) overlooks a scenic tidal cove; the view is best when the tide's in. No surprise that lobster and seafood are featured, but sandwiches, soups, salads, pizza, and a few grilled items make the menu wallet-friendly for anyone.

© HILARY NANGLE

Dreamy views over a boat-filled harbor await diners at Five Islands Lobster Company, in Georgetown.

GEORGETOWN PENINSULA

Just over a mile beyond the turnoff to Reid State Park, you'll reach the end of Route 127 at Five Islands. Here you'll find **Five Islands Lobster Company** (1447 Five Islands Rd., Five Islands, Georgetown, 207/371-2990, www.fiveislandslobster.com, 11:30 A.M.–8 P.M. daily mid-May–mid-October), known for its slogan: "Eat on the dock with the fishermen, but best avoid the table by the bait-shack door." Here you can pig out on lobster rolls, better-than-usual onion rings, crab cakes, and if you must, burgers and hot dogs. It even takes credit cards, a rarity among lobster wharves. Dress down, BYOB, and enjoy the end-of-the-road ambience of this idyllic spot.

Destination Dining

The building alone is worth a visit to chef Michael Gagne's **Robinhood Free Meetinghouse** (210 Robinhood Rd., Georgetown, 207/371-2188, www.robinhood-meetinghouse.com, 5:30–9 P.M. daily in season), a multi-star restaurant in a beautifully restored 1855 building on the Georgetown Peninsula. Most tables are on the main floor; overflow diners go to the 2nd floor, where many of the pews remain. The enormous (more than two dozen entrées, a dozen appetizers) high-quality menu makes it even more enticing. Creativity is the menu byword for Gagne. If you're a chocoholic, save room for Gagne's swoon-worthy signature dessert: Obsession in Three Chocolates with chocolate sauce. Entrées are in the $24–28 range, and portions are large. Reservations are essential. In the off season, ask about special "theme" nights. Gagne sells his famed 72-layer hand-cut cream cheese biscuits frozen, so take a half dozen or so home to enjoy with your leftovers. The restaurant is signed off Route 127. Open year-round.

INFORMATION AND SERVICES

Information

Info is available from the **Southern Midcoast Chamber of Commerce** (2 Main St., Topsham, 877/725-8797, www.midcoastmaine.com). A visitor information center is located in Bath's renovated train station (restrooms available), adjacent to the Bath Iron Works main yard. It's open year-round with brochure racks, and staffed by volunteers from May into October. Request copies of the *City of Bath Downtown Map and Guide* and the *Guide to Southern Midcoast Maine.*

Main Street Bath (4 Centre St., Bath, 207/442-7291, www.visitbath.com) produces a guide and has an informative website. More information is available on the city's website, www.cityofbath.com.

Check out **Patten Free Library** (33 Summer St., Bath, 207/443-5141, www.patten.lib.me.us).

Public Restrooms

Public restrooms are at Bath City Hall (55 Front St.), Patten Free Library (33 Summer St.), Sagadahoc County Courthouse (752 High St.), and (summer only) Waterfront Park (Commercial St.).

GETTING AROUND

The Bath Trolley (207/443-9741, www.bathtrolley.org) circulates through the area, with each one-way trip costing $1. For a schedule, visit City Hall.

Wiscasset Area

Billing itself as "The Prettiest Village in Maine," Wiscasset (pop. 1,200) works hard to live up to its slogan, with quaint street signs, well-maintained homes, and an air of attentive elegance.

Wiscasset ("meeting place of three rivers"), incorporated as part of Pownalborough in 1760, has had its current name since 1802. In the late 18th century, it became the shire town of Lincoln County and the largest seaport north of Boston. Countless tall-masted ships sailed the 12 miles up the Sheepscot River to tie up here, and shipyards flourished, turning out vessels for domestic and foreign trade. The 1807 Embargo Act and the War of 1812 delivered a one-two punch that shut down trade and temporarily squelched the town's aspirations, but Wiscasset yards soon were back at it, producing vessels for the pre–Civil War clipper-ship era—only to face a more lasting decline with the arrival of the railroads and the onset of the Industrial Revolution.

The Davey Bridge, built in 1983, is the most recent span over the Sheepscot. The earliest, finished in 1847, was a toll bridge that charged a horse and wagon $0.15 to cross, pedestrians $0.03 each, and pigs $0.01 apiece. Before that, ferries carried passengers, animals, and vehicles between Wiscasset and Edgecomb's Davis Island (then named Folly Island).

Wiscasset is notorious for midsummer gridlock. Especially on weekends, traffic backs up on Route 1 for miles in both directions—to the frustration of drivers, passengers, and Wiscasset merchants. The state Department of Transportation has tested traffic medians, stoplights, and other devices, but nothing solves the problem. A bypass has been under discussion for years, but not-in-my-backyard opposition to every route has halted progress. (When you stop in town, try to park pointed in the direction you're going; it's impossible to make turns across oncoming traffic.)

SIGHTS

In 1973, a large chunk of downtown Wiscasset was added to the National Register of Historic Places, and a walking tour is the best way to appreciate the Federal, Classical Revival, and even pre-Revolutionary homes and commercial buildings in the Historic District. Listed here are a few of the prime examples. If you do nothing else, be sure to swing by the homes on High Street.

Castle Tucker

Once known as the Lee-Tucker House, Castle Tucker (Lee and High Sts., Wiscasset, 207/882-7169, www.historicnewengland.org, tours on the hour, 11 A.M.–4 P.M. Wed.–Sun. June–Oct. 15,

RURAL RAMBLINGS

Surrounding Wiscasset are the lovely rural inland communities of Dresden, Sheepscot, and Alna, definitely worth a detour.

Begin in Dresden at the 1761 **Pownalborough Court House** (River Rd./Rte. 128, Dresden, 207/882-6817, www.lincolncountyhistory.org, 10 A.M.-4 P.M. Tues.-Sat. July-Aug., Sat. only June and Sept., $4 adults, $2 children 7-17), a pre-Revolutionary riverfront courthouse listed in the National Register of Historic Places. President John Adams once handled a trial here – in a mid-18th-century frontier community (named Pownalborough) established by French and German settlers. During the 30-minute tour of the three-story courthouse, guides delight in pointing out the restored beams, paneling, and fireplaces, as well as the on-site tavern that catered to judges, lawyers, and travelers. Walk a few hundred feet south and you'll find a cemetery with Revolution-era graves. Along the river is a nature trail developed by local Eagle Scouts. From Route 1 in Wiscasset, take Route 27 about nine miles north to the junction with Route 128. Turn left (south) and go 2.5 miles to the courthouse sign. The courthouse is also an easy drive from Bath.

Return to Wiscasset, and follow Route 218 north for about eight miles to Head Tide Village, an eminently picturesque hamlet at the farthest reach of Sheepscot River tides. From the late 18th century to the early 20th, Head Tide (now part of the town of Alna) was a thriving mill town, a source of hydropower for the textile and lumber industries. All that's long gone, but hints of that era come from the handful of well-maintained 18th- and 19th-century homes in the village center.

Up the hill, the stunning 1838 **Head Tide Church,** another fine example of local prosperity, is usually open 2-4 P.M. Saturday in July and August. Volunteer tour guides point out the original pulpit, a trompe l'oeil window, a kerosene chandelier, and walls lined with historic Alna photographs.

Head Tide's most famous citizen was the poet **Edwin Arlington Robinson,** born here in 1869. His family home, at the bend in Route 194 and marked by a plaque, is not open to the public. Perhaps his Maine roots inspired these lines from his poem "New England":

Here where the wind is always north-north-east
And children learn to walk on frozen toes.

Just upriver from the bend in the road is a favorite swimming hole, a millpond where you can join the locals on a hot summer day. Not much else goes on here, and there are no restaurants or lodgings, so Head Tide can't be termed a destination, but it's a village frozen in time – and an unbeatable opportunity for history buffs and shutterbugs.

Also historic, but a bit more lively and fun for kids, is the **Wiscasset, Waterville, and Farmington Railway** (97 Cross Rd., off Rte. 218, Sheepscot, 207/882-4193, www.wwfry.org, 9 A.M.-5 P.M. Sat. year-round and Sun. late May-mid-Oct.), a museum commemorating a two-foot-gauge common carrier railroad that operated in the early part of the 20th century, from Wiscasset in the south to Albion and Winslow in the north. On the grounds are a museum in the old station (free admission) and train rides along the mainline track running north from Cross Road, on the original roadbed ($6 adults, $4 children 4-12). Trains depart Sheepscot hourly 10 A.M.-4 P.M. on weekends. From Route 1 in Wiscasset, take Route 218 north 4.7 miles to a four-way intersection and go left on the Cross Road to the museum.

© HILARY NANGLE

Wiscasset's Castle Tucker is a 19th-century architectural masterpiece that's open for tours during the summer months.

$5) is a must-see. Built in 1807 by Judge Silas Lee, and bought by sea captain Richard Tucker in 1858, the imposing mansion has Victorian wallpaper and furnishings, Palladian windows, an amazing elliptical staircase, and a dramatic view over the Sheepscot River. In 1997, Jane Tucker, Richard's granddaughter, magnanimously deeded the house to Historic New England.

Nickels-Sortwell House

Also owned by Historic New England, the three-story Nickels-Sortwell House (121 Main St., Wiscasset, 207/882-6218, www.historicnewengland.org, tours on the hour 11 A.M.–4 P.M. Fri.–Sun. June–Oct. 15, $5) looms over Route 1, yet it's so close to the road many motorists miss it. Don't make the same mistake. Sea captain William Nickels commissioned the mansion in 1807 but died soon after its completion. For 70 or so years, it was the Belle Haven Hotel, before Alvin and Frances Sortwell's meticulous Colonial Revival restoration in the early 20th century.

Lincoln County Jail and Museum

Wiscasset's Old Jail (207/882-6817, www.lincolncountyhistory.org, 10 A.M.–4 P.M. Tues.–Sat. and noon–4 P.M. Sun. July–August, weekends only June and Sept., $4 adults, $2 children 7–17), completed in 1811, was the first prison in the District of Maine (then part of Massachusetts). Amazingly, it remained a jail—mostly for short-termers—until 1953. Two years after that, the Lincoln County Historical Association took over, so each summer you can check out the 40-inch-thick granite walls, floors, and ceilings; the 12 tiny cells; and historic graffiti penned by the prisoners. Attached to the prison is the 1837 jailer's house, now the Lincoln County Museum, containing antique tools, the original kitchen, and various temporary exhibits. A Victorian gazebo overlooking the Sheepscot River is a great spot for a picnic. From Route 1 (Main St.) in downtown Wiscasset, take Federal Street (Rte. 218) 1.2 miles.

© HILARY NANGLE

Danilo Konvalinka shares his treasures at the Musical Wonder House in Wiscasset.

Musical Wonder House

The treasures in the Musical Wonder House (18 High St., Wiscasset, 207/882-7163, www.musicalwonderhouse.com), an 1852 sea captain's mansion, are indeed astonishing, and eccentric Austrian-born museum founder Danilo Konvalinka delights in sharing them—for a price. The best way to appreciate the collection of hundreds of 19th-century European music boxes, player pianos, and musical rarities is to take a guided tour (available 10 A.M.–5 P.M. Mon.–Sat. and noon–5 P.M. Sun. late May–Oct., reduced schedule spring and fall), including two dozen player-piano and music-box demonstrations. A 35-minute tour is $10; 75-minute tour is $20; a three-hour tour, by appointment only, is $40.

Fort Edgecomb

Built in 1808 to protect the Sheepscot River port of Wiscasset, the Fort Edgecomb State Historic Site (Eddy Rd., Edgecomb, 207/882-7777, 9 A.M.–5 P.M. daily late May–early Sept., $3 nonresident adults, $2 resident adults, $1 children 5–11) occupies a splendid three-acre riverfront spread ideal for picnicking and fishing (no swimming). Many summer weekends, the Revolutionary encampments on the grounds of the octagonal blockhouse make history come alive with reenactments, period dress, craft demonstrations, and garrison drills. It's off Route 1; take Eddy Road just north of Wiscasset Bridge and go one-half mile to Fort Road.

FESTIVALS AND EVENTS

Wiscasset's daylong **Annual Strawberry Festival and Country Fair** (St. Philip's Episcopal Church, Hodge St., 207/882-7184) celebrates with tons of strawberries, plus crafts and an auction on the last Saturday in June. The church also is the site of **Monday-night fish-chowder suppers,** mid-July–mid-August. Reservations are advised (207/882-7184) for these very popular 5:30 P.M. suppers.

A summer highlight at Watershed Center for the Ceramic Arts is its annual **Salad Days,** a fund-raising event held on a July Saturday. For a $25 donation, you choose a handmade pottery plate, fill it from a piled-high buffet of fruit and veggie salads, and be part of an old-fashioned picnic social—and you even get to keep the plate! Afterward, there's plenty of time to explore the center's 32 acres. Call ahead to confirm the date (207/882-6075).

SHOPPING

The oldest commercial building in town is **Wiscasset Hardware** (Water St., Wiscasset, 207/882-6622), built in 1797 as a ship chandlery on the east side of Water Street. These days the store sells more gifty items than hardware and dishes out homemade ice cream downstairs.

Folk-art fans must visit Lois and David Kwantz's **Butterstamp Workshop** (55 Middle St., Wiscasset, 207/882-7825), which creates and sells designs copied from antique molds. Sometimes you can watch the workshop operation, which produces butter and cookie molds, beeswax ornaments, even magnets.

Natural beauty products, bamboo clothing, and fun finds fill Kelley Belanger's fun shop, **In the Clover** (85A Main St., Wiscasset, 207/882-9435, www.intheclover beauty.com).

Antiques and Art

It's certainly fitting that a town filled end-to-end with antique homes should have more than two dozen solo and group antiques shops.

Right downtown, **Blythe House Antiques** (161 Main St., Wiscasset, 207/882-1280) has multiple dealers exhibiting in room settings. French and English antiques are the specialty at **Daybreak Manor** (106 Rte. 1, Wiscasset, 207/882-9786). Both fine art and antiques are sold at **French and Vandyke** (8 Federal St., Wiscasset, 207/882-8302).

European and American 19th- and 20th-century painters are the broad focus at **Wiscasset Bay Gallery** (67 Main St./Rte. 1, Wiscasset, 207/882-7682 or 888/622-9445, www.wiscassetbaygallery.com), which schedules high-quality rotating shows throughout the season.

In the handsome open spaces of an early-

© TOM NANGLE

Antiques and specialty shops line Wiscasset's streets.

19th-century brick schoolhouse, the **Maine Art Gallery** (Warren St., Wiscasset, 207/882-7511, www.maineartgallery.org) was founded in 1954 as a nonprofit organization to showcase contemporary Maine artists.

Two miles south of town is **Avalon Antiques Market** (563 Rte. 1, Wiscasset, 207/882-4239, www.avalonantiquesmarket.com), a huge red barn of a place filled with more than 100 dealers showing on three floors.

ACCOMMODATIONS

Rates are for peak season.

Bed-and-Breakfasts

Named after a famous Maine clipper ship, Paul and Melanie Harris's **Snow Squall Inn** (5 Bradford Rd. at Rte. 1, Wiscasset, 207/882-6892 or 800/775-7245, www.snowsquallinn.com, $107–170) is a renovated mid-19th-century house with four lovely rooms and three family suites, all with phone, air-conditioning, and Wi-Fi, and two with fireplace. Ask Melanie, a licensed massage therapist and a vinyasa yoga instructor, about scheduling a massage or taking a class. It's open all year, but only by reservation November–April.

Then there's a major getaway—**The Squire Tarbox Inn** (1181 Main Rd., Rte. 144, Westport Island, 207/882-7693 or 800/818-0626, www.squiretarboxinn.com, $139–199), an elegantly casual bed-and-breakfast/inn that doubles as a working organic farm. Accomplished Swiss chef-owner Mario De Pietro and his wife, Roni, have continued the inn's reputation for dining excellence. Eleven lovely rooms, some with fireplaces, are divided between the late-18th-century main house and the early-19th-century carriage house; those in the main house are more formal. Rates include breakfast, and the dining room is open to the public by reservation for dinner. Also on the property are walking paths, a rowboat, mountain bikes, a working pottery, and a working farm, with organic vegetable gardens, chickens, and goats. The season stretchs mid-April–December. From downtown Wiscasset, head southwest four miles on Route 1 to Route 144. Turn left and go about 8.5 scenic miles to the inn.

Motels

Fairly close to Route 1 but buffered a bit by century-old hemlocks, the **Wiscasset Motor Lodge** (Rte. 1, Wiscasset, 207/882-7137 or 800/732-8168, www.wiscassetmotorlodge.com, $72–108) is a comfortable, well-maintained motel. Rooms have phone, TV, and air-conditioning, and a light breakfast is included in summer. Ask for a room in the back building if you're sensitive to noise.

FOOD

Hours noted are for peak season, but are subject to change. It's wise to call ahead, especially when traveling off season.

Across Federal Street from the Nickels-Sortwell House in downtown Wiscasset is the lovely **Sunken Garden,** an almost-unnoticed pocket park created around the cellar hole of a long-gone inn. It's a fine place for a picnic.

Local Flavors

Let's start with the obvious, **Red's Eats** (Main and Water Sts., Wiscasset, 207/882-6128, 11 A.M.–11 P.M. Mon.–Sat., noon–6 P.M. Sun., early May–mid-Oct.). This simple take-out stand has garnered national attention through the decades for its lobster rolls stuffed with the meat from a whole lobster. It's easy to spot because of the line. Expect to wait. And wait. And wait, perhaps for an hour or more. Is it worth it? I don't think so, but others rave about the cold lobster rolls, the fried fish, the hot dogs, and the wraps. If you're planning on one of Red's lobster rolls, ask someone who's just bought one the price before you get in line and make sure you have enough cash (no credit cards). The few tables on the sidewalk and behind the building, overlooking the river, are seldom empty (except in bad weather), but it's only a quick walk across Main to picnic tables (and a public restroom) on the Town Wharf, where **Sprague Lobster** (22 Main St., Wiscasset, 207/882-2306) has set up a competing stand. Many locals prefer Sprague's. Lines are rare and the lobster rolls also contain the meat from an entire crustacean.

Back up the street, across a side road from the post office, is **Treat's** (80 Main St., Wiscasset, 207/882-6192, www.treatsofmaine.com, 10 A.M.–6 P.M. Mon.–Sat., noon–5 P.M. Sun.), a superb source of gourmet picnic fixings: sandwiches, soups, wine, cheese, condiments, and artisanal breads.

Family Favorites

Two miles southwest of downtown Wiscasset, **The Sea Basket Restaurant** (303 Rte. 1, Wiscasset, 207/882-6581, www.seabasket.com, 11 A.M.–8 P.M. Wed.–Mon.) has been serving hearty bowls of lobster stew and good-size baskets of eminently fresh seafood since 1981. There's always a crowd—locals eat here, too—so expect to wait. The fried fish is almost healthful, thanks to convection-style frying using trans fat–free oil. Closed January into February.

In a high-visibility location across Route 1 from Red's Eats, **Sarah's Cafe** (Main and

Water Sts., Rte. 1, Wiscasset, 207/882-7504, www.sarahscafe.com, 11 A.M.–8 P.M. daily) is the home of huge "whaleboat" and "dory" sandwiches, homemade soups (self-serve), pizza, vegetarian specials, and an ice-cream fountain. Lobster meat shows up in salads, burritos, quesadillas, wraps, croissants, and more. The deck has front-row seats on the Sheepscot River. Be forewarned that service sometimes is very sluggish, but crayons keep kids busy.

Housed in a big red barn about midway between Bath and Wiscasset, **Montsweag Roadhouse** (942 Rte. 1, Woolwich, 207/443-6563, www.montsweagroadhouse.com, 11 A.M.–9 P.M., to 10 P.M. Fri.–Sat.) gets two thumbs up for reasonably priced foods, from burgers and pizzas to steak and fried fish, and friendly service. The upstairs games room—pool and foosball tables and dart boards—keeps kids busy while the grown-ups chat. This is an especially casual place, with a strong local following. The bar remains open to 1 A.M., with live music both upstairs and down on weekends.

Casual Dining

Overlooking the Kennebec, and just two blocks off Route 1, is **Le Garage** (15 Water St., Wiscasset, 207/882-5409, www.legaragerestaurant.com, 11 A.M.–8:30 P.M. daily), an enduringly popular spot serving traditional fare with flair. Request a porch/deck table, and dine by candlelight. Lamb is a specialty, as is finnan haddie (smoked haddock). Entrée range is $10–27; light suppers are thrifty choices. Reservations are wise on weekends. It's closed January, and Mondays off-season.

Well off the beaten path, on an island connected to the mainland by bridge, is **The Squire Tarbox Inn** (1181 Main Rd., Rte. 144, Westport Island, 207/882-7693 or 800/818-0626, www.squiretarboxinn.com, Wed.–Mon. mid-June–mid-Oct., Thurs.–Sat. mid-April–mid-June and mid-Oct.–Dec.), a working organic farm where Swiss chef Mario De Pietro serves memorable meals. Entrées, such as rack of lamb, Swiss-style veal, and a fish of the day, run $25–30, and are served either on the porch or in an intimate dining room. Off season, Thursday nights are Swiss night, with appropriate cuisine served. Ask about cooking classes.

On the edge of downtown, **Mark Antony's Italian Cuisine** (65 Gardiner Rd., Wiscasset, 207/882-9888, www.markantonysitaliancuisine.com, 5–8 P.M. Wed.–Sun., to 9 P.M. Fri.–Sat.) is a cozy spot that delivers more than its humble exterior promises. Chef and co-owner Mark Buscanera draws on his North End Boston roots to prepare classic Italian fare ($10–25), and he might even serenade your table.

INFORMATION AND SERVICES

Information

The best place pick up Wiscasset info is the display rack at Big Al's Super Values, on Route 1, three miles southwest of downtown. Once you get into town, stop at Wiscasset Hardware for a free walking map of the downtown area.

Check out **Wiscasset Public Library** (21 High St., Wiscasset, 207/882-7161, www.wiscasset.lib.me.us).

Public Restrooms

The Town Wharf, Water Street, and the Lincoln County Court House, on Route 1 next to the sharp curve as you come down the hill from the south, have public restrooms.

Boothbay Peninsula

East of Wiscasset, en route to Damariscotta, only a flurry of signs along Route 1 in Edgecomb (pop. around 1,000) hints at what's down the peninsula bisected by Route 27 and framed by the Sheepscot and Damariscotta Rivers. Drive southward down the Boothbay Peninsula between Memorial Day and Labor Day and you'll find yourself in one of Maine's longest-running summer playgrounds.

The four peninsula towns of **Boothbay** (pop. 2,675), **Boothbay Harbor** (pop. 2,165), **East Boothbay** (pop. 540), and, connected by a bridge, **Southport Island** (pop. 590) are a maze of islands and peninsulas. When Route 27 arrives at the water, having passed through Boothbay Center, you're at the hub, Boothbay Harbor ("the Harbor"), scene of most of the action. The harbor itself is a boat fan's dream, loaded with working craft and pleasure yachts. Ashore are shops and galleries, restaurants and inns, and one-way streets, traffic congestion, and pedestrians everywhere. But don't despair, it's easy to escape the peak season crowds in one of the numerous parks and preserves, fine places for a hike or a picnic. Hop an excursion boat to an offshore island, for a whale watch, or for an evening sail around the bay.

Try to save time for quieter spots: East Boothbay, Ocean Point, Southport Island, the Coastal Maine Botanical Gardens, or even just over the 1,000-foot-long footbridge stretching across one corner of the harbor. Cross the bridge and walk down Atlantic Avenue to the Fishermen's Memorial, a bronze fishing dory commemorating the loss of hardy souls who've earned a rugged living here by their wits and the sea. Across the street is Our Lady Queen of Peace Catholic Church, with shipwright-quality woodwork and its own fishing icon—a lobster trap next to the altar.

Ocean Point, in East Boothbay, is an appealing place to escape the crowds of Boothbay Harbor.

SIGHTS

Boothbay Railway Village

Boothbay Railway Village (Rte. 27, Boothbay, 207/633-4727, www.railwayvillage.org, 9:30 A.M.–5 P.M. daily early June–mid-Oct., $9 adults, $5 children 3–16) feels like a life-size train set. More than two dozen old and new buildings have been assembled here since the museum was founded in 1964, and a restored narrow-gauge steam train makes a 1.5-mile, 20-minute circuit throughout the day. You'll also find more than four dozen antique cars and trucks. Train rides also operate on weekends from late May until daily opening in June and for a Halloween ride on the last weekend in October.

Burnt Island Tour

Visit with a lighthouse keeper's family, climb the tower into the lantern room, and explore an island during a living- and natural-history program presented by the Maine Department of Marine Resources on Burnt Island (207/633-9580, www.maine.gov/dmr/education.htm, $22 adults, $12 children under 12). The tour is offered twice daily in July and August. Travel via excursion boat from 21st-century Boothbay Harbor to Burnt Island, circa 1950, where actors portray the family of lighthouse keeper Joseph Muise, who lived here 1936–1951. During the three-hour program, you'll spend time with the light keeper, his wife, and each of his children, learning about their lifestyles and views on island life. Historical documents, photographs, and lenses, from 1821 to the present, are displayed in the 45-foot covered walkway between the house and tower. You may climb the spiral stairway up to the lantern room and see how the lighthouse actually functions. On an easy hike, a naturalist explains the island's flora, fauna, and geology and recounts legends. During free time, you may hike other trails, listen to a program on present-day lobstering and Maine fisheries, go beachcombing, fish for mackerel off the dock, or just relax and enjoy it all.

Marine Resources Aquarium

A 20-foot touch tank, with slimy but pettable specimens, is a major kid magnet at the Marine Resources Aquarium (McKown Point Rd., West Boothbay Harbor, 207/633-9559, www.maine.gov/dmr/education.htm, 10 A.M.–5 P.M. daily late May–late Aug., 10 A.M.–5 P.M. Wed.–Sun. in Sept., $5 adults, $3 seniors and

© HILARY NANGLE

An inviting beach and a lighthouse await those who venture down Southport Island.

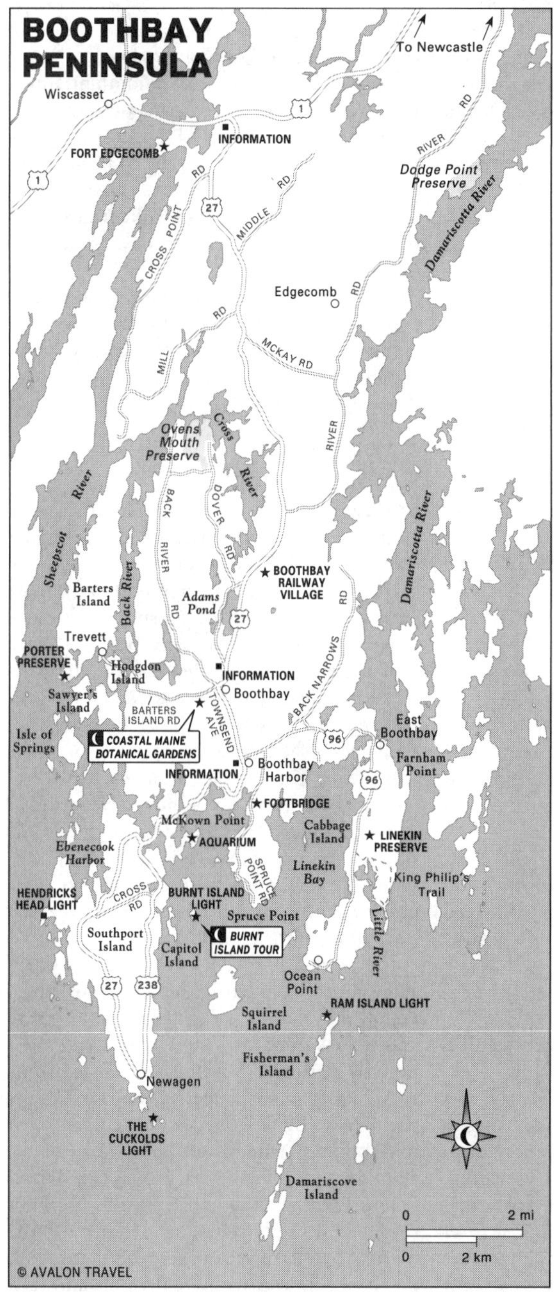

children 5–18), operated by the Maine Department of Marine Resources. Exhibits in the hexagonal aquarium include rare lobsters (oversize, albino, and blue) and other Gulf of Maine creatures, and new residents arrive periodically. Self-guiding leaflets are available. Consider bringing a picnic—it's a great setting. At the height of summer, parking is limited, and it's a longish walk from downtown around the west side of the harbor, so plan to take the free local trolley-bus.

Southport Island

The nautical shortcut of Townsend Gut separates Boothbay Harbor from Southport Island (www.southportislandassociation.org). The island is ideal for a drive-about, following Route 27 south to the island's tip, then returning north on Route 238. En route are plentiful glimpses of island-salted ocean waters, especially if you explore some of the side roads. Here are a few other noteworthy sights.

A historic 1810 Cape-style building, carefully restored, is the 11-room home of the **Hendricks Hill Museum** (Rte. 27, West Southport, 207/633-4831, www.hendrickshill.org, 11 A.M.–3 P.M. Tues., Thurs., and Sat. July–Aug., donation appreciated), a community attic filled with all kinds of workaday tools and utensils and fascinating maritime memorabilia. The museum is about two miles south of the Southport Island bridge, on the right, in the center of West Southport.

From the Southport Village General Store, where you can pick up sandwiches for a picnic, it's just a hop down Beach Road to **Hendricks Head,** with a nice sand beach and lighthouse views.

At the island's tip is the **Southport Memorial Library** (207/633-2741, 9 A.M.–4 P.M. and 7–9 P.M. Tues. and Thurs., 9 A.M.–4 Sat.). Displayed inside is a huge collection of mounted butterflies.

ENTERTAINMENT

The renovated 1894 **Opera House** (86 Townsend Ave., Boothbay Harbor, 207/633-6855, www.boothbayoperahouse.org) hosts concerts, lectures, dramas, and special events. An upstairs bar, in the former Knights of Pythias Hall, is open to adults before performances and for intermission, and often for special events.

The **Boothbay Playhouse** (275 Rte. 27, Boothbay, 207/633-3379, www.boothbayplayhouse.com, $19 adults, $16 children 12 and younger) is a vibrant family-oriented community theater with talent that will amaze you.

The **Lincoln Arts Festival** (207/633-3913, www.lincolnartsfestival.org) presents half a dozen or more concerts—classical, pops, choral, and jazz—and other arts-related events at various locations on the Boothbay Peninsula late June–late September.

Early July through August is a great time for music in Boothbay Harbor. Free **band concerts** at 8 P.M. Thursdays are performed on the Memorial Library lawn. Bring a blanket or folding chair.

EVENTS

The **Fishermen's Festival** is a locally colorful early-season celebration, held the third weekend of April and beginning with a Friday Miss Shrimp Princess pageant. Saturday brings a lobster-crate race and afternoon contests such as trap hauling, scallop- and clam-shucking, fish-filleting, and net mending (plus a real steal—a lobster-eating contest you can enter for $5). Saturday night, church suppers feature fish and shellfish, and on Sunday a chowder luncheon precedes the blessing of the fleet to ensure a successful summer season.

June is the month for **Windjammer Days,** two days of festivities centering on traditional windjammer schooners. Highlights are the Windjammer Parade, harborfront concerts, plenty of food, and a fireworks extravaganza.

In early August, the **Boat Builders Festival** features shipyard and boat tours, food, and kids' activities.

Huge sailboats arrive in the harbor in early September for the **Shipyard Cup** (www.shipyardcup.com), with racing on two days. Hop aboard an excursion boat for a close-up view or drive out to Ocean Point.

RECREATION

Parks and Preserves

BOOTHBAY REGION LAND TRUST

Courtesy of the very active Boothbay Region Land Trust (137 Townsend Ave., Boothbay Harbor, 207/633-4818, www.bbrlt.org), more than 1,700 acres, including six islands, with more than 30 miles of trails available, have been preserved for wildlife, residents, and visitors. Individual preserve maps, as well as a general brochure-map with driving directions, are available at the information centers or at the trust office. Kiosks at the trailheads hold preserve maps. The trust also offers a free series of summertime guided walks and paddles in the various preserves as well as talks. A free guide, available at local businesses and info centers, provides details and access points. Here's just a sampling of the possibilities.

Most popular is the **Porter Preserve,** a 19-acre property bordering the Sheepscot River. Follow the moderately easy 0.86-mile loop trail and be rewarded with spectacular views, especially at sunset. You might even spy some seals lolling in the ledges at low tide. To get there, take Route 27 south to the monument in Boothbay Center. Bear right on Cory Lane and go 0.3 mile, bearing right again on Barters Island Road. Follow it 12.2 miles (perhaps stopping at the Barters Island General Store for lobster rolls or subs to go), and then go left on Kimballtown Road. Go 0.5 mile and turn left at the fork onto Porter Point Road. Park in the small lot just beyond the cemetery.

The 146-acre **Ovens Mouth Preserve** has almost five miles of trails on two peninsulas linked by a 93-foot bridge (wear insect repellent). The 1.6-mile trail on the east peninsula is much easier than the 3.7 miles of trails on the west peninsula. To get there, from the monument in Boothbay Center, travel 1.7 miles north and then go left on Adams Pond Road. Bear right at the fork and then continue 2.2 miles. To get to the east peninsula, bear right at the junction onto the Dover Road Extension. Proceed to the end of the tarred road to the parking lot on the left. To get to the west peninsula, bear left at the junction and continue 0.15 miles to the parking area on the right.

In East Boothbay, on the way to Ocean Point, is the 94.6-acre **Linekin Preserve,** stretching from Route 96 to the Damariscotta River. The 2.3-mile white-blazed River Loop (best done clockwise) takes in an old sawmill site, a beaver dam, and great riverfront views. You'll meet a couple of moderately steep sections on the eastern side, near the river, but otherwise it's relatively easy. To get there, take Route 96 3.8 miles and look for the parking area and trail head on the left.

KNICKERCANE ISLAND

This gem is ideal for a picnic, perhaps with a lobster roll from the Trevett Country Store. The island is connected via bridge, making it a pleasant place to stroll or, if you're brave, swim. Also here is an honest-to-God lobster pound (no, not the kind that serves the tasty crustaceans, but rather the impoundment area for them). The island is off the Barter's Island Road causeway. To find it, from Boothbay Center follow signs for the Coastal Maine Botanical Center, then continue until you come to open water on both sides of the road; the parking area is on the left.

BARRETT PARK

On the east side of the harbor, Barrett Park is an oceanfront park on Linekin Bay, with shade trees, picnic tables, swimming, and restroom. To find it take Atlantic Avenue and turn left on Lobster Cove Road (at the Catholic church).

Coastal Maine Botanical Gardens

Masterful and magical, yet still in their youth, are these shorefront gardens (Barters Island Rd., Boothbay, office Old Firehouse, Rte. 27, Boothbay, 207/633-4333, www.mainegardens.org, 9 A.M.–5 P.M. daily year-round, to 6 P.M. Sat.–Sun., to 8 P.M. Wed. in July–Aug., $10 adults, $8 seniors, $5 children 5–17, $25 family of four). The nonprofit project, designed to preserve more than 125 acres of woodlands with a trail network and landscaped pocket "theme" gardens, has grown to encompass 248 acres, with formal gardens, paths, herb and kitchen gardens, woods walks, a fairy village, five-senses garden, and nearly a mile of waterfront. Artwork is placed throughout. A children's garden, new in 2010, encourages imagination, play, and discovery in a setting drawing from children's literature that's set in Maine, such

It's easy to spend the better part of a day exploring the various gardens at the Coastal Maine Botanical Gardens.

as *Blueberries for Sal* and *Miss Rumphius.* The visitors center has a café (10 A.M.–3 P.M. May 1–Oct. 15), library, and gift shop. Pick up a map and explore on your own, or ask whether a volunteer docent is available to provide a free tour. Allow at least two hours, although you could easily spend a full day here. Entrance to the preserve is on Barters Island Road, about 1.3 miles west of Boothbay Center.

Excursion Boats

Two major fleet operators provide practically every type of sea adventure imaginable. Boothbay Harbor's veteran excursion fleet is **Cap'n Fish's Cruises** (Pier 1, Wharf St., Boothbay Harbor, 207/633-3244, 207/633-2626, or 800/636-3244, www.capnfishmotel.com/boattrips.htm, $17–30 adults, 10–15 children). In addition to whale-watching trips, Cap'n Fish's 150-passenger boats do nine varied, mostly two- to three-hour cruises. There is bound to be a length and itinerary (seal-watching, lobster-trap hauling, lighthouses, Damariscove, puffin cruises, and more) that piques your interest. Pick up a schedule at one of the information centers and call for reservations.

The harbor's other big fleet is **Balmy Days Cruises** (Pier 8, Commercial St., Boothbay Harbor, 207/633-2284 or 800/298-2284, www.balmydayscruises.com), operating three vessels on a variety of excursions. The *Novelty* does about seven daily one-hour harbor tours late June–Labor Day; cost is $14 adults, $7 children under 12. Reservations usually are not necessary. The 31-foot Friendship sloop *Bay Lady* does five 90-minute sailing trips daily in summer. Cost is $22 adults, $16 children. Reservations are wise for the *Bay Lady* as well as for the fleet's most popular cruise, a daylong trip to Monhegan Island on the *Balmy Days II,* departing at 9:30 A.M. and returning at 4:15 P.M. daily early June–late September, plus extended weekends in late May and early October. The three-hour round-trip allows about 3.5 hours ashore on idyllic Monhegan Island. Cost is $32 adults, $18 children.

© HILARY NANGLE

The *Novelty* departs Boothbay Harbor on a cruise.

DAMARISCOVE ISLAND

Summering Wabanakis knew it as Aquahega, but Damerill's Cove was the first European name attributed to the secure, fjordlike harbor at the southern tip of 210-acre Damariscove Island in 1614, when Captain John Smith of the Jamestown Colony explored the neighborhood. By 1622, Damerill's Cove fishermen were sharing their considerable codfish catch with starving Plimoth Plantation colonists desperate for food. Fishing and farming sustained resident Damariscovers during their up-and-down history, and archaeologists have found rich deposits for tracing the story of this early island settlement about seven miles south of Boothbay Harbor.

Rumors persist that the ghost of Captain Richard Pattishall, decapitated and tossed overboard by Indians in 1689, still roams the island, accompanied by the specter of his dog. The fog that often overhangs the bleak, almost-treeless low-slung island makes it easy to fall for the many ghost stories about Pattishall and other onetime residents. In summer, the island is awash with wildflowers, bayberries, raspberries, blackberries, and rugosa roses.

Since 2005, most of 1.7-mile-long Damariscove has been owned by **The Boothbay Region Land Trust** (1 Oak St., 2nd Fl., Boothbay Harbor, 207/633-44818, www.bbrlt.org). Day-use visitors are welcome on the island anytime, but the northern section (called Wood End) is to protect the state's largest nesting colony of eiders – nearly 700 nests. Damariscove Island became a National Historic Landmark in 1978. Dogs are not allowed.

Access to the island is most convenient if you have your own boat. Enter the narrow cove at the southern end of the island. You can disembark at the dock on the west side of the harbor, but don't tie-up here or at the adjacent stone pier. Two guest moorings and two courtesy dinghies are available. Summertime caretakers live in the small cabin above the dock, where a trail map is available. Stay on the trail (watch out for poison ivy) or on the shore and away from any abandoned structures; the former Coast Guard station is privately owned.

Sailing

A trip aboard *Schooner Eastwind,* a 65-foot traditional wooden schooner built in 2004, with **Appledore Cruises** (20 Commercial St. Boothbay Harbor, 207/633-6598, www.fishermanswharfinn.com, $25) is more than a day sail, it's an adventure. Herb and Doris Smith not only built this schooner, they've sailed around the world in their previous boats through the years, providing fodder for many tales. They take passengers on 2.5-hour cruises to the outer islands and Seal Rocks, up to four times daily. The boat departs from Fisherman's Wharf.

Whale- and Puffin-Watching Cruises

Variations in Gulf of Maine whale-migration patterns have added whale-watching to the list of Boothbay Harbor boating options as the massive mammals travel northeastward within reasonable boating distance. **Cap'n Fish's** (Pier 1, Wharf St., Boothbay Harbor, 207/633-3244, 207/633-2626, or 800/636-3244, www.mainewhales.com) is the best choice. Three- to four-hour trips depart daily mid-June–mid-October. Cost is $38 adults, $32 children 11–16, $25 6–10, with a raincheck if the whales don't show up. Reservations are advisable, especially early and late in the season and on summer weekends. No matter what the weather on shore, dress warmly and carry more clothing than you think you'll need. Motion-sensitive children and adults need to plan ahead with appropriate medication.

Cap'n Fish's also runs 2.5-hour puffin-sighting tours to Easter Egg Rock, circling the island once or twice for the best views. Cruises are offered once weekly in June, then three times weekly through late August, for $25 adults, $15 children.

Sea Kayaking

From Memorial Day weekend through September, **Tidal Transit** (18 Granary Way, Chowder House Building, Boothbay Harbor, 207/633-7140, www.kayakboothbay.com), near the footbridge, will get you afloat with two- to three-hour guided lighthouse, wildlife, or sunset tours for around $50. No experience is necessary. Reservations are required. For do-it-yourselfers, Tidal Transit rents single kayaks for $20 an hour or $55 a day, tandems for $45 an hour, $75 a day; other time options are available.

Outdoor Recreation Package

Now here's a deal. For a full day of oceanside play, book a day package at **Linekin Bay Resort** (92 Wall Point Rd., Boothbay Harbor, 207/633-2494 or 866/847-2103, www.linekinbayresort.com, $35 adults, $20 children), a campus of lodges and cabins with an enviable location on Linekin Bay. Day packages provide access to kayaks, canoes, rowboats, heated ocean-view saltwater pool, tennis, Wi-Fi, common rooms with games and books, and even lunch. On Tuesdays, add a lobster bake for $10.

SHOPPING

Artisans' galleries pepper the peninsula. Galleries, boutiques, and T-shirt and novelty shops crowd Boothbay Harbor, providing plenty of browsing for all budgets and tastes. Here are two worth seeking out.

A visit to the **Villard Gallery** (57 Campbell St., Boothbay Harbor, 207/633-3507, www.villardstudios.com) is a must for fans of fine-art crafts. Kim and Philippe Villard split their lives between Boothbay Harbor and southern France, where they live in an abandoned village in the midst of a national park. Philippe is a talented sculptor, Kim an equally talented painter. They collaborate on woodcuts and handmade books, and the results are in collections and museums. Call in advance if you want a demonstration of the process. They have works in all price ranges, from poster prints to the actual woodblocks themselves.

Sea kayaking is a fun way to explore Boothbay Harbor's island-dotted waters.

© HILARY NANGLE

Many of Boothbay Harbor's shops hang over the edge of the working harbor.

Antiques store or museum, you decide. The **Palabra Shop** (53 Commercial St., Boothbay Harbor, 207/633-4225) has 10 chock-full rooms of antiques and collectibles. It's also home to the world's largest collection of Moses bottles.

ACCOMMODATIONS

Here's a hint: If you want to concentrate your time in downtown Boothbay Harbor, shopping or taking boating excursions, stay in town and avoid the parking hassles.

Although the town practically rolls up the sidewalks in the winter, a few businesses do stay open year-round. Lodgings that usually do so are noted; others are seasonal (usually mid-May–mid-October). Rates noted are for peak season.

Classic Inns

To get away from it all, book in at the sigh-producing **Newagen Seaside Inn** (Rte. 27, Southport, 207/633-5242 or 800/654-5242 outside Maine, www.newagenseasideinn.com, $165–285), an unstuffy full-service inn with casual fine dining and views that go on forever. Renovated rooms are split between the Main Inn; the Little Inn, where rooms have private decks, TV, and kitchenettes; and five cottages ($1,600–5,000 per week, with breakfast). Plus there are a long rocky shore, a nature trail, spa, tennis courts, heated oceanfront saltwater pool and hot tub, guest rowboats, game room, candlepin bowling, and porches just for relaxing. Rates include a generous buffet breakfast. The dining room is open to the public by reservation for dinner 5:30–9 P.M. daily; entrées run $18–28. There's also a pub serving lighter fare beginning at 4:30 P.M. It's open mid-May–September. The inn is six miles south of downtown Boothbay Harbor.

Over in East Boothbay, the oceanfront **Ocean Point Inn** (Shore Rd., East Boothbay, 207/633-4200 or 800/552-5554, www.oceanpointinn.com, $135–230) wows guests with spectacular sunset views and an easygoing ambience that keeps guests returning generation after generation. The sprawling complex includes eclectic lodgings: an inn, lodge, motel, apartments, cottages, and others. All rooms have mini-fridge, phone, cable TV, and air-conditioning, and some have kitchenettes. Also on the premises are a restaurant and tavern with fabulous ocean views, a pier, an outdoor heated pool, and Adirondack-style chairs set just so on the water's edge. The best deals are the packages.

For those who require luxury touches, the **Spruce Point Inn and Spa** (Atlantic Ave., Boothbay Harbor, 207/633-4152 or 800/553-0289, www.sprucepointinn.com) is the answer. Accommodations are traditional inn rooms and cottages and condos, all with private decks, mini-fridges, and TV; some have fireplaces, kitchenettes, and whirlpool tubs. Decor and prices vary widely. The inn holds big weddings on many weekends, so try for midweek. Rates begin around $170. Amenities at the 15-acre resort include a full-service spa and fitness center, freshwater and saltwater pools, tennis courts, rocky shorefront, and a shuttle bus to downtown (about 1.5 miles, although it seems farther). A children's program is available 9:30 A.M.–2:30 P.M. for $35 per day, including lunch and snack. Also available is an evening program for ages 4–12 (6–9 P.M. Thurs.–Sun., $25). Dining choices range from poolside to pub-style to fine dining, with prices to match each setting.

Bed-and-Breakfasts

Topping an intown hill with sigh-producing views over the inner and outer harbors and yet just a two-minute walk to shops and restaurants is **Topside Inn** (60 McKown St., Boothbay Harbor, 207/633-5404 or 877/486-7466, www.topsideinn.com, $155–225 d), a solid 19th-century sea captain's home with two motel-style annexes. Innkeepers Brian Lamb and Ed McDermott have completely renovated the three-building complex with an emphasis on comfort. Rooms in the three-story main inn are mostly spacious with nice views. Good books are everywhere, and the rockers on the wraparound porch and Adirondack chairs on the lawn are perfect places to read or relax. The annexes have motelish-type rooms done in bed-and-breakfast style; all have decks and most have at least glimpses of the ocean. All rooms have phone and TV, and there's Wi-Fi access in the main inn. Rates in all buildings include breakfast: a self-serve cold buffet with a hot entrée that's served to the table. Hot beverages are available all day; and some afternoons home-baked cookies appear magically in the living room.

Next door is **The Welch House** (56 McKown St., Boothbay Harbor, 207/633-3431 or 800/279-7313, www.welchhouseinn.com, $140–220), with stunning 180-degree views from the 3rd-floor deck (and not-shabby ones from the lower deck). This 14-room bed-and-breakfast (all private baths, but some are down the hall) is an elegant getaway in a 19th-century shipbuilder's home. All of the rooms have air-conditioning, cable TV-VCR, Wi-Fi, and phone; many have water views; some have fireplaces or whirlpool tubs. Breakfast in the solarium is a treat. It's open year-round.

In town and on the water, the **Blue Heron**

© HILARY NANGLE

Guests at the Topside Inn enjoy some of the best views of Boothbay Harbor's waters.

Inn (65 Townsend Ave., Boothbay Harbor, 207/633-7020 or 866/216-2300, www.blueheronseasideinn.com, $210–265 peak) opened in 2003 and quickly made a name for itself. The Victorian vintage belies the clean, bright interior. Large rooms are accented with antiques and collectibles from Phil and Laura Chapman's years overseas. Each room has a waterfront deck, air-conditioning, fridge, microwave, LCD-HDTV, microwave, Wi-Fi, and phone; some also have a fireplace and whirlpool tub. A dock with kayaks and a paddleboat is available. A full breakfast is elegantly served on Wedgwood china. It's open year-round.

On the east side of the harbor, up a side street but within walking distance of intown shops and restaurants, is Mary Huntington's **Pond House** (7 Bay St., Boothbay Harbor, 207/633-5842, www.pondhousemaine.com, $80–115). The 1920s barn-red home is just one block off the harbor, surrounded by beautiful gardens and edging a pond. The five rooms, some with shared or detached baths, have beautiful oak woodwork and are decorated with a mix of antiques and country pieces, including quilts topping most beds. Rotating artwork covers the walls, and studio space is available to visiting artists. Wi-Fi is available throughout the inn. Mary's breakfasts are legendary.

Escape the hustle and bustle of Boothbay Harbor at the **Five Gables Inn B&B** (107 Murray Hill Rd., East Boothbay, 207/633-4551 or 800/451-5048, www.fivegablesinn.com, $160–235), which began life as a no-frills summer hotel in the late 19th century. It's gone steadily upmarket since then, and well-traveled innkeepers De and Mike Kennedy, owners since 1995, have added their unique touches, including wonderful murals throughout and window seats in the gable rooms. All but one of the 16 light and airy rooms have Linekin Bay views and some have fireplaces. The living room is congenial, the gardens are gorgeous, and the porch goes on forever. Rates include Mike's gourmet buffet breakfast. The inn, on a side road off Route 96 in the traditional boatbuilding hamlet of East Boothbay, is 3.5 miles from downtown Boothbay Harbor. Arriving by boat? One mooring is available for guests.

Marti Booth and Larry Brown give guests a warm welcome to their **Linekin Bay Bed and Breakfast** (531 Ocean Point Rd., 207/633-9900 or 800/596-7420, www.linekinbaybb.com, $145–190). No wonder, considering all the work they did to transform the 1878 home overlooking the bay into an inn. Begin the day with full breakfast on the deck, perhaps watching lobstermen pull their traps. Afternoon refreshments also are served. Guest rooms are spacious and beautifully decorated; all have fireplaces, air-conditioning, phone, TV-VCR, Wi-Fi, and bay views. It's open year-round.

Quiet, private, and out of another era, **Sprucewold Lodge** (4 Nahanada Rd., Boothbay Harbor, 800/732-9778, www.sprucewoldlodge.com, $110) is reputed to be the largest existing log structure east of the Mississippi. The hand-hewn lodge with covered porch was built in the 1920s. Inside are no-frills guest rooms along with a living room anchored by a huge stone fireplace. An expansive hot-and-cold buffet breakfast is served in the dining lodge (available to nonguests by reservation, $11), with large communal tables. Also here are a massive stone fireplace, games, and the property's only TV. General manager Richard Pizer goes all out to make guests welcome. One consideration: The lodge is popular with tour groups.

Motels and Hotels

A great location just 100 feet from the footbridge, a good dining room, a fun lounge, an indoor pool, and harbor views combine to make the **Rocktide Inn** (35 Atlantic Ave., Boothbay Harbor, 207/633-4455 or 800/762-8433, www.rocktideinn.com, $150–250) a popular spot. Rooms are spread out among four buildings, with rates varying according to the view. All have air-conditioning, cable TV, Wi-Fi, and phone, and a full buffet breakfast is included. Even if you don't stay here, pop over for a drink in the tastefully decorated tiki-style lounge (4–11 P.M. daily) or on the expansive decks overhanging the harbor. The dining room, open to the public for dinner (5:30–9 P.M. daily), has both casual and formal areas; men must wear jackets in the latter.

Since 1955, the Lewis family has owned and operated the **Mid-Town Motel** (96 McKown St., Boothbay Harbor, 207/633-2751, www.midtownmaine.com, $89), a spotless, no-frills vintage motel that's within steps of everything. It's a classic: clean, convenient, and relatively cheap, and the owners couldn't be nicer folks.

Every room at the lakefront **Beach Cove Hotel & Resort** (38 Lakeview Rd., Boothbay Harbor, 207/633-0353 or 866/851-0450, www.beachcovehotel.com, $99–199) has a water view, balcony or deck, air-conditioning, mini-fridge, and microwave. The renovated property, about one-mile from downtown, is extremely popular with families who appreciate its beach, dock, outdoor pool, and canoes and rowboats. A light continental breakfast is included.

Campgrounds

With 150 well-maintained wooded and open sites on 45 acres, **Shore Hills Campground** (Rte. 27, Boothbay, 207/633-4782, www.shorehills.com, $27–42) is a popular destination where reservations are essential in midsummer. Be sure to request a wooded site away from the biggest RVs. Leashed pets are allowed. Facilities include a laundry and free use of canoes.

Much smaller and right on the ocean is the **Gray Homestead Oceanfront Camping** (21 Homestead Rd., Southport, 207/633-4612, www.graysoceancamping.com, $35–48), a family-run campground with 40 RV and tenting sites, as well as cottages and apartments. A stone beach, pier, laundry facilities, kayak rentals, and lobsters—live or cooked—are available. There's even a small sand beach.

FOOD

Local Flavors

Right in the center of all the action, **Village Market** (24 Commercial St., Boothbay Harbor, 207/633-0944) makes sandwiches and pizzas to order. Absolutely no atmosphere, but it's cheap and convenient.

It's worth the drive over to Trevett to indulge in a lobster roll from the **Trevett General Store** (207/633-1140), just before the bridge connecting Hodgdon and Barters Islands.

"Free beer tomorrow" proclaims the sign in front of **Bets Famous Fish Fry** (Village Common, Rte. 27, Boothbay), a take-out trailer that's renowned for its ultra-fresh haddock fish-and-chips. Picnic tables are available.

On the east side, the **East Boothbay General Store** (255 Ocean Point Rd., Rte. 96, East Boothbay, 207/633-4503) has been serving locals since 1893. These days, it sells wine and specialty foods in addition to pizzas, sandwiches, and baked goods.

Lots of variety is the key at the seasonal **Boothbay Area Farmers Market** (Town Commons, Boothbay, 9 A.M.–noon Thurs.), with goat cheese, chicken, meats, preserves, breads, and of course fresh produce.

Bakers Way (90 Townsend Ave., Boothbay Harbor, 207/633-1119), a hole-in-the-wall known locally as The Doughnut Shop, turns out the unusual combo of excellent baked goods and Vietnamese food. The breakfast sandwiches are good and the sticky buns are renowned, not only for size but taste. After 11 A.M., Vietnamese dishes are available, most for less than $10. While the inside dining area is purely functional, there's also seating in a pleasant backyard garden. Everything is also available to go.

Tartans and terriers are the dominant motifs at **MacNab's Tea Room** (5 Lu Yu Tea La. off Back River Rd., Boothbay, 207/633-7222 or 800/884-7222, 10 A.M.–5 P.M. Tues.–Sat.), an informal, folksy place where Frances Browne serves lunch, high tea, afternoon tea, and royal tea, all by reservation only.

Reliably good and reasonably priced breakfasts and lunches are turned out by **D'Ellie's** (Pier 1, Boothbay Harbor, 207/633-0277, 9 A.M.–3:30 P.M. daily). Sandwiches come in full and half sizes on a choice of homemade breads (the Anadama is fab!).

Another locals' favorite serving breakfast, lunch, and dinner is the unassuming **Ebb Tide Restaurant** (43 Commercial St., Boothbay

Harbor, 207/633-5692, 6:30 A.M.–9 P.M. daily). Booths line the tiny pine-paneled dining area, where some mighty good homestyle cooking is served. The chowders are renowned, and breakfast is served all day. Look for the red-and-white awning.

Don't tell too many people, but for lunch or a light dinner in an out-of-the-way spot, head to the Boothbay Country Club's **Grille Room** (33 Country Club Rd., Boothbay, 207/633-6085, 11:30 A.M.–7 P.M. daily).

Casual Dining

Real Italian fare prepared by a real Italian chef is on the menu at **Ports of Italy** (47 Commercial St., Boothbay Harbor, 207/633-1011, www.portsofitaly.com, from 5:30 P.M. daily), an upper-level restaurant with deck seating. This isn't a red-sauce place; expect well-prepared and innovative fare, with especially good seafood. Most choices are in the $20 range.

For spectacular sunset views and reliably good food, take a spin out to the **Ocean Point Inn** (Shore Rd., East Boothbay, 207/633-4200 or 800/552-5554, www.oceanpointinn.com, 7:30–10 A.M. and 6–9 P.M. daily, $16–25). Every table in the two-tiered pine-paneled dining room has a view. A children's menu is available.

The tapas menu is fabulous at **Boathouse Bistro** (12 The By-Way, Boothbay Harbor, 207/633-0400, www.theboathousebistro.com, 11:30 A.M.–10 P.M. daily). Best seats in the house are on the 3rd-floor harbor-view deck. There are plenty of other options, but the tapas, pizzas, soups, and salads ($3–15) are the way to go.

One of the most reliable dining experiences in town is at **The Thistle Inn** (55 Oak St., Boothbay Harbor, 207/633-3541, www.thethistleinn.com, from 5 P.M. daily). Everything, from the salad dressings to the desserts, is prepared on-site. It would be easy to make a meal from the appetizers alone—crab cakes, brandied lobster, grilled Caesar salad—but then you wouldn't have room for the main event, perhaps lobster paella or Scottish salmon ($19–30). On a cold night, ask for a table by one of the fireplaces; on a warm night, ask for one on the porch. Lighter fare from a far less pricey menu is served in the pub.

Lobster in the Rough

Boothbay Harbor and East Boothbay seem to have more eat-on-the-dock lobster shacks per square inch than almost anywhere else on the coast, but frankly they're all overcrowded, overpriced, and don't deliver an authentic experience.

Best of the intown lot is **The Lobster Dock** (49 Atlantic Ave., Boothbay Harbor, 207/635-7120, www.thelobsterdock.com, 11:30 A.M.–8:30 P.M. daily), where lobsters are delivered twice daily; now that's fresh. While there are a few choices for landlubbers—even PBJ for kids—lobster and fish are the prime attraction. It's right on the harbor, so the views are superb.

Far more authentic and well worth the splurge is **Cabbage Island Clambakes** (Pier 6, Fisherman's Wharf, Boothbay Harbor, 207/633-7200, www.cabbageislandclambakes.com). Touristy, sure, but it's a delicious adventure. Board the excursion boat *Bennie Alice* at Pier 6 in Boothbay Harbor; cruise for about an hour past islands, boats, and lighthouses; and disembark at 5.5-acre Cabbage Island. Watch the clambake in progress, explore the island, or play volleyball. When the feast is ready, pick up your platter, find a picnic table, and dig in. A cash bar is available in the lodge, as are restrooms. When the weather's iffy, the lodge and covered patio have seats for 100. For $57, you'll get two lobsters (or half a chicken), chowder, clams, corn, egg, onion, potatoes, blueberry cake, beverage, and the boat ride. No credit cards. Clambake season is mid-June–mid-September. The 3.5-hour trips depart at 12:30 P.M. Monday–Friday, at 12:30 and 5 P.M. Saturday, 11:30 A.M. and 1:30 P.M. Sunday.

INFORMATION AND SERVICES

Information

Providing info about their members are the **Boothbay Harbor Region Chamber of**

Commerce (207/633-2353, www.boothbayharbor.com) and the **Boothbay Chamber of Commerce** (207/633-4743, www.boothbay.org).

Check out **Boothbay Harbor Memorial Library** (4 Oak St., Boothbay Harbor, 207/633-3112, www.bmpl.lib.me.us). Thursday evenings in July and August, there are band concerts on the lawn.

Public Restrooms

Public restrooms can be found at the municipal parking lot on Commercial Street (next to Pier 1) and at the municipal lot at the end of Granary Way. Saint Andrews Hospital, the town offices, the library, and the Marine Resources Aquarium also have restrooms.

GETTING AROUND

The Rocktide Inn operates free trolley-buses on continuous scheduled routes during the summer.

Pemaquid Region

At the head of the Pemaquid Peninsula, the riverfront towns of **Damariscotta** and her Siamese twin, **Newcastle,** anchor the western end of the Pemaquid Peninsula; **Waldoboro** anchors the eastern end. Along the peninsula are **New Harbor** (probably Maine's most photographed fishing village), **Pemaquid Point** (site of one of Maine's most photographed lighthouses), and historic ports reputedly used by Captain John Smith, Captain Kidd, and assorted less-notorious types. Here, too, are a restored fortress, Native American historic sites, antiques and craft shops galore, boat excursions to offshore Monhegan, and one of the best pocket-size sand beaches in Mid-Coast Maine.

On Christmas Day 1614, famed explorer Captain John Smith anchored on Rutherford Island, at the tip of the peninsula, and promptly named the spot Christmas Cove. And thus it remains today. Christmas Cove is one of three villages belonging to the town of South Bristol, the southwestern finger of the Pemaquid Peninsula. **South Bristol** and **Bristol** (covering eight villages on the bottom half of the peninsula) were named after the British city.

As early as 1625, settler John Brown received title to some of this territory from the Wabanaki sachem (chief) Samoset, an agreeable fellow who learned snippets of English from British codfishermen. Damariscotta (dam-uh-riss-COT-ta), in fact, is Wabanaki for "plenty of alewives [herring]." The settlement here was named Walpole but was incorporated, in 1847, under its current name.

Newcastle, incorporated in 1763, earned fame and fortune from shipbuilding and brickmaking—which explains the extraordinary number of brick homes and office buildings throughout the town. In the 19th century, Newcastle's shipyards sent clippers, Downeasters, and full-rigged ships down the ways and around the world.

Anchoring the northeastern end of the peninsula is Waldoboro. Route 1 cuts a commercial swath through the town without revealing the attractive downtown—or the lovely Friendship Peninsula, south of the highway. Duck into Waldoboro and then follow Route 220 south 10 miles to Friendship for an off-the-beaten-track drive.

Waldoboro's heritage is something of an anomaly in Maine. It's predominantly German, thanks to 18th-century Teutons who swallowed the blandishments of General Samuel Waldo, holder of a million-acre "patent" stretching as far as the Penobscot River. In the cemetery at the Old German Church, on Route 32, is a 19th-century marker whose inscription sums up the town's early history:

> *This town was settled in 1748, by Germans who emigrated to this place with the prom-*

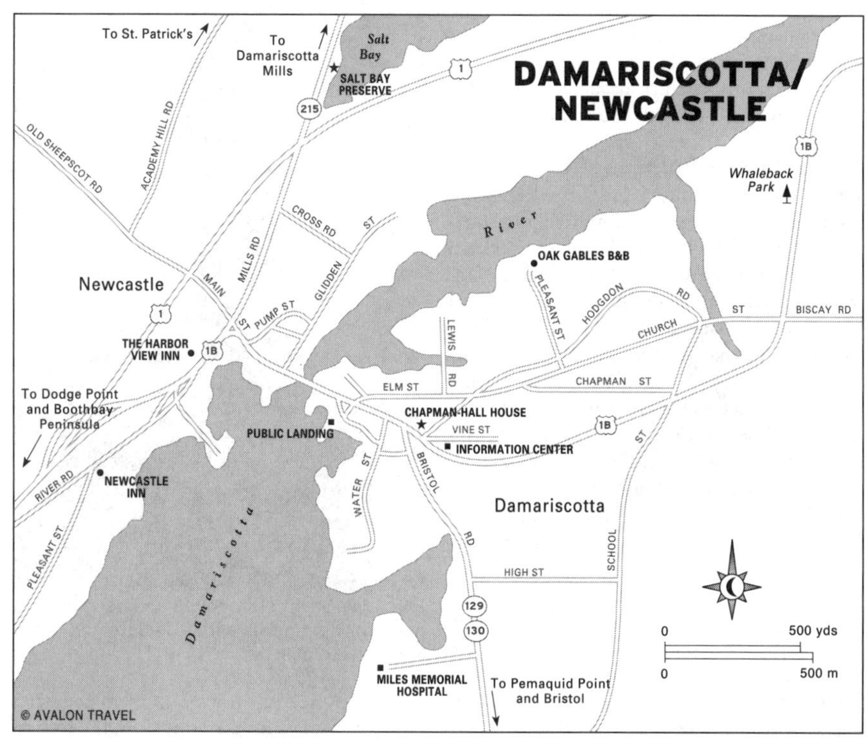

ise and expectation of finding a populous city, instead of which they found nothing but a wilderness; for the first few years they suffered to a great extent by Indian wars and starvation. By perseverance and self-denial, they succeeded in clearing lands and erecting mills. At this time [1855] a large proportion of the inhabitants are descendants of the first settlers.

(Sure makes you wonder why Waldo's name stuck to the town.)

After the mill era, the settlers went into shipbuilding in a big way, establishing six shipyards and producing more than 300 wooden vessels, including the first five-masted schooner, the 265-foot *Governor Ames,* launched in 1888. Although the *Ames*'s ill-supported masts collapsed on her maiden voyage, repairs allowed her to serve as a coal hauler for more than 20 years, and many more five-masters followed in her wake. It's hard to believe today, but Waldoboro once was America's sixth-busiest port. At the Town Landing, alongside the Medomak River, a marker describes the town's shipyards and shipbuilding heritage.

SIGHTS

Chapman-Hall House

Damariscotta's oldest surviving building is the Cape-style Chapman-Hall House (270 Main St., Damariscotta, 10 A.M.–4 P.M. Sat., noon–4 P.M. Sun., late May–mid-Oct.; 10 A.M.–4 P.M. Tues.–Fri. July–Aug., $4), built in 1754 by Nathaniel Chapman, whose family tree includes the legendary John Chapman, a.k.a. Johnny Appleseed. Highlights are a 1754 kitchen and displays of local shipbuilding memorabilia. The National Historic Register house was meticulously restored in the styles of three different eras. Don't miss the antique roses in the back garden. It's now cared for by the Lincoln County Historical Society (207/882-6817, www.lincolncountyhistory.org).

Pemaquid Point Lighthouse

One of the icons of the Maine Coast, Pemaquid Point's lighthouse has been captured for posterity by gazillions of photographers and is depicted on the Maine state quarter. The lighthouse, adjacent keeper's house, and picnic grounds are a town park. Also on the premises is an art gallery. Admission to the grounds, payable at the gatehouse, is $2 for age 12 and older. The lighthouse grounds are accessible all year, even after the museum closes for the season, when admission is free. The point is 15 miles south of Route 1 via winding two-lane Route 130.

Commissioned in 1827, Pemaquid Point Light (www.lighthousefoundation.org) stands sentinel over some of Maine's nastiest shoreline—rocks and surf that can reduce any wooden boat to kindling. Now automated, the light tower is licensed to the American Lighthouse Foundation and is managed by the Friends of Pemaquid Point Lighthouse. Volunteers *aim* to open the tower 10:30 A.M.–5 P.M. daily late May–mid-October, weather permitting. There is no charge for the tower, but donations are appreciated. Still can't get enough? Newcastle Square Vacation Rentals (207/563-6500, www.mainecoastcottages.com) manages a one-bedroom apartment available for weekly rental ($1,150) in the Keeper's House. Proceeds benefit preservation.

The adjacent **Fisherman's Museum** (207/677-2494), in the former light keeper's house, points up the pleasures and perils of the lobstering industry and also has some lighthouse memorabilia. The museum is open 9 A.M.–5 P.M. daily mid-May–mid-October. Museum admission is free (donations appreciated).

While here, visit the **Pemaquid Art Gallery** (207/677-2752), displaying juried works by the Pemaquid Group of Artists since 1928.

Bring a picnic and lounge on the rocks below the light tower, but don't plan to snooze. You'll be busy protecting your food from the dive-bombing gulls and your kids from the treacherous surf.

© TOM NANGLE

Pemaquid Point Lighthouse tips its namesake peninsula and is depicted on the Maine state quarter.

Colonial Pemaquid/ Fort William Henry

At the Colonial Pemaquid State Historic Site (end of Huddle Rd., 207/677-2423, www.friendsofcolonialpemaquid.org, 10 A.M.–7 P.M. daily late May–early Sept., $3 nonresident adults, $2 Maine resident adults, $1 children 5–11), signed off Route 130 in New Harbor, visitors can gain a basic understanding of what life was like in an English frontier settlement. The 19-acre complex, listed on the National Historic Register, comprises a museum–visitors center, Fort William Henry, the Fort House, the remnants of a village, an 18th-century cemetery, picnic area, a pier and boat ramp, and restrooms, all spread out on a grassy point sloping to John's Bay and bordered by McCaffrey's Brook, the Pemaquid River, and Pemaquid Harbor. Bring a picnic, bring a kite, bring a kayak, let the kids run—but do take time to visit the historic sites (a kids' activity book is available for $1). Demonstrations, tours, lectures, and reenactments are part of the site's summer schedule.

Three national flags fly over the ramparts of Fort William Henry, a reconstruction of a fort dating from 1692, the second of three that stood here between 1677 and the late 18th century. The forts were built to defend the English settlement of Pemaquid, settled between 1625 and 1628, from the French. From the rebuilt western tower, you'll have fantastic views of John's Bay and John's Island, named for none other than Captain John Smith; inside are artifacts retrieved from archaeological excavations of the 17th-century trading outpost.

The square, white Fort House, which dates to the late 1700s, houses a research library and archaeology lab as well as a gift shop.

Exhibits at the museum–visitors center focus on regional history, from early Native American life through the colonial period. Selections from the more than 100,000 artifacts uncovered during archaeological digs here are displayed along with a diorama of Pemaquid Village.

Take time to wander the village, 14 cellar holes of 17th- and 18th-century dwellings, a forge, trading post, jail, and other early buildings, all marked with interpretive signs. Also visit the burying ground. Note that no rubbings are permitted, as they could damage the fragile old stones.

Historic Houses of Worship

One of the oldest houses of worship in Maine that still holds services, **The Old Walpole Meeting House** (Rte. 129, Bristol Rd., Walpole), built in 1772, remains remarkably unchanged, with original hand-shaved shingles and handmade nails and hinges. The balcony—where black servants once were relegated—is paneled with boards more than two feet wide. The meetinghouse is 3.5 miles south of Damariscotta and a quarter mile south of where Routes 129 and 130 fork.

The **Harrington Meeting House** (Old

Three national flags fly over the ramparts of reconstructed Fort William Henry.

Harrington Rd., off Rte. 130, 2–4:30 P.M. Mon., Wed., and Fri. July and Aug., donations welcome), begun in 1772 and completed in 1775, now serves as Bristol's local-history museum—town-owned and run by the Pemaquid Historical Association. Behind it is an old cemetery that's fascinating to explore—if you're a fan of that sort of thing.

A remnant of Waldoboro's German connection is the **Old German Church** (Rte. 32, Waldoboro, 207/832-5369 or 207/832-7742, 1–3 P.M. July and Aug.) and its cemetery. The Lutheran church, built in 1772 on the opposite side of the Medomak River, was moved across the ice in the winter of 1794. Inside are box pews and a huge hanging pulpit. One of the three oldest churches in Maine, it lost its flock in the mid-19th century, when new generations no longer spoke German. An annual service is held the first Sunday of August at 3 P.M.

Built in 1808, **St. Patrick's Catholic Church** (Academy Hill Rd., Damariscotta Mills, Newcastle, 207/563-3240, 9 A.M.–sunset daily), a solid brick structure with 1.5-foot-thick walls and a Paul Revere bell, is New England's oldest surviving Catholic church. Academy Hill Road starts at Newcastle Square, downtown Newcastle; the church is 2.25 miles from there, and one mile beyond Lincoln Academy.

St. Andrew's Episcopal Church (Glidden St., Newcastle, 207/563-3533), built in 1883, is nothing short of exquisite, with carved-oak beams, stenciled ceiling, and, for the cognoscenti, a spectacular Hutchings organ.

RETURN OF THE ALEWIVES

If you're in the Damariscotta area in May and early June, don't miss a chance to go to Damariscotta Mills to see the annual **Alewife Run.** During this time more than 250,000 alewives (*Alosa pseudoharengus*, a kind of herring) make their way from Great Salt Bay to their spawning grounds in freshwater Damariscotta Lake, 42 feet higher. Waiting eagerly at the top are ospreys, gulls, cormorants, and sometimes eagles, ready to feast on the weary fish. Connecting the bay and the lake is a man-made stone-and-masonry "fish ladder" (www.damariscottamills.org), a zigzagging channel where you can watch the foot-long fish wriggle their way onward and upward. The ladder was built in 1807; restoration is ongoing. A walkway runs alongside the route, and informative display panels explain the event. It's a fascinating historical ecology lesson. To reach the fishway, take Route 215 for 1.6 miles west of Route 1. When you reach a small bridge, cross it and take a sharp left down a slight incline to a small parking area. Walk behind the fish house to follow the path to the fish ladder. Try to go on a sunny day – the fish are more active and their silvery sides glisten as they go.

The Thompson Ice House

On a Sunday morning in February (weather and ice permitting), several hundred helpers and onlookers gather at Thompson Pond, next to the Thompson Ice House (Rte. 129, South Bristol, 207/644-8551), for the annual ice harvest. Festivity prevails as a crew of robust fellows marks out a grid and saws out 12-inch-thick ice cakes, which are pushed up a ramp to the ice-storage house. More than 60 tons of ice are harvested each year. Sawdust-insulated 10-inch-thick walls keep the ice from melting in this National Historic Register building first used in 1826. In 1990, the house became part of a working museum (1–4 P.M. Wed., Fri., Sat. in July and Aug., donation), with ice tools and a window view of the stored ice cakes. The grounds, including a photographic display board depicting a 1964 harvest, are accessible for free all year. The site is on Route 129, 12 miles south of Damariscotta.

The Gut

At the foot of a hill on Route 129 is the tiny community of **South Bristol,** the heart of the town that stretches along the western edge of the Pemaquid Peninsula. In the village center is a green-painted swing bridge (swinging sideways) spanning a narrow waterway quaintly named The Gut. Separating the mainland from Rutherford Island, The Gut is a busy thoroughfare for local lobster-boat traffic, so the bridge opens and closes often, very often.

Waldoborough Historical Society Museum

The Waldoborough Historical Society Museum (1164 Main St., Waldoboro, 207/832-4713, 1–4:30 P.M. July–Labor Day, free) is a three-building roadside complex just 0.1 mile south of Route 1, at the eastern end of town. On the grounds are the one-room 1857 **Boggs Schoolhouse,** the 1819 **Town Pound** (to detain stray livestock), and two buildings filled with antique tools, toys, and utensils, plus period costumes, antique fire engines, and artifacts from the shipbuilding era.

Maine Antique Toy and Art Museum

Indulge your inner child at the Maine Antique Toy and Art Museum (Rte. 1, Waldoboro, 207/832-7398, 10 A.M.–4 P.M. Thurs.–Mon. late May–mid-Oct., noon–4 P.M. Sat.–Sun. to Christmas, $4). The museum houses an extensive collection of antique toys and original comic art. See how Mickey Mouse first appeared. Browse a collection of Lone Ranger memorabilia. You'll find all the old favorites, from Popeye to Felix the Cat, Betty Boop to Snow White, Pogo to Yoda. Note: This museum is geared to nostalgic adults, not kids.

ENTERTAINMENT

Two struggling arts centers provide year-round concerts, plays, workshops, classes, and exhibits. **River Arts** (170 Business Rte. 1, Damariscotta, 207/563-1507, www.riverartsme.org) doubles as a gallery. Neoclassic on the outside, art deco within, the **Waldo Theatre** (916 Main St., Waldoboro, 207/832-6060, www.thewaldo.org) was built as a cinema in 1936. Restored in the mid-1980s, it now operates as a nonprofit organization, presenting concerts, plays, films, lectures, and other year-round community events.

Lincoln County Community Theater (Theater St., Damariscotta, 207/563-3424, www.lcct.org) owns and operates the historic Lincoln Theater, dating from 1867. It also presents musicals and dramas, concerts, films, and more.

Salt Bay Chamberfest (207/522-3749, www.saltbaychamberfest.org) presents concerts in August.

The local **DaPonte String Quartet** (207/529-4555, www.daponte.org) frequently performs on the peninsula.

FESTIVALS AND EVENTS

July brings the annual **House and Garden Tour,** a peek into some lovely private homes and gardens, and the **St. Andrew's Lawn Party and Auction,** a fun event that always draws a crowd.

In mid-August, **Olde Bristol Days** features a craft show, a parade, road and boat races, live entertainment, and fireworks. At Fort William Henry in Pemaquid, it's a summer highlight on the peninsula.

SHOPPING

Downtown Damariscotta is the region's hub, and it has a nice selection of independent shops, galleries, and boutiques. Downtown parking in summer is a major headache; the municipal lot behind the storefronts has a three-hour limit, and it's almost always full. You'll usually find spots on some of the side streets.

Antiques and Antiquarian Books

Antiques shops are numerous along the Bristol Road (Rte. 130), where many barns have been turned into shops selling everything from fine antiques to old stuff. Serous antiques aficionados will find plenty to browse and buy along this stretch of road.

The multidealer **Nobleboro Antique Exchange** (104 Atlantic Hwy./Rte. 1, Nobleboro, 207/563-6800, www.nobleboroantiqueexchange.com) is housed in a light blue building that goes on and on, with more than

100 display areas on three levels. The selection is diverse, from period antiques to 20th-century collectibles.

Based in a screen-fronted antique carriage house just south of Round Pond Village, **Jean Gillespie Books** (1172 Rte. 32, Round Pond, 207/529-5555) has separate rooms and alcoves, all very user friendly. Specialties are cookbooks, nautical and Maine titles, and illustrated children's books; the "Royalty" category fills six shelves.

Art Galleries

Worth a visit for the building alone, the **Stable Gallery** (26 Water St., Damariscotta, 207/563-1991, www.stablegallerymaine.com), just off Main Street, was built in the 19th-century clipper-ship era and still has original black-walnut stalls—providing a great foil for the work of dozens of Maine craftspeople. Lining the walls are paintings and prints from the gallery's large "stable" of artists.

In his **River Gallery** (79 Main St., Damariscotta, 207/563-6330, www.rivergalleryfineart.com), dealer Geoff Robinson specializes in 19th- and early-20th-century European and American fine art—a connoisseur's inventory.

Showing a high profile ever since it opened in the renovated antique fire station, **The Firehouse Gallery** (1 Bristol Rd., Damariscotta, 207/563-7299, www.thefirehousegallery.com) has a tasteful, well-displayed selection of paintings, sculpture, prints, and jewelry.

Betcha can't leave without buying something from **Pemaquid Craft Co-op** (Rte. 130, New Harbor, 207/277-2077), with 15 rooms filled with quality works by 50 Maine artisans.

Ronna Lugosch bases much of her **Peapod Jewelry** (1794 Rte. 32, Round Pond, 207/529-4411, www.peapodjewelry.com) on that natural peapod form, but instead of peas she uses pearls and gemstones. Also here is her little museum of all things peapod inspired.

Contemporary art is the focus at **Gallery 170** (123 Borland Hill Rd., Damariscotta Mills, 207/332-4014, www.gallery170.com), housed in a restored 1854 church and displaying works by artists both local and afar in rotating shows.

If you are especially interested in arts and crafts, make **Round Pond** part of your itinerary. The small village is home to about a dozen galleries and studios, many within walking distance of one another.

A delightful little off-the-beaten-path find is **Tidemark Gallery** (902 Main St., Waldoboro, 207/832-5109), showing fine arts and crafts from local artists.

Head south from Waldoboro down the Friendship Peninsula to find **Old Point Comfort** (28 Pitcher Rd./Rte. 220 S., Waldoboro, 207/832-8188), the gallery and showroom where weaver Sara Hotchkiss displays her tapestry-woven carpets.

Specialty and Eclectic Shops

The Pemaquid Peninsula is fertile ground for crafts and gifts, and many of the shop locations provide opportunities for exploring off the beaten path.

The inventory at the **Maine Coast Book Shop and Café** (158 Main St., Damariscotta, 207/563-3207) always seems to anticipate customers' wishes, so you're unlikely to walk out empty-handed. You'll find a superb children's section, helpful staff, and always something tempting in the café.

Just off Main Street (turn at Reny's) is **Weatherbird** (72 Courtyard St., Damariscotta, 207/563-8993), a terrifically eclectic shop with an inventory that defies description. Housewares, wines, toys, cards, gourmet specialties, and intriguing women's clothing are all part of the mix. Above it is **Tin Fish Etc.** (207/563-8204). Dana Moses's shop features brilliantly hand-painted tin *objets* made from recycled roofing metal. She also accepts commissions.

All sorts of finds fill the **Walpole Barn** (Rte. 129, Walpole, 207/563-7050, www.walpolebarn.com), Warren and Deb Storch's retirement fun. Browse home and garden products, whimsies, gourmet foods, even wines.

Eric and Sarah Herndon's **Granite Hall**

Store (9 Backshore Rd., off Rte. 32, Round Pond, 207/529-5864) is an old-fashioned country store with merchandise ranging from toys to Irish imports. The "penny" candy, fudge, ice cream, and the old-fashioned peanut-roasting machine capture the kids.

Bells reminiscent of lighthouses, buoys, and even wilderness sounds are crafted by **North Country Wind Bells** (544 Rte. 32, Round Pond, 207/677-2224, www.northcountrybells.com). Factory seconds are a bargain.

A well-chosen selection of silver jewelry fills **Purple Cactus** (107 Huddle Rd., New Harbor, 207/677-2262), Elizabeth Gamage's seasonal shop on the road to Colonial Pemaquid.

Puzzle fans come from all over the country to shop at **I'm Puzzled** (314 Rte. 1, Waldoboro, 207/832-4400), stocked with nearly 2,000 jigsaw puzzles.

Reny's

Whatever you do, don't leave downtown Damariscotta without visiting Reny's (207/563-5757 or 207/563-3011), with stores on each side of Main Street; one sells clothing, the other everything else. This is Reny's hometown, so the selection is huge in both. If you can recognize the edges of cut-out labels, you'll find clothes from major retailers at very discounted prices. Stock up on housewares, munchies, puzzles, shoes, and whatever else floats your boat; the prices can't be beat.

RECREATION

Parks and Preserves

Residents of the Pemaquid Peninsula region are incredibly fortunate to have several foresighted local conservation organizations, each with its own niche and mission: Damariscotta River Association, Pemaquid Watershed Association, Damariscotta Lake Watershed Association, and Medomak Valley Land Trust. In addition, the Nature Conservancy, Maine Audubon, and National Audubon all have holdings on the peninsula, a natural-resource bonanza. For good descriptions of trails throughout Lincoln County, buy a copy of Paula Roberts's *On the Trail in Lincoln County* ($15.75), which describes and provides directions to more than 60 area walking trails. It's available at Salt Bay Farm, which benefits from its sale.

SALT BAY FARM

Headquarters of the **Damariscotta River Association** (DRA, 110 Belvedere Rd., Damariscotta, 207/563-1393, www.draclt.org, 9 A.M.–5 P.M. Mon.–Fri.), founded in 1973, is the Salt Bay Farm Heritage Center, a late-18th-century farmhouse on a farm site. Here you can pick up maps, brochures, and other information on the more than 2,900 acres and 22 miles of shoreline protected and managed by the DRA. More than two miles of trails cover Salt Bay Farm's fields, salt marsh, and shore frontage and are open to the public sunrise–sunset daily year-round. DRA also has a healthy calendar of events, including bird-watching tours, natural-history trips, concerts, and Trail Tamers, an opportunity to work on the trail system. To reach the farm from downtown Newcastle, take Mills Road (Rte. 215) to Route 1. Turn right (north) and go 1.4 miles to the blinking light (Belvedere Rd.). Turn left and go 0.4 mile.

SALT BAY PRESERVE HERITAGE TRAIL

Across Great Salt Bay from the DRA Salt Bay Farm is the trailhead for the Salt Bay Preserve Heritage Trail, a relatively easy three-mile loop around Newcastle's Glidden Point that touches on a variety of habitat and also includes remnants of oyster-shell heaps ("middens") going back about 2,500 years. This part of the trail is protected by the feds; do *not* disturb or remove anything. To reach the preserve from Newcastle Square, take Mills Road (Rte. 215) about two miles to the offices of the *Lincoln County News* (just after the post office). The newspaper allows parking in the northern end of its lot, but stay to the right, as far away from the buildings as possible, and be sure not to block any vehicles or access ways. Walk across Route 215 to the trailhead and pick up a brochure-map.

WHALEBACK PARK

After a decade of push-me, pull-you struggling, the Damariscotta River Association, in conjunction with Maine's Bureau of Parks and Lands, finally acquired all the requisite permits in 2001 to create Whaleback Park, an eight-acre public preserve designed to highlight what remains of the "Glidden Midden," ancient oyster-shell heaps across the river from the park viewpoint. (The midden is also visible, but not as easily, from the Salt Bay Preserve Heritage Trail.) Informational signs explain the history of the midden, allegedly the largest such manmade artifact north of Florida. The "mini mountain" of castoffs was even more vast until the 1880s, when a factory harvested much of it for lime. The trailhead and parking is on Business Route 1 opposite and between the Great Salt Bay School and the CLC YMCA.

DODGE POINT PRESERVE

In 1989, the state of Maine acquired the 506-acre Dodge Point Preserve—one of the stars in its crown—as part of a $35 million bond issue. The Damariscotta River Association, which initiated its protection, helps manage and maintain the property. To sample what the Dodge Point Preserve has to offer, pick up a map at the entrance and follow the Old Farm Road loop trail, and then hook into the Shore Trail (Discovery Trail), heading clockwise, with several dozen highlighted sites. Consider stopping for a riverside picnic and swim at Sand Beach before continuing back to the parking lot. Hunting is permitted in the preserve, so November isn't the best time for hiking here (unless you hike on Sunday, when hunting is banned). The Dodge Point parking area is on River Road, 2.6 miles southwest of Route 1 and 3.5 miles southwest of downtown Newcastle.

TRACY SHORE PRESERVE

Walk through a woodland wonderland that extends to ledgy shorefront along Jones Cove, in South Bristol. Old cellars, moss-covered trails, lichen-covered rocks, a vernal pool, old pasture grounds, and spectacular views highlight this little-known gem, owned by the Nature Conservancy. It has cliffs and lots of slippery rocks, so be extra watchful of children. You can connect to another preserve, the Library Preserve, on a link crossing busy Route 129. The trailhead and parking is at the intersection of Route 129 and the S Road, 8.7 miles south of the split from Route 130.

RACHEL CARSON SALT POND/ LA VERNA PRESERVE

If you've never spent time studying the variety of sealife in a tidal pool, the Rachel Carson Salt Pond is a great place to start. Named after the famed author of *Silent Spring* and *The Edge of the Sea,* who summered in this part of Maine, the salt pond was a favorite haunt of hers. The whole point of visiting a tide pool is to see what the tide leaves behind, so check the tide calendar (in local newspapers, or ask at your lodging) and head out a few hours after high tide. Wear rubber boots and beware of slippery rocks and rockweed. Among the many creatures you'll see in this quarter-acre pond are mussels, green crabs, periwinkles, and starfish. Owned by the Nature Conservancy, the salt pond is on Route 32 in the village of Chamberlain, about a mile north of New Harbor. Parking is limited. Across the road is a trail into a 78-acre inland section of the preserve, most of it wooded. Brochures are available in the registration box.

Golf

The nine-hole **Wawenock Country Club** (Rte. 129, Walpole, 207/563-3938), established in the 1920s, is a challenging and popular public course.

Swimming

Best bet (but also most crowded) on the peninsula for saltwater swimming is town-owned **Pemaquid Beach Park** (www.bristolparks.org), a lovely tree-lined sandy crescent. No lifeguard, but there are showers (cold water) and bathrooms, and the snack bar serves decent food. Admission is $4 for anyone over 12. The gates close at 7 P.M. (restrooms close at 5 P.M.).

The beach is just off Snowball Hill Road, west of Route 130.

A much smaller beach is the pocket-size sandy area in **Christmas Cove,** on Rutherford Island. Take Route 129 around the cove and turn to the right, and then right again down the hill.

One of the area's most popular freshwater swimming holes is **Biscay Pond,** a long, skinny body of water in the peninsula's center. From Business Route 1 at the northern edge of Damariscotta, take Biscay Road (turn at McDonald's) three miles to the pond (on the right, heading east). On hot days, this area sees plenty of cars; pull off the road as far as possible.

Farther down the peninsula, on Route 130 in **Bristol Mills,** is another roadside swimming hole, between the dam and the bridge.

Boat Excursions

At 9 A.M. each day between mid-May and early October, the 60-foot powerboat *Hardy III* departs for **Monhegan,** a Brigadoon-like island a dozen miles offshore, where passengers can spend the day hiking the woods, picnicking on the rocks, bird-watching, and inhaling the salt air. At 3:15 P.M. everyone reboards, arriving in New Harbor just over an hour later. Cost is $32 adults, $18 children 3–11. Reservations are required. Trips operate rain or shine, but heavy seas can affect the schedule. From early June through late September, there's also a second Monhegan trip—used primarily for overnighters—departing New Harbor at 2 P.M. daily. Early and late season, Monhegan trips operate only Wednesday, Saturday, Sunday, and holidays. The *Hardy III* also operates daily 1.5-hour **puffin-watching tours** (5:30 P.M. mid-May–late Aug., $24 adults, $15 children); one-hour **seal-watching tours** (noon daily mid-June–early Sept. and Sept. weekends, $14 adults, $10 children); and one-hour evening **lighthouse cruises** (mid-June–early Sept., $14 adults, $10 children). **Hardy Boat Cruises** (Rte. 32, New Harbor, 207/677-2026 or 800/278-3346, www.hardyboat.com) is 19 miles south of Route 1, based at Shaw's Fish and Lobster Wharf. Parking is $3/day, at the baseball field near Shaw's.

New Harbor, on the Pemaquid Peninsula, is one of the Mid-Coast's numerous picturesque fishing harbors.

Cruise Muscongus Bay aboard the Friendship sloop *Sarah Mead* with **Sail Muscongus** (207/380-5460, www.sailmuscongus.com) on its morning, island, or sunset cruises. Most last about three hours, with rates ranging $30–50 per person; children under 12 are half price. Bring water and snacks. Muscongus Road is off Route 32, north of Round Pond. Parking is $5/day.

Sea Kayaking and Canoeing

Pemaquid Paddlers, a local group, welcomes visitors to its weekly paddles, usually held beginning at 9 A.M. on Saturdays and lasting for about two hours. Check local papers for the schedule.

Midcoast Kayak (45 Main St., Damariscotta, 207/563-5732, www.midcoastkayak.com) has rentals and offers guided tours and lessons on Muscongus Bay and the Damariscotta River. Three-hour to full-day tours range $35–60, and include all sorts of options. If you would rather do it yourself, recreational kayaks rent for $35/day, $25/half day, $20/two hours; sea kayaks (rescue experience required) rent for $45/day, $30/half day, $20/two hours, tandems are $65/full day, $40/half day, $30/two hours. Instruction also is available.

Operating from a base near Colonial Pemaquid is **Maine Kayak** (113 Huddle Rd., New Harbor, 866/624-6351, www.mainekayak.com). Guided options include sunset paddle, wildlife paddle, puffin paddle, paddle-and-sail, half- and full-day trips, and a variety of overnights. Rates begin at $40 for the shorter trips. Rentals begin at $25 single, $35 tandem for two hours, with free delivery in the New Harbor area.

If you have your own boat, or just want to paddle the three-mile length of **Biscay Pond,** you can park at the beach area and put in there. Another good launching site is a state ramp off Route 1 in **Nobleboro,** at the head of eight-mile-long **Lake Pemaquid.**

Two preserves are accessible if you have your own boat. Owned by the Damariscotta River Association, 30-acre **Menigawum Preserve (Stratton Island)** is also known locally as Hodgdon's Island. It's at the entrance to Seal Cove on the west side of the South Bristol peninsula. The closest public boat launch is at The Gut, about four miles downriver—a trip better done *with* (in the same direction as) the tide. The best place to land is Boat House Beach, in the northeast corner—also a great spot for shelling. Pick up a map from the small box at the north end of the island and follow the perimeter trail clockwise. At the northern end, you'll see osprey nests; at the southern tip are Native American shell middens—discards from hundreds of years of marathon summer lunches. (Needless to say, do *not* disturb or remove anything.) You can picnic in the pasture, but camping and fires are not allowed. Stay clear of the abandoned homesite on the island's west side. The preserve is accessible sunrise–sunset.

Named for a 19th-century local woman dubbed "The Witch of Wall Street" for her financial wizardry, **Witch Island Preserve** is owned by Maine Audubon. The wooded 19-acre island has two beaches, a perimeter trail, and the ruins of the "witch's" house. A quarter of a mile offshore, it's accessible by canoe or kayak from the South Bristol town landing, just to the right after the swing bridge over The Gut. Put in, paddle under the swing bridge, and go north to the island.

ACCOMMODATIONS

Inns

Innkeeper Julie Bolthuis has breathed new life into **The Newcastle Inn** (60 River Rd., Newcastle, 207/563-5685 or 800/832-8669, www.newcastleinn.com, $180–255), an 1860s sea captain's home with 14 guest rooms and suites (all with air-conditioning, Wi-Fi, some with fireplaces and whirlpool tubs) spread out between the main inn and carriage house. The lovely grounds descend to the edge of the Damariscotta River. Julie serves a full breakfast and stocks a pantry that includes a bottomless cookie jar. Two rooms are dog friendly.

Within easy walking distance of Pemaquid Light and 16 miles south of Route 1, **The Bradley Inn** (3063 Bristol Rd./Rte. 130, New

Harbor, 207/677-2105 or 800/942-5560, www.bradleyinn.com, $175–250) is a restored late-19th-century three-story building with rooms and a suite (with full kitchen and fireplace) in the inn and carriage house, a separate cottage, and lovely gardens—a great location for a quiet weekend getaway. The inn's restaurant, overlooking the gardens and open to the public, has an ambitious and pricey menu (entrées $25–32). Room rates include full breakfast.

Almost on top of Pemaquid Light is the rambling **Hotel Pemaquid** (3098 Bristol Rd., Rte. 130, New Harbor, 207/677-2312, www.hotelpemaquid.com, $80–160). Seventeen miles south of Route 1 but just 450 feet from the lighthouse (you can't see it from the inn, but you sure can hear the foghorn!), the hotel has been welcoming guests since 1900; it's fun to peruse the old guest registers. Hang out in the large, comfortable parlor or on the wraparound veranda. The owners have gently renovated the property, updating and improving everything without losing the Victorian charm (or quirks) of an old seaside hotel. The inn building has rooms with private and shared baths and suites. Other buildings have motel-style units with private bath. Apartments in the annex are $185–205. A beautiful 2nd-floor suite in the carriage house, with full kitchen and deck, is $250, or $1,400 per week. For the Victorian flavor of the place, request an inn room or suite. No restaurant, but The Bradley Inn and The Sea Gull Shop are nearby. No credit cards. It's open mid-May–mid-October.

Up the eastern side of the peninsula, in the middle of New Harbor, **The Gosnold Arms** (146 Rte. 32, New Harbor, 207/677-3727, off-season 561/575-9549, www.gosnold.com, $115–145 inn, $132–315 cottage) has been here since 1925 and remains deliberately old-fashioned, with pine-paneled rooms and a country-cottage common room. The family-owned operation includes the inn building and eight other buildings (with 14 units), so there's variety in layout, location, and decor. Many of the rooms include water views, but the action at lobster wharf across the street (Shaw's) can preclude an afternoon nap in front rooms. Rates include breakfast. It's open mid-May–mid-October.

Bed-and-Breakfasts

A lovely water-view living room with piano and harp sets the tone for **The Harbor View Inn** (Business Rte. 1, Newcastle, 207/563-2900, www.theharborview.com, $145–195). Another selling point is the huge deck overlooking the twin towns and the river. Joe McEntee's family antiques fill the three beautifully decorated 1st- and 2nd-floor suites. All rooms have phones, Wi-Fi, TV, and comfortable chairs; two have fireplaces. Breakfast is an extravaganza in the formal dining room. It's open all year.

Martha Scudder provides a warm welcome for her guests at **Oak Gables Bed and Breakfast** (Pleasant St., Damariscotta, 207/563-1476 or 800/335-7748, www.oakgablesbb.com, $95). At the end of a pretty lane, this 13-acre hilltop estate overlooks the Damariscotta River. Despite a rather imposing setting, everything's homey, informal, and hospitable. Four 2nd-floor rooms, which can be joined in pairs, share a bath; a guest wing ($875 week) has a full kitchen, private bath, and separate entrance. The heated swimming pool is a huge plus, as is the boathouse deck, on the river. Guests can harvest blackberries from scads of bushes. Also on the grounds are a three-bedroom cottage ($1,200/week), a river-view one-bedroom apartment ($980/week), and a studio apartment ($875/week), usually booked up well ahead. It's open all year.

Wake up with a dip after a restful sleep at the **Mill Pond Inn** (50 Main St., Rte. 215, Damariscotta Mills, Nobleboro, 207/563-8014, www.millpondinn.com, $140). The 1780 colonial was restored and converted into an inn in 1986 by delightful owners Bobby and Sherry Whear. After a full breakfast, snooze in a hammock, watch for eagles and great blue herons, pedal a bicycle into nearby Damariscotta, or canoe the pond, which connects to 14-mile-long Damariscotta Lake. Bobby, a Registered Maine Guide, offers fishing trips and scenic tours of the lake in his restored antique Lyman lapstrake (clinker-built) boat. Use of bicycles and canoe is free to guests. The inn is just a five-minute drive from downtown Damariscotta, but a world away. No credit cards.

The mansard-roofed **Inn at Round Pond** (1442 Rte. 32, Round Pond, 207/529-2004, www.theinnatroundpond.com, $165–195) commands a sea captain's view of the harbor as it presides over the pretty village of Round Pond. It's an easy walk to a waterfront restaurant, two dueling lobster pounds, an old-timey country store, and a handful of galleries and shops. Each of three good-size rooms has harbor views and sitting areas. A full breakfast is included. It's open all year.

You can walk to Christmas Cove from **Sunset Bed and Breakfast** (16 Sunset Loop, South Bristol, 207/644-8849, www.sunsetbnb.com). Kay and Dick Miller have two small rooms under the eaves, one with a full-size bed, the other with twins, sharing one bath in their modest Cape-style house with to-die-for views. Various rates are available, from one room with private bath ($130) to a family of four ($160). Rates include a hearty continental breakfast. Bring a kayak and launch it here. It's open May–October.

About three miles south of town is **Blue Skye Farm** (1708 Friendship Rd., Waldoboro, 207/832-0300, www.blueskyefarm.com), Jan and Peter Davidson's bed-and-breakfast in a gorgeous 18th-century farmhouse, set amid 100 acres with trails, gardens, and lawns. Original wall stencils by Moses Eaton decorate the entry. Breakfast is provided, and guests have full use of the country kitchen to prepare other meals. Other common roams include the dining room, screened-in sun room, and a sitting room with fireplace that's stocked with games. Five rooms, three with private baths, are meticulously decorated. Rates range year-round is $105–145.

Motels and Cottage Colonies

You'll have to plan well in advance to snag one of the humble **Ye Olde Forte Cabins** (18 Old Fort Rd., Pemaquid Beach, 207/677-2261, www.yeoldefortecabins.com, $90–175 per day, $470–665 per week). These no-frills cabins have edged a grassy lawn dropping to John's Bay since 1922. Each has at least a toilet and sink, but a shower house and a well-equipped cookhouse are part of the colony. Although guests are expected to clean up after themselves when using the kitchen, management keeps the place immaculate. The small private beach is a great place to launch a kayak. The cabins are less than 25 yards from Colonial Pemaquid and Fort William Henry. No credit cards.

Tony and Sally Capodilupo have restored four 19th- and 20th-century houses on a 22-acre hilltop, just steps from the village and overlooking the harbor, adding 21st-century amenities while retaining the original village appeal. **The Moorings** (South Side Rd., New Harbor, 207/677-2409 summer, 617/731-4264 winter, www.themooringsnewharbor.com) comprises eight well-equipped weekly rental apartments and a bungalow, all with gas fireplace, TV-DVD, and heat. Also on the premises are a theater, indoor pool, tennis court, hot tub, laundry, cookout area, and billiards room. All are restricted to adults. In-season rates begin at $1,200/week; some units are available for three-day weekend rental for $500.

Just down the road, Dan Thompson is the third-generation innkeeper at **The Thompson House and Cottages** (95 South Side Rd., New Harbor, 207/677-2317, www.thompsoncottages.net, $600–1,700/week), a low-key, old-timey complex of mostly waterfront rooms, apartments, and cottages split among two mini peninsulas. Most have fireplaces. Rowboats are available, and there's a library with games, books, and puzzles.

Now here's a bargain. Up a long winding driveway behind Moody's Diner is **Moody's Motel** (Rte. 1, Waldoboro, 207/832-5362, www.moodysdiner.com, $49–69), in biz since 1927; it's likely little has changed in the meantime. Expect nothing more than a clean and well-run property, and you'll be pleased. The motel and tourist cabins all have screened porches and TV, and a few have kitchenettes.

Campgrounds

A favorite with kayakers is **Sherwood Forest**

Camping (Pemaquid Trail, New Harbor, 800/274-1593, www.sherwoodforestcampsite.com, $32–42). Facilities include a playground, sundeck, and pool, but the campground is just 800 feet from Pemaquid Beach. Two-bedroom rental cabins are $800 per week.

FOOD

Hours noted are for peak season, but are subject to change. It's wise to call ahead, especially when traveling off season.

Local Flavors

DAMARISCOTTA

For breakfast, look no farther than **The Breakfast Place and Bakery** (Business Rte. 1, Main St., 207/563-5434, 7 A.M.–1 P.M. daily), a small place that turns out big breakfasts. Homemade breads, muffins, biscuits, eggs, omelets, pancakes, waffles, and more.

For baked goods, sandwiches, soups, and gourmet goodies to go, head to **Weatherbird** (1168 Elm St., 207/563-8993, 8 A.M.–5:30 P.M. Mon.–Sat.). Eat at one of the handful of tables out front or take it to the waterfront.

The burgers, lobster rolls, and sweet-potato fries earn raves at **Larson's Lunch Box** (430 Main St., 207/563-5755), a no-frills take-out stand with a few picnic tables.

In a barn-style building at the northern edge of Damariscotta, **Round Top Ice Cream** (Business Rte. 1, 207/563-5307) has been dishing out homemade ice cream since 1924.

Rising Tide Natural Foods Market (323 Main St., 207/563-5556, www.risingtide.coop, 8 A.M.–7 P.M. daily), a thriving co-op organization since 1978, has all the natural and organic usuals, plus a self-service deli section with soups, sandwiches, salads, and entrées; indoor seating available.

The **Damariscotta Area Farmers Market** sets up 9 A.M.–noon on Friday mid-May–October at Salt Bay Heritage Center, on Belvedere Road, just off Route 1, and 3–6 P.M. Monday at Rising Tide Market, 323 Main Street. Condiments, baked goods, cheeses, local shellfish, and crafts are always available from about two dozen vendors, and you never know what else will turn up at this major market.

DOWN THE PENINSULA

Homemade ice cream, delicious baked goods, prepared dishes, and sandwiches to go are just a few of the reasons to stop by the seasonal **Island Grocery** (12 West Side Rd., South Bristol, 207/644-8552, www.islandgrocery.net). It also has breads, cheese, and all kinds of gourmet goodies—stock up for a picnic. To find it, take the first right after the swinging bridge.

Just around the corner from Colonial Pemaquid, **The Cupboard Cafe** (137 Huddle Rd., New Harbor, 207/677-3911, www.anchorinnrestaurant.com, 8 A.M.–3 P.M. Tues.–Sat., to noon Sun.) is a homey cabin serving fresh-baked goods, breakfasts, and a nice choice of fresh salads, burgers, sandwiches, and specials. Almost everything is made on the premises; the cinnamon and sticky buns are so popular, they've spurred a mail-order biz.

WALDOBORO

At the corner of Routes 1 and 220, opposite Moody's Diner, is the warehouse-y building that turns out superb **Borealis Breads** (1860 Atlantic Hwy./Rte. 1, 207/832-0655, www.borealisbreads.com, 8:30 A.M.–5:30 P.M. Mon.–Fri., 9 A.M.–4 P.M. Sun.). Using sourdough starters (and no oils, sweeteners, eggs, or dairy products), owner Jim Amaral and his crew produce baguettes, olive bread, lemon fig bread, rosemary focaccia, and about a dozen other inventive flavors (each day has its specialties). A refrigerated case holds a small selection of picnic fixings (sandwich spreads, juices). Great soups and salads, and excellent sandwiches, are available to go.

The **Waldoboro 5&10** (Friendship St., 207/832-4624, 8:30 A.M.–5 P.M. Mon.–Sat.) is one of those old-fashioned, little-of-everything variety stores that disappeared ages ago. Inside are antiques, penny candy, and a deli serving excellent sandwiches and Round Top ice cream. It's a one-man operation, so service can be slow at peak times.

Pick up gourmet picnic fixings at **McKean and Charles** (1587 Rte. 1, 207/832-2221, www.mckeanandcharles.com, 10 A.M.–6 P.M. Mon.–Sat.), and while you're there, ask about any scheduled wine tastings. The store also sells more than 200 different beers and the state's largest selection of single malts.

Each fall around mid-September, a tiny, cryptic display ad appears in local newspapers: "Kraut's Ready." Savvy readers recognize this as the announcement of the latest batch of **Morse's sauerkraut**—an annual ritual since 1918. The homemade kraut is available in stores and by mail order, but it's more fun (and cheaper) to visit the shop, the **Kraut House** (3856 Washington Rd., Rte. 220, 207/832-5569 or 800/486-1605, www.morsessauerkraut.com, 9 A.M.–6 P.M. Thurs.–Tues.), which also has a small restaurant (10:30 A.M.–4 P.M. Mon.–Tues., 8 A.M.–4 P.M. Thurs.–Sun.) serving traditional German fare, including sandwiches such as a classic Reuben, liverwurst, or Black Forest ham; homemade pierogies; sausages; and stuffed cabbage rolls, all less than $10. Big serve-yourself jars of Morse's pickles are on the tables. The red-painted farm store also carries Aunt Lydia's Beet Relish, baked beans, mustard, maple syrup, and other Maine foods as well as a mind-boggling selection of hard-to-find and unusual northern European specialties, cheeses, meats, and preserved fish. It's eight miles north of Route 1.

Truck drivers, tourists, locals, and notables have been flocking to **Moody's Diner** (Rtes. 1 and 220, 207/832-7785, www.moodysdiner.com, 4:30 A.M.–11 P.M. Mon.–Fri., 5 A.M.–11 P.M. Sat., 6 A.M.–11 P.M. Sun.) since the early 1930s, when the Moody family established this classic diner on a Waldoboro hilltop. The antique neon sign has long been a Route 1 beacon, especially on a foggy night, and the crowds continue, with new generations of Moodys and considerable expansion of the premises. It's gone beyond diner-dom. Expect hearty, no-frills fare and such calorific desserts as peanut butter or walnut pie. After eating, you can buy the cookbook.

An even more humble alternative to Moody's is **Deb's Diner** (1495 Rte. 1, 207/832-6144, 6 A.M.–2:30 P.M. Mon.–Sat., 7–11 A.M. Sun.), a tiny spot where the portions are big and the prices are very low. You can easily get out of here for less than $5.

Casual Dining

DAMARISCOTTA

A reliable standby in downtown Damariscotta, next to the Damariscotta Bank and Trust, the **Salt Bay Café** (88 Main St., 207/563-3302, www.saltbaycafe.com, 7:30 A.M.–8 P.M. Mon.–Thurs., to 9 P.M. Fri.–Sat., 8 A.M.–8 P.M. Sun.) has a loyal following—thanks to its imaginative, reasonably priced cuisine and cheerful, plant-filled setting. Vegetarians have their own menu, with more than two dozen choices. Dinner entrées are $11–19; hearty lunch sandwiches run $6–8.

Chef Rick and Jean Kerrigan own **Damariscotta River Grill** (155 Main St., 207/563-2992, www.damariscottarivergrill.com, 11 A.M.–9 P.M. daily), a reliable favorite where the open kitchen offers carefully prepared foods with an emphasis on ultra-fresh seafood. Most entrées $17–27; the artichoke fondue is worth fighting over. Choose a table in the back with a river view, if available.

Bridging the gap between pub and restaurant is the **Newcastle Publick House** (52 Main St., Newcastle, 207/563-3434, www.newcastlepublichouse.com, 11 A.M.–11 P.M. daily, to midnight Fri. and Sat., $8–21). Emphasis is on local foods, including Pemaquid oysters, and pub favorites, such as shepherd's pie, with lamb shanks braised in Geary's London porter.

DOWN THE PENINSULA

The Kerrigans of Damariscotta River Grill also own the **Anchor Inn** (Harbor Rd., Round Pond, 207/529-5584, www.anchorinnrestaurant.com, 11:30 A.M.–9 P.M. daily mid-May–mid-Oct.), tucked away on the picturesque harbor in Round Pond, on the eastern side of the peninsula. Informal and rustic, with a menu that'll surprise you (entrées $18–25), the place always attracts a crowd. Reservations are advisable on summer weekends. After

Labor Day, the schedule can be a bit erratic; call to confirm.

The view's even better at **Coveside Restaurant** (105 Coveside Rd., Christmas Cove, South Bristol, 207/644-8282, www.covesiderestaurant.com, 11 A.M.–9 P.M. daily, $10–28), based at a marina on Rutherford Island, just off the end of the South Bristol peninsula. It's open for lunch and dinner as well as light meals. Grab a seat on the deck and watch a steady stream of boaters and summer vacationers during the cruising season.

Craving a bit o' Southern flavor? **The Samoset** (2477 Rte. 130, New Harbor, 207/677-6771, www.samosetrestaurant.com, 11:30 A.M.–9 P.M. daily, $10–18) delivers, with favorites such as Maine shrimp creole, low-country boil, and chicken-and-sausage gumbo, along with other homestyle classics and the usual fried fare.

Location, location. Right next to Pemaquid Light is **The Sea Gull Shop** (3119 Bristol Rd., Pemaquid Point, 207/677-2374, www.seagullshop.com, 7:30 A.M.–8 P.M. daily mid-May–mid-Oct.), an oceanfront place with touristy prices, but decent food—pancakes and muffins, for instance, overflowing with blueberries. BYOB, and call ahead for hours in spring and fall.

WALDOBORO

Slide into one of the long tables or snag a bar seat at the **Narrows Tavern** (15 Friendship St., 207/832-2210, www.narrowstavern.com, 11:30 A.M.–1 A.M. daily, $8–18) for some homestyle pub grub with a few surprises.

Lobster in the Rough

The Pemaquid Peninsula must have more eat-on-the-dock places per capita than any place in Maine. Some are basic no-frills operations, others are big-time commercial concerns. Each has a loyal following.

The biggest and best-known lobster wharf is **Shaw's Fish and Lobster Wharf** (Rte. 32, New Harbor, 207/677-2200 or 800/772-2209, 11 A.M.–9 P.M. daily). You can also order steak here. And margaritas. And oysters at the wharf raw bar. Fried seafood dinners run $8–17. It's open mid-May–mid-October, closing one hour earlier midweek off-season.

Facing each other across the dock in the hamlet of Round Pond are the **Round Pond Lobster Co-Op** (207/529-5725) and **Muscongus Bay Lobster** (207/529-5528). Both are good, and competition keeps prices low. Muscongus has enlarged in recent years, so it has a bigger menu and covered seating, but tiny Round Pond Lobster keeps it simple and oh-so-fresh. Both usually open around 10 A.M. daily for lunch and dinner and close around sunset.

Other seasonal lobster wharves salting the peninsula are the **New Harbor Co-Op** (Rte. 32, New Harbor, 207/677-2791), **Pemaquid Fishermen's Co-Op** (Pemaquid Harbor Rd., Pemaquid Harbor, 207/677-2801), **South Bristol Fishermen's Co-op** (South Bristol, 207/644-8224), and **Broad Cove Marine Services** (off Rte. 32, Medomak, 207/529-5186), a low-key sleeper with a wowser view.

INFORMATION AND SERVICES

The **Damariscotta Region Chamber of Commerce** (15 Courtyard St., 207/563-8340, www.damariscottaregion.com) publishes a free annual information booklet about the area.

Skidompha Library (Main St., Damariscotta, 207/563-5513, www.skidompha.org) also operates a used-book shop. (Incidentally, if you're puzzled by the name, it comes from the names of the members of a local literary society who founded the library at the turn of the 20th century.) Or check out Waldoboro Public Library (Main St., Waldoboro, 207/832-4484, www.waldoborolibrary.org).

PENOBSCOT BAY

The coastline edging island-studded Penobscot Bay is the image that lures many a vistor to Maine. The rugged and jagged coastline hides protected harbors and links fishing villages with comparatively cosmopolitan towns. Although the state considers this part of the Mid-Coast, this region has a different feel and view, one framed by coastal mountains in Camden and Lincolnville and accented by an abundance of islands.

From Thomaston through Searsport, no two towns are alike except that all are changing, as traditional industries give way to arts- and tourism-related businesses. Thomaston's Museum in the Streets, Rockland's art galleries, Camden's picturesque mountainside harbor, Lincolnville's pocket beach, Belfast's inviting downtown, Searsport's sea captains' homes, and Prospect's Fort Knox all invite exploration, as do offshore islands, many linked to the mainland by ferry.

From salty Port Clyde, take the mail boat to Monhegan, an offshore idyll known as the Artists' Island. From Rockland and Lincolnville Beach, car and passenger ferries depart to Vinalhaven, North Haven, Matinicus, and Islesboro. All are occupied year-round by hardy souls and joined in summer by less-hardy ones. Except for Matinicus, they're great day-trip destinations.

If what appeals to you about a ferry trip is traveling on the water, you can get a taste of the great age of sail by booking a three- or six-day cruise on one of the classic windjammer schooners berthed in Rockland, Rockport, and Camden. Or simply book a day sail or sea-kayak excursion.

HIGHLIGHTS

Monhegan Museum: View an impressive collection of masters at this museum adjacent to the lighthouse, then visit contemporary studios and see where artists find their inspiration by hiking island trails (page 194).

The Farnsworth Art Museum and the Wyeth Center: Three generations of Wyeths are represented in this museum, which also boasts an excellent collection of works by Maine and American masters (page 199).

Owls Head Transportation Museum: View a fabulous collection of vintage airplanes, automobiles, and even bicycles, many of which are flown, driven, or ridden during weekend special events (page 200).

Rockland Breakwater: Take a walk on this nearly mile-long breakwater to the lighthouse at the end (open on weekends). It's an especially fine place to watch the windjammers sail in or out of Rockland Harbor (page 201).

Owls Head Light State Park: The views of Penobscot Bay are spectacular, and it's a great place for a picnic lunch (page 203).

Camden Hills State Park: If you have time, hike the moderate trail to the summit for a gull's-eye view over Camden Harbor and Penobscot Bay. If not, take the easy route and drive (page 223).

Penobscot Marine Museum: Learn what life was *really* like during the Great Age of Sail in a town renowned for the number and quality of its sea captains (page 243).

Fort Knox: A good restoration, frequent events, and secret passages to explore make this late-19th-century fort one of Maine's best (page 243).

Penobscot Narrows Bridge and Observatory: On a clear day, the views from the 420-foot-high tower, one of only three in the world, extend from Mt. Katahdin to Cadillac Mountain (page 244).

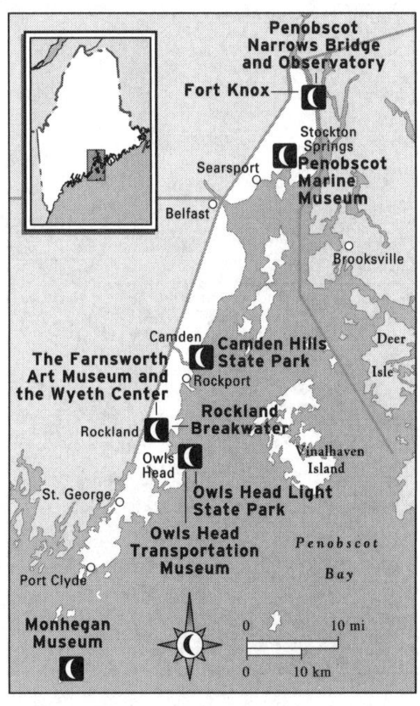

LOOK FOR [icon] TO FIND RECOMMENDED SIGHTS, ACTIVITIES, DINING, AND LODGING.

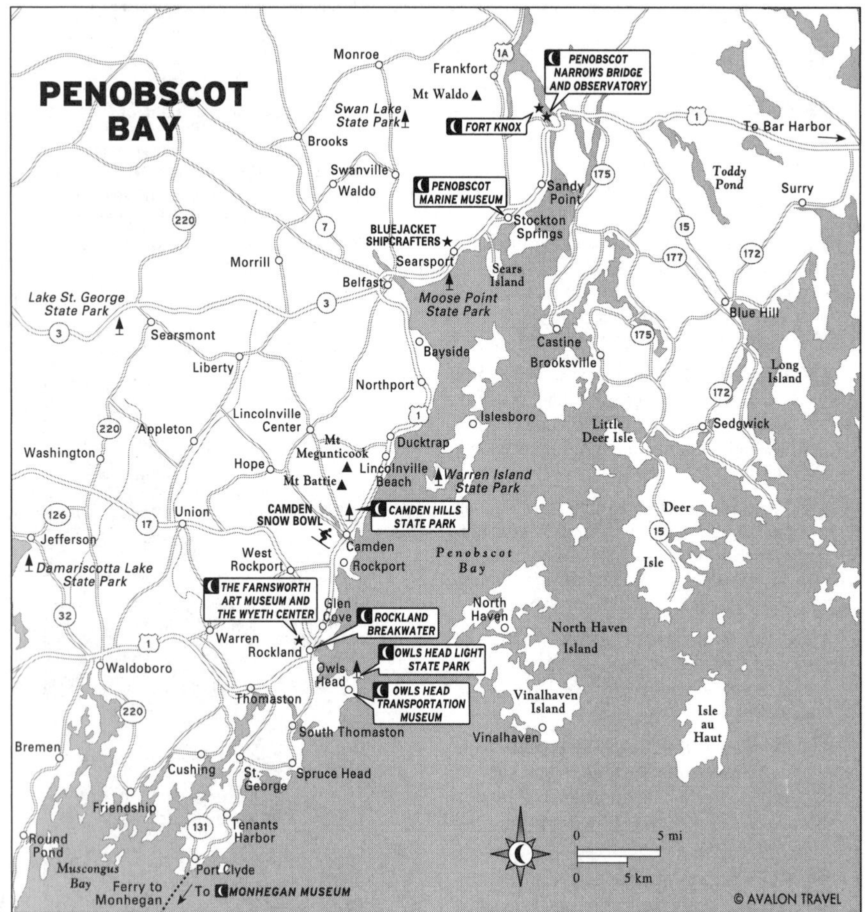

While it's easy to focus on the water, this region is rich in museums and art galleries, antiques and specialty shops, some of the state's nicest inns, and many of its better restaurants.

Most folks arrive in July and August, but autumn, when turning leaves color the hills and reflect in the sea, and the days remain warm and nights are cool, is an ideal season to visit, especially for leaf peepers who want to get off the beaten track. And in winter, when snow blankets the Camden Hills, you can ski while gazing out to Camden Harbor.

PLANNING YOUR TIME

To hit just the highlights, you'll need at least three days. If you want to relax a bit and enjoy the area, plan on 4–5 days. Make it a full week if you plan on overnighting on any of the offshore islands. In general, lodging is less expensive in Rockland, Belfast, and Searsport than it is in Camden. In any case, head for Monhegan or Vinalhaven on a good day and save the museums for inclement ones.

Two-lane Route 1 is the region's central artery, with veins running down the peninsula limbs.

Yes, traffic backs up, especially in Camden (and in Thomaston on the Fourth of July, when it's closed for a parade), but it rarely stops moving. If your destination is Rockland, take I-95 to Augusta and then Route 17 East; if it's Belfast or north, take I-95 to Augusta and then Route 3 East. Route 90 is a nifty bypass around Thomaston and Rockland, connecting Route 1 from Warren to Rockport. For a less direct route, the **Georges River Scenic Byway** is a 50-mile rural inland route, mostly along Route 131, between Port Clyde and Liberty. It parallels the coast, but it meanders through farmlands and tiny villages, and by lakes and rivers, with antiques shops and farmstands along the way. It's simply gorgeous in autumn.

Thomaston Area

Thomaston is a little gem of a town, and getting more so each year thanks to the razing of the old Maine State Prison. It's also the gateway to two lovely fingers of land bordering the St. George River and jutting into the Gulf of Maine—the Cushing and St. George Peninsulas.

In 1605, British adventurer Captain George Waymouth sailed up the river now named after him (the St. George River was originally called the Georges River). A way station for Plymouth traders as early as 1630, Thomaston was incorporated in 1777 and officially named after General John Thomas, a Revolutionary War hero.

Industry began with the production of lime, which was used for plaster. A growing demand for plaster, and the frequency with which the wooden boats were destroyed by fire while carrying loads of extremely flammable lime, spurred the growth of shipbuilding and its related infrastructure. Thomaston's slogan became "the town that went to sea."

Seeing the sleepy harborfront today, it's hard to visualize the booming era when dozens of tall-masted wooden ships slid down the ways. But the town's architecture is a testament and tribute to the prosperous past. All those splendid homes on Main and Knox Streets were funded by wealthy shipowners and shipmasters who well understood how to occupy the idle hands of off-duty carpenters.

SIGHTS

Montpelier

As you head north out of Thomaston on Route 1, you'll come face to face with an imposing colonial hilltop mansion at the junction with Route 131 South. (Behind it, unfortunately, is the rather ugly outline of a huge cement plant.) Dedicated to the memory of General Henry Knox, president George Washington's secretary of war, Montpelier (Rtes. 1 and 131, Thomaston, 207/354-8062, www.generalknox-museum.org, 10 A.M.–3:30 P.M. Tues.–Sat. late May–mid-Oct., $7 adults, $6 seniors, $4 children 5–13, $18 per family) is a 1930s replica of Knox's original Thomaston home. The mansion today contains Knox family furnishings and other period antiques—all described with great enthusiasm during the hour-long tours. A gift shop run by the Friends of Montpelier carries books and other relevant items. Concerts, lectures, and special events occur here periodically throughout the summer; General Knox's birthday is celebrated with considerable fanfare in July.

Museum in the Streets

Montpelier is the starting point for a walking, cycling, or, if you must, driving tour (about three miles) of nearly 70 sites in Thomaston's National Historic District. Pick up a copy of the tour brochure at one of the local businesses. Included are lots of stories behind the facades of the handsome 19th-century homes that line Main and Knox Streets; the architecture here is nothing short of spectacular. Much of this history is also recounted in the Museum in the Streets, a walking tour taking in 25 informative plaques illustrated with old photos throughout town.

EVENTS

Thomaston's **Fourth of July,** an old-fashioned hometown celebration reminiscent of a Norman Rockwell painting, draws huge crowds. A spiffy parade—with bands, veterans, kids, and pets—starts off the morning (11 A.M.), followed by races, craft and food booths, and lots more. If you need to get *through* Thomaston on the Fourth of July, do it well before the parade or well after noon; the marchers go right down Main Street (Rte. 1), and gridlock forces a detour.

SHOPPING

Thomaston has a block-long shopping street (on Rte. 1), with ample free parking out back behind the stores.

If you arrive at Marti Reed's **Personal Book Shop** (78 Main St., Thomaston, 207/354-8058) at the right time, you're likely to run into local writers' groups that gather frequently to swap tips and gossip. That's just the kind of place this is—an independent bookstore with a warm, nurturing feel. Not to mention a dog and cat in residence.

The **Maine State Prison Showroom Outlet** (Main St./Rte. 1, corner of Wadsworth St., Thomaston, 207/354-3131) markets the handiwork of inmate craftsmen. Some of the souvenirs verge on kitsch; the bargains are wooden bar stools, toys (including dollhouses), and chopping boards. You'll need to carry your purchases with you; prison-made goods cannot be shipped.

High-end 17th- and 18th-century American furniture and accessories are the stock-in-trade of **David C. Morey American Antiques** (161 Main St., 207/354-6033).

At the southern end of Thomaston, in a renovated chicken barn, is **Thomaston Place Auction Gallery** (51 Atlantic Hwy./Rte. 1, Thomaston, 207/354-8141 or 888/834-5538, www.thomastonauction.com), the home of Kaja Veilleux, a longtime dealer, appraiser, and auctioneer. Auctions occur frequently, with previews beforehand.

Just south of Thomaston is **Lie-Nielsen Toolworks** (Rte. 1, Warren, 800/327-2520, www.lie-nielsen.com), crafting heirloom-quality hand tools for connoisseurs; tours available.

CAMPING

The best campground is on the Thomaston/Cushing town line at **Saltwater Farm Campground** (Wadsworth St./Cushing Rd., Cushing, 207/354-6735, www.saltwaterfarmcampground.com), a 35-acre Good Sam park 1.5 miles south of Route 1. Thirty-seven open and wooded tent and RV sites ($35–45) overlook the St. George River. Cabins go for $70 a day. Facilities include a bathhouse, pool, hot tub, laundry facilities, store, and a play area. The river is tidal, so swimming is best near high tide; otherwise you're dealing with mudflats.

FOOD

Call to verify days and hours of operation.

Often overlooked by visitors (but certainly not by locals) is casual **Thomaston Café and Bakery** (154 Main St./Rte. 1, Thomaston, 207/354-8589, www.thomastoncafe.com, 7 A.M.–2 P.M. Mon.–Thurs., 7 A.M.–2 P.M. and 5:30–8 P.M. Fri.–Sat., 8:30 A.M.–1:30 P.M. Sun.). German-born chef Herb Peters and his wife, Eleanor, produce superb pastries, breads, and desserts (eat here or take out). Everything's homemade, there are children's options, and the café uses only organic poultry. Try the incredible wild-mushroom hash. Dinner entrées are $16–24. Beer and wine only; reservations essential.

INFORMATION AND SERVICES

The **Rockland-Thomaston Area Chamber of Commerce** (Gateway Center,

Rockland, 207/596-0376 or 800/562-2529, www.therealmaine.com) is the area's best resource.

The **Thomaston Public Library** (42 Main St., Thomaston, 207/354-2453) occupies part of the Greek Revival Thomaston Academy.

Cushing Peninsula

Cushing's recorded history goes back at least as far as 1605, when someone named "Abr [maybe Abraham] King"—presumably a member of explorer George Waymouth's crew—inscribed his name here on a ledge (now private property). Since 1789, settlers' saltwater farms have sustained many generations, and the active Cushing Historical Society keeps the memories and memorabilia from fading away. But the outside world knows little of this. Cushing is better known as "Wyeth country," the terrain depicted by the famous artistic dynasty of N. C., Andrew, and Jamie Wyeth (and assorted talented other relatives).

If you're an Andrew Wyeth fan, visiting Cushing will give you the feeling of walking through his paintings. The flavor of his Maine work is here—rolling fields, wildflower meadows, rocky tidal coves, broad vistas, character-filled farmhouses, and some well-hidden summer enclaves.

SIGHTS

Cushing's town boundary begins 1.3 miles south of Route 1 (take Wadsworth Street at the Maine State Prison Showroom Outlet). Two miles farther, you'll pass giant wooden sculptures in the yard of the late artist **Bernard Langlais,** who died in 1977.

Six miles from Route 1 is the **A. S. Fales**

© TOM NANGLE

The Olson House inspired many of Andrew Wyeth's works.

BEANHOLE BEANS

"To be happy in New England," wrote one Joseph P. MacCarthy at the turn of the 20th century, "you must select the Puritans for your ancestors...[and] eat beans on Saturday night." There is no better way to confirm the latter requirement than to attend a "beanhole" bean supper – a real-live legacy of colonial times, with dinner baked in a hole in the ground.

Generally scheduled, appropriately, for a Saturday night (check local newspapers), a beanhole bean supper demands plenty of preparation from its hosts – and a secret ingredient or two. (Don't even think about trying to pry the recipe out of the cooks.) The supper always includes hot dogs, cole slaw, relishes, home-baked breads, and homemade desserts, but the beans are the star attraction. (Typically, the suppers are also alcohol-free.) Not only are they feasts; they're also bargains, never setting you back more than about $8.

The beans at the Broad Cove Church's annual mid-July beanhole bean supper, served family-style at long picnic tables, are legendary – attracting nearly 200 eager diners. Minus the secrets, here's what happens:

Early Friday morning: Church volunteers load 10 pounds of dry pea and soldier (yellow-eye) beans into each of four large kettles and add water to cover. The beans are left to soak and soften for 6-7 hours. Two or three volunteers uncover the churchyard's four rock-lined beanholes (each about three feet deep), fill the holes with hardwood kindling, ignite the wood, and keep the fires burning until late afternoon, when the wood is reduced to red-hot coals.

Early Friday afternoon: The veteran chefs parboil the beans and stir in the seasonings. Typical additions are brown sugar, molasses, mustard, salt, pepper, and salt pork (much of the secret is in the exact proportions). When the beans are precooked to the cooks' satisfaction, the kettle lids are secured with wire and the pots are lugged outdoors.

Friday midafternoon: With the beans ready to go underground, some of the hot coals are quickly shoveled out of the pits. The kettles are lowered into the pits and the coals replaced around the sides of the kettles and atop their lids. The pits are covered with heavy sheet metal and topped with a thick layer of sand and a tarpaulin. The round-the-clock baking begins, and no one peeks before it's finished.

Saturday midafternoon: Even the veterans start getting nervous just before the pits are uncovered. Was the seasoning right? Did too much water cook away? Did the beans dry out? Not to worry, though – failures just don't happen here.

Saturday night: When a pot is excavated for the first of three seatings (about 5 P.M.), the line is already long. The chefs check their handiwork and the supper begins. No one seems to mind waiting for the second and third seatings – while others eat, a sing-along gets under way in the church, keeping everyone entertained.

and Son Store (locally, just Fales's Store), Cushing's heart and soul—source of fuel, film, gossip, and groceries. Built in 1889, the store has been in the Fales family ever since. You might want to pick up lunch while here. Just beyond the store, take the left fork, continuing down the peninsula toward the Broad Cove Church and the Olson House.

Broad Cove Church

Andrew Wyeth aficionados will recognize the Broad Cove Church as one of his subjects—alongside Cushing Road en route to the Olson House. It's open most days, so step inside and admire the classic New England architecture. The church is also well known as the site of one of the region's best beanhole bean suppers, held on a Saturday mid-July and attracting several hundred appreciative diners. Bear left at the fork after Fales's Store; the church is 0.4 mile farther, on the right.

The Olson House

Many an art lover makes the pilgrimage to the Olson House (11 A.M.–4 P.M. daily late May–mid-Oct., $5), a famous icon near the end of Hathorn Point Road. The early-19th-century farmhouse appears in Andrew Wyeth's 1948 painting *Christina's World* (which hangs in New York's Museum of Modern Art), his best-known image of the disabled Christina Olson, who died in 1968. In 1991, two philanthropists donated the Olson House to the Farnsworth Art Museum in Rockland (a $12 combination ticket includes Farnsworth museum admission), which has retained the house's sparse, lonely, and almost mystical ambience. The clapboards outside remain unpainted, the interior walls bear only a few Wyeth prints (hung close to the settings they depict), and it is easy to sense Wyeth's inspiration for chronicling this place. From Route 1 in Thomaston, at the Maine State Prison Showroom Outlet, turn onto Wadsworth Street and go six miles to Fales's Store. Take the left fork after the store, go 1.5 miles, and turn left onto Hathorn Point Road. Go another 1.9 miles to the house.

St. George Peninsula

Even though the Cushing and St. George Peninsulas face each other across the St. George River, they differ dramatically. Cushing is far more rural, seemingly less approachable—with little access to the surrounding waters; St. George has a slew of things to do and see, and places to sleep and eat, plus shore access in various spots along the peninsula.

The St. George Peninsula is actually better known by some of the villages scattered along its length: **Tenants Harbor, Port Clyde, Wiley's Corner, Spruce Head**—plus the smaller neighborhoods of Martinsville, Smalleytown, Glenmere, Long Cove, Hart's Neck, and Clark Island. Each has a distinct personality, determined partly by the different ethnic groups—primarily Brits, Swedes, and Finns—who arrived to work the granite quarries in the 19th century. Wander through the Seaview Cemetery in Tenants Harbor and you'll see the story: row after row of gravestones with names from across the sea.

A more famous former visitor was 19th-century novelist Sarah Orne Jewett, who holed up in an old schoolhouse in Martinsville, paid a weekly rental of $0.50, and wrote *The Country of the Pointed Firs,* a tale about "Dunnet's Landing" (Tenants Harbor).

Today the picturesque peninsula has saltwater farms, tidy hamlets, a striking lighthouse, spruce-edged tidal coves, an active yachting harbor, and, at the tip, a tiny fishing village (Port Clyde), which serves as a springboard to offshore Monhegan Island.

Port Clyde is likely the best-known community here. (Fortunately, it's no longer called by its unappealing 18th-century name—Herring Gut.) George Waymouth explored Port Clyde's nearby islands in 1605, but you'd never suspect its long tradition. It's a sleepy place, with a general store, low-key inns, a few galleries, and pricey parking.

SIGHTS

Marshall Point Lighthouse Museum

Not many settings can compare with the spectacular locale of the Marshall Point Lighthouse Museum (Marshall Point Rd., Port Clyde, 207/372-6450, www.marshallpoint.org, 1–5 P.M. Sun.–Fri., 10 A.M.–5 P.M. Sat., late May–mid-Oct., free), a distinctive 1857 lighthouse and park overlooking Port Clyde, the harbor islands, and the passing lobster-boat fleet. Bring a picnic and let the kids run on the lawn (but keep them well back from the shoreline). The tiny museum, in the 1895 keeper's house, displays lighthouse and local memorabilia. The grounds are accessible year-round. Take Route 131 to Port Clyde and watch for signs to the museum.

© TOM NANGLE

In the keeper's house at Marshall Point Lighthouse, at the tip of the St. George Peninsula, is a small museum.

SHOPPING

Art

The St. George Peninsula has been attracting artists for decades, and galleries pepper the peninsula. Some have been here for years, others started yesterday; most are worth a stop, so keep an eye out for their signs. In early August, a number of renowned artists usually coordinate an open-studio weekend.

Overlooking the reversing falls in downtown South Thomaston, **The Old Post Office Gallery** (Rte. 73, South Thomaston, 207/594-9396, www.artofthesea.com) has 11 rooms filled with marine art and antiques: ship models, prints, paintings, sculpture, scrimshaw, and jewelry.

Used Books

Drive up to the small parking area at **Lobster Lane Book Shop** (Island Rd., Spruce Head, 207/594-7520), and you'll see license plates from everywhere. The tiny shop, in a crammed but well-organized shed that's been here since the 1960s, has 50,000 or so treasures for used-book fans. For a few dollars, you can stock up on a summer's worth of reading. The shop is just under a mile east of Route 73, with eye-catching vistas in several directions (except, of course, when Spruce Head's infamous fog sets in).

General Store

Despite periodic ownership changes, **Port Clyde General Store** (Rte. 131, Port Clyde, 207/372-6543) remains a characterful destination, a two-century-old country store with ever-increasing upscale touches. Stock up on groceries, pick up a newspaper, order breakfast or a pizza, or buy a sweatshirt (you may need it on the Monhegan boat). Current owner Linda Bean has gussified it even more and added a shop upstairs, and also operates **The Dip Net** out back.

RECREATION

Swimming and Beachcombing

Drift Inn Beach, on Drift Inn Beach Road

(also called Candy's Cove Road), isn't a big deal as beaches go, but it's the best public one on the peninsula, so it gets busy on hot days. The name comes from the Drift Inn, an early-20th-century summer hotel. Drift Inn Beach Road parallels Route 131, and the parking lot is accessible from both roads. Heading south on the peninsula, about 3.5 miles after the junction with Route 73, turn left at Drift Inn Beach Road. The sign frequently disappears; watch for an imposing square granite house and a red farmhouse on your left, turn, then continue 0.2 mile.

Sea Kayaking

The St. George Peninsula is especially popular for sea kayaking, with plenty of islands to add interest and shelter. **Port Clyde Kayaks** (Rte. 131, Port Clyde, 207/372-8128, www.portclydekayaks.com) offers 2.5-hour ($55) and four-hour ($79) guided tours around the tip of the peninsula, taking in Marshall Point lighthouse and the islands. Other options include full moon and sunset tours. Ask about multiday camping or bed-and-breakfast tours.

If you have kayaking experience, you can launch on the ramp just before the causeway that links the mainland with Spruce Head Island, in Spruce Head (Island Rd., off Rte. 73). Parking is limited. A great paddle goes clockwise around Spruce Head Island and nearby Whitehead (there's a lighthouse on its southeastern shore) and Norton Islands. Duck in for lunch at Waterman's Beach Lobster. Around new moon and full moon, plan your schedule to avoid low tide near the Spruce Head causeway, or you may become mired in mudflats.

Excursion Boats

The best boating experience on this peninsula is a passenger-ferry trip from Port Clyde to offshore **Monhegan Island**—for a day, overnight, or longer. Perhaps because the private ferry company has a monopoly on this harbor, the trip isn't cheap, and parking adds

© HILARY NANGLE

For fresh seafood and the best harbor views, visit the Port Clyde General Store.

© HILARY NANGLE

The Monhegan-Thomaston Boat Line ferries passengers to Monhegan Island and also offers scenic cruises.

to the cost, but it's a "must" excursion, so try to factor it into the budget. Port Clyde is the nearest mainland harbor to Monhegan; this service operates all year. **Monhegan-Thomaston Boat Line** (Port Clyde, 207/372-8848, www.monheganboat.com) uses two boats, the *Laura B.* (70 minutes each way) and the newer *Elizabeth Ann* (50 minutes). Round-trip tickets are $32 adults, $18 children 2–12. (Leave your bicycle in Port Clyde; you won't need it on the island.) Reservations are essential in summer, especially for the 10:30 A.M. boat; a $5 per person fee holds the reservation until 75 minutes before departure, so you have to get to the dock early. No deposit is needed for other boats, but show up 30 minutes before departure. Parking in Port Clyde is $4 a day. If a summer day trip is all you can manage, aim for the first or second boat and return on the last one; don't go just for the boat ride.

During the summer, the Monhegan-Thomaston Boat Line also offers 2.5-hour sightseeing cruises, on a varied schedule, including a Puffin/Nature Cruise and Lighthouse Cruise. Each costs $25 adults, $10 children.

ACCOMMODATIONS

Rates noted are for peak season.

Inns

The dreamy island-dotted, oceanfront setting complements **The East Wind Inn** (Mechanic St., Tenants Harbor, 207/372-6366 or 800/241-8439, www.eastwindinn.com, $118–226), the perfect rendition of an old-fashioned country inn—some parts of it more old-fashioned than others. Built in 1860 and originally used as a sail loft, it has a huge veranda, a cozy parlor, harbor-view rooms, and a quiet dining room with a creditable New England menu. Rooms are divided between the main inn, some with shared bath, and the spiffed-up 19th-century Meeting House, a former sea captain's home, which also has one apartment. All rates include a full breakfast. The water-view dining room is open to the public daily for breakfast (7:30–9:30 A.M., to 10 A.M. in July–Aug.) and dinner

(5:30–8:30 P.M., to 9:30 P.M. in July–Aug.). Dinner entrées are $17–26. Reservations are wise. Lunch is available in summer at a dockside take-out. Children are welcome; pets are $15 per visit. The inn is open all year; the dining room is open April–November.

Bed-and-Breakfasts

In the center of South Thomaston village but overlooking the reversing falls on the tidal Wessaweskeag River, the 1830 **Weskeag at the Water** (14 Elm St., Rte. 73, South Thomaston, 207/596-6676 or 800/596-5576, www.weskeag.com, $125–150) has nine rooms, of which four have in-room private baths; one has a whirlpool tub. This place is especially relaxing; congenial innkeepers Gray and Lynne Smith provide guests with games, puzzles, books, a huge video library, a great deck, and a lawn stretching to the river. Bring your sea kayaks and bicycles. It's 1.5 miles from the Owls Head Transportation Museum (the Smiths love vintage cars) and a few more miles from the restaurants of downtown Rockland. It's open all year.

If you stay at the **Ocean House** (Rte. 131, Port Clyde, 207/372-6691 or 800/269-6691, www.oceanhousehotel.com, $110–145), you can plan to roll out of bed, eat breakfast, and head down the hill to the Monhegan boat. Several of the 10 unpretentious rooms (seven with private bath) have great harbor views. No credit cards.

Smack-dab in the middle of Port Clyde, the **Seaside Inn** (5 Cold Storage Rd., Port Clyde, 207/372-0700 or 800/279-5041, www.seasideportclyde.com, $99–159) is an unfussy 1850s sea captain's home with both private and shared baths. A 1st-floor library has books, puzzles, TV, and a fireplace. Rates include a full breakfast.

Every room has a view of Owl's Head Harbor at the **Trinity on the Ocean Bed and Breakfast** (20 Ocean Ave., Owl's Head, 207/596-0071, www.trinityontheocean.com, $180–220), an oceanfront bed-and-breakfast that's within walking distance of Primo restaurant. Hosts Steve and Donna Belyea are Rockland natives, so they know the area well, and they like to share their finds. Donna made the quilts topping the beds in the three guest rooms, each named after a Maine windjammer. A full breakfast is served either inside or on the ocean-view deck.

Camping

The third generation now operates **Lobster Buoy Campsites** (280 Waterman's Beach Rd., South Thomaston, 207/596-7546, www.lobsterbuoycampsites.com, $22–32), an oceanfront campground with 40 sites, 28 with water and electric, all with fire ring and picnic table. You can launch a canoe or kayak from the small sand beach. Most sites are in an open field, and Lookout Beach is reserved for tenting. Every morning in July and August, homemade doughnuts are sold in the office.

FOOD

Call to verify days and hours of operation.

Local Flavors

Don't be surprised to see the handful of tables occupied at the **Keag Store** (Rte. 73, Village Center, South Thomaston, 207/596-6810, 6 A.M.–9 P.M. Mon.–Sat., 7 A.M.–8 P.M. Sun.), one of the most popular lunch stops in the area. (Keag, by the way, is pronounced GIG—short for "Wessaweskeag.") Roast-turkey sandwiches with stuffing are a big draw, as is the pizza, which verges on the greasy but compensates with its flavor—no designer toppings, just good pizza. Order it all to go and head across the street to the public wharf, where you can hang out and observe all the comings and goings.

Casual Dining

The decidedly old-fashioned **Craignair Inn Restaurant** (Clark Island Rd., off Rte. 71, Spruce Head, 207/594-7644, www.craignair.com), built in 1928 to house granite workers, serves dinner in its water-view dining room daily except Sunday, entrées $16–26. Seafood is the specialty. Also in the Main Inn and Vestry Annex are rooms, some with shared baths ($110–153 with breakfast).

© HILARY NANGLE

Waterman's Beach Lobster provides a front-row table on Penobscot Bay.

Lobster in the Rough

These open-air lobster wharves are the best places in the area to get down and dirty and manhandle a steamed or boiled lobster.

Poking right into Wheeler's Bay, **Miller's Lobster Company** (Eagle Quarry Rd., off Rte. 73, Spruce Head, 207/594-7406, www.millerslobster.com, 11 A.M.–7 P.M. daily) is the quintessential lobster pound, a well-run operation that draws crowds all summer long. Lobster rolls, steamed clams, crabmeat rolls, homemade pies—the works. Even hot dogs if you need them. Several picnic tables are under cover for chilly or rainy weather. BYOB.

A broad view of islands in the Mussel Ridge Channel is the bonanza at **Waterman's Beach Lobster** (343 Waterman's Beach Rd., South Thomaston, 207/596-7819, www.watermansbeachlobster.com, 11 A.M.–7 P.M. Wed.–Sun.). This tiny operation has a big reputation: It's won a James Beard Award. It turns out lobster, clam, and mussel dinners, fat lobster and crabmeat rolls, and superb pies (and hot dogs and grilled cheese). Step up to the window and place your order. Service can be slow, but why rush with a view like this? Choose a good day; there's no real shelter from bad weather. BYOB; no credit cards. Next door to the Blue Lupin B&B, the wharf is on a side road off Route 73 between Spruce Head Village and South Thomaston; watch for signs on Route 73.

Monhegan Island

Eleven or so miles from the mainland lies a unique island community with gritty lobstermen, close-knit families, a longstanding summertime artists' colony, no cars, astonishingly beautiful scenery, and some of the best birdwatching on the Eastern Seaboard. Until the 1980s, the island had only radiophones and generator power; with the arrival of electricity and real phones, the pace has quickened a bit—but not much. Welcome to Monhegan Island.

But first a cautionary note: Monhegan has remained idyllic largely because generations of residents, part-timers, and visitors have been ultrasensitive to its fragility. When you buy your ferry ticket, you'll receive a copy of the regulations, all very reasonable, and the captain of your ferry will repeat them. *Heed them or don't go.*

Many of the regulations have been developed by The Monhegan Associates, an island land trust founded in the 1960s by Theodore Edison, son of the inventor. Firmly committed to preservation of the island in as natural a state as possible, the group maintains and marks the trails, sponsors natural-history talks, and insists that no construction be allowed beyond the village limits.

The origin of the name Monhegan remains up in the air; it's either a Maliseet or Micmac name meaning "out-to-sea island" or an adaptation of the name of a French explorer's daughter. In any case, Monhegan caught the attention of Europeans after English explorer John Smith stopped by in 1614, but the island had already been noticed by earlier adventurers, including John Cabot, Giovanni da Verrazzano, and George Waymouth. Legend even has it that Monhegan fishermen sent dried fish to Plimoth Plantation during the Pilgrims' first winter on Cape Cod. Captain Smith returned home and carried on about Monhegan, snagging the attention of intrepid souls who established a fishing/trading outpost here in 1625. Monhegan has been settled continuously since 1674, with fishing as the economic base.

In the 1880s, lured by the spectacular setting and artist Robert Henri's enthusiastic reports, gangs of artists began arriving, lugging their easels here and there to capture the surf, the light, the tidy cottages, the magnificent headlands, fishing boats, even the islanders' craggy features. American, German, French, and British artists have long (and continue to) come here; well-known signatures associated with Monhegan include Rockwell Kent, George Bellows, Edward Hopper, James Fitzgerald, Andrew Winter, Alice Kent Stoddard, Reuben Tam, William Kienbusch, and Jamie Wyeth.

Officially called Monhegan Plantation, the island has about 75 year-rounders. Several hundred others summer here. A handful of students attend the tiny school through eighth grade; high-schoolers have to pack up and move "inshore" to the mainland during the school year.

At the schoolhouse, the biggest social event of the year is the Christmas party, when everyone brings casseroles, salads, and desserts to complement a big beef roast. Kids perform their Christmas play, Santa shows up with presents, and dozens of adults look on approvingly. The islanders turn out en masse for almost every special event at the school, and the adults treat the island kids almost like common property, feeling free to praise or chastise them any time it seems appropriate—a phenomenon unique to isolated island communities.

TEN RULES FOR MONHEGAN VISITORS

1. Smoking is banned everywhere except in the village.
2. Rock climbing is not allowed on the wild headlands on the back side of the island.
3. Preserve the island's wild state – do not remove flowers or lichens.
4. Bicycles and strollers are not allowed on island trails.
5. Camping and campfires are forbidden islandwide.
6. Swim only at Swim Beach, just south of the ferry landing – if your innards can stand the shock. Wait for the incoming tide, when the water is warmest (and this warmth is relative). It's wise not to swim alone.
7. Dogs must be leashed; carry a pooper-scooper to remove their waste.
8. Be respectful of private property; stay on the trails. (As the island visitors guide puts it, "Monhegan is a village, not a theme park.")
9. If you're staying overnight, bring a flashlight; the village paths are very dark.
10. Carry the island trail map when you go exploring; you'll need it.

A strong suggestion: Carry a trash bag, use it, and take it off the island when you leave.

For years, Monhegan's lobster-fishing season—a legislatively sanctioned period—perversely began on December 1 (locally known as Trap Day), but in 2007 that was moved forward to October 1, making it possible for visitors to view the action. An air of nervous anticipation surrounds the dozen or so lobstermen after midnight the day before as they prepare to steam out to set their traps on the ocean floor. Of course, with less competition from mainland fishermen that time of year, and a supply of lobsters fattening up since the previous June, there's a ready market for their catch. But success still depends on a smooth "setting." Meetings are held daily during the month beforehand to make sure everyone will be ready to "set" together. The season ends on June 25.

March brings the annual town meeting, an important community event that draws every able-bodied soul and then some.

Almost within spitting distance of Monhegan's dock (but you'll still need a boat) is whale-shaped **Manana Island,** once the home of an ex–New Yorker named Ray Phillips. Known as the Hermit of Manana, Phillips lived a solitary sheepherding existence on this barren island for more than half a century until his death in 1975. His story had spread so far afield that even the *New York Times* ran a front-page obituary when he died. (Photos and clippings are displayed in the Monhegan Museum.) In summer, youngsters with skiffs often hang around the harbor, particularly Fish Beach and Swim Beach, and you can usually talk one of them into taking you over, for a fee. (Don't try to talk them down too much or they may not return to pick you up.) Some curious inscriptions on Manana (marked with a yellow X near the boat landing) have led archaeologists to claim that Vikings even made it here, but cooler heads attribute the markings to Mother Nature.

One last note: Monhegan isn't for the mobility impaired. There's no public transportation, and roads are rough and hilly.

When to Go

If a day trip is all your schedule will allow, visit Monhegan between Memorial Day weekend and mid-October, when ferries from Port Clyde, New Harbor, and Boothbay Harbor operate daily, allowing 5–8 hours on the island—time enough to do an extensive trail loop, visit the museum and handful of shops, and picnic on the rocks. Other months, there's only one ferry a day from Port Clyde (only three a week Nov.–Apr.), so you'll need to spend the night—not a hardship, but definitely requiring planning.

Almost any time of year, but especially in spring, fog can blanket the island, curtailing photography and swimming (although usually not the ferries). A spectacular sunny day can't be beat, but don't be deterred by fog, which lends an air of mystery you won't forget. Rain, of course, is another matter; some island trails can be perilous even in a misty drizzle.

Other Points to Consider

Monhegan has no bank, but there are a couple of ATMs. Credit cards are not accepted everywhere. Personal checks, travelers checks, or cash will do. The few public telephones in the village require phone credit cards.

The only public restroom unconnected to a restaurant or lodging is on Horn Hill, at the southern end of the village (near the Monhegan House), and it will cost you $1 to use it. Outrageous, perhaps, but the restroom was installed to protect the woods and trails and deter day-trippers from bothering innkeepers. Unfortunately, the fee inspires some people to spurn these facilities and head for the woods. Please spend the dollar and preserve the island.

SIGHTS

Monhegan is a getaway destination, a relaxing place for self-starters, so don't anticipate organized entertainment beyond the occasional lecture or narrated nature tour. Bring sturdy shoes (maybe even an extra pair in case trails are wet), a windbreaker, binoculars, a camera, and perhaps a sketchpad or a journal. If you're staying overnight, bring a flashlight for negotiating the unlighted island walkways, even in the village. For rainy days, bring a book. (If you forget, there's an amazingly good library.) In winter, bring ice skates for use on the Ice Pond.

Monhegan Museum

The National Historic Register **Monhegan Lighthouse**—activated in July 1824 and automated in 1959—stands at the island's highest point, Lighthouse Hill, an exposed summit that's also home to the Monhegan Historical

© HILARY NANGLE

Climb Lighthouse Hill to the Monhegan Museum for panoramic views over the village and Manana Island, beyond.

and Cultural Museum (207/596-7003, www.monheganmuseum.org, 11:30 A.M.–3:30 P.M. daily July–Aug., 12:30–2:30 P.M. daily June and Sept.) in the former keeper's house and adjacent buildings. Overseen by the Monhegan Historical and Cultural Museum Association, the museum contains an antique kitchen, lobstering exhibits, and a fine collection of paintings by noted and not-so-noted artists. Two outbuildings have tools and gear connected with fishing and ice-cutting, traditional island industries. The assistant lightkeeper's house, recently restored top to bottom as a handsome art gallery, provides a climate-controlled environment for the museum's impressive art collection. A volunteer usually is on hand to answer questions. The museum also owns two buildings designed and built by Rockwell Kent and later owned by James Fitzgerald. The house is maintained as a historic house museum; Fitzgerald's works are displayed in the studio. Both are open on a limited basis. Admission is technically free, but donations are encouraged.

Artists' Studios

Nearly 20 artists' studios are open to the public during the summer (usually July and August), but not all at once. At least five are open most days—most in the afternoon (Monday has the fewest choices). Sometimes it's tight timewise for day-trippers who also want to hike the trails, but most of the studios are relatively close to the ferry landing. An annually updated map-schedule details locations, days, and times. It's posted on bulletin boards in the village and is available at lodgings and shops.

Two group galleries worth a visit are **Winter Works,** a craft co-op, and **Lupine Gallery** (207/594-8131), with works by Monhegan artists and artists' supplies.

RECREATION

Hiking and Walking

Just over a half mile wide and 1.7 miles long, barely a square mile in area, Monhegan has 18 numbered hiking trails, most easy to moderate, covering about 11 miles. All are described in the *Monhegan Associates Trail Map* (www.

© HILARY NANGLE

On Monhegan Island, it seems nearly every place you turn, there are artists capturing the iconic scenes.

monheganassociates.org), available at mainland ferry offices and island shops and lodgings or on the website. (The map is not to scale, so the hikes can take longer than you think.)

The footing is uneven everywhere, so Monhegan can present major obstacles to those with disabilities, even on the well-worn but unpaved village roads. Maintain an especially healthy respect for the ocean here, and don't venture too close; through the years, rogue waves on the island's backside have claimed victims young and old.

A relatively easy **day-tripper loop,** with a couple of moderate sections along the backside of the island, takes in several of Monhegan's finest features starting at the southern end of the village, opposite the church. To appreciate it, allow at least two hours. From the Main Road, go up Horn Hill, following signs for the **Burnthead Trail** (no. 4). Cross the island to the **Cliff Trail** (no. 1). Turn north on the Cliff Trail, following the dramatic headlands on the island's backside. There are lots of great picnic rocks in this area. Continue to Squeaker Cove, where the surf is the wildest, but be cautious. Then watch for signs to the **Cathedral Woods Trail** (no. 11), carpeted with pine needles and leading back to the village.

When you get back to Main Road, detour up the **Whitehead Trail** (no. 7) to the museum. If you're spending the night and feeling energetic, consider circumnavigating the island via the **Cliff Trail** (nos. 1 and 1-A). Allow at least 5–6 hours for this route; don't rush it.

Bird-Watching

One of the East Coast's best bird-watching sites during spring and fall migrations, Monhegan is a migrant trap for exhausted creatures winging their way north or south. Avid bird-watchers come here to add rare and unusual species to their life lists, and some devotees return year after year. No bird-watcher should arrive, however, without a copy of the superb *Birder's Guide to Maine.*

Predicting exact bird-migration dates can be dicey, since wind and weather aberrations can skew the schedule. Generally, the best times are mid- to late May and most of September, into early October. If you plan to spend a night (or more) on the island during migration seasons, don't try to wing it—reserve a room well in advance.

Around-the-Island Tour

On most days, the Balmy Days excursion boat makes a half-hour circuit around the island 2–2:30 P.M. for a nominal fee. Ask at the ferry dock.

ACCOMMODATIONS

Rates noted are for peak season.

The island has a variety of lodgings from rustic to comfortable, but none are luxurious. Pickup trucks of dubious vintage meet all the ferries and transport luggage to the lodgings. For cottage renters, Monhegan Trucking charges a small fee for each piece of luggage. Rates are quoted for peak season.

Best lodging is the **Island Inn** (207/596-0371, www.islandinnmonhegan.com, $165–395), an imposing three-story hotel, dating from 1816, that commands a prime chunk of real estate overlooking the harbor. Most rooms have been updated, but retain the simplicity of another era, with painted floors, antique oak furnishings, and comfy beds covered with white down duvets. Just try to resist the siren song of the Adirondack chairs on the expansive veranda and lawns overlooking the ferry landing. Rates for the 32 harbor- and meadow-view rooms and suites (most with private baths) include full breakfast. Add $4 per person daily gratuity and $5 per person for a one-night stay.

In the heart of the village, **Monhegan House** (207/594-7983 or 800/599-7983, www.monheganhouse.com, $77–81 s, $135–165), built in 1870, is a large four-story building with 33 rooms. All but one suite ($215) have shared baths, not always on the same floor as your room. Don't miss the looseleaf notebook in the lobby. Labeled *A Monhegan Novel,* it's the ultimate in shaggy-dog sagas, created by a long string of guests since 1992. Rates include breakfast. There may be a $5 per person surcharge for one-night stays. Children are welcome: Ages 4–12 are $18, ages 13 and older are $28. It's open late May–Columbus Day.

A more modernized hostelry, **Shining Sails** (207/596-0041, www.shiningsails.com, $140–210) lacks the quaintness of the other inns, but the rooms and efficiencies are very comfortable, convenient to the dock, stay open all year, and have private baths. Breakfast (included only in season) is continental. "Well-supervised" children are welcome. An additional four apartments are in a separate building ($165–230). Shining Sails also manages more than two dozen weekly-rental cottages and apartments, with rates beginning around $800/week in season.

The funkiest lodging, and not for everyone, is **The Trailing Yew** (207/596-0440 or 800/592-2520, www.trailingyew.com, $170). Spread among five rustic buildings are 35 rooms, most with shared baths (averaging five rooms per bath and not always in the same building) and lighted with kerosene (about 12 have electricity). Rates include breakfast, dinner, taxes, and gratuities; kids are $45 and up, depending on age. The old-fashioned, low-key 50-seat dining room is open to the public for dinner at 5:45 P.M., served family-style by reservation, and for breakfast at 7:45 A.M. Bring a sleeping bag in spring or fall; rooms are unheated. No credit cards.

FOOD

Most visitors don't arrive on Monhegan expecting gourmet cuisine. Everything is quite casual, and food is hearty and ample. None of the eateries have liquor licenses, so buy beer or wine at one of the stores or the Barnacle Café, or bring it from the mainland. All of the restaurants and food sources are in or close to the village. In most cases hours change frequently, so call first.

Prepared foods, varying from pastries to sandwiches and salads, are available from **Barnacle Café** (207/596-0371), under the same ownership as the nearby Island Inn; **The Novelty,** behind and operated by The Monhegan House; **Carina** (207/594-0837), a boutique grocery; and the **Monhegan Store.**

Casual Dining

The restaurant at the **Island Inn,** open to the public for breakfast and dinner (opens at

6 P.M.), has an excellent dinner menu with creative entrées that range $15–27. It's also open for lunch Thursday–Sunday.

Islanders and visitors flock to the **Monhegan House Café,** overlooking the village, for breakfast and dinner (entrées $13–20).

Lobster in the Rough

You can't get much rougher for lobster in the rough than **Fish House Fish** (on Fish Beach, www.fishbeachmonhegan.com, 11:30 A.M.–7 P.M. daily). Lobster and crabmeat rolls, locally smoked fish, and homemade stews and chowders are on the menu as well as fresh lobster. Take it to the picnic tables on the beach and enjoy.

INFORMATION AND SERVICES

Several free brochures and flyers, revised annually, will answer most questions about planning a day trip or overnight visit to Monhegan. Ferries supply visitors with the *Visitor's Guide to Monhegan Island* and sell the Monhegan Associates Trail Map ($1). Both are also available at island shops, galleries, and lodgings. Info also is available at www.monhegan.com and www.monhegan.info.

Monhegan's pleasant little library, the Jackie and Edward Library, was named after two children who drowned in the surf in the 1920s. The fiction collection is especially extensive, and it's open to everyone.

Also check the Rope Shed, the community bulletin board next to the meadow, right in the village. Monhegan's version of a bush telegraph, it's where everyone posts flyers and notices about nature walks, lectures, excursions, and other special events. You'll also see the current Monhegan Artists Studio Locations map.

GETTING THERE AND AROUND

Ferries travel year-round to Monhegan from Port Clyde, at the end of the St. George Peninsula. Seasonal service to the island is provided from New Harbor by Hardy Boat Cruises and from Boothbay Harbor by Balmy Days Cruises.

Part of the daily routine for many islanders and summer folk is a stroll to the harbor when the ferry comes in, so don't be surprised to see a good-size welcoming party when you arrive. You're the live entertainment.

Monhegan's only vehicles are a handful of pickup trucks owned by local lobstermen and lil' ol' trucks used by Monhegan Trucking. If you're staying a night or longer and your luggage is too heavy to carry, they'll be waiting when you arrive at the island wharf.

Rockland

A "Share the Pride" campaign—kicked off in the 1980s to boost sagging civic self-esteem and the local economy—was the first step in the transformation of Rockland. Once a rundown county seat best known for the aroma of its fish-packing plants, the city has undergone a sea change, most of it for the better. The expansion of the Farnsworth Museum of American Art and the addition of its Wyeth Center was a catalyst. Benches and plants line Main Street (Rte. 1), stores offer appealing wares, coffeehouses and more than a dozen art galleries attract a diverse clientele, and Rockland Harbor is home to more windjammer cruise schooners than neighboring Camden (which had long claimed the title "Windjammer Capital"). If you haven't been to Rockland in the last decade, prepare to be astonished.

Foresighted entrepreneurs had seen the potential of the bayside location in the late 1700s and established a tiny settlement here called "Shore Village" (or "the Shore"). Today's commercial-fishing fleet is one of the few reminders of Rockland's past, when multimasted schooners lined the wharves, some to load volatile cargoes of lime destined to become building material for cities all along the eastern seaboard, others to head northeast—toward the storm-racked Grand Banks and the lucrative cod fishery there. Such hazardous pursuits meant an early demise for many a local seafarer, but Rockland's 5,000 or so residents were enjoying their prosperity in the late 1840s. The settlement was home to more than two dozen shipyards and dozens of lime kilns, was enjoying a construction boom, and boasted a newspaper and regular steamship service. By 1854, Rockland had become a city.

Today, Rockland remains a commercial hub—with Knox County's only shopping plazas (no malls, but the big-box stores have arrived), a fishing fleet that heads far offshore, and ferries that connect nearby islands. Rockland also claims the title of "Lobster Capital of the World," thanks to Knox County's shipment nationally and internationally of 10 million pounds of lobster each year. (The weathervane atop the police and fire department building is a giant copper lobster.)

With just more than 8,000 souls, Rockland is more year-round community than tourist town. But visitors pour in during two big summer festivals—the North Atlantic Blues Festival in mid-July and the Maine Lobster Festival in early August. Highlight of the Lobster Festival is King Neptune's coronation of the Maine Sea Goddess—carefully selected from a bevy of local young women—who then sails off with him to his watery domain.

SIGHTS

The Farnsworth Art Museum and the Wyeth Center

Anchoring downtown Rockland is the nationally respected Farnsworth Art Museum (16 Museum St., 207/596-6457, www.farnsworthmuseum.org), established in 1948 through a trust fund set up by Rocklander Lucy Farnsworth. With an ample checkbook, the first curator, Robert Bellows, toured the country, accumulating a splendid collection of 19th- and 20th-century Maine-related American art, the basis for the permanent "Maine in America" exhibition.

The 6,000-piece collection today includes work by Fitz Hugh Lane, Gilbert Stuart, Eastman Johnson, Childe Hassam, John Marin, Maurice Prendergast, Rockwell Kent, George Bellows, and Marsden Hartley. Best known are the paintings by three generations of the Wyeth family (local summer residents) and sculpture by Louise Nevelson, who grew up in Rockland. Sculpture, jewelry, and paintings by Nevelson form the core of the 3rd-floor Nevelson-Berliawsky Gallery for 20th Century Art. (The only larger Nevelson collection is in New York's Whitney Museum of American Art.) The Wyeth Center, across Union Street in a former church, contains the work of Andrew, N. C., and Jamie Wyeth. The 6,000-square-foot Jamien Morehouse Wing hosts rotating exhibits.

In the Farnsworth's library—a grand, high-ceilinged oasis akin to an English gentleman's reading room—browsers and researchers can explore an extensive collection of art books and magazines. The museum's education department annually sponsors hundreds of lectures, concerts, art classes for all ages, poetry readings, and field trips. Most are open to nonmembers; some require an extra fee. A glitzy gift shop stocks posters, prints, notecards, imported gift items, and art games for children.

Next door to the museum is the mid-19th-century Greek Revival **Farnsworth Homestead,** with original high-Victorian furnishings. Looking as though William Farnsworth's family just took off for the day, the house has been preserved rather than restored.

The Farnsworth also owns the **Olson House,** 14 miles away in nearby Cushing, where the whole landscape looks like a Wyeth diorama. Pick up a map at the museum to help you find the house; it's definitely worth the side trip.

The Farnsworth ($12 adults, $10 seniors and students 17 and older, free children 16 and under and Rockland residents) is open year-round, including summer holidays. Farnsworth hours are 10 A.M.–5 P.M. daily (to 8 P.M. Wed.) in summer, 10 A.M.–5 P.M. Wednesday–Sunday in winter. Call the museum for its current definition of summer and winter. The Homestead (10 A.M.–5 P.M. daily) and the Olson House (11 A.M.–4 P.M. daily) are open late May–mid-October. Note: Admission is free on Wednesdays after 5 P.M.

Owls Head Transportation Museum

Don't miss this place, even if you're not an old-vehicle buff. A generous endowment has made the Owls Head Transportation Museum (Rte. 73, Owls Head, 207/594-4418, www.ohtm.org, 10 A.M.–4 P.M. daily Nov.–Mar., $10 adults, $8 seniors, free children under 18, special events are extra), a premier facility for celebrating wings and wheels; it draws more than 75,000 visitors a year. Scads of eager volunteers help restore the vehicles and keep them running. On weekends May–October, the museum sponsors air shows (often including aerobatic displays) and car and truck meets for hundreds of enthusiasts. The season highlight is the annual rally and aerobatic show (early August), when more than 300 vehicles gather for two days of festivities. Want your own vintage vehicle? Attend the antique, classic, and special-interest auto auction (third Sunday in August). The gift shop carries transportation-related items. If the kids get bored (unlikely), there's a play area outside, with picnic tables. In winter, groomed cross-country-skiing trails wind through the museum's 60-acre site. (Ask for a map at the information desk.)

Maine Discovery Center

The headliner at the Maine Discovery Center (1 Park Dr.) is the **Maine Lighthouse Museum** (207/594-3301, www.mainelighthousemuseum.com, 9 A.M.–5 P.M. Mon.–Fri., 10 A.M.–4 P.M. Sat.–Sun. late May–mid-Oct., closed Sun.–Wed. in winter, $5 adults, $4 seniors, free children under 12), home to the nation's largest collection of Fresnel lenses, along with a boatload-plus of lighthouse-, Coast Guard–, and maritime-related artifacts. On view are foghorns, ships' bells, nautical books and photographs, marine instruments, ship models, scrimshaw, and so much more.

The Owls Head Transportation Museum is a must for fans of vintage wings and wheels and is often the site of air shows.

Project Puffin Visitor Center

If you can't manage a trip to see the puffins, Audubon's Project Puffin Visitor Center (311 Main St., 207/596-5566 or 877/478-3346, www.projectpuffin.org, 10 A.M.–5 P.M. daily, to 7 P.M. Wed., June 1–Oct. 31; call for off-season hours) will bring them to you. Live videos of nesting puffins are just one of the highlights of the center, which also includes interactive exhibits, a gallery, and films, all highlighting successful efforts to restore and protect these clowns of the sea.

Rockland Breakwater

Protecting the harbor from wind-driven waves, the 4,346-foot-long Rockland Breakwater took 18 years to build, with 697,000 tons of locally quarried granite. In the late 19th century, it was piled up, chunk by chunk, from a base 175 feet wide on the harbor floor (60 feet below the surface) to the 43-foot-wide cap. The Breakwater Light—now automated—was built in 1902 and added to the National Historic Register in 1981. The city of Rockland owns the keeper's house, but it's maintained by the Friends of the Rockland Breakwater Lighthouse (www.rocklandlighthouse.com). Member volunteers usually open the lighthouse to the public 9 A.M.–5 P.M. Saturday and Sunday late May–mid-October and for special events. The breakwater provides unique vantage points for photographers, and a place to picnic or catch sea breezes or fish on a hot day, but it is extremely dangerous during storms. Anyone on the breakwater risks being washed into the sea or struck by lightning (ask the local hospital staff: it *has* happened!). Do not take chances when the weather is iffy.

To reach the breakwater, take Route 1 North to Waldo Avenue and turn right. Take the next right onto Samoset Road and drive to the end to **Marie Reed Memorial Park** (tiny beach, benches, limited parking). Or go to the Samoset Resort and take the path to the breakwater from there.

© HILARY NANGLE

A nearly mile-long breakwater connects the Samoset Resort to the lighthouse marking Rockland's harbor.

Sail Power & Steam Museum

Opened in 2009, the Sail Power & Steam Museum (Sharp's Point South, 75 Mechanic St., 207/701-7626, www.sailpowerandsteammuseum.org, 10 A.M.–4 P.M. Wed.–Sat., noon–4 P.M. Sun.) is Captain Jim Sharp's labor of love. Built on the grounds of the former Snow Shipyard, the museum displays highlight Rockland's maritime heritage and include half-models of boats used by shipbuilders in the 19th century, vintage photos, tools of the trade, and other artifacts. Docked nearby is *The Reckord,* a 1914 Norwegian freighter that's used by Sharp for harbor tours.

Main Street Historic District

Rocklanders are justly proud of their Main Street Historic District, lined with 19th- and early-20th-century Greek and Colonial Revival structures, as well as examples of mansard and Italianate architecture. Most now house retail shops on the ground floor; upper floors have offices, artists' studios, and apartments. The chamber of commerce has a map and details.

Flightseeing

Get a gull's-eye view of Coastal Maine riding in an R-44 Raven chopper with **Scenic Helicopters of Maine** (207/596-7006 or 866/596-7006, www.scenic-helicopters.com). Rates begin at $75 per person, minimum two people, for an introductory flight over Rockland and Owl's Head. Flights depart from a heliport on Route 1 at the Thomaston/Rockland line.

For something a bit quieter, soar and swoop on a glider ride with **Spirit Soaring** (207/319-9514, www.spiritsoaring.org). Rates begin at $120 for a half-hour ride over coastal Penobscot Bay. It operates from Knox County Regional Airport in Owls Head, just south of Rockland.

Excursion Train

Ride in restored vintage railcars on the scenic **Maine Eastern Railroad** (207/596-6725 or 800/637-2457, www.maineeasternrailroad.com), operating between Rockland and Brunswick with stops in Wiscasset and Bath. The train operates late May–early November, with special holiday trains in December. Adult fares are $40 round-trip, $25 one-way; seniors $35/$25; children 5–15 $20/$15; family rate $100/$75, covering two adults and two kids. Packages with lodging, meals, and theater are available.

ENTERTAINMENT AND EVENTS

Stop by the **Lincoln Street Center for Arts and Education** (24 Lincoln St., 207/594-6490, www.lincolnstreetcenter.org), a community arts center with exhibitions, performances, and classes, to see what's on the schedule.

The historic **Strand Theater** (339 Main St., 207/594-7266, www.rocklandstrand.com), opened in 1923, underwent an extensive restoration in 2005. Films as well as live entertainment are scheduled. It's also the venue for many **Bay Chamber Concerts** (207/236-2823 or 888/707-2770, www.baychamberconcerts.org) events.

If you're a film buff, you might want to see what the **Saltwater Film Society** (www.saltwaterfilmsociety.org) has on its schedule.

Arts in Rockland (www.artsinrockland.com) coordinates an Art Walk every Wednesday evening in June, July, and August, as well as other special arts events.

In mid-July, the **North Atlantic Blues Festival** means a weekend of festivities featuring big names in blues. Thousands of fans jam Harbor Park for the nonstop music.

August's **Maine Lobster Festival** is a five-day lobster extravaganza, with live entertainment, the Maine Sea Goddess pageant, a lobster-crate race, craft booths, boat rides, a parade, lobster dinners, and megacrowds (the hotels are full for miles in either direction). Tons of lobsters bite the dust during the weekend—despite annual protests by the People for the Ethical Treatment of Animals. (The protests, however, seem only to increase the crowds.)

SHOPPING

Galleries

Piggybacking on the fame of the Farnsworth Museum, or at least working symbiotically, art galleries line Rockland's main and many side streets. Ask around and look around. During the summer, many of them coordinate monthly openings (usually a Wednesday evening) so you can meander and munch (and sip) from one gallery to another.

Across from the Farnsworth's side entrance, the **Caldbeck Gallery** (12 Elm St., 207/594-5935, www.caldbeck.com) has gained a top-notch reputation as a "must-see" (and "must-be-seen") space. Featuring the work of contemporary Maine artists, the gallery mounts more than half a dozen solo and group shows each year, May–September.

Eric Hopkins Gallery (21 Winter St., 207/594-1996, www.erichopkins.com) shows the North Haven artist's colorful aerial-view paintings.

Archipelago (386 Main St., 207/596-0701), on the ground floor of the Island Institute (a nonprofit steward of Maine's 4,617 offshore islands), is an attractive retail outlet for talented craftspeople from 14 year-round islands.

Other eminently browsable downtown Rockland galleries are **Harbor Square Gallery** (374 Main St., 207/594-8700 or 877/594-8700, www.harborsquaregallery.com), **Landing Gallery** (8 Elm St., 888/394-2787), **Playing with Fire! Glassworks & Gallery** (497 Main St., 207/594-7805, www.playingwithfireglassworks.com) and **Nan Mulford Gallery** (313 Main St., 207/594-8481, www.mulfordgallery.com). All are within steps of each other.

Wineries

Head inland on Route 17 and then noodle off on the back roads to discover not one but two wineries. At **Sweetgrass Farm Winery and Distillery** (347 Carroll Rd., Union, 207/785-3024, www.sweetgrasswinery.com, 11 A.M.–5 P.M. daily late May–late Dec.), owner Keith Bodine uses Maine-grown fruits to produce both wines and spirits, and he is eager to show interested folks how. Bring a picnic to enjoy while hiking the winery's trails. Carroll Road is between Shepard Hill Road and North Union Road, both north off Route 17 west of Route 131.

Nearby is **Savage Oakes** (174 Barrett Hill Rd., Union, 207/785-5261, www.savageoakes.com, 11 A.M.–5 P.M. daily, mid-May–late Oct.), where Elmer and Holly Savage and their sons have added winemaking to their second-generation Belted Galloway cattle farm. They grow nine varieties of grapes, both red and white, and produce more than a half dozen wines. Barrett Hill Road is off Route 17 directly opposite Route 131 South.

RECREATION

Parks

OWLS HEAD LIGHT STATE PARK

On Route 73, about 1.5 miles past the junction of Routes 1 and 73, you'll reach North Shore Road in the town of Owls Head. Turn left, toward Owls Head Light State Park. Standing 3.6 miles from this turn, Owls Head Light occupies a dramatic promontory with panoramic views over Rockland Harbor and Penobscot Bay. Don't miss it. The keeper's house and the light tower are off-limits, but the park surrounding the tower has easy walking paths, picnic tables, and a pebbly beach where you can sunbathe or check out Rockland Harbor's boating traffic. (If it's foggy or rainy, don't climb the steps toward the light tower: The view evaporates in the fog, the access ramp can be slippery, and the foghorn is dangerously deafening.) Follow signs to reach the park. From North Shore Road, turn left onto Main Street, then left onto Lighthouse Road, and continue along Owls Head Harbor to the parking area. This is also a particularly pleasant bike route—about 10 miles round-trip from downtown Rockland—although, once again, the roadside shoulders are poor along the Owls Head stretch.

HARBOR PARK

If you're looking for a park with more commotion than quiet green space, spend some time at Harbor Park. Boats, cars, and delivery vehicles come and go, and you can corner a picnic table, a bench, or a patch of grass and watch all the action. During the holidays, a lobster trap Christmas tree presides over the park. Public restrooms (open late May–mid-October) are available. The park is just off Main Street.

Swimming

Lucia Beach is the local name for **Birch Point Beach State Park,** one of the best-kept secrets in the area. In Owls Head, just south of Rockland—and not far from Owls Head Light—the spruce-lined sand crescent (free; outhouses but no other facilities) has rocks, shells, tide pools, and very chilly water. There's ample room for a moderate-size crowd, although parking and turnaround space can get a bit tight on the access road. From downtown Rockland, take Route 73 one mile to North Shore Drive (on your left). Take the next right, Ash Point Drive, and continue past Knox County Regional Airport to Dublin Road. Turn right, go 0.8 mile, then turn left onto Ballyhac Road (opposite the airport landing lights). Go another 0.8 mile, fork left, and continue 0.4 mile to the parking area.

WINDJAMMING

In 1936, Camden became the home of the "cruise schooner" (sometimes called "dude schooner") trade when Captain Frank Swift restored a creaky wooden vessel and offered sailing vacations to paying passengers. He kept at it for 25 years, gradually adding other boats to the fleet – and the rest, as they say, is history. Windjammers have become big business on the Maine coast, with Camden and Rockland sparring for the title of Windjammer Capital. Rockland wrested it from Camden in the mid-1990s and, so far, has held on to it.

Named for their ability to "jam" into the wind when they carried freight up and down the New England coast, windjammers trigger images of the Great Age of Sail. Most are rigged as schooners, with two or three soaring wooden masts; their lengths range from 64 to 132 feet. Nine are National Historic Landmarks; four were built for the trade.

These windjammers head out for 3-6 days, late May-mid-October, tucking into coves and harbors around Penobscot Bay and its islands. The mostly engineless craft set their itineraries by the wind, propelled by stiff breezes to Buck's Harbor, North Haven, and Deer Isle. Everything's totally informal, geared for relaxing.

You're aboard for the experience, not for luxury, so expect basic accommodations with few frills, although newer vessels were built with passenger trade in mind and tend to be a bit more comfy. Down below, cabins typically are small and basic, with paper-thin walls – sort of a campground afloat (earplugs are often available for light sleepers). It may not sound romantic, but be aware that the captains keep track of post-cruise marriages. Most boats have shared showers and toilets. If you're Type-A, given to pacing, don't inflict yourself on the cruising crowd; if you're flexible and ready for whatever, go ahead and sign on. You can help with the sails, eat, curl up with a book, inhale salt air, shoot photos, eat, sunbathe, bird-watch, eat, chat up fellow passengers, sleep, eat, or just settle back and enjoy spectacular sailing you'll never forget.

When you book a cruise, you'll receive all the details and directions, but for a typical six-day trip, you arrive at the boat by 7 P.M. for the captain's call to meet your fellow passengers. You sleep aboard at the dock that night and then depart midmorning Monday and spend five nights and days cruising Penobscot Bay, following the wind, the weather, and the whims of the captain. (Many of the windjammers have no engines, only a motorized yawlboat used as a pusher and a water taxi.) You might anchor in a deserted cove and explore the shore, or you might pull into a harbor and hike, shop, and bar-hop. Then it's back to the boat for chow – windjammer cooks are legendary for creating three hearty, all-you-can-eat meals daily, including at least one lobster feast! When the cruise ends, most passengers find it hard to leave.

On the summer cruising schedule, several weeks coincide with special windjammer events, so you'll need to book a berth far in advance for these: mid-June (Boothbay Harbor's Windjammer Days), July Fourth week (Great Schooner Race), Labor Day weekend (Camden's Windjammer Weekend), and the second week in September (WoodenBoat Sail-In).

Most windjammers offering three- to six-day sails out of Camden, Rockland, and Rockport are members of the **Maine Windjammer Association** (800/807-9463, www.sailmainecoast.com), a one-stop resource for vessel and schedule information. Rates for most schooners begin around $650 for a four-day cruise.

If frigid ocean water doesn't appeal, head for freshwater **Chickawaukee Lake,** on Route 17, two miles inland from downtown Rockland. Don't expect to be alone, though; on hot days, **Johnson Memorial Park**'s pocket-size sand patch is a major attraction. A lifeguard holds forth, and there are restrooms, picnic tables, a snack bar, and a boat-launch ramp. (In winter, iceboats, snowmobiles, and ice-fishing shacks take over the lake.) A signposted bicycle path runs alongside the busy highway, making the park an easy pedal from town.

Golf

The semi-private **Rockland Golf Club** (606 Old County Rd., 207/594-9322, www.rocklandgolf.com, Apr.–Oct.) is an 18-hole course 0.2 mile northeast of Route 17.

For an 18-hole course in an unsurpassed waterfront setting (but with steep rental and greens fees), tee off at the **Samoset Resort** (220 Warrenton St., Rockport, 207/594-2511 or 800/341-1650, www.samoset.com).

Sea Kayaking

Veteran Maine Guide and naturalist Mark DiGirolamo is the sparkplug behind **Breakwater Kayak** (Rockland Public Landing, 207/596-6895 or 877/559-8800, www.breakwaterkayak.com), which has a full range of tours, even multiday ones. A two-hour Rockland Harbor tour (usually offered three times a day at the height of summer) is $50, and the all-day Owls Head Lighthouse tour is $100, including lunch. Reservations are advisable. This outfit is particularly eco-sensitive—Mark has a degree in environmental science—definitely worth supporting. Maine Audubon often taps Mark to lead natural-history field trips. Dress warmly for these tours and be sure to bring a filled water bottle.

Excursion Boats

Marine biologist Captain Bob Pratt is the skipper of ***A Morning in Maine*** (207/594-1844 or 207/691-7245 seasonal boat phone, www.amorninginmaine.com), a classic 55-foot ketch designed by noted naval architect R. D. (Pete) Culler and built by Concordia Yachts. From June through October, *Morning* departs from the middle pier at the Rockland Public Landing three times daily for two-hour sails ($30), with plenty of knowledgeable commentary from Captain Pratt. A 6 P.M. sunset sail is available in July and August. Inquire about boat-and-breakfast overnights, which run $500 per couple and include a sail, lobster dinner, overnight on the boat, and continental breakfast.

Watch Captain Steve Hale set and haul lobster traps during a 1.25-hour cruise aboard the ***Captain Jack*** (Rockland Harbor, 207/594-1048, www.captainjacklobstertours.com), a 30-foot working lobster boat. Cruises depart up to seven times daily, Monday–Saturday May–September; $25 adults, $15 children under 12. Note: There are no toilets aboard. Captain Jack offers a lobster-roll lunch cruise for $45 per person. Reservation required; minimum two people for a trip.

Maine State Ferry Service

Car and passenger ferries service the islands of Vinalhaven, North Haven, and Matinicus. The Vinalhaven and North Haven routes make fantastic day trips (especially with a bike), or you can spend the night; the Matinicus ferry is much less predictable and island services are few.

Bicycling

Rentals ($20), sales, repair, and coffee are provided by **Bikesenjava** (481 Main St., 207/596-1004, www.haybikesenjava.com).

ACCOMMODATIONS

Rates noted are for peak season.

If you're planning an overnight stay in the Rockland area the first weekend in August—during the Maine Lobster Festival—*be sure* to make reservations well in advance. Festival attendance runs close to 100,000, No Vacancy signs extend from Waldoboro to Belfast, and there just aren't enough beds or campsites to go around.

Samoset Resort

The 221-acre waterfront Samoset Resort (220 Warrenton St., Rockport, 207/594-2511 or 800/341-1650, www.samoset.com) straddles the boundary between Rockland and Rockport, the next town to the north. Built on the ashes of a classic 19th-century summer hotel, the Samoset is a top-of-the-line modern resort with knockout ocean views from most of its 178 rooms and suites, all refurbished in

2007 (rates begin around $270), plus 72 separate town houses. Rooms have all the expected bells and whistles, and facilities include indoor and outdoor pools, fitness center, lighted tennis courts, children's day camp ($35, including lunch, ages 5–12), golf simulator, and a fabulous 18-hole waterfront golf course.

Bed-and-Breakfasts

These bed-and-breakfasts are in Rockland's historic district, within easy walking distance of downtown attractions and restaurants, and are members of the **Historic Inns of Rockland Maine** (www.historicinnsofrockland.com), which coordinates the January Pies on Parade event.

Most elegant is **The Berry Manor Inn** (81 Talbot Ave., 207/596-7696 or 800/774-5692, www.berrymanorinn.com, $165–265), on a quiet side street a few blocks from downtown. Cheryl Michaelsen and Michael LaPosta have totally restored the manse built in 1898 by wealthy Rocklander Charles Berry as a wedding gift for his wife (thoughtful fellow). High ceilings and wonderful Victorian architectural touches are everywhere, especially in the enormous front hall and two parlors. Guest rooms and suites are spread between the main house and adjacent carriage house. Most have gas fireplaces and whirlpool tubs. All have air-conditioning, flat-screen TV-DVD, and Wi-Fi. A guest pantry is stocked with free soda and juices and sweets—not that you'll be hungry after the extravagant breakfast.

Opened in 1996, the **Captain Lindsey House Inn** (5 Lindsey St., 207/596-7950 or 800/523-2145, www.lindseyhouse.com, $171–211) is more like a boutique hotel than a bed-and-breakfast. The Barnes family gutted the 1835 brick structure and restored it dramatically, adding such modernities as phones, air-conditioning, Wi-Fi, and TV. The decor is strikingly handsome, not at all fussy or frilly. Don't miss the 1926 safe in the front hall or the hidden-from-the-street garden patio—not to mention the antiques from everywhere that fill the nine comfortable rooms. It's smack downtown, and a few rooms have glimpses of the water. Rates include an extensive hot-and-cold breakfast buffet and afternoon refreshments.

The Limerock Inn (96 Limerock St., 207/594-2257 or 800/546-3762, www.limerockinn.com, $149–229) is a lovely painted lady. The 1890s Queen Anne mansion, with wraparound porch and turret, is listed on the National Historic Register. Each of the eight rooms has its own distinctive flavor—such as the Turret Room with a wedding canopy bed and the Island Cottage Room with a private deck overlooking the back gardens. All are elegantly furnished with an emphasis on guest comfort. Three have whirlpool tubs, one a fireplace; there's Wi-Fi throughout. Breakfast is a treat.

Traveling with Fido and the kiddos? Check into the kid- and pet-friendly **Granite Inn** (546 Main St., Rockland, 800/386-9036, www.oldgraniteinn.com, $150–215), where you can practically roll out of bed and onto an island ferry.

FOOD

Call to verify days and hours of operation.

Local Flavors

A winner for creative breakfasts and lunches is **The Brown Bag** (606 Main St., 207/596-6372 or 800/287-6372, bakery 207/596-6392, 7 A.M.–2:30 P.M., bakery to 4 P.M., Mon.–Sat.). It's *the* place for breakfast, especially weekends, with fantastic baked goods and a full blackboard of other options. Order at the counter; no table service. Find it at the junction of Routes 1 and 17.

Holding down the other end of Main Street is the **Brass Compass Café** (305 Main St., 207/596-5960, 5 A.M.–3 P.M. daily, to 9 P.M. Fri.–Sat.), a great choice for Maine fare. The portions are big, the prices are small, and most of the ingredients are locally sourced. In 2009, celebrity chef Bobby Flay challenged chef-owner Lynn Archer to a lobster club throwdown. Sit indoors or on the dog-friendly patio.

Hot diggity dog! Backed up against an outside wall of The Brown Bag is a longstanding Rockland lunch landmark—**Wasses Hot Dogs** (2 N. Main St., 207/594-7472, 10:30–6 P.M. Mon.–Sat., 11 A.M.–4 P.M. Sun.), source of great chili dogs and creative ice cream (in waffle cones). This onetime lunch wagon is now a permanent modular building—only for takeout, though. It's open all year.

Lots of Rockland-watchers credit Maine's first bookstore-café, **Rock City Books and Coffee** (328 Main St., 207/594-4123, www.rockcitycoffee.com, 6:30 A.M.–8 P.M. Mon.–Sat., from 7 A.M. Sun.), with sparking the designer-food renaissance in town. The menu has expanded greatly since the original coffee, tea, and treats to include frozen drinks, soups, salads, sandwiches, and wraps (including rockin' breakfast wraps, served until 11 A.M.), and plenty of vegetarian choices. Order at the counter and then peruse the shelves of more than 10,000 carefully selected new and "gently used" books while you wait. Frequently there is weekend entertainment.

Scratch-made bread, pastries, and grab-and-go sandwiches have made **Atlantic Baking Co.** (351 Main St., 207/596-0505, www.atlanticbakingco.com, 7 A.M.–6 P.M. Mon.–Sat., 8 A.M.–4 P.M. Sun.) a popular spot for a quick, informal lunch. There are plenty of tables to enjoy your treats, or take it to the waterfront park.

Even closer to Harbor Park is **Sweets & Meats Market** (218 Main St., Rockland, 207/594-2070, www.sweetsandmeatsmarket.com), with a nice selection of sandwiches, including a vegan option, as well as cheeses, meats, and baked goods; there's indoor seating and free Wi-Fi.

If you're craving a decent breakfast or lunch and are up for a little foray "down the peninsula," head for the **Owls Head General Store** (2 S. Shore Dr., Owls Head, 207/596-6038, 6 A.M.–7 P.M. Mon.–Sat., 8 A.M.–3 P.M. Sun.), where the atmosphere is friendly and definitely contagious. If you get lost, the helpful staff will steer you the right way, and they will even take your photograph in front of the store. Despite all the competition from lobster-in-the-rough places, the lobster roll here is among the best around, and more than one critic has proclaimed the burgers the state's best.

The **Rockland Farmers Market** gets underway 9 A.M.–1 P.M. each Thursday June–September at Harbor Park, on Rockland's Public Landing. Wares from more than a dozen vendors include produce, chocolates, crafts, syrup, poultry, mushrooms, baked goods, and cheeses. Every week, there's a special event—music, dancers, lectures, special giveaways, and occasionally a llama or goat for the kids to pet.

Ethnic Fare

Ask local pooh-bah chefs where they go on their night off, and the answer often is Keiko Suzuki Steinberger's **Suzuki's Sushi Bar** (419 Main St., 207/596-7447, www.suzukisushi.com, 11 A.M.–2:30 P.M. and 5–8:30 P.M. Tues.–Sat.). The food matches the decor, simple yet sophisticated. Sashimi, nigiri, *maki,* and *temaki* choices range $6–10; hot entrées are $11–18. Both hot and cold sake are served, or try a saketume, made with gin or vodka, sake, and ume plum. Reservations are essential.

Cassoulet! Moules Provençal! Steak tartare! Chefs Lynette Mosher and Robert Krajewski have created a delicious pocket of France in downtown Rockland at **Lily Bistro** (421 Main St., Rockland, 207/594-4141, www.lilybistromaine.com, 5–9:30 P.M. daily). Most entrées range $16–20.

A small dining area decorated in avocado and gold is the appropriate setting for the Cal-Mex food dished out at **Sunfire Mexican Grill** (488 Main St., 207/594-6196, 11 A.M.–3 P.M. Tues.–Wed., 11 A.M.–3 P.M. and 5–8 P.M. Thurs.–Sat.). You'll find all the usuals, from tacos ($2.95) to a chipotle shrimp tostada ($11.75). Everything is prepared fresh on-site.

When you're *really* famished, the place to go (maybe) is **Conte's Fish Market and Restaurant** (Harbor Park, off Main St., Rockland, no phone), where portions are humongous and prices are not ($10–20). John Conte moved here from New York in 1995, bringing his family's century-old restaurant tradition. Specialties are pasta and seafood—Italian all the way, loaded with garlic. The decor is wildly funky—fishnets, marine relics, old books, even stacks of canned plum tomatoes. Menus are handwritten on paper-towel rolls and in-your-face at the door (order before you sit down), table coverings are yesterday's newspapers, and Edith Piaf chansons or operatic arias sometimes play in the background. Eccentric, unpredictable, not spotless, and definitely not for everyone. Bring your sense of humor and don't be put off by the exterior or the attitude; there's life behind the doors. Beer and wine only. No credit cards. It's open at 4 P.M. daily for dinner, all year (usually, but maybe not). Note: As of early 2010, Conte's future was uncertain; ask locally.

Casual Dining

Big flavors come out of the tiny kitchen at **Café Miranda** (15 Oak St., 207/594-2034, www.cafemiranda.com, 5:30–9 P.M. daily). The menu is overwhelming in size and hard to read, even harder to digest are the flavor contrasts, which will make your brain spin. When it works, it shines, but when it doesn't, it can be painful. Service is irregular. Entrées are $18–27, but many of the appetizers ($6.50–12.50) are enough for a meal. Fresh-from-the-brick-oven focaccia comes with everything. If you sit at the counter, you can watch chef Kerry Altiero's creations emerging from the oven. Beer and wine only. Reservations are essential throughout the summer and on weekends off-season. Patio dining in season.

At the end of a day exploring Rockland, it's hard to beat **In Good Company** (415 Main St., 207/593-9110, from 4:30 P.M. Tues.–Sun., $5–18), a chic and casual wine and tapas bar. Sit at the bar and watch chef-owner Melody Wolfertz, a Culinary Institute of America grad, concoct her creative tapas-style selection of small and large plates. Always a pleasure, and the staff is accommodating and helpful.

Destination Dining

Arriving in Rockland trailing a James Beard Award–winning reputation, chef Melissa Kelly opened **Primo** (Rte. 73, 207/596-0770, www.primorestaurant.com, 5:30–10 P.M. Wed.–Sun.) in the spring of 2000 and hasn't had time to breathe. Since then, she's gone on to open two other restaurants and in 2007 expanded this one in an air-conditioned Victorian home. Fresh local ingredients (many from the restaurant's gardens) are a high priority, and unusual fish specials appear every day. Appetizers are especially imaginative; entrée range is $24–42, but a bar menu with lighter fare and a nightly special also is available ($10–20). Kelly's partner Price Kushner produces an impressive range of breads and desserts. Reservations are essential, usually at least a week ahead on midsummer weekends—and you still may have to wait when you get there. Closed January–May.

INFORMATION AND SERVICES

Information

For information visit the **Penobscot Bay Regional Chamber of Commerce** (Gateway Center, 207/596-0376 or 800/562-2529, www.therealmaine.com, 9 A.M.–5 P.M. Mon.–Fri., 10 A.M.–2 P.M. Sat.) or **Rockland Public Library** (80 Union St., 207/594-0310, www.rocklandlibrary.org).

Public Restrooms

You'll find public restrooms at the Gateway Center; the Knox County Court House, at Union and Masonic Streets; the Rockland Recreation Center, across from the courthouse, next to the playground, at Union and Limerock Streets; the Rockland Public Library; and the Maine State Ferry Service terminal.

GETTING AROUND

All Aboard Trolley Co. (207/594-9300 or 866/594-9300, www.aatrolley.com) offers 40-minute narrated sightseeing tours of downtown Rockland ($8 adults, free children under 12) departing from the Penobscot Bay Regional Chamber of Commerce at the Gateway Center about six times daily.

Vinalhaven and North Haven Islands

Vinalhaven and neighboring North Haven have been known as the Fox Islands ever since 1603, when English explorer Martin Pring sailed these waters and allegedly spotted gray foxes in his search for sustenance. Nowadays, you'll find reference to that name only on nautical charts, identifying the passage between the two islands as the Fox Islands Thorofare—and there's nary a fox in sight.

Each island has its own distinct personality. To generalize, Vinalhaven is the largest and busiest, while North Haven is sedate and exclusive.

VINALHAVEN

Five miles wide, 7.5 miles long, and covering 10,000 acres, Vinalhaven is 13 miles off the coast of Rockland—a 75-minute ferry trip. The shoreline has so many zigs and zags that no place on the island is more than a mile from water.

The island is famed for its granite. The first blocks headed for Boston around 1826, and within a few decades quarrymen arrived from as far away as Britain and Finland to wrestle out and shape the incredibly resistant stone. Schooners, barges, and "stone sloops" left Carver's Harbor carrying mighty cargoes of granite destined for government and commercial buildings in Boston, New York, and Washington, D.C. In the 1880s, nearly 4,000 people lived on Vinalhaven, North Haven, and Hurricane Island. After World War I, demand declined, granite gave way to concrete and steel, and the industry petered out and died. But Vinalhaven has left its mark in ornate columns, paving blocks, and curbstones in communities as far west as Kansas City.

With a full-time population of about 1,300 souls, Vinalhaven is a serious working community, not primarily a playground. Nearly 600 island residents depend on the lobster and

Working boats far outnumber pleasure craft in Vinalhaven's Carver's Harbor.

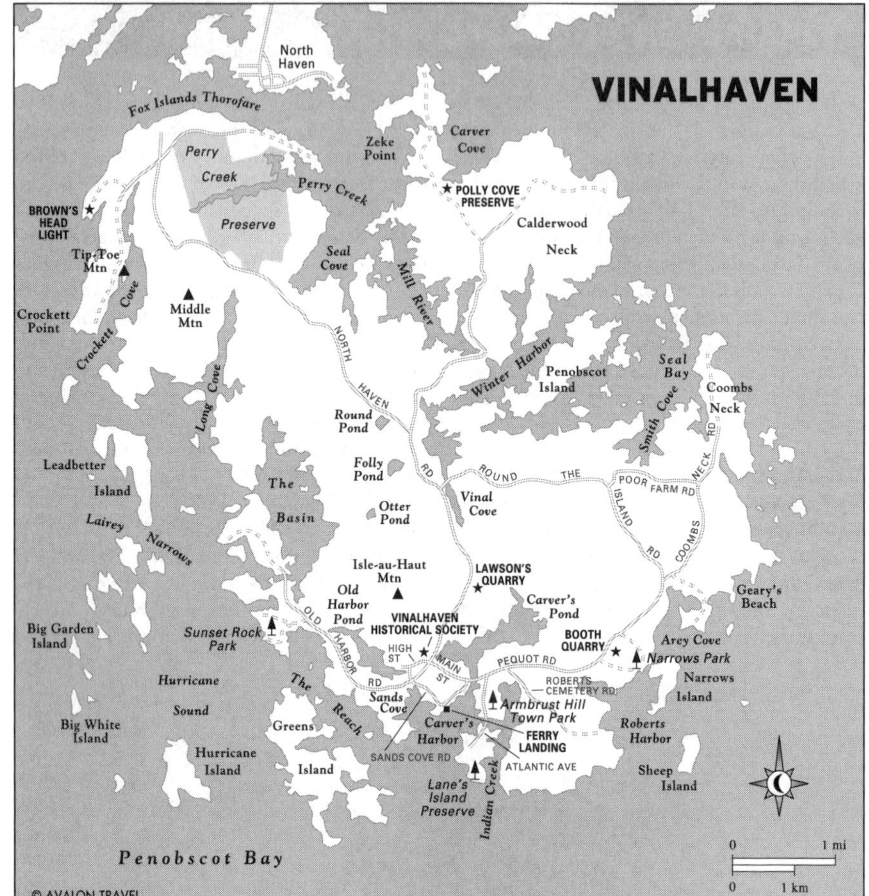

fishing industry. Shopkeepers cater to locals as well as visitors, and increasing numbers of artists and artisans work away in their studios. For day-trippers, there's plenty to do—shopping, picnicking, hiking, biking, swimming—but an overnight stay provides a chance to sense the unique rhythm of life on a year-round island.

Sights

One Main Street landmark that's hard to miss is the three-story cupola-topped **Odd Fellows Hall,** a Victorian behemoth with American flag motifs on the lower windows and assorted gewgaws in the upper ones. Artist Robert Indiana, who first arrived as a visitor in 1969, owns the structure, built in 1885 for the IOOF Star of Hope Lodge. It's not open to the public.

At the top of the hill just beyond Main Street (corner of School and E. Main Sts.) is a greenish-blue replica **galamander,** a massive reminder of Vinalhaven's late-19th-century granite-quarrying era. Galamanders, hitched to oxen or horses, carried the stone from island quarries to the finishing shops. (By the way, the origin of the name remains unexplained.) Next to the galamander is a colorful wooden bandstand, site of very popular evening band concerts held sporadically during the summer.

The **Vinalhaven Historical Society** (207/863-4410, www.vinalhavenhistoricalsociety.org, noon–5 P.M. daily July and Aug. or by appt., free) operates a delightful museum in the onetime town hall on High Street, just east of Carver's Cemetery. The building itself has a tale, having been floated across the bay from Rockland, where it served as a Universalist church. The museum's documents and artifacts on the granite industry are particularly intriguing, and special summer exhibits add to the interest. Donations are welcomed. At the museum, request a copy of *A Self-Guided Walking Tour of the Town of Vinalhaven and Its Granite-Quarrying History,* a handy little brochure that details 17 intown locations related to the late-19th and early-20th-century industry.

Built in 1832 and now owned by the town of Vinalhaven, **Brown's Head Light** guards the southern entrance to the Fox Islands Thorofare. To reach the grounds (no access to the light itself; the keeper's house is a private residence for the town manager), take the North Haven Road about six miles, at which point you'll see a left-side view of the Camden Hills. Continue about another mile to the second road on the left, Crockett River Road. Turn and take the second road on the right, continuing past the Brown's Head Cemetery to the hill overlooking the lighthouse.

Entertainment

No one visits Vinalhaven for nightlife, but concerts (Fox Island series and others), films, and lectures (most organized by the Vinalhaven Land Trust or the Vinalhaven Historical Society) are frequent. Check *The Wind* to see what's on the docket during your visit.

The Saturday-morning anything-goes flea markets are an island must, as much for the browsing and buying as for the gossip.

Brown's Head Light marks the entrance to the Fox Islands Thorofare.

Shopping

Vinalhaven's shops change regularly, but here are a few that have withstood the test of time. **The Paper Store** (Vinal's News Stand, Main St., 207/863-4826) carries newspapers, gifts, film, maps, and odds and ends. **Five Elements Gallery + Studio** (Main St., 207/863-2262) is filled with artist-owner Alison Thibault's jewelry creations and other finds. **New Era Gallery** (Main St., 207/863-9351, www.neweragallery.com) has a well-chosen selection of art in varied media representing primarily island artisans. Don't miss the sculpture garden. A few doors away is **Second Hand Prose,** a used books store run by the Friends of the Vinalhaven Public Library. On the stretch of road between the ferry dock and downtown, **Vinalhaven Candy Co.** (Harbor Wharf, 33 West Main St., 207/863-2031) is a pleaser for both kids and adults.

Parks and Preserves

Vinalhaven is loaded with wonderful hikes and

walks, some deliberately unpublicized. Since the mid-1980s, the foresighted **Vinalhaven Land Trust** (207/863-2543, www.vinalhavenlandtrust.org) has expanded the opportunities. When you reach the island, pick up maps at the land trust's office at **Skoog Memorial Park** (Sands Cove Road, west of the ferry terminal) or inquire at the town office or the Paper Store. The trust also offers a seasonal series of educational walks and talks.

Some hiking options are the Perry Creek Preserve (terrific loop trail), Middle Mountain Park, Tip-Toe Mountain, Polly Cove Preserve, Isle au Haut Mountain, Arey's Neck Woods, Huber Preserve, and Sunset Rock Park.

The Maine chapter of the **Nature Conservancy** (207/729-5181) owns or manages several islands and island clusters near Vinalhaven. **Big Garden** (formerly owned by Charles and Anne Morrow Lindbergh) and **Big White Islands** are easily accessible and great for shoreline picnics if you have your own boat. Other Conservancy holdings in this area are fragile environments, mostly nesting islands off-limits mid-March–mid-August. Contact the Conservancy for specifics.

No, you're not on the moors of Devon, but you could be fooled in the 45-acre **Lane's Island Preserve,** one of the Nature Conservancy's most-used island preserves. Masses of low-lying ferns, rugosa roses, and berry bushes cover the granite outcrops of this sanctuary—and a foggy day makes it even more moorlike and mystical, a Brontë novel setting. The best (albeit busiest) time to come is early August, when you can compete with the birds for blackberries, raspberries, and blueberries. Easy trails wind past old stone walls, an aged cemetery, and along the surf-pounded shore. The preserve is a 20-minute walk (or five-minute bike ride) from Vinalhaven's ferry landing. Set off to the right on Main Street, through the village. Turn right onto Water Street and then right on Atlantic Avenue. Continue across the causeway on Lane's Island Road and left over a salt marsh to the preserve. The large white house on the harbor side of Lane's Island is privately owned.

Next to the ferry landing in Carver's Harbor is **Grimes Park,** a wooded vest-pocket retreat with a splendid view of the harbor. Owned by the American Legion, the 2.5-acre park is perfect for picnics or for hanging out (especially in good weather) between boats.

Just behind the Island Community Medical Center, close to downtown, is 30-acre **Armbrust Hill Town Park,** once the site of granite-quarrying operations. Still pockmarked with quarry pits, the park has beautifully landscaped walking paths and native flowers, shrubs, and trees—much of it thanks to late island resident Betty Roberts, who made this a lifelong endeavor. From the back of the medical center, follow the trail to the summit for a southerly view of Matinicus and other offshore islands. If you're with children, be especially careful about straying onto side paths, which go perilously close to old quarry holes. Before the walk, lower the children's energy level at the large playground off to the left of the trail.

Recreation

SWIMMING

Abandoned quarries are all over the island, and most are on private property, but two town-owned ones are easy to reach from the ferry landing. **Lawson's Quarry,** on the North Haven Road, is one mile from downtown on the North Haven Road; **Booth Quarry** is 1.6 miles from downtown via East Main Street. Both are signposted. You'll see plenty of sunbathers on the rocks and swimmers on a hot day, but there are no lifeguards, so swimming is at your own risk. There are no restrooms or changing rooms. *Note:* Pets and soap are not allowed in the water; camping, fires, and alcohol are not allowed in the quarry areas.

Down the side road beyond Booth Quarry is **Narrows Park,** a town-owned space looking out toward Narrows Island, Isle au Haut, and, on a clear day, Mount Desert Island.

For saltwater swimming, take East Main

Street 2.4 miles from downtown to a crossroads, where you'll see a whimsical bit of local folk art—the Coke lady sculpture. Turn right (east) and go a half mile to **Geary's Beach** (also called **State Beach**), where you can picnic and scour the shoreline for shells and sea glass.

BICYCLING

Even though Vinalhaven's 40 or so miles of public roads are narrow, winding, and poorly shouldered, they're relatively level, so a bicycle is a fine way to tour the island. Bring your own, preferably a hybrid or mountain bike, or rent one at the **Tidewater Motel** (207/863-4618) on Main Street ($15 per day). A wide selection of rental bikes is available on the mainland in Rockport at **Maine Sport Outfitters** (Rte. 1, Rockport, 207/236-8797 or 888/236-8796), but you have to pay extra to bring a bike on the ferry.

A 10-mile, 2.5-hour bicycle route begins on Main Street and goes clockwise out the North Haven Road (rough pavement), past Lawson's Quarry, to Round the Island Road (some sections are dirt), then Poor Farm Road to Geary's Beach and back to Main Street via Pequot Road and School Street. Carry a picnic and enjoy it on Lane's Island; stop for a swim in one of the quarries; or detour down to Brown's Head Light. If you're here for the day, keep track of the time so you don't miss the ferry.

Far more rewarding view-wise, and far shorter, is the one-way-and-back pedal out the Old Harbor Road to The Basin, which is rich in bird and wildlife and serves as a seal nursery. There's also a nice trail at the road's end to The Basin's shorefront and across to an island; ask Phil at the Tidewater Motel for directions.

SEA KAYAKING

Sea kayak rentals are available at the Tidewater Motel for $25 per day including delivery. A guide can be arranged, but it's not necessary to have one to poke around the harbor or, even better, paddle through The Basin, which is especially popular with bird- and wildlife-watchers.

BIRD- AND WILDLIFE-WATCHING

Expert bird guide **John Drury** (207/596-1841, $280) takes bird- and wildlife-watchers on 3.5-hour cruises to spy gannets, Arctic terns, puffins, eagles, and seals. Sightings have even included minke whales and albatross.

Accommodations

If you're planning on staying overnight, don't even consider arriving in summer without reservations. If you're going for the day, pay attention to the ferry schedule and allow enough time to get back to the boat. Islanders may be able to find you a bed in a pinch, but don't count on it. The island has no campsites. Rates listed are for peak season.

Your feet practically touch the water when you spend the night at the **Tidewater Motel and Gathering Space** (12 Main St., Carver's Harbor, 207/863-4618, www.tidewatermotel.com, $165–295), a well-maintained motel in two buildings cantilevered over the harbor. Owned by Phil and Elaine Crossman (she operates the New Era Gallery down the street), the 19-room motel was built by Phil's parents in 1970. It's the perfect place to sit on the deck and watch the lobster boats do their thing. Be aware, though, that commercial fishermen are early risers, and lobster-boat engines can rev up as early as 4:30 on a summer morning—all part of the pace of Vinalhaven. Phil is practically a one-man chamber of commerce. He can recommend hikes and other activities and, since he maintains the island's calendar of events, he always knows what's happening and when. A continental breakfast and use of bicycles are included in the rates; rental sea kayaks are available. Kids 10 and under are free; seven units are efficiencies. It's open all year. Also on the premises is **Island Spirits,** a small gourmet-foods store stocked with wines, beers, cheeses, breads, and other goodies, even picnic baskets to pack it all in. About once a month, the motel hosts a wine tasting in the 2nd-floor Gathering Space, overlooking the harbor. If

© HILARY NANGLE

The Tidewater Motel hangs over Vinalhaven's Carver's Harbor, delivering guests a front-row seat on the action.

you want to get a better sense of island life, pick up a copy of Phil's book *Away Happens,* a collection of humorous essays about island living. You can see a sample from it on the motel's website.

Also convenient to downtown is **The Libby House** (Water St., 207/863-4696, www.libbyhouse1869.com, $75–140), with a two-bedroom apartment and five rooms, three sharing one bath. No breakfast.

Food

Hours listed are for peak season. Expect reduced hours and fewer days of operation at other times.

Baked bean suppers are regularly held at a couple of island locations. Check *The Wind.*

On the harborfront a few minutes walk from the ferry terminal is **Greet's Eats,** a fair-weather takeout for lobster and crab rolls as well as burgers and hot dogs.

The island's best breakfast place is **Surfside** (Harbor Wharf, 207/863-2767, 4 A.M.–1:30 P.M. Mon.–Fri., 4–11 A.M. Sat.–Sun.). Eat inside or on the wharf. The fishcakes earn their raves and are always available on Sundays. It *may* also be open for dinner.

In the morning, **Island Coffee House** (30 Main St., 207/863-4311, 4 A.M.–noon Mon.–Sat., 5–11 A.M. Sun.) serves scrumptious baked goods. In the evening it morphs into **The Pizza Pit** (4–8 P.M. Thurs.–Sun.) serving pizza, wings, pastas, quesadillas, and similar fare; BYOB.

Craving a cappuccino or latte? Vinalhaven's student-run **ARCafé** (39 High St., 207/863-4191, 7 A.M.–6:30 P.M. Mon.–Fri., 10 A.M.–4 P.M. Sat.), next door to the historical society, is the island's best coffee source and provides free Internet access.

Good lunch options are the **Harbor Gawker** (Main St., 207/863-9365, 11 A.M.–8 P.M. Mon.–Sat.), a local landmark since 1975, but now with a nice indoor dining area; **Trickerville Sandwich Shop** (Atlantic St., 207/863-9344, 5 A.M.–4 P.M. Mon.–Sat., 11 A.M.–4 P.M. Sun.), with a few tables inside and out, but no views (lobster dinners served some evenings, ask); and **The Sand Bar** (Main St., 207/863-4500, 11 A.M.–9 P.M. Tues.–Sun.), which has a full bar as well as a good menu of pub-style favorites, soups, salads, and pizza.

For casual dining, book a table at **The Haven Restaurant** (Main St., 207/863-4969), with two options: Harborside (Tues.–Sat., seatings at 6 and 8:15 P.M.) delivers on its name and serves a creative menu that changes nightly. Streetside (6:30–9 P.M., closed Tues.) doesn't take reservations and serves pub-style fare. The restaurant is a one-woman show, and Torry Pratt doubles as a popular local caterer, so it's wise to call.

Newer on the scene is **64 Main** (64 Main St., 207/863-4464, 5:30–9 P.M. Wed.–Sat.), where chef Brett Ackerman draws on his experience at New York City's Union Square Café to create updated versions of vaguely familiar classics. Entrées run $16–20.

Information and Services

Vinalhaven Chamber of Commerce (www.vinalhaven.org) produces a useful little flyer-map showing locations in the Carver's Harbor area. Also helpful for trip planning is a guidebook published by Phil Crossman at the Tidewater Motel (207/863-4618, $3.50). On the island, pick up a copy of Vinalhaven's weekly newsletter, *The Wind,* named after the island's original newspaper, first published in 1884. It's loaded with island flavor: news items, public-supper announcements, editorials, and ads. A year's subscription is $50; free single copies are available at most downtown locales.

Check out the Vinalhaven Public Library (E. Main and Chestnut Sts., 207/863-4401).

Public restrooms are at the ferry landing and the town office (weekdays only).

Getting Around

I can't emphasize this enough: Don't bring a car unless it is absolutely necessary. If you're coming over for a day trip, you can get to parks and quarries, shops, restaurants, and the historical society museum on foot. If you want to explore farther, a bicycle is an excellent option, or you can rent a car or reserve a taxi through the Tidewater Motel (207/863-4618), or Phil will meet you at the ferry landing. Call well ahead to reserve.

NORTH HAVEN

Eight miles long by three miles wide, North Haven is 12 miles off the coast of Rockland—an hour by ferry. The island has sedate summer homes, open fields where hundreds of sheep once grazed, about 350 year-round residents, a yacht club called the Casino, and a village gift shop that's been here since 1954.

Originally called North Island, North Haven had much the same settlement history as Vinalhaven, but, being smaller (about 5,280 acres) and more fertile, it has developed—or not developed—differently. In 1846, North Haven was incorporated and severed politically from Vinalhaven, and by the late 1800s, the Boston summer crowd began buying traditional island homes, building tastefully unpretentious new ones, and settling in for a whole season of sailing and socializing. Several generations later, "summer folk" now come for weeks rather than months, often rotating the schedules among slews of siblings. Informality remains the key, though—now more than ever.

The island has two distinct hamlets—North Haven Village, on the Fox Islands Thorofare, where the state ferry arrives, and Pulpit Harbor, particularly popular with the yachting set. The village is easily explored on foot in a morning.

North Haven doesn't offer a lot for the day visitor, and islanders tend not to welcome them with open arms.

Entertainment

Waterman's Community Center (Main St., 207/867-2100, www.watermans.org) provides a place for island residents and visitors to gather for entertainment, events, and even coffee and gossip. It's home to North Haven Arts & Enrichment. Check the schedule on its website to see what's planned.

© HILARY NANGLE

North Haven's ferry dock is smack downtown.

Shopping

Fanning out from the ferry landing is a delightful cluster of substantial year-round clapboard homes—a marked contrast to the weathered-shingle cottages typical of so many island communities. It won't take long to stroll and shop Main Street.

Anchoring the handful of "downtown" shops and galleries is the **North Haven Gift Shop** (Main St., 207/867-4444), a rabbit warren of rooms that June Hopkins has been running since 1954. You'll have no problem spending money here—everything's tastefully selected, from the pottery to the notecards to the books, jewelry, and gourmet condiments. One room is a gallery with work by Maine artists.

Next door (connected via an elevated corridor) is the **Eric Hopkins Gallery** (Main St., 207/867-2229), owned by June Hopkins's son, a mega-talented painter who's gained repute far beyond Maine. If you can't spring for an original (figure on several thousand dollars), his distinctive work—luminous bird's-eye views of island, sea, and forest—now appears also on notecards, postcards, T-shirts, and one-of-a-kind sweaters. It's open by chance or appointment.

On the main floor of the four-story early-20th-century Calderwood Hall is **North Island Fiber Shop** (Main St.), a huge draw for knitters and hookers. It sells all-natural Maine-made yarns as well as wonderful creations, including quilts, throws, baskets, even candles and pottery, all crafted by Maine artists and artisans. Upstairs is **Herb Parsons Gallery.**

Recreation

North Haven has about 25 miles of paved roads that are conducive to bicycling, but, just as on most other islands, they are narrow, winding, and nearly shoulderless. Starting near the ferry landing in North Haven Village, take South Shore Road eastward, perhaps stopping en route for a picnic at town-owned Mullin's Head Park (also spelled Mullen Head) on the southeast corner of the island. Then follow the road around, counterclockwise, to North Shore Road and Pulpit Harbor.

Accommodations

Within walking distance of the ferry is **Nebo**

© HILARY NANGLE

Renowned artist Eric Hopkins maintains a gallery on North Haven.

Lodge (11 Mullins La., 207/867-2007, www.nebolodge.com, $125–250). Nine rooms (four year-round), some with shared baths, are decorated with island art and many have rugs by Angela Adams. There's Wi-Fi throughout. Rates include a full breakfast and use of inn bikes.

Food

Stop into **Waterman's Coffee Shop** (Waterman Center, 207/867-2100, 7 A.M.–4 P.M. Mon.–Sat., 11:30 A.M.–4 P.M. Sun.) for coffee and sweets and local news.

For a casual meal, on the deck, inside, or take-away (if you've come for the morning, pick up a sandwich for the return ferry), slip into **Sip Ahoy** (207/867-2060, 11 A.M.–11 P.M. daily). For a sit-down meal with a view, head for the **Coal Wharf at H. P. Blake's** (Main St., 207/867-4739, 11 A.M.–11 P.M. daily July–Aug.); it's at Brown's Boatyard. Dinner also is available at **Nebo Lodge** (11 Mullins La., 207/867-2007, www.nebolodge.com).

Information

The best source of information about North Haven is the North Haven Town Office (Upper Main St., 207/867-4433, www.northhavenmaine.org).

GETTING THERE

The Maine State Ferry Service (207/596-2202, www.exploremaine.com) operates six round-trips daily between Rockland and Vinalhaven (75-minute crossing) in summer and three round-trips between Rockland and North Haven (70-minute crossing). Round-trip tickets are $17.50 adults, $8.50 children. Both ferries take cars ($49.50 round-trip, plus $14 reservation fee), but a bicycle ($16.50 round-trip per adult bike, $9.50 per child bike) will do fine unless you have the time or inclination to see every corner of the island. Getting car space on the ferry during midsummer can be a frustrating—and complicated—experience, so *avoid taking a car to the island.* Give yourself time to find a parking space and perhaps to walk from it to the terminal. If you leave a car at the Rockland lot (space is limited and availability varies), it's $10 per 24 hours or $50 per week. You can also park on some of Rockland's side streets and walk, or, for a day trip, in the city lot between Main Street and the water or Harbor Park.

No official ferry service travels between Vinalhaven and North Haven, even though the two islands are almost within spitting distance. Fortunately, the J. O. Brown and Sons boat shop on North Haven provides shuttles 7 A.M.–5 P.M. Call the boat shop (207/867-4621) to arrange a pickup on the Vinalhaven side. Fee is $5 per person round trip. (A handy outdoor pay phone is at the north end of Vinalhaven—at the end of the North Haven Road.) Don't let anyone convince you to return to Rockland for the ferry to North Haven.

Penobscot Island Air (207/596-7500, www.penobscotislandair.net) flies twice daily to Vinalhaven and North Haven, weather permitting, from Knox County Regional Airport in Owls Head, just south of Rockland. Seat availability is dependent on mail volume.

Greater Camden

Camden, flanked by **Rockport** to the south and **Lincolnville** to the north, is one of the Mid-Coast's—even Maine's—prime destinations.

Camden (pop. 5,300), the better known of the three, typifies Maine nationwide, even worldwide, on calendars and postcards, in photo books, you name it. Much of its appeal is its drop-dead-gorgeous setting—a deeply indented harbor with parks, a waterfall, and a dramatic backdrop of low mountains. That harbor is a summer-long madhouse, jammed with dinghies, kayaks, windjammers, mega-yachts, minor yachts, and a handful of fishing craft.

Driven apart by a local squabble in 1891, Camden and Rockport (pop. 3,500) have been separate towns for more than a century, but they're inextricably linked. They share school and sewer systems and an often-hyphenated partnership. On Union Street, just off Route 1, a white wooden arch reads Camden on one side and Rockport on the other. Rockport has a much lower profile, and its harbor is relatively peaceful—with yachts, lobster boats, and a single windjammer schooner.

Two distinct enclaves make up Lincolnville (pop. 2,000): oceanfront Lincolnville Beach ("the Beach") and, about five miles inland, Lincolnville Center ("the Center"). Lincolnville is laid-back and mostly rural; the major activity center is a short strip of shops and restaurants at the Beach, and few visitors realize there's anything else.

SIGHTS

Self-Guided Historical Tour

Historic Downtown Camden is an illustrated map and brochure detailing historical sites and businesses in and around downtown. To cover it all, you'll want a car or bike; to cover segments and really appreciate the architecture, don your walking shoes. Pick up a copy of the brochure at the chamber of commerce.

Old Conway Homestead and Cramer Museum

Just inside the Camden town line from Rockport, the Old Conway Homestead and Cramer Museum (Conway Rd., Camden, 207/236-2257, www.crmuseum.org, 11 A.M.–3 P.M. Tues.–Fri. July–Aug., $5 adults, $2 children) is a six-building complex owned and run by the Camden-Rockport Historical Society. The 18th-century Cape-style Conway House, on the National Register of Historic Places, contains fascinating construction details and period furnishings; in the barn are carriages and farm tools. Two other buildings—a blacksmith shop and a 19th-century sap house used for making maple syrup—have been moved to the grounds and restored. In the contemporary Mary Meeker Cramer Museum (named for the prime benefactor) are displays from the historical society's collection of ship models, old documents, and period clothing. For local color, don't miss the Victorian outhouse. Also here is an education center for workshops and seminars. The museum and sap house are also open for maple-syrup demonstrations on Maine Maple Sunday (fourth Sunday in March).

Vesper Hill

Built and donated to the community by a local benefactor, the rustic open-air **Vesper Hill Children's Chapel** is dedicated to the world's children. Overlooking Penobscot Bay and surrounded by gardens and lawns, the nondenominational chapel is an almost mystical oasis in a busy tourist region. Except during weddings or memorial services, there's seldom a crowd, and if you're lucky, you might have the place to yourself. From Central Street in downtown Rockport, take Russell Avenue east to Calderwood Lane (fourth street on right). On Calderwood, take the second right (Chapel St.) after the

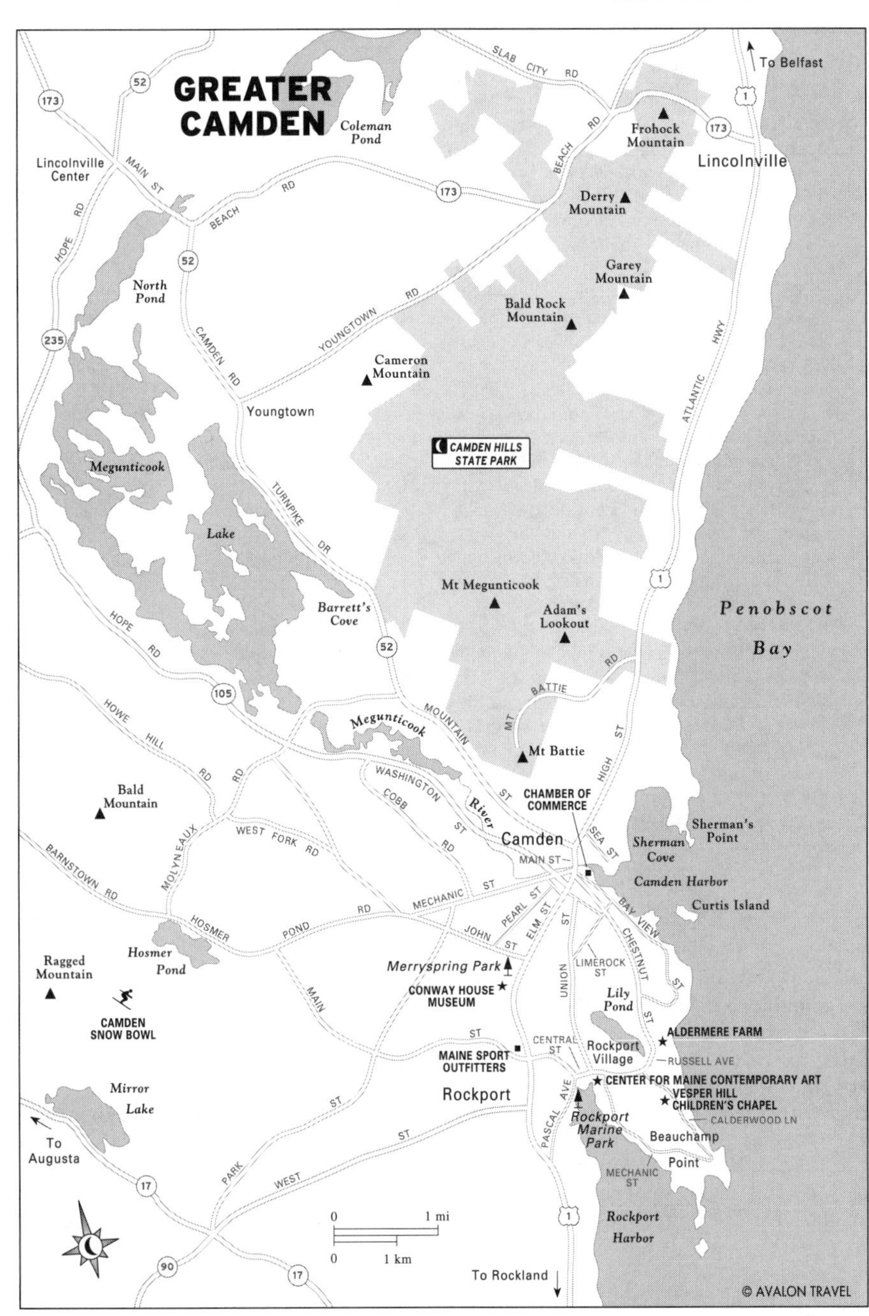

PENOBSCOT BAY

ISLESBORO

Lying three miles offshore from Lincolnville Beach, via 20-minute car ferry, is 12-mile-long Islesboro, a year-round community with a population of about 600 – beefed up annually by a sedate summer colony. Car ferries are frequent enough to make Islesboro an ideal day-trip destination – and that's the choice of most visitors, partly because food options are few and overnight lodging isn't available. The only camping is on nearby Warren Island State Park – and you have to have your own boat to get there.

The best way to get an island overview is to do an end-to-end auto or bike tour. Pick up an island map at the ferry terminal and explore, heading down to Dark Harbor and Town Beach at the island's bottom then up to Pripet and Turtle Head at its top. You won't see all the huge "cottages" tucked down long driveways, and you won't absorb island life and its rhythms, but you'll scratch the surface of what Islesboro is about.

En route, you'll pass exclusive summer estates, workaday homes, spectacular seaside vistas, a smattering of shops, and the **Historical Society Museum** (388 Main St., 207/734-6744, 12:30-4:30 P.M. Sat.-Wed., July-Aug. and by appt.). On the up-island circuit, watch for a tiny marker on the west side of the road (0.8 mile north of the Islesboro Historical Society building). It commemorates the 1780 total eclipse witnessed here – the first recorded in North America. At the time, British loyalists still held Islesboro, but they temporarily suspended hostilities, allowing Harvard astronomers to lug their instruments to the island and document the eclipse.

Allow time before the return ferry to visit the **Sailors' Memorial Museum,** a town-owned museum filled with seafaring memorabilia and allegedly home to a benevolent ghost or two. It's in the keeper's house adjacent to **Grindle Point Light** (207/734-2253, www.lighthouse.cc/grindle), built in 1850, rebuilt in 1875, and now automated.

The car ferry *Margaret Chase Smith* (207/789-5611, Islesboro 207/734-6935, www.exploremaine.org) departs Lincolnville Beach almost every hour on the hour, 8 or 9 A.M. to 5 P.M., and Islesboro on the half hour, 7:30 A.M.-4:30 P.M. Round-trip fares are $25 for car, $8.50 adults, $3.25 children, $7 adult bicycles, and $4 child bikes. Reservations are $5 extra. A slightly reduced schedule prevails late October-early May. The 20-minute trip crosses a stunning three-mile stretch of Penobscot Bay, with views of islands and the Camden Hills. In summer, avoid the biggest bottlenecks: Friday afternoon (to Islesboro), and Sunday afternoon and Monday holiday afternoons (from Islesboro). The *Smith* remains on Islesboro overnight, so don't miss the last run to Lincolnville Beach.

(private) golf course. If the sign is down, look for a boulder with Vesper Hill carved in it. From downtown Camden, take Chestnut Street to just past Aldermere Farm; turn left at Calderwood Lane and take the second right after the golf course.

Aldermere Farm (20 Russell Ave., Rockport, 207/236-2739, www.aldermere.org), by the way, is the home of America's original herd of Belted Galloway cattle—Angus-like beef cattle with a wide white midriff. First imported from Scotland in 1953, the breed now shows up in pastures all over the United States. The animals' startling "Oreo-cookie" hide pattern never fails to halt passersby—especially in spring and early summer, when the calves join their mothers in the pastures. Maine Coast Heritage Trust, a state conservation organization based in Brunswick, owns the 136-acre farm. Call for information on tours or other events.

Center for Maine Contemporary Art

Once a local firehouse, this attractive building has been totally rehabbed to provide display space for the work of Maine's best contemporary artists. The nonprofit Center for Maine Contemporary Art (62 Russell Ave., Rockport, 207/236-2875, www.artsmaine.org, 10 A.M.–5 P.M. Tues.–Sat., 1–5 P.M. Sun., $5) mounts as many as a dozen shows each summer, along with special lectures, a wildly popular art auction (early August), an annual juried art exhibition featuring more than 100 selections, and an annual juried craft show (mid-October) spotlighting several dozen artisans. An exceptional gift shop carries high-end crafts.

ENTERTAINMENT

At 8 P.M. Wednesday and Thursday in July and August, and once a month the rest of the year, **Bay Chamber Concerts** (207/236-2823 or 888/707-2770, www.baychamberconcerts.org) draw sell-out audiences to the beautifully restored (and air-conditioned) Rockport Opera House and Rockland's Strand Theatre. Founded in the 1960s as a classical series, the summer concerts feature a resident quartet, prominent guest artists, and outstanding programs. It has expanded to include world music, jazz, and dance. The first week in August ("Next Generation Week") is devoted to classes and concerts for and by talented teenagers. Seats are reserved for summer concerts ($25–34 adults, $8 children 18 and younger, plus $5 processing fee per order); open seating is the rule in winter, when tickets are less expensive and programs vary from classical to pops to jazz. (Season tickets and flex passes are available.)

The beautifully renovated **Camden Opera House** (29 Elm St., Camden, 207/236-7963, box office 207/236-4884, www.camdenoperahouse.com) is the site of many performances by renowned performers.

The Lincolnville Band, one of the oldest town bands in the country, often plays in the park's Bicentennial Bandstand, built to commemorate the town's 200th birthday.

FESTIVALS AND EVENTS

One weekend in February is given over to the **Camden Conference,** an annual three-day foreign-affairs conference with nationally and internationally known speakers. The first weekend in February marks the **National Toboggan Championships,** two days of races and fun at the nation's only wooden toboggan chute at the Camden Snow Bowl.

The third Thursday of July is **House and Garden Day,** when you can take a self-guided tour (10 A.M.–4:30 P.M.) of significant homes and gardens in Camden and Rockport. Proceeds benefit the Camden Garden Club. **HarborArts,** on the third weekend in July, draws dozens of artists and craftspeople displaying and selling their wares at the Camden Amphitheatre, Harbor Park.

Labor Day weekend is also known as **Windjammer Weekend** here, with cruises, windjammer open houses, fireworks, and all kinds of live entertainment in and around Camden Harbor. Twenty top artisans open their studios for the annual **Country Roads Artists and Artisans Tour** in September.

Dozens of artists and craftspeople display and sell their wares at the **Fall Festival and Arts and Crafts Show,** the first weekend in October at the Camden Amphitheatre, Harbor Park.

A who's who of entrepreneurs show up for the annual **PopTech** conference in late October.

Christmas by the Sea is a family-oriented early-December weekend featuring open houses, special sales, concerts, and a visit from Santa Claus.

SHOPPING

New and Old Books

The Owl and Turtle Bookshop (32 Washington St., Camden, 207/236-4769 or 800/876-4769), one of Maine's best independent new-books stores, has thousands of books and a wonderful children's room. It's just off Main Street in the Knox Mill Center.

Another source for books and a whole lot more is **Sherman's** (Main St., Camden, 207/236-2223), part of a small Maine chain.

If you want a good read at a great price, **Stone Soup Books** (33 Main St., Camden, no phone), a tiny 2nd-floor shop across from the Lord Camden Inn, is Camden's best source for contemporary used fiction.

Dolls

Antique and hand-crafted museum-quality dolls and doll houses fill **Lucy's Doll House** (49 Bay View St., Camden, 207/236-4122).

Art, Crafts, and Gifts

You'll need to wander the streets to take in all the gift and craft shops, particularly in Camden. Some are obvious; others are tucked away on side streets and back alleys. Explore.

A downtown Camden landmark since 1940, **The Smiling Cow** (41 Main St., Camden, 207/236-3351 or 800/646-6169) is as good a place as any to pick up Maine souvenirs—a few slightly kitschy, but most reasonably tasteful. Before or after shopping here, head for the rear balcony for coffee and a knockout view of the harbor and the Megunticook River waterfall.

Also downtown is **Ducktrap Bay Trading Co.** (37 Bayview St., Camden, 207/236-9568), source of decoys, wildlife, and marine art and other fine craft.

Just off Route 90, less than two miles from the Rockport intersection with Route 1, is **Carver Hill Gallery** (264 Meadow St., Rockport, 207/236-0745, www.carverhillgallery.com), exhibiting fine art and craft in a center-chimney cape, barn, and gardens.

At **Danica Candleworks** (Rte. 90, West Rockport, 207/236-3060), owner Erik Laustsen learned the hand-dipping trade from his Danish relatives.

The **Messler Gallery** (25 Mill St., Rockport, 207/594-5611), just off Route 90 and on the campus of the Center for Furniture Craftsmanship, presents rotating shows that focus on woodworking.

Handsome dark wood buildings 0.2 mile north of the Beach are home to **Windsor Chairmakers** (Rte. 1, Lincolnville, 207/789-5188 or 800/789-5188). You can observe the operation, browse the display area, or order some of the well-made chairs, cabinets, and tables.

Professional boatbuilder Walt Simmons has branched out into decoys and wildlife carvings, and they're just as outstanding as his boats. Walt and his wife, Karen, run **Duck Trap Decoys** (Duck Trap Rd., Lincolnville, 207/789-5363), a gallery-shop that also features the work of nearly five dozen other woodcarvers.

It's a lot easier to get soft, wonderful handwoven and hand-dyed **Swans Island Blankets** (231 Rte. 1, Northport, 297/338-9691) since the company moved its sales operation off the island near Mount Desert to the mainland, just 2.7 miles north of Lincolnville Beach. Such quality comes at a sky-high price.

Wine

Gaze out the backdoor of the **Cellardoor Vineyard** (367 Youngtown Rd., Lincolnville, 207/763-44778, www.mainewine.com), and it's possible to convince yourself you're in Sonoma Valley. Tucked in the folds of the rolling hills, just inland of Lincolnville Beach, Cellardoor occupies a farmhouse and barn overlooking six acres of grapes. Inside the barn, the retail shop offers free tastings, and you can pick up cheeses and other munchies for an impromptu picnic on the deck. The winery also has a retail shop at the intersection of Route 1 and 90 in Rockport.

Discount Shopping

How could anyone resist a thrift shop with the name **Heavenly Threads** (57 Elm St./Rte. 1, Camden, 207/236-3203)? Established by Camden's community-oriented First Congregational Church (next door to the shop), Heavenly Threads carries high-quality pre-owned clothing, books, and jewelry. It's staffed by volunteers, with proceeds going to such local ecumenical causes as Meals on Wheels.

RECREATION

Parks and Preserves

For more than a century, the Camden-Rockport area has benefited from the providence of conscientious year-round and summertime conservationists. Thanks to their benevolence, countless acres of fragile habitat, woodlands, and scenic viewpoints have been preserved. Nowadays, the most active organization is the **Coastal Mountains Land Trust** (CMLT, 101 Mt. Battie St., Camden, 207/236-7091, www.coastalmountains.org), founded in 1986. It has protected nearly 6,000 acres. Maps and information about trails open to the public are available from CMLT. Check the website for guided hikes and other events.

A Rockland-based group, **The Georges River Land Trust** (207/594-5166, www.grlt.org), whose territory covers the Georges (St. George) River watershed, is the steward for The Georges Highland Path, a low-impact hiking trail that reaches Rockport and Camden from the back side of the surrounding hills.

CAMDEN HILLS STATE PARK

A five-minute drive and a small fee gets you to the top of **Mt. Battie,** centerpiece of 5,650-acre Camden Hills State Park (Belfast Rd./Rte. 1, 207/236-3109, www.parksandlands.com, $4.50 nonresident adults, $3 resident adults, $1.50 nonresident seniors, free resident seniors, $1 children 5–11) and the best place to understand why Camden is "where the mountains meet the sea." The summit panorama is breathtaking, and reputedly the inspiration for Edna St. Vincent Millay's poem "Renascence" (a bronze plaque marks the spot); information boards identify the offshore islands. Climb the summit's stone tower for an even better view. The 20 miles of hiking trails (some for every ability) include two popular routes up Mt. Battie—an easy hour-long hike from the base parking lot (Nature Trail) and a more

© HILARY NANGLE

Camden Harbor Park was designed by Frederick Law Olmsted in 1931 and is now listed on the National Register of Historic Places.

strenuous 45-minute one from the top of Mt. Battie Street in Camden (Mt. Battie Trail). Or drive up the paved Mt. Battie Auto Road. The park has plenty of space for picnics. In winter, ice climbers use a rock wall near the Maiden's Cliff Trail, reached via Route 52 (Mountain St.). The park entrance is two miles north of downtown Camden. Request a free trail map. The park is open mid-May–mid-October. Hiking trails are accessible all year, weather permitting.

MERRYSPRING PARK

Straddling the Camden-Rockport boundary, 66-acre Merryspring Park (Conway Rd., Camden, 207/236-2239, www.merryspring.org) is a magnet for nature lovers. More than a dozen well-marked trails wind through woodlands, berry thickets, and wildflowers; near the preserve's parking area are lily, rose, and herb gardens. Admission is free, but donations are welcomed. Also free are family programs. Special programs (fee charged) include lectures, workshops, and demonstrations. The entrance is on Conway Road, 0.3 mile off Route 1, at the southern end of Camden. Trails are open dawn to dusk daily.

INTOWN PARKS

Just behind the Camden Public Library is the **Camden Amphitheatre** (also called the Bok Amphitheatre, after a local benefactor), a sylvan spot resembling a set for *A Midsummer Night's Dream* (which, yes, has been performed here). Concerts, weddings, and all kinds of other events take place in the park. Across Atlantic Avenue, sloping to the harbor, is **Camden Harbor Park,** with benches, a couple of monuments, and some of the best waterfront views in town. The noted landscape firm of Frederick Law Olmsted designed the park in 1931 and it is listed on the National Register of Historic Places. Both the park and amphitheatre were restored to their original splendor in 2004.

Rockport's in-town parks include **Marine Park,** off Pascal Avenue, at the head of the harbor; **Walker Park,** on Sea Street, west side of the harbor; **Mary-Lea Park,** overlooking the harbor next to the Rockport Opera House; and **Cramer Park,** alongside the Goose River just west of Pascal Avenue. At Marine Park are the remnants of 19th-century lime kilns, an antique steam engine, picnic tables, a boat-launching ramp, and a polished granite sculpture of André, a harbor seal adopted by a local family in the early 1960s. André had been honorary harbormaster, ringbearer at weddings, and the subject of several books and a film—and even did the honors at the unveiling of his statue—before he was fatally wounded in a mating skirmish in 1986, at the age of 25.

CURTIS ISLAND

Marking the entrance to Camden Harbor is town-owned Curtis Island, with a 26-foot automated light tower (and adjoining keeper's house) facing into the bay. Once known as Negro Island, it's a sight (and site) made for photo ops; the views are stunning in every direction. A kayak or dinghy will get you out to the island, where you can picnic (take water; there are no facilities), wander around, gather berries, or just watch the passing fleet. Land on the Camden (west) end of the island, allowing for the tide change when you beach your boat. Respect the privacy of the keeper's house in summer; it's occupied by volunteer caretakers.

FERNALD'S NECK

Three miles of Megunticook Lake shoreline, groves of conifers, and a large swamp ("the Great Bog") are features of 328-acre Fernald's Neck Preserve, on the Camden-Lincolnville line (and the Knox–Waldo County line). Shoreline and mountain views are stupendous, even more so during fall-foliage season. The easiest trail is the 1.5-mile Blue Loop, at the northern end of the preserve; from it, you can access the 1-mile Orange Loop. From the Blue Loop, take the 0.2-mile Yellow Trail offshoot to Balance Rock for a great view of the lake and hills. Some sections can be wet; wear boots or rubberized shoes, and use insect repellent. From Route

1 in Camden, take Route 52 (Mountain St.) about 4.5 miles to Fernald's Neck Road, about 0.2 mile beyond the Youngtown Inn. Turn left and then bear left at the next fork and continue to the parking lot at the road's end. Pick up a map-brochure at the trailhead register. A map is also available at the chamber of commerce office. No dogs. Note: The preserve closes and the gate is locked at 7:30 P.M.

AVENA BOTANICALS MEDICINAL HERB GARDEN

Visitors are welcome to visit Deb Soule's one-acre medicinal herb gardens (519 Mill St., Rockport, 207/594-2403, www.avenabotanicals.com, 9 A.M.–5 P.M. Mon.–Fri., free), part of an herbal and healing arts teaching center. Pick up a garden map and guide at the entrance, then stroll the paths. More than 125 species of common and medicinal herbs are planted, and everything is labeled. Mill Street is just shy of one mile south of the intersection of Routes 17 and 90 in West Rockport. Turn left on Mill Street and continue for almost one mile. Avena is on the right, down a long dirt driveway.

Recreation Centers

More than an alpine ski area, the **Camden Snow Bowl** (207/236-3438, www.camdensnowbowl.com) is a four-season recreation area with tennis courts, public swimming in Hosmer Pond, and hiking trails as well as alpine trails for day and night skiing and riding and the only toboggan chute in Maine.

Bicycling and Sea Kayaking

Local entrepreneurs Stuart and Marianne Smith have made **Maine Sport Outfitters** (Rte. 1, Rockport, 207/236-8797 or 888/236-8796, www.mainesport.com) a major destination for anyone interested in outdoor recreation. The knowledgeable staff can lend a hand and steer you in almost any direction, for almost any summer or winter sport. Nothing seems to stump them. The store sells and rents canoes, kayaks, bikes, skis, and tents, plus all the relevant clothing and accessories. A bicycle rents for $20 per day, calm-water canoes and kayaks are $30–40 per day. Sea kayaks are $50 per day single, $65 per day tandem.

Maine Sport Outdoor School (800/722-0826, a division of Maine Sport) has a full schedule of canoeing, kayaking, and camping trips. A two-hour guided Camden Harbor tour departs at least three times daily in summer and costs $35 adult, $30 children 10–15. A four-hour guided harbor-to-harbor tour (Rockport to Camden) is offered once each day for $75 adults, $60 children, including a picnic lunch. Multiday instructional programs and tours are available. The store is a half mile north of the junction of Routes 1 and 90.

Ducktrap Kayak (2175 Rte. 1, Lincolnville Beach, 207/236-8608) runs guided coastal tours, with rates beginning at $30 per person. Rentals are also available for $20–30, depending upon type and size, and delivery can be arranged.

If you have your own boat, good saltwater launch sites include Eaton Point, at the end of Sea Street, in Camden, and Marine Park, in Rockport; for freshwater paddling, put in at Megunticook Lake, west and east sides; Bog Bridge, on Route 105, about 3.5 miles from downtown Camden; Barrett's Cove, on Route 52, also about 3.5 miles from Camden; or in Lincolnville, Norton Pond and Megunticook Lake. (You can even paddle all the way from the head of Norton Pond to the foot of Megunticook Lake, but use care navigating the drainage culvert between the two.)

Hiking

There's enough hiking in **Camden Hills State Park** to fill any vacation, but many other options exist. For instance, there's **Bald Mountain,** northwest of downtown Camden, for magnificent views of Penobscot Bay. From Route 1 at the southern end of town (between Subway and Exxon), take John Street for 0.8 mile. Turn left and go 0.2 mile to a fork. Continue on the left fork (Hosmer Pond Road) for two miles. Bear left onto Barnestown Road (passing the Camden Snow Bowl) and go 1.4 miles to the trailhead on the right, signposted Georges Highland Path Barnestown Access. Maps are available in the box; the parking lot holds half a dozen cars. The blue-blazed trail is relatively easy, requiring just over an hour round-trip; the summit views are spectacular, especially in fall. Carry a picnic and enjoy it at the top. Avoid this in late May and early June, however, when the blackflies take command. Depending on the season, you may encounter squishy areas, although trail stewards have installed some well-placed boardwalks.

The boundaries of both Camden Hills State Park and Fernald's Neck extend into Lincolnville, where the major state-park hike follows the **Ski Shelter Trail** to the **Bald Rock Trail.** From Route 1 in Lincolnville Beach, take Route 173 west about 2.5 miles to the marked parking area just beyond the junction of Youngtown Road. The 1,200-foot summit—with great views of Penobscot Bay (weather permitting)—is about two miles one-way, easy to moderate hiking. The route links with the rest of the state-park trail network, but unless you've arranged for a shuttle, it's best to do Bald Rock as a round-trip hike.

The Georges Highland Path eventually will wind through the Georges (St. George) River watershed from the source in Liberty to the outlet in Port Clyde. Spearheaded by members of the Georges River Land Trust (207/594-5166, www.grlt.org), the blue-blazed trail currently has 40 miles of connected trails in four main sections, including Ragged Mountain Area. Contact the Rockland-based land trust for an up-to-date map, or pick it up from a trailhead box.

Swimming

FRESHWATER

The Camden area is blessed with several locales for freshwater swimming—a real boon, since Penobscot Bay can be mighty chilly, even at summer's peak. **Shirttail Point,** with limited parking, is a small sandy area on the Megunticook River. It's shallow enough for young kids and has picnic tables and a play area. From Route 1 in Camden, take Route 105 (Washington Street) 1.4 miles; watch for a small sign on the right. **Barrett's Cove,** on Megunticook Lake, has more parking spaces, usually more swimmers, and restrooms, picnic tables, and grills, as well as a play area. Diagonally opposite the Camden Public Library, take Route 52 (Mountain Street) about three miles; watch for the sign on the left. To cope with the parking crunch on hot summer days, bike to the beaches. You'll be ready for a swim after the uphill stretches, and it's all downhill on the way back.

Lincolnville has several ponds (some would call them lakes). On Route 52 in Lincolnville Center is Breezemere Park, a small town-owned swimming and picnic area on **Norton Pond.** Other Lincolnville options are **Coleman Pond, Pitcher Pond,** and **Knight's Pond.**

SALTWATER

The region's best ocean swimming is **Lincolnville Beach,** where Penobscot Bay flirts with Route 1 on a sandy stretch of shorefront in the congested hamlet of Lincolnville Beach. On a hot day, the sand is wall-to-wall people; during one of the coast's legendary northeasters, it's quite a wild place.

Another place for an ocean dip is **Laite Beach Park,** on Bay View Street about 1.5 miles from downtown Camden. It edges Camden Harbor and has a strip of sand, picnic tables, a playground, and children's musical events 1–3 P.M. every Wednesday in July and August. Check the local papers or contact Camden Parks and Recreation (207/236-3438) for the schedule.

In Rockport, dip your toes in the ocean at **Walker Park,** tucked away on the west side of the harbor. From Pascal Avenue, take Elm Street, which becomes Sea Street. Walker Park is on the left, with picnic tables, a play area, and a small, pebbly beach.

Golf

On a back road straddling the Camden-

Rockport line, the nine-hole **Goose River Golf Club** (50 Park St., Rockport, 207/236-8488) competes with the best for outstanding scenery.

Day Sails and Excursions

Most day sails and excursion boats operate late May–October, with fewer trips in the spring and fall than in July and August. You can't compare a two-hour day sail to a weeklong cruise on a Maine windjammer, but at least you get a hint of what could be—and it's a far better choice for kids, who aren't allowed on most windjammer cruises.

The classic wooden schooner ***Olad*** (207/236-2323, www.maineschooners.com, $31 adults, $19 children under 12) does several two-hour sails daily from Camden's Public Landing, weather permitting, late May–mid-October. Captain Aaron Lincoln is a Rockland native, so he's got the local scoop on the all the sights.

Another historic Camden day sailer is the 57-foot, 18-passenger schooner ***Surprise*** (207/236-4687, www.camdenmainesailing.com, $35) built in 1918 and skippered by congenial educator Jack Moore and his wife, Barbara. Between May and October, they do daily two-hour sails, departing from Camden's Public Landing. Minimum age is 12.

The 49-passenger ***Appledore*** (207/236-8353, www.appledore2.com), built in 1978 for round-the-world cruising, sails from Bay View Landing beginning around 10 A.M. 3–4 times daily June–October. Most cruises last two hours and cost $35 adults, $25 children. Cocktails, wine, and soft drinks are available.

Over in Rockport, the schooner ***Heron*** (207/236-8605 or 800/599-8605, www.woodenboatco.com) is a 65-foot John Alden–designed wooden yacht launched in 2003. Sailing options include a lobster-roll lunch sail ($65), lighthouse sail ($45), and sunset sails with hors d'oeuvres ($55).

For a short cruise—but a great way to see Camden and Rockport and their lighthouses and shorelines—head down to the Camden Public Landing and buy a ticket for the 30-passenger converted lobster boat ***Betselma*** (207/236-4446, www.betselma.com). Reservations usually aren't needed. Retired schooner captain Les Bex knows these waters, the wildlife, and the history. He does about eight hour-long trips daily, beginning at 10:30 A.M. June–September, for $10 adults, $5 children under 12. The last trip is at 7:30 P.M. He also does two two-hour trips—one in the morning, one in the afternoon—for $20 adults, $10 children under 12. A three-hour combo ($30 adults, $15 children) also is available. Pets are welcome.

If the kids are bombarding you with FAQs about lobsters, here's the solution. Take a two-hour trip aboard Captain Alan Philbrick's ***Lively Lady Too*** (207/236-6672, www.livelyladytoo.com, $25 adults, $5 children under 15), berthed at Camden's Bay View Landing. He hauls in a trap, takes out a lobster, explains all its parts, and generally provides all the answers. As a former biology teacher, he's a whiz at natural history, so there's also information about seabirds, seals, and lots more. Trips depart Monday–Saturday.

ACCOMMODATIONS

The region is loaded with lodgings—from basic motels to cottage complexes to elegant inns and bed-and-breakfasts. Many of Camden's most attractive accommodations (especially bed-and-breakfasts) are on Route 1 (variously disguised as Elm St., Main St., and High St.), heavily trafficked in summer. If you're extra-sensitive to nighttime noises, request a room facing away from the street. Rates noted here are for peak season.

Camden

BED-AND-BREAKFASTS

A baker's dozen of Camden's finest bed-and-breakfasts have banded together in the **Camden Bed and Breakfast Association** (www.camdeninns.com), with an attractive brochure and website. Some of them are described here. Rates reflect peak season.

The 1874 **Camden Harbour Inn** (83

© HILARY NANGLE

Most of the rooms at the Camden Harbour Inn have at least a glimpse of Camden's harbor.

Bayview St., 207/236-4200 or 800/236-4200, www.camdenharbourinn.com, $300–700) underwent a masterful renovation and restoration by new Dutch owners, partners Raymond Brunyanszki and Oscar Verest, reopening in 2007 as a boutique bed-and-breakfast complete with 21st-century amenities. It retains the bones of a 19th-century summer hotel, but the decor is contemporary European, with worldly accent pieces and velour furnishings in purples, reds, and silvers. Guest rooms, some with fireplaces, patios, decks, or balconies, have at least a glimpse of Camden's harbor or Penobscot Bay. All have air-conditioning, Wi-Fi, flat-screen TV, refrigerator, and king-size bed. Service is five-star, right down to chocolates and slippers at turndown. At breakfast, included, the menu includes choices such as lobster Benedict as well as a buffet with fresh baked items, smoked salmon, and other goodies. Snacks are always available. And their restaurant, Natalie's, is one of the state's best. The owners also speak Dutch, German, some French, and rudimentary Indonesian and Thai.

The **Hartstone Inn** (41 Elm St., 207/236-4259 or 800/788-4823, www.hartstoneinn.com, $125–275) is Michael and Mary Jo Salmon's imposing mansard-roofed Victorian close to the heart of downtown. Although some rooms face the street (and these are insulated with triple-pane windows), most do not, and all have air-conditioning. Once inside, you're away from it all. Even more removed are rooms in two other buildings under the Hartstone's umbrella. Suites in the Manor House, tucked behind the main inn, have contemporary decor. Rooms and suites in The Hideaway, in a residential neighborhood about a block away, have country French flair. All are elegant (Wi-Fi, air-conditioning); some have fireplaces and whirlpools. Be *sure* to make reservations for dinner. And then, there's the incredible breakfast. If you get hooked, the Salmons organize culinary classes during the winter, and you can even arrange for a one-on-one cooking experience with Michael.

Opened to guests in 1901, the **Whitehall Inn** (52 High St./Rte. 1, 207/236-3391 or 800/789-6565, www.whitehall-inn.com, $149–199) retains its century-old genteel air. Lovely gardens, rockers on the veranda, a tennis court, and attentive service all add to the appeal of this historic country inn. Ask to see the Millay Room, commemorating famed poet Edna St. Vincent Millay, who graduated from Camden High School and first recited her poem "Renascence" to Whitehall guests in 1912. It also played a role in *Peyton Place,* and enlarged movie photos are displayed throughout. Spread out between the main inn and the annex are 45 comfortable, unpretentious rooms, all with flat-screen TV, Internet access, and imported linens; a few share baths. Rates include a full menu breakfast. The dining room, Vincent's, is open to the public for breakfast (7–10 A.M. daily) and dinner (6–9 P.M. Wed.–Mon.). Also on the premises is Gossip, a bar serving pub fare. It's open mid-May–late October.

Claudio and Roberta Latanza, both natives of Italy, became the fourth innkeepers at the **Camden Maine Stay** (22 High St./Rte. 1, 207/236-9636, www.mainestay.com, $155–290) in 2009. Like their predecessors, they do everything right, from the comfortable yet elegant decor to the delicious breakfasts and afternoon snacks to the welcoming window candles and garden retreats. The stunning residence, built in 1802, faces busy Route 1 and is just a bit uphill from downtown, but inside and out back, behind the carriage house and barn, you'll feel worlds away.

In the heart of downtown Camden, **The Lord Camden Inn** (24 Main St./Rte. 1, 207/236-4325 or 800/336-4325, www.lordcamdeninn.com, $199–299) is a hotel alternative in a historic four-story downtown building (with elevator). Top-floor rooms have harbor-view balconies. Rates include a breakfast buffet. Pooches are pampered in pet-friendly rooms for $25 per night, including bed, biscuits, bowls, and local dog info.

One of Maine's most unusual (and priciest) bed-and-breakfasts, **Norumbega** (61 High St./Rte. 1, 207/236-4646 or 877/363-4646, $195–525, www.norumbegainn.com) is an 1886 turreted stone castle overlooking Camden's outer harbor. Provided your wallet can stand the crunch, splurge for a night (or two) here—if only to feel like temporary royalty. Twelve rooms and suites, most named after European castles, are strikingly decorated, filled with antiques, and have all the expected amenities. Rates include a full breakfast.

ECLECTIC PROPERTIES

A hybrid of an inn, bed-and-breakfast, motel, and cottage, **The High Tide Inn on the Ocean** (Rte. 1, 207/236-3724 or 800/788-7068, www.hightideinn.com, $75–230), three miles north of town, has enough variety for every budget—all in an outstanding seven-acre oceanfront setting with a private pebbly beach. Accommodations are a bit rustic, and some are dated. The two-story, eight-unit "Oceanfront" motel unit is closest to the water and farthest from Route 1. Rates include continental breakfast with fabulous popovers on the water-view porch. Pets can be accommodated in some rooms.

Step back in time at family-owned **Beloin's on the Maine Coast** (245 Belfast Rd./Rte. 1, 207/236-3262, www.beloins.com, $80–175). Don't judge this place from the roadside motel; down the road is another motel and cottages with spectacular oceanfront settings. Agnes Beloin keeps everything tidy, but it's all a bit old-fashioned and rustic (think 1950s). All rooms have TV and phone, some have refrigerators or kitchenettes, and all guests have access to a private sand beach. A two-bedroom shorefront cottage is $160–240. Extra guests in rooms are $5 per night; pets are $10 per stay.

MOTEL

It's a short stroll into Merryspring Gardens from the **Cedar Crest Motel** (115 Elm St./Rte. 1, 207/236-4839, www.cedarcrestmotel.com, $129–144), a nicely maintained property on 3.5 wooded and landscaped acres on the southern edge of downtown. Each of the 37 rooms has air-conditioning, Wi-Fi, phone, and TV. Some have mini-fridges. On the premises are a guest computer, outdoor heated pool, playground, laundry, and restaurant serving all meals and live jazz on Friday evenings.

CAMPING

Camden Hills State Park (Belfast Rd./Rte. 1, 207/236-3109, $3 adults, $1 children 5–11,

$25 nonresidents, $15 residents for basic site; $37.45 nonresidents, $26.75 residents with water and electric) has a 112-site camping area and is wheelchair-accessible. Pets are allowed, showers are free, and the sites are large.

Rockport

MOTELS AND COTTAGE COLONIES

One of the area's spiffiest motels also has terrific Penobscot Bay views. In the Glen Cove section of Rockport (three miles south of downtown Rockport, three miles north of downtown Rockland, next door to Penobscot Bay Medical Center), the **Glen Cove Motel** (Rte. 1, Glen Cove, 207/594-4062 or 800/453-6268, www.glencovemotel.com, $89–299) sits on a 17-acre bluff with a lovely trail leading to the rocky shore. Many of the 34 units boast water views; all have air-conditioning, phone, Wi-Fi, cable TV, and refrigerator. A continental breakfast is included. The pool is heated. Request a room set back from Route 1.

Step back in time at the oceanfront **Oakland Seashore Motel & Cottages** (112 Dearborn Ln., 207/594-8104, www.oaklandseashorecabins.com, $77–122), a low-key throwback on 70 mostly wooded acres that dates back more than a century. It was originally a recreational park operated by a trolley company, but its heyday passed with the arrival of the automobile. In the late 1940s, shorefront cabins were added, and in the 1950s the dance pavilion was renovated into a motel. The rooms and cabins are simple, comfortable, clean, and right on the ocean's edge; some have kitchenettes, a few have full kitchens. Bathrooms are tiny. No phones or TVs. The grounds are gorgeous, with big shade trees, grassy lawns, and well-placed benches and chairs, and there's a rocky beach that's ideal for launching a kayak. Note: This place isn't for those who need attentive service or fluffy accommodations, but it's a gem for those who appreciate quiet simplicity with a big view.

Clean rooms, a convenient location, lovely ocean views from most rooms, and reasonable prices have made the Beale family's **Ledges by the Bay** (930 Rte. 1, Glen Cove, 207/594-894, www.ledgesbythebay.com, $89–169) a favorite among budget-conscious travelers. Rooms have air-conditioning, TV, Wi-Fi, and phone; most have private balconies. Other pluses include private shorefront, small heated pool, and light continental breakfast. Pets are welcome in some rooms. Kids under 13 stay free in parents' room.

The family-owned and -operated all-suites **Country Inn** (8 Country Inn Way/Rte. 1, 207/236-2725 or 888/707-3945, www.countryinnmaine.com, $179–219 d) is an especially good choice for families, thanks to an indoor pool, play areas, guest laundry, and fitness room. Rooms are divided between a main inn and cottage suites. Some units have fireplaces, whirlpool tubs, and microwaves; all have air-conditioning, phone, fridge, Wi-Fi, and TV. A continental breakfast buffet, afternoon snacks, and evening chocolate-chip cookies are included. Kids 6–16 are $5 per night; those older are $10. On-site massage and yoga classes are available.

Lincolnville

BED-AND-BREAKFASTS

Private, secluded, and surrounded by 22 acres of gardens, the oceanfront shingle-style **Inn at the Ocean's Edge** (Rte. 1, Lincolnville Beach, 207/236-0945, www.innatoceansedge.com, $280–475) is splurge worthy. Every room has a king-size bed, fireplace, and whirlpool tub for two, as well as TV, air-conditioning, Wi-Fi, and superb ocean views. The grounds are lovely, with an infinity pool and chairs placed just so to take in the views. There's also a good restaurant on the premises. Rates include breakfast; packages with dinner are available.

Even more private and secluded is **The Inn at Sunrise Point** (Rte. 1, Lincolnville, Camden, 207/236-7716 or 800/435-6278, www.sunrisepoint.com, $200–525), an elegant retreat with all the whistles and bells you'd expect at these rates. The three handsome rooms in the main lodge, four separate cottages, two lofts, and two suites are all named after Maine authors or artists. Breakfast in the conservatory is divine.

© HILARY NANGLE

The views from the summit of Ducktrap Mountain, at Point Lookout Resort, take in the panorama of Penobscot Bay.

MOTEL

The family-run **Mount Battie Inn** (2158 Atlantic Hwy./Rte. 1, Lincolnville, 207/236-3870 or 800/224-3870, www.mountbattie.com, $160–180) has 22 charming motel-style rooms with air-conditioning, TV, phone, Wi-Fi, fridge, and continental breakfast, including home-baked treats.

Another family-run gem, the **Ducktrap Motel** (12 Whitney Rd., Lincolnville, 207/789-5400 or 877/977-5400, www.ducktrapmotel.com, $85–115) is set back from Route 1 and screened by trees. Both the grounds and the rooms are meticulously maintained. All rooms have TV, fridge, coffeemaker, and air-conditioning; deluxe rooms have microwaves; the cottage has an efficiency kitchen.

COTTAGE RESORT

It's hard to categorize **Point Lookout Resort and Conference Center** (Rte. 1, Lincolnville, 800/515-3611, www.visitpointlookout.com, $125–275 per cabin), but by any definition it's a good value and a tremendous property spread out on Ducktrap Mountain. Once a corporate retreat center, it was purchased by the Erickson Foundation and now doubles as an education and conference center as well as offering well-outfitted accommodations to leisure travelers. The 106 one- to three-bedroom cabins are decorated in a Ralph Lauren–does-summer-camp motif (leather chairs, comfy beds, nice linens). All have screened porches, phones, individual Wi-Fi, TV, fridges, microwaves, heat, and air-conditioning. Some have fireplaces, a second bathroom, and full kitchen. All are tucked in the woods on the 100-plus-acre property. Also on the premises are an amazing fitness-wellness center with testing programs, gym, virtual golf, squash, racquetball, a full array of equipment, and a bowling alley with video arcade; mapped hiking trails, tennis courts, softball field, and artificial turf soccer field; a casual restaurant; and full conference facilities. Use of most facilities is free for guests. The views over Penobscot Bay from the summit are stupendous.

FOOD

Call to verify days and hours of operation.

Local Flavors

ROCKPORT

The best source for health foods, homeopathic remedies, and fresh, seasonal produce is **Fresh Off the Farm** (495 Rte. 1, 207/236-3260, 8 A.M.–7 P.M. Mon.–Sat., 9 A.M.–5:30 P.M. Sun.), an inconspicuous red-painted roadside place that looks like an overgrown farmstand (it is). Watch for one of those permanent-temporary signs highlighting latest arrivals (Native Blueberries, Native Corn, etc.). The shop is 1.3 miles south of the junction of Routes 1 and 90.

At the southern entrance to Rockport, a sprawling red building is the home of **The Rockport Marketplace and The State of Maine Cheese Company** (461 Commercial St./Rte. 1, 207/236-8895 or 800/762-8895, 9 A.M.–5 P.M. Mon.–Sat., noon–4 P.M. Sun.). Inside are locally made varieties of cows'-milk hard cheeses, all named after Maine locations (Aroostook Jack, Allagash Caraway, St. Croix Black Pepper, and so on) as well as hundreds of Maine-made products, from food to crafts. Among the items are blueberry chutneys, maple syrup, designer breads, great jams—a one-stop-shopping (and tasting) site.

At the junction of Routes 1 and 90, a colorfully painted barn is the home of **The Market Basket** (Rte. 1, 207/236-4371, 7 A.M.–6:30 P.M. Mon.–Sat., 9 A.M.–4 P.M. Sun.), the best takeout source for creative sandwiches, homemade soups, cheeses, exotic condiments, pastries, wine (large selection), beer, and entrées-to-go. The market will also do boat provisioning. In winter, it sponsors weeklong cooking classes.

A combination market, farm, and café, with regular tastings, lectures, and events, **Farmers Fare** (Rte. 90 at Cross St., Rockport, 207/236-3273, www.farmersfare.com, 7 A.M.–6 P.M. Mon.–Sat., 9 A.M.–3 P.M. Sun.) focuses on what's fresh and mostly local. Go for lunch or Sunday brunch, and while there, pick up all kinds of farm-produced products.

CAMDEN

The **Camden Farmers Market** (3:30–5:30 P.M. Wed. mid-June–late Sept. and 9 A.M.–noon Sat. early May–late Oct.), one of the best in the state, holds forth at the Knox Mill Complex on Washington Street. It continues through the winter inside the Knox Mill.

The **Camden Bagel Cafe** (Brewster Mill, 26 Mechanic St., 207/236-2661, 6:30 A.M.–2 P.M. Mon.–Sat., 7:30 A.M.–2 P.M. Sun.) has a hugely loyal clientele, drawn by *real* coffee, fresh bagels, fast service, daily newspapers, and a casual air. No credit cards.

Good coffee is a draw at the **Camden Deli** (37 Main St., 207/236-8343, 7 A.M.–10 P.M. daily), in the heart of downtown, but its biggest asset is the windowed seating overlooking the Megunticook River waterfall. The view doesn't get much better than this (go upstairs for the best angle). Made-to-order sandwiches and wraps, homemade soups, veggie burgers, and subs all add to the mix.

Since the early 1970s, **Scott's Place** (85 Elm St./Rte. 1, 207/236-8751, 10:30 A.M.–4 P.M. Mon.–Fri., to 3 P.M. Sat.), a roadside lunch stand near Reny's at the Camden Marketplace, has been dishing up inexpensive ($2–10) burgers and dogs, nowadays adding veggie burgers and salads. Call ahead and it'll be ready.

Peek behind the old-fashioned facade at **Boynton-McKay Food Company** (30 Main St., 207/236-2465, 7 A.M.–5 P.M. Tues.–Sat., 8 A.M.–4 P.M. Sun., kitchen closes 3 P.M. daily) and you'll see an old-fashioned soda fountain, early-20th-century tables, antique pharmacy accessories, and a thoroughly modern café menu. Restored and rehabbed in 1997, Boynton-McKay had been *the* local drugstore for more than a century. The new incarnation features bagels, creative salads, homemade soups, superb wrap sandwiches, an espresso bar, and the whole works from the soda fountain. It's open for breakfast and lunch.

Facing downtown Camden's five-way intersection, **French and Brawn** (1 Elm St., 207/236-3361, 6 A.M.–8 P.M. Mon.–Sat., 8 A.M.–8 P.M. Sun.) is an independent market that earns the description *super.* Ready-made sandwiches, soups, and other goodies complement the oven-ready takeout meals, high-cal frozen desserts, esoteric meats, and a staff with a can-do attitude.

LINCOLNVILLE

No question, the **Northport Diner** (Rte. 1, Northport, 207/338-1524, 5 A.M.–2 P.M. daily) looks like a dive from the exterior, but this is the kind of home-cookin' gem chowhounds love to stumble upon and devour. It's a homey Mom-and-Pop operation (literally, just Pop in the kitchen and Mom out front), where the breads, muffins, doughnuts, and biscuits are all homemade; the portions are generous and prices low. Little, if anything, is more than $10, and most choices are less than $6. Breakfast is served all day, and the crabmeat omelet is alone worth the stop.

Family Favorites

CAMDEN

Elm Street Grille (Cedar Crest Motel, 115 Elm St./Rte. 1, 207/236-4839, www.cedarcrestmotel.com) is a favorite for great breakfasts, lunch, and dinner Tuesday–Sunday. The pizzas get high marks. It's all very reasonably priced and served in a comfortable dining room, with a handful of seats on a deck. On Friday nights, there's live jazz.

In the heart of Camden, **Cappy's** (1 Main St., 207/236-2254, www.cappyschowder.com, 11 A.M.–midnight daily, $10–21) is small, a bit cramped, reliably good (it's been here for more than 25 years), and very popular with locals and out-of-towners alike, despite being a bit pricey. In summer, request a table in the 2nd-floor Crow's Nest, where you'll be less squished; microbrew tastings are held here 4–6 P.M. daily in season. It's a burger-and-sandwich menu with some heartier seafood choices; clam chowder is a specialty. During summer, Cappy's operates a bakery with takeout pastries, sandwiches, and other goodies underneath, facing on the alley that runs down to the public parking lot.

LINCOLNVILLE

French flair without the attitude is why **Chez Michel** (Rte. 1, Lincolnville Beach, 207/789-5600, 4:30–9 P.M. Tues.–Sat., 11:30 A.M.–9 P.M. Sun., $18–25) is a perennial favorite, even for families (kids' menu). Try for one of the window tables with water views. Early-bird specials are served before 5:45 P.M.

Casual Dining

CAMDEN AND ROCKPORT

Chef-owner Brian Hill has created one of the region's hottest restaurants with **Francine Bistro** (55 Chestnut St., Camden, 207/230-0083, www.francinebistro.com, 5:30–10 P.M. Tues.–Sat.). The well-chosen menu (entrées $24–30) is short and focused on whatever's fresh and (usually) locally available that day. In addition to the dining room, there's also seating at the bar and, when the weather cooperates, on the front porch.

Down on the harbor is the informal, art-filled **Atlantica** (1 Bay View Landing, Camden, 207/236-6011 or 888/507-8514, www.atlanticarestaurant.com, 11:30 A.M.–2 P.M. and 5–9 P.M. daily, $25–36), two floors of culinary creativity with an emphasis on seafood. In summer, try for a table on the deck hanging over the water. Be forewarned: Service can be iffy.

The Waterfront Restaurant (Bay View St., Camden, 207/236-3747, 11:30 A.M.–9:30 P.M. daily, $16–26) has the biggest waterside dining deck in town, but you'll need to arrive early to snag one of the tables. Lunches are the most fun, overlooking lots of harbor action; at high tide, you're eye to eye with the boats. Most folks rave about the place, but I've found it inconsistent.

Food as art is the idea behind the **Gallery Café** (297 Commercial St./Rte. 1, Rockport, 207/230-0061, www.prismglassgallery-cafe.com, 11 A.M.–3 P.M. and 5–9 P.M. Wed.–Sat., 10 A.M.–3 P.M. and 4–8 P.M. Sun., $15–24), a restaurant that's part of **Prismglass,** a fine-art glass gallery and working studio representing more than 50 glass artists. The Italian-leaning menu changes seasonally. Brunch is $8–14.

LINCOLNVILLE

Appropriately named, **The Edge** (Inn at the Ocean's Edge, Rte. 1, Lincolnville Beach, 207/236-4430, www.innatoceansedge.com, 4–8:30 P.M. daily, $16–30) provides a front-row seat on Penobscot Bay, whether you're in the cozy dining room or on the deck. The menu features familiar foods with creative touches and an emphasis on fresh and local. Sunday night is pizza night, with fancy pies.

Fine Dining

CAMDEN

Reservations are a must for chef Michael Salmon's five-course fixed-price extravaganzas at the **Hartstone Inn** (41 Elm St., 207/236-4259 or 800/788-4823, www.hartstoneinn.com, $45). Michael, named Caribbean chef of the year when they lived in Aruba, has cooked at the Beard House by invitation. Even Julia Child dined here. The menu changes weekly to use the freshest ingredients.

Since opening in 2007 to rave reviews, **Natalie's at the Camden Harbour Inn** (83 Bayview St., 207/236-4200, www.nataliesrestaurant.com, 5–9:30 P.M. daily) has become one of the state's top tables. Chef Lawrence Klang's French-accented menu, which complements the dining room, was designed to be reminiscent of the Left Bank in Paris a century ago. Instead of looking out at the Seine, you're gazing over Camden Harbor. Entrées begin in the high $20s, a five-course tasting menu is $65, and a four-course grand lobster menu reflects market prices. Lighter fare is served in the bar and lounge.

LINCOLNVILLE

For a romantic, classic French experience, head a bit inland to **Youngtown Inn and Restaurant** (581 Youngtown Rd., 207/763-4290 or 800/291-8438, www.youngtowninn.com, 6–9 P.M. Tues.–Sun., $22–28), where chef-owner Manuel Mercier draws on his Parisian heritage and European training. Upstairs are six guestrooms ($160–175, with breakfast; $250 with breakfast and dinner).

© HILARY NANGLE

The Lobster Pound Restaurant is a huge barn of a place, right on Lincolnville Beach.

Lobster in the Rough

Lincolnville's best-known landmark is **The Lobster Pound Restaurant** (Rte. 1, Lincolnville Beach, 207/789-5550, www.lobsterpoundmaine.com, 11:30 A.M.–8 P.M. daily, to 9 P.M. in July and Aug., $12–35). About 300 people—some days, it looks like more than that—can pile into the restaurant and enclosed patio, so be sure to make reservations on summer weekends. Despite the crowds, food and service are reliably good. Lobster, of course, is king, but the huge menu will satisfy everyone.

INFORMATION AND SERVICES

Information

For planning, contact **Camden-Rockport-Lincolnville Chamber of Commerce** (207/236-4404 or 800/223-5459, www.visitcamden.com). Also handy is a directory published by the **Lincolnville Business Group** (www.lincolnville.org).

Check out **Camden Public Library** (Main St./Rte. 1, Camden, 207/236-3440, www.camden.lib.me.us) or **Rockport Public Library** (1 Limerock St., Rockport, 207/236-3642, www.rockport.lib.me.us).

Public Restrooms

Public restrooms are available at Camden's Public Landing, near the chamber of commerce, and at the Camden Public Library. In Rockport, there are restrooms at Marine Park. In Lincolnville, there are restrooms at the ferry terminal.

Belfast

With a population of about 6,400, Belfast is relatively small as cities go, but it's officially cool: *Budget Travel* magazine named it one of the top 10 coolest towns in America. Even before that, Belfast was one of those off-the-beaten-track destinations popular with tuned-in travelers. Chalk that up to its status as a magnet for leftover back-to-the-landers and enough artistic types to earn the city a nod for cultural cool. Belfast has a curling club, a food co-op and a green store, meditation centers, an increasing number of art galleries and boutiques, dance and theater companies, the oldest shoe store in America, and half a dozen different 12-step self-help groups. It even has a poet laureate.

This eclectic city is a work in progress, a study in Maine-style diversity. It's also a gold mine of Federal, Greek Revival, Italianate, and Victorian architecture. Take the time to stroll the well-planned backstreets, explore the shops, and hang out at the gussied-up waterfront.

Separating Belfast from East Belfast, the Passagassawakeag River (Puh-sag-gus-uh-WAH-keg) fortunately is known more familiarly as "the Passy." The Indian name has been translated as both "place of many ghosts" and the rather different "place for spearing sturgeon by torchlight." You choose. No matter, you can cross it via a pedestrian bridge.

Many travelers make Belfast a day stop on their way between Camden and Bar Harbor. Truly, Belfast is worth more time than that. Spend a full day or two here, and it's likely you'll be charmed, like many of the other urban refugees, into resettling here.

SIGHTS

Historic Walking Tour

No question, the best way to appreciate Belfast's fantastic architecture is to tour by ankle express. At the Belfast Area Chamber of Commerce, pick up the well-researched *Belfast Historic Walking Tour* map-brochure. Among more than 40 highlights on the mile-long self-guided route are the 1818 Federal-style **First Church,** handsome residences on **High** and **Church Streets,** and the 1840 **James P. White House** (corner of Church St. and Northport Ave., now an elegant bed-and-breakfast), New England's finest Greek Revival residence. Amazing for a community of this size, the city actually has three distinct National Historic Districts: Belfast Commercial Historic District (47 downtown buildings), Church Street Historic District (residential), and Primrose Hill Historic District (also residential). Another walking tour is presented by the Belfast Historical Society's **Museum in the Streets,** comprising two large panels and 30 smaller ones highlighting historic buildings and people. Signs are in English and French.

Bayside

Continuing the focus on architecture, just south of Belfast, in Northport, is the Victorian enclave of Bayside, a neighborhoody sort of place with small, well-kept gingerbreaded cottages cheek-by-jowl on pint-size lots. Formerly known as the Northport Wesleyan Grove Campground, the village took shape in the mid-1800s as a summer retreat for Methodists. In the 1930s, the retreat was disbanded and the main meeting hall was razed, creating the waterfront park at the heart of the village. Today, many of the colorfully painted homes are rented by the week, month, or summer season, and their tenants are more likely to indulge in athletic rather than religious pursuits. The camaraderie remains, though, and a stroll (or cycle or drive) through Bayside is like a visit to another era. Bayside is four miles south of Belfast, just east of Route 1. If you want to join the fun, try **Bayside Cottage Rentals** (539 Bluff Rd., Northport, 207/338-5355, www.baysidecottagerentals.com).

Temple Heights

Continue south on Shore Road from Bayside to **Temple Heights Spiritualist Camp** (Shore Rd., Northport, 207/338-3029, www.templeheightscamp.org), yet another religious enclave—this one still going. Founded in 1882, Temple Heights has become a shadow of its former self, reduced primarily to the funky 12-room Nikawa Lodge on Shore Road ($35 d, $25 s, shared bath, some with ocean view), but the summer program continues, thanks to prominent mediums from all over the country. Even a temporary setback in 1996—when the camp president was suspended for allegedly putting a hex on Northport's town clerk—failed to derail the operation. Camp programs, mid-June–Labor Day, are open to the public; a schedule is published each spring. Spiritualist church services, séances, and group healing sessions are free; Saturday-morning workshops are $20. Better yet, sign up for a 1.5-hour or longer **group message circle,** when you'll sit with a medium and a dozen or so others and receive insights—often uncannily on target—from departed relatives or friends. Message circles occur at 7:30 P.M. Wednesday and Saturday (arrive a half hour early). Suggested donation is $15 per person and reservations are necessary. Private half-hour readings can be arranged for a donation of $40.

ENTERTAINMENT AND EVENTS

Entertainment

It's relatively easy to find nightlife in Belfast—not only are there theaters and a cinema, but there usually are a couple of bars open at least until midnight, and sometimes later. Some spots also feature live music, particularly on weekends.

If you don't feel like searching out a newspaper to check the entertainment listings, just go to the **Belfast Co-op Store** (123 High St., 207/338-2532) and study the bulletin board. You'll find notices for more activities than you could ever squeeze into your schedule.

Open mic nights, jazz jams, classes, and lectures pepper the calendar for **Waterfall Arts** (265 High St., 207/338-2222, www.waterfallarts.org).

Just south of Belfast, the funky **Blue Goose Dance Hall** (Rte. 1, Northport, 207/338-3003) is the site for folk concerts, contra dances, auctions, and other events. Check local papers or the Belfast Co-op Store bulletin board.

About a dozen galleries participate in Belfast

OFF THE BEATEN PATH IN LIBERTY

Seventeen miles west of Belfast, off Route 3, is Liberty, a tiny town with a funky tool store, quirky museum, a bargain T-shirt shop, and a great state park. Everything is seasonal, running roughly mid-May through mid-October or so. Call before visiting if you want to be sure everything's open.

It's a store! It's a museum! It's amazing! More than 10,000 "useful" tools – plus used books and prints and other tidbits – fill the three-story **Liberty Tool Company** (Main St., 207/589-4771). Drawn by nostalgia and a compulsion for handmade adzes and chisels, thousands of vintage-tool buffs arrive at this eclectic emporium each year; few leave empty-handed. Nor do the thousands of everyday home hobbyists looking to pick up a hammer or find a missing wrench to fill out a set. Nor do the antiques-seekers, who browse the trash and treasures on the upper floors. The collection is beyond amazing, especially in its organization. Owner Skip Brack brings back vanloads of finds almost every week, and after sorting and cleaning, many make it into this store.

The best-of-the-best make it into Brack's **Davistown Museum** (Main St., 207/589-4900, www.davistownmuseum.org), on the 3rd floor of the building housing Liberty Graphics, across the street. The museum houses not only a history of Maine and New England hand tools, but also local, regional, Native American, and environmental artifacts and information and an amazing collection of contemporary art, highlighted by works by artists such as Louise Nevelson (who used to buy tools across the street), Melitta Westerlund, and Phil Barter.

Downstairs is **Liberty Graphics Outlet Store** (1 Main St., 207/589-4035), selling the eco-sensitive company's overstocks, seconds, and discontinued-design T-shirts. Outstanding silk-screened designs are done with water-based inks, and many of the shirts are organic cotton; prices begin at $5.

Just down Main Street is the old **Liberty Post Office,** a unique octagonal structure that looks like an oversize box. It was built in 1867 as a harnessmaker's shop and later used as the town's post office.

You'll find practically every tool possible, and then some, at Liberty Tool Company.

Two miles west of downtown, **Lake St. George State Park** (Rte. 3, 207/589-4255, $6 nonresident adults, $4 resident adults, $1 children 5-11) is a refreshing find. This 360-acre park has wooded picnic sites with grills along the lake, a beach, rental boats, playground, volleyball and basketball courts, and five miles of hiking trails. Also available are campsites, $25 for nonresidents, $15 residents. Afterward, head to **John's Ice Cream** (Rte. 3, 207/589-3700) for amazing flavors handcrafted (homemade is too pedestrian to describe it) on the premises.

If you're up for more inland exploring, weave your way along the **Georges River Scenic Byway,** a 50-mile auto route along the St. George River (a.k.a. Georges River) from its inland headwaters to the sea in Port Clyde. The official start is at the junction of Routes 3 and 220 in Liberty, but you can follow the trail in either direction, or pick it up anywhere along the way. Road signs are posted, but it's far better to obtain a map-brochure at a chamber of commerce or other information locale. Or contact the architects of the route, **The Georges River Land Trust** (207/594-5166, www.grlt.org).

Arts' **Friday Gallery Walk,** held every Friday night in July and August, and every first Friday September–December.

An old-fashioned downtown cinema—recently restored to its art deco splendor—shows first-run films for moderate ticket prices. The **Colonial Theatre** (163 High St., 207/338-1930, www.colonialtheatre.com) has three screens, each with 1–2 showings a night and matinees Saturday, Sunday, and sometimes Wednesday. It's open all year.

Check local papers for the schedule of the **Belfast Maskers** (43 Front St., 207/338-9668, www.belfastmaskerstheater.com), a community theater group that never fails to win raves for its interpretations of contemporary and classical dramas. In winter wear an extra pair of socks; the floor is drafty.

Also worth checking out is the **Northport Music Theater** (851 Rte. 1, Northport, 207/338-8383, www.northportmusictheater.com, $20–25), a 128-seat theater presenting shows mid-June–late August.

© HILARY NANGLE

America's oldest shoe store is in downtown Belfast.

Events

The Belfast Garden Club sponsors **Open Garden Days** once a week mid-May–mid-September at the homes of club members and friends in and around Belfast. Gardens are open 10 A.M.–3 P.M. rain or shine; a $3 per person donation is requested to benefit local beautification projects. Check local newspapers or ask at the chamber of commerce for the schedule.

Every Friday evening during July and August, more than 20 mostly downtown galleries open their doors for the **Friday Gallery Walk.**

In early July, soon after the Fourth of July, the **Arts in the Park** festival gets underway at Heritage Park, on the Belfast waterfront. It's a weekend event, with two days of music, juried arts and crafts, children's activities, and lots of food booths.

The **Belfast Bay Festival,** usually the third week of July, has music, carnival rides, fireworks, food, and more.

SHOPPING

It's easy and fun to shop in downtown Belfast, a town that has so far managed to keep the big boxes away, providing fertile ground for entrepreneurs. Downtown shops reflect the city's population, with galleries and boutiques, thrift and used-goods stores, and eclectic shops.

Books

Mr. Paperback (1 E. Belmont Ave., 207/338-2084), in the Reny's Plaza, is also home to an excellent café, **Bell the Cat** (207/338-2084, 9 A.M.–8 P.M. Mon.–Sat., to 6 P.M. Sun.).

Specialty Shops

Even if shoes aren't on your shopping list, stop in at "the oldest shoe store in America." Founded in the 1830s(!), **Colburn Shoe Store** (81 Main St., 207/338-1934 or 877/338-1934) may be old, but it isn't old-fashioned.

Brambles (69 Main St., 207/338-3448) is

a gardener's delight, with fun, whimsical, and practical garden-themed merchandise.

Wooden toys are just one reason to visit **Out of the Woods** (48 Main St., 207/338-2692), which specializes in Maine-made wood products.

Just over the Belfast bridge is **Cherished Home** (31 Searsport Ave./Rte. 1, 207/338-4111), where Genie Francis (a.k.a. Laura of the famed Luke and Laura on the soap opera *General Hospital*) sells a nice selection of home-oriented merchandise.

About two miles east of Belfast's bridge, on the right, is the small roadside shop of **Mainely Pottery** (181 Searsport Ave./Rte. 1, 207/338-1108). Since 1988, Jeannette Faunce and Jamie Oates have been marketing the work of more than two dozen Maine potters, each with different techniques, glazes, and styles. It's the perfect place to select from a wide range of reasonably priced work.

© HILARY NANGLE

Kayakers, sailboats, and cruise ships share Belfast's harbor.

The Green Store

Calling itself a "general store for the 21st century," The Green Store (71 Main St., 207/338-4045) carries a huge selection of environmentally friendly products. Whether you're thinking of going off the grid, need a composting toilet, or just want natural-fiber clothing or other natural-living products, this is the place. A very knowledgeable staff can answer nearly any question on environmentally sustainable lifestyles.

RECREATION

Belfast is rich in parks and picnic spots. One of the state's best municipal parks is just on the outskirts of downtown. Established in 1904, **Belfast City Park** (87 Northport Ave., 207/338-1661, free) has lighted tennis courts, an outdoor pool, a pebbly beach, plenty of picnic tables, an unusually creative playground, lots of green space for the kids, and fantastic views of Islesboro, Blue Hill, and Penobscot Bay. For more action, right in the heart of Belfast, head for **Heritage Park,** at the bottom of Main Street, with front-row seats on waterfront happenings. Bring a picnic, grab a table, and watch the yachts, tugs, and lobster boats. Every street between the two parks that ends at the ocean is a public right of way.

Golf

Just south of Belfast is the nine-hole **Northport Golf Club** (581 Bluff Rd., Northport, 207/338-2270), established in 1916.

Bicycling

The **Belfast Bicycle Club** (www.belfastbicycleclub.org) invites folks on group rides. Check the website for a current schedule.

Excursion Boats

Sail aboard the Friendship sloop ***Amity*** (evenings 207/469-0849, daytime 207/323-1443, www.friendshipsloopamity.com), based at the Belfast Public Landing, for 90-minute morning ($20) or 2.5-hour afternoon ($30) sails; age 15 and younger are half price. The classic

Friendship sloop, built in 1901 in Friendship, was originally used for lobstering. Now beautifully restored, it carries up to six passengers. Home-baked cookies and hot coffee and tea are served on all cruises. Captain Stephen O'Connell, a former journalist, explains the boat's history and its role in lobstering and regales passengers, when asked, with tales of his experiences living in exotic locations around the world.

Take a day trip to Castine aboard the ***Good Return,*** operated by Belfast Bay Cruises (207/322-5530, www.belfastbaycruises.com), departing from Thompson Wharf (between Belfast Maskers theater and the pedestrian bridge). Captain Melissa Terry, a fifth-generation descendent of a whaling captain from New Bedford, Massachusetts, is a Maine Maritime Academy graduate who enjoys sharing her love of the sea. The 4.5-hour Castine Lunch Cruise ($30 adults, $17 children 5–15) provides time for exploring Castine and lunch (on your own); an extended 7.25-hour Castine trip is the same fee. Other options include a 1.5-hour educational lobstering cruise, during which traps are hauled ($25 adults, $12.50 children), and a 1.25-hour harbor cruise ($15 adults, $7 children).

If you don't have your own kayak, **Water Walker** (152 Lincolnville Ave., 207/338-6424, www.kayak-tour-maine.com) has a full range of options. Owner Ray Wirth, a Registered Maine Guide and ACA-certified open-water instructor, will arrange customized trips from a few hours to multiple days, as well as provide instruction. Two-hour Belfast Harbor tours are $35 per person; subtract $10 if you have your own boat.

Winter Sports

The Scottish national sport of curling has dozens of enthusiastic supporters at Maine's only curling rink, the **Belfast Curling Club** (Belmont Ave., Rte. 3, 207/338-9851, www.belfastcurlingclub.org), an institution here since the late 1950s. Leagues play regularly on weeknights, and the club holds tournaments *(bonspiels)* and open houses several times during the season, which runs early November–early April.

ACCOMMODATIONS

Bed-and-Breakfasts and Inns

On a quiet side street, **The Jeweled Turret** (40 Pearl St., 207/338-2304 or 800/696-2304, www.jeweledturret.com, $115–159) is one of Belfast's pioneer bed-and-breakfasts. Carl and Cathy Heffentrager understand the business and go out of their way to make guests comfortable. The 1898 Victorian inn is loaded with handsome woodwork and Victorian antiques—plus an astonishing stone fireplace. Carl can even fix your bike, if necessary, and he's up on all the local byways.

The White House (1 Church St., 207/338-1901 or 888/290-1901, www.mainebb.com, $175–250), the handsomest manse in Belfast, is the star of the Church Street Historic District. Built in the mid-19th century, the Greek Revival building is elegant inside and out—parlors, library, and guest rooms are accented with plaster ceiling medallions; it features marble fireplaces and a magnificent stairway. New owners Diana and Santiago Rich have added fancy linens, Wi-Fi, plasma TVs, and other upscale touches. A giant copper beech tree dominates the parklike grounds and gardens. Box lunches are available.

Over three years, beginning in 2005, professional innkeepers Ed and Judy Hemmingsen renovated adjacent mid-19th-century row houses into an elegant boutique hotel, the **Belfast Bay Inn & Luxury Suites** (72 Main St., 207/338-5600, www.belfastbayinn.com, $198–350). The two rooms and six suites differ in size and design, some with fireplaces, others with balconies, but all have original art, expanded wet bars, and quality furnishings that invite relaxation. In-room spa services are available. A full breakfast is served to each room. The Hemmingsens delight in surprising guests with unexpected extras.

Motels

The 61 rooms at the oceanfront **Belfast**

Harbor Inn (91 Searsport Ave., 207/338-2740 or 800/545-8576, www.belfastharborinn.com, $59–159) have TV, air-conditioning, free Wi-Fi and local calls; there's an outdoor heated pool—a real plus for families, as is the laundry. Pets are allowed in some rooms for $10 per night. Rates include a continental breakfast buffet. If you can swing it, request an ocean-view room.

Campground

Every one of the 44 mostly open sites at the **Moorings Oceanfront RV Resort** (191 Searsport Ave./Rte. 1, 207/338-6860, www.mooringscamp.com) has an ocean view and hookups. Views are fabulous, and the rocky beach has a pocket of sand; swimming is only for the hardy. The downsides: Many sites feel crowded, and there's often a wait for showers. Sites in midsummer are $42–58 (two adults plus three kids under 17). Facilities include laundry, play area, kayak launch, game room, Wi-Fi, and on-site restaurant.

FOOD

Call to verify days and hours of operation.

Local Flavors

Wraps are fast food at **Bay Wrap** (20 Beaver St., 207/338-9757, www.baywrap.com, 11 A.M.–7 P.M. Mon.–Fri., to 4 P.M. Sat.). There's no limit to what the staff can stuff into various flavors of tortillas. Eat here or get them to go. Another plus: **John's Ice Cream,** one of Maine's best homemade treats, is available here, too.

The **Belfast Co-op Store** (123 High St., 207/338-2532, www.belfast.coop, 7:30 A.M.–8 P.M. daily) is an experience in itself. You'll have a good impression of Belfast after one glance at the clientele and the bulletin board. Open to members and nonmembers alike (with lower prices for members), the co-op is a full-service organic and natural foods grocery, with a deli-café serving lunches daily and weekend brunches.

The Belfast Farmers Market (Washington St. parking lot downtown, 9 A.M.–1 P.M. Fri.) provides the perfect opportunity for stocking up for a picnic. In addition to plentiful veggies, you'll find breads, meats, cheeses, sweets, and other goodies.

Ethnic Fare

Don't be put off by the lackluster exterior of **Seng Thai** (160 Searsport Ave./Rte. 1, 207/338-0010, 11 A.M.–9 P.M. Tues.–Sun.), a small, low building across from the Comfort Inn. Inside the ambience is pleasant, the service is good, everything's available for takeout if you prefer, and best of all, it's decent Thai food (entrées $8–14).

Casual Dining

A longtime standby for creative (including vegetarian) world cuisine, **Darby's Restaurant and Pub** (155 High St., 207/338-2339, www.darbysrestaurant.com, 11:30 A.M.–3:30 P.M. and 5–9 P.M. daily) served tofu before tofu was cool. This place has been providing food and drink since just after the Civil War; the tin ceilings and antique bar are reminders of that. Entrées $11–20.

Fresh food prepared in creative ways has earned **Chase's Daily** (96 Main St., 207/338-0555, 7 A.M.–5 P.M. Tues.–Sat., to 8 P.M. Fri., 8 A.M.–2 P.M. Sun.) a devoted local following. The emphasis is on vegetarian fare, and most of the produce comes from the Chase family farm in nearby Freedom. Most choices are in the $7–12 range; dinner entrées $15–22. The restaurant doubles as an art gallery, farmers market, and bakery. It's not the place for a quiet dinner, as the space is large and tends to be loud.

Industrial chic, casual, and laid-back best describe **Three Tides** (2 Pinchy La., on Marshall Wharf, 207/338-1707, www.3tides.com, 4 P.M.–1 A.M. Tues.–Sat., to 9 P.M. Sun.). Grab a booth inside, a seat at the bar, or a table on the deck overlooking the working harbor, and then choose from the tapas-style menu ($3.50–12). You might even play a game of bocce while waiting. Beers and ales are brewed on the premises. Also part of the operation is

LB, a lobster pound, so lobster is almost always on the menu.

It doesn't look like much from the outside, but **Papa J's and the Lobster Bar** (193 Searsport Ave., 207/338-6464, 4–10 P.M. Tues.–Sat.) is warm and welcoming inside, with nice water views, a casual style, and—most important—well-prepared food ($12–25) complemented by a surprisingly good wine list. Order the lobster and feta pizza; you won't be disappointed.

Lobster in the Rough

Young's Lobster Pound (2 Fairview St., 207/338-1160, 8 A.M.–8 P.M. daily May–Nov.) is a classic eat-on-the-dock lobster place overlooking the bay. Dress down, relax, and pile into the crustaceans. BYOB. No credit cards. From downtown, cross the bridge to East Belfast and turn right at Jed's Restaurant. Continue to the end of the street.

Marshall Wharf is home to both a lobster pound and a brewery, both adjacent to the Three Tides restaurant, where you can order from either.

INFORMATION AND SERVICES

Information

The **Belfast Area Chamber of Commerce** (16 Main St., 207/338-5900, www.belfastmaine.org) produces a regional guide.

Check out **Belfast Free Library** (106 High St., 207/338-3884, www.belfast.lib.me.us).

Public Restrooms

Facilities are at the waterfront Public Landing, in the railroad station, at the Waldo County Court House, and at the Waldo County General Hospital.

Searsport Area

Five miles northeast of downtown Belfast, you're in the heart of Searsport, a name synonymous with the sea, thanks to an enduring oceangoing tradition that's appropriately commemorated here in the state's oldest maritime museum. The seafaring heyday occurred in the mid-19th century, but settlers from the Massachusetts Colony had already made inroads here 200 years earlier. By the 1750s, Fort Pownall, in nearby **Stockton Springs,** was a strategic site during the French and Indian War (the American phase of Europe's Seven Years' War).

Shipbuilding was underway by 1791, reaching a crescendo between 1845 and 1866, with six year-round shipyards and nearly a dozen more seasonal ones. By 1885, 10 percent of all full-rigged American-flag ships on the high seas were under the command of Searsport and Stockton Springs captains—a significant number bearing the name of Pendleton, Nichols, or Carver. Many of these were involved in the perilous China trade, rounding notorious Cape Horn with great regularity.

All this global contact shaped Searsport's culture, adding a veneer of cosmopolitan sophistication. Imposing mansions of seafaring families were filled with fabulous Oriental treasures, many of which eventually made their way to the Penobscot Marine Museum. Brick-lined Main Street is more evidence of the mid-19th-century wealth, and local churches reaped the benefits of residents' generosity. The Second Congregational Church, known as the Safe Harbor Church and patronized by captains and shipbuilders (most ordinary seamen attended the Methodist church), boasts recently restored Tiffany-style windows and a Christopher Wren steeple.

Another inkling of this area's oceangoing superiority comes from visits to local burial grounds: Check out the headstones at Gordon, Bowditch, and Sandy Point cemeteries. Many have fascinating tales to tell.

Today the Searsport area has a population of just under 2,600, and its major draws are the Penobscot Marine Museum, the still-handsome brick Historic District, several bed-and-breakfasts, a couple of special state parks, and wall-to-wall antiques shops and flea markets.

The Maine Historic Preservation Commission considers the buildings in Searsport's Main Street Historic District the best examples of their type outside of Portland—a frozen-in-time mid-19th-century cluster of brick and granite structures. The ground floors of most of the buildings are shops or restaurants; make time to stop in and admire their interiors.

SIGHTS

Penobscot Marine Museum

Exquisite marine paintings, historical photographs, ship models, boats, and unusual China-trade *objets* are just a few of the 10,000 treasures at the Penobscot Marine Museum (5 Church St., at Rte. 1, Searsport, 207/548-2529, www.penobscotmarinemuseum.org, 10 A.M.–5 P.M. Mon.–Sat., noon–5 P.M. Sun., $8 adults, $3 children 7–15, or $18 per family), Maine's oldest maritime museum—founded in 1936. Allow several hours to explore the exhibits, housed in five separate buildings on the museum's downtown campus. For a start, you'll see one of the nation's largest collections of paintings by marine artists James and Thomas Buttersworth. And the 1830s Fowler-True-Ross House is filled with exotic artifacts from foreign lands. Call or check the website for the schedule of lectures, concerts, and temporary exhibits. This isn't a very sophisticated museum, but it is a treasure. It's open late May–mid-October.

Fort Knox

Looming over Bucksport Harbor, the *other* Fort Knox (Rte. 174, Prospect, 207/469-7719, www.fortknox.maineguide.com, 9 A.M.–sunset May 1–Nov. 1, $4.50 nonresident adults, $3 residents, $1 children 5–11) is a 125-acre state historic site just off Route 1. Named for Major General Henry Knox, George Washington's first secretary of war, the sprawling granite fort was begun in 1844. Built to protect the upper Penobscot River from attack, it was never finished and never saw battle. Still, it was, as guide Kathy Williamson said, "very

© HILARY NANGLE

Construction on Fort Knox began in 1844. Today Rodman cannons are among the prizes at the sprawling granite fort.

well thought out and planned, and that may have been its best defense." Begin your visit at the Visitor and Education Center, operated by the Friends of Fort Knox, a nonprofit group that has partnered with the state to preserve and interpret the fort. Guided tours are available Memorial Day–Labor Day, and well worth it, as guides point out some of the fort's distinguishing features, including two complete Rodman cannons. Wear rubberized shoes and bring a flashlight to explore the underground passages; you can set the kids loose. The fort hosts Civil War reenactments several times a summer, a Renaissance Fair, a paranormal-psychic fair, and other events (check the website). The Halloween Fright at the Fort is a ghoulish event for the brave. The grounds are accessible all year. Bring a picnic; views over the river to Bucksport are fabulous.

Penobscot Narrows Bridge and Observatory

Do not miss the Penobscot Narrows Bridge and Observatory (9 A.M.–5 P.M. late May–Nov. 1, to 6 P.M. in July and Aug., $7.50 nonresident adults, $5 resident adults, $3 children 5–11, includes fort admission), accessible via Fort Knox. The observatory tops the 420-foot-high west tower of the new bridge spanning the Penobscot River. It's one of only three such structures in the world and the only one in the States. You'll zip up in an elevator, and when the doors open you're facing a wall of glass (yes, it's a bit of a shocker, downright terrifying for anyone with a serious fear of heights). Ascend two more flights (elevator available), and you're in the glass-walled observatory; the views on a clear day extend from Mt. Katahdin to Mount Desert Island. Even when it's hazy, it's still a neat experience.

BlueJacket Shipcrafters

Complementing the collections at the museum are the classic and contemporary models built by BlueJacket Shipcrafters (160 E. Main St./Rte. 1, Searsport, 800/448-5567, www.bluejacketinc.com), which boasts Maine's largest selection of ship models and nautical gifts.

© HILARY NANGLE

The Penobscot Narrows Bridge and Observatory tower rises out of Fort Knox.

Even if you're not a hobbyist, stop in to see the incredibly detailed models on display. Shipcrafters is renowned for building one-of-a-kind museum-quality custom models—it's the official modelmaker for the U.S. Navy—but don't despair, there are kits here for all abilities (and budgets). It's easy to find: Just look for the inland lighthouse on Route 1.

SHOPPING

The word "shopping" in Searsport usually applies to antiques—from 25-cent flea-market collectibles to well-used tools to high-end china, furniture, and glassware. The town has more than a dozen separate businesses—and some of those are group shops with multiple dealers. Searsport vies with Wells and Wiscasset as Maine's "Antiques Capital."

More than two dozen dealers supply the juried inventory for Bob and Phyllis Sommer's **Pumpkin Patch** (15 W. Main St./Rte. 1, Searsport, 207/548-6047)—with a heavy emphasis on Maine antiques. Specialties include quilts (at least 80 are always on hand), silver, paint-decorated furniture, Victoriana, and nautical and Native American items.

In excess of 70 dealers sell their antiques and collectibles at **Searsport Antique Mall** (149 E. Main St./Rte. 1, Searsport, 207/548-2640), making it another worthwhile stop for those seeking oldies but goodies.

The **Waldo County Craft Co-op** (307 E. Main St./Rte. 1, Searsport, 207/548-6686) features the work of about 30 Mainers: quilts, jams, bears, dolls, jewelry, baskets, pottery, floorcloths, and lots else.

Are you a hooker? Thirteen rooms full of hooked rugs, and supplies, fill **Searsport Rug Hooking** (396 E. Main St./Rte. 1, Searsport, 207/548-6100, www.searsportrughooking.com), in the midst of antiques shops and flea markets at the eastern end of town. The mother-daughter team of Christine Sherman and Julie Mattison, along with a talented staff, not only sell rugs, patterns, wool, and all the other supplies and necessities of the craft, they also design the patterns, dye the wools, teach, and demonstrate.

If you're a fan of jams and jellies, a must-stop is **Colleen's** (Rte. 1, Searsport, 207/548-6613). Colleen forages for wild berries for her wild strawberry and wild raspberry jams. Then there's her rose jelly, made not from hips but petals. And her maple spread, and . . .

A local fixture in Stockton Springs since 1960, **The Book Barn** (E. Main St., Stockton Springs, 207/567-3351) is jam-packed with used and antiquarian books.

RECREATION

Parks

MOOSE POINT STATE PARK

Here's a smallish park with a biggish view—183 acres wedged between Route 1 and a dramatic Penobscot Bay panorama. Moose Point State Park (Rte. 1, Searsport, 207/548-2882, $3 nonresident adults, $2 resident adults, $1 children 5–11) is 1.5 miles south of downtown Searsport. Bring a picnic, let the kids hang out and play (there's no swimming, but good tide-pooling at low tide), or walk through the woods or along the meadow trail. It's officially open late May–October 1, but since it's alongside the highway the park is accessible, weather permitting, all year.

MOSMAN PARK

Southeast of busy Route 1, the four-acre town-owned Mosman Park has picnic tables, a traditional playground, lots of grassy space, a pocket-size pebbly beach, seasonal toilets, and fabulous views of the bay. Turn off Route 1 at Water Street and continue to the end.

SEARS ISLAND

After almost two decades of heavy-duty squabbling over a proposed cargo port.on Searsport's 936-acre Sears Island (www.protectsearsisland.org), the state bought the island for $4 million in November 1997. The squabbling continued, but in 2009 a conservation easement was created that will protect 601 acres on one of the largest uninhabited islands on the East Coast for posterity. The island is a fine place for bird-watching, picnicking, walking, fishing, and cross-country skiing. It's linked to the mainland by a causeway. From downtown Searsport, continue northeast on Route 1 two miles to Sears Island Road (on your right). Turn and go 1.2 miles to the beginning of the island, where you can pull off and park before a gate (cars aren't allowed on the island). An easy 1.5-mile walk will take you to the other side of the island, overlooking Mack Point (site of a rather unattractive cargo port) and hills off to the left. Bring a picnic and binoculars—and a swimsuit if you're hardy enough to brave the water.

FORT POINT STATE PARK

Continuing northeast on Route 1 from Sears Island will get you to the turnoff for Fort Point State Park (Fort Point Rd., Stockton Springs, 207/567-3356, $3 nonresident adults, $2 resident adults, $1 children 5–11) on Cape Jellison's eastern tip. Within the 154-acre park are the earthworks of 18th-century **Fort Pownall** (a British fortress built in the French and Indian War), **Fort Point Light** (a square 26-foot 19th-century tower guarding the mouth of the Penobscot River) and adjacent bell tower, shoreline trails, and a 200-foot pier where you can fish or bird- or boat-watch. (Bird-watchers can spot waterfowl—especially ruddy ducks, but also eagles and osprey.) Bring picnic fixings, but stay clear of the keeper's house—it's private. At the Route 1 fork for Stockton Springs, bear right onto Main Street and continue to Mill Road, in the village center. Turn right and then left onto East Cape Road, then another left onto Fort Point Road, which leads to the parking area. Officially, the park is open late May–Labor Day, but it's accessible all year, weather permitting.

Bicycling

Birgfeld's Bicycle Shop (184 E. Main St./Rte. 1, Searsport, 207/548-2916 or 800/206-2916), in business since the 1970s, is a mandatory stop for any cyclist, novice or pro. Local information on about 15 biking loops, supplies, maps, weekly group rides with the **Belfast Bicycle Club** (www.belfastbicycleclub.org), sales (also skateboards and scooters), and excellent repair services are all part of the Birgfeld's mix.

An especially good ride in this area is the **Cape Jellison** loop in Stockton Springs. Park at Stockton Springs Elementary School and do the loop from there. Including a detour to Fort Point, the ride totals less than 10 miles from downtown Stockton Springs.

ACCOMMODATIONS

Searsport's gorgeous and monstrous homes seem likely prospects as inns, and indeed many have tried, but few succeed. Most only last a season or two before reverting to private homes.

Bed-and-Breakfasts

The **1794 Watchtide** (190 W. Main St./Rte. 1, Searsport, 207/548-6575 or 800/698-6575, www.watchtide.com, $140–190) occupies a sprawling late-18th-century sea captain's home formerly known as The College Club Inn. Each of the four rooms and one suite has a historic-name connection; the Eleanor Roosevelt Suite acknowledges visits by former first ladies in decades past. All have air-conditioning, TVs, and mini-fridges. Two rooms have whirlpool tubs. Rooms in the back have the nicest views and are most quiet. Breakfasts are fabulous. Collapse on the 60-foot sun porch, overlooking the bay, and you may never want to leave.

A budget find for vegetarians and vegans, **Elm Cottage** (5 Elm St., Searsport, 207/548-2941, www.elmcottageinsearsport.com, $85–90), an 1840 cape, has two rooms, one with water view, tucked under the eaves. The full vegetarian breakfast can be tailored to meet restrictive diets. Reiki is offered, and there's Wi-Fi.

Motel

The **Yardarm** (172 E. Main St./Rte. 1, Searsport, www.searsportmaine.com, $65–125), a small motel set back from the road, is next door to BlueJacket Shipcrafters. Each of the 18 pine-paneled units has TV, air-conditioning, Wi-Fi, and phone; suites (perfect for families) have a dinette, microwave, and small fridge. A continental breakfast is served in a cheery breakfast room in the adjacent farmhouse. Two rooms are pet friendly. It's open May–late October.

Here's a find. **Bait's Motel** (215 E. Main St./Rte. 1, Searsport, 207/548-7299, www.baitsmotel.com, $79–119) doesn't look like much from the exterior, but inside the recently renovated rooms are outfitted with quality comfortable furniture, down duvets and pillows, and nice toiletries. Add fridges, cable TV, free local calls and Wi-Fi, and individually controlled heat and air-conditioning. Standard rooms are pet friendly. It's adjacent to Angler's Restaurant.

Campground

How can you beat 1,100 feet of tidal oceanfront and unobstructed views of Islesboro, Castine, and Penobscot Bay? **Searsport Shores Camping Resort** (216 W. Main St./Rte. 1, Searsport, 207/548-6059, www.campocean.com) gets high marks for its fabulous setting. About 100 good-size sites (including walk-in oceanfront tenting sites) go for $39–68 a day. Facilities include a private beach, small store, free showers, laundry, play areas, recreation hall, nature trails, and volleyball court. Request a site away from organized-activity areas. Bring a sea kayak and launch it here. Leashed pets are allowed. In early September, the campground hosts Fiber Arts College, a weekend of classes, demonstrations, and camaraderie for spinners, hookers, weavers, and the like.

FOOD

Call to verify days and hours of operation.

The **Anglers Restaurant** (215 E. Main St./Rte. 1, Searsport, 207/548-2405, www.anglersrestaurant.net, 11 A.M.–8 P.M. daily) is probably the least assuming and one of the most popular restaurants around. Expect hearty New England cooking, hefty portions, local color, no frills, and a bill that won't dent your wallet. Big favorites are the chowders and stews and lobster rolls. Dinner entrées are $9–14, although lobsters are higher. The "minnow menu" for smaller appetites runs $6–13. Desserts are a specialty: The gingerbread with whipped cream is divine; kids love the "bucket o' worms." If it's not too busy, and you've ordered a lobster, ask owner Buddy Hall if he'll demonstrate hypnotizing it. It's adjacent to the Bait's Motel, 1.5 miles northeast of downtown Searsport.

Good home cooking with an emphasis on fried food has made **Just Barb's** (Main St./Rte. 1, Stockton Springs, 207/567-3886, 6 A.M.–8 P.M. daily) a dandy place for an unfussy meal at a low price. Fried clams and scallop stew are both winners; finish up with a slab of pie or shortcake. The $7.99 all-you-can-eat fish fry is available daily after 11 A.M.

INFORMATION AND SERVICES

The **Belfast Area Chamber of Commerce** (207/338-5900, www.belfastmaine.org) and **Waldo County Marketing Association** (800/870-9934, www.waldocountymaine.com) have information about the Belfast area.

Searsport's small self-serve info center is in a shed-like building on Route 1 (at Norris St.), across from the Pumpkin Patch antiques shop.

Check out the **Carver Memorial Library** (Mortland Rd. at Union St., Searsport, 207/548-2303, www.carver.lib.me.us).

Bucksport Area

The new Penobscot Narrows Bridge provides an elegant entry to the Bucksport area, a longtime rough-and-ready river port and papermaking town that's slowly gentrifying. Bucksport is no upstart. Native Americans first gravitated to these Penobscot River shores in summers, finding here a rich source of salmon for food and grasses for basketmaking. In 1764, it was officially settled by Colonel Jonathan Buck, a Massachusetts Bay Colony surveyor who modestly named it Buckstown and organized a booming shipping business here. His remains are interred in a local cemetery, where his tombstone bears the distinct outline of a woman's leg; this is allegedly the result of a curse by a witch Buck ordered executed, but in fact it's probably a flaw in the granite. (The monument is across Route 1 from the Hannaford supermarket, on the corner of Hinks Street.)

Just south of Bucksport, at the bend in the Penobscot River, Verona Island is best known as the mile-long link between Prospect and Bucksport. Just before you cross the bridge from Verona to Bucksport, hang a left and then a quick right to a small municipal park with a boat launch and broad views of Bucksport Harbor (and the paper mill). In the Buck Memorial Library is a scale model of Admiral Robert Peary's Arctic exploration vessel, the *Roosevelt,* built on this site.

Bucksport has a nice riverfront walkway, a historical theater, and the best views of Fort Knox. Route 1 east of Bucksport leads to **Orland,** with an idyllic setting on the banks of the Narramissic River. It's also the site of a unique service organization called H.O.M.E. (Homeworkers Organized for More Employment). East Orland (officially part of Orland) claims the Craig Brook National Fish Hatchery and Great Pond Mountain (you can't miss it, jutting from the landscape on the left as you drive east on Route 1).

SIGHTS

Alamo Theatre

Phoenix-like, the 1916 Alamo Theatre (85 Main St., Bucksport, 207/469-0924 or 800/639-1636, event line 207/469-6910, www.alamotheatre.org) has been retrofitted for a new life—focusing on films about New England produced and/or revived by the unique Northeast Historic Film (NHF), which is headquartered here. Stop in, survey the restoration, visit the displays (donation requested), and browse the Alamo Theatre Store for antique postcards, T-shirts, toys, and reasonably priced videos on ice harvesting, lumberjacks, maple sugaring, and other traditional New England topics. A half mile west of Route 1, it's open 9 A.M.–4 P.M. Monday–Friday all year. The Alamo has also become an active cinema, screening classic and current films regularly in the 120-seat theater, usually on weekends. Each summer there's also a silent film festival.

Bucksport Waterfront Walkway

Stroll the one-mile paved walkway from the Bucksport/Verona Bridge to Webber Docks. Along the way are historical markers, picnic tables, a gazebo, a restroom, and expansive views of the harbor and Fort Knox.

H.O.M.E.

Adjacent to the flashing light on Route 1 in Orland, H.O.M.E. (207/469-7961, www.homecoop.net) is tough to categorize. Linked with the international Emmaus Movement founded by a French priest, H.O.M.E. (Homeworkers Organized for More Employment) was started in 1970 by Lucy Poulin, still the guiding force, and two nuns at a nearby convent. The quasi-religious organization shelters refugees and the homeless, operates a soup kitchen and a car-repair service, runs a day-care center, and teaches work skills in a variety of hands-on cooperative programs. Seventy percent of its income comes from sales of crafts, produce, and services. At the Route 1 store (corner of Upper Falls Rd., 9 A.M.–4:30 P.M. daily) you can buy handmade quilts, organic produce, maple syrup, and jams—and support a worthwhile effort. You can also tour the crafts workshops on the property.

Craig Brook National Fish Hatchery

For a day of hiking, picnicking, swimming, canoeing, and a bit of natural history, pack a lunch and head for 135-acre Craig Brook National Fish Hatchery (306 Hatchery Rd., East Orland, 207/469-2803), on Alamoosook Lake. Turn off Route 1 six miles east of Bucksport and continue 1.4 miles north to the parking area just above the visitors center. The visitors center (8:30 A.M.–3:30 P.M. Mon.–Fri., 8 A.M.–3:30 P.M. Sat.–Sun. in summer, free) offers interactive displays on Atlantic salmon (don't miss the downstairs viewing area), maps, and a restroom. The grounds are accessible 6 A.M. to sunset daily year-round. Established in 1889, the U.S. Fish and Wildlife Service hatchery raises sea-run Atlantic salmon for stocking six Maine rivers. The birch-lined shorefront has picnic tables, a boat-launching ramp, an Atlantic salmon display pool, additional parking, and a spectacular cross-lake view. Watch for eagles, osprey, and loons. Also on the premises is the small **Atlantic Salmon Museum** (noon–3 P.M. Thurs., Sat., and Sun. or by arrangement with the hatchery), housed in a circa-1896 ice house and operated by the Friends of Craig Brook. Inside are salmon and fly-fishing artifacts and memorabilia.

SHOPPING

Locals come just as much for the coffee and conversation as the selection of new and used reads at **BookStacks** (71 Main St., Bucksport, 207/469-8992).

RECREATION

Great Pond Mountain Conservation

The Great Pond Mountain Conservation Trust (207/469-6772, www.greatpondtrust.org) acts as conscientious local steward for Great Pond Mountain and Great Pond Wildlands. It also hosts hikes and other activities.

Encompassing two parcels of land and nearly 4,300 acres, the Great Pond Wildlands is a jewel. The larger parcel totals 3,420 acres and surrounds Hothole Valley, including Hothole Brook, prized for its trout, and shoreline on Hothole Pond. The smaller, 875-acre tract includes two miles of frontage on the Dead River (not to be confused with the Dead River of rafting fame in northwestern Maine) and reaches up Great Pond Mountain and down to the ominously named Hell Bottom Swamp. The land is rich with wildlife: black bear, moose, bobcat, and deer, just to name a few species, plus with the pond, swamp, and river it's ideal for birdwatching. With 14 miles of woods roads lacing the land, it's prime territory for walking, mountain biking, and snowshoeing, and the waterways invite fishing and paddling. Avoid the area during hunting season. Snowmobiling is permitted; ATVs are banned. Access to the Dead River tract is from the Craig Brook National Fish Hatchery; follow Don Fish Road to the Dead River Gate and Dead River Trail. The South Gate to Hothole Pond Tract is on Route 1, just southwest of Route 176. You can drive in along Valley Road about 2.5 miles to a parking area.

The biggest rewards for the 1.8-mile easy-to-moderate hike up 1,038-foot **Great Pond Mountain** are 360-degree views and lots of space for panoramic picnics. On a clear day, Baxter State Park's Katahdin is visible from the peak's north side. In fall, watch for migrating hawks. Access to the mountain is via gated private property beginning about a mile north of Craig Brook National Fish Hatchery on Hatchery Road, East Orland. Roadside parking is available near the trailhead, but during fall-foliage season you may need to park at the hatchery. Pick up a brochure from the box at the trailhead, stay on the trail, and respect the surrounding private property.

Canoeing

If you've brought a canoe, **Silver Lake,** just

two miles north of downtown Bucksport, is a beautiful place for a paddle. There's no development along its shores, and the bird-watching is excellent. No swimming ($500 fine); this is Bucksport's reservoir. To get to the public launch, take Route 15 north off Route 1 after crossing the Verona-Bucksport Bridge. Go 0.5 mile and turn right on McDonald Road, which becomes Silver Lake Road, and follow it 2.1 miles to the launch site.

Golf

Bucksport Golf Club (Duck Cove Rd., Rte. 46, 1.5 miles north of Rte. 1, 207/469-7612, mid-Apr.–Sept.), running 3,397 yards, prides itself on having Maine's longest nine-hole course.

River Cruise

See Fort Knox and the bridges from the water and learn about the region's history and lore on a narrated trip aboard *Lil' Toot* with **Bucksport Harbor Tours** (96 Main St., Bucksport, 207/469-7498, www.littletoottours.com). Wildlife sightings, including osprey, eagles, and seals, are a possibility. The 75-minute tours depart from the Bucksport Town Dock four times on Friday, Saturday, and most Sundays in July and August. An evening cruise lasts two hours. Buy tickets ($15–20 adults, $7.50–10 children 2–12) at **Bittersweet Gift Shop** (81 Main St., Bucksport).

ACCOMMODATIONS

Inns and Bed-and-Breakfasts

The **Orland House** (10 Narramissic Dr., Orland, 207/469-1144, www.orlandhousebb.com, $85–125), Alvion and Cindi Kimball's elegant yet comfortable 1820 Greek Revival home, overlooks the Narramissic River. It's been beautifully restored, preserving the architectural details but adding plenty of creature comforts. Cindi heads the local chamber of commerce, so she's a wealth of info.

Location, location, location. If only the six simple rooms at the old-timey **Alamoosook Lakeside Inn** (off Rte. 1, Orland, 207/469-6393 or 866/459-6393, www.alamoosooklakesideinn.com, $125) actually overlooked the lake, then it would be the perfect rustic lakeside lodge. The property is gorgeous, and the location well-suited for exploring the area, but the rooms are so-so, with tiny bathrooms. All have

© HILARY NANGLE

For a different perspective on Fort Knox and the Penobscot Narrows Bridge, book a trip aboard the *Lil' Toot* out of Bucksport.

windows and doors opening onto a long sun porch overlooking the lake. Now the upside: The lodge has a quarter mile of lakefront, and guests have access to canoes and kayaks. Paddle across the lake to the fish hatchery for a hike up Great Pond Mountain. A full breakfast is served; free Wi-Fi. It's open year-round.

Motels

In downtown Bucksport, the **Fort Knox Inn** (64 Main St., Bucksport, 207/469-3113 or 800/528-1234, $115–199) is a four-story Best Western nudged right up to the harbor's edge. Forty modern rooms have phones, air-conditioning, free Wi-Fi, and cable-satellite TV. Be sure to request a water view, or you'll be facing a parking lot.

Camping

The rivers, lakes, and ponds between Bucksport and Ellsworth make the area especially appealing for camping, and sites tend to be cheaper than in the Bar Harbor area. During July and August, especially on weekends, reservations are wise.

Six miles east of Bucksport, across from Craig Pond Road, is Back Ridge Road, leading to **Balsam Cove Campground** (286 Back Ridge Rd., East Orland, 207/469-7771 or 800/469-7771, www.balsamcove.com, $22–42). From Route 1, take Back Ridge Road 1.5 miles to the left turn for the campground on the shores of 10-mile-long Toddy Pond. Facilities on the 50 acres include 60 wooded waterfront or water-view tent and RV sites, a one-room rental cabin ($54–68), on-site rental trailers ($65–80), a dump station, a store, laundry, free showers, boat rentals, and freshwater swimming. Open late May to late September. Dogs are welcome on camping sites for $2 per day.

The same season holds for 10-acre **Whispering Pines Campground** (Rte. 1, East Orland, 207/469-3443, www.campmaine.com/whisperingpines/, $36 for two people, $2 per child over age 7), also on Toddy Pond, but with access directly from Route 1. Facilities include 50 tent and RV sites (request one close to the pond), free use of canoes and rowboats, freshwater swimming, a playground, free showers, and a recreation hall. Whispering Pines is 6.5 miles east of Bucksport.

FOOD

MacLeod's (Main St., Bucksport, 207/469-3963, 11 A.M.–9 P.M. Tues.–Sat.) is Bucksport's most popular and enduring restaurant. Some tables in the pleasant dining room have glimpses of the river and Fort Knox. The wide-ranging menu has choices for all tastes and budgets. Reservations are wise for Saturday nights.

In what passes as downtown Orland (hint: don't blink), **Orland Market and Pizza** (Rte. 175/91 Castine Rd., Orland, 207/469-9999, www.orlandmarket.com, 7 A.M.–9 P.M. daily) is a delight. Established in 1860, the old-fashioned country store has a little of this and a bit of that along with breakfast sandwiches, hot and cold sandwiches, grilled foods, salad, and all kinds of pizza. Call or drop by to find out the day's homemade specials, perhaps lasagna or spaghetti and meatballs. Smoked ribs are the specialty every other Thursday, weather permitting.

INFORMATION AND SERVICES

The **Bucksport Bay Area Chamber of Commerce** (52 Main St., Bucksport, 207/469-6818, www.bucksportchamber.org) is right next to the municipal office in downtown Bucksport. Office hours are 9 A.M.–5 P.M. Monday–Friday, but the side door is always open for access to an extensive array of brochures, newspapers, and other publications, plus bulletin board notices. The local *Enterprise* newspaper and the Bucksport Chamber of Commerce produce a very helpful annual, *The Guide,* covering Bucksport, Orland, and Verona Island.

Public Restrooms

In Bucksport, public restrooms next to the town dock (behind the Bucksport Historical Society) are open spring, summer, and fall. Restrooms are open year-round in the Bucksport Municipal Office (weekdays) on Main Street.

BLUE HILL PENINSULA AND DEER ISLE

The Blue Hill Peninsula, once dubbed "The Fertile Crescent," is unique. Few other Maine locales harbor such a high concentration of artisans, musicians, and on-their-feet retirees juxtaposed with top-flight wooden-boat builders, lobstermen, and umpteenth-generation Mainers. Perhaps surprisingly, the mix seems to work.

Anchored by the towns of Bucksport to the east and Ellsworth to the west, the peninsula comprises several enclaves with markedly distinct personalities. Blue Hill, Castine, Orland, Brooklin, Brooksville, and Sedgwick are stitched together by a network of narrow, winding country roads. Thanks to the mapmaker-challenging coastline and a handful of freshwater ponds and rivers, there's a view of water around nearly every bend.

You can watch the sun set from atop Blue Hill Mountain; tour the home of the fascinating Jonathan Fisher; stroll through the village of Castine (charming verging on precious), whose streets are lined with dowager-like homes; visit *WoodenBoat* magazine's world headquarters in tiny Brooklin; and browse top-notch studios and galleries throughout the peninsula. Venture a bit inland of Route 1, and you find lovely lakes for paddling and swimming and another hill to hike.

After weaving your way down the Blue Hill Peninsula and crossing the soaring pray-as-you-go bridge to Little Deer Isle, you've entered the realm of island living. Sure, bridges and causeways connect the points, but the farther down you drive, the more removed from civilization you'll feel. The pace slows; the population

© TOM NANGLE

HIGHLIGHTS

Parson Fisher House: More than just another historic house, the Parson Fisher House is a remarkable testimony to one man's ingenuity (page 255).

Blue Hill Mountain: It's a relatively easy hike for fabulous 360-degree views from the summit of this local landmark (page 257).

Flash! In the Pans Community Steel Band: Close your eyes while listening to this phenomenal steel-pan band, and you just might think you're on a Caribbean island rather than in Maine (page 264).

Holbrook Island Sanctuary State Park: Varied hiking trails and great bird-watching are the rewards for finding this off-the-beaten-path preserve (page 267).

Castine Historic Tour: A turbulent history detailed on signs throughout town makes Castine an irresistible place to tour on foot or bike (page 270).

Sea Kayaking: Hook up with "Kayak Karen" to see Castine from the water (page 273).

Haystack Mountain School of Crafts: Arrange your schedule to visit the spectacular architect-designed campus of this renowned oceanfront school (page 279).

Art and Craft Galleries: The Haystack crafts school has inspired dozens of world-class artisans to set up shop on Deer Isle (page 283).

Guided Island Tours: Join Captain Walter Reed for a boat tour amidst the islands customized to your interests (page 288).

Acadia National Park: Tipping sparsely populated **Isle au Haut** is a remote section of the national park, perfect for a day trip or longer (page 293).

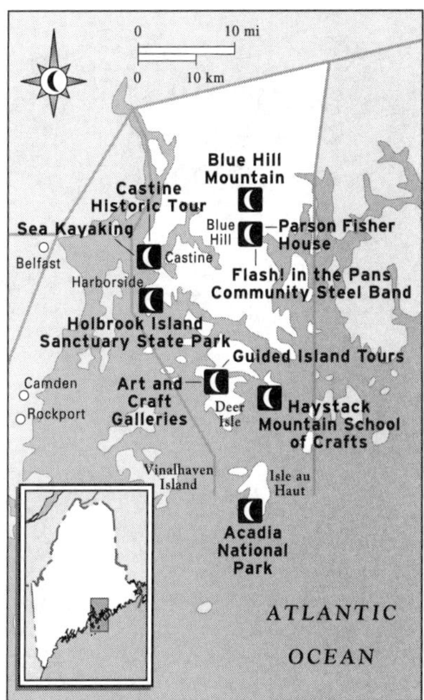

LOOK FOR ☾ TO FIND RECOMMENDED SIGHTS, ACTIVITIES, DINING, AND LODGING.

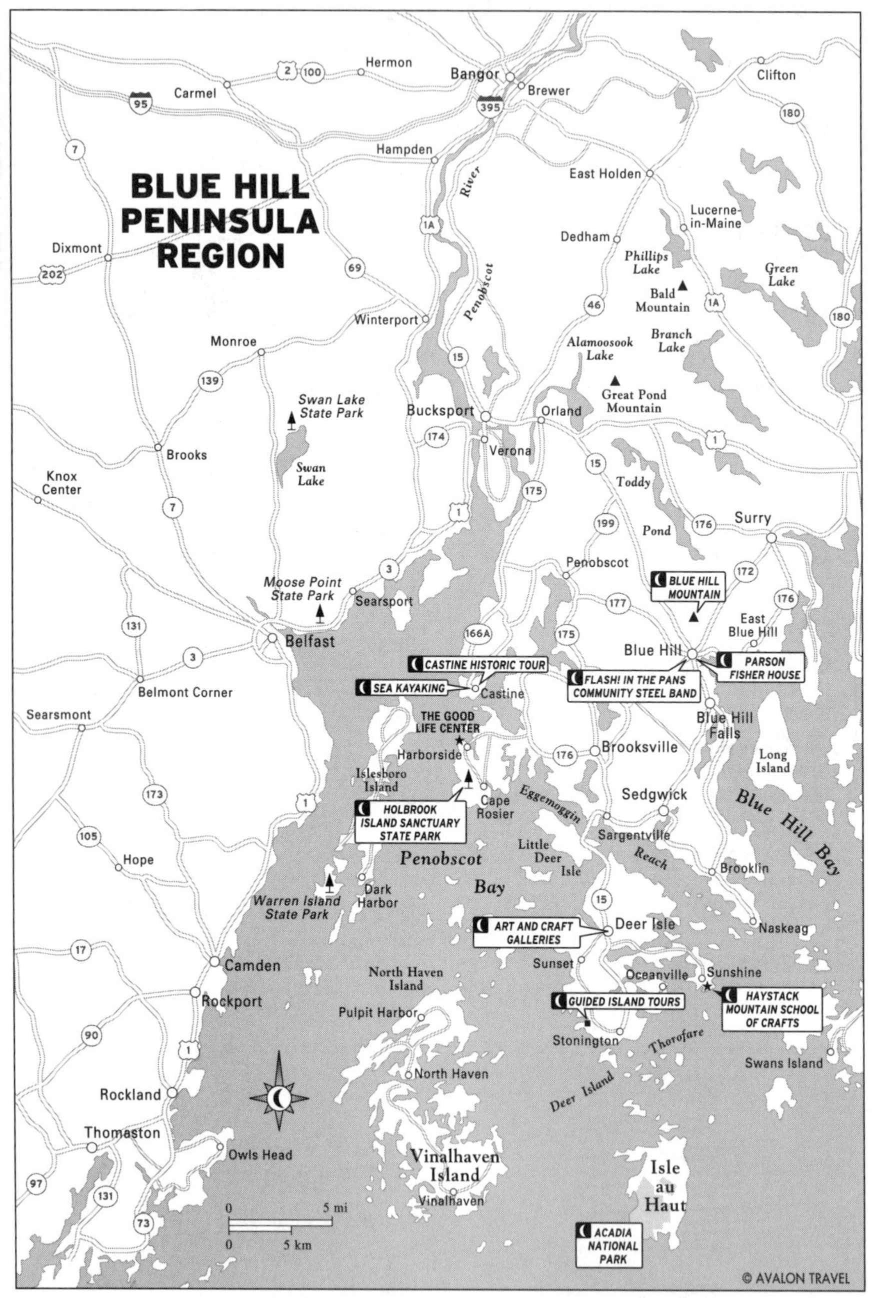
BLUE HILL PENINSULA REGION
Bangor
Brewer
Hermon
Carmel
Clifton
Hampden
East Holden
Lucerne-in-Maine
Dedham
Phillips Lake
Green Lake
Bald Mountain
Branch Lake
Alamoosook Lake
Great Pond Mountain
Dixmont
Winterport
Monroe
Penobscot River
Bucksport
Orland
Verona
Swan Lake State Park
Swan Lake
Brooks
Knox Center
Toddy Pond
Surry
Penobscot
BLUE HILL MOUNTAIN
East Blue Hill
Blue Hill
PARSON FISHER HOUSE
Moose Point State Park
Searsport
Belfast
CASTINE HISTORIC TOUR
SEA KAYAKING
Castine
FLASH! IN THE PANS COMMUNITY STEEL BAND
Belmont Corner
Searsmont
THE GOOD LIFE CENTER
Harborside
Blue Hill Falls
Brooksville
Long Island
Islesboro Island
Cape Rosier
Sedgwick
Blue Hill Bay
HOLBROOK ISLAND SANCTUARY STATE PARK
Eggemoggin Reach
Sargentville
Hope
Penobscot Bay
Little Deer Isle
Brooklin
Warren Island State Park
Dark Harbor
Deer Isle
ART AND CRAFT GALLERIES
Naskeag
Camden
Sunset
North Haven Island
Oceanville
Sunshine
Rockport
HAYSTACK MOUNTAIN SCHOOL OF CRAFTS
Pulpit Harbor
GUIDED ISLAND TOURS
Stonington
Thorofare
Swans Island
North Haven
Rockland
Deer Island
Thomaston
Owls Head
Vinalhaven Island
Isle au Haut
Vinalhaven
ACADIA NATIONAL PARK
0 5 mi
0 5 km
© AVALON TRAVEL

dwindles. Fishing and lobstering are the mainstays; lobster boats rest near many homes and trap fences edge properties. If your ultimate destination is the section of Acadia National Park on Isle au Haut, the drive down Deer Isle serves to help disconnect you from the mainland. To reach the park's acreage on Isle au Haut, after wending your way through Little Deer Isle and Deer Isle, you'll board the Isle au Haut ferryboat for the trip down Merchant Row to the island.

PLANNING YOUR TIME

To truly enjoy this region, you'll want to spend at least three or four days here, perhaps splitting your lodging between two or three locations. The region is designed for leisurely exploring; you won't be able to zip from one location to another. Traveling along the winding roads, discovering galleries and country stores, and lodging at traditional inns are all part of the experience.

Arts fans will want to concentrate their efforts in Blue Hill, Deer Isle, and Stonington. Outdoor-oriented folks should consider Deer Isle, Stonington, or Castine as a base for sea kayaking or exploring the area preserves. For architecture and history buffs, Castine is a must.

No visit to this region is complete without at least a cruise by if not a visit to Isle au Haut, an offshore island that's home to a remote section of Acadia National Park. Allow at least a few hours for a ride on the mail boat, but if you can afford the time, spend a full day hiking the park's trails. Don't forget to pack food and water.

Blue Hill

Twelve miles south of Route 1 is the hub of the peninsula, Blue Hill (pop. 2,390), exuding charm from its handsome old homes to its waterfront setting to the shops, restaurants, and galleries that boost its appeal.

Eons back, Native American summer folk gave the name Awanadjo ("small, hazy mountain") to the mini-mountain that looms over the town and draws the eye for miles around. The first permanent settlers arrived after the French and Indian War, in the late 18th century, and established mills and shipyards. More than 100 ships were built here between Blue Hill's incorporation, in 1789, and 1882—bringing prosperity to the entire peninsula.

Critical to the town's early expansion was its first clergyman, Jonathan Fisher, a remarkable fellow who's been likened to Leonardo da Vinci. In 1803, Fisher founded Blue Hill Academy (predecessor of today's George Stevens Academy), then built his home (now a museum), and eventually left an immense legacy of inventions, paintings, engravings, and poetry.

Throughout the 19th century and into the 20th, Blue Hill's granite industry boomed, reaching its peak in the 1880s. Scratch the Brooklyn Bridge and the New York Stock Exchange and you'll find granite from Blue Hill's quarries. Around 1879, the discovery of gold and silver brought a flurry of interest, but little came of it. Copper was also found here, but quantities of it, too, were limited.

At the height of industrial prosperity, tourism took hold, attracting steamboat-borne summer boarders. Many succumbed to the scenery, bought land, and built waterfront summer homes. Thank these summer folk and their offspring for the fact that music has long been a big deal in Blue Hill. The Kneisel Hall Chamber Music School, established in the late 19th century, continues to rank high among the nation's summer music colonies. New York City's Blue Hill Troupe, devoted to Gilbert and Sullivan operettas, was named for the longtime summer home of the troupe's founders.

SIGHTS

Parson Fisher House

Named for a brilliant Renaissance man who

arrived in Blue Hill in 1794, the Parson Fisher House (Rte. 15/176, 44 Mines Rd., 207/374-2459, www.jonathanfisherhouse.org, 1–4 P.M. Thurs.–Sat. early July–mid-Oct., $5) immerses visitors in period furnishings and Jonathan Fisher lore. And Fisher's feats are breathtaking: He was a Harvard-educated preacher who also managed to be an accomplished painter, poet, mathematician, naturalist, linguist, inventor, cabinetmaker, farmer, architect, and printmaker. In his spare time, he fathered nine children. Fisher also pitched in to help build the yellow house on Tenney Hill, which served as the Congregational Church parsonage. Now it contains intriguing items created by Fisher, memorabilia that volunteer tour guides delight in explaining, including a camera obscura. Don't miss it.

Historic Houses

A few of Blue Hill's elegant houses have been converted to museums, inns, restaurants, and even some offices and shops, so you can see them from the inside out. To appreciate the private residences, you'll want to walk, bike, or drive around town. Also ask at the Holt House about village walking tours.

In downtown Blue Hill, a few steps off Main Street, stands the **Holt House** (3 Water St., 207/326-8250, www.bluehillhistory.org, 1–4 P.M. Tues. and Fri., 11 A.M.–2 P.M. Sat., July–mid-Sept., $3 adults, free children 12 and under), home of the Blue Hill Historical Society. Built in 1815 by Jeremiah Holt, the Federal-style building contains restored stenciling, period decor, and masses of memorabilia contributed by local residents. In the carriage house are even more goodies, including old tools, a sleigh, carriages, and so forth.

Walk or drive up Union Street (Route 177), past George Stevens Academy, and wander **The Old Cemetery,** established in 1794. If gnarled trees and ancient headstones intrigue you, there aren't many good-sized Maine cemeteries older than this one.

Bagaduce Music Lending Library

At the foot of Greene's Hill in Blue Hill is one of Maine's more unusual institutions, a library where you can borrow from a collection of more than one million scores and pieces of sheet music (3 Music Library La., Rte. 172, 207/374-5454, www.bagaducemusic.org, 10 A.M.–3 P.M. Mon.–Fri. or by appointment). Somehow this seems so appropriate for a community that's a magnet for music lovers. Annual membership is $10 ($5 for students); fees range $1–4 per piece.

Scenic Routes

Parker Point Road (turn off Route 15 at the Blue Hill Library) takes you from Blue Hill to Blue Hill Falls the back way, with vistas en route toward Acadia National Park. For other great views, drive the length of **Newbury Neck,** in nearby Surry, or head west on Route 15/176 toward Sedgwick, Brooksville, and beyond.

ENTERTAINMENT

Variety and serendipity are the keys here. Check local calendar listings and tune in to radio station WERU (89.9 and 102.9 FM, www.weru.org), the peninsula's own community radio; there might be announcements of concerts by local resident pianist Paul Sullivan or the Bagaduce Chorale, or maybe a contra dance or a tropical treat from Flash! In the Pans Community Band (www.flashinthe-pans.org). The George Stevens Academy has a free Tuesday evening lecture series in July and August.

Music

Since 1922, chamber-music students have been spending summers perfecting their skills and demonstrating their prowess at the **Kneisel Hall Chamber Music School** (Pleasant St., Rte. 15, 207/374-2811, www.kneisel.org). Faculty concerts run Friday evenings and Sunday afternoons late June–late August. The concert schedule is published in the spring, and reserved-seating tickets ($30 inside, $20 on the veranda outside, nonrefundable) can be ordered by phone. Other opportunities to hear the students and faculty exist, including young artist concerts, children's concerts, open rehearsals, and more. Kneisel Hall is about a half mile from the center of town.

The Blue Hill Congregational Church is the site for the **Vanderkay Summer Music Series** (207/374-2891), which ranges from choral music from the Middle Ages to gospel. Tickets are $15.

Chamber music continues in winter thanks to the volunteer **Blue Hill Concert Association** (207/326-4666, www.bluehillconcerts.org), which presents five concerts between January and March at the Congregational Church. Recommended donation is $20.

EVENTS

WERU's annual Full Circle Fair is usually held in mid-August at the Blue Hill Fairgrounds (Rte. 172, north of downtown Blue Hill). Expect world music, good food, crafts, and socially and environmentally progressive talks.

On Labor Day weekend, the **Blue Hill Fair** (Blue Hill Fairgrounds, Rte. 172, 207/374-9976) is one of the state's best agricultural fairs.

SHOPPING

Boutiques, antiques, galleries, and even two downtown bookstores make shopping a pleasure in Blue Hill.

Antiques

Blue Hill Antiques (8 Water St., 207/374-2199 or 207/326-4973) specializes in 18th- and 19th-century French and American furniture—it attracts a high-end clientele. The same patrons seek out neighboring Brad Emerson's **Emerson Antiques** (33 Water St., 207/374-5140), concentrating on early Americana, such as hooked rugs and ship models.

Books

Blue Hill's literate population manages to support two full-service, year-round independent bookstores.

Ever-helpful Bonnie Myers provides free advice on the region with a money-back guarantee at **North Light Books** (Main St., 207/374-5422). It's a delight to browse, the children's book selection is terrific, and out back is Blue Hill Hearth, with all sorts of treats.

Around the corner is **Blue Hill Books** (26 Pleasant St., Rte. 15, 207/374-5632, www.bluehillbooks.com), which organizes an "authors series" during the summer.

Wine

Blue Hill Wine Shop (138 Main St., 207/374-2161), tucked into a converted horse barn, carries more than 1,000 wines, plus teas, coffees, and blended tobaccos and unusual pipes for diehard, upscale smokers. Monthly wine tastings (usually 2:30–6 P.M. last Saturday of the month) are always an adventure.

PARKS AND RECREATION

Blue Hill Mountain

Mountain seems a fancy label for a 943-footer, yet Blue Hill Mountain stands alone, visible from Camden and even beyond. On a clear day, head for the summit and take in the wraparound view encompassing Penobscot Bay, the hills of Mount Desert, and the Camden Hills. Climb the fire tower and you'll see even more. In mid-June, the lupines along the way are breathtaking; in fall, the colors are spectacular—with reddened blueberry barrens added to the variegated foliage. Go early in the day; it's a popular easy-to-moderate hike. A short loop on the lower slopes takes only half an hour. Take Route 15 (Pleasant Street) to Mountain Road. Turn right and go 0.8 mile to the trailhead (on the left) and the small parking area (on the right). You can also walk (uphill) the mile from the village.

Blue Hill Heritage Trust

This fine organization (101 Union St., 207/374-5118, www.bluehillheritagetrust.org, 8 A.M.–5 P.M. Mon.–Fri.) works hard at preserving the region's landscape. It also presents a Walks 'n' Talks series, with offerings such as kayaking by preservation land along Eggemoggin Reach, a full-moon hike up Blue Hill Mountain, and walks through other trust properties, such as 700-acre Kingdom Woods

GALLERY HOPPING IN BLUE HILL

Perhaps it's Blue Hill's location near the renowned Haystack Mountain School of Crafts. Perhaps it's the way the light plays off the rolling countryside and onto the twisting coastline. Perhaps it's the inspirational landscape. Whatever the reason, numerous artists and artisans call Blue Hill home, and top-notch galleries are abundant.

Judith Leighton knows contemporary art, and her **Leighton Gallery** (24 Parker Point Rd., 207/374-5001, www.leightongallery.com) is a real treat. The airy two-story-plus-basement space, in a converted barn on the Parker Point Road, is filled with a great selection. Be sure to visit the equally spectacular and extremely peaceful backyard sculpture garden. The **Liros Gallery** (14 Parker Point Rd., 207/374-5370 or 800/287-5370, www.lirosgallery.com) has been dealing in Russian icons since the mid-1960s. Prices are high, but the icons are fascinating. The gallery also carries Currier and Ives prints, antique maps, and 19th-century British and American paintings. From here, it's a short walk to **Blue Hill Bay Gallery** (Main St., 207/374-5773, www.bluehillbaygallery.com), which represents contemporary artists in various media and has a permanent collection of earlier works.

Don't miss the spacious, well-lit intown gallery of **Jud Hartmann** (Main St. at Rte. 15, 207/359-2544, www.judhartmanngallery.com), who makes limited-edition bronze sculptures of the Woodland tribes of the northeast. Hartmann often can be seen working on his next model in the gallery – a real treat. He's a wealth of information about his subjects, and he loves sharing the fascinating – even mesmerizing – stories he's uncovered during his meticulous research.

Also on Main Street are three other fun, artsy gallery-shops. **Handworks Gallery** (Main St., 207/374-5613, www.handworksgallery.org) sells a range of fun, funky, utilitarian and fine-art crafts by more than 50 Maine artists and craftspeople, including jewelry, furniture, rugs, wall hangings, and clothing. Browse **North Country Textiles** (Main St., 207/374-2715, www.northcountrytextiles.com) for fine handwoven throws, rugs, clothing, and table linens as well as other fine crafts.

Pottery is abundant in Blue Hill. **Rackliffe Pottery** (Rte. 172, 207/374-2297 or 888/631-3321, www.rackliffepottery.com), noted for its vivid blue wares, also makes its own glazes and has been producing lead-free pottery since 1969.

About two miles from downtown is another don't-miss. **Mark Bell Pottery** (Rte. 15, 207/374-5881), in a tiny building signaled only by a small roadside sign, is the home of exquisite award-winning porcelain by the eponymous potter. It's easy to understand why his wares were displayed at the Smithsonian Institution's Craft Fair as well as other juried shows across the country. The delicacy of each vase, bowl, or other item is astonishing, and the glazes are gorgeous. Twice each summer he has kiln openings – they're must-attend events for collectors and fans. Call for details.

Conservation Preserve and Cooper Farm at Caterpillar Hill. Many include talks by knowledgeable folks on complementary topics.

Blue Hill Town Park

At the end of Water Street is a small park with a terrific view. It has a small pebble beach, picnic tables, portable toilet, and a playground.

MERI Center

A great way to raise kids' environmental consciousness is to enroll them in summer activities sponsored by the MERI Center for Marine Studies (55 Main St., 207/374-2135, www.meriresearch.org). MERI (the Marine Environmental Research Institute), a nonprofit marine-ecology organization, schedules **island excursions** and **"eco-cruises"** geared to different age groups ($20–60); cruises are limited to 12 passengers. The MERI Center has a touch tank, a marine lending library, and exhibit space. A Thursday-evening Ocean

Environment lecture series is offered once or twice monthly. On Fridays during fall, winter, and spring, MERI offers a movie night, with refreshments, during which it screens marine-related films. It's free, but a $3 donation is appreciated. MERI is open Monday–Friday year-round and also Saturdays in July and August.

Outfitter

The Activity Shop (61 Ellsworth Rd., 207/374-3600, www.theactivityshop.com) rents bicycles for $35 per week and Old Town canoes and kayaks at rates beginning at $25 per day, including delivery within a reasonable area.

ACCOMMODATIONS

Inns and Bed-and-Breakfasts

If you're trying to imagine a classic country inn, **The Blue Hill Inn** (Union St., Rte. 177, 207/374-2844 or 800/826-7415, www.bluehillinn.com, $175–205, mid-May–late Oct.) would be it. Sarah Pebworth graciously welcomes guests to her antiques-filled inn, open since 1840 and located steps from Main Street's shops and restaurants. Ten air-conditioned rooms and a suite have real chandeliers, four-poster beds, down comforters, fancy linens, and braided and Oriental rugs; three have wood-burning fireplaces. Rear rooms overlook the extensive cutting garden, with chairs and a hammock. A three-course breakfast is served by candlelight in the elegant dining room (also available to the public, $12.95). Afternoon refreshments with sweets and superb hors d'oeuvres are served 6–7 P.M. in two elegant parlors or the garden. Also available are two year-round accommodations in the elegant Cape House ($270–295).

What's old is new at **Barncastle** (125 South St., 207/374-2330, www.barncastlehotel.com, $125–175), a late-19th-century shingle-style cottage that's listed on the National Register. It opens to a two-story foyer with a split stairway and balcony. Rooms and suites open off the balcony, and all are spacious, minimally decorated, and have contemporary accents,

© TOM NANGLE

The Blue Hill Inn is a classic country inn.

including flat-screen TVs, Wi-Fi, fridge, and microwave. Rates include a continental breakfast. Downstairs are a games room with pool table and a tavern, serving lighter fare.

Two miles north of town, at Marcia and Jim Schatz's **Blue Hill Farm Country Inn** (Rte. 15, 207/374-5126, www.bluehillfarminn.com, $95–115), a huge refurbished barn serves as the gathering spot for guests. If the weather is lousy, you can plop down in front of the oversize woodstove and start in on cribbage or other games. Antique sleigh-runner banisters lead to the barn's seven 2nd-floor rooms—all with private baths, skylights, hooked rugs, and quilts. A wing of the farmhouse has seven more rooms with shared baths. Breakfast is generous continental. On the inn's 48 acres are well-cleared nature trails, an 18th-century cellar hole, and a duck pond. It's open year-round.

FOOD

As always, hours are listed for peak season; call to verify days and hours of operation before making a special trip.

Local Flavors

Picnic fare and pizza are available at **Merrill & Hinckley** (11 Union St., 207/374-2821, 6 A.M.–9:30 P.M. Mon.–Fri., 7 A.M.–10 P.M. Sat., 8 A.M.–9 P.M. Sun.), a quirky 150-year-old family-owned grocery and general store.

The **Blue Hill Co-op and Cafe** (4 Ellsworth Rd., Rte. 172, 207/374-2165, cafe 207/374-8999, 7 A.M.–9 P.M. daily) sells organic and natural foods. Breakfast items, sandwiches, salads, and soups—many with ethnic flavors—are available in the café.

Tucked behind North Light Books is **Blue Hill Hearth** (58 Main St., 207/610-9090, 8 A.M.–7 P.M. Mon.–Fri., 9 A.M.–3 P.M. Sat.–Sun.). The breads are outstanding, but you can also pick up ready-made sandwiches, soups, and irresistible baked goods, including 15 different types of chocolate chip cookies. Vegan options are available, and these are made using completely separate utensils.

Local gardeners, farmers, and craftspeople peddle their wares at the **Blue Hill Farmers Market** (9–11:30 A.M. Sat. and 3–5 P.M. Wed. late May–mid-Oct.). It's a particularly enduring market, well worth a visit. Demonstrations by area chefs and artists are often on the agenda. From late May to late August, the Saturday market is at the Blue Hill Fairgrounds, then it moves to the First Congregational Church. The Wednesday market is at the church.

Here's a double hit: **Bird Watcher's Store & Cafe** (37 Water St., 207/374-3740, 9 A.M.–5 P.M. Mon.–Sat.). Half the store is a café, serving baked goods, soups, salads, and sandwiches; the other half is a store catering to bird-watchers. Choose from tables inside on the water-view deck, or just take it down the street to the park.

The chowder earns raves at **The Pantry** (27 Water St., 207/374-2229, 8 A.M.–2 P.M. Mon.–Fri., 8 A.M.–2 P.M. Sat.–Sun.), a no-frills source of inexpensive meals.

Pop into **Millbrook Company** (103 Main St., 207/359-8344, 8 A.M.–7 P.M. Mon.–Thurs., 8 A.M.–8 P.M. Fri., 1–8 P.M. Sat., 1–6 P.M. Sun.) for baked goods and wonderful homemade ice creams in flavors such as blueberry pear.

Family Favorites

The first choice for families or anyone looking for a casual but very good meal is **The Blue Moose** (50 Main St., 207/374-3274, www.thebluemooserestaurant.com, 10 A.M.–3 P.M. and 5–9 P.M. Mon.–Fri., 7:30 A.M.–3 P.M. and 5–9 P.M. Sat.–Sun.), which has two menus and welcomes kids. Most choices are in the $9–21 range, reflecting pub fare and small and large portions available for most dishes. Kids' menu ranges $6–7. It's open daily for breakfast, lunch, and dinner.

Very popular with local folks is **Marlintini's Grill** (83 Mines Rd., 207/374-2500, 11:30 A.M.–9 P.M. daily, bar stays open until 1 A.M.). Inside, half is a sports bar, the other half a restaurant. You can sit in either, but the bar side can get raucous. Best bet: the screened-in porch. The menu ranges from soups, salads, and burgers to fried seafood, ribeye, and nightly homestyle specials; there's a kids' menu, too. The portions are big; the service is good; the food is okay.

Just south of town is **Barncastle** (125 South St., 207/374-2300, www.barncastlehotel.com, 11:30 A.M.–8 P.M. daily), serving a creative selection of wood-fired pizzas in three sizes, as well as sandwiches, subs, paninis, calzones, and salads, in a lovely shingle-style cottage. There are vegetarian options. Expect to wait for a table; this is one popular spot.

Fine Dining

Here's a double header: **Arborvine** and **The Vinery** (Main St., www.arborvine.com). For a light lunch or dinner, head to The Vinery (207/374-2441, 5:30–9 P.M. Wed.–Sun.), a piano and wine bar–bistro in a beautifully renovated barn, with live music. Entrées are $7–15. If you're up for something fancier, make reservations at the Arborvine (207/374-2119, 5:30–9 P.M. Tues.–Sun. summer, Fri.–Sun. winter), a conscientiously renovated two-century-old Cape-style house with four dining areas, each with a different feel and understated decor. Most entrées are in the $26–35 range. The wine list is small but select. Chef-owner John Hikade and his wife, Beth, operate both establishments.

Beard nominee Rich Hanson, chef-owner of the popular Cleonice in Ellsworth, is bringing new life to the historic old forge building that hangs over the river downtown. The two-level **Table A Farmhouse Bistro** (66 Main St., 207/374-5677, www.farmkitchentable.com, 11:30 A.M.–9 P.M. daily, no lunch Mon.) serves a casual bistro menu upstairs ($12–28). It's a bit more formal downstairs, where the entrées begin at $22. Request a table on the porch, and you'll be serenaded by the water rushing (or, during dry spells, at least attempting to gurgle) underneath as you dine.

Seafood

For lobster, fried fish, and the area's best lobster roll, head to **The Fish Net** (Main St., 207/374-5240, 11 A.M.–8 P.M. Sun.–Thurs., until 9 P.M. Fri.–Sat.), an inexpensive mostly take-out joint on the eastern end of town.

It's not easy to find **Perry Long's Lobster Shack and Pier** (1076 Newbury Neck Rd., Surry, 207/667-1955, 10 A.M.–7 P.M. daily), but for a classic lobster shack experience, make the effort. Expect lobster, rolls, corn, chips, mussels, and clams and a few picnic tables on the water's edge. Do call first. Oh, and save room for the homemade ice cream sandwiches.

INFORMATION AND SERVICES

Information

The **Blue Hill Peninsula Chamber of Commerce** (207/374-3242, www.bluehillpeninsula.org) has information on Blue Hill and the surrounding area. You can also find information (although some is outdated) at www.bluehillme.com. One interesting feature on this site is a section on wildlife sightings.

At the **Blue Hill Public Library** (5 Parker Point Rd., 207/374-5515, www.bluehill.lib.me.us), ask to see the armored vest, which *may* have belonged to Magellan. The library also sponsors a summer lecture series.

Public Restrooms

Public buildings with restrooms are the Blue Hill Town Hall (Main Street), Blue Hill Public Library (Main Street), and Blue Hill Memorial Hospital (Water Street).

Brooklin/Brooksville/Sedgwick

Nestled near the bottom of the Blue Hill Peninsula and surrounded by Castine, Blue Hill, and Deer Isle, this often-missed area offers superb hiking, kayaking, and sailing, plus historic homes and unique shops, studios, lodgings, and personalities.

The best-known town is Brooklin (pop. 841), thanks to two magazines: the *New Yorker* and *WoodenBoat*. Wordsmiths extraordinaire E. B. and Katharine White "dropped out" to Brooklin in the 1930s and forever afterward dispatched their splendid material for the *New Yorker* from here. (The Whites' former home, a handsome colonial not open to the public, is on Route 175 in North Brooklin, 6.5 miles from the Blue Hill Falls bridge.) In 1977, *WoodenBoat* magazine moved its headquarters to Brooklin, where its 60-acre shoreside estate attracts builders and dreamers from all over the globe. Nearby Brooksville (pop. 911) drew the late Helen and Scott Nearing, whose *Living the Good Life* made them role models for back-to-the-landers. Their compound now verges on "must-see" status. Buck's Harbor, a section of Brooksville, is the setting for *One Morning in Maine,* one of Robert McCloskey's beloved children's books. Oldest of the three towns is Sedgwick (pop. 1,175, incorporated in 1789), which once included all of Brooklin and part of Brooksville. Now wedged *between* Brooklin and Brooksville, it includes the hamlet of Sargentville, the Caterpillar Hill scenic overlook, and a well-preserved complex of historic buildings. The influx of pilgrims—many of them artists bent on capturing the spirit that has proved so enticing to creative types—continues in this area.

SIGHTS

WoodenBoat Publications

On Naskeag Point Road, 1.2 miles from downtown Brooklin (Rte. 175), a small sign marks the turn to the world headquarters of the *WoodenBoat* empire (Naskeag Point Rd., Brooklin, 207/359-4651, www.woodenboat.com). Buy magazines, books, clothing, and all manner of nautical merchandise at the handsome new store, stroll the grounds, or sign up for one of the dozens of one- and two-week spring, summer, and fall courses in seamanship, navigation, boatbuilding, sailmaking, marine carving, and more. Special courses are geared to kids, women, pros, and all-thumbs neophytes; the camaraderie is legendary, and so is the cuisine. School visiting hours are 8 A.M.–5 P.M. Monday–Saturday June–October.

Historical Sights

Now used as the museum/headquarters of the Sedgwick-Brooklin Historical Society, the 1795 **Reverend Daniel Merrill House** (Rte. 172, Sedgwick, 207/359-8086, 2–4 P.M. Sun. July–Aug., or by appt., donations welcomed) was the parsonage for Sedgwick's first permanent minister. Inside the house are period furnishings, old photos, toys, and tools; a few steps away are a restored 1874 schoolhouse, an 1821 cattle pound (for corralling wandering bovines), and a hearse barn. Pick up a brochure during open hours and guide yourself around the buildings and grounds. The **Sedgwick Historic District,** crowning Town House Hill, comprises the Merrill House and its outbuildings, plus the imposing 1794 Town House and the 23-acre Rural Cemetery (the oldest headstone dates from 1798) across Route 172.

The Good Life Center

Forest Farm, home of the late Helen and Scott Nearing, is now the site of The Good Life Center (372 Harborside Rd., Harborside, 207/326-8211, www.goodlife.org). Advocates of simple living and authors of 10 books on the subject, the Nearings created a trust to perpetuate their farm and philosophy. Resident stewards lead tours (usually 1–4 P.M. Thurs.–Mon. late June–early Sept., but call ahead), $5 donation suggested. Ask about the schedule for the

© TOM NANGLE

Shop for all things wooden boat related at the *WoodenBoat* school's shop.

traditional Monday-night meetings (7 P.M.), featuring free programs by gardeners, philosophers, musicians, and other guest speakers. Occasional work parties, workshops, and conferences are also on the docket. The farm is on Harborside Road, just before it turns to dirt. From Route 176 in Brooksville, take Cape Rosier Road, go eight miles, passing Holbrook Islands Sanctuary. At the Grange Hall, turn right and follow the road 1.9 miles to the end. Turn left onto Harborside Road and continue 1.8 miles to Forest Farm, across from Orrs Cove.

Four Season Farm

About a mile beyond the Nearings' place is Four Season Farm (609 Weir Cove Rd., Harborside, 207/326-4455, www.fourseasonfarm.com, 1–5 P.M. Mon.–Sat., June–Sept.), the lush organic farm owned and operated by internationally renowned gardeners Eliot Coleman and Barbara Damrosch. Both have written numerous books and articles and starred in TV gardening shows. Coleman is a driving force behind the use of the word "authentic" to mean "beyond organic," demonstrating a commitment to food that is local, fresh, ripe, clean, safe, and nourishing. He's successfully pioneered a "winter harvest," developing environmentally sound and economically viable systems for extending fresh vegetable production from October through May in cold-weather climates. The farm is a treat for the eyes as well as the taste buds—you've never seen such gorgeous produce. Ask about dinners on the farm and other events. Also here is the **Cape Rosier Artist Collective,** a gallery showing works by local artisans.

Scenic Routes

No one seems to know how **Caterpillar Hill** got its name, but its reputation comes from a panoramic vista of water, hills, and blueberry barrens—with a couple of convenient picnic tables where you can stop for lunch, photos, or a ringside view of sunset and fall foliage. From the 350-foot elevation, the views take in Walker Pond, Eggemoggin Reach, Deer Isle, Swans Island, and even the Camden Hills. The signposted rest area is on Route 175/15, between Brooksville and Sargentville, next to

The Flash! In the Pans Community Steel Band performs somewhere on the peninsula nearly every Monday night.

a gallery; watch out for the blind curve when you pull off the road. If you want to explore on foot, the one-mile Cooper Farm Trail loops through the blueberry barrens and woods. From the scenic overlook, walk down to and out Cooper Farm Road to the trailhead.

Between Sargentville and Sedgwick, Route 175 offers nonstop views of Eggemoggin Reach, with shore access to the Benjamin River just before you reach Sedgwick village.

Two other scenic routes are **Naskeag Point,** in Brooklin, and **Cape Rosier,** the westernmost arm of the town of Brooksville. Naskeag Point Road begins off Route 175 in "downtown" Brooklin, heads down the peninsula for 3.7 miles past the entrance to WoodenBoat Publications, and ends at a small shingle beach (limited parking) on Eggemoggin Reach. Here you'll find picnic tables, a boat launch, a seasonal toilet, and a marker commemorating the 1778 Battle of Naskeag, when British sailors came ashore from the sloop *Gage,* burned several buildings, and were run off by a ragtag band of local settlers. Cape Rosier's roads are poorly marked, perhaps deliberately, so keep your DeLorme atlas handy. The Cape Rosier loop takes in Holbrook Island Sanctuary, Goose Falls, the hamlet of Harborside, and plenty of water and island views. Note that some roads are unpaved, but they usually are well maintained.

ENTERTAINMENT AND EVENTS

Flash! In the Pans Community Steel Band

If you're a fan of steel-band music, the Flash! In the Pans Community Steel Band (207/374-2172, www.flashinthepans.org) usually performs somewhere on the peninsula on Monday nights (7:30–9 P.M.) mid-June–early September. Local papers carry the summer schedule for the nearly three-dozen-member band, which deserves its devoted following. Admission is usually a small donation to benefit a local cause. It's worth every penny to join the fun.

Brooksville Open Mic Nights

Meet locals, savor soup and bread, and share your talents at the Tinder Hearth open mic nights (207/326-9266, www.tinderhearth.org, 5–8 P.M. Sun.), held in the barn during the warmer months. Check Tinder Hearth's website for other programs and workshops.

Eggemoggin Reach Regatta

Wooden boats are big attractions hereabouts, so when a huge fleet sails in for this regatta (usually the first Saturday in August, but the schedule can change), crowds gather. Don't miss the parade of wooden boats. The best locale for watching the regatta itself is on or near the bridge to Deer Isle or near the Eggemoggin Landing grounds on Little Deer Isle. For details, see www.erregatta.com.

SHOPPING

Most of these businesses are small, owner-operated shops, which means they're often catch as catch can. If you want to be sure, call ahead.

Antiques

When you need a slate sink, a clawfoot tub, brass fixtures, or a Palladian window, **Architectural Antiquities** (52 Indian Point La., Harborside, 207/326-4938, www.arch-antiquities.com), on Cape Rosier, is just the ticket—a restorer's delight. Prices are reasonable for what you get, and they'll ship your purchases. Open all year by appointment; ask for directions when you call. Antiques dating from the Federal period through the turn of the 20th century are the specialties at **Sedgwick Antiques** (775 N. Sedgwick Rd./Rte. 172, Sedgwick, 207/359-8834). Early furniture, handmade furniture, and a full range of country accessories and antiques can be found at **Thomas Hinchcliffe Antiques** (26 Cradle Knolls La., off Rte. 176, West Sedgwick, 207/326-9411). Painted country furniture, decoys, and unusual nautical items are specialties at Peg and Olney Grindall's **Old Cove Antiques** (106 Caterpillar Rd./Rte. 15, Sargentville, 207/359-2031 or 207/359-8585), a weathered-gray shop across from the Eggemoggin Country Store.

Artists' and Artisans' Galleries

Small studio-galleries pepper Route 175 (Reach Road) in Sedgwick and Brooklin; most are marked only by small signs, so watch carefully. First up is **Eggemoggin Textile Studio** (off Rte. 175/Reach Rd., Sedgwick, 207/359-5083, www.chrisleithstudio.com), where the incredibly gifted Christine Leith weaves scarves, wraps, hangings, and pillows with hand-dyed silk and wool; the colors are magnificent. You might catch her at work on the big loom in her studio shop, a real treat.

Continue along the road to find **Reach Road Gallery** (Reach Rd., Sedgwick, 207/359-8803), where Holly Meade sells her detailed woodblock prints as well as prints from the children's books she's illustrated.

Only a few doors down is **Mermaid Woolens** (Reach Rd., Sedgwick, 207/359-2747, www.mermaidwoolens.com), source of Elizabeth Coakley's wildly colorful hand knits—vests, socks, and sweaters. They're pricey but worth every nickel. She also does seascape paintings. Clever woman.

Continue over to Brooklin, where Virginia G. Sarsfield handcrafts paper products, including custom lampshades, calligraphy papers, books, and lamps, at **Handmade Papers** (Rte. 175 at Center Harbor Rd., Brooklin, 207/359-8345, www.handmadepapersonline.com). She shares the address with Ken Carpenter's **Maine Hooked Rugs** (207/359-9878, www.maine-hookedrugs.com).

Just a bit farther is **Naskeag Gallery** (Rte. 175, Brooklin, 207/359-4619), where talented glass artist Sihaya Hopkins has a studio gallery.

In Brooksville, more treasures await on Route 176. You'll need to watch carefully for the sign marking the long drive to **Paul Heroux and Scott Goldberg Pottery** (2032 Coastal

E. B. WHITE: SOME WRITER

Since the mid-1940s, every child has heard of E. B. White – author of the memorable *Stuart Little, Charlotte's Web,* and *Trumpet of the Swan* – and every college kid for decades has been reminded to consult his *Elements of Style* – but how many realize that White and his wife, Katharine, were living not in the Big City but in the hamlet of North Brooklin, Maine? It was Brooklin that inspired Charlotte and Wilbur and Stuart, and it was Brooklin where the Whites lived very full, creative lives.

Abandoning their desks at the *New Yorker* in 1938, Elwyn Brooks White and Katharine S. White bought an idyllic saltwater farm on the Blue Hill Peninsula and moved here with their young son, Joel, who became a noted naval architect and yachtbuilder in Brooklin before his untimely death in 1997. Andy (as E. B. had been dubbed since his college days at Cornell) produced 20 books, countless essays and letters to editors, and hundreds (maybe thousands?) of "newsbreaks" – those wry clipping-and-commentary items sprinkled through each issue of the *New Yorker*. Katharine continued wielding her pencil as the magazine's standout children's-book editor, donating many of her review copies to Brooklin's Friend Memorial Library, one of her favorite "causes." (The library also has two original Garth Williams drawings from *Stuart Little*, courtesy of E. B., and a lovely garden dedicated to the Whites.) Katharine's book, *Onward and Upward in the Garden*, a collection of her *New Yorker* gardening pieces, was published in 1979, two years after her death.

Later in life, E. B. sagely addressed the young readers of his three award-winning children's books:

> *Are my stories true, you ask? No, they are imaginary tales, containing fantastic characters and events. In real life, a family doesn't have a child who looks like a mouse; in real life, a spider doesn't spin words in her web. In real life, a swan doesn't blow a trumpet. But real life is only one kind of life – there is also the life of the imagination. And although my stories are imaginary, I like to think that there is some truth in them, too – truth about the way people and animals feel and think and act.*

E. B. White died on October 1, 1985, at the age of 86. He and Katharine and Joel left large footprints on this earth, but perhaps nowhere more so than in Brooklin.

Rd./Rte. 176, Brooksville, 207/326-9062). The small gallery is a treat for pottery fans.

Continue southwest on Route 176 and watch closely for signs for **Bagaduce Forge** (140 Ferry Rd., Brooksville, 207/326-9676); this isn't easy to find. Joseph Meltreder is both blacksmith and farrier, and his small forge, with big views, is the real thing. He turns out whimsical pieces. Especially fun are the nail people—you'll know them when you see them.

Wine and Gifts

Three varieties of English-style hard cider are specialties at **The Sow's Ear Winery** (Rte. 176 at Herrick Rd., Brooksville, 207/326-4649), a minuscule operation in a funky gray-shingled building. Winemaker Tom Hoey also produces sulfite-free blueberry, chokecherry, and rhubarb wines; he'll let you sample it all. Ask to see his cellar, where everything happens. No credit cards.

Nautical books, T-shirts, gifts, food (including homemade bread and key lime pie), and boat gear line the walls and shelves of the shop at **Buck's Harbor Marine** (on the dock, South Brooksville, 207/326-8839, www.bucksharbor.com).

PARKS, PRESERVES, AND RECREATION

Holbrook Island Sanctuary State Park

In the early 1970s, foresighted benefactor Anita Harris donated to the state 1,230 acres in Brooksville that would become the Holbrook Island Sanctuary (207/326-4012, www.state.me.us/doc/parks, free). From Route 176, between West Brooksville and South Brooksville, head west on Cape Rosier Road, following brown-and-white signs for the sanctuary. Trail maps and bird checklists are available in boxes at trailheads or at park headquarters. The easy Backshore Trail (about 30 minutes) starts here, or go back a mile and climb the steepish trail to **Backwoods Mountain** for the best vistas. Other attractions include shorefront picnic tables and grills, four old cemeteries, and super bird-watching during spring and fall migrations. Leashed pets are allowed, but no bikes on the trails and no camping. Officially open May 15–October 15, but the access road and parking areas are plowed for cross-country skiers.

Swimming

A small, relatively little-known beach is Brooklin's **Pooduck Beach.** From the Brooklin General Store (Route 175), take Naskeag Point Road about half a mile, watching for the Pooduck Road sign on the right. Turn right and drive to the end. You can also launch a sea kayak into Eggemoggin Reach here.

Bicycling

Bicycling in this area is hazardous. Roads here are particularly narrow and winding, with poor shoulders. If you're determined to pedal, consider either the Naskeag scenic route or around Cape Rosier, where traffic is light.

Sailing

Captain LeCain Smith sails ***Perelandra*** (Buck's Harbor, 207/326-4279), a 44-foot steel-hulled ketch, in the waters of Penobscot Bay. Rates begin at $40 per person for a two-hour sail and increase to $100 per person for a full day. The boat holds a maximum of six passengers.

Ensign-class Antares day sailboats are available for rental at **Buck's Harbor Marine** (on the dock, South Brooksville, 207/326-8839, www.bucksharbor.com). The full-keel boats rent for $135 per day. Buck's Harbor also charters bareboat sail and power yachts to qualified skippers.

Picnicking

You can take a picnic to the **Bagaduce Ferry Landing,** in West Brooksville off Route 176, where there are picnic tables and cross-river vistas toward Castine.

ACCOMMODATIONS

Cottage Colony

The fourth generation manages the **Hiram Blake Camp** (220 Weir Cove Rd., Harborside, 207/326-4951, www.hiramblake.com, Memorial Day–late Sept.), but other generations pitch in and help with gardening, lobstering, maintenance, and kibitzing. Thirteen cottages and a duplex line the shore of this 100-acre property, which has been in family hands since before the Revolutionary War. The camp itself dates from 1916. Don't bother bringing reading material: The dining room has ingenious ceiling niches lined with countless books. Guests also have the use of rowboats. The rate includes home-cooked breakfasts and dinners served family style; lobster is always available at an additional charge. Much of the fare is grown in the expansive gardens. Other facilities include a dock, a recreation room, a pebble beach, and an outdoor chapel. There's a one-week minimum (beginning Sat. or Sun.) in July and August, when cottages go for $600–2,850 a week (including breakfast, dinner, and linens). Off-season rates (no meals or linens, but cottages have cooking facilities) are $630–895 a week. The best chances for getting a reservation are in June and September. Dogs are welcome. No credit cards accepted.

Bed-and-Breakfasts

The **Dragonflye Inn** (Naskeag Point Rd.,

Brooklin, 207/359-808, www.dragonflyeinn.com, $175), an 1874 mansard-roofed Victorian in what passes as downtown Brooklin, is a casual put-your-feet-up kind of place, with a special invitation issued to WoodenBoat school students, gallery fans (lots of work by local artisans), and kayakers. Owner Joe Moore's goal is sustainability: Towels and linens are made from organic cotton; soaps and shampoos are local and all natural; cleaning products are all natural, biodegradable, and earth friendly. Breakfast is light continental.

Best known for its restaurant and pub, **The Brooklin Inn** (Rte. 175, Brooklin, 207/359-2777, www.brooklininn.com, $105–135 with breakfast; add $10 for a one-night stay) also has five comfortable bedrooms; two share a bath. It's open year-round.

FOOD

As always, hours are listed for peak season; call to verify days and hours of operation.

Cooking Classes

In summer, chef Terence Janericco (617/426-7458, or, after July 1, 207/359-2068, www.terencejanericcocookingclasses.com), author of a dozen cookbooks, moves his cooking school from Boston to Brooklin. The demonstration-only three-hour classes are $70 per person, which includes dining on the foods prepared.

Local Flavors

Competition is stiff for lunchtime seats at the **Morning Moon Cafe** (junction of Rte. 175 and Naskeag Point Rd., Brooklin, 207/359-2373, 7 A.M.–2 P.M. Thurs.–Sun.), mostly because WoodenBoat staffers consider it an annex to their offices. "The Moon" is a friendly hangout for coffee, pizza, or great sandwiches and salads.

Across the street from the Morning Moon Cafe, the **Brooklin General Store** (1 Reach Rd., junction of Rte. 175 and Naskeag Point Rd., Brooklin, 207/359-8817, 5 A.M.–7 P.M. Mon.–Sat., 7 A.M.–5 P.M. Sun.), vintage 1872, carries groceries, beer and wine, newspapers, take-out sandwiches, and local chatter.

In North Brooksville, where Route 175/176 crosses the Bagaduce River, stands the **Bagaduce Lunch,** named an "American Classic" by the James Beard Foundation in 2008. Owners Judy and Mike Astbury buy local fish and clams. Check the tide calendar and go when the tide is changing; order a clam roll or a hamburger, settle in at a picnic table, and watch the reversing falls. If you're lucky, you might sight an eagle, osprey, or seal. The food is so-so, but the setting is tops. The popular takeout stand (outdoor tables only) is open 11 A.M.–7 or 8 P.M. daily, but closes at 3 P.M. Wednesday, from early May to mid-September.

Lunch is the specialty at **Buck's Harbor Market** (Rte. 176, South Brooksville, 207/326-8683, 7 A.M.–7 P.M. Mon.–Fri., 8 A.M.–7:30 P.M. Sat., 8 A.M.–6 P.M. Sun., year-round), a low-key, marginally yuppified general store popular with yachties in summer.

Ethnic Fare

El El Frijoles (41 Caterpillar Rd./Rte. 15, Sargentville, 207/359-2486, www.elelfrijoles.com, 11 A.M.–8 P.M. Wed.–Sun.) gets good marks for its California-style empanadas, burritos, and tacos. It's a small, somewhat funky operation housed in a barn behind Coast to Coast Fine Arts.

Casual Dining

Behind the Buck's Harbor Market is **Buck's Restaurant** (6 Cornfield Hill Rd., Brooksville, 207/326-8688, 5:30–8:30 P.M. daily, $15–24), an outpost of fiery colors calmed down by white tablecloths. Respected chefs Jonathan Chase and Nancy McMillan create comfort foods with a dash of creativity.

All the meat and produce is organic and most is sourced locally at **The Brooklin Inn** (Rte. 175, Brooklin, 207/359-2777, www.brooklininn.com, 5:30–9 P.M. daily, $19–40). The chef tries to know "who raised, grew, picked, or caught all the food," and all the fish are wild, free swimming, and locally caught. A children's menu is available.

Downstairs an **Irish pub** (5:30–10 P.M. daily) serves burgers, Guinness stew, pizza, and, on Fridays, all the fresh baked haddock you can eat for $10.

Country Inn Dining

The chef seems to change annually at **The Lookout** (455 Flye Point Rd., off Rte. 175, North Brooklin, 207/359-2188, www.thelookoutinn.biz, 5:30–8 P.M. Wed.–Sun., $18–24). The inn and restaurant, at the tip of Flye Point, have a knockout view of Herrick Bay (as long as there's no fog). It's been owned and operated by Flye family descendants for more than 110 years (judging from the look of the place, little has changed in that period); ask around about its current reputation.

INFORMATION AND SERVICES

The best source of information about the region is the **Blue Hill Peninsula Chamber of Commerce** (207/374-2281, www.bluehillpeninsula.org).

Libraries

Friends Memorial Library (Rte. 175, Brooklin, 207/359-2276) has a lovely Circle of Friends Garden, with benches and a brick patio. It's dedicated to the memory of longtime Brooklin residents E. B. and Katharine White. Also check out **Free Public Library** (1 Town House Rd., Rte. 176, Brooksville, 207/326-4560) and Sedgwick Village Library (Main St., Sedgwick, 207/359-2177).

Castine

Castine (pop. 1,343) is a gem—a serene New England village with a tumultuous past. It tips a cape, surrounded by water on three sides, including the entrance to the Penobscot River, which made it a strategic defense point. Once beset by geopolitical squabbles, saluting the flags of three different nations (France, Britain, and Holland), its only crises now are local political skirmishes. This is an unusual community, a National Historic Register enclave that many people never find. The town celebrated its bicentennial in 1996. Today a major presence is Maine Maritime Academy, yet Castine remains the quietest imaginable college town. Students in search of a party school won't find it here; naval engineering is serious business.

What visitors discover is a year-round community with a busy waterfront, an easy-to-conquer layout, a handful of traditional inns, wooded trails on the outskirts of town, an astonishing collection of splendid Georgian and Federalist architecture, and water views nearly every which way you turn. If you're staying in Blue Hill or even Bar Harbor, spend a day here. Or book a room in one of the town's lovely inns, and use Castine as a base for exploring here and beyond. Either way, you won't regret it.

HISTORY

Originally known as Fort Pentagoet, Castine received its current name courtesy of Jean-Vincent d'Abbadie, Baron de St.-Castin. A young French nobleman manqué who married a Wabanaki princess named Pidiwamiska, d'Abbadie ran the town in the second half of the 17th century and eventually returned to France.

A century later, in 1779, occupying British troops and their reinforcements scared off potential American seaborne attackers (including Colonel Paul Revere), who turned tail up the Penobscot River and ended up scuttling their more than 40-vessel fleet—a humiliation known as the Penobscot Expedition and still regarded as one of America's worst naval defeats.

When the boundaries for Maine were finally set in 1820, with the St. Croix River marking the east rather than the Penobscot River, the last British Loyalists departed, some floating their homes north to St. Andrews, in New Brunswick, Canada, where they can still be seen today. For a while, peace and prosperity became the bywords for Castine—with lively commerce in fish and salt—but it all collapsed during the California Gold Rush and the Civil War trade embargo, leaving the town down on its luck.

Of the many historical landmarks scattered around town, one of the most intriguing must be the sign on "Wind Mill Hill," at the junction of Route 166 and State Street:

> *On Hatch's Hill there stands a mill. Old Higgins he doth tend it. And every time he grinds a grist, he has to stop and mend it.*

In smaller print, just below the rhyme, comes the drama:

> *Here two British soldiers were shot for desertion.*

Castine has quite a history indeed.

SIGHTS

Castine Historic Tour

To appreciate Castine fully, you need to arm yourself with the Castine Merchants Association's visitors brochure-map (all businesses and lodgings in town have copies) and follow the numbers on bike or on foot. With no stops, walking the route takes less than an hour, but you'll want to read dozens of historical plaques, peek into public buildings, shoot some photos, and perhaps even do some shopping.

Highlights of the tour include the late-18th-century **John Perkins House,** moved to Perkins Street from Court Street in 1969 and restored with period furnishings. It's open in July and August for guided tours (2–5 P.M. Sun. and Wed., $5).

Next door, **The Wilson Museum** (107 Perkins St., 207/326-8545, www.wilsonmuseum.org, 2–5 P.M. Tues.–Sun. late May–late Sept., free), founded in 1921, contains an intriguingly eclectic two-story collection of prehistoric artifacts, ship models, dioramas,

© TOM NANGLE

You can tour the John Perkins House, which is adjacent to the Wilson Museum.

baskets, tools, and minerals assembled over a lifetime by John Howard Wilson, a geologist-anthropologist who first visited Castine in 1891 (and died in 1936). Among the exhibits are Balinese masks, ancient oil lamps, cuneiform tablets, Zulu artifacts, pre-Inca pottery, and assorted local findings.

Open the same days and hours as the Perkins House are the **Blacksmith Shop,** where a smith does demonstrations, and the **Hearse House,** containing Castine's 19th-century winter and summer funeral vehicles. Both have free admission.

At the end of Battle Avenue stands the 19th-century **Dyce's Head Lighthouse,** no longer operating; the keeper's house is owned by the town. Alongside it is a public path (signposted; pass at your own risk) leading via a wooden staircase to a tiny patch of rocky shoreline and the beacon that has replaced the lighthouse.

The highest point in town is **Fort George State Park,** site of a 1779 British fortification. Nowadays, little remains except grassy earthworks, but there are interpretive displays and picnic tables.

Main Street, descending toward the water, is a feast for historic architecture fans. Artist Fitz Hugh Lane and author Mary McCarthy once lived in elegant houses along the elm-lined street (neither building is open to the public). On Court Street between Main and Green stands turn-of-the-20th-century **Emerson Hall,** site of Castine's municipal offices. Since Castine has no official information booth, you may need to duck in here (it's open weekdays) for answers to questions.

Across Court Street, **Witherle Memorial Library,** a handsome early-19th-century building on the site of the 18th-century town jail, looks out on the Town Common. Also facing the Common are the Adams and Abbott Schools, the former still an elementary school. The **Abbott School** (10 A.M.–4 P.M. Tues.–Sat., 1–4 P.M. Sun. July–Labor Day, reduced schedule spring and fall, free but donations welcome), built in 1859, has been carefully restored for use as a museum and headquarters for the **Castine Historical Society**

MAINE MARITIME ACADEMY

The state's only merchant-marine college (and one of only seven in the nation) occupies 35 acres in the middle of Castine. Founded in 1941, the academy awards undergraduate and graduate degrees in such areas as marine engineering, ocean studies, and marina management, preparing a student body of about 750 men and women for careers as ship captains, Naval architects, and marine engineers.

The academy owns a fleet of 60 vessels, including the historic research schooner *Bowdoin,* flagship of Arctic explorer Admiral Donald MacMillan, and the 499-foot training vessel *State of Maine,* berthed down the hill at the waterfront. In 1996 and 1997, the *State of Maine,* formerly the U.S. Navy hydrographic survey ship *Tanner,* underwent a $12 million conversion for use by the academy. It is still subject to deployment, and, in 2005, the school had to quickly find alternative beds for students using the ship as a dormitory when it was called into service in support of rescue and rebuilding efforts after Hurricane Katrina in New Orleans. Midshipmen conduct free 30-minute tours of the vessel on weekdays in summer (about mid-July to late August). The schedule is posted at the dock, or call 207/326-4311 to check; photo ID is required.

Weekday tours of the campus can be arranged through the admissions office (207/326-2206 or 800/227-8465 outside Maine, www.mainemaritime.edu). Campus highlights include the three-story Nutting Memorial Library in Platz Hall (open daily during the school year, weekdays in summer and during vacations); the Henry A. Scheel Room, a cozy oasis in Leavitt Hall containing memorabilia from late Naval architect Henry Scheel and his wife, Jeanne; and the well-stocked bookstore (Curtis Hall, 207/326-9333, 8 A.M.–3 P.M. Mon.–Fri.).

(207/326-4118, www.castinehistoricalsociety.org). A big draw at the volunteer-run museum is the 24-foot-long Bicentennial Quilt, assembled for Castine's 200th anniversary in 1996. The historical society, founded in 1966, organizes lectures, exhibits, and special events (some free) in various places around town.

On the outskirts of town, across the narrow neck between Wadsworth Cove and Hatch's Cove, stretches a rather overgrown canal (signposted "British Canal") scooped out by the occupying British during the War of 1812. Effectively severing land access to the town of Castine, the Brits thus raised havoc, collected local revenues for eight months, then departed for Halifax with enough funds to establish Dalhousie College (now Dalhousie University). Wear waterproof boots to walk the canal route; the best time to go is at low tide.

If a waterfront picnic sounds appealing, buy the fixings at Bah's Bakehouse and settle in on the grassy earthworks along the harborfront at **Fort Madison,** site of an 1808 garrison (then Fort Porter) near the corner of Perkins and Madockawando Streets. The views from here are fabulous, and it's accessible all year. A set of stairs leads down to the rocky waterfront.

ENTERTAINMENT AND EVENTS

Possibilities for live music include **Dennett's Wharf** (15 Sea St., 207/326-9045), where some performances require a ticket, and **The Reef** (on the wharf, tucked underneath the bank facing the parking area and harbor).

The Castine Town Band often performs free concerts on the Common. Check www.castine.org for its schedule.

The community-based **Castine Arts Association** (www.castinearts.org) presents concerts, exhibits, workshops, and other performances at various locations around town each summer.

The Wilson Museum (107 Perkins St., 207/326-8545, www.wilsonmuseum.org) frequently schedules concerts, lectures, and demonstrations.

The Trinitarian Church often brings in high-caliber musical entertainment.

Celebrate Castine (www.celebratecastine.com) is a town-wide event in mid-July.

SHOPPING

Antiques and Galleries

Tucked into the back of the 1796 Parson Mason House, one of Castine's oldest residences, **Leila Day Antiques** (53 Main St., 207/326-8786, www.leiladayantiques.com) is a must for anyone in the market for folk art, period furniture, and quilts.

Traditional American craftwork is sold at **Castine Historical Handworks** (9 Main St., Castine, 207/326-4460, www.castinehistoricalhandworks.com).

Oil paintings by local artists Joshua and Susan Adam are on view at **Adam Gallery** (140 Battle Ave., 207/326-8272, www.adamgalleryonline.com).

Books

Driving toward Castine on Route 166, watch on your right for a small sign for **Dolphin Books and Prints** (314 Castine Rd., 207/326-0888, www.dolphin-book.com), where Pete and Liz Ballou have set up their antiquarian business with more than 10,000 books as well as framed prints and art.

In downtown Castine, a block up from the waterfront, **The Compass Rose Bookstore and Café** (3 Main St., 207/326-9366 or 800/698-9366, www.compassrosebooks.com) carries an ever-expanding selection of new books, cards, games, and prints chosen by owner Sharon Biggie. In the back of the shop is a café serving hot and cold drinks (espresso, too), soup, sandwiches, and tasty baked goods.

Furniture

Bench-made Windsor chairs are the specialty at **M&E Gummel Chairworks** (600 Shore Rd., 207/326-8122, www.gummelchairworks.com). The father-and-son team use 18th-century methods when handcrafting the chairs, colonial dining tables, and bowls, one at a time in their late-19th-century barn workshop.

RECREATION

Witherle Woods

This 152-acre preserve, owned by Maine Coast Heritage Trust (maps available via email from info@mcht.org), is a popular walking area with a maze of trails and old woods roads leading to the water. Many Revolutionary War–era relics have been found here; if you see any, do *not* remove them. Access to the preserve is via a shaded old woods road on Battle Avenue, located between the water district property (at the end of the wire fence) and the Manor's exit driveway and diagonally across from La Tour Street.

Sea Kayaking

Right near Dennett's Wharf is **Castine Kayak Adventures** (17 Sea St., 207/326-9045, www.castinekayak.com), spearheaded by Maine Guide Karen Francoeur. All skill levels are accommodated; "Kayak Karen," as she's known locally, is particularly adept with beginners, delivering wise advice from beginning to end. Three-hour half-day trips are $55; six-hour full-day tours are around $105 including lunch. Two-hour sunset tours are $40; the sunrise tour includes a light breakfast for $55. Friday nights, there are special two-hour phosphorescence tours, under the stars (weather permitting), for $55 per person. Longer trips are available for $150 per day. If you have your own boat, call Karen for advice; she knows these waters. She also offers instruction for all levels as well as a Maine Sea Kayak Guide course.

Swimming

Backshore Beach, a crescent of sand and gravel on Wadsworth Cove Road (turn off Battle Avenue at the Castine Golf Club), is a favorite saltwater swimming spot, with views across the bay to Stockton Springs. Be forewarned, though, that ocean swimming in this part of Maine is not for the timid. The best time to try it is on the incoming tide, after the sun has had time to heat up the mud. At mid- to high tide, it's also the best place to put in a sea kayak.

© HILARY NANGLE

Kayaking provides a different perspective on Castine's harbor.

Golf

The nine-hole **Castine Golf Club** (200 Battle Ave., 207/326-8844, www.castinegolfclub.com) dates to 1897, when the first tee required a drive from a 30-step-high mound. It was redesigned in 1921 by Willie Park Jr.

EXCURSION BOATS

Glide over Penobscot Bay aboard the wooden motorsailor **Guildive** (207/701-1421, www.guildivecruises.com), captained by Kata Kana and Zander Parker. The two-hour sails coast $30–35 adults, $25 children under 12, and depart Dennett's Wharf four times daily, including a sunset BYOB cocktail cruise.

Several times weekly, Captain Melissa Terry's **Belfast Bay Cruises** (207/322-5530, www.belfastbaycruises.com, $15 adults, $6 children 5–15) offers a one-hour Castine Harbor Tour aboard the *Good Return,* passing by Dyce's Head Lighthouse and Holbrook and Nautilus Islands. Also ask about a day trip to Belfast ($30 adult, $17 children).

ACCOMMODATIONS

Inns

Castine is blessed with three fine traditional inns. This is not the place to come if you require in-room phones, air-conditioning, or fancy bathrooms. Rather, the pace is relaxed and the accommodations reflect the easy elegance of a bygone era.

The three-story Queen Anne–style **Pentagöet Inn** (26 Main St., 207/326-8616 or 800/845-1701, www.pentagoet.com, May–late Oct., $115–245 peak) is the perfect Maine summer inn, right down to the lace curtains billowing in the breeze, the soft floral wallpapers, and the intriguing curiosities that accent, but don't clutter, the rooms. Congenial innkeepers Jack Burke, previously with the foreign service, and Julie Van de Graaf, a pastry chef, took over the century-old inn in 2000 and have given it new life, upgrading rooms and furnishing them with Victorian antiques, adding handsome gardens, and carving out a niche as a dining destination. Their enthusiasm for the area is contagious. The inn's 16 rooms are spread out between the main house (with Wi-Fi service) and the adjoining house. A hot buffet breakfast and afternoon refreshments are provided. Jack holds court in Passports Pub (chock-full of vintage photos and prints and exotic antiques) every afternoon, advising guests on activities and opportunities. Borrow one of the inn's bikes and explore around town or simply walk—the Main Street location is convenient to everything Castine offers. Better yet, just sit on the wraparound porch and take it all in.

Once the summer "cottage" of Arthur Fuller, a South Boston Yacht Club commodore, **The Manor Inn** (Battle Ave., 207/326-4861 or 877/626-6746, www.manor-inn.com, $115–275) overlooks town and harbor from five mostly wooded acres elevated above Battle Avenue. Though the atmosphere is informal, there are lots of elegant architectural touches. Nancy Watson and Tom Ehrman, innkeepers here since 1998, continue to improve the inn each year. The 14 2nd- and 3rd-floor rooms are an eclectic mix: Some have canopied beds and fireplaces, some are especially family friendly. A separate guest building has a TV and games as well as Nancy's yoga studio; guests are welcome to join her morning Iyengar classes (Mon., Wed., Fri., $12 drop-ins). Wi-Fi is available. The trailhead for Witherle Woods is close by. The inn is often the site of weddings and receptions; ask before you book unless you don't mind being the odd man out. It's open mid-February–late December. Well-behaved pets are $25 per stay.

© TOM NANGLE

The yellow Victorian Pentagöet Inn stands out in a town of white houses.

FOOD

As always, hours are listed for peak season; call to verify days and hours of operation.

Local Flavors

Since 1920, locals have been buying lunch and ice cream at **Castine Variety** (1 Main St., 207/326-8625, 7 A.M.–8 P.M.). Go for the vintage feeling and the inexpensive breakfasts, lunches, and ice cream.

Another institution is **The Breeze** (Town Dock, 207/326-9200, 9 A.M.–7 P.M. daily), a waterfront takeout stand with reliably good basics like burgers, fried clams, and ice cream. You can't beat the location or the view.

When everything else in town is closed, your best bet for late-night eats is **The Reef** (8 Sea St., on the wharf, tucked underneath the bank facing the parking area and harbor, 207/326-4040, 11 A.M.–1 A.M. daily). The hand-tossed gourmet pizzas are available in three sizes. There are plenty of pub-style favorites, too. The atmosphere is more bar than restaurant, with a pool table in the back and a small stage area for live entertainment.

Casual Dining

Here's a doubleheader: **Bah's Bakehouse** (26 Water St., 207/326-9510, www.bahsworld.com, 7 A.M.–3 P.M. daily) and, sharing the same location, **Stella's Jazz Nocturnal** (207/326-9710, 5:30–11 P.M. Tues.–Sun., food service to 10 P.M.). Upstairs is Bah's, a higgledy-piggledy eatery of three rooms and a deck at the end of an alleyway tucked between Main and Water Streets. Its slogan is "creative flour arrangements," and creative it is. Stop here for coffee, cold juices, pastries, interesting snacks and salads, homemade soups, wine or beer, good sandwiches, and, if you're lucky, fish cakes. Be forewarned: If it's crowded, go elsewhere—the kitchen is quickly overwhelmed and service can be slow to frustrating. Underneath the deck is Stella's ($9–18), an intimate dining room and lounge where live jazz is performed Thursday through Sunday.

On a warm summer day, it's hard to find a better place to while away a few hours than **Dennett's Wharf** (15 Sea St., 207/326-9045, www.dennettswharf.com, 11 A.M.–midnight daily, May–Columbus Day), and that's likely what you'll do here, as service can be slow. Next to the town dock, it's a colorful barn of

© HILARY NANGLE

Dennett's Wharf hangs over Castine Harbor and is a good spot for a brew and a burger.

a place with outside deck and front-row windjammer-watching seats in summer. Best advice is to keep your order simple.

The Pine Cone Pub at the Manor Inn (76 Battle Ave., 207/326-4861, from 5 A.M. Tues.–Sat.) serves a light menu, with such choices as Caesar salad and fish-and-chips.

Fine Dining

Jazz music plays softly and dinner is by candlelight at the **Pentagoet** (26 Main St., 207/326-8616 or 800/845-1701, www.pentagoet.com, opens at 6 P.M. Tues.–Sat.). In fine weather, you can dine on the porch. Choices vary from roasted *loup de mer* to slow-cooked lamb shank, or simply make a meal of small plates, such as lamb lollipops and crab cakes and a salad. Don't miss the lobster bouillabaisse or the chocolate *budino,* a scrumptious warm Italian pudding that melts in your mouth (a must for chocoholics). Most entrées are in the $18–29 range.

The bi-level dining room at **The Manor Inn** (76 Battle Ave., 207/326-4861, 6–8:30 P.M. Tues.–Sat. in summer, Thurs.–Sat. off-season) overlooks the gardens and lawn. Dinner is served from an extensive menu accented with Asian tastes, Indian curries, and other world flavors, accompanied by home-baked breads, and always including vegetarian choices (most entrées $16–24). Reservations are essential on weekends. It's open from Valentine's Day to late December.

INFORMATION AND SERVICES

Castine has no local information office, but all businesses and lodgings in town have copies of the Castine Merchants Association's visitors brochure-map. For additional information, go to the **Castine Town Office** (Emerson Hall, 67 Court St., 207/326-4502, www.castine.me.us, 8 A.M.–3:30 P.M. Mon.–Fri.).

Libraries

Check out **Witherle Memorial Library** (41 School St., 207/326-4375, www.witherle.lib.me.us). Also accessible to the public is the Nutting Memorial Library, in Platz Hall on the Maine Maritime Academy campus.

Public Restrooms

Castine has public restrooms on the town dock, at the foot of Main Street.

Deer Isle

"Deer Isle is like Avalon," wrote John Steinbeck in *Travels with Charley*—"it must disappear when you are not there." Deer Isle (the name of both the island and its midpoint town) has been romancing authors and artisans for decades, but it's unmistakably real to the quarrymen and fishermen who've been here for centuries. These long-timers are a sturdy lot, as even Steinbeck recognized: "I would hate to try to force them to do anything they didn't want to do."

Early-18th-century maps show no name for the island, but by the late 1800s, nearly 100 families lived here, supporting themselves first by farming, then by fishing. In 1789, when Deer Isle was incorporated, 80 local sailing vessels were scouring the Gulf of Maine in pursuit of mackerel and cod, and Deer Isle men were circling the globe as yachting skippers and merchant seamen. At the same time, in the once-quiet village of Green's Landing (now called Stonington), the shipbuilding and granite industries boomed, spurring development, prosperity, and the kinds of rough hijinks typical of commercial ports the world over.

Green's Landing became the "big city" for an international crowd of quarrymen carving out the terrain on Deer Isle and nearby Crotch Island, source of high-quality granite for Boston's Museum of Fine Arts, the Smithsonian Institution, a humongous fountain for John D. Rockefeller's New York

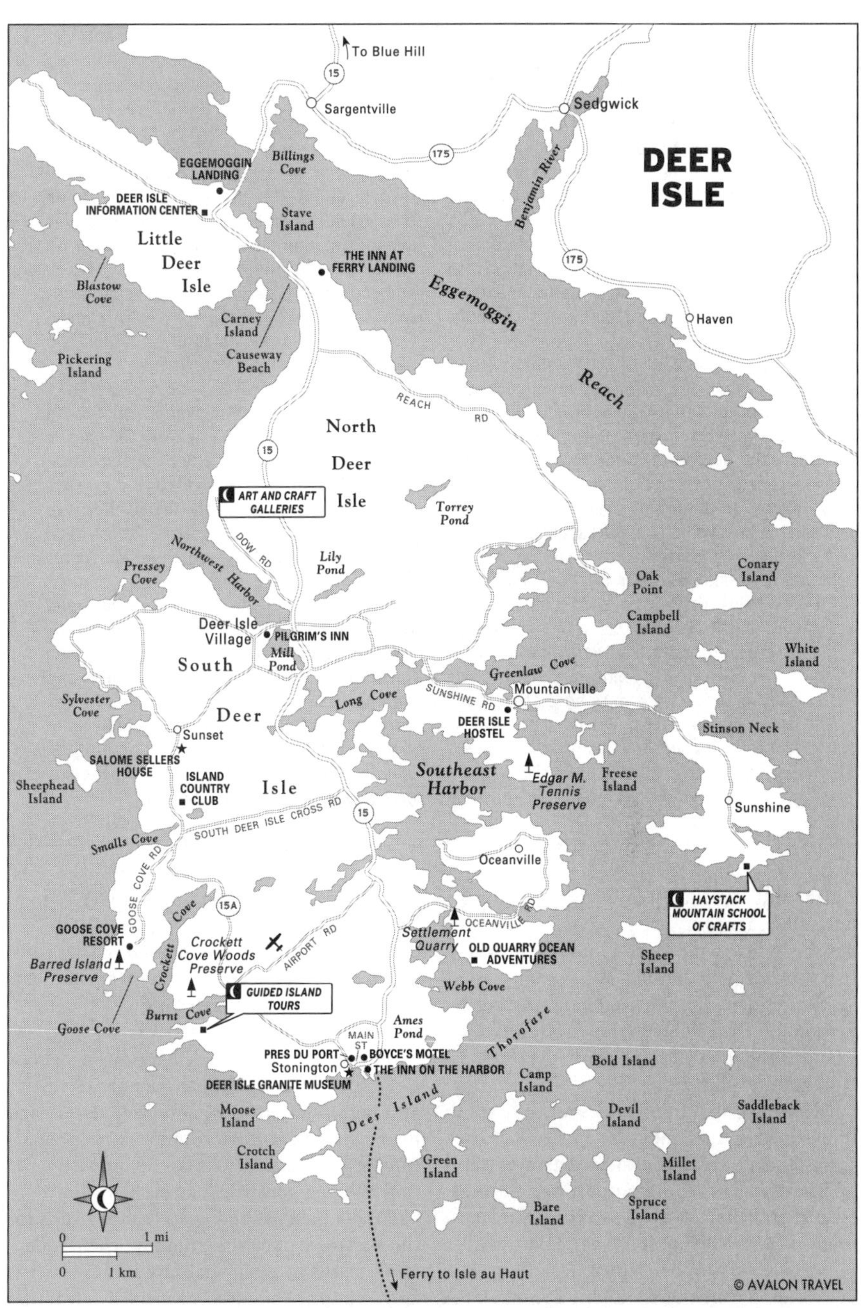
To Blue Hill
15
Sargentville
Sedgwick
175
DEER ISLE
Benjamin River
EGGEMOGGIN LANDING
Billings Cove
DEER ISLE INFORMATION CENTER
Stave Island
Little Deer Isle
THE INN AT FERRY LANDING
Eggemoggin
Reach
Blastow Cove
Carney Island
Causeway Beach
Haven
Pickering Island
REACH RD
North Deer Isle
ART AND CRAFT GALLERIES
Torrey Pond
DOW RD
Lily Pond
Northwest Harbor
Pressey Cove
Oak Point
Conary Island
Campbell Island
Deer Isle Village
PILGRIM'S INN
Mill Pond
South Deer Isle
White Island
Greenlaw Cove
Mountainville
SUNSHINE RD
Long Cove
Sylvester Cove
DEER ISLE HOSTEL
Stinson Neck
Sunset
SALOME SELLERS HOUSE
Southeast Harbor
Edgar M. Tennis Preserve
Freese Island
Sheephead Island
ISLAND COUNTRY CLUB
SOUTH DEER ISLE CROSS RD
Sunshine
Smalls Cove
GOOSE COVE RD
Oceanville
15A
HAYSTACK MOUNTAIN SCHOOL OF CRAFTS
OCEANVILLE RD
GOOSE COVE RESORT
Crockett Cove
Crockett Cove Woods Preserve
AIRPORT RD
Settlement Quarry
OLD QUARRY OCEAN ADVENTURES
Barred Island Preserve
Sheep Island
Webb Cove
GUIDED ISLAND TOURS
Burnt Cove
Goose Cove
Ames Pond
MAIN ST
Thorofare
PRES DU PORT
BOYCE'S MOTEL
Stonington
THE INN ON THE HARBOR
DEER ISLE GRANITE MUSEUM
Bold Island
Camp Island
Moose Island
Deer Island
Devil Island
Saddleback Island
Crotch Island
Green Island
Millet Island
Bare Island
Spruce Island
0 1 mi
0 1 km
Ferry to Isle au Haut
© AVALON TRAVEL

THE MAINE ISLAND TRAIL

In the early 1980s, a "trail" of coastal Maine islands was only the germ of an idea. By the end of the millennium, the **Maine Island Trail Association** (MITA, 207/596-6456, www.mita.org) counted some 4,000 members dedicated to conscientious (i.e., low- or no-impact) recreational use of about 150 public and private islands along 350 miles of Maine coastline between Kennebunkport and Machias, and it continues to grow.

More than a dozen of these islands (each year new ones are added and others are subtracted) are in the Acadia region – between Isle au Haut and Schoodic Point. In fact, one of the best island clusters along the entire trail is in the waters off Stonington on Deer Isle.

Access to the trail is only by private boat, and the best choice is a sea kayak, to navigate shallow or rock-strewn coves. Sea kayak rentals are available in Bar Harbor, Southwest Harbor, Blue Hill, Castine, and Stonington, and several outfitters offer island tours. The best source of information is the Maine Association of Sea Kayaking Guides and Instructors (MASKGI), whose members agree to adhere to the Leave No Trace philosophy.

The trail's publicly owned islands – supervised by the state Bureau of Public Lands – are open to anyone; the private islands are restricted to MITA members, who pay $45 per individual or $65 per family annually for the privilege (and, it's important to add, the responsibility). With the fee comes the ***Maine Island Trail Guidebook,*** providing directions and information for each of the islands. With membership comes the expectation of care and concern. "Low impact" means different things to different people, so MITA experienced acute growing pains when enthusiasm began leading to "tent sprawl."

To cope with and reverse the overuse, MITA has created an "adopt-an-island" program, in which volunteers become stewards for specific islands and keep track of their use and condition. MITA members are urged to pick up trash, use tent platforms where they exist, and move on if an island has already reached its assigned capacity (stipulated on a shoreline sign and/or in the guidebook).

A superb complement to the *Maine Island Trail Guidebook* is a copy of *Hot Showers!* by Lee Bumsted, a former MITA staff member. Recognizing the need for alternating island camping and warm beds (and hot showers), Bumsted has almost single-handedly alleviated island stress and strain. Some of the bed-and-breakfasts and inns listed in her guide give discounts to MITA members.

estate, and less showy projects all along the Eastern Seaboard. The heyday is long past, but the industry did extend into the 20th century (including a contract for the pink granite at President John F. Kennedy's Arlington National Cemetery gravesite). Today, Crotch Island is the site of Maine's only operating island granite quarry.

Measuring about nine miles north to south (plus another three miles for Little Deer Isle), the island of Deer Isle today has a handful of hamlets (including **Sunshine, Sunset, Mountainville,** and **Oceanville**) and two towns—**Stonington** and **Deer Isle**—with a population just under 3,000. Road access is via Route 15 on the Blue Hill Peninsula. A huge suspension bridge, built in 1939 over Eggemoggin Reach, links the Sargentville section of Sedgwick with Little Deer Isle; from there, a sinuous 0.4-mile causeway connects to the northern tip of Deer Isle.

Deer Isle remains an artisans' enclave, anchored by the Haystack Mountain School of Crafts. Studios and galleries are plentiful, although many require noodling along back roads to find them. Stonington, a rough-and-tumble fishing port with an idyllic setting, is slowly being gentrified, as each season more and more galleries and upscale shops open for the summer. Locals are holding their collective breaths, hoping that any improvements don't change the town too much (although most visitors could do without the car racing on Main Street at night). Already, real-estate prices and accompanying taxes have escalated way past the point where many a local fisherman can hope to buy, and in some cases maintain, a home.

SIGHTS

Sightseeing on Deer Isle means exploring back roads, browsing the galleries, walking the trails, hanging out on the docks, and soaking in the ambience.

Haystack Mountain School of Crafts

The renowned Haystack Mountain School of Crafts (Sunshine Rd., Deer Isle, 207/348-2306, www.haystack-mtn.org) in Sunshine is open to the public on a limited basis, but if it fits in your schedule, go. Anyone can visit the school store or walk down the central stairs to the water; to see more of the campus, take a tour (1 P.M. Wed., $5), which includes a video, viewing works on display, and the opportunity to visit some studios. Beyond that, there are slide programs, lectures, demonstrations, and concerts, presented by faculty and visiting artists, starting at 8 P.M. on varying weeknights from early June to late August. Perhaps the best opportunities are the End-of-Session auctions, held on Thursday nights every two or three weeks, when you can tour the studios for free 4–6 P.M. and view the works the teachers and students have produced, then return for the auction preview at 7:30 P.M., followed by the auction at 8 P.M. It's a great opportunity to buy craftwork at often very reasonable prices.

Historic Houses and Museums

There's more to the 1830 **Salome Sellers House** (416 Sunset Rd./Rte. 15A, Sunset Village, 207/348-2897, 1–4 P.M. Wed. and Fri. July–early Sept., free but donations appreciated) than first meets the eye. A repository of local memorabilia, archives, and intriguing artifacts, it's also the headquarters of the **Deer**

Architect Edward Larrabee Barnes designed the oceanfront Haystack Mountain School of Crafts on Deer Isle.

GETTING CRAFTY

Internationally famed artisans – sculptors and papermakers, weavers and jewelers, potters and printmakers – become the faculty each summer for the unique **Haystack Mountain School of Crafts.** Founded in 1950 by Mary Beasom Bishop (1885–1972) and a group of talented Maine artisans as a studio research and study program, Haystack has grown into one of the top craft schools in the country.

Under the direction of beloved former director Francis Merritt, the school opened its first campus near Haystack Mountain, in Montville, Maine, in 1951. Ten years later, when the state unveiled plans to build a new highway (Route 3) that would bisect that campus, the school moved to its present 40-acre oceanfront location at the end of the Sunshine Road in Deer Isle. Good move.

You would be hard-pressed to find a more artistically stimulating and architecturally stunning environment. Architect Edward Larrabee Barnes's award-winning campus perfectly complements its dramatic setting. The angular cedar-shingled buildings are connected via walkways and teaching decks and a central staircase that cascades like a waterfall down the wooded hillside to the rocky coast below. The visual impression is one of spruce and ledge, glass and wood, islands and water.

One thing that makes Haystack work is its diverse student body. Students of all abilities, from beginners through advanced professionals, come from around the globe for the two- to three-week summer sessions, taking weekday classes and enjoying round-the-clock studio access to follow their creative muses. In a recent year, students ranged in age from 18 to 75, and in professions from a retired teacher to a physicist. What brings them all here, says current director Stuart Kestenbaum, is the "direct making experience." That experience draws not only those who make but also those who collect. For a collector of fine craft, he says, taking a class is a "great way to get insight into the making process; it gives a different relationship with the craft being collected." Each session also includes a range of crafts. These may include blacksmithing, drawing, metals, wood, beads, clay, fibers, printmaking, glass, weaving, mixed media, paper, and baskets.

Isle-Stonington Historical Society. Sellers, matriarch of an island family, was a direct descendent of Mayflower settlers. She lived to be 108, a lifetime spanning from 1800 to 1908, earning the record for oldest recorded Maine resident. The house contains Sellers's furnishings, and in a small exhibit space in the rear is a fine exhibit of baskets made by Maine's Native American tribes. Behind the house are the archives, heritage gardens, and an exhibit hall filled with nautical artifacts. Bringing all this to life are enthusiastic volunteer guides, many of them island natives. They love to provide tidbits about various items; seafarers' logs and ship models are particularly intriguing, and don't miss the 1920s peapod, the original lobster boat on the island. The house is just north of the Island Country Club and across from Eaton's Plumbing.

Close to the Stonington waterfront, the **Deer Isle Granite Museum** (51 Main St., Stonington, 207/367-6331) was established to commemorate the centennial of the quarrying business hereabouts. The best feature of the small museum is a 15-foot-long working model of Crotch Island, center of the industry, as it appeared at the turn of the 20th century. Flatcars roll, boats glide, and derricks move—it all looks very real. The museum is open in July and August, but it's best to call for current days and hours of operation. The recommended donation is $5 per family.

Another downtown Stonington attraction is a Lilliputian complex known as the **Miniature Village.** Some years ago, the late Everett Knowlton created a dozen and a half replicas of local buildings and displayed them on granite blocks in his yard. Since his death, they've been restored and put on display each summer in town—along with a donation box to support the upkeep. The village is set up on East Main Street (Route 15), below Hoy Gallery.

Pumpkin Island Light

A fine view of Pumpkin Island Light can be had from the cul-de-sac at the end of the Eggemoggin Road on Little Deer Isle. If heading south on Route 15, bear right at the information booth after crossing the bridge and continue to the end.

Penobscot East Resource Center

The purpose of the Penobscot East Resource Center, in Stonington (207/367-2708, www.penobscoteast.org), is "to energize and facilitate responsible community-based fishery management, collaborative marine science, and sustainable economic development to benefit the fishermen and the communities of Penobscot Bay and the Eastern Gulf of Maine." Bravo to that! It operates a **Lobster Hatchery** (Stonington Lobster Coop No. 1, 51 Indian Point Rd.), which was constructed by volunteers from the lobster industry in donated space with $25,000 raised locally and a matching grant. Lobster production began in 2006. Guided tours are offered ($10 adults, $5 children); call the resource center for the schedule.

The man behind both ventures is Ted Ames, who won a $500,000 MacArthur Foundation "genius grant" in 2005.

ENTERTAINMENT AND EVENTS

Stonington's National Historic Landmark, the 1912 **Opera House** (207/367-2788, www.operahousearts.org), is home to Opera House Arts, which hosts films, plays, lectures, concerts, family programs, and workshops year-round.

Mid-June, when lupine in various shades of pink and purple seem to be blooming everywhere, brings the **Lupine Festival** (207/348-2676 or 207/367-2420). The weekend festival includes art openings and shows, boat rides, a private garden tour, and entertainment ranging from a contra dance to movies.

© TOM NANGLE

The lights are on once again in Stonington's Opera House.

July through September is the season for **First Friday,** an open-house night held on the first Friday evening of each month, with demonstrations, music, and refreshments, sponsored by the Stonington Galleries (www.stoningtongalleries.com).

Seamark Community Arts (207/348-2333, www.seamarkcommunityarts.com) hosts arts workshops for children and adults in areas such as book arts, nature crafts, pottery, drawing and painting, film and video, printmaking, basketry, textile arts, and more. The summer highlight is the themed annual auction; in 2009, local artists contributed artistic serving trays keeping with that year's theme, "At Your Service."

Mid-July brings the **Stonington Lobsterboat Races** (207/348-2804), very popular competitions held in the harbor, with lots of possible vantage points. Stonington is one of the major locales in the lobster-boat race circuit.

TED AMES, GENIUS

Ted Ames, the man behind the Penobscot East Resource Center and the Lobster Hatchery in Stonington, is a genius. In 2005, he was awarded a $500,000 MacArthur Fellowship. These prestigious "genius grants" are awarded to "talented individuals who have shown extraordinary originality and dedication in their creative pursuits and a marked capacity for self-direction." The foundation credited Ames with fusing "the roles of fisherman and applied scientist in response to increasing threats to the fishery ecosystem resulting from decades of overharvesting." Criteria for selection are: exceptional creativity, promise for important future advances based on a track record of significant accomplishment, and potential for the fellowship to facilitate subsequent creative work. No question, they found the right guy in Ted Ames.

A humble, soft-spoken man with dogged determination, Ames found little time to bask in the limelight from the award. While he certainly appreciated the money and the attention paid to his causes, the numerous interviews with TV, radio, and newspaper reporters took up valuable time, time he would rather use researching fisheries, collecting data, and devising ways to develop community-based fisheries management.

Ames is a fascinating guy, a combination of fisherman, lobsterman, and research scientist with deep Maine roots. "My family were some of the original settlers of Vinalhaven," he says. Ancestors on his father's side arrived in 1757, on the island off Rockland in Maine's mid-coast. "My mother's side came from Mount Desert." They were the original settlers on Bartlett's Island. When King George told the family to leave, they refused and stayed put. Ames grew up in a fishing family on Vinalhaven and went on to earn a master's degree in biochemistry from the University of Maine. But fishing was in his blood, and he eventually returned to the sea as a lobsterman and groundfisherman.

His years on the water gave him firsthand experience watching the changes in Maine's fisheries. He watched Maine's coastal economy change as fishing ports became more gentrified: Commercial piers gave way to oceanfront homes, and marine-related businesses gave way to fancy boutiques. His education combined with his experiences gave him tools and the insight needed to work toward developing new fisheries management practices and supporting fishing communities. He studied fishing patterns in the Gulf of Maine, noting spawning and habitat, and he complemented his research by listening to the stories and experiences of aging fishermen. By doing so, he was able to establish a fishing timeline beginning with historical patterns and following their evolution to current ones.

The Penobscot East Resource Center, which he founded with his wife, Robin, a former marine resources commissioner, and the Lobster Hatchery both are designed as research facilities as well as places for community members and others to learn more about fishing, meet commercial fishermen and women, and learn about their lifestyles in order to help support them and preserve the tradition and the economy. Ames, a master at gaining community support (due perhaps to his impeccable Maine credentials), managed to raise $25,000 from local fishing families, businesses, and individuals in an area not known for wealth.

Ames is using the unrestricted MacArthur Fellows Program money to continue his fisheries research and to develop "community-based groundfishing management to make it sustainable, so coastal fishing communities can survive into the next century. That's a challenge, but we're in the midst of it." There's no better person to be at the forefront than Ted Ames.

In early October is **Peninsula Potters Open Studios** (207/348-5681), during which more than two dozen potters welcome visitors.

Want to meet locals and learn more about the area? **Island Heritage Trust** sponsors a series of walks, talks, and tours from mid-June through mid-September. For information and reservations, call 207/348-2455.

ART AND CRAFT GALLERIES

Thanks to the presence and influence of Haystack Mountain School of Crafts, megatalented artists and artisans lurk in every corner of the island. Most galleries are tucked away on back roads, so watch for roadside signs. Many have studios open to the public where you can watch the artists at work. Here's just a sampling.

North End of Deer Isle

Although **Ronald Hayes Pearson** has died, his innovative and beautiful jewelry lives on in his eponymous studio and gallery (29 Old Ferry Rd., 207/348-2535), where artisans continue to create his designs under the watchful eye of his wife.

The nearby **Greene-Ziner Gallery** (73 Reach Rd., 207/348-2601, www.melissagreene.com) is a double treat. Melissa Greene turns out incredible painted and incised pottery (she's represented in the Smithsonian's Renwick Gallery) and Eric Ziner works magic in metal sculpture and furnishings. Your budget may not allow for one of Melissa's pots (in the four-digit range), but I guarantee you'll covet them. The gallery also displays the work of several other local artists.

Deer Isle Village Area

One of the island's premier galleries is Elena Kubler's **The Turtle Gallery** (61 N. Deer Isle Rd., Rte. 15, 207/348-9977, www.turtlegallery.com), in a handsome space formerly known as the Old Centennial House Barn (owned by the late Haystack director Francis Merritt) and the adjacent farmhouse. Group and solo shows of contemporary paintings, prints, and crafts are hung upstairs and down in the barn; works by gallery artists are in the farmhouse; and there's usually sculpture in the gardens both in front and in back. It's just north of Deer Isle Village—across from the Shakespeare School, oldest gallery on the island.

After the death of its founder, Mary Nyburg, the future of the famed **Blue Heron Gallery** (207/348-2267, www.blueherondeerisle.com) was blowing in the wind. Supporters, Haystack alumni, and friends rose to the occasion, and now the gallery is secure, even if its location moves every season. It remains a retail outlet for the work of the school's internationally renowned faculty—printmakers, blacksmiths, potters, weavers, papermakers, glassworkers, and more; seek it out.

Just a bit south is **Dockside Quilt Gallery** (33 Church St., 207/348-2531, www.docksidequiltgallery.com), where Nancy Knowlton, her daughter Kelly Pratt, and daughter-in-law Rebekah Knowlton stitch heirloom-quality quilts. Also here are Re-Bears, one-of-a-kind teddy bears handcrafted from vintage furs and fabrics by ninth-generation islander Heather Cormier. Custom quilts and bears can be ordered.

The **Deer Isle Artists Association** (13 Dow Rd., 207/348-2330, www.deerisleartists.com) is headquartered less than a mile northwest of the village. The co-op gallery features two-week exhibits of paintings, prints, drawings, and photos by local pros. Horse fans won't want to miss Penelope Plumb's upstairs gallery, **Equine Art** (207/348-6892, www.penelopeplumb.com).

The **RED DOT Gallery** (3 Main St., 207/348-2733, www.reddotgallery.net) shows the works of 10 artists creating in varied media.

Sunshine Road

Now for a bit of whimsy. From Route 15 in Deer Isle Village, take the Sunshine Road east 2.9 miles to **Peter Beerits Sculpture** (600 Sunshine Rd., 800/777-6845, www.nervousnellies.com). The meadows and woods surrounding the studio teem with whimsical wood and metal sculptures, including

© HILARY NANGLE

Peter Beerits's whimsical sculptures accent the grounds of Nervous Nellie's.

dragons, Huns on horseback, moose, a blues joint and a western saloon, a general store, and more. The property is also home to Beerits's other enterprise, **Nervous Nellie's Jams and Jellies,** known for outstandingly creative condiments; sampling is encouraged. The best time to come is from May to early October, 9 A.M.–5 P.M., when the shop operates the ultra-casual **Mountainville Cafe,** serving tea, coffee, and delicious scones—with, of course, delicious Nervous Nellie's products. Stock up, because they're sold in only a few shops.

Stonington

Cabinetmaker Geoffrey Warner features his work as well as that of other local woodworkers in rotating shows at **Geoffrey Warner Studio** (431 N. Main St., 207/367-6555, www.geoffreywarnerstudio.com). Warner mixes classic techniques with contemporary styles and Eastern, nature-based, and Arts and Crafts accents to create some unusual and rather striking pieces.

Bright and airy **Isalos Fine Art** (Main St., Stonington, 207/367-2700, www.isalosart.com) shows the work of local artists in rotating shows.

Debi Mortenson shows her paintings, photography, and sculptures at **D Mortenson Gallery** (10 W. Main St., 207/367-5875, www.debimortenson.com) year-round.

The **g.Watson Gallery** (68 Main St., 207/367-2900) is a fine art gallery representing a number of top-notch artists working in varied media.

More paintings, many in bold, bright colors, can be found at Jill Hoy's **Hoy Gallery** (E. Main St., 207/367-2368, www.jillhoy.com).

A bit off the beaten path, but worth seeking out, is the **Siri Beckman Studio** (115 Airport Rd., 207/367-5037, www.siribeckman.com), Beckman's home studio–gallery featuring her woodcuts, prints, and watercolors.

SHOPPING

The greatest concentration of shops is in Stonington, where galleries, clothing boutiques, and eclectic shops line Main Street.

© HILARY NANGLE

If you're in need of a good read, pop into Dockside Books & Gifts, on Stonington's waterfront.

Antiques, Books, and Gifts

In "downtown" Deer Isle Village, you'll find **The Periwinkle** (8 Main St., Deer Isle, 207/348-2256), where Neva Beck carries a fine inventory of Maine books, as well as crafts, notecards, and gifts. Look for Neva's hand-braided rugs and chair pads and her baby quilts.

The eclectic selection at **Bayside Antiques and Gifts** (131 Main St., Stonington, 207/367-8714) includes antiques, decorative accessories, and gifts, but the specialty is quality 18th- and 19th-century furniture and accessories from the northeast.

In downtown Stonington, below the Opera House, **Dockside Books & Gifts** (62 W. Main St., Stonington, 207/367-2652) carries just what its name promises, with a specialty in marine and Maine books. The rustic two-room shop has spectacular harbor views.

In 2008, Janice Glenn moved her browsers' emporium, **Old Schoolhouse Antiques at Burnt Cove** (194 Burnt Cove Rd., Stonington, 207/367-2849), to Burnt Cove, across from the grocery store. It's a funky shop jam-packed with vintage clothing, kitchenware (organized by color), textiles, cookbooks, and other collectibles, with an especially nice collection of quilts, rugs, and samplers. No credit cards.

Eclectic Shops

If you're looking for Maine pottery, weaving, metalwork, pewterware, imported tiles, or walking sticks, go directly to the **Harbor Farm Store** (Rte. 15, Little Deer Isle, 207/348-7755 or 800/342-8003, www.harborfarm.com), one of the state's best gift shops.

At the bottom of the island, **The Seasons of Stonington** (6 Thurlow's Hill Rd., Stonington, 207/367-6348) sells wine, fine foods, art, and other finds.

RECREATION

Parks and Preserves

Foresighted benefactors have managed to set aside precious acreage for respectful public use on Deer Isle. The Nature Conservancy (207/729-5181, www.nature.org) owns two properties, **Crockett Cove Woods Preserve** and **Barred Island Preserve.** The conscientious steward of other local properties is the **Island Heritage Trust** (420 Sunset Rd., Sunset, 207/348-2455, www.islandheritagetrust.org). At the office, open daily in summer and 1–4 P.M. Wednesday and Friday in winter, you can pick up notecards, photos, T-shirts, and helpful maps and information on hiking trails and nature preserves. Proceeds benefit the IHT's efforts; donations are much appreciated.

SETTLEMENT QUARRY

Here's one of the easiest, shortest walks in the area, leading to an impressive vista. From the parking lot on Oceanville Road (just under a mile off Route 15), marked by a carved granite sign, it's about five minutes to the top of the old quarry, where the viewing platform (a.k.a. the "throne room") takes in the panorama—all the way to the Camden Hills on a good day. In early August, wild raspberries are an additional enticement. Three short loop trails lead into the surrounding woods from here. A map is available in the trailhead box.

EDGAR TENNIS PRESERVE

The 145-acre Tennis Preserve, off the Sunshine Road, has very limited parking, so don't try to squeeze in if there isn't room; schedule your visit for another hour or day. But do go, and bring at least a snack if not a full picnic to enjoy on one of the convenient rocky outcroppings (be sure to carry out what you carry in, though). Allow at least 90 minutes to enjoy the walking trails, one of which skirts Pickering Cove, providing sigh-producing views. Another trail leads to an old cemetery. Parts of the trails can be wet, so wear appropriate footwear. Bring binoculars for bird-watching. The preserve is open sunrise–sunset. To find it, take the Sunshine Road 2.5 miles to the Tennis Road, and follow it to the preserve.

SHORE ACRES PRESERVE

The 38-acre preserve, a gift in 2000 from Judy Hill to the Island Heritage Trust, comprises old farmland, woodlands, clam flats, a salt marsh, and granite shorefront. Three walking trails connect in a 1.5-mile loop, with the Shore Trail section edging Greenlaw Cove. As you walk along the waterfront, look for the islands of Mount Desert rising in the distance and seals basking on offshore ledges. Do not walk across the salt marsh and try to avoid stepping on beach plants. To find the preserve, take the Sunshine Road 1.2 miles and then bear left at the fork onto the Greenlaw District Road. The preserve's parking area is just shy of one mile down the road. Park only in the parking area, not on the paved road.

CROCKETT COVE WOODS PRESERVE

Donated to the Nature Conservancy by benevolent, eco-conscious local artist Emily Muir, 98-acre Crockett Cove Woods Preserve is Deer Isle's natural gem—a coastal fog forest laden with lichens and mosses. Four interlinked walking trails cover the whole preserve, starting with a short nature trail. Pick up the helpful map-brochure at the registration box. Wear rubberized shoes or boots and respect adjacent private property. The preserve is open sunrise–sunset daily all year. From Deer Isle Village, take Route 15A to Sunset Village. Go 2.5 miles to Whitman Road and then to Fire Lane 88. The local contact phone number is 207/367-2674.

BARRED ISLAND PRESERVE

Owned by the Nature Conservancy but managed by the Island Heritage Trust, Barred Island Preserve was donated by Carolyn Olmsted, grandniece of noted landscape architect Frederick Law Olmsted, who summered nearby. A former owner of Goose Cove Lodge donated an additional 48 acres of maritime boreal fog forest. A single walking trail, one mile long, leads from the parking lot to the point. At low tide, and when eagles aren't nesting, you can continue out to Barred Island. Another trail skirts the shoreline of Goose Cove, before retreating inland and rejoining with the main trail. From a high point on the main trail, you can see more than a dozen islands, many of which are protected from development, as well as Saddleback Ledge Light, 14 miles distant. To get to the preserve, follow Route 15A to Goose Cove Road and then continue to the parking area on the right. If it's full, return another day.

HOLT MILL POND PRESERVE

The Stonington Conservation Commission administers this town-owned preserve, where more than 47 bird species have been identified (bring binoculars). It comprises four habitats: upland spruce forest, lowland spruce/mixed forest, freshwater marsh, and saltwater marsh. A self-guiding nature trail is accessible off the Airport Road (off Route 15 at the intersection with Lily's Café). Look for the Nature Trail sign just beyond the medical center. The detailed self-guiding trail brochure, available at the trailhead registration kiosk, is accented with drawings by noted artist Siri Beckman.

AMES POND

Ames Pond is neither park nor preserve, but it might as well be. On a back road close to Stonington, it's a mandatory stop in July and August, when the pond wears a blanket of pink and white water lilies. From downtown Stonington, take Indian Point Road east, just under a mile, to the pond.

CAUSEWAY BEACH AND SCOTT'S LANDING

If you're itching to dip your toes in the water, stop by Causeway Beach along the causeway linking Little Deer Isle to Deer Isle. It's popular for swimming and is also a significant habitat for birds and other wildlife. On the other side of Route 15 is Scott's Landing, with more than 20 acres of fields, trails, and shorefront.

Sporting Outfitters and Guided Trips

The biggest operation is **Old Quarry Ocean Adventures** (Stonington, 207/367-8977 or 877/479-8977, mobile 207/266-7778, www.oldquarry.com), with a broad range of outdoor adventure choices. Bill Baker's ever-expanding enterprise rents canoes, kayaks, sailboats, bikes, moorings, platform tent sites, and cabins. Bicycle rentals are $20 per day or $100 per week. Sea kayak rentals are $57 per day for a single, $67 for a tandem. Half-day rates (based on a four-hour rental) are $42 and $52, respectively. Overnight 24-hour rental is available for a 10 percent surcharge. Other options include canoes, rowboats, and sailboats; check the website for details. For all boat rentals, you must demonstrate competency in the vessel. They'll deliver and pick up anywhere on the island for a fee of $22. All-day guided tours in single kayaks are $105; tandems are $175. Half-day tours are $55 and $110, respectively. Plenty of other options are available, including sunset tours, family trips, and gourmet picnic paddles.

Overnight kayaking camping trips on nearby islands are led by a Registered Maine Guide. Rates, including meals, begin at $285 per adult for one night; three-person minimum. If you're bringing your own kayak, you can park your car ($7 per night up to two nights, $6 per night for three or more nights) and launch from here ($5 per boat for launching); they'll take your trash and any trash you find. Old Quarry is off the Oceanville Road, less than a mile from Route 15, just before you reach the Settlement Quarry preserve. It's well signposted.

Next to the restaurant of the same name, and owned by the same family, is **Finest Kind** (Center District Crossroad, about halfway between Routes 15 and 15A, 207/348-7714). Bicycle rentals here are $15 per day or $75 per week. Kayak or canoe rentals are $35 per day for a single, $45 for a tandem, including paddles, life jackets, spray skirts, delivery, and pickup.

Guided Walks

The Island Heritage Trust (402 Sunset Rd., Sunset, 207/348-2455, www.islandheritagetrust.org), along with the Stonington and Deer Isle Conservation Commissions, sponsors a Walks and Talks series. Guided walks cover topics such as Birds and Bird Calls for Beginners, The Geology of Deer Isle, and Migrating Shorebird Walk. Call for information and reservations.

Sea Kayaking

The waters around Deer Isle, with lots of islets and protected coves, are extremely popular for sea kayaking, especially off Stonington.

If you sign up with the **Maine Island Trail Association** (207/761-8225, www.mita.org, $45/year), you'll receive a handy manual that steers you to more than a dozen islands in the Deer Isle archipelago where you can camp, hike, and picnic—eco-sensitively, please. Boat traffic can be a bit heavy at the height of summer, so to best appreciate the tranquility of this area, try this in September, after the Labor Day holiday. Nights can be cool, but days are likely to be brilliant. Do remember this is a working harbor.

The six-mile paddle from Stonington to Isle au Haut is best left to experienced paddlers, especially since fishing folks refer to kayakers as "speed bumps."

For equipment rentals or guided trips, Old Quarry Ocean Adventures (Stonington, 207/367-8977 or 877/479-8977, mobile 207/266-7778, www.oldquarry.com) is especially helpful and provides many services for kayakers. Old Quarry is off the Oceanville Road, less than a mile from Route 15, just before you reach the Settlement Quarry preserve. It's well signposted.

Swimming

The island's only major freshwater swimming hole is the **Lily Pond,** northeast of Deer Isle Village. Just north of the Shakespeare School, turn into the Deer Run Apartments complex. Park and take the path to the pond, which has a shallow area for small children.

Golf and Tennis

About two miles south of Deer Isle Village, watch for the large sign (on the left) for the **Island Country Club** (Rte. 15A, Sunset, 207/348-2379, early June–late Sept.), a nine-hole public course that's been here since 1928. Also at the club are three beautifully maintained tennis courts. Note: The club's cheeseburgers and salads are among the island's best bargain lunches.

Excursion Boats

ISLE AU HAUT BOAT COMPANY

If you're not up for self-propulsion, board the *Miss Lizzie,* which from mid-June through late August departs at 2 P.M. Monday–Saturday from the Isle au Haut Boat Company (Seabreeze Ave., Stonington, 207/367-5193 or 207/367-6516, www.isleauhaut.com) dock in Stonington for a narrated one-hour trip among the islands; on morning tours, the crew hauls a string of lobster traps. Cost is $18 adults, $8 children under 12. Another option is to cruise over and back to Isle au Haut, without stepping foot off the boat, for half of the usual round-trip fare ($35 adults, $18 children). Reservations are advisable, especially in July and August. Day parking is available at the pier for $4, or find a spot in town and save the surcharge.

GUIDED ISLAND TOURS

Captain Walter Reed's Guided Island Tours (207/348-6789, www.guidedislandtours.com) aboard the *Gael* are custom designed for a maximum of four passengers. Walt is a Registered Maine Guide and professional biologist who also is a steward for Mark Island Lighthouse and several uninhabited islands in the area. He provides in-depth perspective and the local scoop. The cost is $35 per person for the first hour plus $25 per person for each additional hour; kids under 12 are half price. Reservations required; box lunches are available for an additional fee.

OLD QUARRY OCEAN ADVENTURES

Yet another aspect of the Old Quarry Ocean Adventures (Stonington, 207/367-8977 or 877/479-8977, mobile 207/266-7778, www.oldquarry.com) empire are sightseeing tours on the *Nigh Duck.* The three-hour trips, one in the morning (9 A.M.–noon) and one in the afternoon (1–4 P.M.), are $40 for adults and $24 for children under 12. Both highlight the natural history of the area as Captain Bill navigates the boat through the archipelago. Lobster traps are hauled on both trips (but not on Sunday); the morning trip visits Isle au Haut. The afternoon excursion features an island swimming break in a freshwater quarry. Also available is a 1.5-hour sunset cruise, departing half an hour before sunset, for $34 adults and $24 children under 12. And if that's not enough, Old Quarry also offers puffin, lighthouse, whale-watching, and island cruises, with rates beginning at $55 per adult, $35 per child. Of course, if none of this floats your boat, you can also arrange for a custom charter for $140 per hour.

Old Quarry also offers a number of special trips in conjunction with Island Heritage Trust. Most are noted on Old Quarry's website, but for reservations or more info, call 207/348-2455.

ACCOMMODATIONS

Inns and Bed-and-Breakfasts

Pilgrim's Inn (20 Main St., Deer Isle, 207/348-6615, www.pilgrimsinn.com, $129–239) is a beautifully restored colonial building and newer cottages overlooking the peaceful Mill Pond. The National Historic Register inn began life in 1793 as a boardinghouse named The Ark; be sure to check out the fascinating guestbook, with names dating back to 1901. A bit of a disconnect from the peacefulness is the recently added TV room (request a room far away from it, as the noise carries) and the downstairs tavern (formerly a fine-dining restaurant). It's open from early May to mid-October.

The Inn on the Harbor (45 Main St., Stonington, 207/367-2420 or 800/942-2420, www.innontheharbor.com, $139–225) is exactly as its name proclaims—its expansive deck hangs right over the harbor. Although recently updated, the 1880s complex still has an air of unpretentiousness. Most of the 14 rooms and suites, each named after a windjammer, have fantastic harbor views and private or shared decks where you can keep an eye on lobster boats, small ferries, windjammers, and pleasure craft. (Binoculars are provided.) Streetside rooms can be noisy at night. Rates include a continental buffet breakfast. An espresso bar is open 11 A.M.–4:30 P.M. Nearby are antiques, gift, and craft shops; guest moorings

© HILARY NANGLE

The view from the back decks at the Inn on the Harbor is first rate.

are available. The inn is open all year, but call ahead off-season, when rates are lower.

In downtown Stonington, just up the hill from the Inn on the Harbor and convenient for walking to everything (even a small sandy beach a mile away), is **Pres du Port** (W. Main St. and Highland Ave., Stonington, 207/367-5007, www.presduport.com, $125–150), a bright bed-and-breakfast run by amiable innkeeper Charlotte Casgrain. After many summers at a Deer Isle French summer camp and a career as a Connecticut French teacher, she's settled here. Three rooms have detached baths, one has a private bath; there are vanity sinks in the rooms. Children are welcome, and there's even a toy cupboard to entertain them. Adults can relax in the water-view hot tub, or climb to Charlotte's Folly, a rooftop lookout, for the extensive views. No credit cards.

Eggemoggin Reach is almost on the doorstep at **The Inn at Ferry Landing** (77 Old Ferry Rd., Deer Isle, 207/348-7760, www.ferrylanding.com, $130–178), overlooking the abandoned Sargentville–Deer Isle ferry wharf. The view is wide open from the inn's great room, where guests gather to read, play games, talk, and watch passing windjammers. Professional musician Gerald Wheeler has installed two grand pianos in the room; it's a treat when he plays. His wife, Jean, is the hospitable innkeeper, managing three water-view guest rooms and a suite. A harpsichord and a great view are big pluses in the suite. The Mooring, an annex that sleeps five, is rented by the week ($1,700, without breakfast). The inn is open all year except Thanksgiving and Christmas; Wi-Fi is available throughout.

Motels

Right in downtown Stonington, just across the street from the harbor, is **Boyce's Motel** (44 Main St., Stonington, 207/367-2421 or 800/224-2421, www.boycesmotel.com, $65–130). Eleven units all have TV, phones, and refrigerators; some have kitchens and living rooms, and one has two bedrooms. Across the street, Boyce's has a private harborfront deck for its guests. Ask for rooms well back from Main Street to lessen the noise of locals cruising the street at night. It's open year-round.

Resort

In 2009, **Goose Cove Resort** (Goose Cove Rd., Sunset, 207/348-2600, www.goosecovelodgemaine.com, $125–550) reopened the rustic cabins and guestrooms on this fabulous oceanfront property adjacent to the Barred Island Preserve. Many have ocean views, some have kitchenettes, most have either decks or granite ledge patios. There's a beach, nature trails, and the **Cocatoo Restaurant** serves lunch and dinner daily in season. The location is remote, secluded, and fabulous for those who enjoy communing with nature.

Hostels

In 2009, the rustic-bordering-on-primitive **Deer Isle Hostel** (65 Tennis Rd., Deer Isle, 207/348-2308, www.deerislehostel.com, $25 adults, $15 children under 12) opened near the Tennis Preserve. Owner Dennis Carter, a Surry, Maine, native and local stoneworker and carpenter, modeled it on The Hostel in the Forest in Brunswick, Georgia. It's completely off the grid, with a pump in the kitchen for water and an outhouse. Carter expects guests to work in the extensive organic gardens, using produce for shared meals prepared on a wood stove, the sole source of heat. The three-story timber-frame design is taken from a late-17th-century home in Massachusetts. Carter hand-cut the granite for the basement, and the timbers in the nail-free frame are hand-hewn from local blown-down spruce. Frills are limited to a sauna and a solar shower. The goal is sustainability, not profit. No credit cards.

Camping

Plan ahead if you want to camp at **Old Quarry Ocean Adventures Campground** (130 Settlement Rd., Stonington, 207/367-8977, www.oldquarry.com), with both oceanfront and secluded platform sites for tents and just three RV sites. Rates range $35–50 for two, plus $17 for each additional person, varying with location and hook-ups. Children younger than 12 are $6, under 5 are free. Leashed pets are permitted. Parking is designed so that vehicles are kept away from most campsites, but you can use a garden cart to transport your equipment between your car and your site. The campground is adjacent to Settlement Quarry Park.

FOOD

As always, hours are listed for peak season; call to verify days and hours of operation.

Local Flavors

After browsing the shops, you just might need a double-dip cone from **Harbor Ice Cream,** across the street from the Periwinkle in Deer Isle Village. Or a scoop of farm-made Smiling Hill Farm ice cream from **Stonington Cow Ice Cream,** on the main drag in Stonington.

The hickory-smoked salmon, unsliced, made by **Stonington Sea Products** (100 N. Main St., Stonington, 207/367-2400 or 888/402-2729, www.stoningtonseafood.com) was named in the May 2005 issue of the *Rosengarten Report* as one of the "25 Best Products" the noted food critic has ever recommended, describing it in terms including "Wow!" and "Bravo!" See for yourself, or try any of the company's other smoked products.

Craving sweets? Head to **Susie Q's Sweets and Curiosities** (40 School St., Stonington, 207/367-2415, 8 A.M.–3 P.M. Thurs.–Mon.). Susan Scott bakes a fine selection of cookies and pies, offers a limited selection of breakfast and lunch choices, and also carries antiques, books, quilts, toys, and other fun items. It's a Wi-Fi hotspot.

Burnt Cove Market (Rte. 15, Stonington, 207/367-2681, 6 A.M.–9 P.M. Mon.–Sat., 9 A.M.–9 P.M. Sun.) sells pizza, fried chicken, and sandwiches, plus beer and wine.

Creativity defines the menu at **Lily's Cafe and Wine Bar** (450 Airport Rd. at Rte. 15, Stonington, 207/367-5936, 7 A.M.–5 P.M. Mon.–Thurs., to 8 P.M. Fri.), mercifully expanded in 2008. It's all very casual; order at the counter and find a table either inside, on the upstairs deck, or outside in the garden. Or assemble an haut gourmet picnic from veggie and meat sandwiches, Mediterranean salads, cheeses, and homemade soups and breads. Upstairs is the Chef's Attic, with a smattering of antiques as well as works by local artists. Alas, it's closed on weekends. Beer and wine are served. Most lunch entrées are about $9.

The Island Community Center (6 Memorial La., just off School St., Stonington) is the locale for the lively **Island Farmers Market** (10 A.M.–noon Fri. late May–late Sept.), selling smoked and organic meats, fresh herbs and flowers, produce, gelato and yogurt, maple syrup, jams and jellies, fabulous breads and baked goods, chocolates, ethnic foods, crafts, and so much more. Go early; items sell out quickly.

Family Favorites

In July or August, don't show up at **Finest Kind Dining** (70 Center District Crossroad, Deer Isle, 207/348-7714, www.finestkindenterprises.com, 5–8:30 P.M. Mon.–Sat. May–Oct.) without a dinner reservation. This log-cabin family restaurant serves home-style all-American food in a come-as-you-are setting. Pizza, pasta, prime rib, and seafood are all available, and there's a salad bar, too; most items are in the $8–20 range. And save room for dessert. The restaurant, owned by the Perez family, is halfway between Route 15 and Sunset Road (Route 15A). The enterprising Perezes also own the adjacent **Round the Island Mini Golf** (same phone, open the same months) and rent canoes, kayaks, and bicycles.

Harbor Cafe (Main St., Stonington, 207/367-5099, 6 A.M.–8 P.M. Mon.–Thurs., to 9 P.M. Fri.–Sat., to 2 P.M. Sun.) is *the* place to go for breakfast (you can eavesdrop on the local fisherfolk if you're early enough), but it's also reliable for lunch and dinner (especially on Friday nights for the seafood fry, with free seconds).

The views are top-notch from the harborfront **Fisherman's Friend Restaurant** (5 Atlantic Ave., Stonington, 207/367-2442, 11 A.M.–9 P.M. Sun.–Thurs., to 10 P.M. Fri.–Sat.). The restaurant gets high marks for respectable food, generous portions, ultra-fresh seafood, outstanding desserts, and consistency, but it seems to have lost its soul when it moved from its old digs to this larger and more modern space. Still, where else can you get lobster prepared 30 different ways? Prices are reasonable—the Friday-night fish fry, with free seconds, is $9.99. It's open from early May to late October.

Casual Dining

Families are welcome at the **Whale's Rib Tavern** (20 Main St./Sunset Rd., Deer Isle Village, 207/348-5222, 5–8:30 P.M. daily, closed Tues. in May, Sept., and Oct.), a comfy white-tablecloth tavern in the lower level of the Pilgrim's Inn. Everyone can find something that appeals and is within their budget, from burgers to beef tenderloin, fish-and-chips to scampi. Ask about the Friday-night three-course special.

You have a front seat—and a comfortable one at that—for all the harbor action at **Maritime Cafe** (27 Main St., Stonington, 207/367-2600, www.maritimecafe.com, 11:30 A.M.–3:30 P.M. and 5–8:30 P.M. daily, $18–28). Big windows frame the harbor from the dining room, and there's also lunch seating on the harborside deck. The menu emphasizes seafood (no surprise), but there are other choices and always a vegetarian selection.

In 2007 **The Cockatoo Portuguese Restaurant** (Goose Cove Rd., Sunset, 207/348-2300, noon–9 P.M. daily) opened in the lovely Goose Cove Lodge. The views are the best on the island, and there is both indoor and outdoor seating and a full bar. Chef Suzen Carter prepares fresh, fresh, fresh seafood, most of it caught by her husband, Bradley, as well as chicken and meat. She was brought up in the Azores, so Portuguese-inspired preparations are the specialty, but you can get a classic Maine shore dinner here, too. Frankly, the Portuguese paella is the way to go. An order for two includes scallops, shrimp, mussels, and clams, most still in their shells, as well as a whole lobster, all served over Mozambique rice in a fabulous and slightly spicy sauce. Unless you're really big eaters, you'll likely have leftovers. Equally delicious is the Bacalhau ha Braz, shredded codfish with onions and crispy potatoes and peppers. Everything is cooked to order, and while service and timing has improved from the interminable wait times of the place's early operation, you should go prepared for a leisurely meal. With this location and these views, sit back and relax. Most choices are $18–38, although lunch rolls (fish, crabmeat, scallop) begin at $8.

INFORMATION AND SERVICES

The **Deer Isle-Stonington Chamber of Commerce** (207/348-6124, www.deerisle-maine.com) has a summer information booth on a grassy triangle on Route 15 in Little Deer Isle, a quarter of a mile after crossing the bridge from Sargentville (Sedgwick).

Across from the Pilgrim's Inn is the **Chase Emerson Memorial Library** (Main St., Deer Isle Village, 207/348-2899). At the tip of the island is the **Stonington Public Library** (Main St., Stonington, 207/367-5926).

Public Restrooms

Public restrooms are at the Atlantic Avenue Hardware pier and at the Stonington Town Hall, Main Street; at the Chase Emerson Library in Deer Isle Village; and behind the information booth on Little Deer Isle.

Isle au Haut

Eight miles off Stonington lies 4,700-acre Isle au Haut, roughly half of which belongs to Acadia National Park. Pronounced variously as "I'll-a-HO" or "I'LL-a-ho," the island has nearly 20 miles of hiking trails, excellent birdwatching, and a tiny village.

About 60 souls call 5,800-acre Isle au Haut home year-round, most of them eking out a living from the sea. Each summer, the population temporarily swells with day-trippers, campers, and cottagers—then settles back in fall to the measured pace of life on an offshore island.

Samuel de Champlain, threading his way through this archipelago in 1605 and noting the island's prominent central ridge, came up with the name of Isle au Haut—High Island. Appropriately, the tallest peak (543 feet) is now named Mount Champlain.

More recent fame has come to the island thanks to island-based author Linda Greenlaw, of *Perfect Storm* fame, who wrote *The Lobster Chronicles.* Although that book piqued interest, Isle au Haut remains uncrowded and well off the beaten tourist track.

Most of the southern half of the six-mile-long island belongs to Acadia National Park, thanks to the wealthy summer visitors who began arriving in the 1880s. It was their heirs who, in the 1940s, donated valuable acreage to the federal government. Today, this offshore division of the national park has a well-managed 18-mile network of trails, a few lean-tos, several miles of unpaved road, and summertime passenger-ferry service to the park entrance.

In the island's northern half are the private residences of fisherfolk and summer folk, a minuscule village (including a market and post office), a five-mile paved road, and a lighthouse. The only vehicles on the island are owned by residents.

If spending the night on Isle au Haut sounds appealing (it is), you'll need to plan well ahead; it's no place for spur-of-the-moment sleepovers. (Even spontaneous day trips aren't always possible.) The best part about staying overnight on Isle au Haut is that you'll have so much more than seven hours to enjoy this idyllic island.

ACADIA NATIONAL PARK

Mention Acadia National Park and most people think of Bar Harbor and Mount Desert Island, where more than three million visitors arrive each year. The Isle au Haut section of the park sees maybe 5,000 visitors a year—partly because only 48 people a day (not counting campers) are allowed to land here. But the remoteness of the island and the scarcity of beds and campsites also contribute to the low count.

Near the town landing, where the year-round mail boat and another boat dock, is the **Park Ranger Station** (207/335-5551), where you can pick up trail maps and park information—and use the island's only public facilities. (Do yourself a favor, though: Make your plans

© HILARY NANGLE

The Isle au Haut lighthouse, built in 1907, is now listed on the National Historic Register.

by downloading Isle au Haut maps and information from the Acadia National Park website, www.nps.gov/acad.)

Hiking

Hiking on Acadia National Park trails is the major recreation on Isle au Haut, and even in the densest fog you'll see valiant hikers going for it. A loop road circles the whole island; an unpaved section goes through the park, connecting with the mostly paved non-park section. Walking on that is easy. Beyond the road, none of the park's 18 miles of trails could be labeled "easy"; the footing is rocky, rooty, and often squishy. But the park trails *are* well marked, and the views—of islets, distant hills, and ocean—make the effort worthwhile. Go prepared with proper footwear.

The most-used park trail is the four-mile one-way **Duck Harbor Trail,** connecting the town landing with Duck Harbor. (You can either use this trail or follow the island road—mostly unpaved in this stretch—to get to the campground when the summer ferry ends its Duck Harbor runs.)

Even though the summit is only 314 feet, **Duck Harbor Mountain** is the island's toughest trail. Still, it's worth the 1.2-mile one-way effort for the stunning 360-degree views from the summit. Option: Rather than return via the trail's steep, bouldery sections, cut off at the Goat Trail and return to the trailhead that way.

For terrific shoreline scenery, take **Western Head** and **Cliff Trails** at the island's southwestern corner. They form a nice loop around Western Head. The route follows the coastline, ascending to ridges and cliffs and descending to rocky beaches, with some forested sections. Options: Close the loop by returning via the Western Head Road. If the tide is out (and *only* if it's out), you can walk across the tidal flats to the quaintly named Western Ear for views back toward the island. Western Ear is private, so don't linger. The **Goat Trail** adds another four miles (round-trip) of moderate coastline hiking east of the Cliff Trail; views are fabulous and bird-watching is good, but if you're here only for a day, you'll need to decide whether there's time to do this and still catch the return mail boat. If you do have the time and the energy, you can connect from the Goat Trail to the **Duck Harbor Mountain Trail.**

OTHER RECREATION

Biking

Pedaling is limited to the 12 or so miles of mostly unpaved, hilly roads, and while it is a way to get around, frankly, the terrain is neither exciting, fun, nor view-worthy. Mountain bikes are not allowed on the park's hiking trails, and rangers try to discourage park visitors from bringing them to the island. If you're staying at the Inn at Isle au Haut, you can borrow a bike, which is handy around the "village" and for going swimming in Long Pond. You can also rent a bike (about $23 per day) on the island from the Isle au Haut Ferry Service or Old Quarry Ocean Adventures. It costs $18 round-trip to bring your own bike aboard the Isle au Haut Ferry. Both boats carry bikes *only* to the town landing, not to Duck Harbor.

Swimming

For superb **freshwater swimming,** head for Long Pond, a skinny 1.5-mile-long swimming hole running north–south on the east side of the island, abutting national park land. You can bike over there, clockwise along the road, almost five miles, from the town landing. Or bum a ride from an island resident. There's a minuscule beachlike area on the southern end with a picnic table and a float. If you're here only for the day, though, there's not enough time to do this *and* get in a long hike. Opt for the hiking—or do a short hike and then go for a swim (the shallowest part is at the southern tip).

ACCOMMODATIONS AND FOOD

Options for food are extremely limited on Isle au Haut, so if you're coming for a day trip, bring sufficient food and water.

Inn

On the east side of the island is **The Inn at**

Isle au Haut (Lighthouse Point, Isle au Haut, off-island 207/335-5141, www.innatisleauhaut.com, $300–375), a mansard-roofed waterfront Victorian home that Diana Santospago has turned into an inn. An accomplished cook, Diana whips up fabulous breakfasts, lunches, and dinners for her guests; bring your own beer or wine. Open to the public for dinner by reservation. The downstairs room with private bath is most spacious. Three rather small rooms on the 2nd floor share one bath; all but one have water views. Single-speed bikes are provided for guests, and it's an easy pedal to Long Pond for swimming or to connect with park trails. Special early- and late-summer packages at the inn include cruises, tours, and cooking classes with Linda Greenlaw. The inn is open from early June to late September.

Camping

You'll need to get your bid in early to reserve one of the five six-person lean-tos at the national park's **Duck Harbor Campground,** the only camping on Isle au Haut, open May 15 to October 15. Before April 1, contact the park for a reservation request form (Acadia National Park, 207/288-3338, www.nps.gov/acad). From April 1 on *(not before, or the park people will send it back to you),* return the completed form, along with a check for $25, to reserve camping for up to six people for a maximum of five nights May 15–June 14, three nights June 15–September 15, and five nights again September 16–October 15. Mark the envelope "Attn: Isle au Haut Reservations." Competition is stiff in the height of summer, so list alternate dates. The park refunds the check if there's no space; otherwise, it's nonrefundable and you'll receive a "special-use permit" (*do not* forget to bring it along). There's no additional camping fee.

Unless you don't mind backpacking nearly five miles to reach the campground, try to plan your visit between mid-June and Labor Day, when the mail boat makes a stop in Duck Harbor. It's wise to call the Isle au Haut Company for the current ferry schedule before choosing dates for a lean-to reservation.

Trash policy is carry-in/carry-out, so pack a trash bag or two with your gear. Also bring a container for carting water from the campground pump, since it's 0.3 mile from the lean-tos. It's a longish walk to the general store for food—when you could be spending your time hiking the island's trails—so bring enough to cover your stay.

The three-sided lean-tos are big enough (8 by 12 feet, 8 feet high) to hold a small (two-person) tent, so bring one along if you prefer being fully enclosed. A tarp will also do the trick. (Also bring mosquito repellent—some years, the critters show up here en masse.) No camping is permitted outside of the lean-tos, and nothing can be attached to trees.

Food

Isle au Haut is pretty much a BYO place—and for the most part, that means BYO food. Although the Inn at Isle au Haut is open to the public for dinner by reservation, you need to get there and back, only possible if you're staying in a rental cottage with a car.

Thanks to the seasonal **Isle au Haut General Store** (207/335-5211, www.theislandstore.net), less than a five-minute walk from the town landing, you won't starve. The inventory isn't extensive, but it can be intriguing, due to the store manager who travels worldwide and stocks the shop with her finds. On the other hand, food probably won't be your prime interest here—the island itself is as good as it gets.

Even more intriguing is **Black Dinah Chocolatiers** (207/335-5010, www.blackdinahchocolatiers.com), just shy of a mile from the town landing. Steve and Kate Shaffer's little shop doubles as a café, serving pastries, organic coffees and teas, a few lunch-type offerings, and, of course, decadent handmade chocolates. It also has free Wi-Fi.

GETTING THERE

Isle au Haut Boat Company

The Isle au Haut Boat Company (Seabreeze Ave., Stonington, 207/367-5193, www.isleauhaut.com) generally operates five daily trips

Monday–Saturday, plus two on Sunday from mid-June to early September. Other months, there are 2–3 trips Monday–Saturday.

Round-trips from April to mid-October are $35 adults, $19 children under 12 (two bags per adult, one bag per child). Round-trip surcharges include bikes ($18), kayaks/canoes ($38 minimum), and pets ($8). If you're considering bringing a bike, be sure to inquire about on-island bike rentals ($23 per day). Weather seldom affects the schedule, but be aware that ultra-heavy seas could cancel a trip.

There is twice-daily ferry service, from mid-June to Labor Day, from Stonington to Duck Harbor, at the edge of Isle au Haut's Acadia National Park campground. For a day trip, the schedule allows you 6.5 hours on the island Monday–Saturday and 4.5 hours on Sunday. No boats or bikes are allowed on this route, and no dogs are allowed in the campground. A ranger boards the boat at the town landing and goes along to Duck Harbor to answer questions and distribute maps. Before mid-June and after Labor Day, you'll be off-loaded at the Isle au Haut town landing, about five miles from Duck Harbor. The six-mile passage from Stonington to the Isle au Haut town landing takes 45 minutes; the trip to Duck Harbor is 75 minutes.

Ferries depart from the Isle au Haut Boat Company dock (Seabreeze Ave., off E. Main St. in downtown Stonington). Parking ($9 per day outside, $11 indoors) is available next to the ferry landing.

Old Quarry Ocean Adventures

The new kid on the block offering seasonal service to Isle au Haut, Old Quarry Ocean Adventures (Stonington, 207/367-8977 or 877/479-8977, mobile 207/266-7778, www.oldquarry.com) transports passengers on the renovated *Nigh Duck.* The boat usually leaves Old Quarry at 9 A.M. and arrives at the island's town landing one hour later. It departs from the same point at 5 P.M., arriving back at Old Quarry around 6 P.M. The fee is $35 round-trip for adults, $18 for children under 12. You can add an island bike rental for an additional $20. Old Quarry also offers a taxi service to Isle au Haut for $140 per hour for up to six people.

ACADIA REGION

Summer folk have been visiting Mount Desert Island (MDI) for millennia. The earliest Native Americans discovered fabulous fishing and clamming, good hunting and camping, and invigorating salt air here. Today's arrivals find variations on the same theme: thousands of lodgings and campsites, hundreds of restaurant seats, dozens of shops, plus 40,000 acres of Acadia National Park.

It's no coincidence that artists were a large part of the 19th-century vanguard here: The dramatic landscape, with both bare and wooded mountains descending to the sea, still inspires everyone who sees it. Once the word got out, painterly images began confirming the reports, and the surge began. Even today, no saltwater locale on the entire eastern seaboard can compete with the variety of scenery on Mount Desert Island.

Those pioneering artists brilliantly portrayed this area, adding romantic touches to landscapes that really need no enhancement. From the 1,530-foot summit of Cadillac Mountain, preferably at an off hour, you'll sense the grandeur of it all—the slopes careening toward the bay and the handful of islands below looking like the last footholds between Bar Harbor and Bordeaux.

For nearly four centuries, controversy has raged about the pronunciation of the island's name, and we won't resolve it here. French explorer Samuel de Champlain apparently gets credit for naming it l'Ile des Monts Deserts, "island of bare mountains," when he sailed by

HIGHLIGHTS

Park Loop Road: If you do nothing else on Mount Desert, drive this magnificent road that takes in many of Acadia National Park's highlights (page 308).

The Carriage Roads: Whether you walk, bike, or ride in a horse-drawn carriage, do make it a point to see Mr. Rockefeller's roads and bridges (page 308).

Jordan Pond House: For more than a century, afternoon tea and popovers on the lawn of the Jordan Pond House have been a tradition. Make reservations for an afternoon pick-me-up, perhaps after walking or biking the many carriage roads that lead here (page 312).

Abbe Museum: The downtown Abbe Museum and its seasonal museum at Sieur de Monts Springs are fascinating places to while away a few hours and learn about Maine's Native American heritage (page 316).

Oceanarium: A fabulous introduction to the coastal ecology is provided at this low-tech, kid-friendly site (page 316).

Dive-In Theater Boat Cruise: Got kids? Don't miss this tour, where Diver Ed brings the undersea world aboard (page 322).

Asticou Azalea Garden and Thuya Garden: "Magical and enchanting" best describes these two peaceful gardens. While Zen-like Asticou is best seen in spring, Thuya delivers color through summer and also has hiking paths (page 331).

Wendell Gilley Museum: Gilley's intricately carved birds, from miniature shorebirds to life-size birds of prey, are a marvel to behold (page 337).

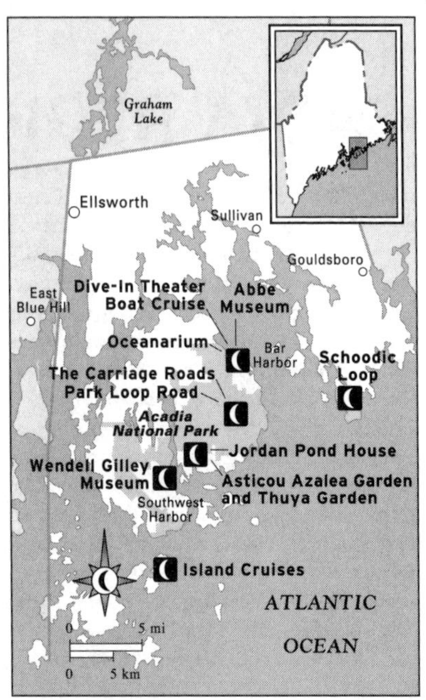

LOOK FOR TO FIND RECOMMENDED SIGHTS, ACTIVITIES, DINING, AND LODGING.

Island Cruises: Kim Strauss shares his deep knowledge of island ways and waters on the lunchtime cruise that allows time to explore Frenchboro (page 340).

Schoodic Loop: An ultra-scenic six-mile road edging the pink-granite shores of Acadia National Park's only mainland section and accessing hiking trails and picnic spots (page 352).

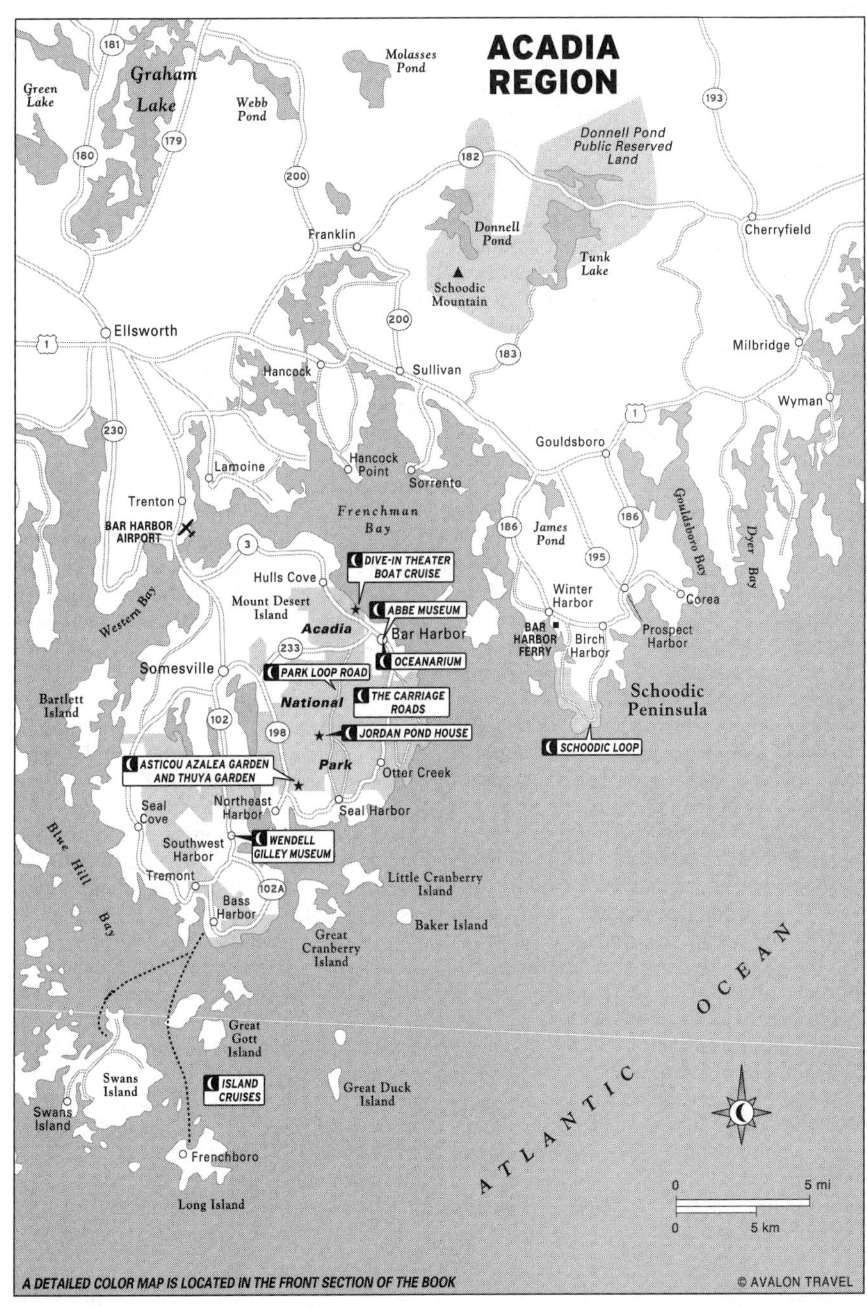
ACADIA REGION
Molasses Pond
Graham Lake
Green Lake
Webb Pond
Donnell Pond Public Reserved Land
Donnell Pond
Tunk Lake
Schoodic Mountain
Franklin
Cherryfield
Ellsworth
Milbridge
Hancock
Sullivan
Wyman
Gouldsboro
Lamoine
Hancock Point
Sorrento
Trenton
Frenchman Bay
BAR HARBOR AIRPORT
James Pond
Gouldsboro Bay
Dyer Bay
Hulls Cove
DIVE-IN THEATER BOAT CRUISE
Winter Harbor
Corea
Mount Desert Island
ABBE MUSEUM
Western Bay
Acadia
Bar Harbor
BAR HARBOR FERRY
Birch Harbor
Prospect Harbor
OCEANARIUM
Somesville
PARK LOOP ROAD
National
THE CARRIAGE ROADS
Schoodic Peninsula
Bartlett Island
JORDAN POND HOUSE
SCHOODIC LOOP
ASTICOU AZALEA GARDEN AND THUYA GARDEN
Park
Otter Creek
Seal Cove
Northeast Harbor
Seal Harbor
Blue Hill Bay
Southwest Harbor
WENDELL GILLEY MUSEUM
Tremont
Little Cranberry Island
Bass Harbor
Baker Island
Great Cranberry Island
Great Gott Island
Swans Island
ISLAND CRUISES
Great Duck Island
ATLANTIC OCEAN
Frenchboro
Long Island
0 5 mi
0 5 km
A DETAILED COLOR MAP IS LOCATED IN THE FRONT SECTION OF THE BOOK
© AVALON TRAVEL

in 1604. The accent in French would be on the second syllable, but today "Mount De-SERT" and "Mount DES-ert" both have their advocates, although the former gets the accuracy nod. In any case, the island is anything but deserted today. Even as you approach it, via the shire town of Ellsworth and especially in Trenton, you'll run the gauntlet of a minor-league Disneyland, with water slides, bumper cars, and enough high-cholesterol eateries to stun the surgeon general. Don't panic: Acadia National Park lies ahead. Even on the most crowded days, if you venture more than a few steps into the park you'll find you have it nearly to yourself.

As you drive or bike around Mount Desert—vaguely shaped like a lobster claw and indented by Somes Sound (the only fjord on the United States' east coast)—you'll cross and recross the national-park boundaries, reminders that Acadia National Park, covering a third of the island, is indeed the major presence here. It affects traffic, indoor and outdoor pursuits, and, in a way, even the climate.

The other major presence is Bar Harbor, largest and best known of the island's communities. It's the source of just about anything you could want (if not need), from T-shirts to tacos, books to bike rentals. The contrast with Acadia is astonishing as the park struggles to maintain its image and character.

Bar Harbor shares the island with Southwest Harbor, Tremont, and a number of small villages: Bass Harbor, Bernard, Northeast Harbor, Seal Harbor, Otter Creek, Somesville, and Hall Quarry. From Bass, Northeast, and Southwest Harbors, private and state ferries shuttle bike and foot traffic to offshore Swans Island, Frenchboro (Long Island), and the Cranberry Isles (and cars to Swans Island).

Stay on Route 1, instead of taking Route 3 to the island, and the congestion disappears. The towns lining the eastern shore of Frenchman Bay have some of the best views of all: front-row seats facing the peaks of Mount Desert Island. It's no wonder many artists and artisans make their homes here—for the inspiring scenery, no doubt. And at the tip of the Schoodic Peninsula, a stunning pocket of Acadia National Park sees only a fraction of the visitors who descend on the main part of the park.

PLANNING YOUR TIME

So much to do, so little time—that's the lament of most visitors. While you can circumnavigate Mount Desert Island in a day, hitting the highlights along the Park Loop with just enough time to ooh and ah at each, to appreciate Acadia you need time to hike the trails, ride the carriage roads, get afloat on a whale-watching cruise or a sea kayak, visit museums, and explore an offshore island or two. A week or longer is best, but you can get a taste of Acadia in 3–4 days.

The region is very seasonal, with most restaurants, accommodations, and shops open mid-May–mid-October. May and June bring the new greens of spring and blooming rhododendrons and azaleas in Northeast Harbor's Asticou Garden, but mosquitoes and blackflies are at their worst, and weather is temperamental—perhaps sunny and hot one day, damp and cold the next, a packing nightmare. July and August bring summer at its best, along with the biggest crowds. September is a gem of a time to visit: no bugs, fewer people, less fog, and the golden light of fall. Foliage usually begins turning in early October, making it an especially beautiful time to visit (the Columbus Day holiday weekend brings a spike in visitors). Winter is Acadia's silent season, best left for independent travelers who don't mind making do or perhaps making a meal of peanut-butter crackers if an open restaurant can't be found.

The only way onto Mount Desert Island is Route 3. Unless you're traveling in the wee hours of the morning or late at night, expect traffic. Avoid it during shift changes on-island, 8–9 A.M. and 3–4 P.M. weekdays, when traffic slows to a crawl. On the island, use the Island Explorer bus system to avoid parking hassles.

Ellsworth

The punchline to an old Maine joke is "Ya cahn't get they-ah from he-ah." The truth is, you can't get to Acadia without going through Ellsworth and Trenton. Indeed, when you're crawling along in bumper-to-bumper traffic, it might seem as if all roads lead to downtown Ellsworth. And the truth is, many do. Route 1, the main thoroughfare along the coast, and Route 1A, which connects to Bangor, meet in downtown Ellsworth. Route 172 leads to the Blue Hill Peninsula and on to Deer Isle, Stonington, and the mail boat to Isle au Haut. Route 1 continues north, providing access to the Schoodic Peninsula and a remote section of the park. And the Bar Harbor Road (Route 3) is something of an Achilles heel—often a summertime bottleneck as it funnels all traffic to Mount Desert Island.

While there are ways to skirt around a few of the worst bottlenecks, the region does have its calling cards. Ellsworth, Hancock County's shire town, has mushroomed with the popularity of Acadia National Park, but you can still find handsome architectural remnants of the city's 19th-century lumbering heyday (which began shortly after its incorporation in 1800). Brigs, barks, and full-rigged ships—built in Ellsworth and captained by local fellows—loaded lumber here and carried it round the globe. Despite a ruinous 1855 fire that swept through downtown, the lumber trade thrived until late in the 19th century, along with factories and mills turning out shoes, bricks, boxes, and butter.

These days, Ellsworth is the region's shopping mecca. Antiques shops and small stores line Main Street, which doubles as Route 1 in the downtown section; supermarkets, strip malls, and big-box stores line Routes 1 and 3 between Ellsworth and Trenton.

One more plus for the area is the Bar Harbor Chamber of Commerce Information Center, on Route 3 in Trenton. If you're day-tripping to Mount Desert Island, you can leave your car here and hop aboard the free Island Explorer bus, eliminating driving and parking hassles.

SIGHTS

Woodlawn

Very little has changed at the Woodlawn (Surry Rd./Rte. 172, 207/667-8671, www.woodlawnmuseum.com, 10 A.M.–5 P.M. Tues.–Sat., 1–4 P.M. Sun. June–Sept., 1–4 P.M. Tues.–Sun. May and Oct., $10 adults, $3 children 5–12, grounds are free) since George Nixon Black donated his home, also known as "the Black Mansion," to the town in 1928. Completed in 1828, the Georgian house is a marvel of preservation—one of Maine's best—filled with Black family antiques and artifacts. Enthusiastic docents lead hour-long tours, beginning on the hour, to point out the circular staircase, rare books and artifacts, canopied beds, a barrel organ, and lots more. Afterward, plan to picnic

© HILARY NANGLE

Ellsworth's city hall is just one of many buildings in the shire town with interesting architecture.

Take a break in downtown Ellsworth, where there are plenty of interesting shops and restaurants.

on the manicured grounds, then explore two sleigh-filled barns, the Memorial Garden, and the two miles of mostly level trails in the woods up beyond the house. On several Wednesday afternoons in July and August, there are elegant teas in the garden (or in the carriage house if it's raining), with china, silver, linens, special-blend tea, sandwiches, pastries, and live music—all for $20 per person; reservations are required. On Route 172, a quarter mile southwest of Route 1, watch for the small sign and turn into the winding uphill driveway.

Birdsacre

En route to Bar Harbor, watch carefully on the right for the sign that marks Birdsacre (Rte. 3, Bar Harbor Rd., 207/667-8460, www.birdsacre.com), a 200-acre urban sanctuary. Wander the trails in this peaceful preserve—spotting wildflowers, birds, and well-labeled shrubs and trees—and you'll have trouble believing you're surrounded by prime tourist territory. One trail, a boardwalk loop through woods behind the nature center, is wheelchair- and stroller-accessible. The sanctuary is open all year, from sunrise to sunset. At the sanctuary entrance is the 1850 **Stanwood Homestead Museum,** with period furnishings and wildlife exhibits. Once owned by noted ornithologist Cordelia Stanwood, the volunteer-operated museum is open for tours by chance or appointment, from mid-May to mid-October. Admission to the preserve and the homestead is free, but donations are needed and greatly appreciated. Birdsacre is also a wildlife rehabilitation center, so expect to see all kinds of winged creatures, especially hawks and owls, in various stages of rescue. Some will be returned to the wild, while others remain here for educational purposes. Stop by the Nature Center for even more exhibits.

Kisma Preserve

I can't stress this enough: Kisma Preserve (446 Bar Harbor Rd., Rte. 3, Trenton, 207/667-3244, www.kismapreserve.org, 9:30 A.M.–dusk daily mid-May–late fall, $13) is *not* a zoo; it's a nonprofit educational facility, and

© TOM NANGLE

Kisma Preserve is a sanctuary for retired or relocated exotic animals.

everything revolves around preserving and protecting the animals, most of which are either rescues or retirees. Rules are strictly enforced—no running, loud voices, or disruptive behavior is permitted. The only way to view the animals is on a guided tour. Guides educate visitors about the biology of the animals, how they came to be here, and whether they'll be returned to the wild. For serious animal lovers, the preserve offers behind-the-scenes tours and close-ups for fees beginning around $25 per person; there even are options for staying in the preserve overnight. It truly is a special place, with more than 100 exotic and not-so-exotic creatures—reindeer, bison, wolves, moose, big cats, and more. Donations are essential to Kisma's survival. Yes, it's pricey, but so too is feeding and caring for these animals.

The New England Museum of Telephony

What was life like before cell phones or touch-tone dialing? Find out at the New England Museum of Telephony (166 Winkumpaugh Rd., 207/667-9491, www.ellsworthme.org/ringring, 1–4 P.M. Thurs.–Sun. July.–Sept., $5 adults, $2.50 children), a hands-on museum with the largest collection of old-fashioned switching systems in the East, including many from Maine. Place a call to see how these old systems work. To find the museum, head 10 miles north on Route 1A (toward Bangor), then go left on Winkumpaugh Road for one mile.

Downeast Scenic Railroad

The all-volunteer Downeast Rail Heritage Preservation Trust (800/449-7245, www.downeastscenicrail.org) is rehabilitating the tracks between Ellsworth/Washington Junction and Green Lake in anticipation of operating a scenic excursion train. If you're a rail enthusiast, you might want to check the progress or perhaps even volunteer to assist.

Aerial Touring

Two businesses provide a variety of ways to get an eagle's-eye view of the area. Both are based on the Route 3 side of Hancock County/Bar Harbor Airport, just north of Mount Desert Island and 12 miles north of downtown Bar Harbor.

Scenic Flights of Acadia (Bar Harbor Rd., Rte. 3, Trenton, 207/667-6527, www.mainecoastalflight.com) offers low-level flightseeing services in the Mount Desert Island region. Flights range 22–60 minutes and begin around $50 per person, with a two-passenger minimum.

Scenic Biplane and Glider Rides (968 Bar Harbor Rd./Rte. 3, Trenton, 207/667-7627, www.acadiaairtours.com) lets you soar in silence with daily glider flights. The one- or two-passenger gliders are towed to at least an altitude of 2,500 feet and then released. An FAA-certified pilot guides the glider. Rates begin at $199 for a 20-minute flight for two, $149 for one. Or ride in a biplane: A 20-minute ride in an open-cockpit plane is $225 for two, $175 for one. All flights are subject to an airport fee.

ENTERTAINMENT

Ellsworth has three free summer series. The **Ellsworth Concert Band** performs Wednesday evenings in the plaza outside Ellsworth City Hall. If it rains, it's held inside City Hall. Practice begins at 6:30 P.M., concerts start at 8 P.M., and the 50-member community band even welcomes visitors with talent and instruments—just show up at practice time. **Outdoor family movies** (www.ellswortharts.org) are shown Thursdays at sunset on the lawn of the Knowlton School. **Concerts** (www.downtownellsworth.com) are staged at Harbor Parks on Fridays at 6 P.M.

Ace lumberjack "Timber" Tina Scheer has been competing around the world since she was seven, and she shows her prowess at **The Great Maine Lumberjack Show** (Rte. 3, 207/667-0067, www.mainelumberjack.com, 7 P.M. daily mid-June–late Aug., $8.75 adults, $6.75 children 4–11). During the 75-minute "Olympics of the Forest," you'll watch two teams compete in 14 events, including ax throwing, cross-cut sawing, log rolling, speed climbing, and more. Some are open to participation. (Kids can learn log rolling by appointment.) Performances are held rain or shine. Seating is under a roof, but dress for the weather if it's inclement. The ticket office opens at 6 P.M.

The carefully restored art deco **Grand Auditorium** of Hancock County (100 Main St., 207/667-9500, www.grandonline.org) is the year-round site of films, concerts, plays, and art exhibits.

SHOPPING

Specialty Shops

You're unlikely to meet a single soul who has left the **Big Chicken Barn Books and Antiques** (Rte. 1, 1768 Bucksport Rd., 207/667-7308) without buying *something.* You'll find every kind of collectible on the vast 1st floor, courtesy of more than four dozen dealers. Climb the stairs for books, magazines, old music, and more. With 21,000 square feet, this place is addictive, with free coffee, restrooms, and hassle-free browsing. The Big Chicken is 11 miles east of Bucksport, 8.5 miles west of Ellsworth.

Just south of downtown, in a National Historic Register property, the 1838 courthouse at the corner of Court Street and Route 1 is **Courthouse Gallery Fine Art** (6 Court St., 207/667-6611, www.courthousegallery.com), showcasing works by some of Maine's top contemporary artists.

A fine collection of antiquarian and used books fills the shelves of **Apple Tree Books** (71 Main St., 207/667-7999).

The 40-plus-dealer **Old Creamery Antique Mall** (13 Hancock St., 207/667-0522) fills 6,000 square feet on two jam-packed floors.

Around the corner is **Atlantic Art Glass** (25 Pine St., 207/664-0222), where you can watch Linda and Ken Perrin demonstrate glass blowing and buy their contemporary creations.

Don't miss **Rooster Brother** (29 Main St./Rte. 1, 207/667-8675 or 800/866-0054, www.roosterbrother.com) for gourmet cookware, cards, and books on the main floor; coffee, tea, candy, cheeses, a huge array of exotic condiments, fresh breads, and other gourmet items on the lower level; and discounted merchandise on the 2nd floor, open seasonally. You can easily pick up all the fixings for a fancy picnic here.

It's hard to categorize **J&B Atlantic Company** (142 Main St./Rte. 1, 207/667-2082). It takes up a good part of the block, with room after room filled with furniture, home accessories, gifts, books, and antiques.

John Edwards Market (158 Main St., 207/667-9377) is a two-fold find. Upstairs is a natural-foods store. Downstairs is the Wine Cellar Gallery, a terrific space showcasing Maine artists throughout the year.

Discount Shopping

You can certainly find bargains at the **L. L. Bean Factory Store** (150 High St./Rte. 1, 207/667-7753), but this is an outlet, so scrutinize the goods for flaws and blemishes before buying.

Across the road is **Reny's Department Store** (Ellsworth Shopping Center, 185 High St./Rte. 1, 207/667-5166, www.renys.com), a Maine-based discount operation with a you-never-know-what-you'll-find philosophy. Trust me, you'll find something here.

In an adjacent shopping plaza is **Marden's** (225 High St./Rte. 1A, 207/669-6036, www.mardenssurplus.com), another Maine bit-of-this, bit-of-that enterprise with the catchy slogan "I shoulda bought it, when I saw it." Good advice.

ACCOMMODATIONS

Motels and Inns

Acadia Birches (20 Thorsen Rd., facing Rte. 1, 207/667-3621 or 800/435-1287, www.acadiabirchesmotel.com, $99–199, children 16 and younger free) is a clean, generic, somewhat dated motel with 67 air-conditioned rooms, all with kitchenettes. It's popular with tour groups. Request a room overlooking the nine-hole course. Rooms have phones and cable TV; some have air-conditioning. It's open all year.

Family-owned, nicely landscaped, and meticulously maintained, the **Open Hearth Inn** (Rte. 3, Trenton, 207/667-2930 or 800/655-0234, www.openhearthinn.com, $85–150 d) is on the Island Explorer bus route, less than a quarter mile from the bridge connecting Trenton to Mount Desert, and within walking distance of four lobster restaurants. Choose an inn room with a three-course breakfast or opt for a tourist court–style cottage or motel room (both with continental buffet breakfast), or apartment with kitchen. All have TV, fridge, air-conditioning, and Wi-Fi. Also on the premises is an enclosed family hot tub. The only drawback might be traffic noise. Kids under 12 are free; two pet-friendly rooms are an additional $25. Free pickup at Bar Harbor Airport. Open year-round.

Campgrounds

Equally convenient (or not) to the Schoodic Region and Mount Desert Island is the 55-acre **Lamoine State Park** (23 State Park Rd., Rte. 184, Lamoine, 207/667-4778, www.parksandlands.com). Park facilities include a pebble beach and a picnic area with a spectacular view, a boat-launch ramp, and a children's play area. Day-use admission is $4.50 nonresident adults, $3 resident adults, $1 children 5–11. Camping (62 sites) is $25 per site per night for nonresidents ($15 for Maine residents), plus a $2-per-night fee for reservations. No hookups are available; two-night minimum stay, 14-night maximum. (Camping season is mid-May–mid-Sept. Reserve online at www.state.me.us/doc/parks/reservations using a credit card, or call 207/624-9950 or 800/332-1501 in Maine, weekdays.) Leashed pets are allowed, but not on the beach, and cleanup is required.

FOOD

Local Flavors

Order breakfast anytime at **The Riverside Café** (151 Main St., 207/667-7220, 6 A.M.–2 P.M. Mon.–Thurs., to 8 P.M. Fri., 7 A.M.–8 P.M. Sat., 7 A.M.–2 P.M. Sun.). Lunch service begins at 11 A.M. On weekend nights there's often entertainment. And the café's name? It used to be down the street, overlooking the Union River.

Less creative but no less delicious are the home-style breakfasts at **Martha's Diner** (Reny's Plaza, 151 High St., 207/664-2495, 6 A.M.–2 P.M. Mon.–Sat., 7 A.M.–1 P.M. Sun.), where lunch is also served weekdays 11 A.M.–2 P.M. Almost everything on the menu is less than $5, booths are red leatherette and Formica, and the waitresses likely will call you "doll."

Jordan's Snack Bar (200 Down East Hwy./Rte. 1, 207/667-2174, 10:30 A.M.–9 P.M. daily) has almost a cult following for its crabmeat rolls and fried clams. Wednesday Cruise-Ins, beginning at 6 P.M., usually feature live entertainment and draw up to 50 vintage cars.

Breakfast and deli sandwiches, salads and wraps, smoothies and sweets are served at **The Maine Grind** (192 Main St., 207/667-0011, www.mainegrind.com, 7:30 A.M.–5:30 P.M. Mon.–Sat., 8 A.M.–4 P.M. Sun.). There's free Wi-Fi service, too.

Ice cream doesn't get much finer than that sold at **Morton's Ice Cream** (13 School St., 207/667-1146), a small shop with a deservedly giant reputation for homemade Italian gelato, sorbet, and ice cream. It's well worth the slight detour.

In 2008, hugely popular **Pectic Seafood** (367 Rte. 3, Bar Harbor Rd., Trenton, 207/667-7566, www.pecticseafood.com) opened, complete with indoor and outdoor seating and restrooms. The menu ranges from burgers and subs to fried seafood dinners and fresh lobster rolls at prices ranging $4–16. In addition, Pectic sells prepared heat-and-eat foods such as seafood Newberg, baked stuffed haddock, vegetable lasagna, and chicken soup, and it sells a wide array of fresh fish and specialty foods.

Casual Dining

Cleonice Mediterranean Bistro (112 Main St., 207/664-7554, www.cleonice.com, 11:30 A.M.–9 P.M. daily in summer, call ahead in the off-season) is named for chef-owner Richard Hanson's mother, Cleonice Renzetti. (It helps if you learn how to pronounce it: klee-oh-NEESE.) Gleaming woodwork and brass lighting fixtures combine for a golden glow in the long dining room, lined with wooden booths on one side and a 32-foot wooden bar, dating from 1938, on the other. The tapas and meze selection alone, served 2:30–5 P.M., is worth the trip—covering the Mediterranean circuit (spanakopita, hummus, manchego cheese with pear sauce, and even *brandade de morue*); most are around $5. Dinner runs $13–30.

Lobster

Hard to say which is better—the serene views or the tasty lobster—at Brian and Jane Langley's **Union River Lobster Pot** (8 South St., 207/667-5077, www.lobsterpot.com, 4–9 P.M. daily June–mid-Sept.). It's tucked behind Rooster Brother, right on the banks of the Union River. Remember to save room for the pie—especially the blueberry.

Far more touristy is **Trenton Bridge Lobster Pound** (Rte. 3, Bar Harbor Rd., Trenton, 207/667-2977, www.trentonbridgelobster.com, 11 A.M.–7:30 P.M. Mon.–Sat. late May–mid-Oct.), on the right, next to the bridge leading to Mount Desert Island. Watch for the "smoke signals"—steam billowing from the huge vats.

INFORMATION AND SERVICES

The **Ellsworth Area Chamber of Commerce** (163 High St., 207/667-5584, www.ellsworthchamber.org) has information and an area guidebook.

En route from Ellsworth on Route 3, and shortly before you reach Mount Desert, you'll see (on your right) the **Bar Harbor Chamber of Commerce** (Rte. 3, Trenton, 207/288-5103 or 888/540-9990, www.barharbormaine.com). You'll find all sorts of info on the island and other locations, plus restrooms, phones, and a helpful staff.

George Nixon Black, grandson of the builder of the Woodlawn Museum, donated the National Historic Register–listed Federalist **Ellsworth Public Library** (46 State St., 207/667-6363, www.ellsworth.lib.me.us) to the city in 1897.

GETTING AROUND

Route #1 of the **Island Explorer** bus system, which primarily serves Mount Desert Island with its fleet of propane-fueled fare-free vehicles, connects the Hancock County/Bar Harbor Airport in Trenton with downtown Bar Harbor. Operated by Downeast Transportation, the Island Explorer runs late June–mid-October.

Acadia National Park on Mount Desert Island

Rather like an octopus, or perhaps an amoeba, Acadia National Park extends its reach here and there and everywhere on Mount Desert Island. America's first national park east of the Mississippi River, and the only national park in the northeastern United States, was created from donated parcels—a big chunk here, a tiny chunk there—and slowly but surely fused into its present-day size of more than 46,000 acres. Within the boundaries of this splendid space are mountains, lakes, ponds, trails, fabulous vistas, and several campgrounds. Each year, more than two million visitors bike, hike, and drive into and through the park. Yet even at the height of summer, when the whole world seems to have arrived here, it's possible to find peaceful niches and less-trodden paths.

Acadia's history is unique among national parks and indeed fascinating. Several books have been written about some of the high-minded (in the positive sense) and high-profile personalities who provided the impetus (and wherewithal) for the park's inception and never flagged in their interest and support. Just to spotlight a few, we can thank the likes of George B. Dorr, Charles W. Eliot, and John D. Rockefeller Jr. for what we have today.

The most comprehensive guide to the park and surrounding area is *Moon Acadia National Park.*

NATIONAL PARK INFORMATION

Anyone entering the park by any means should buy a pass. Entrance fees, covering pedestrians, bicyclists, and motorized vehicles, are $20 late June–early October; $10 May 1–late June and most of October. That covers one vehicle for seven days. If you're traveling alone, an individual seven-day pass is $5. An annual pass to Acadia is $40, the America the Beautiful pass covering all federal recreation sites is $80, a lifetime senior pass is $10, and an access pass for disabled citizens is free. Passes are available at the visitors centers.

Hulls Cove Visitor Center

The modern Hulls Cove Visitor Center (Rte. 3, Hulls Cove, 207/288-3338, 8 A.M.–4:30 P.M. daily mid-April–late Oct., to 6 P.M. July–Aug., to 5 P.M. in Sept.) is eight miles southeast of the head of Mount Desert Island and well signposted. Here you can buy your park pass, make reservations for ranger-guided natural- and cultural-history programs, watch a 15-minute film about Acadia, study a relief map of the park, buy books, park souvenirs, and CD or cassette guides, and use the restrooms. Pick up a copy of the ***Beaver Log,*** the tabloid-format park newspaper that lists the schedule of park activities, plus tide calendars and the entire schedule for the excellent **Island Explorer** shuttle-bus system, which operates late June–Columbus Day. The Island Explorer is supported by entrance fees (park pass required), as well as by Friends of Acadia and L. L. Bean. If you have children, enroll them in the park's **Junior Ranger Program** (a nominal fee may be charged). They'll receive a booklet. To earn a Junior Ranger Patch, they must complete the activities and join one or two ranger-led programs or walks.

Thompson Island Visitor Center

As you cross the bridge from Trenton toward Mount Desert Island, you might not even notice that you arrive first on tiny Thompson Island, site of a visitors center (8 A.M.–6 P.M. daily mid-May–mid-Oct.) established jointly by the chambers of commerce of Mount Desert Island's towns and Acadia National Park. In season, a park ranger usually is posted here to answer questions and provide basic advice on hiking trails and other park activities, but consider this a stopgap—be sure to also continue to the park's main visitors center.

Acadia National Park Headquarters

From November to April, information is available at Acadia National Park Headquarters

(Eagle Lake Rd./Rte. 233, 8 A.M.–4:30 P.M. daily), about 3.5 miles west of downtown Bar Harbor. During the summer, it's open weekdays only.

SIGHTS

Park Loop Road

The 27-mile Park Loop Road takes in most of the park's big-ticket sites. It begins at the visitors center, winds past several of the park's scenic highlights (with parking areas), ascends to the summit of **Cadillac Mountain,** and provides overlooks to magnificent vistas. Along the route are trailheads and overlooks, as well as **Sieur de Monts Spring** (Acadia Nature Center, Wild Gardens of Acadia, Abbe Museum summer site, and the convergence of several spectacular trails), **Sand Beach, Thunder Hole, Otter Cliffs, Fabbri picnic area** (there's one wheelchair-accessible picnic table), **Jordan Pond House, Bubble Pond, Eagle Lake,** and the summit of **Cadillac Mountain.** Just before you get to Sand Beach, you'll see the Park Entrance Station, where you'll need to buy a pass if you haven't already done so. (If you're here during nesting/fledging season—April–mid-August—be sure to stop in the Precipice Trailhead parking area.)

Start at the parking lot below the Hulls Cove Visitor Center and follow the signs; part of the loop is one-way, so you'll be doing the loop clockwise. Traffic gets heavy at midday in midsummer, so aim for an early-morning start if you can. Maximum speed is 35 mph, but be alert for gawkers and photographers stopping without warning, and pedestrians dashing across the road from stopped cars or tour buses. If you're out here at midday in midsummer, don't be surprised to see cars and RVs parked in the right lane in the one-way sections; it's permitted.

Allow a couple of hours so you can stop along the way. You can rent an audio tour on cassette or CD for $12.95 (including directions, instruction sheet, and map) at the Hull's Cove Visitor Center. Another option is to pick up the drive-it-yourself tour booklet ***Motorist Guide: Park Loop Road*** ($1.50), available at the Thompson Island and Hulls Cove Visitor Centers.

The Carriage Roads

In 1913, John D. Rockefeller Jr. began laying out what eventually became a 57-mile carriage-road system, overseeing the project through the 1940s. Motorized vehicles have never been allowed on these lovely graded byways, making them real escapes from the auto world. Devoted now to multiple uses, the "Rockefeller roads" see hikers, bikers, baby strollers, horse-drawn carriages, even wheelchairs. Fortunately, a $6 million restoration campaign, undertaken during the 1990s, has done a remarkable job of upgrading surfaces, opening overgrown panoramas, and returning the roads to their original 16-foot width.

Pick up a free copy of the carriage-road map at any of the centers selling park passes. Busiest times are 10 A.M.–2 P.M.

The most crowded carriage roads are those closest to the visitors center—the Witch Hole Pond Loop, Duck Brook, and Eagle Lake.

Seventeen unique bridges accent Acadia's famed carriage roads.

WITH A LITTLE HELP FROM OUR FRIENDS . . .

Every park in America needs a safety net like **Friends of Acadia (FOA),** a dynamic organization headquartered in Bar Harbor. Propane-powered shuttle-bus service needs expanding? FOA finds a multimillion-dollar donor. Well-used trails need maintenance? FOA organizes volunteer work parties. New connector trails needed? FOA gets them done. No need seems to go unfilled.

FOA – one of Acadia National Park's greatest assets – is both reactive and proactive. It's an amazingly symbiotic relationship. When informed of a need, the Friends stand ready to help; when they themselves perceive a need, they propose solutions to park management and jointly figure out ways to make them happen. It's hard to avoid sounding like a media flack when describing this organization.

Friends of Acadia was founded in 1986 to preserve and protect the park for resource-sensitive tourism and myriad recreational uses. Since 1995, FOA has contributed more than $13.5 million to the park and surrounding communities for trail upkeep, carriage road maintenance, seasonal park staff funding, and conservation projects. Plus FOA cofounded the Island Explorer bus system and instigated the Acadia Trails Forever program, a joint park-FOA partnership for trail rehabilitation. In 2003, for instance, FOA and the park announced the reopening (after considerable planning and rebuilding) of the Homans Path, on the east side of Dorr Mountain. The trail, built around 1916 and named after Eliza Homans, a generous benefactor, fell into disuse in the 1940s. It ascends via a granite stairway to a ledge with a commanding view of the Great Meadow and Frenchman Bay. More recently, FOA reconstructed the East Cliffs Trail on Sargent Mountain and reopened the abandoned Penobscot Mountain Trail. As part of its Tranquility Project to reduce traffic congestion on the island, FOA purchased land in Trenton for an off-island transit and welcome center and has sold approximately 150 acres to the Maine Department of Transportation for the facility.

The Schoodic Committee of Friends of Acadia (www.friendsofschoodic.org) does much of the same type of work to preserve and protect the Schoodic section of the park. It conducts roadside and shoreline cleanups, helps maintain trails, and assists with advocacy.

You can join FOA and its 3,000 members and support this worthy cause for $35 a year; gifts of any amount are welcome (43 Cottage St., Bar Harbor, 207/288-3340 or 800/625-0321, www.friendsofacadia.org). You can also lend a hand (or two) while you're here. FOA and the park organize volunteer work parties for Acadia trail, carriage road, and other outdoor maintenance three times weekly between June and Columbus Day: 8:20 A.M.–12:30 P.M. Tuesday, Thursday, and Saturday. Call the recorded information line (207/288-3934) for the work locations, or 207/288-3340 or 800/625-0321 for answers to questions. The meeting point is Park Headquarters (Eagle Lake Rd., Rte. 233, Bar Harbor), about three miles west of town. This is a terrific way to give something back to the park, and the camaraderie is contagious. Be sure to take your own water, lunch, and bug repellent. Dress in layers and wear closed-toe shoes. More than 8,000 volunteer hours a year go toward this effort.

Each summer, Friends of Acadia also sponsors a handful of **Ridge Runners,** who work under park supervision and spend their days out and about on the trails repairing cairns, explaining the Leave No Trace philosophy to visitors, and assisting with research projects.

If you plan to be in the region on the first Saturday in November, call the FOA office in advance to register for the annual carriage road cleanup, which usually draws 250 or so volunteers. Bring water and gloves; there's a free hot lunch at midday for everyone who participates. It's dubbed Take Pride in Acadia Day – indeed an apt label.

Avoid these, opting instead for roads west of Jordan Pond. Or go early in the morning or late in the day. Better still, go off-season, when you can enjoy the fall foliage (late September–mid-October) or winter's cross-country skiing.

If you need a bicycle to explore the carriage

roads, you can rent one in Bar Harbor or Southwest Harbor. Be forewarned that hikers are allowed on the carriage roads that spill over onto private property south of the Jordan Pond House, but they are off-limits to bicyclists. The no-biking areas are signaled with Green Rock Company markers. The carriage-road map clearly indicates the biking/no-biking areas. *Bicyclists must be especially speed-sensitive on the carriage roads, keeping an eye out for hikers, horseback riders, small children, and the hearing impaired.*

To recapture the early carriage-roads era, take one of the horse-drawn open-carriage tours run by **Carriages of Acadia,** based at Wildwood Stables (Park Loop Rd., Seal Harbor, 877/276-3622), a mile south of the Jordan Pond House. Six one- and two-hour trips start at 9 A.M. daily mid-June–Columbus Day. Reservations are not required, but they're encouraged, especially in midsummer. Best outing is the two-hour **Day Mountain Summit** ($25 adults, $10 children 6–12, $7 ages 2–5) sunset ride. Other routes are around $20 adults, $10 children, $6 little kids. If you take the two-hour carriage ride to Jordan Pond House, departing at 1:15 P.M. daily ($18 adults, not counting food and beverage), you're guaranteed a reserved lawn chair for tea and popovers.

Bass Harbor Light

At the southern end of Mount Desert's western "claw," follow Route 102A to the turnoff toward Bass Harbor Head. Drive or bike to the end of Lighthouse Road, walk down a steep wooden stairway, and look up and to the right. Voilà! Bass Harbor Head Light—its red glow automated since 1974—stands sentinel at the eastern entrance to Blue Hill Bay. Built in 1858, the 26-foot tower and lightkeeper's house are privately owned, but the dramatic setting is a photographer's dream.

Baker Island

The best way to get to—and to appreciate—history-rich Baker Island is on the ranger-narrated Acadia National Park Baker Island Tour aboard the *Miss Samantha,* booked through **Bar Harbor Whale Watch Co.** (1 West St., Bar Harbor, 207/288-2386 or 888/942-5374, www.barharborwhales.com, $43 adults, $20 children 6–14, $5 age 5 and younger). The half-day tours depart Monday–Saturday late June–mid-September and include access via skiff to the 130-acre island with farmstead, lighthouse, and intriguing rock formations. The return trip provides a view of Otter Cliffs (bring binoculars and look for climbers), Thunder Hole, Sand Beach, and Great Head from the water.

RECREATION

Hikes

If you're spending more than a day on Mount Desert Island, plan to buy a copy of *A Walk in the Park: Acadia's Hiking Guide,* by Tom St. Germain, which details more than 60 hikes, including some outside the park. Remember that pets are allowed on park trails, but only on leashes no longer than six feet. Four of the Island Explorer bus routes are particularly useful for hikers, alleviating the problems of backtracking and car-jammed parking lots. Here's a handful of favorite Acadia hikes, from easy to rugged.

These three easy trails are ideal for young families. **Jordan Pond Nature Trail:** Start at the Jordan Pond parking area. This is an easy wheelchair-accessible one-mile wooded loop trail; pick up a brochure. Include Jordan Pond House (for tea and popovers) in your schedule. **Ship Harbor Nature Trail:** Start at the Ship Harbor parking area, on Route 102A between Bass Harbor and Seawall Campground, in the southwestern corner of the island. The easy 1.3-mile loop trail leads to the shore; pick up a brochure at the trailhead. Ship Harbor is particularly popular among bird-watchers seeking warblers, and you just might spot an eagle while you picnic on the rocks. **Wonderland:** An even easier trail, with its parking area just east of the Ship Harbor parking area, Wonderland is 1.4 miles round-trip.

Great Head Trail: This moderately easy

1.4-mile loop trail starts at the eastern end of Sand Beach, off the Park Loop Road. Park in the Sand Beach parking area and cross the beach to the trailhead. Or take Schooner Head Road from downtown Bar Harbor and park in the small area where the road dead-ends. There are actually two trail loops here, both of which have enough elevation to provide terrific views.

Gorham Mountain: Another moderate hike with great views is this 1.8-mile round-trip. It's a great family hike, as kids especially love the Cadillac Cliffs section. Access is off the Park Loop Road, just beyond Thunder Hole.

Beech Mountain: A moderate hike, Beech Mountain's summit has an abandoned fire tower, from which you can look out toward Long Pond and the Blue Hill Peninsula. A knob near the top is a prime viewing site for the migration of hawks (and other raptors) in September. Round-trip on the wooded route is about 1.2 miles, although a couple of side trails can extend it. You'll have less competition here, in a quieter part of the park. Take Route 102 south from Somesville, heading toward Pretty Marsh. Turn left onto Beech Hill Road and follow it to the parking area at the end.

Beehive Trail and **Precipice Trail:** These two are the park's toughest routes, with sheer faces and iron ladders; Precipice often is closed (usually mid-Apr.–late July) to protect nesting peregrine falcons. If challenges are your thing and these trails are open (check beforehand at the visitors center), go ahead. But a fine alternative in the difficult category is the **Beachcroft Trail** on Huguenot Head. Also called the Beachcroft Path, the trail is best known for its 1,500 beautifully engineered granite steps. Round-trip is about 2.2 miles, or you can continue a loop at the top, taking in the **Bear Brook Trail** on Champlain Mountain, for about 4.4 miles. The parking area is just north of Route 3, near Sieur de Monts Spring.

Rock Climbing

Acadia has a number of splendid sites prized by climbers: the sea cliffs at Otter Cliffs and Great Head; South Bubble Mountain; Canada Cliff (on the island's western side); and the South Wall and the Central Slabs on Champlain Mountain. If you haven't tried climbing, *never* do it yourself, without instruction. **Acadia Mountain Guides Climbing School** (198 Main St., Bar Harbor, 207/288-8186 or 888/232-9559, www.acadiamountainguides.com) and **Atlantic Climbing School** (ACS, 24 Cottage St., 2nd fl., Bar Harbor, 207/288-2521, www.climbacadia.com) both provide instruction and guided climbs. Costs depend upon the site, experience, session length, and number of climbers; call for details.

Swimming

Slightly below the Park Loop Road (take Island Explorer Route #3/Sand Beach), **Sand Beach** is the park's (and the island's) biggest sandy beach. Lifeguards are on duty during the summer, and even then, the biggest threat can be hypothermia. The salt water is terminally glacial—in mid-July, it still might not reach 60°F. The best solution is to walk to the far end of the beach, where a warmer, shallow stream meets the ocean. On a hot August day, arrive early; the parking lot fills up.

The park's most popular freshwater swimming site, staffed with a lifeguard and inevitably crowded on hot days, is **Echo Lake,** south of Somesville on Route 102 and well signposted (take Island Explorer Route #7/Southwest Harbor).

If you have a canoe, kayak, or rowboat, you can reach swimming holes in **Seal Cove Pond** and **Round Pond,** both on the western side of Mount Desert. The eastern shore of **Hodgdon Pond** (also on the western side of the island) is accessible by car (via Hodgdon Road and Long Pond Fire Road). **Lake Wood,** at the northern end of Mount Desert, has a tiny beach, restroom, and auto access. To get to Lake Wood from Route 3, head west on Crooked Road to unpaved Park Road. Turn left and continue to the parking area, which will be crowded on a hot day, so arrive early.

© HILARY NANGLE

Don't miss an opportunity to take part in one of Acadia National Park's ranger-led programs.

PARK RANGER PROGRAMS

When you stop at the Hulls Cove Visitor Center and pick up the current issue of the park's *Beaver Log* newspaper (or download it ahead of time at www.nps.gov/acad), you'll find a whole raft of possibilities for learning more about the park's natural and cultural history.

The park ranger programs, lasting 1–3 hours, are great—and most are free. During July and August, there are about 100 programs each week, all listed in the *Log*. Included are early-morning (7 A.M.) bird-watching walks; mountain hikes (moderate level); tours of the historic Carroll Homestead, a 19th-century farm; Cadillac summit natural-history tours; children's expeditions to learn about tide pools and geology (an adult must accompany kids); trips for those in wheelchairs; and even a couple of tours a week in French. Some tours require reservations, most do not; a few, including boat tours, have fees.

Park rangers also give the evening lectures during the summer in the amphitheaters at Blackwoods and Seawall Campgrounds.

CAMPING

Mount Desert Island has at least a dozen private (commercial) campgrounds, but there are only two—Blackwoods and Seawall—within park boundaries on the island; neither has hookups. Both have seasonal restrooms (no showers) and dumping stations. Both also have seasonal amphitheaters, where rangers present evening programs.

Blackwoods Campground

With more than 300 campsites, Blackwoods, just off Route 3, five miles south of Bar Harbor, is open all year. Because of its location on the east side of the island, it's also the more popular of the two campgrounds. Reservations (877/444-6777, www.recreation.gov, credit card required) are suggested May 1–October 31, when the fee is $20 per site per night. Reservations can be made up to six months prior. In April and November, camping is $10; December–March it's free.

Seawall Campground

Reservations are not accepted at Seawall Campground, on Route 102A in the Seawall district, four miles south of Southwest Harbor—it's first-come, first-served. But in midsummer, you'll need to arrive as early as 8:30 A.M. (when the ranger station opens) to secure one of the 200 or so sites. Seawall is open from late May through September. The cost is $20 per night for drive-up sites and $14 per night for walk-in sites.

RV length at Seawall is limited to 35 feet, with the width limited to an awning extended no more than 12 feet. Generators are not allowed in the campground.

JORDAN POND HOUSE

The only restaurant within the park is the Jordan Pond House (Park Loop Rd., 207/276-3316, 11:30 A.M.–8 P.M. daily mid-May–late

JORDAN POND HOUSE

In the late 19th century, when Bar Harbor was in the throes of becoming "the great new place" to escape the heat of Washington, New York, Philadelphia, and the Midwest, gentle ladies and men patronized an unassuming farmhouse/teahouse on the shores of Jordan Pond. By 1895 or 1896, under the stewardship of Thomas McIntire, it became Jordan Pond House – a determinedly rustic establishment, with massive fieldstone fireplaces, serving afternoon tea and leisurely luncheons during the summer and fall.

And rustic it remained, well into the late 20th century – until leveled by a disastrous fire in the summer of 1979. At that point, it was owned by Acadia National Park – John D. Rockefeller Jr. had bought it in the 1930s and donated it to the park in the early 1940s. Since then, it's been managed on behalf of the park by concessionaires – at present the Acadia Corporation (which also operates gift shops in several locations).

Today, Jordan Pond House, the only restaurant within Acadia National Park, must rely on its framed antique photos to conjure a bit of nostalgia for the bygone era. The building is modern and open, the pace in summer is frenetic, and the food is average. But the view from the lawn over Jordan Pond and the astounding Bubbles is incredible. Surely *it* hasn't changed.

So...at least once, brave the crowds and have afternoon tea on the lawn at Jordan Pond House. Order tea or Oregon chai or even cappuccino and fresh popovers (two) with extraordinary strawberry jam.

If you think you'll need a popover fix when you return home, you can always buy a package of the mix along with the jam in the gift shop, or make them from scratch. Here's the Jordan Pond House recipe:

JORDAN POND HOUSE POPOVERS

2 large eggs
1 cup whole milk
1 cup all-purpose flour (presifted)
½ teaspoon salt
⅛ teaspoon baking soda

Preheat oven to 425°F. Beat eggs with electric mixer at high speed three minutes. Reduce mixer speed to lowest setting and very gradually pour in half the milk. In separate bowl, combine sifted flour, salt, and baking soda and sift again.

With mixer still running at slowest speed, add dry ingredients to egg-and-milk mixture. Turn off mixer and use rubber spatula to blend mixture thoroughly.

Set mixer to medium speed and very gradually pour in remaining milk, blending one minute. Raise mixer speed to highest setting and beat 10 minutes.

Strain batter through fine-mesh strainer to remove lumps and then pour into well-buttered popover or custard cups. Bake 15 minutes. Without opening the oven, reduce heat to 350°F and bake 15 more minutes (20 minutes if oven door has a window).

Serve immediately with fresh jam and room-temperature butter.

Hint: Popovers turn out significantly better if baked in ovenproof cups rather than in metal or glass.

The recipe makes two popovers. Increase as desired, but be sure to measure carefully.

Oct., to 9 P.M. late June–early Sept.), a modern facility in a spectacular waterside setting. Jordan Pond House began life as a rustic 19th-century teahouse; wonderful old photos still line the walls of the current incarnation, which went up after a disastrous fire in 1979. Afternoon tea is still a tradition, with tea, popovers, and extraordinary strawberry jam served on the lawn until 5:30 P.M. daily in summer, weather permitting. Not exactly a bargain at nearly $10, but it's worth it. However, Jordan Pond is far from a secret, so expect to wait for seats at the height of summer. Better yet, plan ahead and make reservations.

© TOM NANGLE

Tea and popovers on the lawn at the Jordan Pond House is a long-standing island tradition.

Jordan Pond House is on the Island Explorer's Route #5. *A health note:* Perhaps because of all the sweet drinks and jam served outdoors, patrons at the lawn tables sometimes find themselves pestered by bees. They don't usually sting unless you pester them back, but be alert if anyone in your party is hyperallergic to bee stings.

Bar Harbor and Vicinity

In 1996, Bar Harbor celebrated the bicentennial of its founding (as the town of Eden). In the late 19th century and well into the 20th, the town grew to become one of the East Coast's fanciest summer watering holes.

In those days, ferries and steam yachts arrived from points south, large and small resort hotels sprang up, and exclusive mansions (quaintly dubbed "cottages") were the venues of parties thrown by summer-resident Drexels, DuPonts, Vanderbilts, and prominent academics, journalists, and lawyers. The "rusticators" came for the season, with huge entourages of servants, children, pets, and horses. The area's renown was such that by the 1890s, even the staffs of the British, Austrian, and Ottoman embassies retreated here from summers in Washington, D.C.

The establishment of the national park in 1919 and the arrival of the automobile changed the character of Bar Harbor and Mount Desert Island; two World Wars and the Great Depression took an additional toll in myriad ways; but the coup de grâce for Bar Harbor's era of elegance came with the Great Fire of 1947.

Nothing in the history of Bar Harbor and Mount Desert Island stands out like the Great Fire of 1947, a wind-whipped conflagration that devastated more than 17,000 acres on the

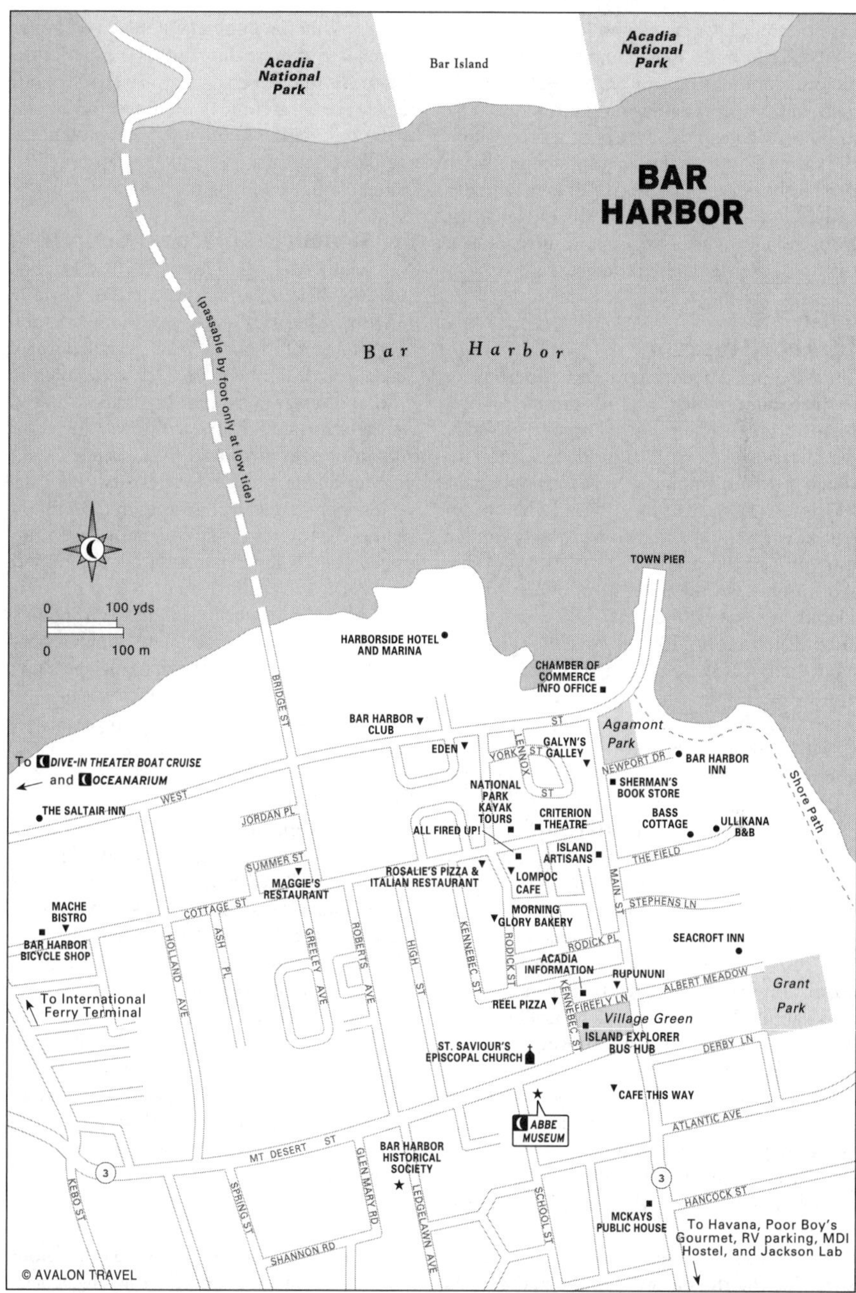

BAR HARBOR
Acadia National Park
Bar Island
Acadia National Park
Bar Harbor
(passable by foot only at low tide)
0 100 yds
0 100 m
TOWN PIER
HARBORSIDE HOTEL AND MARINA
CHAMBER OF COMMERCE INFO OFFICE
BAR HARBOR CLUB
EDEN
GALYN'S GALLEY
Agamont Park
BAR HARBOR INN
NEWPORT DR
SHERMAN'S BOOK STORE
Shore Path
To DIVE-IN THEATER BOAT CRUISE and OCEANARIUM
THE SALTAIR INN
WEST ST
YORK ST
LENNOX ST
NATIONAL PARK KAYAK TOURS
CRITERION THEATRE
BASS COTTAGE
ULLIKANA B&B
JORDAN PL
ALL FIRED UP!
ISLAND ARTISANS
THE FIELD
SUMMER ST
ROSALIE'S PIZZA & ITALIAN RESTAURANT
LOMPOC CAFE
MAGGIE'S RESTAURANT
BRIDGE ST
MAIN ST
STEPHENS LN
MACHE BISTRO
COTTAGE ST
MORNING GLORY BAKERY
BAR HARBOR BICYCLE SHOP
RODICK PL
SEACROFT INN
HOLLAND AVE
ASH PL
GREELEY AVE
ROBERTS AVE
HIGH ST
KENNEBEC ST
RODICK ST
ACADIA INFORMATION
RUPUNUNI
ALBERT MEADOW
Grant Park
To International Ferry Terminal
REEL PIZZA
FIREFLY LN
Village Green
ISLAND EXPLORER BUS HUB
ST. SAVIOUR'S EPISCOPAL CHURCH
DERBY LN
CAFE THIS WAY
ABBE MUSEUM
ATLANTIC AVE
MT DESERT ST
BAR HARBOR HISTORICAL SOCIETY
3
KEBO ST
SPRING ST
GLEN MARY RD
LEDGELAWN AVE
SCHOOL ST
HANCOCK ST
MCKAYS PUBLIC HOUSE
To Havana, Poor Boy's Gourmet, RV parking, MDI Hostel, and Jackson Lab
SHANNON RD
© AVALON TRAVEL

eastern half of the island and leveled gorgeous mansions, humble homes, and more trees than anyone could ever count. Only three people died, but property damage was estimated at $2 million. Whole books have been written about the October inferno; fascinating scrapbooks in Bar Harbor's Jesup Memorial Library dramatically relate the gripping details of the story. Even though some of the elegant cottages have survived, the fire altered life here forever.

SIGHTS

Abbe Museum

The fabulous Abbe Museum is a superb place to introduce children (and adults) to prehistoric, historic, and contemporary Native American tools, crafts, and other cultural artifacts, with an emphasis on Maine's Micmac, Maliseet, Passamaquoddy, and Penobscot tribes. Everything about this privately funded museum, established in 1927, is tasteful. It has two campuses. The main campus (26 Mount Desert St., Bar Harbor, 207/288-3519, www.abbemuseum.org, 10 A.M.–6 P.M. daily late May.–early Nov., call ahead for off-season and winter hours, which vary year to year, $6 adults, $2 children 6–15) is home to a collection spanning nearly 12,000 years. Museum-sponsored events include craft workshops, hands-on children's programs, archaeological field schools, and the **Native American Festival** (held at the College of the Atlantic; usually the first Saturday after July 4). The museum's gift shop has an especially nice selection of Native American–made baskets.

Admission to the intown Abbe also includes admission to the museum's original site in the park, about 2.5 miles south of Bar Harbor, at Sieur de Monts Spring, where Route 3 meets the Park Loop Road (9 A.M.–4 P.M. mid-May–mid-Oct.). Inside a small but handsome National Historic Register building are displays from a 50,000-item collection. Admission to only the Sieur de Monts Spring Abbe is $3 adults, $2 children 6–15 (admission here can be credited to main museum fees).

While you're at the original Abbe Museum site, take the time to wander the paths in the adjacent **Wild Gardens of Acadia,** a 0.75-acre microcosm of more than 400 plant species native to Mount Desert Island. Twelve separate display areas, carefully maintained and labeled by the Bar Harbor Garden Club, represent native plant habitats; pick up the map-brochure that explains each.

St. Saviour's Episcopal Church

St. Saviour's (41 Mt. Desert St., Bar Harbor, 207/288-4215, 7 A.M.–dusk daily), close to downtown Bar Harbor, boasts Maine's largest collection of Tiffany stained-glass windows. Ten originals are here; an 11th was stolen in 1988 and replaced by a locally made window. Of the 32 non-Tiffany windows, the most intriguing is a memorial to Clarence Little, founder of the Jackson Laboratory and a descendant of Paul Revere. Images in the window include the laboratory, DNA, and mice. In July and August, volunteers regularly conduct free tours of the Victorian-era church (completed in 1878); call for the schedule or make an appointment for an off-season tour. The church is open for self-guided tours (8 A.M.–8 P.M.)—pick up a brochure in the back. If old cemeteries intrigue you, spend time wandering the 18th-century town graveyard next to the church.

Oceanarium

At the northern edge of Mount Desert Island, 8.5 miles northwest of downtown Bar Harbor, is this understated but fascinating spot, also called the **Maine Lobster Museum and Hatchery** (1351 Rte. 3, Bar Harbor, 207/288-5005, www.theoceanarium.com, 9 A.M.–5 P.M. Mon.–Sat. mid-May–mid-Oct.). This low-tech, high-interest operation awes the kids, and it's pretty darn interesting for adults, too. David and Audrey Mills have been at it since 1972 and are determined to educate visitors while showing them a good time. Visitors on tour view thousands of tiny lobster hatchlings, enjoy a museum, finger sealife in a touch tank, and meander along a salt marsh walk, where you can check out tidal creatures and vegetation. All tours begin on the hour and half hour. Allow 1–2 hours to see everything. Tickets are

$12 adults, $7 children 4–12, covering admission to the lobster hatchery, lobster museum, and touch tank; an expanded program includes a 45-minute Marsh Walk for $14 adults, $8 children.

College of the Atlantic

A museum, a gallery, and a pleasant campus for walking are reasons to visit the College of the Atlantic (105 Eden St., Rte. 3, Bar Harbor, 207/288-5015, www.coa.edu), which specializes in human ecology, or humans' interrelationship with the environment. In a handsome renovated building, the **George B. Dorr Natural History Museum** showcases regional birds and mammals in realistic dioramas made by COA students. The biggest attraction for children is the please-touch philosophy, allowing kids to reach into a touch tank and to feel fur, skulls, and even whale baleen. Suggested donation is $3.50 adults, $2.50 seniors, $1.50 teenagers, and $1 ages 3–12. The museum is open 10 A.M.–5 P.M. Tuesday–Saturday mid-June to Labor Day; off-season by appointment. The museum also sponsors an excellent and very popular **Family Nature Camp**—six full-week programs—between late June and mid-August; it's essential to register well in advance (800/597-9500, www.coa.edu/summer). Families are housed and fed on the campus ($900 adults, $450 children 5–15; covers almost everything; ask about early-season discounts). The museum gift shop has a particularly good collection of books and gifts for budding naturalists.

Across the way is the **Ethel H. Blum Gallery** (207/288-5015, ext. 254, 10 A.M.–4 P.M. Tues.–Sat. in summer, 9 A.M.–4 P.M. Mon.–Fri. during the academic year), a small space that hosts some intriguing exhibits.

Also on campus is the **Beatrix Farrand Garden,** which is undergoing restoration. The garden, designed in 1928, contained more than 50 varieties of roses and was the prototype for the rose garden at Dumbarton Oaks in Washington, D.C. Both are known for Farrand's use of garden rooms, such as the terraces in this garden.

Also open is the 1st floor of **The Turrets,** a magnificent 1895 seaside cottage that's now an administration building. Don't miss the gardens in front, either.

The college and its museum are a half mile northwest of downtown Bar Harbor; take Island Explorer Route #2/Eden Street.

Bar Harbor Whale Museum

For a whale of a good time, don't miss the small but jam-packed Bar Harbor Whale Museum (52 West St., Bar Harbor, 207/288-0288, www.barharborwhalemuseum.org, 10 A.M.–8 P.M. in June, Sept., Oct., 9 A.M.–9 P.M. July–Aug., hours may vary off-season), operated by research associates affiliated with College of the Atlantic's Allied Whale program. Features include a life-sized model of a prehistoric walking whale, a 29.5-foot humpback whale skeleton, seals, marine birds, a 22-foot-long minke porpoise, and interactive exhibits on whales and climate change. There's also a mesmerizing video of whales in their habitat. Admission is free, but donations support marine mammal research and conservation. While here, ask about COA's **Adopt a Finback or Humpback Whale** program. Biologists from Allied Whale have identified more than 1,000 finbacks and more than 6,000 humpbacks. Your $40–50 contribution supports research and nets you a color photo of your whale, a brief history of it, and a book, as well as an adoption certificate and newsletter subscription. The museum's gift shop is green—lots of good choices here for budding naturalists—and the museum uses no plastic. Note: The museum may be moving in 2010; call for details.

The Bar Harbor Historical Society

The Bar Harbor Historical Society (33 Ledgelawn Ave., Bar Harbor, 207/288-0000, www.barharborhistorical.org, 1–4 P.M. Mon.–Sat. mid-June–mid-Oct., free), in its own National Historic Register building, has fascinating displays, stereopticon images, and a scrapbook about the 1947 fire that devastated the island. The photographs alone are worth the visit. Also here are antique maps, Victorian-era hotel registers, and other local memorabilia. In winter, it's open by appointment.

For a sample of Bar Harbor before the great fire, wander over to upper West Street, which is on the National Historic Register thanks to the remaining grand cottages that line it.

Hulls Cove Tool Barn and Sculpture Garden

Part shop, part nature center, part art gallery, the Hulls Cove Tool Barn and Sculpture Garden (17 Breakneck Rd., behind Hulls Cove General Store, Hulls Cove, 207/288-5126, www.jonesport-wood.com, 9 A.M.–5 P.M. Wed.–Sat., noon–5 P.M. Sun.) is just one of creative Skip Brack's enterprises. Inside the barn is an extensive selection of old tools, with an emphasis on woodworking hand tools. Paths lace through perennial gardens, woods, and fields at the Davistown Museum Sculpture Garden, which surrounds the barn and continues across the street. Throughout the garden are sculptures by noted Maine artists and found-object creations by Brack. Take the Island Explorer Route #1/Campgrounds and request a stop at the Hulls Cove General Store, then walk up the road.

Research Laboratories

Some of the world's top scientists live here year-round or come to Bar Harbor in summer to work at two prominent scientific laboratories.

World-renowned in genetic research, scientists at **The Jackson Laboratory for Mammalian Research** (600 Main St., Rte. 3, Bar Harbor, 207/288-6000, www.jax.org) study cancer, diabetes, muscular dystrophy, heart disease, Alzheimer's disease, and other diseases—with considerable success. The nonprofit research institution, locally called JAX or just "the lab," is also renowned for its genetics databases and for producing genetically defined laboratory mice, which are shipped to research labs worldwide. Free scheduled public tours (limited to 15, call for details, preregistration required) begin in the lab's visitors lobby and visit the lab's three main research wings. These show the evolution of facilities over the decades, beginning with the 1980s, and the guide discusses the genetic research occurring in each. The lab is 1.5 miles south of downtown Bar Harbor.

No less impressive is the **Mount Desert Island Biological Laboratory** (159 Old Bar Harbor Rd., Salisbury Cove, 207/288-3605, www.mdibl.org), one of the few scientific research institutions in the world dedicated to studying marine animals to learn more about human health and environmental health. It is the only comprehensive effort in the country to sequence genomes. Family-oriented public programs include **Splash!** (late June–late Aug., call for schedule). This hands-on program introduces genetics and marine life using MDIBL's MIT-designed LEGO sets to see how DNA divides and mutates, then progresses to the touch tanks and aquarium. To avoid crowds, go on a nice day. The lab also presents **Science Fridays** about once a month, a two-hour program that includes lunch with a scientist followed by lab time; it's limited to 15 participants and minimum age is 16. **Family Science Night,** held once or twice each summer, is an interactive program of performances, demonstrations, and hands-on science; reservations recommended. The lab also presents a symposium and lectures by top scientists. The lab is six miles north of Bar Harbor off Route 3.

Bar Harbor and Park Tours

The veteran of the Bar Harbor–based bus tours is **Acadia National Park Tours** (tickets at Testa's Restaurant, Bayside Landing, 53 Main St., Bar Harbor, 207/288-3327, www.acadiatours.com, $27.50 adults, $15 children 12 and younger), operating May–October. A 2.5- to 3-hour naturalist-led tour of Bar Harbor and Acadia departs at 10 A.M. and 2 P.M. daily from downtown Bar Harbor (Testa's is across from Agamont Park, near the Bar Harbor Inn). Reservations are wise in midsummer and during fall-foliage season (late September and early October); pick up reserved tickets 30 minutes before departure.

If you have a time crunch, take the one-hour trolley-bus tour operated by **Oli's Trolley** (ticket office at 1 West St., Bar Harbor, 207/288-9899 or 866/987-6553, www.acadiaislandtours.com), which departs downtown Bar Harbor five times daily (between 10 A.M. and 6 P.M.) in July and August, including Bar Harbor mansion drive-bys and the Cadillac summit. Purchase tickets at Harbor Place, 1 West Street, next to the town pier on the waterfront. Dress warmly if the air is at all cool; it's an open-air trolley. Cost is $15 adults, $10 children under 12. Reservations are advisable. The trolley also does 2.5-hour park tours at 10 A.M. and 2 P.M. May–October. Tickets are $29 adults, $10 children under 12. The bus and trolley routes both include potty stops.

Note: While the Island Explorer buses do reach a number of key park sights, they are not tour buses. There is no narration, the bus cuts off the Park Loop at Otter Cliffs, and it excludes the summit of Cadillac Mountain.

Costumed guides lead small groups on **Historic Bar Harbor Walking Tours** (207/408-3578, 9 A.M. Mon.–Sat., $12 adults, $8 children 12 and younger, reservations required). The two-hour tours cover about 1.3 miles, and guides share tales of Bar Harbor during its Victorian heyday. Tours run rain or shine and depart from the fountain in Agamont Park.

Bird-Watching and Nature Tours

For private tours of the park and other parts of the island, contact Michael Good at **Down East Nature Tours** (150 Knox Rd., Bar Harbor, 207/288-8128, www.downeastnaturetours.com). A biologist and Maine Guide, Good is simply batty about birds. He's spent more than 25 years studying the birds of North America, and he's even turned his home property on Mount Desert Island into a bird sanctuary. Good specializes in avian ecology in the Gulf of Maine, giving special attention to native and migrating birds. Whether you're a first-timer wanting to spot eagles, peregrine falcons, shorebirds, and warblers or a serious bird-watcher seeking to add to your life list, perhaps with a Nelson's sharptailed sparrow, Good's your man. Prices begin at $75 per person for four hours and include transportation from your lodging; family rates are available. Bring your own binoculars, but Good supplies a spotting scope.

ENTERTAINMENT

The **Bar Harbor Town Band** performs free Monday and Thursday evenings (8 P.M.) July to mid-August on the Village Green (Main St. and Mount Desert St., Bar Harbor).

Above Rupununi restaurant, **Carmen Verandah** (119 Main St., Bar Harbor, 207/288-2766) is the weekend place to be and be seen, with music, dancing, and more.

You never know quite what's going to happen at **Improv Acadia** (15 Cottage St., Bar Harbor, 207/288-2503, www.improvacadia.com, $15 adults, $10 children 12 and younger). Every show is different, as actors use audience suggestions to create comedy sketches. Shows are staged once or twice a night, late May to mid-October. Dessert, snacks, and drinks are available.

The **Bar Harbor Music Festival** (207/288-5744 in July and August, 212/222-1026 off-season, www.barharbormusicfestival.org), a summer tradition since 1967, emphasizes up-and-coming musical talent in a series of classical, jazz, and pop concerts and even an opera, usually Fridays and Sundays early July to early August, at various island locations including local inns and an annual outdoor concert in Acadia National Park. Tickets are $25–35 adults, $15 students, and can be purchased at the festival office building (59 Cottage St., Bar Harbor). Pre-concert dinners are also sometimes available at $35. Reservations are wise.

Theaters

Built in 1932 and listed on the National Register of Historic Places, the beautifully refurbished **Criterion Theatre and Arts Center** (35 Cottage St., Bar Harbor, 207/288-3441 for films, 207/288-5829 for concerts, www.criteriontheatre.com) is a gem. In 2007 it gained nonprofit status, with a mission to make arts and theater more accessible through diverse programs. Now, in addition to screening films, the Criterion puts on concerts, plays, and other special events. You'll soak up the nostalgia in this art deco classic with 877 seats (including an elegant floating balcony).

Combine pizza with your picture show at **Reel Pizza Cinerama** (33 Kennebec Pl., Bar Harbor, 207/288-3811 for films, 207/288-3828 for food, www.reelpizza.net). Two films are screened nightly on each of two screens. All tickets are $6; pizzas are $9–22. Doors open at 4:30 P.M.; get there early for the best seats.

Create Your Own Art

Definitely worthy of the entertainment category is **All Fired Up!** (44 Cottage St., Bar Harbor, 207/288-3130, www.acadiaallfiredup.com), the perfect answer to "What do we do in the rain?" Solution: Paint your own pottery, make mosaics, or create a critter (stuffed animal). Studio time (including all the supplies) is $10 adults, $7 children.

EVENTS

Bar Harbor is home to numerous special events; here's just a sampling. For more, call 207/288-5103 or visit www.barharbormaine.com.

In mid-June, the annual **Acadia Birding Festival** attracts bird-watchers with guided walks, boating excursions, tours, talks, and meals.

In late June, **Legacy of the Arts** is a weeklong celebration of music, art, theater, dance, and history, with tours, exhibits, workshops, concerts, lectures, demonstrations, and more.

The **Fourth of July** is always a big deal in Bar Harbor, celebrated with a blueberry-pancake breakfast (6 A.M.), a parade (10 A.M.), a seafood festival (11 A.M. on), a band concert, and fireworks. A highlight is the Lobster Race, a crustacean competition drawing contestants such as Lobzilla and Larry the Lobster in a four-lane saltwater tank on the Village Green. Independence Day celebrations in the island's smaller villages always evoke a bygone era.

The Abbe Museum, the College of the Atlantic, and the Maine Indian Basketmakers Alliance sponsor the annual **Native American Festival** (10 A.M.–4 P.M. first Sat. after July 4, free), featuring baskets, beadwork, and other handicrafts for sale, and Indian drumming and dancing (held at College of the Atlantic, Bar Harbor).

In even-numbered years, the **Mount Desert Garden Club Tour** presents a rare chance to visit some of Maine's most spectacular private gardens on the second or third Saturday in July (confirm the date with the Bar Harbor Chamber of Commerce).

The **Directions Craft Show** fills a weekend in late July or early August with extraordinary displays and sales of crafts by members of the Maine Crafts Guild. You'll find it at Mount Desert Island High School (Rte. 233, Eagle Lake Rd., Bar Harbor). Hours are Friday 5–9 P.M., Saturday and Sunday 10 A.M.–5 P.M.

SHOPPING

Bar Harbor's boutiques—running the gamut from attractive to kitschy—are indisputably visitor oriented; many shut down for the winter.

Downtown Bar Harbor's best craft gallery is **Island Artisans** (99 Main St., Bar Harbor, 207/288-4214, www.islandartisans.com). More than 100 Maine artists are represented here, and the quality is outstanding. Don't miss it. You'll find basketwork, handmade paper, wood carvings, blown glass, jewelry, weaving, metalwork, ceramics, and more.

For more than three decades, **Alone Moose Fine Crafts** (78 West St., Bar Harbor, 207/288-4229, www.finemainecrafts.com) has lured collectors and browsers with its selection of sculpture, pottery, jewelry, and other works.

Toys, cards, and newspapers blend in with the new-book inventory at **Sherman's Book Store** (56 Main St., Bar Harbor, 207/288-3161). It's just the place to pick up maps and trail guides for fine days and puzzles for foggy days.

RECREATION

Walks

A real treat is a stroll along downtown Bar Harbor's **Shore Path,** a well-trodden granite-

© TOM NANGLE

Bar Harbor's famed Shore Path edges the waterfront.

edged byway built around 1880. Along the craggy shoreline are granite-and-wood benches, town-owned **Grant Park** (great for picnics), birch trees, and several handsome mansions that escaped the 1947 fire. Offshore are the four Porcupine Islands. The path is open 6:30 A.M.–dusk, and leashed pets are okay. Allow about 30 minutes for the mile loop, beginning next to the town pier and the Bar Harbor Inn and returning via Wayman Lane.

Check local newspapers or the Bar Harbor Chamber of Commerce visitor booklet for the times of low tide, then walk across the gravel bar to wooded **Bar Island** (formerly Rodick's Island) from the foot of Bridge Street in downtown Bar Harbor. Shell heaps recorded on the eastern end of the island indicate that Native Americans enjoyed this turf in the distant past. You'll have the most time to explore the island during new-moon or full-moon low tides, but no more than four hours—about two hours before and two hours after low tide. Be sure to wear a watch so you don't get trapped (for up to 10 hours). The foot of Bridge Street is also an excellent kayak-launching site.

About a mile from downtown, along Main Street, Route 3, is **Compass Harbor,** a section of the park where you can stroll through woods to the water's edge and explore the overgrown ruins of Acadia National Park cofounder George Dorr's home.

Bear right at the fork just after the Thompson Island Visitor Center on Route 102/198 to reach **Indian Point/Blagden Preserve,** a lovely preserve owned by the Nature Conservancy. Five trails wind through forested 110-acre Indian Point/Blagden Preserve, a rectangular parcel with island, hill, and bay vistas. Seal-watching and bird-watching are popular—harbor seals on offshore rocks and woodpeckers (plus 130 other species) in blowdown areas. To spot the seals, plan your hike around low tide, when they'll be sprawled on the rocks close to shore. Wear rubberized shoes. Bring binoculars or use the telescope installed here for the purpose. To keep from disturbing the seals, watch quietly and avoid jerky movements. Park near the preserve entrance and follow the Big Woods Trail, which runs the length of the preserve. A second parking area is further in, but then you'll miss much of the preserve. When you reach the second parking area, just past an old field, bear left along the Shore Trail to see the seals. Register at the caretaker's house (just beyond the first parking lot, where you can pick up bird and flora checklists), and respect private property on either side of the preserve. It's open dawn–6 P.M. daily year-round. From the junction of Routes 3 and 102/198, continue 1.8 miles to Indian Point Road and turn right. Go 1.7 miles to a fork and turn right. Watch for the preserve entrance on the right, marked by a Nature Conservancy oak leaf.

Bicycling

With all the great biking options, including 33 miles of carriage roads open to bicycles and some of the best roadside bike routes in Maine, you'll want to bring a bike or rent one here.

The Minutolo family's **Bar Harbor Bicycle Shop** (141 Cottage St., Bar Harbor, 207/288-3886, www.barharborbike.com), on the corner with Route 3, has been in business since 1977 and has earned an excellent reputation. If you have your own bike, stop here for advice on routes—the Minutolos have cycled everywhere on the island and can suggest the perfect mountain-bike or road-bike loop based on your ability and schedule. The shop organizes free Sunday-morning group road rides, usually 9 A.M.–noon, with a longer option for more experienced cyclists. The shop has rentals varying from standard mountain bikes to full-suspension models and even tandems as well as all the accessories and gear you might need; rates begin about $22 per day. Hours in summer are 8 A.M.–6 P.M. daily, 9 A.M.–5:30 P.M. Tuesday–Saturday other months.

Sea Kayaking

National Park Kayak Tours (39 Cottage St., Bar Harbor, 207/288-0342 or 800/347-0940, www.acadiakayak.com) limits its Registered Maine Guide–led tours to a maximum of six tandem kayaks per trip. Four-hour morning, midday, afternoon, or sunset paddles are offered, including shuttle service, a paddle/safety lesson, and a brief stop, for $48 per person in July and August, $44 off-season. Most trips cover about six miles. Multiday camping trips also are offered. Try to make reservations at least one day in advance.

Golf

Duffers first teed off in 1888 at **Kebo Valley Golf Club** (100 Eagle Lake Rd., Rte. 233, Bar Harbor, 207/288-5000, www.kebovalleyclub.com, May–Oct.), Maine's oldest club and the eighth-oldest in the nation. The 17th hole became legendary when it took president William Howard Taft 27 tries to sink the ball in 1911.

Excursion Boats

DIVE-IN THEATER BOAT CRUISE

You don't have to go diving in these frigid waters; others will do it for you. When the kids are clamoring to touch slimy sea cucumbers and starfish at various touch tanks in the area, they're likely to be primed for Diver Ed's Dive-In Theater Boat Cruise (207/288-3483 or 800/979-3370, www.divered.com), departing from the College of the Atlantic pier (105 Eden St., Bar Harbor). Former Bar Harbor harbormaster and College of the Atlantic grad Ed Monat heads the crew aboard the 46-passenger *Starfish Enterprise,* which goes a mile or two offshore where Ed, professional diver, goes overboard with a video camera and a mini-Ed, who helps put things in proportion. You and the kids stay on deck, all warm and dry, along with Captain Evil, who explains the action on a TV screen. There's communication back and forth, so the kids can ask questions as the divers pick up urchins, starfish, crabs, lobsters, and other sea life. When Ed resurfaces, he brings a bag of touchable specimens—another chance to pet some slimy creatures (which go back into the water after show-and-tell). Great concept. Watch the kids' expressions—this is a big hit. The two-hour trips depart three times daily Monday–Friday, twice daily Saturday, and once on Sunday, from early July through early September; fewer trips are made in spring and fall. Cost is $35 adults, $30 seniors, $25 children ages 5–12, $10 younger than five. Usually twice weekly there's a park ranger or naturalist

© TOM NANGLE

Excursion boats depart from Bar Harbor's piers.

on board and the tour lasts for three hours—check the park's *Beaver Log* newspaper or Diver Ed's website for the schedule and reservation information—these trips cost an additional $5. Advance reservations are strongly encouraged.

WHALE-WATCHING AND PUFFIN-WATCHING

Whale-watching boats go as far as 20 miles offshore, so no matter what the weather in Bar Harbor, dress warmly and bring more clothing than you think you'll need—even gloves, if you're especially sensitive to cold. I've been out on days when it's close to 90°F on island, but feels more like 30°F in a moving boat on open ocean. Motion-sensitive children and adults should plan in advance for appropriate medication, such as seasickness pills or patches. Adults are required to show a photo ID when boarding the boat.

Whale-watching, puffin-watching, and combo excursions are offered by **Bar Harbor Whale Watch Company** (1 West St., Bar Harbor, 207/288-2386 or 800/942-5374, www.barharborwhales.com), sailing from the town pier (1 West Street) in downtown Bar Harbor. The company operates under various names, including Acadian Whale Watcher, and has a number of boats. Most trips are accompanied by a naturalist (often from Allied Whale at the College of the Atlantic), who regales passengers with all sorts of interesting trivia about the whales, porpoises, seabirds, and other marine life spotted along the way. In season, some trips go out as far as the puffin colony on Petit Manan Light. Trips depart daily from late May through late October, but with so many options it's impossible to list the schedule—call for the latest. Tickets are $52–56 adults, $28 children 6–14, $8 children under six. A portion of the ticket price benefits Allied Whale, which researches and protects marine animals in the Gulf of Maine.

Trips may extend longer than the time advertised, so don't plan anything else too tightly around the trip. However, do try to visit the Whale Museum either before or after.

Scenic Nature Cruises (1.5–2 hours) and kid-friendly Lobster and Seal Watch Cruises (1.5 hours) also are offered. Rates for these are around $27 for adults, $16 children, $5 kiddies.

SAILING

Captain Steve Pagels, under the umbrella of **Downeast Windjammer Cruises** (207/288-4585 or 207/288-2373, www.downeastwindjammer.com), offers 1.5- to 2-hour day sails on the 151-foot steel-hulled *Margaret Todd,* a gorgeous four-masted schooner with tanbark sails that he designed and launched in 1998. Trips depart daily at 10 A.M. and 2 P.M. and around sunset mid-May to mid-October (weather permitting) from the Bar Harbor Inn pier, just east of the town pier in downtown Bar Harbor. You'll get the best wildlife sightings on the morning trip, but better sailing on the afternoon trip; there's live music on the sunset one. Some morning sails are narrated by a park ranger. Buy tickets either at the pier or at 27 Main Street or online with a credit card; plan to arrive at least half an hour early. Cost is $35 adults, $33 seniors, $25 children 6–11, $5 ages 2–5. Dogs are welcome on all sails.

SEA VENTURE

Captain Winston Shaw's custom boat tour by Sea Venture (207/288-3355, www.svboattours.com) lets you design the perfect trip aboard *Reflection,* a 20-foot motor launch. Captain Shaw, a Registered Maine Guide and committed environmentalist, specializes in nature-oriented tours. He's the founder and director of the Coastal Maine Bald Eagle Project, and he was involved in the inaugural Earth Day celebration in 1970. He's been studying coastal birds for more than 25 years. You can pick from 10 recommended cruises lasting from one to eight hours, or design your own. In any case, the boat is yours. Boat charter rate is $95 per hour for one or two people, $110 for three or four, and $150 for five or six. Captain Shaw can also arrange for picnic lunches. On longer trips, restroom stops are available. The boat departs from the Atlantic Oakes Motel pier, off Route 3, in Bar Harbor.

LOBSTER CRUISE

When you're ready to learn The Truth about lobsters, sign up for a two-hour cruise aboard Captain John Nicolai's *Lulu* (56 West St., Bar Harbor, 207/963-2341 or 866/235-2341, www.lululobsterboat.com), a traditional Maine lobster boat that departs up to four times daily from the Harborside Hotel and Marina. Captain Nicolai provides an entertaining commentary on anything and everything, but especially about lobsters and lobstering. He hauls a lobster trap and explains intimate details of the hapless critters. (Lobstering is banned on Sundays June–August; the cruises operate, but there's no hauling that day.) Reservations are required. Cost is $30 adults, $27 seniors and military, $17 children 2–12. Free parking is available in the hotel's lot.

ACCOMMODATIONS

Unless otherwise noted, properties are seasonal. Most are open May into October. Rates listed are for peak season.

Hotels and Motels

One of the town's best-known and best-situated hotels is the **Bar Harbor Inn** (Newport Dr., Bar Harbor, 207/288-3351 or 800/248-3351, www.barharborinn.com, $199–379), a sprawling complex on eight acres overlooking the harbor and Bar Island. The 153 rooms and suites vary considerably in style, from traditional inn to motel, and are in three different buildings. Continental breakfast is included. Frills aplenty including restaurants, a heated outdoor pool, and a full-service spa.

The appropriately named **Harborside Hotel & Marina** (55 West St., Bar Harbor, 207/288-5033 or 800/238-5033, www.theharborsidehotel.com, from $280) fronts the water in downtown Bar Harbor. Almost all of the 187 rooms and suites have a water view and semiprivate balconies. Some have whirlpool tubs; deluxe rooms have marble baths, and some have large outdoor hot tubs. A fine-dining restaurant and full-service spa are located in the beautifully restored Bar Harbor Club. An Italian restaurant is in the hotel. Facilities also include an outdoor heated pool and hot tub and a pier.

On the edge of downtown, across from College of the Atlantic, are two adjacent, sister properties tiered up a hillside, **Wonder View Inn & Suites** (55 Eden St., Bar Harbor, 888/439-8439, www.wonderviewinn.com) and the **Bluenose Hotel** (90 Eden St., Bar Harbor, 207/288-3348 or 800/445-4077, www.barharborhotel.com). The pet-friendly (for $20 per night) Wonder View comprises four older motels on estate-like grounds with grassy lawns and mature shade trees. On the premises are an outdoor pool and a restaurant. Rooms vary, with rates beginning at $109 in season, including afternoon cookies and tea. The Bluenose, one of the island's top properties, comprises two buildings. Mizzentop is newest, and rooms and suites are quite elegant, many with fireplaces, all with fabulous views and balconies. Also here is a spa, fitness center, indoor and outdoor pools, and a lounge with live music every evening. Stenna Nordica rooms are more modest and have outdoor corridors, but still have views. Rates range $189–529.

In town, the family-owned **Villager** (207 Main St., Bar Harbor, 207/288-3211 or 888/383-3211, winter 207/288-2270, www.barharborvillager.com, $79–148) delivers clean standard motel rooms (air-conditioning, phone, TV, Wi-Fi) with an outdoor pool and friendly service and advice. The location puts all of downtown's sights within walking distance, and the Bangor bus stop is here.

Also on the lower end of the budgetary scale are two neighboring motels: **Edenbrook Motel** (96 Eden St., Rte. 3, Bar Harbor, 207/288-4975 or 800/323-7819, www.edenbrookmotelbh.com, $70–100), with panoramic views of Frenchman Bay from some rooms, and the wee bit fancier **Highbrook Motel** (94 Eden St., Rte. 3, Bar Harbor, 207/288-3591 or 800/338-9688, www.highbrookmotel.com, $99–139). Both are about 1.5 miles from Acadia's main entrance, one mile from downtown.

If all you want is a room with a bed, **Robbins Motel** (396 Rte. 3, Bar Harbor, 207/288-4659 or 800/858-0769, $58 d), an older motel, has 30 small, unadorned (some might call them dismal) but clean queen-bedded rooms (air-conditioning, TV, Wi-Fi) and an outdoor pool. No charm, not quiet, but cheap.

Inns and Bed-and-Breakfasts

Few innkeepers have mastered the art of hospitality as well as Roy Kasindorf and Hélène Harton, owners of the **Ullikana Bed and Breakfast** (16 The Field, Bar Harbor, 207/288-9552, www.ullikana.com, $195–340), a 10-room Victorian Tudor inn built by Alpheus Hardy, Bar Harbor's first "cottager" in 1885. They genuinely enjoy their guests. Hélène's a whiz in the kitchen; after one of her multicourse breakfasts, usually served on the water-view patio, you won't be needing lunch. She's also a decorating genius, blending antiques and modern art, vibrant color with soothing hues, folk art and fine art, with a result like a finely tuned orchestra. Roy excels at helping guests select just the right hike, bike route, or other activity. Afternoon refreshments provide a time for guests to gather and share experiences. The comfortable rooms all have private baths; many have working fireplaces, and some have private terraces with water views. Hélène and Roy also own The Yellow House, next door, with six lovely rooms decorated in old Bar Harbor style and a huge living room filled with antique wicker. They're in a quiet downtown location close to Bar Harbor's Shore Path. French spoken.

Right next door is the gorgeously renovated and rejuvenated **Bass Cottage** (14 The Field, Bar Harbor, 207/288-1234 or 866/782-9224, www.basscottage.com, $225–365). Corporate refugees Teri and Jeff Anderholm purchased the 26-room 1885 cottage in 2003 and spent a year gutting it, salvaging the best of the old and blending in new to turn it into a luxurious and stylish 10-room inn. It retains its Victorian bones, yet it is most un-Victorian in style. Guest rooms are soothingly decorated with cream and pastel-colored walls and have phones, Wi-Fi, and TV with DVD (a DVD library is available—a godsend on a stormy day); many rooms have fireplaces and whirlpool tubs. The spacious and elegant public rooms—expansive living rooms, cozy library,

© HILARY NANGLE

The Ullikana Bed and Breakfast is tucked in a quiet downtown location, just steps from Main Street or the waterfront.

porches—flow from one to another. Teri puts her culinary degree to use preparing baked goods, fruits, and savory and sweet entrées for breakfast and evening refreshments. A guest pantry is stocked with tea, coffee, and snacks. Plans call for dinner to be served, too.

Situated on one oceanfront acre in the West Street Historical District, **The Saltair Inn** (121 West St., Bar Harbor, 207/288-2882, www.saltairinn.com, $240–355) was originally built in 1887 as a guesthouse. Innkeepers Kristi and Matt Losquadro and their young family now welcome guests in five spacious rooms, three of which face Frenchman Bay. Frills vary by room but might include whirlpool tubs, fireplaces, and balconies. All have TV and Wi-Fi. A full breakfast is served either in the dining room or on the water-view deck. It's steps from downtown, but really, with a location like this, why leave?

Outside of town, in a serene location with fabulous views of Frenchman Bay, is Jack and Jeani Ochtera's ☾ **Inn at Bay Ledge** (150 Sand Point Rd., Bar Harbor, summer 207/288-4204, winter 207/875-3262, www.innatbayledge.com, $150–475), an oasis of calm tucked under towering pines and atop an 80-foot cliff. Terraced decks descend to a pool and hot tub and onto the lawn, which stretches to the cliff's edge. Stairs descend to a private stone beach below. It's an elegant, casual retreat. Almost all guest rooms have water views. Beds are topped with down comforters and feather beds; some rooms have whirlpool tubs, and 2nd-floor rooms have private decks. A sauna and steam shower are available. Also available are cottages; hillside ones lack the view but have use of the inn's facilities; the Summer House at Bay Ledge is a shingled cottage with a deck 25 feet from the edge of Frenchman Bay.

Much less pricey and a find for families is the **Seacroft Inn** (18 Albert Meadow, Bar Harbor, 207/288-4669 or 800/824-9694, www.seacroftinn.com, $99–139), well situated just off Main Street and near the Shore Path. All rooms in Bunny and Dave Brown's white multi-gabled cottage have air-conditioning, phone, TV, refrigerator, and microwave; a continental breakfast is available for $5 per person. Housekeeping is $10 per day. Some rooms can be joined as family suites.

Hostels

The **Bar Harbor/Mount Desert Island Hostel** (321 Main St., Bar Harbor, 207/288-5587, www.barharborhostel.com, $25 dorm bed, $80 private room, $15 for tent platform), in a beautifully renovated building on the edge of town, has a well-equipped kitchen and a laundry. Linens are provided. No smoking, no liquor, no credit cards, midnight curfew. Reservations are essential, as this is a popular location.

FOOD

You won't go hungry in Bar Harbor, and you won't find chain fast-food places. The island's best collection of good, inexpensive restaurants are along Rodick Street, from Reel Pizza down to Rosalie's, which actually fronts on Cottage Street. You'll find a good ethnic mix here, from Mexican to Thai to Italian. For sit-down restaurants, make reservations as far in advance as possible. Hours listed are for peak season; expect reduced operations during spring and fall; few places (the greatest concentration is on Rodick Street) are open in winter.

Local Flavors

Only a masochist could bypass **Ben and Bill's Chocolate Emporium** (66 Main St., Bar Harbor, 207/288-3281 or 800/806-3281), a long-running taste experience in downtown Bar Harbor. The homemade candies and more than 50 ice cream flavors (including a dubious lobster flavor) are nothing short of outrageous; the whole place smells like the inside of a chocolate truffle. It opens daily at 10 A.M., with closing dependent upon season and crowds, but usually late in the evening.

If ice cream is your passion, a must-stop is **Mt. Desert Ice Cream** (325 Main St. and 7 Firefly La., Bar Harbor, 207/460-5515) for wildly creative flavors.

Probably the least-expensive lunch or ice cream option in town is **West End Drug Co.** (105 Main St., Bar Harbor, 207/288-3318), where you can get grilled cheese sandwiches, PBJ, and other white-bread basics as well as frappes (a Maine-ism—frappes are made with ice cream, milk shakes aren't) and sundaes at the fountain.

Equally inexpensive, but with a healthful menu, is the **Blair Dining Hall** at College of the Atlantic (105 Eden St., Bar Harbor, 207/288-5015, www.coa.edu). Known as Take-A-Break, the hall serves breakfast, lunch, and dinner weekdays during the school year. While there are individual choices, the best deal is the all-you-can eat breakfast, lunch, or dinner ($5–10). There are always vegetarian, vegan, and meat choices, and the selection includes organic and local foods whenever possible.

For more natural flavors, head to the **Alternative Community Market** (16 Mount Desert St., Bar Harbor, 207/288-8225, 8 A.M.–8 P.M. Mon.–Sat., 10 A.M.–6 P.M. Sun.), with a deli where you can purchase breakfast bagels and wraps, sandwiches and paninis, espresso, or even fruit smoothies. There's limited seating indoors and on the deck.

Between Mother's Day and late October, the **Eden Farmers Market** operates out of the YMCA parking lot off Lower Main Street in Bar Harbor 9 A.M.–noon each Sunday. You'll find fresh meats and produce, local cheeses and maple syrup, yogurt and ice cream, bread, honey, preserves, and even prepared Asian foods.

Efficient, friendly cafeteria-style service makes **EPI's Pizza** (8 Cottage St., Bar Harbor, 207/288-5853, 11 A.M.–8 P.M. daily, to 8:30 P.M. July–Aug.) an excellent choice for subs, salads, pizzas, and even spaghetti. If the weather closes in, there are always the pinball machines in the back room.

When it comes to pub-grub favorites, such as burgers and fish sandwiches, **The Thirsty Whale Tavern** (40 Cottage St., Bar Harbor, 207/288-9335, 7 A.M.–7 P.M. daily) does it right.

For breakfast or brunch, you can't beat **2 Cats** (130 Cottage St., Bar Harbor, 207/288-2808 or 800/355-2828, www.2catsbarharbor.com, 7 A.M.–1 P.M.). "Fun," "funky," and "fresh" best describe both the restaurant and the food ($8–12). Dine inside or on the patio. Dinner is also served at 2 Cats—call for nights and hours. Three upstairs guest rooms are available for $165–195, less in winter—with breakfast, of course.

Picnic Fare

Althouh a few of these places have some seating, most are for the grab-and-go crowd.

For a light, inexpensive meal, you can't go wrong at **Morning Glory Bakery** (39 Rodick St., Bar Harbor, 207/288-3041, www.morningglorybakery.com, 7 A.M.–7 P.M. Mon.–Fri., 8 A.M.–7 P.M. Sat.–Sun.). Fresh-baked goodies, breakfast and regular sandwiches, soups and salads are all made from scratch. Planning a day in the park? Call ahead for a boxed lunch.

Also earning high marks is **Michelle's Brown Bag Cafe** (164 Main St., Bar Harbor, 207/288-5858, 9 A.M.–8 P.M.) for its paninis, salads, and sandwiches.

The (Spot) Grill (33 Cottage St., Bar Harbor, 207/288-1233, 7 A.M.–9 P.M. daily, to 2 A.M. Fri.–Sat., opens at 8 A.M. Sat.–Sun.) is just the spot to pick up breakfast, lunch, dinner, or nibbles. The order-at-the-counter menu leans toward the Mediterranean, but the options are many. Take it to go or eat here. Box lunches also are available.

If you happen to be on Route 102 in the Town Hill area around lunchtime, plan to pick up picnic fare at **Mother's Kitchen** (Rte. 102, Town Hill, Bar Harbor, 207/288-4403, www.motherskitchenfoods.com, 8 A.M.–2 P.M. Mon.–Fri.). The plain, minuscule building next to Salsbury's (look for the Real Good Food sign) is deceiving—it's been operating since 1995 and turns out 20 different sandwiches, as well as deli salads, scones, breakfast sandwiches, great cookies, and pies.

Brewpubs and Microbreweries

Bar Harbor's longest-lived brewpub is the **Lompoc Cafe** (36 Rodick St., Bar Harbor, 207/288-9392, www.lompoccafe.com, 11:30 A.M.–9 P.M. late Apr.–mid-Dec.), with ales from Atlantic Brewing Co. on tap. Go for pizzas, salads, and entrées ($10–18), along with bocce in the beer garden and live entertainment on weekends. After 9 P.M., there's just beer and thin-crust pizza until about 1 A.M.

Lompoc's signature Bar Harbor Real Ale and five or six others are brewed by the **Atlantic Brewing Company** (15 Knox Rd., Town Hill, in the upper section of the island, 207/288-2337 or 800/475-5417, www.atlanticbrewing.com). Free brewery tours, including tastings, are given daily at 2, 3, and 4 P.M. late May through mid-October. Also operating here in summer is **Mainely Meat Bar-B-Q** (207/288-9200, 11:30 A.M.–8 P.M. daily, $8–16), offering pulled pork, chicken, ribs, and similar fare for lunch and dinner.

Atlantic also owns **Bar Harbor Brewing Company & Soda Works** (8 Mt. Desert St., Bar Harbor, 207/288-4592, www.barharborbrewing.com). Tours and tastings are held most afternoons; stop by or call for the schedule. Kids can sample Bar Harbor Blueberry Soda or Root Beer.

Family Favorites

An unscientific but reliable local survey gives the best-pizza ribbon to **Rosalie's Pizza & Italian Restaurant** (46 Cottage St., Bar Harbor, 207/288-5666, www.rosaliespizza.com, 4–10 P.M. daily), where the Wurlitzer jukebox churns out tunes from the 1950s. Rosalie's earns high marks for consistency with its homemade pizza (in four sizes or by the slice), calzones, and subs—lots of vegetarian options. If you need something a bit heartier, try the Italian dinners—spaghetti, eggplant parmigiana, and others—all less than $10, including a garlic roll. Beer and wine are available. Here's a hint: Avoid the downstairs lines by heading upstairs and ordering at that counter, or call in your order.

Route 66 Restaurant (21 Cottage St., Bar Harbor, 207/288-3708, www.bhroute66.com, 7 A.M.–8 P.M. or so daily, $8–22), filled with '50s memorabilia and old toys, is a fun restaurant that's a real hit with kids (check out the train running around just below the ceiling). The wide-ranging menu includes sandwiches, burgers, pizza, steak, chicken, seafood, and kids' choices.

Casual Dining

You can't go wrong at **Galyn's Galley** (17 Main St., Bar Harbor, 207/288-9706, www.galynsbarharbor.com, 11:30 A.M.–10 P.M. daily, Mar.–Nov.). Once a Victorian boarding house and later a 1920s speakeasy, Galyn's has been a popular restaurant since 1986. Lots of plants, modern decor, reliable service, a great downtown location, and several indoor and outdoor dining areas contribute to the loyal clientele. The cuisine is consistently good if not outstandingly creative (dinner entrées $15–31). Reservations are advisable in midsummer.

Set back from the road behind a garden is the very popular **McKays Public House** (231 Main St., Bar Harbor, 207/288-2002, www.mckayspublichouse.com, 4:30–10 P.M. daily, $8–22), a comfortable pub with seating indoors, in small dining rooms or at the bar, or outdoors, in the garden. Classic pub fare includes Reuben sandwiches, shepherd's pie, burgers, and fish-and-chips. Fancier entrées, such as seafood risotto, are also available.

Good food at a fair price reels them into **Poor Boy's Gourmet** (300 Main St., Bar Harbor, 207/288-4148, www.poorboysgourmet.com, from 4:30 P.M. daily). Until 6 P.M. it serves an Early Bird menu with a half dozen entrées as well as another 10 all-you-can-eat pasta choices for $8.95. The price jumps just a bit after that, with most entrées running $11–15. There's even an el-cheapo lobster feast.

Casual, friendly, creative, and reliable defines **Cafe This Way** (14 Mount Desert St., Bar Harbor, 207/288-4483, www.cafethisway.com, 7–11 A.M. Tues., 7–11 A.M. and 5:30–9 P.M. Wed.–Mon., $15–25), where it's easy to make a meal out of the appetizers alone. Not a choice for quiet dining.

Chef-owner Karl Yarborough is putting **Mache Bistro** (135 Cottage St., Bar Harbor, 207/288-0447, www.machebistro.com, from 5:30 P.M. Mon.–Sat., $16–28) on the must-dine list. His interpretations of "French food with local flair" are creative, without being over the top.

Views! Views! Views! Savor the panoramic views over Bar Harbor, Frenchman Bay, and the Porcupine Islands along with breakfast or dinner ($10–33) at the **Looking Glass Restaurant** (Wonder View Inn, 50 Eden St., Bar Harbor, 207/288-5663, www.wonderviewinn.com, 7 A.M.–1 P.M. daily). It's quite casual, and there's a children's menu, too.

Ethnic and Vegetarian Fare

For Thai food, **Siam Orchard** (30 Rodick St., Bar Harbor, 207/288-9669, 11 A.M.–9 P.M. daily) gets the locals' nod. House specials run $14–18; curries and noodle dishes, such as pad Thai, $11–15. Lunch specials are around $8 and a sushi two-for-one happy hour runs 3–5 P.M. There are plenty of choices for vegetarians. Siam Orchard serves beer and wine only and is open all year.

Sharing the same building is **Gringo's** (30 Rodick St., Bar Harbor, 207/288-2326, 11 A.M.–10 P.M. daily), a Mexican hole-in-the-wall specializing in takeout burritos, wraps, homemade salsas, and smoothies, with almost everything—margaritas and beer, too—less than $8. For a real kick, don't miss the jalapeño brownies.

For "American fine dining with Latin flair," head to **Havana** (318 Main St., Bar Harbor, 207/288-2822, www.havanamaine.com, 5–10 P.M. daily May–late Oct., Wed.–Sat. the rest of the year), where the innovative Cuban-esque menu (entrées $16–35) changes frequently to take advantage of what's locally available. Inside, bright orange walls and white tablecloths set a tone that's equally festive and accomplished.

Italian with pizzazz is served in both half and full portions at **Guinness and Porcelli's** (191 Main St., Bar Harbor, 207/288-0300, www.guinnessporcellis.com, 4:30 P.M.–close daily). Pizzas, creative soups and salads, and entrées please all appetites and tastes.

Fancy to Fine Dining

Fresh, fresh, fresh seafood—that's what you'll

find at **Maggie's Restaurant** (6 Summer St., Bar Harbor, 207/288-9007, www.maggiesbarharbor.com, 5–9:30 P.M. Mon.–Sat. June–Oct.). The restaurant grew out of owner Maggie O'Neil's experiences as a fishmonger, and much of the equally fresh produce comes from Maggie's own farm. Most entrées, such as halibut with orange chive beurre blanc or bronzed salmon with ginger lime butter, run $16–24; a notable exception are the lobster crepes, which reflect market rates and may be around $30—but oh, my, are they worth it! Soft music and good service complement the dining experience.

Five miles south of Bar Harbor, in the village of Otter Creek (which itself is in the town of Mount Desert), is the inauspicious-looking **Burning Tree** (Rte. 3, Otter Creek, 207/288-9331, 5–10 P.M. Wed.–Mon. late June–early Oct., also closed Mon. after Labor Day), which is anything but nondescript inside. Chef-owners Allison Martin and Elmer Beal Jr. have created one of Mount Desert Island's best restaurants. Bright and airy, with about 16 tables crowded in three areas, it serves a casually chic crowd. Reservations are essential in summer. Specialties are imaginative seafood entrées and vegetarian dishes ($19–25). The homemade breads and desserts are delicious. At the height of summer, service can be a bit rushed and the kitchen runs out of popular entrées. Solution: Plan to eat early; it's worth it.

INFORMATION AND SERVICES

The **Bar Harbor Chamber of Commerce** (1201 Bar Harbor Rd./Rte. 3, Trenton, 207/288-5103 or 888/540-9990, www.barharbormaine.com) is open daily in summer, weekdays off-season. From late May to mid-October, the chamber usually operates a downtown branch.

Once you're on Mount Desert, if you manage to bestir yourself early enough to catch sunrise on the Cadillac summit (you won't be alone—it's a popular activity), stop in at the Chamber of Commerce office later and request an official membership card for the **Cadillac Mountain Sunrise Club** (they'll take your word for it).

Libraries

Jesup Memorial Library (34 Mount Desert St., Bar Harbor, 207/288-4245, www.jesup.lib.me.us) is open all year.

Public Restrooms

Downtown Bar Harbor has public restrooms in the Harbor Place complex at the town pier, in the municipal building (fire/police station) across from the Village Green, and on the School Street side of the athletic field, where there is RV parking. Restrooms are also at the Mount Desert Island Hospital and the International Ferry Terminal.

Parking

Make it easy on yourself, help improve the air quality, and reduce stress levels by leaving your car at your lodging (or if day-tripping, at the Bar Harbor Chamber of Commerce on Route 3 in Trenton) and taking the Island Explorer.

RVs are not allowed to park near the town pier; designated RV parking is alongside the athletic field, on Lower Main and Park Streets, about eight blocks from the center of town.

Northeast Harbor

Ever since the late 19th century, the upper crust from the City of Brotherly Love has been summering in and around Northeast Harbor. Sure, they also show up in other parts of Maine, but it's hard not to notice the preponderance of Pennsylvania license plates surrounding Northeast Harbor's elegant "cottages" mid-July–mid-August.

Actually, even though Northeast Harbor is a well-known name with special cachet, it isn't even an official township; it's a zip-coded village within the town of Mount Desert, which collects the breathtaking property taxes and doles out the municipal services.

The attractive boutiques and eateries in Northeast Harbor's small downtown area cater to a casually posh clientele, while the well-protected harbor attracts a tony crowd of yachties. For their convenience, a palm-size annual directory, *The Redbook,* discreetly lists owners' summer residences and winter addresses—but no phone numbers.

SIGHTS

Somes Sound

As you head toward Northeast Harbor on Route 198 from the northern end of Mount Desert Island, you'll begin seeing cliff-lined Somes Sound on your right. Experts disagree as to whether Somes is a true fjord, but in any case, it's a lovely chunk of real estate. The glacier-sculpted sound juts five miles into the interior of Mount Desert Island from its mouth, between Northeast and Southwest Harbors. Watch for the right-hand turn for Sargent Drive (no RVs allowed), and follow the lovely granite-lined route along the east side of the sound. Halfway along, a marker explains the geology of this spectacular natural inlet. There aren't many pullouts en route, and traffic can be fairly thick in midsummer, but don't miss it. An ideal way to appreciate Somes Sound is from the water—sign up for an excursion out of Northeast or Southwest Harbor.

Asticou Azalea Garden and Thuya Garden

If you have the slightest interest in gardens (even if you don't, for that matter), allow time for Northeast Harbor's two marvelous public gardens. Both are operated by the nonprofit Mount Desert Land and Garden Preserve (207/276-3727, www.gardenpreserve.org). If gardens are extra-high on your priority list, inquire locally about visiting the private Rockefeller garden, accessible on a very limited basis.

One of Maine's best spring showcases is the **Asticou Azalea Garden,** a 2.3-acre pocket where about 70 varieties of azaleas, rhododendrons, and laurels—many from the classic Reef Point garden of famed landscape designer Beatrix Farrand—burst into bloom. When Charles K. Savage, beloved former innkeeper

© HILARY NANGLE

Northeast Harbor's Asticou Azalea Garden is spectacular in spring, when the azaleas are in full bloom.

THE MAINE SEA COAST MISSION

Remote islands and other isolated communities along Maine's rugged coastline may still have a church, but few have a full-time minister; fewer yet have a health-care provider. Yet these communities aren't entirely shut off from either preaching or medical assistance.

Since 1905, the Maine Sea Coast Mission (127 West St., Bar Harbor, 207/288-5097 or 888/824-7258, www.seacoastmission.org), a nondenominational, nonprofit organization rooted in a Christian ministry, has offered a lifeline to these communities. The mission serves nearly 2,800 people on eight different islands, including Frenchboro, the Cranberries, Swans, and Isle au Haut, as well as others living in remote coastal locations on the mainland. Its numerous much-needed services include a Christmas program, youth programs, emergency financial assistance, food and clothing assistance, ministers to island and coastal communities, scholarships, health services, even work on fisheries management.

Many of these services are delivered via the mission's *Sunbeam V*, a 75-foot diesel boat that has no limitation on when it can travel and few on where it can travel. In winter, it even serves as an icebreaker, clearing harbors and protecting boats from ice damage.

A nurse and a minister usually travel on the *Sunbeam*. The minister may conduct services on the island, or on the boat, which also functions as a gathering place for fellowship, meals, and meetings. The minister also reaches out to those in need, marginalized, or ill, and often helps with island funerals. Onboard telemedicine equipment enables the nurse to provide much-needed health care, including screening clinics for diabetes, cholesterol, and prostate and skin cancer; and providing flu and pneumonia vaccines and tetanus shots.

During your travels in the Acadia region, you might see the *Sunbeam* homeported in Northeast Harbor or on its island rounds.

of the Asticou Inn, learned the Reef Point garden was being undone in 1956, he went into high gear to find funding and managed to rescue the azaleas and provide them with the gorgeous setting they have today, across the road and around the corner from the inn. Serenity is the key—with a Japanese sand garden, stone lanterns, granite outcrops, pink gravel paths, and a tranquil pond. Try to visit early in the season and early in the morning, to savor the effect. Blossoming occurs here from May through August, but the prime time for azaleas is roughly mid-May to mid-June. The garden is on Route 198, at the northern edge of Northeast Harbor, immediately north of the junction with Peabody Drive (Route 3). Watch for a tiny sign on the left (if you're coming from the north), marking access to the parking area. A small box suggests a $1 donation, and another box contains a garden guide ($2). Pets are not allowed in the garden. Take Island Explorer Route #5/Jordan Pond or Route #6/Brown Mountain and request a stop.

Behind a carved wooden gate on a forested hillside not far from Asticou lies an enchanted garden also designed by Charles K. Savage, and inspired by Beatrix Farrand. Special features of **Thuya Garden** are perennial borders and sculpted shrubbery. On a misty summer day, when few visitors appear, the colors are brilliant. Adjacent to the garden is **Thuya Lodge** (207/276-5130), former summer cottage of Joseph Curtis, donor of this awesome municipal park. The lodge, with an extensive botanical library and quiet rooms for reading, is open 10 A.M.–4:30 P.M. Monday–Saturday and noon–4:30 P.M. Sunday from late June to Labor Day. The garden is open 7 A.M.–7 P.M. daily. A collection box next to the front gate requests a $5 donation per adult. To reach Thuya, continue on Route 3 beyond Asticou Azalea Garden and watch for the Asticou Terraces parking area (no RVs; two-hour limit) on the right. Cross the road and climb the Asticou Terraces Trail (0.4 mile) to the garden. Or drive 0.2 mile beyond the Route 3 parking area, watching for a minuscule Thuya Garden sign on the left. Go half a mile up the steep, narrow, and curving driveway to the parking area. Or take Island Explorer Route #5/Jordan Pond and request a stop.

After you've visited Thuya Garden open the back gate, where you'll see a sign for the **Eliot Mountain Trail,** a moderately difficult (lots of exposed roots) 1.4-mile round-trip trail. Near the summit, Northeast Harbor spreads out before you. If you're here in August, sample the wild blueberries. Much of the Eliot Mountain Trail is on private land, so stay on the path and be respectful of private property.

Petite Plaisance

On Northeast Harbor's quiet South Shore Road, Petite Plaisance is a special-interest museum commemorating noted Belgian-born author and college professor Marguerite Yourcenar (pen name of Marguerite de Crayencour), the first woman elected to the prestigious Académie Française. From the early 1950s to 1987, Petite Plaisance was her home, and it's hard to believe she's no longer here; her intriguing possessions and presence fill the two-story house—of particular interest to Yourcenar devotees. Free hour-long tours of the 1st floor are given in French or English, depending on visitors' preferences. (French-speaking visitors often make pilgrimages here.) The house is open for tours daily June 15–August 31. No children under 12 are allowed. Call 207/276-3940 at least a day ahead, between 9 A.M.–4 P.M., for an appointment and directions, or write: Petite Plaisance Trust, P.O. Box 403, Northeast Harbor 04662. Yourcenar admirers should request directions to Brookside Cemetery in Somesville, seven miles away, where she is buried.

Great Harbor Maritime Museum

Annual exhibits focusing on the maritime heritage of the Mount Desert Island area are held in the small, eclectic Great Harbor Maritime Museum (124 Main St., Northeast Harbor, 207/276-5262, 10 A.M.–5 P.M. Tues.–Sat. late June to Labor Day, plus Sun. Sept.–Oct., $3), housed in the old village fire station and municipal building. ("Great Harbor" refers to the Somes Sound area—Northeast, Southwest, and Seal Harbors, as well as the Cranberry Isles.) Yachting, coastal trade, and fishing receive special emphasis. Look for the canvas rowing canoe, built in Veazie, Maine, between 1917 and 1920; it's the only one of its kind known to exist today. Special programs and exhibitions are held during the summer.

RECREATION

Excursion Boats

Northeast Harbor is the starting point for a couple of boat services headed for the **Cranberry Isles.** The vessels leave from the commercial floats at the end of the concrete municipal pier on Sea Street. (Other boats depart from Southwest Harbor, and there's also regular ferry/mail-boat service between Northeast Harbor and the Cranberries, both described later.)

The 75-foot ***Sea Princess*** (207/276-5352, www.barharborcruises.com) carries visitors as well as an Acadia National Park naturalist on a 2.5-hour morning trip around the mouth of Somes Sound and out to Little Cranberry Island (Islesford) for a 50-minute stopover. The boat leaves Northeast Harbor at 10 A.M. daily mid-May to mid-October ($25). A narrated afternoon trip departs at 1 P.M. on the same route. A scenic 1.5-hour Somes Sound cruise departs at 3:45 P.M. daily from late June to early September. The same months, two sunset cruises are offered. The three-hour sunset dinner cruise departs for the Islesford Dock Restaurant on Little Cranberry (Islesford) at 5:15 P.M. Dinner is on your own at the restaurant. A 1.5-hour sunset cruise of Somes Sound departs at 7 P.M. Cost for all tours is $20–25 adults, $15 children 5–12, $5 for children under five. Reservations are advisable for all trips, although even that provides no guarantee, since the cruises require a 15-passenger minimum.

SHOPPING

Upscale shops, galleries, and boutiques, with clothing, artworks, housewares, antiques, and antiquarian books, line both sides of Main Street, making for intriguing browsing and expensive buying (but be sure to check the sale rooms of the clothing shops for bona fide bargains). The season is short, though, with some shops open only in July and August.

One must-visit is **Shaw Contemporary Jewelry** (100 Main St., 207/276-5000 or 877/276-5001, www.shawjewelry.com). Besides the spectacular silver and gold beachstone jewelry created by Rhode Island School of Design alumnus Sam Shaw, the work of more than 100 other jewelers is displayed exquisitely. Plus there are sculptures, Asian art, and rotating art exhibits. It all leads back toward a lovely light-filled garden. Prices are in the stratosphere, but appropriately so. As one well-dressed customer was overheard sighing to her companion: "If I had only one jewelry store to go to in my entire life, this would be it." It's open year-round.

ENTERTAINMENT

Mount Desert Festival of Chamber Music

Since 1964, the Mount Desert Festival of Chamber Music (207/276-3988, www.mtdesertfestival.org) has presented concerts in the century-old Neighborhood House on Main Street at 8:15 P.M. Tuesdays mid-July–mid-August. Tickets ($25 general admission, $10 student) are available at the Neighborhood House box office on Mondays and Tuesdays during the concert season or by phone reservation.

ACCOMMODATIONS

Rates are listed for peak season.

Inns

If money's no object and an old-timey yet haute ambience appeals, spring for the **Asticou Inn** (Rte. 3, Northeast Harbor, 207/276-3344 or 800/258-3373, www.asticou.com, $235–280). Built in 1883 and refurbished periodically, the classic harbor-view inn has 31 2nd-, 3rd-, and 4th-floor rooms and suites in the main building, plus 16 rooms and suites in several more modern cottages. Rooms vary widely, from tiny to luxe, but all retain old-fashioned charm (if you love it; it'll just seem outdated if you don't). No in-room TV, phone, or air-conditioning. Facilities include a dining room, clay tennis courts, an outdoor pool, and access to the Northeast Harbor Golf Club. Packages with breakfast and dinner run $322–422 in July and August. Try to plan a late May or early June visit; you're practically on top of the Asticou Azalea Garden, and the rates are lowest, $140–215. The Asticou is a popular wedding venue, so if you're looking for a quiet weekend, check the inn's wedding schedule before you book a room.

Bed-and-Breakfasts

Less pricey and far less formal, **The Maison Suisse Inn** (144 Main St., Northeast Harbor, 207/276-5223 or 800/624-7668, www.maisonsuisse.com, $195–395) is a lovely shingle-style inn set off the street behind a rustic garden. Ten rooms and suites are in the main inn, another five in the guest cottage behind it. All have private bath, TV, and phone; some have a fireplace or porch. Breakfast is provided at a restaurant across the street.

The casual elegance of a bygone era still exists at **Grey Rock Inn** (Rte. 3/198, Northeast Harbor, summer 207/276-9360, winter 207/244-4437, www.greyrockinn.com, $185–375, mid-May–late Oct.), an antiques-filled mansion with to-die-for views over Northeast Harbor to the outer islands. Guest rooms are comfortable and large; many have fireplaces. Common rooms, most with fireplaces, flow from one to another. Trails lace the property's seven acres, which are bordered by Acadia National Park on two sides. Head out for a hike, perhaps to the summit of Norumbega Mountain, or stroll down the street to downtown Northeast Harbor. Rates include a full breakfast.

In 1888, architect Fred Savage designed the two shingle-style buildings that make up the three-story **Harbourside Inn** (Main St., Northeast Harbor, 207/276-3272, www.harboursideinn.com, $125–295, mid-June–mid-Sept.). The Sweet family has preserved the old-fashioned feel by decorating the 11 spacious rooms and three suites with antiques, yet modern amenities include some kitchenettes

© HILARY NANGLE

The classic Asticou Inn overlooks yacht-filled Northeast Harbor.

and phones. Most rooms have working fireplaces. A continental breakfast is served. Trails to Norumbega Mountain and Upper Hadlock Pond leave from the back of the property. Do note that over the years the waterfront property has been sold, so despite the inn's name only glimpses of the harbor can be seen.

Three miles from Northeast Harbor, in equally tony Seal Harbor, is a true bargain, the **Lighthouse Inn and Restaurant** (12 Main St./Rte. 3, Seal Harbor, 207/276-3958, www.lighthouseinnandrestaurant.com, $50–75). Sure, the three rooms are a bit dated and dowdy, but at these prices, who cares! All have private baths, and downstairs is a restaurant (8 A.M.–9 P.M. Mon.–Sat., to 4 P.M. Sun.), serving all meals at equally reasonable prices. It's a short walk to Seal Harbor Beach and the Seal Harbor entrance to the Park Loop Road.

Motels

Although it's overdue for an overhaul—every room has two double beds and the decor is uninspired—you can't beat the location of the **Kimball Terrace Inn** (10 Huntington Rd., Northeast Harbor, 207/276-3383 or 800/454-6225, www.kimballterraceinn.com, $175–195). The three-story motel faces the harbor, and every room has a patio or private balcony (ask for a harbor-facing room). Do bring binoculars for yacht-spotting. The motel has a pool, a restaurant serving three meals daily, and a lounge, and it is a short walk to Northeast Harbor's downtown. It is a popular wedding venue, so ask if there are any groups in-house before you book if that's a concern. The best deals are early and late season, when rates plummet, and there are some wallet-friendly packages.

FOOD

Hours listed are for peak season, early July through early September. If you're visiting at other times, call, as most restaurants are open fewer days and hours during slower periods.

Local Flavors

In the **Pine Tree Market** (121 Main St., Northeast Harbor, 207/276-3335, 7 A.M.–7 P.M. Mon.–Sat., 8 A.M.–6 P.M. Sun.), you'll find gourmet goodies, a huge wine selection, a resident butcher, fresh fish, a deli, homemade breads, pastries, sandwiches, and salads. The market offers free delivery to homes and boats.

Pop into **Full Belli Deli** (5 Sea St., Northeast Harbor, 207/276-4299, 8 A.M.–4 P.M. Mon.–Sat., to 2 P.M. Sun.) for soups, fat sandwiches, and breakfast fare.

From June well into October, the **Northeast Harbor Farmers Market** is set up each Thursday, 9 A.M.–noon, across from the Kimball Terrace Inn on Huntington Road. Look for the usuals, as well as cheeses, cider, maple syrup, breads, cookies, yarns and related fiber products, and prepared Asian foods.

Casual Dining

Tucked in a shady corner of a parking lot behind Shaw's Jewelry is a taste of the Mediterranean. **Bassa Cocina de Tapeo** (3 Old Firehouse La., Northeast Harbor, 207/276-0555, www.bassacocina.com), a perfect choice for a hot, sultry night, lets you pick and choose from a tapas menu ($6–12) or splurge on entrées ($15–35), all representing the flavors of the Mediterranean. A wine bar serves grappas, sherries, and Mediterranean wines. Dine inside or on the patio. It opens for dinner at 5:30 P.M. daily in season.

Casual yet sophisticated, **Redbird Provisions** (11 Sea St., Northeast Harbor, 207/276-3006, www.redbirdprovisions.com, 11:30 A.M.–2 P.M. and 6–9 P.M. daily) is the perfect neighborhood restaurant—if your neighbors are the yachting type. Inspired lunches and dinners ($20–35) reflecting seasonally available ingredients are served in a renovated house and on the weatherized patio.

Fine Dining

The elegant mural-lined dining room at the **Asticou Inn** (Rte. 3, 207/276-3344 or 800/258-3373, 7–9 A.M., 11:30 A.M.–2 P.M., and 6–9 P.M. daily) is open to the public for breakfast, lunch, Sunday brunch, and dinner ($22–35). Lunch is served on the harborside deck, with serene views over Northeast Harbor. Jackets and ties are advised for dinner.

INFORMATION AND SERVICES

The harborfront Chamber Information Bureau (also called the Yachtsmen's Building) of the **Mount Desert Chamber of Commerce** (18 Harbor Rd., Northeast Harbor, 207/276-5040, 8 A.M.–5 P.M. daily mid-June–mid-Oct.) covers the villages of Somesville, Northeast Harbor, Seal Harbor, Otter Creek, Pretty Marsh, Hall Quarry, and Beech Hill.

Public Restrooms

Restrooms are at the end of the building housing the Great Harbor Maritime Museum, in the town office on Sea Street, and at the harbor.

GETTING AROUND

Northeast Harbor is serviced by Route #5/Jordan Pond and Route #6/Brown Mountain of the Island Explorer bus system.

The Quiet Side

Southwest Harbor considers itself the hub of Mount Desert Island's "quiet side." In summer, its tiny downtown district is probably the busiest spot on the whole western side of the island (west of Somes Sound), but that's not saying a great deal. "Southwest" has the feel of a settled community, a year-round flavor that Bar Harbor sometimes lacks. And it competes with the best in the scenery department. The Southwest Harbor area serves as a very convenient base for exploring Acadia National Park, as well as the island's less-crowded villages and offshore Swans Island, Frenchboro, and the Cranberry Isles.

The quirky nature of the island's four town boundaries creates complications in trying to categorize various island segments. Officially, the town of Southwest Harbor includes only the villages of **Manset** and **Seawall,** but nearby is the precious (really!) hamlet of **Somesville.** The Somesville National Historic District, with its distinctive arched white footbridge, is especially appealing, but traffic gets congested here along Route 102, so rather than just rubbernecking, plan to stop and walk around.

The "quiet side" of the island becomes even more quiet as you round the southwestern edge into **Tremont,** which includes the villages of **Bernard; Bass Harbor,** home of Bass Harbor Head Light and ferry services to offshore islands; and **Seal Cove.** Tremont occupies the southwesternmost corner of Mount Desert Island. It's about as far as you can get from Bar Harbor, but the free Island Explorer bus service's Route #7/Southwest Harbor comes through here regularly.

Be sure to visit these small villages. Views are fabulous, the pace is slow, and you'll feel as if you've stumbled upon "the real Maine."

SIGHTS

Wendell Gilley Museum

In the center of Southwest Harbor, the Gilley Museum (Herrick Rd., corner of Rte. 102, Southwest Harbor, 207/244-7555, www.wendellgilleymuseum.org, 10 A.M.–4 P.M. Tues.–Sun. June–Oct., to 5 P.M. July–Aug., Fri.–Sun. in May, Nov., and Dec., $5 adults, $2 children 5–12) was established in 1981 to display the life work of local woodcarver Wendell Gilley (1904–1983), a onetime plumber who had gained a national reputation for his carvings by the time of his death. The modern, energy-efficient museum houses more than 200 of his astonishingly realistic bird specimens carved over more than 50 years. Summer exhibits also feature other wildlife artists. Many days, a local artist gives woodcarving demonstrations, and members of the local carving club often can be seen whittling away. The gift shop carries an ornithological potpourri—from books to binoculars to carving tools. Kids over eight appreciate this more than younger ones. If you're bit by the carving bug, workshops are available, ranging from 90-minute introductory lessons for adults and children ($25), offered most weekdays during the summer, to multiday classes on specific birds ($70).

Mount Desert Island Historical Society Museum

This tiny museum (Rte. 102, Somesville, 207/276-9323, 1–4 P.M. Tues.–Sat., seasonal) is adjacent to the gently curving white bridge in Somesville, so there's a good chance you're going to stop nearby, if just for a photo. In season, the heirloom garden, filled with flowering plants and herbs of the 19th and early 20th centuries, is worth a photo or two in and of itself. The one-room museum has local artifacts and memorabilia displayed in a themed exhibit that changes annually. You can purchase a walking tour guide to Somesville in the museum. If you're especially interested in history, ask about the museum's programs, which include speakers, demonstrations, and workshops. No admission fee, but donations are welcomed.

Charlotte Rhoades Park and Butterfly Garden

It's easy to miss the Charlotte Rhoades Park and Butterfly Garden (Rte. 102, Southwest Harbor, 207/244-5405), but that would be a mistake. This tiny seaside park was donated to the town in 1973, and the butterfly garden was established and is maintained entirely by volunteers. The park is seldom busy, and it's a delightful place for a picnic. A kiosk is stocked with butterfly observation sheets. The park is located on the water side of Route 102 between the Causeway Golf Club and the Seal Cove Road.

Country Store Museum

Stepping inside the former general store that's now headquarters for the Tremont Historical Society (Shore Rd., Bass Harbor, 207/244-9753, www.tremontmainehistory.us) is like stepping into the 1800s. Displays highlight the local heritage. If you're lucky, seventh-generation islander Muriel Davidson might be on duty and regale you with stories about her aunt, author Ruth Moore. You can buy copies of Moore's books here—good reads all. The museum, across from the Seafood Ketch, is open July to mid-October, but hours vary by season so call first; donations appreciated.

The Seal Cove Auto Museum

The late Richard C. Paine Jr.'s Brass Era (1905–1917) car collection, one of the largest in the country, is nicely displayed and identified in the Seal Cove Auto Museum (Pretty Marsh Rd., Rte. 102, Seal Cove, 207/244-9242, www.sealcoveautomuseum.org, 10 A.M.–5 P.M. daily late May–mid-Oct., $5 adults, $4.50 seniors, $2 children 12 and younger). All vehicles are in as-found condition; this ranges from fresh-from-the-barn to meticulously restored. It's easy for kids of any age to spend an hour here, reminiscing or fantasizing. Among the highlights are a 1907 Chadwick Touring Car and a 1910 Chadwick Racer, two of only three Chadwicks still in existence; a 1915 F.R.P., the fifth of only nine built and the only one still in existence; an original 1903 Ford Model A, the first car commercially produced by the Ford Motor Co., and a 1909 Ford Model T "Tin Lizzie," from the first year of production. The oldest car in the collection is an 1899 DeDion-Bouton, one of the earliest cars produced in the world. The museum is about six miles southwest of Somesville. Or, if you're coming from Southwest Harbor, take Route 102 north to Seal Cove Road (partly unpaved) west to the other side of Route 102 (it makes a giant loop) and go north about 1.5 miles. This is not on the Island Explorer route.

ENTERTAINMENT

Life Is a Cabaret

It's not too far to drive from Southwest Harbor to Bar Harbor for dinner and evening entertainment, but Southwest has a cabaret theater that draws customers in the reverse direction for great entertainment and so-so food: **The Deck House Restaurant and Cabaret Theater** (Great Harbor Marina, 11 Apple La., off Rte. 102, Southwest Harbor, 207/244-5044, www.thedeckhouse.com). Try to arrive for dinner by 6:30 P.M. to enjoy the spectacular harbor view and order your meal (entrées are $18–27). The table is yours for the evening for an additional $10 per person cover charge (reservations are essential in midsummer). At about 7:45 P.M., the young waitstaff, chameleonlike, unveil their other talents—singing, dancing, even storytelling and puppetry. After hearing the dozen or so numbers, you won't be surprised to learn that many Deck House staff have moved on to Broadway and beyond. The performers aren't compensated, so be prepared to leave a tip. The Deck House is open mid-June to mid-September; closed Mondays.

Repertory Theater

Somesville is home to the **Acadia Repertory Theatre** (Rte. 102, Somesville, 207/244-7260 or 888/362-7480, www.acadiarep.com, $23 adults, $18 seniors, students, and military, $10 children under 16), which has been providing first-rate professional summer stock on the stage of Somesville's antique Masonic Hall since the 1970s. Classic plays by Wilde, Neil

Simon, and even Moliere have been staples, as has the annual Agatha Christie mystery. Performances in the 144-seat hall run from late June to late August, Tuesday–Sunday at 8:15 P.M., with 2 P.M. matinees on the last Sunday of each play. Special children's plays occur Wednesday and Saturday at 10:30 A.M. in July and August. Tickets for children's theater programs are $8 adults, $5 children. (No credit cards are accepted; pay at the box office before the performance.)

Lecture Series

During July and August, the Claremont hotel (22 Claremont Rd., Southwest Harbor, 207/244-5036 or 800/244-5036, www.theclaremonthotel.com) sponsors a free weekly lecture series on Thursday evenings at 8 P.M. Past topics have ranged from Arab-Israeli peace possibilities to wildlife on Mount Desert Island.

EVENTS

During July and August, the Wednesday **Pie Sale** at the Somesville Union Meeting House is always a sellout. Go early; the doors open at 10 A.M.

In early August, the annual **Claremont Croquet Classic,** held on the grounds of the classic Claremont hotel, is open to all ages.

In September, Smuggler's Den Campground, on Route 102 in Southwest Harbor, is home to the annual **MDI Garlic Festival,** with entertainment and opportunities to savor the stinking rose, and in October the campground hosts the annual **Oktoberfest and Food Festival** (207/244-9264 or 800/423-9264, www.acadiachamber.com), a one-day celebration with crafts, food, games, music, and about two dozen Maine microbrewers presenting about 80 different brews.

SHOPPING

Southwest Harbor

Fine art of the 19th and early 20th century is the specialty at **Clark Point Gallery** (46 Clark Point Rd., Southwest Harbor, 207/244-0920, www.clarkpointgallery.com). Most works depict Maine and Mount Desert Island.

Jewelry approaches fine art at **Aylen & Son Jewelers** (332 Main St., Rte. 102, Southwest Harbor, 207/244-7369, www.peteraylen.com). For more than 25 years, Peter and Judy Aylen have been crafting and selling jewelry in 18-karat gold and sterling silver and augmenting it with fine gemstones or intriguing beads.

In the middle of Southwest Harbor's small shopping area is **Sand Castle Ocean and Nature Store** (360 Main St., Southwest Harbor, 207/244-4118), a delightful shop with a huge range of handcrafted items, most with a marine theme.

More than 50 coastal Maine artisans sell their crafts at **Flying Mountain Artisans** (28 Main St., Rte. 102, Southwest Harbor, 207/244-0404), a cooperatively owned shop with a good range of creative goods from quilts to blown glass. Also here is a gallery showing the works of more than 20 artists. Consider stopping in after a hike on Flying Mountain.

Bernard and Seal Cove

It's fun to poke around **Ravenswood** (McMullen Ave., Bass Harbor, 207/669-4287), a musty shop filled with old books, nautical gifts, model ship kits, and marvelous birds carved on site.

Stop in at **E. L. Higgins** (Bernard Rd., Bernard, 207/244-3983, www.antiquewicker.com), where in two one-time classrooms in an 1890s schoolhouse Edward Higgins has the state's best collection of antique wicker furniture, about 400 pieces at any given time.

Right next door is **Linda Fernandez Handknits** (Bernard Rd., Bernard, 207/244-7224), with beautiful hand-knit sweaters, mittens, hats, socks, Christmas stockings, and embroidered pillowcases all handcrafted by the talented and extended Fernandez family. The kids' lobster sweaters are especially cute.

When a psychic told A. Jones more than 30 years ago that she would move to an island, she thought: Wrong. Actually, the psychic was right. Continue down Bernard Road, then hang a left on Columbia Avenue to find **A. Jones Gallery** (Columbia Ave., Bernard, 207/244-5634). Inside is a double find: artworks in a variety of media and styles and a working studio in the barn; country antiques and folk-art finds in the garage.

Potters Lisbeth Faulkner and Edwin Davis can often be seen working in their studio at **Seal Cove Pottery & Gallery** (Kelleytown Rd., Seal Cove, 207/244-3602, www.sealcovepottery.com). In addition to their functional hand-thrown or hand-built pottery, they exhibit Davis's paintings as well as crafts by other island artisans.

RECREATION

Hiking

At the Southwest Harbor/Tremont Chamber of Commerce office, or at any of the area's stores, lodgings, and restaurants, pick up a free copy of the Trail Map/Hiking Guide, a very handy foldout map showing more than 20 hikes on the west side of Mount Desert Island. Trail descriptions include distance, time required, and skill levels (easy to strenuous).

Bicycle Rentals

Southwest Cycle (370 Main St., Southwest Harbor, 207/244-5856 or 800/649-5856, www.southwestcycle.com) rents bikes by the day and week and is open all year (June–Sept. hours are 8:30 A.M.–5:30 P.M. Mon.–Sat., 9:30 A.M.–4 P.M. Sun.). The staff will fix you up with maps and lots of good advice for three loops (10–30 miles) on the western side of Mount Desert. Rentals begin around $16 for a half day and $22 for a full day. The shop also rents every imaginable accessory, from baby seats to jogging strollers.

Golf

Play a quick nine at the **Causeway Club** (Fernald Point Rd., 207/244-3780), which edges the ocean. Be forewarned: It's more challenging than it looks.

Excursion Boats

ISLAND CRUISES

High praise goes to Captain Kim Strauss's Island Cruises (Little Island Marine, Shore Rd., Bass Harbor, 207/244-5785, www.bassharborcruises.com) for its narrated 3.5-hour **lunch cruise to Frenchboro.** The 49-passenger *R. L. Gott,* which Strauss built, departs at 11 A.M. daily during the summer. Kim has been navigating these waters for more than 55 years, and his experience shows not only in his boat handling, but also in his narration. Expect to pick up lots of local heritage and lore about once-thriving and now abandoned granite-quarrying and fishing communities, the sardine industry, and lobstering, and to see seals, cormorants, guillemots, and often eagles, too. The trip allows enough time on Frenchboro for a picnic (or lunch at the summertime deli on the dock) and a short village stroll, then a return through the sprinkling of islands along the 8.3-mile route. Kim also hauls a few traps and explains lobstering. He also earns major points for maneuvering the boat so that passengers on both sides get an up-close view of key sights. It's an excellent, enthralling tour for all ages. Round-trip cost is $27 adults, $17 children 11 and younger. Be sure to make reservations, and if the weather looks iffy, call ahead to confirm. Most of the trip is in sheltered water, but rough seas can put the kibosh on it. Island Cruises also does a two-hour **afternoon nature cruise** among the islands that covers the same topics but spends a bit more time at seal ledges and other spots ($23 adults, $17 children). On either trip, don't forget to bring binoculars. You'll find the Island Cruises dock by following signs to the Swans Island Ferry and turning right at the sign shortly before the state ferry dock.

FRIENDSHIP SLOOP CHARTERS

Charter a traditional Friendship sloop with **Downeast Friendship Sloop Charters** (Dysert's Great Harbor Marina, Apple Lane, Southwest Harbor, 207/266-5210, www.downeastfriendshipsloop.com). Private charters start at $125 per hour, including an appetizer; shared trips are $50 per person for two hours, $75 per person for three hours. A sunset sail is a lovely way to end a day. One of the boats used is the oldest known Friendship sloop still sailing.

DEEP-SEA FISHING

Go fishing with the **Masako Queen Fishing Company** (Beal's Wharf, Clark Point Rd., Southwest Harbor, 207/244-5385, www.masakoqueen.com, $59 adults, $39 children 5–12) aboard the 43-foot *Vagabond,* and you might return with a lobster. The boat goes 8–20 miles offshore for mackerel, bluefish, codfish, and more. All equipment is included. Dress warmly.

Boat Rentals and Lessons

Mansell Boat Rental Co. (135 Shore Rd., Manset, next to Hinckley, 207/244-5625, www.mansellboatrentals.com) rents sailboats and power boats by the day or week, including a keel day sailor for $195 per day, and a 13.6 Boston Whaler for $175 per day. Also available are sailing lessons: $195 for a two-plus-hour sail lesson cruise for two, which includes rigging and unrigging the boat; $100 per hour for private lessons, minimum two hours.

Paddling

SEA KAYAKING

On the outskirts of Southwest Harbor's downtown is **Maine State Kayak** (254 Maine St., Southwest Harbor, 207/244-9500 or 877/481-9500, www.mainestatekayak.com). Staffed with experienced, environmentally sensitive kayakers (several are Registered Maine Guides), the company offers four-hour guided trips, departing at 8:30 and 10 A.M. and 2 P.M. and a sunset tour, with a choice of half a dozen routes (depending on tides, visibility, and wind conditions). Rate is $48 per person ($44 in June and September). Most trips include island or beach breaks. Maximum group size is six tandems; minimum age is 12. Neophytes are welcome.

If you have your own boat, consider putting in at either the park's Pretty Marsh picnic area, off Route 102 in Pretty Marsh, or at the public boat launch at the end of Bartlett's Landing Road, off the Indian Point Road near the Route 102 end.

CALM-WATER PADDLING

Just west of Somesville (take the Pretty Marsh Road), and across the road from Long Pond, the largest lake on Mount Desert Island, **National Park Canoe & Kayak Rental** (145 Pretty Marsh Rd., Rte. 102, Mount Desert, 207/244-5854 or 877/378-6907, www.nationalparkcanoerental.com, mid-May–mid-Oct.) makes canoeing and kayaking a snap. Just rent the boat, carry it across the road to Pond's End, and launch it. Be sure to pack a picnic. Rates begin at $45 for a three-hour canoe rental, $24 for a solo kayak, and $52 for a tandem kayak. A do-it-yourself sunset canoe or kayak tour (from 5 P.M. to sunset) is $17 per person. Late fee is $10 per half hour. Reservations are essential in July and August.

If you've brought your own canoe (or kayak), launch it here at Pond's End and head off. It's four miles to the southern end of the lake. If the wind kicks up, skirt the shore; if it *really* kicks up from the north, don't paddle too far down the lake, as you'll have a devil of a time getting back.

Almost the entire west side of Long Pond is Acadia National Park property, so plan to picnic and swim along there; tuck into the sheltered area west of Southern Neck, a crooked finger of land that points northward from the western shore. Stay clear of private property on the east side of the lake.

ACCOMMODATIONS

Rates are listed for peak season.

Inn

When you're ready to splurge, **The Claremont** (22 Claremont Rd., Southwest Harbor, 207/244-5036 or 800/244-5036, www.theclaremonthotel.com) may well be your choice. The most popular time here is the first week in August, during the annual Claremont Croquet Classic. An elegant grande dame dressed in mustard yellow clapboard, the Claremont dominates a six-acre hilltop with stupendous views over Somes Sound. Guests have access to croquet courts, a clay tennis court, bikes, rowboats, and a library. Dating from 1884, the main building has 24 rooms, most of them refurbished yet pleasantly old-fashioned and neither fussy nor fancy. Additional rooms are in the Phillips House and Cole Cottage. Rooms in these buildings are $185–255 including buffet breakfast. Also on the premises are 14 cottages ($203–308); they can go for as high as $3,675 a week in midsummer. A hefty 15 percent service charge is added to all rates. Children are welcome. The hotel and dining room are open early June to mid-October; cottages are open late May to mid-October.

Bed-and-Breakfasts

Many of Southwest Harbor's bed-and-breakfasts are clustered downtown, along Main Street and the Clark Point Road.

Set on a corner, well back from the Clark Point Road, is **Harbour Cottage Inn** (9 Dirigo Rd., Southwest Harbor, 207/244-5738 or 888/843-3022, www.harbourcottageinn.com), appealingly revamped in 2002 when Javier Montesinos and Don Jalbert took over the reins. Built in 1870, it was the annex for the island's first hotel and housed the increasing numbers of rusticators who patronized this part of the island. It has evolved into a lovely bed-and-breakfast with eight rooms ($187–197) and three suites ($248–294), decorated in a colorful and fun cottage style. Most rooms have whirlpool baths or steam-sauna showers, some have fireplaces, and all have TV and Wi-Fi. Rates include a multicourse breakfast. Also part of Harbour Cottage is **Pier One,** which offers five weekly truly waterfront suites ($1,414–1,624), including a studio cottage. All were renovated in 2009 in a comfortable cottage style; all have kitchens, TV, and phone. Guests have private use of a 150-foot pier, and they can dock or launch canoes, kayaks, or other small boats from right outside their doors; dockage is available for larger boats. It's all within walking distance of downtown.

The linden-blossom fragrance can be intoxicating in summer at the **Lindenwood Inn** (118 Clark Point Rd., Southwest Harbor, 207/244-5335 or 800/307-5335, www.lindenwoodinn.com, $155–295). Jim King, the Australian owner, has imaginatively decorated the inn's nine rooms and poolside bungalow with artifacts from everywhere in a style that's sophisticated yet comfortable. After you hike Acadia's trails, the heated pool and hot tub are especially welcome, and after that, perhaps enjoy a drink while shooting pool or playing darts. Some rooms have harbor views.

In 2004, Ann and Charlie Bradford sold the family home that had housed their long-time bed-and-breakfast and reopened a petite version of the **Island House** (36 Freeman Ridge, Southwest Harbor, 207/244-5180, www.islandhousebb.com) in their new custom home, built atop a ridge in a quiet neighborhood about a mile from downtown. They've downsized the guest space to just two comfy rooms ($130), plus a guest living-dining room, all on one level (a great place for anyone with mobility problems, although it's not wheelchair-accessible). Anne's warm hospitality and delicious full breakfasts remain the same. The Bradfords also rent a separate two-bedroom apartment above the garage ($185), with a tiny deck offering glimpses of distant islands. The Island House is open all year.

Even glimpsed through the trees from the road, **The Birches** (46 Fernald Point Rd., Southwest Harbor, 207/244-5182, www.thebirchesbnb.com, $105–150) is appealing. A wooded drive winds down to the large home fronting the ocean, near the mouth of Somes Sound. It's just 350 yards to the Causeway Golf Club and a short walk to the Flying Mountain trailhead. Built as a summer cottage in 1916, The Birches retains that causal summer ease, right down to the stone fireplace in the living room and the croquet court on the lawn. Guest rooms are large and minimally decorated. Hosts Dick and Rocky Homer serve a full breakfast.

In Manset, adjacent to the Hinckley Yacht complex and with jaw-dropping views down Somes Sound, is **The Moorings** (133 Shore Rd., Manset, 207/244-5523 or 800/596-5523, www.mooringsinn.com, $110–195), owned and operated by the King family since 1960. The oceanfront complex is part motel, part cottage rental, and part old-fashioned bed-and-breakfast. Rooms are named after locally built sailing vessels. The motel-style rooms in the Lighthouse View Wing have refrigerators, microwaves, waterfront decks, and incredible views (spend the afternoon counting the Hinckley yachts). Also on the property or nearby are cottage units ($125–200). Bikes, canoes, and kayaks are available for guests, so you can paddle around the harbor; Mansell Boat Rental Co. is also on the premises. Dogs are permitted with permission.

When price is no object and you *really* want pampering, check into **Ann's Point Inn & Spa** (79 Anns Point Rd., Bass Harbor, 207/244-9595, www.annspointinn.com, $275–345), an oceanfront inn at the tip of Ann's Point. Each of four rooms has a king-size bed covered in luxurious linens, a gas fireplace, and all the amenities you might expect, including robes and slippers, in-room TV-DVD players, phones, Wi-Fi, CD players, and air-conditioning. Rooms are huge, and all have ocean views. If that's not enough, there's an indoor pool, hot tub, and sauna, plus afternoon hors d'oeuvres and evening sweets. All this is on two acres with 690 feet of shorefront. The inn is open year-round.

Motels and Cottages

Right smack on the harbor and just a two-minute walk from downtown is the appropriately named **Harbor View Motel & Cottages** (11 Ocean Way, Southwest Harbor, 207/244-5031 or 800/538-6463, www.harborviewmotelandcottages.com). The family-owned complex comprises motel rooms ($55–126/night, $335–805/week) spread out in two older one-story buildings and a newish three-story structure that fronts the harbor. A continental breakfast is served to motel guests from July 1 through early Sept. Also on the premises are seven housekeeping cottages with kitchenettes (weekly rentals only; $485–1,225), ranging from studios to two-bedrooms. Pets are welcome in some units.

Right across from the famed seawall and adjacent to the park is the **Seawall Motel** (566 Seawall Rd./Rte. 102A, Southwest Harbor, 207/244-9250 or 800/248-9250, www.seawallmotel.com, $110). The no-surprises two-story motel (upstairs rooms have the best views) has free Wi-Fi, in-room phones, and cable TV. A continental breakfast is included mid-May–October. Kids 12 and younger stay free. The location's excellent for bird-watchers.

Camping

On the eastern edge of Somesville, just off Route 198, at the head of Somes Sound, the **Mount Desert Campground** (516 Somes Sound Dr., Rte. 198, Somesville, 207/244-3710, www.mountdesertcampground.com, $36–49) has 152 wooded tent sites, about 45 on the water, spread out on 58 acres. Reservations are essential in midsummer—one-week minimum for waterfront sites, three days for off-water sites in July and August. (Campers book a year ahead for waterfront sites here.) This deservedly popular and low-key campground gets high marks for maintenance, noise control, and convenient tent platforms. Electrical hookups are available for $2 per night. No pets July–early September. No trailers over 20 feet. Kayak and canoe rentals available.

Built on the site of an old quarry, on a hillside descending to rocky frontage on Somes Sound, **Somes Sound View Campground** (86 Hall Quarry Rd., Mount Desert, 207/244-3890, off-season 207/244-7452, www.ssvc.info, $29–55) is among the smallest campgrounds on the island, with fewer than 60 sites, all geared to tents and vans. Facilities include hot showers (if you're camping on the lowest levels, it's a good hike up to the bathhouse), a heated pool, a boat launch, kayak and paddleboat rentals, and a fishing dock. You can swim in the sound from a rocky beach. Leashed pets are allowed. No credit cards are accepted. The campground is open from late May to mid-October. It's two miles south and east of Somesville and a mile east of Route 102.

For RVs and big rigs, **Smuggler's Den Campground** (Rte. 102, Southwest Harbor, 207/244-3944, www.smugglersdencampground.com, $31–51) is a midsized campground between Echo Lake and downtown Southwest Harbor. Facilities include a heated pool and a kiddie pool, laundry, free hot showers, lobster and ice cream sales, and entertainment. Well-behaved pets are a possibility.

FOOD

Local Flavors

Lots of goodies for picnics can be found at **Sawyer's Market** (Main St., Southwest Harbor, 207/244-7061, 5:30 A.M.–7:30 P.M. Mon.–Sat.); for wine and cheese head across the street to **Sawyer's Specialties** (Main St., Southwest Harbor, 207/244-3317), open daily.

The students at College of the Atlantic run **Beech Hill Farm** (Beech Hill Rd., Mount Desert, 207/244-5204, 8 A.M.–5 P.M. Tues.–Sat.), a five-acre MOFGA-certified organic farm that also has acres of heirloom apple trees and 65 acres of forestland. (MOFGA stands for Maine Organic Farmers and Gardeners Association.) Visit the farmstand for fresh produce as well as other organic or natural foods, such as cheeses and baked goods.

Ethnic Fare

Craving a taste of Mexico? **XYZ Restaurant** (80 Seawall Rd., Rte. 102A, Manset, 207/244-5221, 5:30–9 P.M.) specializes in the flavors of interior Mexico: Xalapa, Yucatán, and Zacatecas (hence "XYZ"). Most popular dish? *Cochinitas*—citrus-marinated pork rubbed with achiote paste (it's worthy of its reputation). Entrées are $24. The margaritas are classic—requiring, allegedly, 1,100 pounds of fresh limes each year. For dessert, try the XYZ pie. Dine inside or on the porch. Note: There's a bit of attitude here.

From the outside, it doesn't look like much, but locals know you can count on **DeMuro's Top of the Hill** (Rte. 102, Southwest Harbor, 207/244-0033, www.topofthehilldining.com, 4:30 P.M.–close daily) for a good meal at a fair price. The Italian-influenced menu has something in all price ranges ($10–25). Early-bird specials are served 4:30–6:30 P.M.

Craving authentic Asian-French fusion fare? Chiaolin and Ken Korona's **Chow Maine Cafe** (19 Clark Point Rd., Southwest Harbor, 207/699-4142, www.chow-maine.com, 11:30 A.M.–9:30 P.M. Mon.–Sat.) delivers. Plus, you can pick up both Asian meals and Pectic Seafoods prepared entrées to go. BYOB. It's adjacent to the post office.

Casual Dining

By day, **Eat-a-Pita** (326 Main St., Southwest Harbor, 207/244-4344, 8 A.M.–4 P.M. daily, to 9 P.M. Tues.–Sun.) is a casual, order-at-the-counter restaurant serving breakfast and lunch. At night it morphs into **Cafe 2,** a full-service restaurant. The dining room, furnished with old oak tables and chairs, has a funky, artsy 'tude; there's also patio seating outside and an outdoor bar (think pink flamingoes). Start the day with a Greek or Acapulco omelet. Lunch emphasizes pita sandwiches, burgers, paninis, and salads (delicious—call in advance for take-out); dinner choices ($9–26) include salads, light meals, a half-dozen pastas, and entrées.

Good food, good coffee, and good wine mix with a Mediterranean-influenced menu at **Sips** (4 Clark Point Rd., Southwest Harbor, 207/244-4550, 6:30 A.M.–9:30 P.M. daily). Small- and large-plate and tapas-style choices range $8–25; the risottos are especially good. Service can be iffy.

Earning high praise for its internationally accented fare, good service, fabulous views over the harbor, and incredible martinis is **Fiddlers' Green** (411 Main St., Southwest Harbor, 207/244-9416, www.fiddlersgreenrestaurant.com, 5:30 P.M.–close Tues.–Sun.). House specialties, such as Asian vegetable hot pot, tempura scallops, and steaks, range $16–32, but you can also make a meal of small plates, soups, and salads.

Fine Dining

The dreamy views from **Xanthus** (22 Claremont Rd., 207/244-5036 or 800/244-5036, 6–9 P.M. daily), at the Claremont hotel, descend over the lawns and croquet courts, boathouse and dock, to the water backed by mountains. It's truly a special place for an elegant meal complemented by an old-fashioned grace. Unfortunately the chefs seem to change annually, so it's hard to predict the quality; it's best to ask locally, but when it's on, it sings. Jackets not required, but gentlemen won't feel out of place wearing one, entrées $24–30. Dining-room reservations are wise in midsummer. In July and August, informal lunches and cocktails are served in the shorefront Boat House, also open to the public.

Red sky at night, diners delight. Gold walls, artwork, wood floors, and a giant hearth set a chic tone for **Red Sky** (14 Clark Point Rd., 207/244-0476, www.redskyrestaurant.com, 5:30–9 P.M. daily), one of the island's tonier restaurants. The creative fare (entrées $19–30) emphasizes fresh seafood, hand-cut meats, and local organic produce, and there's always a vegetarian choice. The restaurant is open Valentine's Day–New Year's Eve.

Seafood and Lobster in the Rough

If you have a penchant for puns—or can tune them out—head for the family-run **Seafood Ketch Restaurant** (McMullin Ave., Bass Harbor, 207/244-7463, 11 A.M.–9 P.M. daily). The corny humor begins with "Please no fishing from dining room windows or the deck" and "What foods these morsels be," and goes up (or down, depending on your perspective) from there. But there's nothing corny about the seafood roll, an interesting change from the usual lobster or crab roll. There are a few "landlubber delights," but mostly the menu has fresh seafood dishes—including the baked lobster-seafood casserole (a recipe requested by *Gourmet*). Most entrées run $19–24, but sandwiches and lighter fare are available. This is a prime family spot (with a kids' menu), where the best tables are on the flagstone patio overlooking Bass Harbor (bring bug dope). Follow signs for the Swans Island ferry terminal.

Few restaurants have as idyllic a setting as **Thurston's Lobster Pound** (Steamboat Wharf Rd., Bernard, 207/244-7600, www.thurstonslobster.com, 11 A.M.–8:30 P.M. daily), which overlooks lobster boat–filled Bass Harbor. The screened dining room practically sits in the water. Family-oriented Thurston's also has chowders, sandwiches, and terrific desserts. Beer and wine are available. Be sure to read the directions at the entrance and order before you find a table on one of two levels.

The appropriately named **Gilley's Head of the Harbor** (433 Main St., Southwest Harbor, 207/244-5222, 11 A.M.–9 P.M. daily) serves lobster and a whole lot more in a pleasant dining room, with big windows overlooking the harbor.

INFORMATION AND SERVICES

Information

Near the public parking lots and fire station (behind Sawyer's Market) is the **Southwest Harbor/Tremont Chamber of Commerce** (Village Green Way, Southwest Harbor, 207/244-9264 or 800/423-9264, www.acadiachamber.com).

Check out **Southwest Harbor Public Library** (338 Main St., Southwest Harbor, 207/244-7065, www.swhplibrary.org).

Public Restrooms

In downtown Southwest Harbor, public restrooms are at the southern end of the parking lot behind the Main Street park and near the fire station. Across Main Street, Harbor House also has a restroom, and there are portable toilets at the town docks. There's also a public restroom at the Swans Island ferry terminal.

GETTING AROUND

Southwest Harbor, Tremont, and Bass Harbor are serviced by Route #7/Southwest Harbor of the Island Explorer bus system.

Islands near Mount Desert

Sure, Mount Desert is an island, but for a sampling of real island life, you'll want to make a day trip to one of the offshore islands. Most popular are the Cranberry Isles and Swans Island, but don't overlook Frenchboro, an off-the-radar-screen gem.

CRANBERRY ISLES

The Cranberry Isles, south of Northeast and Seal Harbors, comprise Great Cranberry, Little Cranberry (called Islesford), Sutton, Baker, and Bear Islands. Islesford and Baker include property belonging to Acadia National Park. Bring a bike and explore the narrow, mostly level roads on the two largest islands (Great Cranberry and Islesford), but *remember to respect private property.* Unless you've asked permission, *do not* cut across private land to reach the shore.

The Cranberry name has been attributed to 18th-century loyalist governor Francis Bernard, who received these islands (along with all of Mount Desert) as a king's grant in 1762. Cranberry bogs (now long gone) on the two largest islands evidently caught his attention. Permanent European settlers were here in the 1760s, and there was even steamboat service by the 1820s.

Lobstering and other fishing industries are the commercial mainstay, boosted in summer by the various visitor-related pursuits. Artists and writers come for a week, a month, or longer; day-trippers spend time on Great Cranberry and Islesford.

Largest of the islands is **Great Cranberry,** with a general store, a small historical museum with café, and a gift shop, but not much else except pretty views.

The second-largest island is **Little Cranberry,** locally known as Islesford. It's easy to spend the better part of a day here exploring. Begin at **The Islesford Historical**

Big windows and a deck take in the harbor views from the Islesford Dock restaurant.

FRENCHBORO, LONG ISLAND

Since Maine has more Long Islands than anyone cares to count, most of them have other labels for easy distinction. Here's a case in point – a Long Island known universally as Frenchboro, the name of the village that wraps around Lunts Harbor. With a year-round population hovering around 70, Frenchboro has had ferry service only since 1960. Since then, the island has acquired phone service, electricity, and satellite TV, but don't expect to notice much of that when you get here. It's a very quiet place where islanders live as islanders always have – making a living from the sea and proud of it. In 1999, when more than half the island (914 acres, including 5.5 miles of shorefront) went up for sale by a private owner, an incredible fundraising effort collected nearly $3 million, allowing purchase of the land in January 2000 by the Maine Coast Heritage Trust. Some of the funding has been put toward restoration of the village's church and one-room schoolhouse; islanders and visitors will still have full access to all the acreage, and interested developers will have to look elsewhere.

Frenchboro is a delightful day trip. A good way to get a sense of the place is to take the 3.5-hour lunch cruise run by Captain Kim Strauss of **Island Cruises** (207/244-5785, www.bassharborcruises.com). For an even longer day trip to Frenchboro, plan to take the passenger ferry *R. L. Gott* during her weekly run for the Maine State Ferry Service. Each Friday from early April to late October, the *Gott* departs Bass Harbor at 8 A.M., arriving in Frenchboro at 9 A.M. The return trip to Bass Harbor is at 6 P.M., allowing nine hours on the island. The Maine State Ferry Service uses the ferry *Captain Henry Lee* (same one used on the Swans Island route) for service to Frenchboro on Wednesday, Thursday, and Sunday, but the service is only over-and-back (50 minutes each way) – no chance to explore the island.

When you go, take a picnic with you, or stop at **Lunt's Dockside Deli** (207/334-2922), open in July and August only. It's a very casual establishment – order at the window, grab a picnic table, and wait for your name to be called. Lobster rolls and fish chowder are the specialties, but there are plenty of other choices, including sandwiches, hot dogs, and even vegetable wraps. Of course, you can get lobster, too. Prices are low, the view is wonderful, and you might even get to watch lobsters being unloaded from a boat. You can also purchase treats at the Frenchboro Bakery (207/460-2099) and the Offshore Store (207/334-2943).

The **Frenchboro Historical Society Museum,** just up from the dock, has interesting old tools, other local artifacts, and a small gift shop. It's usually open afternoons from Memorial Day to Labor Day. The island has a network of maintained trails through the woods and along the shore, easy and not-so-easy; some can be squishy and some are along bouldery beachfront. The trails are rustic and most are unmarked, so proceed carefully. In the center of the island is a beaver pond. (You'll get a sketchy map on the boat, but you can also get one at the Historical Society.)

Frenchboro is the subject of *Hauling by Hand,* a fascinating, well-researched "biography" published in 1999 by eighth-generation islander Dean Lunt, now a journalist in Portland. His website (www.frenchboroonline.com) has helpful info for visiting the island; another good site is www.frenchboromaine.com.

There's a restroom above the Dockside Deli and two others near the museum. If you're captivated by the island, you can rent a harborfront cottage on the property of the Israel B. Lunt House (207/334-2973 or 207/334-2991).

In August, Frenchboro hosts its annual **Lobster Festival** (Lunt & Lunt Lobster Company, 207/334-2922), a midday meal comprised of lobster, chicken salad, hot dogs, coleslaw, homemade pies, and more, served rain or shine, with proceeds benefiting a local cause. Islanders and hundreds of visitors gather in the village for the occasion. The Maine State Ferry makes a special run that day.

Museum (207/288-3338, 9 A.M.–noon and 12:30–3:30 P.M. Mon.–Sat., 10:45 A.M.–noon and 12:30–3:30 P.M. Sun. mid-June–late Sept., free), operated by the National Park Service. The exhibits focus on local history, much of it maritime, so displays include ship models, household goods, fishing gear, and other memorabilia. Also on Islesford are public restrooms (across from the museum), a handful of galleries, and a general store. For lunch, bring a picnic or head to **The Islesford Dock** (207/244-7494, www.islesford.com/idcbusiid.html, 5–9 P.M. Mon., 11 A.M.–3 P.M. and 5–9 P.M. Tues.–Sun., late June–Labor Day), where prices are moderate, the food is home-cooked, and the views across to Acadia's mountains are incredible. If you want to spend the night, Evelyn Boxley operates the **Islesford House B&B** (207/244-9309, $125), with four rooms sharing one bath.

Getting There

Decades-old family-run **Beal and Bunker** (P.O. Box 33, Cranberry Isles 04625, 207/244-3575) provides year-round mail-boat/passenger service to the Cranberries from Northeast Harbor. The schedule makes it possible to do both islands in one day. The summer season, with more frequent trips, runs late June–Labor Day. The first boat departs Northeast Harbor's municipal pier at 7:30 A.M. Monday–Saturday; first Sunday boat is 10 A.M. The last boat for Northeast Harbor leaves Islesford at 6:30 P.M. and leaves (Great) Cranberry at 6:45 P.M. The boats do a bit of to-ing and fro-ing on the three-island route (including Sutton in summer), so be patient as they make the circuit. It's a people-watching treat. If you just did a round-trip and stayed aboard, the loop would take about 1.5 hours. Round-trip tickets (covering the whole loop, including intra-island if you want to visit both Great Cranberry and Islesford) are $24 adults, $12 children 3–11, free children under three. Bicycles are $7 round-trip. The off-season schedule operates early May through mid-June and early September through mid-October; the winter schedule runs mid-October through April. In winter, the boat company advises phoning ahead on what Mainers quaintly call "weather days."

Hop a passenger ferry to the Cranberry Isles.

The **Cranberry Cove Ferry** (upper town dock, Clark Point Rd., Southwest Harbor, 207/244-5882 or cell 207/460-1981, www.downeastwindjammer.com) operates a summertime service to the Cranberries, mid-May–mid-October, aboard the 47-passenger *Island Queen.* The ferry route begins at the upper town dock (Clark Point Road) in Southwest Harbor, with stops in Manset and Great Cranberry before reaching Islesford an hour later. (Stops at Sutton can be arranged.) In summer (mid-June–mid-September), there are six daily round-trips, with two additional evening trips Wednesday–Saturday. The first departure from Southwest Harbor is 7 A.M.; last departure from Islesford is 6 P.M. Round-trip fares are $24 adults, $16 children, $6 bicycle.

The **MDI Water Taxi** (207/244-7312), a converted lobster boat, makes frequent on-demand trips to the Cranberries.

Captain John Dwelley (207/244-5724) also operates a water-taxi service to the Cranberries. His six-passenger ***Delight*** makes the run from Northeast, Southwest, or Seal Harbor for $55–70 per trip, depending upon time of day, early June–late September. Reservations are required for trips 6–11 P.M. and 6–8 A.M. Custom cruises are available, including excursions to Baker's Island.

SWANS ISLAND

Six miles off Mount Desert Island lies scenic roughly 7,000-acre Swans Island (pop. 327), named after Colonel James Swan, who bought it and two dozen other islands as an investment in 1786. (Unfortunately the island's library, home to its historical society collection, burned to the ground in 2008.) As with the Cranberries, fishing is the year-round way of life here, with lobstering being the primary occupation. In summer, the population practically triples with the arrival of artists, writers, and other seasonal visitors. The island has no campsites, few public restrooms, and only a handful of guest rooms. Visitors who want to spend more than a day tend to rent cottages by the week.

You'll need either a bicycle or a car to get around on the island, as the ferry comes in on one side and the village center is on the other. Should you choose to bring a car, it's wise to make reservations for the ferry, especially for the return trip. Bicycling is a good way to get around, but be forewarned that the roads are narrow, lacking shoulders, and hilly in spots.

If you can be flexible, wait for a clear day, then pack a picnic and catch the first ferry (7:30 A.M.) from Bass Harbor. At the ferry office in Bass Harbor, request a Swans Island map. Keep an eye on your watch so you don't miss the last ferry (4:30 P.M.) back to Bass Harbor.

The ferry arrives in the northeast corner of the island. Head off down the main road toward Burnt Coat Harbor. (The island has three villages—Atlantic, Minturn, and Swans Island.)

Pedal or drive around to the west side of the harbor and down the peninsula to **Hockamock Head Light** (officially Burnt Coat Harbor Light). From the ferry landing, Hockamock Head is 4.5 miles. The distinctive square lighthouse, built in 1872 and now automated, sits on a rocky promontory overlooking Burnt Coat Harbor, Harbor Island, lobster-boat traffic, and crashing surf. The keeper's house is unoccupied; the grounds are great for picnics.

If it's hot, ask for directions to one of two prime island swimming spots: **Fine Sand Beach** (saltwater) or **Quarry Pond** (freshwater). Fine Sand Beach is on the west side of Toothacher Cove; you'll have to navigate about a mile of unpaved road to get there, but it's worth the trouble. Be prepared for chilly water, however. Quarry Pond is in Minturn, on the opposite side of Burnt Coat Harbor from the lighthouse. Follow the one-way loop around, and you'll see it on your right as you're rounding the far side of the loop.

Shopping options are few on Swans, but there is one worth noting. If you head left at the end of Ferry Terminal Road, you'll come to **Saturn Press** (463 Atlantic Rd., 207/526-4000), where designer Jane Goodrich and printer James Van Pernis create notecards and papers using antique letterpresses. The shop is usually open 9 A.M.–5 P.M. Monday–Friday, and the informal tours explain the letterpress process (you can usually see them in action) and visit the studios where the designs, based on the company's library of tens of thousands of graphic image ephemera, are created. Afterwards, pick up some notecards in the small shop or at least a catalog. Saturn has few retail outlets, as most of its products are carried by museums and fine paper stores.

A Swans Island summer highlight is the **Sweet Chariot Music Festival,** a three-night midweek extravaganza in early August. Windjammers arrive from Camden and Rockland, enthusiasts show up on their private boats, and the island's Oddfellows Hall is standing-room-only for three evenings of folk singing, storytelling, and impromptu hijinks. In mid-afternoon of the first two days (about 3:30 P.M.), musicians go from boat to boat in Burnt Coat Harbor, entertaining with sea chanteys. Along the route from harbor to concert, enterprising local kids peddle lemonade, homemade brownies, and kitschy craft items. It's all very festive, but definitely a "boat thing," not very convenient for anyone without waterborne transport.

Overnight accommodations are available at **The Harbor Watch Motel** (111 Minturn Rd., 207/526-4563 or 800/532-7928, www.swansisland.com, $95–120). Swans has one small, struggling grocery store, **Carrying Place Market** (Minturn Rd., 207/526-4043), plus **Island Bake Shop** (73 Ferry Terminal Rd., 207/526-4123, 9 A.M.–2 P.M. Mon.–Sat.) and **Boathouse Take-Out** (207/526-4201), clinging to a cliffside overlooking the harbor on the way to the lighthouse.

Getting There and Around

Swans Island is a six-mile 40-minute trip on the state-operated car ferry *Captain Henry Lee,* operated by the **Maine State Ferry Service** (207/244-3254, daily recorded info 800/491-4883, www.exploremaine.org). The ferry makes up to six round-trips a day, the first from Bass Harbor at 7:30 A.M. (Sunday 9 A.M.) and the last from Swans Island at 4:30 P.M. Round-trip fares are around $17.50 adults, $8.50 children 5–11; bikes are $16.50 adults, $9.50 children; vehicles are $49.50. Reservations are accepted only for vehicles (be in line at least 15 minutes before departure, or you risk forfeiting your space).

To reach the Bass Harbor ferry terminal on Mount Desert Island, follow the distinctive blue signs, marked Swans Island Ferry, along Routes 102 and 102A.

Southwest Cycle (Main St., Southwest Harbor, 207/244-5856 or 800/649-5856) rents bikes by the day and week and is open all year. It also has ferry schedules and Swans Island maps. (For the early-morning ferry, you'll need to pick up bikes the day before; be sure to reserve them if you're doing this in July or August.)

Schoodic Peninsula

Slightly more than 2,366 of Acadia National Park's acres are on the mainland Schoodic Peninsula—the rest are all on islands (including Mount Desert). World-class scenery and the relative lack of congestion, even at the height of summer, are just two reasons to sneak around to the eastern side of Frenchman Bay. Others are abundant opportunities for outdoor recreation, two scenic byways, and dozens of artists' and artisans' studios tucked throughout this region.

Still, the biggest attractions in this area are the spectacular vignettes and vistas—of offshore lighthouses, distant mountains, and close-in islands—and the unchanged villages. **Winter Harbor** (pop. 988), known best as the gateway to Schoodic, shares the area with an old-money, low-profile Philadelphia-linked summer colony on exclusive Grindstone Neck.

Gouldsboro (pop. 1,941)—including the not-to-be-missed villages of **Birch Harbor, Corea,** and **Prospect Harbor**—earned its own minor fame from Louise Dickinson Rich's 1958 book *The Peninsula,* a tribute to her summers on Corea's Cranberry Point, "a place that has stood still in time." Since 1958, change has crept into Corea, but not so as you'd notice. It's still the same quintessential lobster-fishing community, perfect for photo ops. A new section of the Maine Coastal Islands National Wildlife Reserve, the 431-acre **Corea Heath Unit,** has taken over former Navy lands along Route 195 in Corea. Plans call for developing trails, including one along the shorefront (call 207/546-2124 for updated information). In another initiative, the Frenchman Bay Conservancy is seeking to acquire the 600-acre Northern Corea Heath, across the highway, home to Grand Marsh and Grand Marsh Bay.

Between Ellsworth and Gouldsboro are **Hancock, Sullivan,** and **Sorrento.** Venture down the ocean-side back roads and you'll discover an old-timey summer colony at Hancock Point, complete with library, post office, yacht club, and tennis courts.

Meander inland to find the lakes for boating and fishing and peaks for hiking.

SCHOODIC SECTION OF ACADIA NATIONAL PARK

The Schoodic section of Acadia is much smaller, less busy, and provides fewer recreational opportunities than that on Mount Desert Island, but it's still magnificent and well worth visiting.

As with so much of Acadia's acreage on Mount Desert Island, the Schoodic section became part of the park largely because of the deft diplomacy and perseverance of George B. Dorr. No obstacle ever seemed too daunting to Dorr. In 1928, when the owners objected to donating their land to a national park tagged with the Lafayette name (geopolitics being involved at the time), Dorr even managed to obtain congressional approval for the 1929 name change to Acadia National Park—and Schoodic was part of the deal.

To reach the park boundary from Route 1 in Gouldsboro, take Route 186 south to Winter Harbor. Continue through town, heading east, and then turn right and continue to the park entrance sign, just before the bridge over Mosquito Harbor.

Lobster traps, ropes, and buoys are piled on the working wharves edging Corea's harbor.

You can also tour the park using the free Island Explorer bus, which circulates through Winter Harbor, around the Schoodic Loop, and on to Prospect Harbor, with stops along the way. It's an efficient and environmentally friendly way to go.

Perhaps one of the best ways to get to know the park is to become involved with the **Friends of Schoodic** (www.friendsofschoodic.org), which supports the park with cleanup projects, trail and building maintenance, and staffing the visitors information booth at the Gatehouse.

Schoodic Loop

The major sights of Acadia's Schoodic section lie along the six-mile one-way road that meanders counterclockwise around the tip of the Schoodic Peninsula. You'll discover official and unofficial picnic areas, hiking trailheads, offshore lighthouses, and turnouts with scenic vistas. Also named the Park Loop Road, it's best referred to as the Schoodic Loop, to distinguish it from the one on Mount Desert.

The first landmark is **Frazer Point Picnic Area,** with lovely vistas, picnic tables, and wheelchair-accessible restrooms. Other spots are fine for picnics, but this is the only official one. If you've brought bikes, leave your car here and do a counterclockwise 12.2-mile loop through the park and back to your car via Birch Harbor and Route 186. It's a fine day trip.

From the picnic area, the road becomes one-way. Unlike on the Park Loop Road on Mount Desert, no parking is allowed in the right lane. There are periodic pullouts, but not many cars can squeeze in. Despite the fact that this is far from the busiest section of Acadia, it can still be frustrating to be unable to find a space in the summer months. The best advice, therefore, is to stay in the area and do this loop early in the morning or later in the afternoon, perhaps in May or June. (The late September and early October foliage is gorgeous, but traffic *does* increase then.) While you're driving, if you see a viewpoint you like (with room to pull off), stop; it's a long way around to return.

From this side of Frenchman Bay, the vistas

© HILARY NANGLE

The Schoodic Education and Research Center, on the old Navy base on Schoodic Point, hosts lectures year-round.

SCENIC BYWAYS

This region boasts not one but two designated scenic byways: the **Schoodic National Scenic Byway,** which wraps around the peninsula, and the **Blackwoods Scenic Byway** (formerly the State Route 182 Scenic Byway), an inland blue highway cutting through the Donnell Pond Public Reserved Lands. If time permits, drive at least one of these two routes. Ideally, you'd do both, because the scenery differs greatly. Best idea yet: Connect the two via Route 1, creating a route that includes lakes and forests, mountains and fields, ocean and rocky coast. If you only have one day to explore this region, this takes in the best of it. In early to mid-October, when the foliage is at its peak, the vistas are especially stunning.

The 29-mile Schoodic National Scenic Byway stretches from Sullivan on Route 1 to Gouldsboro and then southward on Route 186 and around the Schoodic Peninsula, ending in Prospect Harbor. A detailed guide is available online at www.schoodicbyway.org. Other information is available at www.byways.org.

The 12.5-mile Blackwoods Scenic Byway meanders along State Route 182 inland of Route 1, from Franklin to Cherryfield, edging lakes and passing through small villages. You'll find access to trailheads and boat launches at Donnell Pond and Tunk Lake. Although Cherryfield is beyond the Schoodic region, it's a beautiful town to visit, filled with stately Victorian homes, and it's also the self-proclaimed wild blueberry capital of the world. Maps and information are available from www.exploremaine.com.

of Mount Desert's summits are gorgeous, behind islands sprinkled here and there.

Drive 1.6 miles from the picnic area to Raven's Head, a Thunder Hole–type cliff with sheer drops to the churning surf below (no fences, so not a good place for little ones) and fabulous views. The trail is unmarked, but there's a small pullout on the left side of the road opposite it. Be extremely careful here, stay on the path (the environment is very fragile and erosion is a major problem), and stay well away from the cliff's edge.

At 2.2 miles past the picnic area, watch for a narrow, unpaved road on the left, across from an open beach vista. It winds for a mile (keep left at the fork) up to a tiny parking circle, from which you can follow the trail (signposted Schoodic Trails) to the open ledges on 440-foot Schoodic Head. From the circle, there's already a glimpse of the view, but it gets much better. If you bear right at the fork, you'll come to a grassy parking area with access to the Alder Trail and the Schoodic Head Trail.

Continue on the Schoodic Loop Road, and hang a right onto a short two-way spur to **Schoodic Point.** Just before it is a small info center, staffed by volunteers and park rangers. It's located on the site of a former top-secret U.S. Navy base that became part of the park in 2002. The campus is now the Schoodic Education and Research Center (locally called by its acronym, SERC); occasional lectures and programs are held here.

From Schoodic Point, return to the Loop Road. Look to your right, and you'll see Little Moose Island, which can be accessed at low tide. Be careful though, and don't get stranded here. Continue to the **Blueberry Hill** parking area (about one mile from the Schoodic Point/Loop Road intersection), a moorlike setting where the low growth allows almost 180-degree views of the bay and islands. There are a few trails in this area—all eventually converging on **Schoodic Head,** the highest point on the peninsula. (Don't confuse this with Schoodic Mountain, which is well north of here.) Across the road and up the road a bit is the trailhead for the 180-foot-high **Anvil** headland.

As you continue along this stretch of road, keep your eyes peeled for eagles, which frequently soar here. There's a nest on the northern end of Rolling Island; you can see it with binoculars from some of the roadside pullouts.

GALLERY HOPPING

Artist and artisan studios and galleries are numerous, and it's easy to while away a foggy day browsing and buying. Begin by picking up copies of the *Artist Studio Tour Map*, which details and provides directions to about a dozen galleries in Franklin, Sullivan, and Hancock, and the *Schoodic Peninsula* brochure, which notes galleries and shops on the peninsula. Both are widely available and free. Hours and days of operation vary; it's best to call first if you really want to visit a gallery. Here's a sampling to get you started.

HANCOCK AND SULLIVAN

Take the Point Road 2.5 miles to find Russell and Akemi Wray's **Raven Tree Gallery** (536 Point Rd., Hancock, 207/422-8273). Russell specializes in wood sculpture, bronzes, prints, and jewelry; Akemi crafts pottery. Out front is a small sculpture gallery.

Return to Route 1 and take Eastside Road, just before the Hancock-Sullivan Bridge, and drive 1.5 miles south to **Gull Rock Pottery** (325 Eastside Rd., Hancock, 207/422-3990), where Torj and Kurt Wray (Russell's parents) have a magical waterfront setting and sculpture gallery. Inside is wheel-thrown, hand-painted dishwasher-safe pottery decorated with blue-and-white motifs representing local landscapes.

Cross the Hancock-Sullivan Bridge and then take your first left off Route 1 onto Taunton Drive to find the next three galleries. Drawing from her experiences as an oil painter and from her life in Japan, Peg McAloon creates masterful one-of-a-kind quilts at **Wildfire Run Quilt Boutique** (148 Taunton Dr., Sullivan, 207/422-3935, www.maineus.com/wildfirerun).

Nearby **Lunaform** (Cedar La., West Sullivan, 207/422-0923, www.lunaform.com) is in a class by itself. First there's the setting – the beautifully landscaped grounds surrounding an abandoned granite quarry. Then there's the realization that many of the wonderfully aesthetic garden ornaments created here look like hand-turned *pottery*, when in fact they're hand turned but made of steel-reinforced concrete. It takes a bit of zigging and zagging to get here. Go right onto Track Road; after a half mile, go left onto Cedar Lane.

Bet you can't keep from smiling at the whimsical animal sculptures and fun furniture of talented sculptor-painter Philip Barter. His work is the cornerstone of the eclectic **Barter Family Gallery** (Shore Rd., Sullivan, 207/422-3190, www.barterfamilygallery.com). But there's more: Barter's wife and seven children have put their considerable skills to work producing hooked and braided rugs, jewelry, and other craft items. Follow Taunton Road 2.5 miles from Route 1.

Continue north on Taunton Road, as it loops around Hog Bay and onto Route 200, for the next three stops. Charles and Susanne Grosjean's **Hog Bay Pottery** (245 Hog Bay Rd., Rte. 200, Franklin, 207/565-2282) is another double treat. Inside the casual, laid-back showroom are Charles's functional nature-themed pottery and Susanne's stunning handwoven rugs.

Handwoven textiles are the specialty at

From Blueberry Hill, continue 1.2 miles to a pullout for the East Trail, the shortest and most direct route to Schoodic Head. From here, it's about another mile to the park exit, in Wonsqueak Harbor. It's another two miles to the intersection with Route 186 in Birch Harbor. (If you didn't bring a picnic lunch or dinner, Bunker's Wharf Restaurant is an excellent, if a bit pricey, stop, with views of a working wharf.)

ENTERTAINMENT AND EVENTS

Winter Harbor's biggest wingding is the annual **Lobster Festival** (www.acadia-schoodic.org) the second Saturday in August. The gala daylong event includes a parade, live entertainment, lobster-boat races (a serious competition in these parts), crafts fair, games, and more crustaceans than you could ever consume.

Acadia Partners for Science and Learning

Moosetrack Studio (388 Bert Gray Rd./Rte. 200, Sullivan, 207/422-9017), where the selections vary from handwoven area rugs to shawls woven from merino wool and silk. Camilla Stege has been weaving since 1969 and her work reflects her experience and expertise.

Paul Breeden, best known for the remarkable illustrations, calligraphy, and maps he's done for *National Geographic,* Time-Life Books, and other national and international publications, displays and sells his paintings at the **Spring Woods Gallery and Willowbrook Garden** (40A Willowbrook La., Sullivan, 207/422-3007, www.springwoodsgallery.com, www.willowbrookgarden.com). Also filling the handsome modern gallery space are paintings by Ann Breeden and metal sculptures and silk scarves by the talented Breeden offspring. Be sure to allow time to meander through the sculpture garden, where there's even a playhouse for kids.

SCHOODIC PENINSULA

From Route 1, loop down to Winter Harbor and back up on Route 186 through Prospect Harbor to find these galleries.

Architectural stoneware, with a specialty in sinks, is the drawing card at **Maine Kiln Works** (115 S. Gouldsboro Rd./Hwy. 186, Gouldsboro, 207/963-5819, www.waterstonesink.com), but you'll also find functional pottery in the shop. You might also see Dan Weaver at work on the wheel in the back room.

Every piece handcrafted at **Gypsy Moose Glass Studio** (20 Williamsbrook Rd., South Gouldsboro, 207/963-2674) is made from a single glass rod, which means no two are alike. You'll find glass beads, fused-glass earrings, swan weather predictors, and much more at this working studio just off Route 186.

If you're lucky, you might catch Susan Dickson-Smith throwing a pot at **Stave Island Gallery/Proper Clay Stoneware** (Rte. 186, South Gouldsboro, 207/963-2040, www.properclay.com).

An old post office houses **Lee Art Glass** (679 S. Gouldsboro Rd./Rte. 196, Gouldsboro, 207/963-7280). Although Rod Lee has died, his works live on thanks to Wayne Tucker and Sheldon R. Bickford, who bought the business after training with Lee. The fused-glass tableware is created by taking two pieces of window glass and firing them on terra-cotta or bisque molds at 1,500°F. What makes the end result so appealing are the colors and the patterns – crocheted doilies or stencils – impressed into the glass. The almost-magical results are beautiful, delicate-looking yet functional.

Visiting the **U.S. Bells Foundry and Watering Cove Pottery** (56 W. Bay Rd., Rte. 186, Prospect Harbor, 207/963-7184, www.usbells.com) is a treat for the ears, as browsers try out the many varieties of cast-bronze bells made in the adjacent foundry by Richard Fisher. If you're lucky, he may have time to explain the process – particularly intriguing for children and a distraction from their instinctive urge to test every bell in the shop. The store also carries quilts by Dick's wife, Cindy, and wood-fired stoneware and porcelain by their daughter-in-law Liza Fisher. U.S. Bells is 0.25 mile up the hill from Prospect Harbor's post office.

(207/288-1326, www.acadiapartners.org) is working with Acadia National Park to create a scientific research center at **Schoodic Education and Research Center** (www.nps.gov/acad/serc.htm) on the old Navy base on Schoodic Point, locally called SERC. In 2007 it launched a biennial international sculpture symposium, with the aim of creating granite sculptures to place within coastal communities throughout the region. A lecture series, presented in Moore Auditorium every second Saturday evening year-round (and more often in summer), features speakers, usually researchers or nationally known experts, addressing environmental topics related to the park and its surroundings.

In 2009 local benefactor Edith Robb Dixon donated $1 million to Acadia Partners in the name of her late husband, Fritz Eugene Dixon Jr., to renovate the Rockefeller Building, the

French Norman Revival–style mansion near the SERC's entrance. Initial plans call for a welcome center on the 1st floor and executive offices and accommodations for researchers and faculty on the upper floors.

The **Pierre Monteux School for Conductors and Orchestra Musicians** (Rte. 1, Hancock, 207/422-3280, www.monteuxschool.org), a prestigious summer program founded in 1943, has achieved international renown for training dozens of national and international classical musicians. It presents two well-attended concert series starting in late June and running through July. The Wednesday series (7:30 P.M., $10 adults, $5 children) features chamber music; the Sunday concerts (5 P.M., $15 adults, $5 students) feature symphonies. An annual children's concert usually is held on a Monday (1 P.M.) in early to mid-July. All concerts are held in the school's Forest Studio.

Concerts, art classes, coffeehouses, workshops, and related activities are presented year-round by **Schoodic Arts for All** (207/963-2569, www.schoodicarts.org). Many are held at historic Hammond Hall in downtown Winter Harbor. A summer series presents monthly concerts on Friday evenings May–October. In early August, the two-week **Schoodic Arts Festival** is jam-packed with daily workshops and nightly performances for all ages.

Seeking to add more vibrancy and diversity to the peninsula's entertainment offerings and to indulge their own interests in music and the sciences, the owners of Oceanside Meadows Inn created the **Innstitute for the Arts and Sciences** (207/963-5557, www.oceaninn.com), which presents a series of Thursday-night events late June–late September, with a break during the Schoodic Arts Festival. The wide-ranging calendar includes lectures and concerts as well as art shows. Some are free, others are $10 in advance or $12 at the door.

During July, **Hancock County Friends of the Arts** (Rte. 1, East Sullivan, 207/422-3615, www.hcfafarmsteadbarn.org) presents a free entertainment series for children in a barn that Ginia Davis Wexler, a former singer, and her husband, Morris, turned into a theater in the late 1960s for just this purpose. Two shows are presented. Admission is free, but donations are much appreciated. The barn is three miles south of the Gouldsboro Post Office.

SHOPPING

Art, Books, and Antiques

Winter Harbor Antiques and Works of Hand (424–426 Main St., Winter Harbor, 207/963-2547) is a double treat: Antiques fill one building and works by local craftspeople and artists fill the other. It's across from Hammond Hall and set behind colorful well-tended gardens.

Barbara Noel makes most of the sea-glass jewelry, mobiles, and other creations at **Harbor Treasures** (358 and 368 Main St., Winter Harbor, 207/963-7086).

Here's a nifty place: **Chapter Two** (611 Corea Rd., Corea, 207/963-7269, www.chaptertwocorea.com) is home to the Corea Rug Hooking Company and Accumulated Books Gallery. Spread out in three buildings are a nice selection of used and antiquarian books, fine crafts, and Rosemary's hand-hooked rugs. Sip on tea or coffee while browsing. Yarn, rug-hooking supplies, and lessons are available. Ask Garry for info on hiking local preserve trails, and don't miss the short trail behind the shop.

Ever seen a palmara, durian jack, pangium edule, or dompaum? Even know what they are? **Coastal Antiques** (Rte. 186, Prospect Harbor, 207/963-5546) has the original nut collection from Perry's Nut House in Belfast, which pulled in tourists from around the globe until its demise. Some specimens are amazing to see. The shop, which also sells antiques, shares a building with DeMarco Realty at the intersection with the Corea Road/Route 195.

Need a good read? Duck into **Scottie's Bookhouse** (209 Rte. 1, Hancock, 207/667-6834) and choose from a wide-ranging selection of about 35,000 used books.

Food and Wine

German and Italian presses, Portuguese corks, and Maine fruit all contribute to the creation of Bob and Kathe Bartlett's award-winning dinner and dessert wines. Not ones to rest on their many laurels, in 2008 the Bartletts introduced grape wines. Founded in 1982, **Bartlett Maine Estate Winery** (175 Chicken Mill Pond Rd., Gouldsboro, 207/546-2408, 10 A.M.–5 P.M. Mon.–Sat. late May–mid-Oct.) produces more than 20,000 gallons annually in a handsome wood-and-stone building designed by the Bartletts. No tours, but you're welcome to sample the wines. Reserve wines and others of limited vintage are sold only on-premises. Bartlett's is a half mile south of Route 1 in Gouldsboro.

Organic fruit and honey wines are produced at family-operated **Shalom Orchard Organic Winery and Bed and Breakfast** (158 Eastbrook Rd., Franklin, 207/565-2312, www.shalomorchard.com). The certified-organic farm is well off the beaten path but worth a visit not only for the wines, but also for yarns, pelts, fleece, and especially the views of Frenchman Bay from the hilltop orchard. The farm also has two simple guest rooms, sharing one bath and kitchenette. A full farm breakfast is included in the $55–70 rate. Pets and kids are welcome. To find the farm, take Route 182 to Route 200/Eastbrook Road, and go 1.6 miles.

This and That

You can find just about anything at the **Winter Harbor 5 and 10** (Main St., Winter Harbor, 207/963-7927, www.winterharbor5and10.com). It's the genuine article, an old fashioned five-and-dime that's somehow still surviving in the age of Wal-Mart.

RECREATION

Preserves

The very active Frenchman Bay Conservancy (FBC, 207/422-2328, www.frenchmanbay.org) manages a number of small preserves dotting the region, and most have at least one trail providing access. The Conservancy publishes a free Short Hikes map, available locally, that provides directions to seven of these.

TIDAL FALLS PRESERVE

FBC's four-acre Tidal Falls Preserve (off Eastside Rd., Hancock) overlooks Frenchman Bay's only reversing falls (roiling water when

© HILARY NANGLE

At low tide, watch for clam diggers on the Schoodic Peninsula's tidal flats.

the tide turns). There's no longer a lobster pound, but there are still picnic tables on the lawn overlooking the falls and ledges where seals often slumber. It's an idyllic spot. Concerts and other activities are sometimes offered.

COREA HEATH

In 2008, FBC purchased 600 acres of land known as the Corea Heath, and that summer volunteers began cutting trails. "Heath" is a local word for peatland or bog, and this one is a rare coastal plateau bog, distinguished because it rises above the surrounding landscape. It's a spectacular property, with divergent ecosystems including bogs, ledges, and mixed-wood forest. Natural features include pitcher plants, sphagnum mosses, rare vascular plants, and jack pines. It's a fabulous place for bird-watching, too, and the preserve borders a section of the Maine Coastal Islands National Wildlife Refuge. Check with the Conservancy or stop into Chapter Two (611 Corea Rd., Corea, 207/963-7269, www.chaptertwocorea.com) for more info. Trail access is off the Corea Road and parking is limited.

DONNELL POND PUBLIC RESERVED LAND

More than 14,000 acres comprising remote forests, ponds and lakes, and mountains have been preserved for public access in Donnell Pond Public Reserved Land (Maine Bureau of Parks and Lands, 207/827-1818, www.parksandlands.com), north and east of Sullivan. Hikers can climb Schoodic, Black, and Caribou Mountains; paddlers and anglers have Donnell Pond, Tunk Lake, Spring River Lake, Long Pond, Round Pond, and Little Pond, among others. There are primitive campsites, too. Route 182, an official Scenic Highway, cuts right through the Donnell Pond preserve. Hunting is permitted, so take special care during hunting season.

The hiking isn't easy here, but it isn't technical, and the options are many. The interconnecting trail system takes in Schoodic Mountain, Black Mountain, and Caribou Mountain. Follow the Schoodic Mountain Loop clockwise, heading westward first. To make a day of it, pack a picnic and take a swimsuit (and don't forget a camera and binoculars for the summit views). On a brilliantly clear day, you'll see Baxter State Park's Katahdin, the peaks of Acadia National Park, and the ocean beyond. And in late July/early August, blueberries are abundant on the summit. For such rewards, this is a popular hike, so don't expect to be alone, especially on fall weekends, when the foliage colors are spectacular.

The Black Mountain ascent begins easily enough and then climbs steadily through the woods, easing off a bit before reaching bald ledges. Continue to the true summit by taking the trail past Wizard Pond. Views take in the forested lands, nearby lakes and peaks, and out to Acadia's peaks. You can piggyback it with Schoodic Mountain, using that trailhead base for both climbs. Another possibility is to add Caribou Mountain. That loop exceeds seven miles, making a full day of hiking.

Trailheads are accessible by either boat or vehicle. To reach the vehicle-access trailhead for Schoodic Mountain from Route 1 in East Sullivan, drive just over four miles northeast on Route 183 (Tunk Lake Road). Cross the Maine Central Railroad tracks and turn left at the Donnell Pond sign onto an unpaved road (marked as a jeep track on the USGS map). Go about 0.25 mile and then turn left for the parking area and trailhead for Schoodic Mountain, Black Mountain, Caribou Mountain, and a trail to Schoodic Beach. If you continue straight, you'll come to another trailhead for Black and Caribou Mountains. Water-access trailheads are at Schoodic Beach and Redman's Beach.

Bicycling

The best choices for cycling are the **Schoodic Loop** and the quiet roads of **Grindstone Neck** and **Corea.**

SeaScape Kayaking (18 E. Schoodic Dr., Birch Harbor, 207/963-5806) rents bicycles on a 24-hour basis ($20); weekly rates are available.

Paddling

Experienced sea kayakers can explore the coastline throughout this region. Canoeists can paddle the placid waters of Jones Pond on the Schoodic Peninsula. In Donnell Pond Public Reserved Land, the major water bodies are **Donnell Pond** (big enough by most gauges to be called a lake) and **Tunk** and **Spring River Lakes;** all are accessible for boats (even, alas, powerboats).

To reach the boat-launching area for Donnell Pond from Route 1 in Sullivan, take Route 200 north to Route 182. Turn right and go about 1.5 miles to a right turn just before Swan Brook. Turn and go not quite two miles to the put-in; the road is poor in spots but adequate for a regular vehicle. The Narrows, where you'll put in, is lined with summer cottages ("camps" in the Maine vernacular); keep paddling eastward to the more open part of the lake. Continue on Route 182 to find the boat launches for Tunk Lake and Spring River Lake (hand-carry only). Canoeists and kayakers can access Tunk Stream from Spring River Lake.

Still within the preserve boundaries, but farther east, you can put in a canoe at the northern end of Long Pond and paddle southward into adjoining Round Pond. In early August, Round Mountain, rising a few hundred feet from Long Pond's eastern shore, is a great spot for gathering blueberries and huckleberries. The put-in for Long Pond is on the south side of Route 182 (park well off the road), about two miles east of Tunk Lake.

OUTFITTERS AND TRIPS

Paddle around the waters of Schoodic or Flanders Bay with **SeaScape Kayaking** (18 E. Schoodic Dr., Birch Harbor, 207/963-5806). Guided three- to four-hour tours are $50 per person, including fortification: homemade blueberry scones for morning trips and blueberry–white chocolate chip cookies in the afternoon. Canoe rental for lake usage is $50 per day; kayaks are $40 double, $30 single.

Master Maine Guides Darrin Kelly and Megan Gahl are committed to sustainability and education—they not only talk the talk, they walk the walk, living off the grid in a yurt surrounded by protected lands. Their enthusiasm and knowledge come through on their trips. **Ardea EcoExpeditions** (34 Hacmatack Rd., Gouldsboro, 207/460-9731, www.ardea-ecoexpeditions.com) offers a wide range of sea kayaking options, from half- and full-day trips to camping or inn-to-inn overnights to research expeditions. A half-day coastal exploration and introduction to sea kayaking is $65; a full day of island hopping is $105, including lunch. Family trips are available ($65 adults, $55 accompanying children), as are instructional trips, a first-light sunrise tour geared to bird-watchers, and a sunset tour that can be combined with a lobster bake. Custom overnights begin at $145 per person per day. Ask about "voluntourism" research expeditions, including island inventory and monitoring and seabird surveys. Ardea donates 1 percent of sales to local nonprofits—all the more reason to choose this outfitter.

Antonio Blasi, a Registered Maine Sea Kayak and Recreational Guide, leads guided tours of Frenchman or Taunton Bay and hiking and camping expeditions through **Hancock Point Kayak Tours** (58 Point Rd., Hancock, 207/422-6854, www.hancockpointkayak.com). A three-hour paddle, including all equipment, safety and paddling demonstrations, and usually an island break, is $45. Overnight kayak camping trips are $150 per person. Antonio also leads overnight backpacking trips for $125 per person, and cross-country skiing and snowshoe tours are available in winter.

Swimming

The best freshwater swimming in the area is at **Jones Beach,** a community-owned recreation area on Jones Pond in West Gouldsboro. Here you'll find restrooms, a nice playground, picnic facilities, boat launch, swim area with a float, and a small beach. It's at the end of Recreation Road, off Route 195, which is 0.3 mile south of Route 1.

Two beach areas on Donnell Pond are also popular for swimming—**Schoodic Beach** and **Redman's Beach**—and both have picnic tables, fire rings, and pit toilets. It's a half-mile hike to Schoodic Beach from the parking lot. Redman's Beach is accessible only by boat. Other pocket beaches are also accessible by boat, and there's a rope swing (use at your own risk) by a roadside pullout for Fox Pond.

Golf

Play a nine-hole round at the **Grindstone Neck Golf Course** (Grindstone Ave., Winter Harbor, 207/963-7760, www.grindstonegolf.com), just for the dynamite scenery and for a glimpse of this exclusive late-19th-century summer enclave.

ACCOMMODATIONS

Rates noted are for peak season.

Country Inns

Le Domaine (1513 Rte. 1, Hancock, 207/422-3395 or 800/554-8498, www.ledomaine.com) has gained a five-star reputation for its restaurant, founded in 1946—long before fine dining had cachet here. But that's only part of the story. Above the restaurant is a charming five-room French country inn. The 80-acre inn property, nine miles east of Ellsworth, is virtual Provence, an oasis transplanted magically to Maine. On the garden-view balconies, or on the lawn out back, you're oblivious to the traffic whizzing by. Better yet, follow the lovely wooded trail to a quiet pond. Three guest rooms ($150) and two suites ($225) all are named after locales in Provence. Continental breakfast is included and guests receive a 10 percent discount on dinners. Alert the inn if you'll be arriving after 5:30 P.M., when the staff has to focus on dinner. The restaurant is open to the public 6–9 P.M. Tuesday–Sunday. Reservations are essential, especially in July and August.

Follow Hancock Point Road 4.8 miles south of Route 1 to the three-story, gray-blue **Crocker House Country Inn** (967 Point Rd., Hancock, 207/422-6806, www.crockerhouse.com, $110–160), Rich and Liz Malaby's antidote to Bar Harbor's summer traffic. Built as a summer hotel in 1884, the inn underwent rehabbing a century later, but it retains a decidedly old-fashioned air despite now offering Wi-Fi. Breakfast is included. Guests can relax in the common room or reserve spa time in the carriage house. One kayak and a few bicycles are available; clay tennis courts are nearby. If you're arriving by boat, request a mooring. The inn's dining room is a draw in itself.

Bed-and-Breakfasts

Overlooking the Gouldsboro Peninsula's only sandy saltwater beach, **Oceanside Meadows Inn** (Rte. 195, Corea Rd., Prospect Harbor, 207/963-5557, www.oceaninn.com, $149–209, May–mid-Oct.) is a jewel of a place on 200 acres with organic gardens, wildlife habitat, and walking trails. The elegant 1860s captain's house has seven attractive rooms, and the 1820 Shaw farmhouse next door has another seven. Breakfast is an impressive four-course event, usually featuring herbs and flowers from the inn's gardens. Energetic husband-and-wife team Ben Walter and Sonja Sundaram seem to have thought of everything—hot drinks available all day, a guest fridge, beach toys, even detailed guides to the property's trails and habitats (great for entertaining kids). As if all that weren't enough, Sonja and Ben have totally restored the 1820 timber-frame barn out back—creating the **Oceanside Meadows Innstitute for the Arts and Sciences.** Local art hangs on the walls, and, from June to September the 125-seat barn has a full schedule of concerts and lectures on natural history, Native American traditions, and more, usually on Thursday nights. Some are free, some require tickets; all require reservations. The inn's website is also a phenomenal resource on area activities. Oceanside Meadows is six miles off Route 1.

Watch lobster boats unload their catch at the dock opposite **Elsa's Inn on the Harbor** (179 Main St., Prospect Harbor, 207/963-7571, www.elsasinn.com, $115–165). Jeffrey and Cynthia Alley; their daughter, Megan; her husband, Glenn Moshier; and grandsons Andrew and Emmett have turned the home of

Jeff's mother, Elsa, into a warm and welcoming inn. The Alley family roots in the area go back more than 10 generations, so you're guaranteed to receive solid information on where to go and what to do. Every room has an ocean view, and Megan pampers guests with sumptuous linens, down duvets, terry robes, Wi-Fi, and a hearty hot breakfast. After a day exploring, settle into a rocker on the veranda and gaze over the boat-filled harbor out to Prospect Harbor Light. And afterward? Well, perhaps a lobster bake. Upon request, Megan's dad will bring over some fresh lobster and Megan will prepare a complete lobster dinner—corn on the cob, coleslaw, homemade rolls, and a seasonal dessert, all for about $25 per person, depending upon market rates.

Set well back from Route 1, **Acadia View Bed and Breakfast** (175 Rte. 1, Gouldsboro, 207/963-7457 or 866/963-7457, www.acadiaview.com, $139–169) is built on a bluff with views across Frenchman Bay to the peaks of Mount Desert and a path down to the shorefront. Pat and Jim Close built the oceanfront house as a bed-and-breakfast, opening it in 2005. The building may be new, but it's filled with antique treasures from the Closes' former life in Connecticut. Each of the four guest rooms has a private deck. The Route 1 location, while next to nothing, is convenient for everything.

Off the beaten path is Bob Travers and Barry Canner's **Black Duck Inn on Corea Harbor** (Crowley Island Rd., Corea, 207/963-2689, www.blackduck.com, $140–200, May–mid-Oct.), literally the end of the line on the Gouldsboro Peninsula. Set on 12 acres in this timeless fishing village, the bed-and-breakfast has four handsomely decorated rooms and plenty of common space. Across the way, perched on the harbor's edge, are two little seasonal cottages, one rented by the day (three-night minimum) and one by the week. The inn and Corea are geared to wanderers, readers, and anyone seeking serenity (who isn't?). Rocky outcrops dot the property and a nature trail meanders to a millpond; in early August, the blueberries are ready. If the fog socks in, the large parlor has comfortable chairs and loads of books.

Something of a categorical anomaly, **The Bluff House Inn** (Rte. 186, Gouldsboro, 207/963-7805, www.bluffinn.com, $75–130) is part motel, part hotel, part bed-and-breakfast—a seemingly successful mix in a contemporary building overlooking Frenchman Bay, on the west side of the Gouldsboro Peninsula. Verandas wrap around the 1st and 2nd floors, so bring binoculars for sighting osprey and bald eagles. Pine walls and flooring give a lodge feeling to the open 1st floor. Settle by the stone fireplace or grab a seat by the window. Breakfast is a generous continental. On Friday nights, a lobster bake is served (market rates, usually around $25). The eight 2nd-floor rooms are decorated "country" fashion, with quilts on the very comfortable beds. (In hot weather, request a corner room.) Wi-Fi is available. The inn is open all year; pet-friendly rooms are available ($15 cleaning fee).

Machias native Dottie Mace operated a bed-and-breakfast in Virginia before returning to Maine to open **Taunton River Bed & Breakfast** (19 Taunton Dr., Sullivan, 207/422-2070, www.tauntonriverbandb.com, $115–125) in a 19th-century farmhouse with river views. Rooms are carefully decorated; they're warm and inviting, formal without being stuffy. Two of the three bedrooms share a bath. It would be easy to spend the day just sitting on the porch swing, but it's an easy pedal or drive to local art galleries. The inn is just a stone's throw off Route 1, so traffic noise might bother the noise sensitive.

Sustainable living is the focus of Karen and Ed Curtis's peaceful **Three Pines Bed and Breakfast** (274 East Side Rd., Hancock, 207/460-7595, www.threepinesbandb.com, $100–125, year-round), fronting on Sullivan Harbor, just below the Reversing Falls. Their quiet off-the-grid 40-acre oceanfront organic farm faces Sullivan Harbor and is home to a llama, rare-breed chickens and sheep, ducks, and bees, as well as a large organic garden, berry bushes, an orchard, and greenhouses. Photovoltaics provide electricity; appliances are primarily propane-powered; satellite technology operates the phone, TV, and Internet systems. Two inviting guest rooms have private entrances and water views. A full vegetarian breakfast (with fresh eggs from the farm) is served. Bicycles and a canoe are available. You can walk or pedal along an abandoned railway line down to the point, and you can launch a canoe or kayak from the back—or is it the front?—yard. Children are welcome; pets are a possibility.

Innkeeper Carolyn Bucklin is determined to create the perfect bed-and-breakfast experience at **Cottage by the Sea** (38 Kilkenny Cove, Hancock, 207/422-6783, www.cottagebytheseamaine.com, $145–165, June 1–mid-Oct.). Top-quality linens, fully equipped rooms (satellite TV, irons and ironing boards, hair dryers, telephones), evening turndown service, and air-conditioning make it hard to tear yourself away from the oceanfront inn. Three rooms are available, one with a view of Kilkenny Cove. Breakfast is a multicourse affair; afternoon refreshments are served. No pets, as there is a resident dog.

Cottages

Roger and Pearl Barto, whose family roots in this region go back five generations, have four rental accommodations on their Henry's Cove oceanfront property, **Main Stay Cottages** (66 Sargent St., Winter Harbor, 207/963-2601, www.awa-web.com/stayinn, $80–115). Most unusual is the small one-bedroom Boat House, which has stood since the 1880s. It hangs over the harbor, with views to Mark Island Light, and you can hear the water gurgling below you at high tide. Other options include a very comfortable efficiency cottage, a one-bedroom cottage, a 2nd-floor suite with a private entrance, and a four-bedroom house ($250/night). All have big decks and fabulous views over the lobster boat–filled harbor; watch for the eagles that frequently soar overhead. Main Stay is on the Island Explorer bus route and just a short walk from where the Bar Harbor Ferry docks.

Also rustic, but in need of attention and charming in a sweet, old-fashioned way, are **Albee's Shorehouse Cottages** (Rte. 186, Prospect Harbor, 207/963-2336 or 800/963-2336, www.theshorehouse.com, $85–130/night, May–mid-Oct.), a cluster of 10 vintage cottages decorated with braided rugs, fresh flowers, and other homey touches. Two things make this place special: the waterfront location—and it's truly waterfront; many of the cottages are just a couple of feet from the high-tide mark—and the management. Owner Richard Rieth goes out of his way to make guests feel welcome. Pick up lobsters and say what time you want dinner, and they'll be cooked and delivered to your cottage. Richard sometimes brings home-baked sweets and other treats to cottages when he has the time and inclination. He's slowly fixing up the simple cottages, first tackling much-needed new roofs and exterior painting. Now he's beginning to turn his attention to the interiors. In peak season, cottages rent on a Saturday-to-Saturday basis, but shorter rentals are often available. Wi-Fi throughout. Dogs are welcome.

Donnell Pond Public Reserved Land

A handful of authorized, primitive campsites can be found on Tunk Lake (southwestern corner) and Donnell Pond (at Schoodic Beach and Redman's Beach), all accessible by foot or boat. Each has a table, fire ring, and nearby pit toilet. Many of the sites are lakefront. All are first-come, first-served (no fees or permits required), and are snapped up quickly on midsummer weekends. You can camp elsewhere within this public land, excepting day-use areas, but fires are not permitted in unauthorized sites.

FOOD

Local Flavors

Make a point to attend one of the many **public suppers** held throughout the summer in this area and so many other rural corners of Maine. Typically benefiting a worthy cause, these usually feature beans, chowder, or spaghetti and the serendipity of plain potluck. Everyone saves room for the homemade pies. Notices of such suppers are usually posted on public bulletin boards in country stores and in libraries, on signs in front of churches, and at other places people gather.

This area has two excellent smokehouses. Defying its name, **Sullivan Harbor Smokehouse** (Rte. 1, Hancock, 207/422-3735 or 800/422-4014, www.sullivanharborfarm.com) has moved to spacious, modern new digs in Hancock. Big interior windows allow visitors to see into the production facility and watch the action. The newer **Grindstone Neck of Maine** (311 Newman St., Rte. 186, just north of downtown Winter Harbor, 207/963-7347 or 866/831-8734, www.grindstoneneck.com) also earns high marks for its smoked salmon, shellfish, spreads, and pâtés, all made without preservatives or artificial ingredients. Also available are fresh fish, wine, and frozen foods for campers. In summer you can purchase fresh lobster and crab rolls.

Eat while you shop or vice versa at **Harbor Girl Emporium & Cafe** (4 Duck Pond Rd., Winter Harbor, 207/963-5900, 9 A.M.–9 P.M. daily), a pleasant little spot near the beginning of the Schoodic Loop. Inside are Prospect Harbor Soap Co. products and works by local crafters, as well as a menu ranging from pizza to lobster.

Pick up veggies, meats, eggs, cheeses, and handcrafted fiber products as well as jams, preserves, and baked goods at the **Winter Harbor Farmers Market** (parking lot, corner Newman St. and Rte. 186, Winter Harbor, 9 A.M.–noon Tues. late June–early Sept.).

Once a true old-fashioned country store with a classic traditional soda fountain and penny candy, **Gerrish's Store** (352 Main St., Winter Harbor, 207/963-6100, 7 A.M.–7 P.M. daily) has undergone many changes in recent years. It seems to come under new management every summer. In its latest incarnations it's been more of an upscale bakery and deli spot with espresso and ice cream, too.

Craving curry? Call in your order 24 hours in advance, and **Tandoor Downeast** (119 Eastbrook Rd., Franklin, 207/565-3598, www.tandoordowneast.com, 5–8 P.M. Mon.–Fri., 1–8 P.M. Sat.–Sun.) will prepare authentic Indian cuisine for you to take away. Chef Gunjan Gilbert's menu is extensive, and prices are reasonable, with most choices $6–8. Or take your chances and simply stop by and choose from whatever's available. If you have a cottage, in-house preparation—they come and cook in your kitchen—is available. A selection is usually also available at the Winter Harbor Farmers Market. In 2009, Tandoor began offering sit-down dinners at the Franklin Veteran's Club once a week; call for details.

From India, step into Italy at Buzzy Gioia's **Maple Knoll Pizza** (132 Blackswoods Rd./Rte. 182, Franklin, 207/565-2068, 2–8 P.M. Wed.–Sun.), on the eastern edge of "intown" Franklin. Buzzy draws on his Italian heritage—his parents came from the Old Country—to craft authentic pizzas, submarine sandwiches, and calzones.

Family Favorites

The best place for grub and gossip in Winter Harbor is **Chase's Restaurant** (193 Main St., Winter Harbor, 207/963-7171, 7 A.M.–8 P.M. daily, to 2 P.M. Sun.), a seasoned no-frills booth-and-counter operation that turns out first-rate fish chowder, fries, onion rings, wraps, home-style dinners, and downright cheap breakfasts.

In "downtown" Prospect Harbor, the **Downeast Deli** (at the corner of Rtes. 186 and 195, Prospect Harbor, 207/963-2700, 11 A.M.–8 P.M. Mon.–Sat.) will fix you right up with hot or cold hoagies, deli-style sandwiches, and good pizza with a wide array of mix-and-match choices. The biggest seller is the homemade ice cream sandwich.

Don't be put off by the lobster "sculpture" outside **Ruth & Wimpy's Kitchen** (792 Rte. 1, Hancock, 207/422-3723, www.ruthandwimpys.com, 11 A.M.–9 P.M. Mon.–Sat.); you'll probably see a crowd as well. This family-fare standby serves hefty sandwiches, lobster prepared 30 ways, pizza, pasta, and steak. Prices begin at less than $3 for a cheeseburger and climb to about $25 for a twin lobster dinner. Locals praise the lobster roll as the cheapest and best around. Antique license plates and collections of miniature cars and trucks accent the interior. It's five miles east of Ellsworth, close to the Hancock Point turnoff.

Good food served by friendly folks is what pulls the locals into **Chester Pike's Galley** (2336 Rte. 1, Sullivan, 207/422-8200, 6 A.M.–2 P.M. Tues.–Thurs., 6 A.M.–2 P.M. and 4:30–8:30 P.M. Fri. and Sat., 7 A.M.–2 P.M. Sun., $6–15). The prices are low, the portions big. If you're on a diet, don't even *look* at the glass case filled with fresh-baked pies, cakes, and cookies. Go early if you want to snag one of the homemade doughnuts (and order dessert first). It's also open Friday nights for a fish fry with free seconds, and Saturday nights for prime rib.

Here's a surprise: You can't get much farther from Mexico than coastal Maine and still be in the States, but **The Mexican Restaurant** (1166 Rte. 1, Hancock, 207/422-3723, 8 A.M.–9 P.M. daily, closed Dec.) has earned a reputation for being a hot spot for authentic Mexican and Central American fare. Originally in Harrington, where it catered to the region's migrant blueberry pickers, this multi-generation family operation now shares a huge log building with a motorcycle shop. Everything's made on the premises, even the tortilla chips. The interior is bright and cheerful, and there also are tables on the porch and a few picnic tables on the lawn. Almost everything on the menu is $3–10, and the choices are plentiful. BYOB.

Casual Dining

The Fisherman's Inn (7 Newman St., Rte. 186, Winter Harbor, 207/963-5585, 11:30 A.M.–2 P.M. and 4:30–9 P.M. Mon.–Sat., 10 A.M.–2 P.M. and 4:30–9 P.M. Sun., late May–mid-Oct.) has been an institution in these parts since 1947. Kathy Johnson runs the front of the house; her husband, Carl, is the master in the kitchen. He's also the brains behind Grindstone Neck of Maine, the smoked seafood operation just up the road, and diners are welcomed with a sample of smoked salmon spread and a cheese spread. That's followed up with Carl's focaccia bread and the house dipping sauce, a tasty blend of romano cheese, fresh garlic, red pepper, and parsley with olive oil. And that all comes before any appetizers. Seafood is the specialty here, and there's a good chance that the guy at the neighboring booth caught your lobster or fish. Asian influences are evident, too. Entrée range is $17–28, and some dishes can top that given seasonal market rates, but early-dining specials, usually around $13, are available 4:30–5:30 P.M. A three-course Sunday brunch is $15.

It's easy to miss **Chipper's** (Rte. 1, Hancock, 207/422-8238, 5–9 P.M. Tues.–Sun.), a simple Cape-style building hard by Route 1 (that's "very close to" Route 1 in Maine lingo), but that would be a mistake, as Chipper Butterwick definitely knows his way around the kitchen. The wide-ranging menu includes rack of lamb and even chateaubriand, but the emphasis is on seafood; the crab cakes earn rave reviews. Meals include a sampling of tasty haddock chowder and a salad, but save room for the homemade ice cream for dessert. Entrées are in the $16–30 range, but some appetizer-salad combos provide budget options.

Fine Dining

Le Domaine (1513 Rte. 1, Hancock, 207/422-3395 or 800/554-8498, www.ledomaine.com, 6–9 P.M. Tues.–Sun. mid-June–mid-Oct. and 10:30 A.M.–1:30 P.M. Sun. mid-June–early Oct.) has gained a five-star reputation for *très* French fare, an excellent wine cellar, and lovely Provençal decor. Reservations are essential, especially in July and August. Opt for the five-course fixed-price menu for $35; otherwise the tab may dent your budget (entrées $27–32), but stack that up against plane fare to France.

The unpretentious dining rooms at the **Crocker House Country Inn** (967 Point Rd., Hancock Point, 207/422-6806, www.crockerhouse.com, 5:30–9 P.M. daily) provide a setting for well-prepared Continental fare with flair, crafted from fresh and local ingredients (entrées $22–32); reservations are essential as this is one of the area's most consistent and popular dining spots. The dining room is open daily May 1–October 31 and Friday–Sunday in April, November, and December.

INFORMATION AND SERVICES

For advance information about eastern Hancock County, contact the **Schoodic Peninsula Chamber of Commerce** (P207/963-7658, www.acadia-schoodic.org).

To plan ahead, see the Acadia website (www.nps.gov/acad), where you can download a Schoodic map.

Libraries

Check out **Dorcas Library** (Rte. 186, Prospect Harbor, 207/963-4027, www.dorcas.lib.me.us) or **Winter Harbor Public Library** (18 Chapel La., Winter Harbor, 207/963-7556, www.winterharbor.lib.me.us), in the 1888 beach stone and fieldstone Channing Chapel.

The inviting octagonal **Hancock Point Library** (Hancock Point Rd., Hancock Point, 207/422-6400, summer only, call for hours) was formed in 1899. More than a library, it's a center for village activities. Check the bulletin boards by the entrance to find out what's happening when.

GETTING AROUND

The passenger-only **Bar Harbor Ferry** (207/288-2984, www.barharborferry.com, round-trip $29.50 adults, $19.50 children, $6 bike) operates five-times daily late June–late September and coordinates with the free **Island Explorer** (www.exploreacadia.com) bus's summertime Schoodic route, making a super car-free excursion in either direction.

THE DOWN EAST COAST

The term "Down East" is rooted in the direction the wind blows—the prevailing southwest wind that powered 19th-century sailing vessels along this rugged coastline. But to be truly Down East, in the minds of most Mainers, you have to be physically here, in Washington County—a stunning landscape of waterways, forests, blueberry barrens, rocky shoreline dotted with islands and lighthouses, and independent pocket-size communities, many still dependent upon fishing or lobstering for their economies.

At one time, *most* of the Maine coast used to be as underdeveloped as this part of it. You can set your clock back a generation or two while you're here; you'll find no giant malls, only a couple of fast-food joints, and two—count 'em—traffic lights. While there are a handful of restaurants offering fine dining, for the most part your choices are limited to family-style restaurants specializing in home cooking with an emphasis on fresh (usually fried) seafood and lobster rolls. Nor will you find grand resorts or even not-so-grand hotels. Motels, tourist cabins, and small inns and bed-and-breakfasts dot the region. The upside is that prices, too, are a generation removed. If you're searching for the Maine of your memories or your imagination, this is it.

When eastern Hancock County flows into western Washington County, you're on the Down East Coast (sometimes called the Sunrise Coast). From Steuben eastward to Jonesport, Machias, and Lubec—then "around the corner" to Eastport, and Calais—Washington County is twice the size of Rhode Island, covers

HIGHLIGHTS

Maine Coastal Islands National Wildlife Refuge: More than 300 birds have been sighted at Petit Manan Point, but even if you're not a bird-watcher, come for the hiking and, in August, the blueberries (page 370).

Great Wass Island Preserve: The finest natural treasure in this part of Maine is the Great Wass Archipelago, partly owned by the Nature Conservancy, with opportunities for hiking and bird-watching (page 376).

Machias Seal Island Puffin Tour: Excursion boats depart from Jonesport and Cutler for Machias Seal Island, home to Atlantic puffins (the clowns of the sea), as well as razorbill auks, Arctic terns, and common murres (pages 376 and 385).

West Quoddy Head State Park: This candy-striped lighthouse is a Maine Coast icon and even a short hike along the paths edging the cliffs reaps big rewards (page 387).

Roosevelt Campobello International Park: Make it an international vacation by venturing over to this New Brunswick park, home to the Roosevelt Cottage and miles of hiking trails, jointly managed by the United States and Canada (page 394).

Shackford Head State Park: The reward for this easy hike are panoramic views over Cobscook Bay, from Eastport to Campobello (page 400).

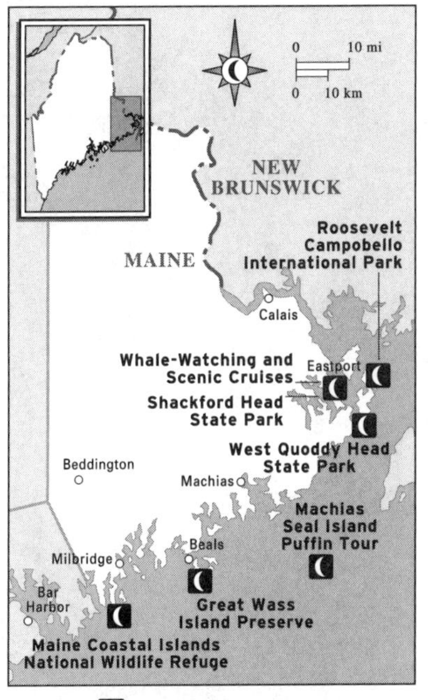

LOOK FOR ☾ TO FIND RECOMMENDED SIGHTS, ACTIVITIES, DINING, AND LODGING.

Whale-Watching and Scenic Cruises: Cruise into Passamaquoddy Bay, pass the Old Sow Whirlpool, and ogle seabirds and whales (page 403).

2,528 square miles, has about 35,000 residents, and stakes a claim as the first U.S. real estate to see the morning sun. The region also includes handfuls of offshore islands—some accessible by ferry, charter boat, or private vessels. (Some, with sensitive bird-nesting sites, are off-limits during the summer.) At the uppermost point of the coast, and conveniently linked to Lubec by a bridge, New Brunswick's Campobello Island is a popular day-trip destination—the locale of Franklin D. Roosevelt's summer retreat. Other attractions in this area include festivals, concert series, art and antiques galleries, lighthouses, two Native American reservations, and the great outdoors for hiking, biking, birding, sea kayaking, whale-watching, camping, swimming, and fishing. Hook inland to Grand Lake Stream to find a remote, wild land of lakes famed for fishing and old-fashioned family-style summer vacations.

One of the Down East Coast's millennial buzzwords has been eco-tourism, and local conservation organizations and chambers of commerce have targeted and welcomed visitors

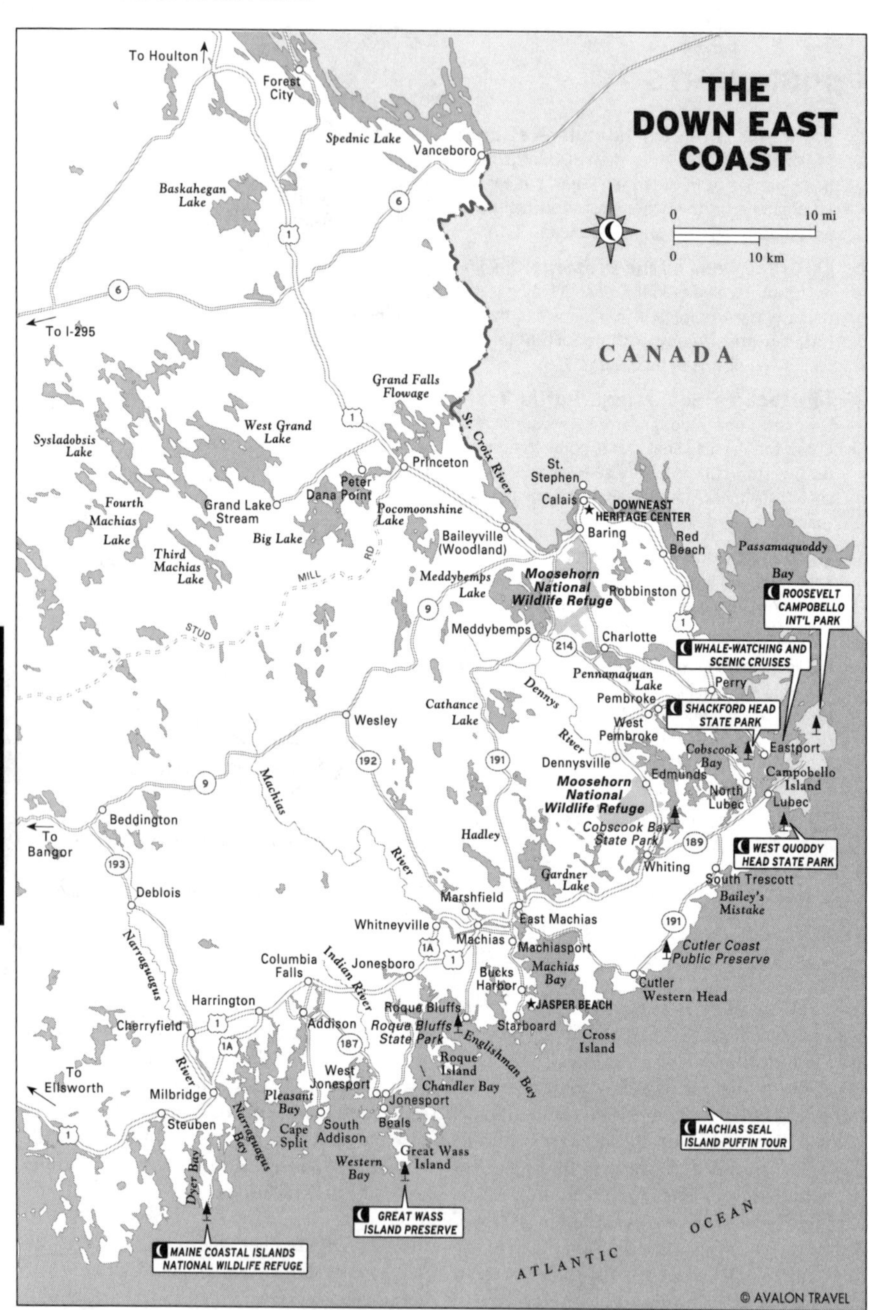
THE DOWN EAST COAST
0 10 mi
0 10 km
CANADA
To Houlton
Forest City
Spednic Lake
Vanceboro
Baskahegan Lake
To I-295
Grand Falls Flowage
West Grand Lake
Sysladobsis Lake
Princeton
Peter Dana Point
Fourth Machias Lake
Grand Lake Stream
Third Machias Lake
Big Lake
Pocomoonshine Lake
Baileyville (Woodland)
St. Croix River
St. Stephen
Calais
DOWNEAST HERITAGE CENTER
Baring
Red Beach
Passamaquoddy Bay
MILL RD
STUD
Meddybemps Lake
Moosehorn National Wildlife Refuge
Robbinston
ROOSEVELT CAMPOBELLO INT'L PARK
Meddybemps
Charlotte
WHALE-WATCHING AND SCENIC CRUISES
Dennys River
Pennamaquan Lake
Perry
Pembroke
SHACKFORD HEAD STATE PARK
Cathance Lake
Wesley
West Pembroke
Cobscook Bay
Eastport
Dennysville
Campobello Island
Edmunds
Moosehorn National Wildlife Refuge
North Lubec
Lubec
Machias River
Beddington
To Bangor
Hadley
Cobscook Bay State Park
WEST QUODDY HEAD STATE PARK
Whiting
Deblois
Gardner Lake
South Trescott
Bailey's Mistake
Marshfield
East Machias
Whitneyville
Machias
Machiasport
Cutler Coast Public Preserve
Narraguagus River
Columbia Falls
Indian River
Jonesboro
Bucks Harbor
Machias Bay
Cutler
Western Head
Harrington
JASPER BEACH
Roque Bluffs
Cherryfield
Addison
Roque Bluffs State Park
Starboard
Englishman Bay
Cross Island
Roque Island
To Ellsworth
West Jonesport
Chandler Bay
Milbridge
Pleasant Bay
Jonesport
Narraguagus Bay
Steuben
Cape Split
South Addison
Beals
MACHIAS SEAL ISLAND PUFFIN TOUR
Dyer Bay
Western Bay
Great Wass Island
GREAT WASS ISLAND PRESERVE
MAINE COASTAL ISLANDS NATIONAL WILDLIFE REFUGE
ATLANTIC OCEAN
© AVALON TRAVEL

willing to be careful of the fragile ecosystems here—visitors who will contribute to the economy while respecting the natural resources and leaving them untrammeled, visitors who don't cross the fine line between light use and overuse. Low-impact tourism is essential for this area. However, outfitters and canoe-, kayak-, and bicycle-rental outlets are few and far between.

One natural phenomenon no visitor can affect is the tide—the inexorable ebb and flow, predictably in and predictably out. If you're not used to it, even the 6- to 10-foot tidal ranges of southern Maine may surprise you. But along this coastline, the tides are astonishing—as much as 28 feet difference in water level within six hours. Old-timers tell stories of big money lost betting on horses racing the fast-moving tides.

Another surprise to visitors may be how early the sun rises—and sets—on the Sunrise Coast. Keep in mind that if you cross into Canada in either Lubec or Calais, you enter Atlantic time, and you'll need to set your clock ahead one hour.

Yet another distinctive natural feature of Washington County is its blueberry barrens (fields). Depending on the time of year, the fields will be black (torched by growers to jump-start the crop), blue (ready for harvest), or maroon (fall foliage, fabulous for photography). In early summer, a million rented bees set to work pollinating the blossoms. By August, when a blue haze forms over the knee-high shrubs, bent-over bodies use old-fashioned wooden rakes to harvest the ripe berries. It's backbreaking work, but the employment lines usually form quickly when newspaper ads announce the advent of the annual harvest.

One bit of advice you might not receive from the tourism people is that warm clothing is essential in this corner of Maine. It may be nicknamed the Sunrise Coast, but it also gets plenty of fog, rain, and cool temperatures. Temperatures tend to be warmer, and the fog diminishes, as you head toward the inland parts of the county, but you can *never* count on that. Mother Nature is an accomplished curveball pitcher, and el Niño and la Niña periodically provide an assist.

PLANNING YOUR TIME

Down East Maine is not for those in a hurry. Traffic ambles along. Towns are few and far between. Nature is the biggest calling card here, and to appreciate it you'll need time to hike, bike, canoe, sea kayak, or take an excursion boat. Although Route 1 follows the coast in general, it's often miles from the water. You'll want to ramble down the peninsulas to explore the seaside villages, see lighthouses, or hike in parks and preserves, and perhaps wander inland to the unspoiled lakes. You'll need at least three days to begin to cover the territory, ideally five days or longer if you want to really explore it.

Milbridge

The pace begins to slow a bit by the time you've left Hancock County and entered western Washington County, the beginning of the Down East Coast. In this little pocket are the towns of Steuben, Milbridge, Cherryfield, and Harrington.

Nowadays life can be tough here, where once great wooden ships slid down the ways and brought prosperity and trade to shippers, builders, and barons of the timber industry, of which Cherryfield's stunning houses are evidence enough. The barons now control the blueberry fields, covering much of the inland area of western Washington County and annually shipping millions of pounds of blueberries out of headquarters in Milbridge (pop. 1,330) and Cherryfield (pop. 1,200). The big names here are Jasper Wyman and Sons and Cherryfield Foods.

Milbridge straddles Route 1 and the Narraguagus River (Nar-ra-GWAY-gus, a Native American name meaning "above the boggy place"), once the state's premier source of Atlantic salmon. Cherryfield is at the tidal limit of the Narraguagus. Even though Route 1A trims maybe three miles off the trip from Milbridge to Harrington (pop. 900), resist the urge to take it. Take Route 1 from Milbridge to Cherryfield—the Narraguagus Highway—and then continue to Harrington. You just shouldn't miss Cherryfield.

Steuben's claim to fame is the Petit Manan section of the Maine Coastal Islands National Wildlife Refuge.

SIGHTS

Maine Coastal Islands National Wildlife Refuge

Occupying a 2,166-acre peninsula in Steuben with 10 miles of rocky shoreline (and three offshore islands) is the refuge's outstandingly scenic Petit Manan Point Division (Pigeon Hill Rd., Steuben, 207/546-2124, www.fws.gov/northeast/mainecoastal). The remote location means it sees only about 15,000 visitors a year, most of those likely bird-watchers, as more than 300 different birds have been sighted here. The refuge's primary focus is restoring colonies of nesting seabirds. Among the other natural highlights here are stands of jack pine, coastal raised peatlands, blueberry barrens, fresh- and saltwater marshes, granite shores, and cobble beaches. When asking directions locally, you might hear it called 'tit Manan.

The moderately easy four-mile round-trip Birch Point Trail and easy 1.5-mile round-trip Hollingsworth or Shore Trail provide splendid views and opportunities to spot wildlife along the shore and in the fields, forests, and marshland. The Hollingsworth Trail, leading you to the shoreline, is the best. On clear days, you can see the 123-foot lighthouse on Petit Manan Island, 2.5 miles offshore. The Birch Point Trail heads through blueberry fields to Dyer Bay and loops by the waterfront, with much of the trail passing through woods.

From Route 1, on the east side of Steuben, take Pigeon Hill Road. Six miles down is the first parking lot, for the Birch Point Trail; another half mile takes you to the parking area for the Hollingsworth Trail; space is limited at both parking areas. If you arrive in August, help yourself to blueberries. The refuge is open sunrise–sunset daily all year; cross-country skiing is permitted in winter.

Milbridge Historical Society Museum

A group of energetic residents worked tirelessly to establish the Milbridge Historical Society Museum (S. Main St., Milbridge, 207/546-4471, www.milbridgehistoricalsociety.org, 1–4 P.M. Sat.–Sun. June–Sept. and also Tues. July–Aug., donations accepted). Displays in the large exhibit room focus on Milbridge's essential role in the shipbuilding trade, but kids will enjoy such oddities as an amputation knife used by a local doctor and a re-created country kitchen.

Scenic Fall-Foliage Routes

In fall—roughly early September–early October in this part of Maine—the postharvest blueberry fields take on brilliant scarlet hues, then maroon. They're gorgeous. The best barren-viewing road is Route 193 between Cherryfield and Beddington, via Deblois, the link between Routes 1 and 9—a 21-mile stretch of granite outcrops, pine windscreens, and fiery-red fields.

Cherryfield Historic District

Imagine a little town this far Down East having a 75-acre National Register Historic District with 52 architecturally significant buildings. If architecture appeals, don't miss Cherryfield. The **Cherryfield-Narraguagus Historical Society** (88 River Rd., Cherryfield, 207/546-2076, www.cherryfieldhistorical.com, 1–4 P.M. Sat. in summer) has produced a free brochure-map, *Guide to the Cherryfield Historic District,* which you can download. Architectural styles included on the route are Greek Revival, Italianate, Queen Anne, Colonial Revival, Second Empire, Federal, and Gothic Revival—dating from 1803 to 1940, with most being late 19th century. Especially impressive for such a small town are the Second Empire–style homes.

© TOM NANGLE

Cherryfield's National Register Historic District has 52 architecturally significant buildings.

ENTERTAINMENT AND EVENTS

The biggest event in this end of Washington County, and even beyond, is the **Milbridge Anniversary Celebration,** the last weekend in July, drawing hundreds of visitors. The Saturday-afternoon highlight is the codfish relay race—hilarious enough to have been featured in *Sports Illustrated* and on national television. The four-member teams, clad in slickers and hip boots, *really do* hand off a greased cod instead of the usual baton. Race rules specify that runners must be "reasonably sober" and not carry the codfish between their teeth or legs. Also on the schedule are blueberry pancake breakfasts, a fun parade, kids' games, auction, dance, beano and cribbage tournaments, craft booths, and a lobster bake. You have to be there. The relay race has been going since the mid-1980s; the festival has been going for a century and a half.

Check locally for the concert schedule of the **Cherryfield Band,** an impressive community group with about three dozen enthusiastic members. They're in demand May–December, but best of all are their concerts, usually Tuesday evenings, in the lovely downtown bandstand overlooking the Narraguagus River.

The Humboldt Field Research Institute (59 Eagle Hill Rd., Steuben, 207/546-2821, www.eaglehill.us, 7:30 P.M. Thurs. and Sat. early July–late Aug., $8) offers lectures, sometimes preceded by optional dinners (fee), by guest lecturers, authors, and scholars on wide-ranging natural history and cultural history topics with a scientific focus. Call for the current schedule. The institute is four miles off Route 1. Take Dyer Bay Road off Route 1, bearing left at the fork onto Mogador Road for a total of 3.6 miles, then left on Schooner Point Road, then right on Eagle Hill Road. Programs take place in the dining hall lecture room.

SHOPPING

Arthur Smith (Rogers Point Rd., Steuben, 207/546-3462) is the real thing when it comes to chainsaw carvings. He's an extremely talented folk artist who looks at a piece of wood and sees an animal in it. His carvings of great blue herons, eagles, wolves, porcupines, flamingoes, and other creatures are incredibly detailed, and his wife, Marie, paints them in lifelike colors. Don't expect a fancy studio; much of the work can be viewed roadside.

Also in Steuben, but on the other end of the spectrum, is **Ray Carbone** (460 Pigeon Hill Rd., Steuben, 207/546-2170), whose masterful wood, stone, and bronze sculptures and fine furniture are definitely worth stopping to see, if not buy. Don't miss the granite sculptures and birdbaths in the garden.

In the barn of Steuben's second-oldest house, the historical Shaw Shaw farm, is **The Shaw Place Antiques** (Village Loop, 207/546-2330), where Jan Whelan sells antiques, treasures, and her magnificent handmade sweaters, made using only the highest-quality yarns. Whelan delight in telling visitors the history of the house and the area, and often weaves in her own heritage—she believes knitting is in her blood, as her 15th-century ancestors were

British wool merchants. Check out the guestbook: Shoppers have included Robert Redford and Tom Selleck.

BOATING EXCURSIONS

Captain Jaime Robertson's **Robertson Sea Tours and Adventures** (Milbridge Marina, Fickett's Point Rd., 207/546-3883 or 207/461-7439, www.robertsonseatours.com, May 15–Oct. 1) offers cruises from the Milbridge Marina aboard the *Mairi Leigh,* a classic Maine lobster boat. A puffins and seabirds cruise lasts three hours and is $70 for adults, $55 for children 12 and younger, with a $200 boat minimum. The island lobster cruise ($60 adults, $45 children, $150 boat minimum) lasts 2–2.5 hours and passes seven islands and lobster-trap hauling.

Captain Harry "Buzzy" Shinn's **Downeast Coastal Cruises** (207/546-7720 or cell 207/598-7740, www.downeastcoastalcruises.com) depart from the Milbridge Landing aboard the comfortable *Alyce K.* for island cruises, lighthouse cruises, puffin cruises, lobster cruises (complete with meal), sunset cruises, and charters. Cruises last 2–3.5 hours and cost $45–75 per adult, $35–65 per child; boat minimums apply.

ACCOMMODATIONS

Rates noted are for peak season.

Bed-and-Breakfasts and Motels

One of Cherryfield's 52 Historic Register buildings, the 1793 Archibald-Adams House is now the **Englishman's Bed and Breakfast** (122 Main St., Cherryfield, 207/546-2337, www.englishmansbandb.com, $95–155). The magnificently restored Federal-style home borders the Narraguagus River and makes a superb base for exploring inland and Down East Maine. The lovely grounds have gardens and a screened-in gazebo. Owners Peter (the Englishman) and Kathy Winham are archaeologists and serious tea drinkers—they also sell fine teas online (www.teasofcherryfield.com) and in area specialty stores; afternoon tea is a treat (reservation required). Two guest rooms in the main house have river views. One has a private half bath but shares a full bath. A riverside guesthouse, built in the 1990s, melds beautifully with the inn's architecture and is self-catering; pets are allowed here for $7 per night.

Although **The Red Barn Motel** (5 N. Main St., Milbridge, 207/546-7721, $60) has seen better days, all rooms have air-conditioning, Wi-Fi, and TV. Ask for one facing the Narraguagus River. Pets are welcome.

Campgrounds

Since 1958, the Ayr family has opened its quiet, well-off-the-beaten-path property on Joy Cove to campers. With a convenient location 15 minutes from Petit Manan National Wildlife Refuge and 20 minutes from Schoodic Point, **Mainayr Campground** (321 Village Rd., Steuben, 207/542-2690, www.mainayr.com, late May–mid-Oct., $27–32) has 35 tenting and RV sites (five with full hookups). Also on the premises are a playground, a laundry, a beach for tidal swimming, clamming flats, a grassy launch area for kayaks and canoes, a camp store, berries for picking, and fresh lobsters. If that's not enough, David Ayr enjoys regaling campers with stories.

FOOD

Call to verify days and hours of operation.

Local Flavors

You can easily pick up enough goodies for a picnic lunch or to stock a cottage kitchen at the Saturday-morning **Milbridge Farmers Market** (9 A.M.–noon Sat. early June–mid-Oct.), which sets up downtown, across from Kelco. Choose from fresh baked goods, goat cheese, organic veggies and meats, and eggs as well as wool products, soaps, and skin lotions.

Cinnamon doughnut muffins, chocolate-pecan cookies, multigrain breads, and English muffins are just a few of the reasons to dip off Route 1 to **Wildflour Bakery** (314 Village Rd., Steuben, 207/546-0978, 8 A.M.–4 P.M. Fri., 8 A.M.–1 P.M. Sat.), the tiny bakery where auto mechanic turned baker Rich Chevalier turns out hearty, creative breads and sweets. It's a great spot to catch the local gossip, too. Hours can vary; call for current days and hours of operation.

At the end of a long driveway winding through the woods in the back of beyond is **Painted Pepper Farm** (Good's Point Rd., Steuben, 207/546-9777, www.paintedpepperfarm.com), an organic farm operated by Lisa Reilich and Jordan Godino and their children. At the self-serve farm store you can purchase their maple syrup (you pass the sugar house on the drive), granola, preserves, applesauces, and, for a real treat, their yogurts, gelatos (the lemon zest is to die for), and cheese produced from their herd of Nigerian goats. From Route 1, take the Dyers Bay Road three miles to Good's Point Road. The farm is on the right. It's open daily, except Thursday and Sunday, from 10 A.M.–4 P.M., but it's wise to call before making a special trip.

Family Favorites

If you're heading out to Petit Manan National Wildlife Refuge, trust me on this. Ignore the exterior and venture into **Country Charm** (336 Pigeon Hill Rd., Steuben, 207/546-3763, 5 A.M.–8 P.M. Wed.–Sat., 5:30 A.M.–7 P.M. Sun.). The fried fish is fabulously fresh, crispy, light, and cheap, even by local standards. You easily can get out of here for less than $10 per person, far less if you're on a tight budget. The original dining room has, well, country charm (sit here if you want to listen in on the local gossip); the newer ones (added when a real kitchen replaced the original blue trailer) are purely functional. Hungry? Order the Charm Special: two eggs, bacon, sausages, pancakes, toast, and coffee all for a whopping $5; omelets begin around $3.

In Milbridge, the best choice is **44 Degrees North** (17 Main St., Milbridge, 207/546-4440, www.44-degrees-north.com, 11 A.M.–9 P.M. Tues.–Sun., to 3 P.M. Mon.). The front room is family oriented, with booths, tables, and cheerful decor. The back room doubles as a bar and has a big-screen TV. Expect home cooking, with a few surprises, and, as is usually the case in this part of Maine, mouthwatering desserts. Most heartier choices are less than $16.

More good home cooking, from shepherd's pie to fried fish, comes out of the kitchen at **Scovils Millside Dining** (1276 Main St./Rte. 1, Harrington, 207/483-6544, 7 A.M.–7 P.M. daily), a cheerful family-run restaurant near the intersections of Routes 1 and 1A.

INFORMATION

The best source for area info is the **Machias Bay Area Chamber of Commerce** (207/255-4402, www.machiaschamber.org).

Jonesport/Beals Area

Between western Washington County and the Machias Bay area is the molar-shaped Jonesport Peninsula, reached from the west via the attractive little town of Columbia Falls, bordering Route 1. Rounding the peninsula are the picturesque towns of Addison, Jonesport, and Beals Island. First settled around 1762, Columbia Falls (pop. about 550) still has a handful of houses dating from the late 18th century, but its best-known structure is the early-19th-century Ruggles House.

On the banks of the Pleasant River, just south of Columbia Falls, Addison (pop. 1,150) once had four huge shipyards cranking out wooden cargo vessels that circled the world. Since that 19th-century heyday, little seems to have changed, and the town today may be best known as the haunt of painter John Marin, who first came to Maine in 1914.

Jonesport and Beals Island, with a combined population of about 2,185, are traditional hard-working fishing communities—old-fashioned, friendly, and photogenic. Beals, connected to Jonesport via an arched bridge over Moosabec Reach, is named for Manwarren Beal Jr. and his wife, Lydia, who arrived around 1773 and quickly threw themselves into the Revolutionary War effort. But that's not all they did—the current phone book covering Jonesport and Beals Island lists dozens of Beal descendants (as well as dozens of Alleys and Carvers, other early names).

Even more memorable than Manwarren Beal was his six-foot, seven-inch descendent Barnabas, dubbed "Tall Barney" for obvious reasons. The larger-than-life fellow became the stuff of legend all along the Maine coast—and a popular Jonesport restaurant preserves his name.

Also legendary here is the lobster-boat design known as the Jonesport hull. People from away won't recognize its distinctive shape, but count on the fishing pros to know it. The harbor here is jam-packed with Jonesport lobster boats, and souped-up versions are consistent winners in the summertime lobsterboat-race series.

SIGHTS

Ruggles House

Behind a picket fence on a quiet street in Columbia Falls stands the remarkable Ruggles House (Main St., Columbia Falls, 207/483-4637, www.ruggleshouse.org, 9:30 A.M.–4:30 P.M. Mon.–Sat., 11 A.M.–4:30 P.M. Sun., June 1–Oct. 15, $5 adults, $2 children). Built in 1818 for Judge Thomas Ruggles—lumber baron, militia captain, even postmaster—the tiny house on a grand scale boasts a famous flying (unsupported) staircase, intricately carved moldings, Palladian window, and unusual period furnishings. Rescued in the mid-20th century and maintained by the Ruggles House Society, this gem has become a magnet for savvy preservationists. A quarter mile east of Route 1, it's open for hour-long guided tours.

At the house, pick up a copy of the Columbia Falls walking-tour brochure, which details the intriguing history of other houses in this hamlet.

Maine Central Model Railroad

Here's nirvana for model-train enthusiasts. Harold ("Buz") Beal and his wife, Helen, have created a fantastic model railroad layout—the

The Ruggles House is an architectural masterpiece.

Maine Central Model Railroad—covering about 900 square feet in a building next to their house. It features 4,000 trees, 407 train cars, 3,000 feet of track, 11 bridges and trestles, and 200 switches. The trains wind through towns modeled on real Maine places. Look for Stephen King's house in Bangor. Buz Beal, a 26-year Coast Guard veteran, figures railroading is in his blood; his grandfather was a Canadian Pacific engineer. Visitors are welcome any day of the year, but it's best to call ahead (207/497-2255) to be sure someone's home. Look for the sign on Route 187, about four miles northeast of downtown Jonesport. (Route 187 makes a loop through the peninsula; the Beals are on the easternmost side of the loop—7.7 miles south of Route 1.) There's no charge, but donations are welcomed. Buzz will usually run at least one train for visitors, but it takes three people to operate the full model. That usually occurs on Sunday evenings.

Maine Coast Sardine History Museum

In the first half of the 20th century, sardine processing was big business in Maine, with more than 400 factories along the coast, and Jonesport was home to 15 of them. Ronnie Peabody, director of the Maine Coast Sardine History Museum (24 Mason Bay Rd., Jonesport, 207/497-2961, 10 A.M.–4 P.M. Tues.–Fri. and Sun., $4 adults, $2 students) and his wife, Mary, began collecting sardine artifacts and memorabilia in 2001, and opened this museum in 2008. Ronnie is a passionate guide who brings life to the photos, equipment, and even the cans displayed. You can zip through on your own in about 20 minutes, but start asking Ronnie questions or ask him to guide you through, and you'll wonder where the hour went.

Downeast Institute for Applied Marine Research and Education

University of Maine at Machias professor Brian Beals founded the Beals Island Regional Shellfish Hatchery, now the Downeast Institute (Black Duck Cove, Great Wass Island, 207/497-5769, www.downeastinstitute.org), a marine field station for the University of Maine at Machias. Learn everything there is to know about shellfish, especially soft-shell clams, on this eight-acre property, with two natural coves. Tours are by appointment.

Wild Salmon Research Center

Established in 1922, this center (Columbia Falls, 207/483-4336, www.mainesalmonrivers.org, 8 A.M.–4 P.M. Mon.–Fri., free) has a few educational displays and a library. In the basement is a volunteer-run fish hatchery that raises 50,000 Atlantic salmon fry annually. Staff welcome visitors and explain the efforts to save Maine's endangered salmon. You might also ask about the status of the East Machias Aquatic Research Center, a new facility under development by the Downeast Salmon Federation. Hatchery operations began in 2009. Also planned are laboratories, a resources center, and small museum.

ENTERTAINMENT AND EVENTS

For a taste of real Maine, don't miss the early April **Fried Smelt Dinner.**

The biggest annual event hereabouts is the wingding Jonesport **Fourth of July** celebration, with several days of special activities, including barbecues, beauty pageant, kids' games, fireworks, and the famed **Jonesport Lobsterboat Races** in Moosabec Reach.

Peabody Memorial Library presents bimonthly art shows and sponsors a summer music series.

SHOPPING

Flower-design majolica pottery and whimsical terra-cotta items are April Adams' specialties at **Columbia Falls Pottery** (150 Main St., Columbia Falls, 207/483-4075 or 800/235-2512, www.columbiafallspottery.com), an appealing shop in a rehabbed country store next to the Ruggles House. A two-bedroom apartment is available for rent upstairs either as one unit by the week for $700 or, when available, by the room, for $120–150 per night.

Allow time to browse **Gray Wolf Gift, Gallery & Frame Shop** (280 Water St., Addison, 207/483-6567). Owner and artist Beth Ferriero has filled it with work by more than 30 area artists and artisans, and the quality is top notch.

Two adjacent antiques shops brighten Jonesport's waterfront. Maureen Hart sells antiques, paintings by Audrey Soule, and whimsies at **Harbor House on Sawyer Cove** (32 Sawyer Sq., 207/497-5417). Eclectic finds await browsers at **Moospecke Antiques** (Sawyer Sq., 207/497-2457).

In downtown Jonesport, **Church's True Value** (Main St., Rte. 187, Jonesport, 207/497-2778) carries all the usual hardware items, plus gifts, souvenirs, and sportswear. Helpful owners John and Sharon Church can also answer any question about the area and solve most any problem.

Nelson Decoys Downeast Gallery (Cranberry La., Jonesport, 207/497-3488) is equal parts shop, gallery, and museum. Inside are not only hand-carved decoys, but also creations by other area artists and artisans. It's in an old schoolhouse, just off Main Street downtown.

RECREATION

Great Wass Island Preserve

Allow a whole day to explore 1,576-acre Great Wass Island, an extraordinary preserve, even when it's drenched in fog—a not-infrequent event. Owned by the Nature Conservancy (207/729-5181, www.nature.org), the preserve is at the tip of Jonesport's peninsula. Easiest hiking routes are the wooded two-mile Little Cape Point and 1.5-mile Mud Hole Trails, retracing your path for each. (Making a loop by connecting the two along the rocky shoreline adds considerably to the time and difficulty, but do it if you have time; allow about six hours and wear waterproof footwear.) Expect to see beach-head iris (like a blue flag) and orchids, jack pine, a peat bog, seals, pink granite, pitcher plants, lots of warblers, and maybe some grouse. Carry water and a picnic; wear bug repellent. No camping, fires, or pets; no toilet facilities. Daytime access only. To reach the preserve from Route 1, take Route 187 to Jonesport (12 miles) and then cross the arched bridge to Beals Island. Continue across Beals to the Great Wass causeway (locally called "the Flying Place") and then go three miles on Black Duck Cove Road to the parking area (on the left). Watch for the Nature Conservancy oak-leaf symbol. At the parking area, pick up a trail map and a bird checklist.

Also owned by the Nature Conservancy is 21-acre **Mistake Island,** accessible only by boat. Low and shrubby, Mistake has a Coast Guard–built boardwalk from the landing at the northwest corner to **Moose Peak Light,** standing 72 feet above the water at the eastern end of the island. The only negative on this lovely island is rubble left behind when the government leveled the keeper's house.

Machias Seal Island Puffin Tour

A great-grandson of legendary local "Tall Barney" Beal, Captain Barna Norton began offering puffin-watching trips to Machias Seal Island (MSI) in 1940 in a 33-foot boat incautiously named *If.* Now his descendents have taken over the helm of **Norton of Jonesport** (118 Main St., Jonesport, 207/497-5933 or 207/497-5933, www.machiassealisland.com, $100). The *Chief* heads 20 miles offshore to an island claimed by both the United States and Canada—a colorful saga. To preserve the fragile nesting sites of Atlantic puffins and arctic terns, access to the 15-acre island is restricted. Passengers are off-loaded into small boats, but sea swells sometimes prevent landing. (The captain supplies wristbands to queasy passengers.) The trip is *not* appropriate for small children or unsteady adults. The boat departs Jonesport around 7 A.M. and returns around noon. Wear waterproof hiking boots, take a hat, and pack some munchies.

Scenic Cruises

Operating as **Coastal Cruises** (Kelley Point Rd., Jonesport, 207/497-3064 or 207/497-2699), Captain Laura Fish and her brother

PUFFINS

The chickadee is the Maine state bird, and the bald eagle is our national emblem, but probably the best-loved bird along the Maine coast is the Atlantic puffin *(Fratercula arctica)*, a member of the auk (Alcidae) family. Photographs show an imposing-looking creature with a quizzical mien; amazingly, this larger-than-life seabird is only about 12 inches long. Black-backed and white-chested, the puffin has bright orange legs, "clown-makeup" eyes, and a distinctive, rather outlandish red-and-yellow beak. Its diet is fish and shellfish.

Almost nonexistent in this part of the world as recently as the 1970s, the puffin (or "sea parrot") has recovered dramatically thanks to the unstinting efforts of Cornell University ornithologist Stephen Kress and his Project Puffin (www.projectpuffin.org). Starting with an orphan colony (of two) on remote Matinicus Rock, Kress painstakingly transferred nearly a thousand puffin chicks (also known fondly as "pufflings") from Newfoundland and used artificial nests and decoys to entice the birds to adapt to and reproduce on Eastern Egg Rock in Muscongus Bay.

In 1981, thanks to the assistance and persistence of hundreds of interns and volunteers, and despite the predations of great black-backed gulls, puffins finally were fledged on Eastern Egg, and the rest, as they say, is history. Within 20 years, more than three dozen puffin couples were nesting on Eastern Egg Rock, and still more had established nests on other islands in the area. Kress's methods have received international attention, and his proven techniques have been used to reintroduce bird populations in remote parts of the globe. In 2001, *Down East* magazine singled out Kress to receive its prestigious annual Environmental Award.

HOW AND WHERE TO SEE PUFFINS

Puffin-watching, like whale-watching, involves heading offshore, so be prepared with warm clothing, rubber-soled shoes, a hat, sunscreen, binoculars, and, if you're motion sensitive, appropriate medication.

© ABLESTOCK PREMIUM/123RF

Colorful beaks have earned puffins the nickname "clowns of the sea."

The Maine Audubon Society undertakes evening excursions from New Harbor to Eastern Egg Rock 2-3 times a summer, and Hardy Boat Cruises has puffin-watching trips from New Harbor daily early June-mid-August, but the best daily up-close-and-personal opportunities for puffin-watching along the Down East Coast – specifically, on Machias Seal Island – are aboard boats departing from Cutler and Jonesport. Both **Bold Coast Charters** (207/259-4484, www.boldcoast.com) and **Norton of Jonesport** (207/497-5933 www.machiassealisland.com) operate May into August and cost about $100 per person. Weather permitting, you'll be allowed to disembark on the 20-acre island.

ADOPT-A-PUFFIN PROGRAM

Stephen Kress's Project Puffin has devised a clever way to enlist supporters via the Adopt-a-Puffin program (www.projectpuffin.org). For a $100 donation, you'll receive a certificate of adoption, vital statistics on your adoptee, annual updates, and a T-shirt.

Harry Fish, a certified dive master, offer three-hour Moosabec Reach cruises in the 23-foot powerboat *Aaron Thomas.* Among the sights are Great Wass Island and Mistake Island. Rates begin at $50 per person, varying with number of passengers; six-person maximum. Dive trips begin at $100 per person for two or more. Reservations are required. Trips depart from Jonesport and operate May–mid-October.

ACCOMMODATIONS

Rates noted are for peak season.

Bed-and-Breakfasts

How about staying in a beautiful, modern farmhouse overlooking the water—with llamas lolling outside? At **Pleasant Bay Bed and Breakfast and Llama Keep** (338 West Side Rd., Addison, 207/483-4490, www.pleasantbay.com, $50–135), Joan and Lee Yeaton manage to pamper more than 40 llamas and a herd of red deer as well as their two-legged guests. Three miles of trails wind through the 110 acres, and a canoe is available for guests. Three lovely rooms (private and shared baths) and one suite, with microwave and refrigerator, all have water views. Rates include a delicious breakfast. Arrange in advance for a llama walk ($15 per llama). It's open all year. The farm borders Pleasant Bay, 3.9 miles southwest of Route 1.

The fanciest digs in Jonesport are at **Harbor House on Sawyer Cove** (Sawyer Sq., Jonesport, 207/497-5417, www.harborhs.com, $135), hospitably run by Maureen and Gene Hart—she an ex-nurse, he an ex-engineer. They've been sharing their passion for Jonesport with Harbor House guests for more than a dozen years. Two very comfortable and spacious 2nd-floor rooms—named Beach Rose and Lupine and decorated accordingly—have incredible views of Moosabec Reach. Binoculars are provided so you can watch the action. The rooms also have TV and Wi-Fi, and a guest phone, fridge, and microwave are provided. The Harts operate an antiques shop, selling what they call "curiosities," on the 1st floor of this fascinating old building, once Jonesport's telegraph office. Maureen serves a great breakfast—early enough for bird-watchers—on the harbor-view porch. Harbor House is open all year.

Cottages and Apartments

Proprietor Dorothy Higgins's **Cranberry Cove Cottages** (56 Kelley Point Rd., Jonesport, 207/497-2139, ddhiggi@hotmail.com, $135) comprise two second-story apartments, each distinctively furnished in cottage style and with TV, phone, and harbor view. Both have kitchenettes provisioned with all sorts of goodies, from fresh eggs to wine and cheese. Pets are welcome. Rates decrease with length of stay.

Abigail Oates-Alley has two carefully decorated, nicely appointed, and well-equipped two-bedroom units in a harborfront duplex called **Moose-a-bec** (34 Old House Point, Jonesport, 207/497-2121, $135). Both have big views, full baths with laundries, dishwashers, and TV. Really, Abigail has thought of just about everything, right down to kitchen supplies such as foil, plastic wrap, and napkins. Outside are lovely gardens, a children's playset, and stairs leading to a small pebble beach. It's adjacent to a working wharf, so expect to see and hear the boats going out and returning each day. The downstairs unit is wheelchair accessible. The second bedroom upstairs is more bed than room.

Campgrounds

The town of Jonesport operates the low-key, no-frills **Jonesport Campground** (Henry Point, Kelley Point Rd., Jonesport) on two acres with fabulous views over Sawyer Cove and Moosabec Reach. Basic facilities include outhouses, picnic tables, and fire rings; three power poles provide hookups. Showers and washing machines are available across the cove at Jonesport Shipyard (207/497-2701). The campground is exposed to wind off the water, so expect nights to be cool. Sites are allocated on a first-come, first-served basis. It's open early May–Labor Day. Avoid the campground during Fourth of July festivities; it's jam-packed. From Route 187 at

©HILARY NANGLE

Harbor House on Sawyer Cove is both a bed-and-breakfast and an antiques shop.

the northeastern edge of Jonesport, turn right onto Kelley Point Road and then right again to Henry Point.

FOOD

Call to verify days and hours of operation.

Craving carbs? Head for Lois Hubbard's home bakery, called **The Farm** (1561 Mason's Bay Rd., Rte. 187, Jonesport, 207/497-5949). In addition to specialty breads, Lois produces 15 flavors of whoopie pies, including blueberry. The bakery, 3.3 miles south of the Jonesboro end of Route 1, is open all year.

For local color, start at **Tall Barney's** (52 Main St., Rte. 187, Jonesport, 207/497-2403, www.tallbarneys.com), where you'll find homemade baked beans and chowders, pizza, and more—and you won't break the bank. Sit back and watch the servers chat up the lobstermen regulars camped out at the big center table, known locally as the Liars' Table. Join them, if you dare. No credit cards. Days and hours of operation change frequently, so call.

Another possibility for breakfast or lunch is **The Lighthouse Cafe** (Main St., Jonesport, 207/497-5650), which usually opens in the wee hours for the local fishermen.

INFORMATION AND SERVICES

The **Machias Bay Area Chamber of Commerce** (12 E. Main St., Machias, 207/255-4402, www.machiaschamber.org) handles inquires for the Machias area as well as Jonesport.

In downtown Jonesport, two reliable sources for local information are **Church's True Value** (Main St., Rte. 187, Jonesport, 207/497-2778), open every day but Sunday, and Maureen Hart at **Antiques on the Harbor** (Sawyer Square, 207/497-5417).

Machias Bay Area

The only negative thing about **Machias** (Muh-CHY-us, pop. about 2,500) is its Micmac Indian name, meaning "bad little falls" (even though that's accurate—the midtown waterfall here *is* treacherous). A contagious local esprit pervades this shire town of Washington County, thanks to antique homes, a splendid river-valley setting, Revolutionary War monuments, and a small but busy university campus.

If you regard crowds as fun, an ideal time to land here is during the renowned annual Machias Wild Blueberry Festival, third weekend in August, when harvesting is under way in Washington County's blueberry fields and you can stuff your face with blueberry everything—muffins, jam, pancakes, ice cream, pies. You can also collect blueberry-logo napkins, T-shirts, magnets, pottery, and jewelry. Biggest highlight: the annual summer musical parody.

Among the other summer draws are a chamber-music series, art shows, and semiprofessional theater performances. Within a few miles are day trips galore—options for hiking, biking, golfing, swimming, and sea kayaking.

Also included within the Machias sphere are the towns of **Roque Bluffs, Jonesboro, Whitneyville, Marshfield, East Machias,** and **Machiasport.** Just to the east, between Machias and Lubec, are the towns of **Whiting** and **Cutler.**

HISTORICAL SIGHTS

History is a big deal in this area, and since Machias was the first settled Maine town east of the Penobscot River, lots of enthusiastic amateur historians have helped rescue homes and sites dating from as far back as the Revolutionary War.

English settlers, uprooted from communities farther west on the Maine coast, put down permanent roots here in 1763, harvesting timber to ensure their survival. Stirrings of revolutionary discontent surfaced even at this remote outpost, and when British loyalists in Boston began usurping some of the valuable harvest, Machias patriots plotted revenge. By 1775, when the armed British schooner *Margaretta* arrived as a cargo escort, local residents aboard the sloop *Unity,* in a real David-and-Goliath episode, chased and captured the *Margaretta.* On June 12, 1775, two months after the famed Battles of Lexington and Concord (and five days before the Battle of Bunker Hill), Machias Bay was the site of what author James Fenimore Cooper called "The Lexington of the Sea"—the first naval battle of the American Revolution. The name of patriot leader Jeremiah O'Brien today appears throughout Machias—on a school, a street, a cemetery, and a state park. In 1784, Machias was incorporated; it became the shire town in 1790.

Museums

One-hour guided tours vividly convey the atmosphere of the 1770 **Burnham Tavern** (Main St., Rte. 192, Machias, 207/255-6930, www.burnhamtavern.com, 9:30 A.M.–4 P.M. Mon.–Sat. mid-June–late Sept., or by appt., $5 adults, $0.25 children under 12), one of 21 homes in the *country* designated as most significant to the American Revolution. Upstart local patriots met here in 1775 to plot revolution against the British. Job and Mary Burnham's tavern-home next served as an infirmary for casualties from the Revolution's first naval battle, just offshore. Lots of fascinating history lies in this National Historic Site maintained by the Daughters of the American Revolution. Hanging outside is a sign reading, "Drink for the thirsty, food for the hungry, lodging for the weary, and good keeping for horses, by Job Burnham."

Headquarters for the Machiasport Historical Society and one of the area's three

TWO SCENIC ROUTES

The drives described below can also be bike routes (easy to moderately difficult), but be forewarned that the roads are narrow and shoulderless, so caution is essential. Heed biking etiquette.

ROUTE 191, THE CUTLER ROAD

Never mind that Route 191, between East Machias and West Lubec, is one of Maine's most stunning coastal drives – you can still follow the entire 27-mile stretch and meet only a handful of cars. **East Machias** even has its own historic district, with architectural gems dating from the late 18th century along High and Water Streets. Further along Route 191, you'll find fishing wharves, low moorlands, a hamlet or two, and islands popping over the horizon. The only peculiarly jarring note is the 26-tower forest of North Cutler's Naval Computer and Telecommunications Station, nearly 1,000 feet high – monitoring global communications – but you'll see this only briefly. (At night, the skyscraping red lights are really eerie, especially if you're offshore aboard a boat.) Off Route 191 are minor roads and hiking trails worth exploring, especially the coastal trails of the Cutler Coast Public Preserve. About three miles south of the Route 191 terminus, you can also check out **Bailey's Mistake,** a hamlet with a black-sand (volcanic) beach. And the name? Allegedly it stems from one Captain Bailey who, misplotting his course and thinking he was in Lubec, drove his vessel ashore here one night in the late 19th century. Unwilling to face the consequences of his lapse, he and his crew off-loaded their cargo of lumber and built themselves dwellings. Whether true or not, it makes a great saga. Even though it's in the town of **Trescott,** and the hamlet is really South Trescott, everyone knows this section as Bailey's Mistake.

ROUTE 92, STARBOARD PENINSULA

Pack a picnic and set out on Route 92 (beginning at Elm Street in downtown Machias) down the 10-mile length of the Starboard Peninsula to a stunning spot known as the Point of Maine. Along the way are the villages of Larrabee, Bucks Harbor, and Starboard, all part of the town of Machiasport. In Bucks Harbor is the turnoff (a short detour to the right) to **Yoho Head,** a controversial upscale development overlooking Little Kennebec Bay.

South of the Yoho Head turnoff is the sign for **Jasper Beach.** From the Jasper Beach sign, continue 1.4 miles to two red buildings (the old Starboard School House and the volunteer fire department). Turn left onto a dirt road and continue to a sign reading Driveway. Go around the right side of a shed and park on the beach. (Keep track of the tide level, though.) You're at **Point of Maine,** a quintessential Down East panorama of sea and islands. On a clear day, you can see offshore **Libby Island Light,** the focus of Philmore Wass's entertaining narrative *Lighthouse in My Life: The Story of a Maine Lightkeeper's Family.*

oldest residences, the 1810 **Gates House** (344 Port Rd., Machiasport, 207/255-8461, 12:30–4:30 P.M. Tues.–Fri. July–Aug., donation appreciated) was snatched from ruin and restored in 1966. The National Historic Register building overlooking Machias Bay contains fascinating period furnishings and artifacts, many related to the lumbering and shipbuilding era. The museum, four miles southeast of Route 1, has limited parking on a hazardous curve.

O'Brien Cemetery

Old-cemetery buffs will want to stop at O'Brien Cemetery, resting place of the town's earliest settlers. It's next to Bad Little Falls Park, close to downtown, off Route 92 toward Machiasport. A big plus here is the view, especially in autumn, of blueberry barrens, the waterfall, and the bay.

Fort O'Brien State Memorial

The American Revolution's first naval battle

© TOM NANGLE

Discover Machias's significant role in the American Revolution at the Burnham Tavern museum.

was fought just offshore from Fort O'Brien in June 1775. Now a State Historic Site, the fort was built and rebuilt several times—originally to guard Machias during the Revolutionary War. Only Civil War–era earthworks now remain, plus well-maintained lawns overlooking the Machias River. Steep banks lead down to the water; keep small children well back from the edge. No restrooms or other facilities, but there's a playground at the Fort O'Brien School, next door. Officially, the park is open Memorial Day weekend–Labor Day, but it's accessible all year. Admission is free. Take Route 92 from Machias about five miles toward Machiasport; the parking area is on the left.

OTHER SIGHTS

Maine Sea Salt Company

Season your visit with a tour of the Maine Sea Salt Co. (11 Church La., Marshfield, 207/255-3310, www.maineseasalt.com), which produces sea salt in its solar green houses and shallow pools using evaporation and reduction of sea water. Free tours (available most days 9 A.M.–5 P.M., call first) explain the process and include tastings of natural, seasoned, and smoked salts.

University of Maine at Machias

Founded in 1909 as Washington State Normal School, University of Maine at Machias (9 O'Brien Ave., Machias, 207/255-1200, www.umm.maine.edu) is now part of the state university system. The **UMM Art Galleries** (Powers Hall, 9 A.M.–4 P.M. Mon.–Fri.) feature works from the university's expanding permanent collection of Maine painters—including John Marin, William Zorach, Lyonel Feininger, and Reuben Tam. Rotating exhibits occur throughout the school year.

UMM's **Center for Lifelong Learning** has a state-of-the-art fitness center, six-lane heated pool, and the George Simpson Murdock Bookstore, which stocks more than textbooks. The pool and fitness room are open to the public ($7); call for schedule.

Also open to the public is **Merrill Library** (207/255-1284).

ENTERTAINMENT AND EVENTS

The University of Maine at Machias is the cultural focus in this area, particularly during the school year. **Stage Front: The Arts Downeast** puts on an annual series of concerts, plays, recitals, and other events in the Performing Arts Center at the university. The summer series, once a month, usually features classical and pops concerts, including at least one performance by the energetic Steuben-based Opera Maine organization. Contact UMM (207/255-1384) for schedule information.

If the UMM Ukulele Club is performing anywhere, don't miss them.

Machias Bay Chamber Concerts (207/255-3849, www.machiasbaychamberconcerts.com) occur at 7:30 P.M. Tuesday evenings early July–mid-August at the Centre Street Congregational Church. Art exhibits accompany concerts. Tickets are $15 adults, $8 students, free children age 12 and younger.

The **Machias Wild Blueberry Festival** (www.machiasblueberry.com) is the summer highlight, running Friday–Sunday the third weekend in August and featuring a pancake breakfast, road races, concerts, a craft show, a baked-bean supper, a homegrown musical, and more. The blueberry motif is everywhere. It's organized by Centre Street Congregational Church in downtown Machias.

SHOPPING

Influenced by traditional Japanese designs, Connie Harter-Bagley markets her dramatic raku ceramics at **Connie's Clay of Fundy** (Rte. 1, Box 345, East Machias, 207/255-4574, www.clayoffundy.com), on the East Machias River, four miles east of Machias. If she's at the wheel, you can also watch her work.

A number of regional artists and artisans show and sell their wares at **Unique Possibilities** (300 E. Main St./Rte. 1, Machias, 207/255-3337), in the Causeway Common building (same complex as Dunkin' Donuts). Also here, but well hidden, is **The Country Tea Room** (207/255-3337, 11 A.M.–4 P.M. Tues.–Sun.), a relaxing place to have lunch or sip tea and snack on sweets.

Need a read? **Jim's Books, etc.** (8 Elm St., Machias, 207/255-9058), at the third house on the left on Route 32, just beyond the university campus, is open by chance or appointment.

RECREATION

Parks and Preserves

Just as dedicated as the historical preservationists are the hikers, bird-watchers, and other eco-sensitive outdoors enthusiasts who've helped preserve thousands of acres in this part of Maine for public access and appreciation.

At **Bad Little Falls Park,** alongside the Machias River, stop to catch the view from the footbridge overlooking the roiling falls (especially in spring). Bring a picnic and enjoy this midtown oasis tucked between Routes 1 and 92.

Thanks to a handful of foresighted year-round and summer residents, spectacular crescent-shaped **Jasper Beach**—piled high with ocean-polished jasper and other rocks—has been preserved by the town of Machiasport. No sand here, just stones, in intriguing shapes and colors. Resist the urge to fill your pockets with souvenirs. Parking is limited; no facilities. From Route 1 in downtown Machias, take Route 92 (Machias Road) 9.5 miles southeast, past the village of Bucks Harbor. Watch for a large sign on your left. The beach is on Howard's Cove, 0.2 mile off the road, and accessible all year.

Southwest of Machias, six miles south of Route 1, is **Roque Bluffs State Park** (Roque Bluffs Rd., Roque Bluffs, 207/255-3475, www.parksandlands.com). Saltwater swimming this far north is for the young and brave, but this park also has a 60-acre freshwater pond warm and shallow enough for toddlers and the old and timid. Facilities include primitive changing rooms, outhouses, a play area, and picnic tables (no food or lifeguards). Views go on forever from the wide-open mile-long sweep of sand beach. Admission is $4.50 nonresident adults, $3 resident adults, $1 children 5–11. The fee box relies on the honor system. The park is open daily May 15–September 15, but the beach is accessible all year.

On Route 191, about 4.5 miles northeast of the center of Cutler, watch for the parking area (on the right) for the **Cutler Coast Public Preserve,** a 12,000-acre preserve with nearly a dozen miles of beautifully engineered hiking trails on the seaward side of Route 191. Easiest is the 2.8-mile round-trip Coastal Trail through a cedar swamp and spruce-fir forest to an ocean promontory and back. Allow 5–6 hours to continue with the 5.5-mile Black Point Brook Loop, which progresses along a stretch of moderately rugged hiking southward along dramatic tree-fringed shoreline cliffs. Then head back via the Black Point Brook cutoff and connect with the Inland Trail to return to your car (or bicycle). Bring binoculars and a camera; the views from this wild coastline are fabulous. Also bring insect repellent—inland boggy stretches are buggy. Carry a picnic and commandeer a granite ledge overlooking the surf. Precipitous cliffs and narrow stretches can make the shoreline section of this trail perilous for small children or insecure adults, so use extreme caution and common sense. There are no facilities in the preserve. If you're here in August, you can stock up on blueberries and even some wild raspberries. Another option, the 9.1-mile Fairy Head Loop, starts the same way as the Black Point Brook Loop but continues southward along the coast, leading to three primitive campsites (stoves only, no fires), available on a first-come, first-served basis. There's no way to reserve these, so you take your chances. Unless you have gazelle genes, the longer loop almost demands an overnight. Information on the preserve, including a helpful map, is available from the **Maine Bureau of Parks and Lands** (207/287-3821, www.parksandlands.com). Originally about 2,100 acres, this preserve was quintupled in 1997, when several donors, primarily the Richard King Mellon Foundation, deeded to the state 10,055 acres of fields and forests across Route 191 from the trail area, creating a phenomenal tract that now runs from the ocean all the way back to Route 1. Mostly in Cutler but also in Whiting, it was Maine's second-largest public-land gift—after Baxter State Park.

Hiking

Eventually, the **Down East Sunrise Trail** (www.sunrisetrail.org), a rails-to-trails conversion, will stretch 85 miles from Ellsworth to Ayers Junction, in Charlotte, just west of Calais. The 30-mile section between Machias to Ayers Junction opened in 2009. Check the website for updates and a map.

Golf

With lovely water views, and tidal inlets serving as obstacles, the nine-hole **Great Cove Golf Course** (387 Great Cove Rd., off Roque Bluffs Rd., Jonesboro, 207/434-7200) is a good challenge. Or, play a quick nine at **Barren View Golf Course** (Rte. 1, Jonesboro, 207/434-6531, www.barrenview.com).

Canoeing, Sea Kayaking, and Bicycling

If you've brought your own sea kayak, there are public launching ramps in Bucks Harbor (east of the main Machias Road) and at Roque Bluffs State Park. You can also put in at Sanborn Cove, beyond the O'Brien School on Route 92, about five miles south of Machias, where there's a small parking area. Before setting out, be sure to check the tide calendar and plan your strategy so you don't have to slog through acres of muck when you return.

Sunrise Canoe and Kayak (0.02 mile off Rte. 1 on an unsigned road, behind Margaretta Motel, Machias, 207/255-3375 or 877/980-2300, www.sunrisecanoeandkayak.com) rents canoes and kayaks for $25–35 per day, and offers half-day sea-kayak excursions on Machias Bay, including one to a petroglyph site ($48 pp). Hybrid mountain bike rentals are $20 per day. Pickup and delivery service is available. It also offers guided day trips and fully outfitted multiday canoeing and kayaking excursions on the Machias and St. Croix Rivers and along the Bold Coast.

The spectacular **Machias River,** one of Maine's most technically demanding canoeing rivers, is a dynamite trip mid-May–mid-June, but no beginner should attempt it. The best advice is to sign on with an outfitter/guide. The run lasts 4–6 days, the latter if you start from Fifth Machias Lake. Expect to see such wildlife as osprey, eagles, ducks, loons, moose, deer, beaver, and snapping turtles. Be aware, though, that the Machias is probably the buggiest river in the state, and blackflies will form a welcoming party. In addition to Sunrise Canoe and Kayak, Bangor-based **Sunrise Expeditions** (207/942-9300 or 800/748-3730, www.sunrise-exp.com) also offers fully outfitted trips.

Machias Seal Island Puffin Tour

Andy Patterson, the skipper of the 40-footer *Barbara Frost,* operates the **Bold Coast Charter Company** (207/259-4484, www.boldcoast.com), homeported in Cutler Harbor. Andy provides knowledgeable narration, answers questions in depth, and shares his considerable enthusiasm for this pristine corner of Maine. He's best known for his five-hour puffin-sighting trips to Machias Seal Island (departing between 7 and 8 A.M. mid-May–Aug., $100); the trip is unsuitable for small children or unsteady adults. Daily access to the island is restricted, and swells can roll in, so passengers occasionally cannot disembark, but the curious puffins often surround the boat, providing plenty of photo opportunities. A seabird tour, without an island visit, is available for $100 adults, $60 children 14 and younger. No matter what the air temperature on the mainland, be sure to dress warmly, and wear sturdy shoes. The *Barbara Frost*'s wharf is on Cutler Harbor, just off Route 191. Look for the Little River Lobster Company sign; you'll depart from the boat-launching ramp. All trips are dependent on weather and tide conditions, and reservations are required. No credit cards.

ACCOMMODATIONS

Rates noted are for peak season.

Bed-and-Breakfasts and Inns

The first two bed-and-breakfasts listed here also have dining rooms open to the public.

The beautifully restored 1797 **Chandler River Lodge** (654 Rte. 1, Jonesboro, 207/434-2540, www.chandlerriverlodge.com, $100–175) sits well off the highway and overlooks treed lawns that roll down to the Chandler River. It's an idyllic spot, with Adirondack-style chairs positioned just where you want to sit and take in the views. Rates include a continental breakfast.

Victoriana rules at the **Riverside Inn** (Rte. 1, East Machias, 207/255-4134, www.riversideinn-maine.com, $99–135), a meticulously restored early-19th-century sea captain's home with two rooms and two suites (one with kitchenette). Relax on the deck overlooking the East Machias River or sit in the lovely terraced perennial gardens and you'll forget you're a few steps from a busy highway.

The barn-red **Inn at Schoppee Farm** (Rte. 1, Machias, 207/255-4648, www.schoppeefarm.com, $110) fronts on the tidal Machias River. The 19th-century farm operated as a dairy for three generations before Machias natives David and Julie Barker returned home to operate it as a bed-and-breakfast. They welcome guests with two rooms, each furnished with antiques and such niceties as air-conditioning, Wi-Fi, whirlpool baths, satellite TV, and soft down comforters in addition to river views and a full breakfast. Just east of the causeway, it's a healthy walk to downtown diversions.

The second generation now operates **Micmac Farm Guesthouses** (Rte. 92, Machiasport, 207/255-3008, www.micmacfarm.com, $85–95/night, $550–595/week). Stay in one of Anthony and Bonnie Dunn's three rustic but comfortable and well-equipped cottages, and you'll find yourself relaxing on the deck overlooking the tidal Machias River and watching for seabirds, seals, and eagles. No breakfast is provided, but each wood-paneled cottage has a kitchenette and dining area. Pets and children are welcome. There's also a river-view room in the restored 18th-century Gardner House, with a private bath with whirlpool tub. Guests have use of the farmhouse, including a library. A light breakfast is provided for Gardner House guests.

Motels

The best feature of the two-story **Machias Motor Inn** (109 Main St./Rte. 1, Machias, 207/255-4861, www.machiasmotorinn.com, $99) is its location overlooking the tidal Machias River; sliding doors open onto decks with a view. Twenty-eight guest rooms and six efficiencies have extra-long beds, plus cable TV, air-conditioning, Wi-Fi, and phone. Next door is Helen's Restaurant—famed for seasonal fruit pies and an all-you-can-eat weekend breakfast buffet. Pets ($5 fee) are welcome at the motel. The motel is within easy walking distance to downtown; perfect if you're here for the Blueberry Festival. It's open all year.

For inexpensive digs, you can't beat the **Blueberry Patch** (550 Rte. 1, Jonesboro, 207/434-5411, $55–75), a clean and bright motel and tourist cabins, with three efficiency units. Mark and Norma Lyons provide homespun hospitality with a few extras. All rooms have satellite TV, air-conditioning, Wi-Fi, and phones, and there's even a pool and small playground. If you're taller than six feet, choose a motel room rather than a cabin (cabin bathrooms are tiny). A light continental breakfast is available.

FOOD

Call to verify days and hours of operation.

Watch the local papers for listings of **public suppers, spaghetti suppers,** or **baked bean suppers,** a terrific way to sample the culinary talents of local cooks. Most begin at 5 P.M., and it's wise to arrive early to get near the head of the line. The suppers often benefit needy individuals or struggling nonprofits, and where else can you eat nonstop for less than $10?

Local Flavors

Ask locals where to get the best pizzas, sandwiches, and salads, and the answer is always **Fat Cat Deli** (11 Main St., Machias, 207/255-6777, 11 A.M.–8 P.M. Mon.–Fri., opens noon on Sat.).

Craving something healthful? The **Whole Life Market** (4 Colonial Way, Machias, 207/255-8855, www.wholelifemarket.com, 9 A.M.–6 P.M. Mon.–Sat., 10 A.M.–2 P.M. Sun.) has a pleasant café serving salads, soups, sandwiches, and baked goods made from organic fruits, vegetables, and grains and hormone-free dairy products.

Another source for fresh, healthful foods is the **Machias Valley Farmers Market** (8 A.M.–3 P.M. Sat. May–Oct. and daily during peak season). It's held on "the dike," a low causeway next to the Machias River. It's usually a good source for blueberries in late July and August.

Family Favorites

Family-owned, and very popular all day long, is **The Blue Bird Ranch Family Restaurant** (78 Main St./Rte. 1, Machias, 207/255-3351, www.bluebirdranchrestaurant.com, 6 A.M.–8 P.M. daily), named for the Prout family's other enterprise, Blue Bird Ranch Trucking Company. Service is efficient, food is hearty, and portions are ample in the three dining rooms.

Helen's (111 Main St./Rte. 1, Machias, 207/255-8423, 6 A.M.–8:30 P.M. Mon.–Sat., 7 A.M.–8 P.M. Sun.) is renowned for its blueberry pie. A new generation has spruced up the restaurant, an institution in these parts since 1950. Beyond pie, it's a source of inexpensive fare.

Fine Dining

When you want to splurge, reserve a table at one of these two inns with dining rooms open to the public.

Oak furnishings and lacy white tablecloths set the tone at the **Riverside Inn** (Rte. 1, East Machias, 207/255-4134, www.riversideinn-maine.com, 5–8 P.M. Tues.–Sun., $24–29), one of the region's most consistent and long-lasting fine-dining spots. The well-prepared fare ranges from trout meunière to beef Wellington. Reservations are required.

Gaze out at the river while dining fireside at the **Chandler River Lodge** (654 Rte. 1, Jonesboro, 207/434-2540, 11:30 A.M.–2 P.M. Thurs.–Fri., 5–8 P.M. Tues.–Sat.), and be sure to stroll the grounds either before or afterward. At dinner, entrées ($28–35) might include filet mignon or veal Oscar.

INFORMATION AND SERVICES

The **Machias Bay Area Chamber of Commerce** (12 E. Main St., Machias, 207/255-4402, www.machiaschamber.org) stocks brochures, maps, and information on area hiking trails. The office is generally open 10 A.M.–3 P.M. Monday–Friday.

Lubec and Vicinity

Literally the beginning of America—at the nation's easternmost point—Lubec (pop. 1,730) can serve as a base for exploring New Brunswick's Campobello Island, the Cutler coastline, and territory to the west. With a couple of appealing bed-and-breakfasts and more than 90 miles of meandering waterfront, Lubec conveys the aura of realness: a hardscrabble fishing community that extends a welcome to visitors. Lubec residents love to point out that the closest traffic light is 50 miles away.

Settled in 1780 and originally part of Eastport, Lubec was split off in 1811 and named for the German port of Lübeck (for convoluted reasons still not totally clear). The town's most famous resident was Hopley Yeaton, first captain in the U.S. Revenue-Marine (now the U.S. Coast Guard), who retired here in 1809.

Along the main drag (Water Street), a number of shuttered buildings reflect the town's roller-coaster history. Once the world's sardine capital, Lubec no longer has a packing plant, but aquaculture has come to the forefront, and new businesses are slowly arriving.

SIGHTS

West Quoddy Head State Park

Beachcombing, hiking, picnicking, and an up-close look at Maine's only red-and-white-striped lighthouse are the big draws at 480-acre Quoddy Head State Park (West Quoddy Head Rd., Lubec, 207/733-0911, www.parksandlands.com, 9 A.M.–sunset May 15–Oct. 15, $3 nonresident adults, $2 Maine resident adults, $1 children), the easternmost point of U.S. land. Begin with a visit to the **Visitor Center** (207/733-2180, www.westquoddy.com, 10:10 A.M.–4 P.M. daily late May–mid-Oct., free), located in the 1858 keeper's house and operated by the enthusiastic all-volunteer West Quoddy Head Light Keepers Association. Inside are exhibits on lighthouse memorabilia, local flora and fauna, and area heritage; a gallery displaying local works; and a staffed information desk.

The current **West Quoddy Head Light,** towering 83 feet above mean high water, was built in 1857. (Its counterpart, East Quoddy Head Light, is on New Brunswick's Campobello Island.) Views from the lighthouse grounds are fabulous, and whale sightings are common in summer. The lighthouse tower is open annually for one day in June or early July, during Lighthouse Week, and other times when the Coast Guard is on-site.

The cliffs of Canada's Grand Manan Island

© TOM NANGLE

Candy-striped West Quoddy Head Light, in Lubec, is a regional icon.

are visible from the park's grounds. A 1.75-mile moderately difficult trail follows the 90-foot cliffs to Carrying Place Cove, and an easy mile-long boardwalk winds through a unique moss and heath bog designated as a National Natural Landmark. Be forewarned that the park gate is locked at sunset. In winter, the park is accessible for snowshoeing. From Route 189 on the outskirts of Lubec, take South Lubec Road (well signposted) to West Quoddy Head Road. Turn left and continue to the parking area.

Mulholland Market and McCurdy Smokehouse

Lubec Landmarks (207/733-2197, www.mccurdyssmokehouse.org) is working to preserve these two local landmarks. The smokehouse complex, the last herring-smoking operation in the country (closed in 1991), can be seen on the water side of Water Street. In 2007, after years of effort, it finally reopened to the public for tours. Mulholland Market is the organization's headquarters. Inside are displays about the smokehouses and exhibits of local art. It's volunteer operated, so hours change frequently; call for current schedule.

Lubec Historical Society

The society's small museum in the **Old Columbian Store** (135 Main St., 207/733-2274, 9 A.M.–3 P.M. Mon., Wed., and Fri., free) doubles as a visitors information center. Among the historical and genealogical displays is a working model of the machine used in the infamous Gold from Seawater swindle of 1898. Volunteers will gladly fill you in on that or you can pick up a brochure. While here, also pick up the *Lubec Historic Walking Tour* brochure, which highlights about a dozen historical sites in downtown Lubec. The museum is on the left as you're entering town, just beyond Uncle Kippy's restaurant.

Lubec Breakwater

Even the humongous tides and dramatic sunsets over Johnson Bay can get your attention if you hang out at the breakwater. Across the channel on Campobello Island is red-capped **Mulholland Point Lighthouse,** an abandoned beacon built in 1885. As the tide goes out—18 or so feet—you'll also see hungry harbor seals dunking for dinner. And if you're lucky, you might spot the eagle pair that nests on an island in the channel (bring binoculars).

Quoddy Mist

The old RJ Peacock factory is now home to **Quoddy Mist** (72 Water St., Lubec, 207/733-4847, www.quoddymist.com), which produces all-natural sea salt in about a dozen flavors. Tastings are available, and free tours explain the process. It's tucked behind Dianne's Glass Gallery.

ENTERTAINMENT AND EVENTS

Classical music is the focus (for the most part) at **SummerKeys** (207/733-2316 or off-season 973/316-6220, www.summerkeys.com), a music camp for adults, no prior

© HILARY NANGLE

Lubec Landmarks has restored McCurdy Smokehouse and opened it for tours.

experience required, with weeklong programs in piano, voice, oboe, flute, clarinet, guitar, violin, and cello. Free concerts by visiting artists, faculty, and students are held at 7:30 P.M. Wednesday evenings late June–early September in the Congregational Christian Church, on Church Street.

Live music is usually on tap on weekends at Cohill's Inn and Annabell's Pub, both on Water Street.

During summer, concerts are usually held Thursday evenings at the town bandstand on Main Street.

An ambitious grassroots group has launched **Cobscook Community Learning Center** (207/733-2233, Timber Cove Rd., Trescott, www.thecclc.org). Two timber-frame buildings house CCLC's year-round programs, an open pottery studio, fiber-arts studio, and multiuse classrooms. Festivals, adult education, indigenous education, sustainable and value-added eco-ventures, youth programs, and more are offered. Open-jam music nights, held on the second, fourth, and fifth Mondays each month (7–10 P.M., donation appreciated), bring in as many as 20 musicians and a good crowd of listeners.

Bird-watching is big here, and spring brings **The Down East Spring Birding Festival** (207/733-2201, www.downeastbirdfest.org) to the Cobscook Bay Area, held annually in late May. Guided and self-guided explorations, presentations, and tours fill the schedule, and participation is limited, so register early.

SHOPPING

Two downtown shops are within strolling distance of each other. Dianne Larkin sells her handcrafted hot-fused glass jewelry, plates, and other creations at **Dianne's Glass Gallery** (72 Water St., Lubec, 207/733-2458, www.diannesglass.com); she also operates a one-room bed-and-breakfast in her home, $50 with morning muffins. **Northern Tides** (24 Water St., Lubec, 207/733-2500) carries intriguing works by local artisans such as sea-glass creations, pottery crafted with finds from the sea, felt work, and weaving.

TIDES

Nowhere in Maine is the adage "Time and tide wait for no man" more true than along the Washington County coastline. The nation's most extreme tidal ranges occur in this area, so the hundreds of miles of tidal shore frontage between Steuben and Calais provide countless opportunities for observing tidal phenomena. Every six hours or so, the tide begins either ebbing or flowing. The farther Down East you go, the higher (and lower) the tides. Although tides in Canada's Bay of Fundy are far higher, the highest tides in New England occur along the St. Croix River, at Calais.

Tides govern coastal life – particularly Down East, where average tidal ranges may be 10–20 feet and extremes approach 28 feet. Everyone is a slave to the tide calendar, which coastal-community newspapers diligently publish. Boats tie up with extra-long lines; clammers and wormdiggers schedule their days by the tides; hikers have to plan for shoreline exploring; and kayakers need to plan their routes to avoid getting stuck in the muck.

Tides, as we all learned in elementary school, are lunar phenomena, created by the gravitational pull of the moon; the tidal range depends on the lunar phase. Tides are most extreme at new and full moons – when the sun, moon, and Earth are all aligned. These are spring tides, supposedly because the water springs upward (the term has nothing to do with the season). And tides are smallest during the moon's first and third quarters – when the sun, Earth, and moon have a right-angle configuration. These are neap tides ("neap" comes from an Old English word meaning "scanty"). Other lunar/solar phenomena, such as the equinoxes and solstices, can also affect tidal ranges.

The best time for shoreline exploration is on a new-moon or full-moon day, when low tide exposes mussels, sea urchins, sea cucumbers, starfish, periwinkles, hermit crabs, rockweed, and assorted nonbiodegradable trash. Rubber boots or waterproof, treaded shoes are essential on the wet, slippery terrain.

Caution is also essential in tidal areas. Unless you've carefully plotted tide times and heights, don't park a car, bike, or boat trailer on a beach; make sure your sea kayak is lashed securely to a tree or bollard; don't take a long nap on shoreline granite; and don't cross a low-tide land spit without an eye on your watch.

A perhaps apocryphal but almost believable story goes that one flatlander stormed up to a ranger at Cobscook Bay State Park one bright summer morning and demanded indignantly to know why they had had the nerve to drain the water from her shorefront campsite during the night. When it comes to tides...you have to go with the flow.

En route to West Quoddy Head, stop at **Crow Town Gallery** (406 S. Lubec Rd., Lubec, 207/733-8860) to view a fine selection of locally inspired art.

Lighthouse buffs must stop at **West Quoddy Gifts** (Quoddy Head Rd., one mile before the lighthouse, 207/733-2457). It's stocked with souvenirs and gifty items, most with a lighthouse theme.

RECREATION

Tours

Native Lubec residents, often with roots going back generations and with specialties as diverse as wildlife, bird-watching, photography, and diving, deliver insights and share their knowledge on **Tours of Lubec and Cobscook** (135 Main St., Lubec, 207/733-2997 or 888/347-9302, www.toursoflubecandcobscook.com). Credit enthusiastic Lubec resident Ruta Jordans for creating the nonprofit Association to Promote and Protect the Lubec Environment (APPLE) to help visitors learn more about Lubec. APPLE sponsors personalized interpretive tours covering area art, culture, the environment, history, and heritage. Suggested donations range $20–45 per person. Call or visit the website to create an itinerary that works for you.

Hiking and Walking

Tag along with Lubec's **Pathfinders Walking Group,** enthusiastic area residents who go exploring every Sunday year-round, usually meeting at 2 P.M. for a two-hour ramble; check local papers for schedule. Nonmembers are welcome, there's no fee, and you'll see a Lubec (and more) that most visitors never encounter.

Two Maine Coast Heritage Trust preserves are fine places for a walk. The 376-acre **Hamilton Cove Preserve**'s 1.5 miles of ocean frontage are highlighted by cobble beaches, rocky cliffs, and jaw-dropping views (on a clear day) of Grand Manan. To find it, take Route 189 to the South Lubec Road toward Quoddy Head, but bear right at the fork on Boot Cove Road and continue 2.4 miles to a small parking lot on the left. There's a kiosk with maps about 100 feet or so down the trail. It's about one mile to an observation platform and another half mile to the bench at the trail's end. Continue on Boot Cove Road another 1.5 miles to find **Boot Head Preserve,** with dramatic cliffs and ravines that epitomize Maine's Bold Coast reputation. The trail passes through a rare coastal raised peatland before continuing to a viewing platform on the coast. From the parking lot to Boot Cove via the Coastal Trail it's 1.25 miles; return via the Interior Trail for another 0.75 mile.

For information on other hikes in the area, pick up a copy of *Cobscook Trails,* a guidebook with maps and trail details. It's available for $7 at local stores. Another resource available locally is *Self-Guided Birding Explorations, Washington County, Maine,* published in conjunction with the Down East Spring Birding Festival. It lists and maps walks and hikes and notes habitats and bird species.

Biking and Kayaking

The Wharf (60 Johnson St., Lubec, 207/733-4400, www.wharfrentals.com) rents bikes for $18 per day, $12 half day, and kayaks for $25–35.

ACCOMMODATIONS

Rates noted are for peak season.

Many visitors use Lubec as a base for day trips to Campobello Island, so it's essential to make reservations at the height of summer. Several lodgings are also available on Campobello.

Bed-and-Breakfasts and Inns

Built in 1860 by a British sea captain, **Peacock House Bed and Breakfast** (27 Summer St., Lubec, 207/733-2403 or 888/305-0036, www.peacockhouse.com, $95–135) has long been one of Lubec's most prestigious residences. Among the notables who have stayed here are Donald MacMillan, the famous Arctic explorer; and U.S. senators Margaret Chase Smith and Edmund Muskie. It has three rooms and four suites; suites have TV and sitting area; one has a gas fireplace and a refrigerator. One room is wheelchair-accessible.

Unusual antiques fill the guest and sitting rooms of the 19th-century **Home Port Inn** (45 Main St., Lubec, 207/733-2077 or 800/457-2077 outside Maine, www.homeportinn.com, $95–115), ensconced on a Lubec hilltop. Each of the seven rooms has a private bath, although some are detached; some have water views. Rates include a generous continental breakfast. The inn also serves dinner by reservation.

Piano students at SummerKeys often practice on the living room piano at **BayViews** (6 Monument St., Lubec, 207/733-2181, $60–100), providing impromptu concerts for other guests. The 1824 Victorian house sits on two acres edging Johnson Bay. It's a relaxed bed-and-breakfast, filled with eclectic antiques, art, and books. (Owner Kathryn Rubeor has a master's in English literature.) It's an easy walk to town if you can tear yourself away from the back deck or lawn chairs or hammock. Breakfast is a

© HILARY NANGLE

The former Coast Guard station at West Quoddy Head has been restored and now welcomes guests.

bountiful continental, with fresh fruit and juice, home-baked bread, and homemade granola and toppings. One huge suite perfect for a family and one twin room, with a piano, have private baths; two doubles and one single share a bath.

Ellen and Jack Gearrin extend a warm, Irish welcome to guests at **Cohill's Inn** (7 Water St., 207/733-4300, www.cohillsinn.com, $95–125), which overlooks the Bay of Fundy out one side, and the Narrows out the other. There are no frills or fuss in the simply but nicely furnished guest rooms; each has a fan and TV, beds are covered with comforters and quilts, and a continental breakfast is included in the rate. Downstairs is a popular and reliable pub, but service ends at 8 P.M. so it's quiet at night.

Motel

The lackluster **Eastland Motel** (385 County Rd., Rte. 189, Lubec, 207/733-5501, www.eastlandmotel.com, $70–80) has 20 rooms with cable TV, Wi-Fi, and air-conditioning. Request one of the 12 rooms in the newer section. Free continental breakfast. Small pets possible ($10).

Apartments, Suites, and Houses

The farmhouse on the Bell family's 200-year-old saltwater farm, **Tide Mill Farms** (40 Tide Mill Rd., Edmunds, two miles north of Rte. 189, 207/733-2110, www.tidemillfarm.com), is available for weekly rental. Ocean views are available from throughout the century-old farmhouse, which has five bedrooms and 1.5 baths. Amenities include a TV-VCR, washer-dryer, and gas grill. Linens are provided. Original settler Robert Bell built a tidal gristmill here, and one of the stones still lies on the point. Explore the farm's 1,600 acres, including six miles of shorefront as well as forest and mountain trails. Watch for eagles, seals, and loons. The property is home to the organic farm of the same name, and you'll see farm animals and operations.

Bill Clark has rescued the former Coast Guard station at West Quoddy Head and restored, renovated, and reopened it as **West Quoddy Station** (S. Lubec Rd., Lubec, 207/733-4452 or 877/535-4714, www.quoddyvacation.com), with five one-bedroom units (four in the lodge and one separate cabin), plus the five-bedroom, 2.5-bath Station House. All have kitchens, Wi-Fi, and DirecTV. Views are stupendous and extend to East Quoddy Head on Campobello; West Quoddy Head is about a half-mile walk. Rates begin at $90 per night, when available, but weekly rentals ($600–1,700) get first preference.

Another reclamation project is taking place at a former sardine factory. Judy and Victor Trafford are renovating the truly waterfront complex into **The Wharf** (60 Johnson St., Lubec, 207/733-4400, www.wharfrentals.com). Rooms ($100/night, $550/week) have use of a common kitchen and dining area. Two-bedroom, two-bathroom apartments ($150/night, $850/week) have full kitchens and laundry facilities. All have incredible views and Wi-Fi. Also on the premises are a yoga studio and bike and kayak rentals. A water taxi to Eastport was expected to begin operation in 2010, and an on-site restaurant is planned.

Campgrounds

A 3.5-mile network of nature trails, picnic spots, great bird-watching and berry picking, hot showers, a boat launch, and wooded shorefront campsites make **Cobscook Bay State Park** (Rte. 1, Edmunds Township, 207/726-4412, www.parksandlands.com), on the 888-acre Moosehorn Reserve, one of Maine's most spectacular state parks. It's even entertaining just to watch the 24-foot tides surging in and out of this area at five or so feet an hour; there's no swimming because of the undertow. Reserve well ahead to get a place on the shore. No hookups, but there's a dump station for RVs. To guarantee a site in July and August, using MasterCard or Visa, call 207/624-9950 (800/332-1501 in Maine) or visit www.campwithme.com; reservation fee is $2 per site per night, two-night minimum. The park is open daily mid-May–mid-October; trails are groomed in winter for cross-country skiing, and one section goes right along the shore. Summer day-use fees are $4.50 nonresident adults, $3 resident adults, $1.50 nonresident seniors, free resident seniors, $1 children 5–11. The nonresident camping fee is $24 per site per night; the fee for Maine residents is $14.

FOOD

Local Flavors

You can't go wrong with a stop at **Bold Coast Smokehouse** (224 County Rd./Rte. 189, Lubec, 207/733-8912 or 888/733-0807, www.boldcoastsmokehouse.com). Vinny Gartmayer is a master of the smoking process, creating delectable hot and cold smoked salmon, smoked fish spreads, smoked salmon sticks (great for picnics; try the garlic-pepper), and other goodies.

Monica's (56 Pleasant St., Lubec, 866/952-4500, www.monicaschocolates.com) gives meaning to the term sinfully delicious. Monica Elliott creates sumptuous handmade gourmet chocolates using family recipes from her native Peru. Visitors can sample chocolates before buying. (Smart move: You're guaranteed to buy after you taste.)

Stave off a midday hunger attack with home-baked goodies with an organic twist from **Sun Porch Industries** (99 Johnson St., Lubec, 207/733-7587, 11 A.M.–5 P.M. Wed.–Sun.), a tiny natural and organic foods store.

Dining

Dining in Lubec is a bit of a crapshoot. It's wise to ask locally about current reputations, although often you'll find mixed reviews even then.

Depending on your source, **Uncle Kippy's** (County Rd./Rte. 189, Lubec, 207/733-2400, www.unclekippys.com, 11 A.M.–8 P.M. Tues.–Sun., to 9 P.M. Fri.–Sat.) gets high and higher marks in Lubec for wholesome cooking. A sign out front announces, "Stop in or we'll both starve." Steak and seafood are specialties—at unfancy prices—and the pizza is the area's best. Don't be put off by the For Sale sign; it's been there for more than a decade.

Good burgers, chowders, and other choices from the daily chalkboard menu as well as Guinness, Smithwick's, and microbrews have earned **Cohill's Inn** (7 Water St., Lubec, 207/733-4300, www.cohillsinn.com, 11:30 A.M.–9 P.M. daily, $8–22) an enthusiastic two thumbs-up from locals and visitors alike. The dining room has fabulous water views, and there's often entertainment on Saturday afternoons.

The nicest dining room in the area is at the **Home Port Inn** (45 Main St., Lubec, 207/733-2077 or 800/457-2077 outside Maine, www.homeportinn.com, 5–8 P.M. daily). Reservations are advisable for this very popular restaurant, which has a sunken dining room with tables for 30. The specialty is seafood (entrées run $16–26), but the food often doesn't match the setting. Open in summer only.

INFORMATION AND SERVICES

The **Cobscook Bay Area Chamber of Commerce** (www.cobscookbay.com) covers the Cobscook Bay region, including Lubec. Another good resource is the Tourist Information link on the Lubec town website (www.lubecme.govoffice2.com). Local sources of information include: **The Puffin Pines** (240 Rte. 1, Whiting); the **Old Columbian Store** (Main St., Lubec, 207/733-4696, 9 A.M.–3 P.M. Mon., Wed., and Fri.); and the **Visitor Center at West Quoddy Head Lighthouse** (207/733-2180, www.westquoddy.com, 10:10 A.M.–4 P.M. daily late May–mid-Oct.).

Lubec Memorial Library (corner of Water and School Sts., Lubec, 207/733-2491) has a public restroom.

GETTING AROUND

To & Fro Water Taxi, at The Wharf (69 Johnson St., 207/733-4400, $16 round-trip), planned to operate between Lubec and Eastport. Call for current status and schedule.

Campobello Island

ROOSEVELT CAMPOBELLO INTERNATIONAL PARK

Just over the Franklin D. Roosevelt Memorial Bridge from Lubec lies nine-mile-long Campobello Island, in Canada's New Brunswick province. Since 1964, 2,800 acres of the island have been under joint U.S. and Canadian jurisdiction as Roosevelt Campobello International Park, commemorating U.S. president Franklin D. Roosevelt. FDR summered here as a youth, and it was here that he contracted infantile paralysis (polio) in 1921. The park, covering most of the island's southern end, has well-maintained trails, picnic sites, and dramatic vistas, but its centerpiece is the imposing Roosevelt Cottage, a mile northeast of the bridge. It's interesting to note that before becoming a summer retreat for wealthy Americans, Campobello was the feudal fiefdom of a Welsh family. King George III awarded the grant to Captain William Owen in 1767, and he arrived in 1770.

Roosevelt Cottage/Visitor Centre

Little seems to have changed in the 34-room red-shingled Roosevelt "Cottage" overlooking Passamaquoddy Bay since President Roosevelt last visited in 1939. The Roosevelt Cottage (459 Rte. 774, Welshpool, Campobello, NB, Canada, 506/752-2922 seasonal, www.fdr.net) grounds are beautifully landscaped, and the many family mementos—especially those in the late president's den—bring history alive. It all feels very personal, far less stuffy than most presidential memorials.

Stop first at the park's Visitor Centre, where you can pick up brochures (including a trail map, bird-watching guide, and bog guide), use the restrooms, and see a short video setting the stage for the cottage visit. Then walk across to the house-museum (10 A.M.–6 P.M. Atlantic daylight time, 9 A.M.–5 P.M. eastern daylight time, last tour at 5:45 P.M., mid-May–mid-Oct., free). Guides are stationed in various rooms to explain and answer questions. Be sure to also visit the neighboring **Hubbard**

Roosevelt's summer cottage on Campobello appears as though the former U.S. president just left.

Cottage, open July 1–early September whenever it isn't in use by conferences. Free outside walking tours of the estate and on-site presentations on local ecology are given, weather and staff permitting.

The Park by Car

If time is short, or you're unable to hike, at least take some of the park's driving routes—**Cranberry Point Drive,** 5.4 miles round-trip from the Visitor Centre; **Liberty Point Drive,** 12.4 miles round-trip, via Glensevern Road, from the Visitor Centre; and **Fox Hill Drive,** a 2.2-mile link between the other two main routes. Even with a car, you'll have access to beaches, picnic sites, spruce and fir forests, and great views of lighthouses, islands, and the Bay of Fundy.

Just west of the main access road from the bridge is the **Mulholland Point picnic area,** where you can spread out your lunch next to the distinctive red-capped lighthouse overlooking Lubec Narrows.

Hiking and Picnicking

Within the international park are 8.5 miles of walking/hiking trails, varying from dead easy to moderately difficult. Easiest is the 1.2-mile (round-trip) walk from the Visitor Centre to **Friar's Head picnic area,** named for its distinctive promontory jutting into the bay. For the best angle, climb up to the observation deck on the "head." Grills and tables are here for picnickers. Pick up a brochure at the Visitor Centre detailing natural sights along the route.

The most difficult—and most dramatic—trail is a 2.4-mile stretch from **Liberty Point to Raccoon Beach,** along the southeastern shore of the island. Precipitous cliffs can make parts of this trail chancy for small children or insecure adults, so use caution. Liberty Point is incredibly rugged, but observation platforms make it easy to see the tortured rocks and wide-open Bay of Fundy. Along the way is the SunSweep Sculpture, an international art project by David Barr. At broad Raccoon Beach, you can walk the sands, have a picnic, or watch for whales, porpoises, and osprey. To avoid returning via the same route, park at Liberty Point and walk back along Liberty Point Drive from Raccoon Beach. If you're traveling with nonhikers, arrange for them to meet you with a vehicle at Con Robinson's Point.

A fascinating boardwalk, perfect for those in wheelchairs, is **Eagle Hill Bog,** 1.8 miles (2.9 km) down the Glensevern Road. Interpretive signs explain the lichens, scrub pines, pitcher plants, and other flora and fauna within the bogs. A spur trail leads to a trail that climbs quickly to an observation deck.

You can also walk the park's perimeter, including just more than six miles of shoreline, but only if you're in good shape, have waterproof hiking boots, and can spend an entire day on the trails. Before attempting this, however, inquire at the Visitor Centre about trail conditions and tide levels.

CAMPOBELLO BEYOND THE INTERNATIONAL PARK

Take a day or two and explore Campobello beyond the park. You can also continue by ferry from here to New Brunswick's Deer Island and on to Eastport.

Herring Cove Provincial Park

New Brunswick's provincial government does a conscientious job of running Herring Cove Provincial Park (506/752-2396 or 800/561-0123, www.campobello.com/herring.html), with picnic areas, 91 campsites (506/752-7010), a four-mile trail system, a mile-long sandy beach, freshwater Glensevern Lake, a restaurant with fabulous views, and the nine-hole championship-level **Herring Cove Golf Course** (506/752-2467). The park is open early June–September.

East Quoddy Head Light

Consult the tide calendar before planning your assault on East Quoddy Head Light (also known as Head Harbour Light), at Campobello's northernmost tip. It's on an islet accessible only at low tide. The distinctive white light tower bears a huge red cross. (You're likely to pass near it on whale-watching trips out of Eastport.) From the Roosevelt Cottage, follow Route 774 through the village of Wilson's Beach and continue to the parking area. A stern Canadian Coast Guard warning sign tells the story:

> *Extreme Hazard. Beach exposed only at low tide. Incoming tide rises 5 feet per hour and may leave you stranded for 8 hours. Wading or swimming are extremely dangerous due to swift currents and cold water. Proceed at your own risk.*

So there. It's definitely worth the effort for the bay and island views from the lighthouse grounds, often including whales and eagles. Allow about an hour before and after dead low tide (be sure your watch coincides with the Atlantic-time tide calendar).

In 2005, **The Friends of the Head Harbour Lightstation** (916 Rte. 774, Welshpool, NB, Canada, www.campobello.com/lighthouse), a local group, took over maintenance of the station to preserve it. It now charges access fees to support the efforts. You can see the light from the nearby grounds at no charge, but if you want to hike out to the island or visit the light, suggested donations are $5–10 Canadian. The Friends hope to eventually open it to the public with an interpretive center highlighting the lighthouse's history, maritime ecosystems in the Bay of Fundy, and whale-rescue efforts. In the meantime, work parties provide an opportunity to peek inside. You can support the efforts with a membership, available for US$15 individual or US$25 family.

Whale-Watching

Island Cruises (506/752-1107 or 888/249-4400) departs three times daily from Head Harbour Wharf for scenic whale-watching cruises aboard the *Mister Matthew,* a 37-foot traditional Bay of Fundy fishing boat that carries 20 passengers. Captain Mac Greene is a member of the Fundy Whale Rescue Team, so he has great insights and stories to share.

© HILARY NANGLE
East Quoddy Head Light is easily recognized by its distinctive red cross marking.

ACCOMMODATIONS AND FOOD

In midsummer, if you'd like to overnight on the island, be sure to reserve lodgings well in advance; Campobello is a popular destination. The nearest backup beds are in Lubec, and those fill up, too. Rates noted are for peak season.

The Owen House (11 Welshpool St., Welshpool, Campobello Island, NB, Canada, 506/752-2977, www.owenhouse.ca, late May–mid-Oct., $104–210 Canadian) is the island's best address, a comfortably elegant early-19th-century inn on 10 acres on Deer Point overlooking Passamaquoddy Bay and Eastport in the distance. Nine guest rooms (two with shared baths) on three floors are decorated with antiques and family treasures along with owner Joyce Morrel's paintings (Joyce grew up in this house) and assorted handmade quilts. There's a 1st-floor room that's ideal for those with mobility problems. Joyce and innkeeper Jan Meiners are very active in the lighthouse preservation efforts. Just north of the inn is the Deer Island ferry landing.

The Lupine Lodge (610 Rte. 774, Welshpool, Campobello Island, NB, Canada, 506/752-2555, www.lupinelodge.com, early June–mid-Oct., $100–165 Canadian), a log lodge complex, is only a quarter mile from the Roosevelt Cottage. Bay views from the 11-acre grounds and a few of the 11 rooms are terrific, but rooms have no frills and thin walls. The adjacent restaurant serves breakfast, lunch, and dinner. Out the back door are the Adams Estate trails of the provincial park.

Campsites and tent cabins are available at **Herring Cove Provincial Park** (506/752-7010).

Don't expect culinary creativity on Campobello, but you won't starve—at least during the summer season. Best choice is **Family Fisheries** (1977 Rte. 774, Wilson's Beach, Campobello Island, NB, Canada, 506/752-2470, 10:30 A.M.–8 or 9 P.M. daily), a seafood restaurant and fish market toward the northern end of the island. Portions are huge, service is okay, the fish is super-fresh, and the homemade desserts are decent. BYOB. The only island restaurant with a liquor license is Lupine Lodge, which has more atmosphere.

INFORMATION AND SERVICES

To visit Campobello, you'll have to pass customs checkpoints on the U.S. and Canada ends of the Franklin D. Roosevelt Memorial Bridge (Lubec, U.S., Customs 207/733-4331; Campobello, Canada, Customs 506/752-2091). Be sure to have required identification: passport or passport card.

Be aware that crossing this short little bridge takes an hour, because there's a one-hour time difference between Lubec and Campobello. Lubec (like the rest of Maine) is on eastern standard time; Campobello, like the rest of Canada's Maritime Provinces, is on Atlantic time, an hour later. As soon as you reach the island, set your clock ahead an hour.

There is no need to convert U.S. currency to Canadian for use on Campobello; U.S. dollars are accepted everywhere on the island, but prices tend to be quoted in Canadian dollars.

Off the bridge, stop at the **Tourist Information Centre** (44 Rte. 774, Welshpool, NB, Canada, 506/752-7043, May–Oct.) on your right for an island map, trail maps of the international park, tide info for lighthouse visits, and New Brunswick propaganda.

For information on Campobello Island, contact **Campobello Island Tourism Association** (506/752-7010, www.campobelloislandtourism.com).

Eastport and Vicinity

When you leave Whiting, the gateway to Lubec and Campobello, and continue north on Route 1 around Cobscook Bay, it's hard to believe that life could slow down any more than it already has, but it does. The landscape's raw beauty is occasionally punctuated by farmhouses or a convenience store, but little else.

Edmunds Township's claims to fame are its splendid public lands—Cobscook Bay State Park and a unit of Moosehorn National Wildlife Refuge. Just past the state park, loop along the scenic shoreline before returning to Route 1.

Pembroke, once part of adjoining Dennysville, claims Reversing Falls Park, where you can watch (and hear) ebbing and flowing tides draining and filling Cobscook Bay.

If time allows a short scenic detour, especially in fall, turn left (northwest) on Route 214 and drive 10 miles to quaintly named Meddybemps, allegedly a Passamaquoddy word meaning "plenty of alewives [herring]." Views over Meddybemps Lake, on the north side of the road, are spectacular, and you can launch a canoe or kayak into the lake here, less than a mile beyond the junction with Route 191 (take the dead-end unpaved road toward the water).

Backtracking to Route 1, heading east from Pembroke, you'll come to Perry, best known for the Sipayik (Pleasant Point) Indian Reservation, a Passamaquoddy settlement, two miles east of Route 1, that's been here since 1822. Route 191 cuts through the reservation's heart.

The city (yes, it's officially a city) of Eastport (pop. 1,900) is on Moose Island, connected by causeway to the mainland at Sipayik (Pleasant Point). Views are terrific on both sides, especially at sunset, as you hopscotch from one blob of land to another and finally reach this mini city, where the sardine industry was introduced as long ago as 1875. Five sardine canneries once operated here, employing hundreds of local residents who snipped the heads off herring and stuffed them into cans—one of those esoteric skills not easily translatable to other tasks. In the 1990s, the focus was on fish farming. In the new century, entrepreneurs and artisans seem to be leading the way.

Settled in 1772, Eastport has had its ups and downs, mostly mirroring the fishing industry. It's now on an upswing, as people "from

© TOM NANGLE

The fisherman statue on Eastport's waterfront is a souvenir of the coastal village's role as a set for a TV series.

away" have arrived to soak up the vibe of a small town with a heavy Down East accent. Artists, artisans, and antiques shops are leading the town's rejuvenation as a tourist destination, with The Tides Institute at the forefront. A big push came in 2001, when the Fox Network reality-TV series *Murder in Small Town X* was filmed here; the city morphed into the village of Sunrise, Maine, and local residents eagerly filled in as extras. The huge waterfront statue of a fisherman is a remnant of the filming.

Until 1811, the town also included Lubec, which is about 2.5 miles across the water in a boat, but 40-something miles in a car. A Lubec-based passenger ferry was planned for 2010 operation.

SIGHTS

Historic Walking Tour

The best way to appreciate Eastport's history is to pick up and follow the route in *A Walking Guide to Eastport,* available locally for $2. The handy map-brochure spotlights the city's 18th-, 19th-, and early-20th-century homes, businesses, and monuments, many now on the National Register of Historic Places. Among the highlights are historic homes converted to bed-and-breakfasts, two museums, and a large chunk of downtown Water Street, with many handsome brick buildings erected after a disastrous fire swept through in 1886. A free walking map, with far fewer details, also is available.

Raye's Mustard Mill Museum

How often do you have a chance to watch mustard being made in a turn-of-the-20th-century mustard mill? Drive by J. W. Raye and Co. (83 Washington St., Rte. 190, Eastport, 207/853-4451 or 800/853-1903, www.rayesmustard.com, 9 A.M.–5 P.M. Mon.–Fri., 10 A.M.–5 P.M. Sat.–Sun.), at the edge of Eastport, and stop in for a free 15-minute tour (offered as schedule permits, call first). You'll get to see the granite millstones, the mustard seeds being winnowed, and enormous vats of future mustard. Raye's sells mustard under its own label and produces it for major customers under their labels. The shop stocks all of Raye's mustard varieties (samples available), other Maine-made food, and gift items, and it also has a small café where you can buy coffee, tea, and snacks. Both Martha Stewart and Rachael Ray have discovered Raye's, which took home both gold and bronze medals from the 2007 World Wide Mustard Competition.

The Tides Institute and Museum of Art

One of the most promising additions to Eastport's downtown is The Tides Institute (43 Water St., 207/853-4047, www.tidesinstitute.org, 10 A.M.–4 P.M. Tues.–Sat., free), housed in a former bank that's being restored. The institute's impressive goals are to build significant cultural collections and to produce new culturally important works employing printmaking, letterpress, photography, bookmaking, oral history, and other media. For its collection, the institute is focusing on works by artists

THE QUODDY LOOP

It's easy to make it a two-nation vacation and avoid backtracking along Route 1 by looping through Canada. In July and August, **East Coast Ferries** (Deer Island, New Brunswick, Canada, 506/747-2159 or 877/747-2159, www.eastcoastferries.nb.ca) operates funky, bargelike car ferries between Eastport and Deer Island, and then on to Campobello Island – and vice versa. The ferry schedule is in Atlantic time, so adjust for the one-hour time distance when planning, since Eastport is on eastern time and the two Canadian islands are on Atlantic time. Campobello departures are on the hour, beginning at 9 A.M. Atlantic time (8 A.M. eastern time). Eastport departures are on the half hour, beginning at 9:30 A.M. Atlantic time (8:30 A.M. eastern time). Check the schedule carefully to avoid missing the last boat back to Eastport. (If you take a car, you can drive back to Eastport from Campobello via Lubec. It's 1.5 miles by water and almost 50 miles by road.) The ferry landing in Eastport is just off Water Street, 0.3 mile north of Washington Street, next to the Eastport Chowder House Restaurant. Fees for car and driver, in Canadian dollars, are $16 for Deer Island/Campobello, $13 for Deer Island/Eastport, no charge for kids 12 and younger, and non-driving passengers are $3 (no credit cards, fare collected on board); car maximum is $23 for Deer Island/Campobello, $18 for Deer Island/Eastport; a fuel surcharge may be added. It all seems very informal, and the trip is an adventure, but remember that you're crossing the Canadian border. United States citizens need a passport; most non-Europeans also need a Canadian visa.

associated with the U.S.-Canada northeast coast, but with an eye to the broader world. Already, it has significant works by artists such as Martin Johnson Heade and photographers such as Paul Caponigro, a fine selection of baskets by Native Americans, and two organs made by the local Pembroke organ company in the 1880s. A series of rotating shows during the summer highlight both the permanent collections and loaned works. The research and reference library has more than 4,000 volumes. The institute also offers programs in a range of topics and workshops by visiting artists. These are open to the public by reservation. Definitely stop in for a visit.

Passamaquoddy Indian Reservation

To get to Eastport, you pass through the Passamaquoddy's Sipayik or Pleasant Point Reservation (www.wabanaki.com). Ask locally or check the website to find basket makers and other traditional artists who might sell from their homes. The fancy and work baskets are treasures, constantly escalating in price. It's a real treat to be able to buy one from the maker.

PARKS AND PRESERVES

Shackford Head State Park

Ninety-acre Shackford Head (off Deep Cove Rd., Eastport, trailhead and parking area just east of the Washington County Community College Marine Technology Center at the southern end of town, www.parksandlands.com, free) is on a peninsula that juts into Cobscook Bay. It has five miles of wooded trails, with the easiest being the 1.2-mile round-trip to Shackford Head Overlook and its continuation onto the steeper Ship Point Trail, which adds another half mile, rising gently to a 175-foot-high headland with wide-open views of Eastport and, depending on weather, Campobello Island, Lubec, Pembroke, and even Grand Manan. This state preserve is a particularly good family hike. There's a toilet near the parking area, but no other facilities. Also here is a memorial with plaques detailing the history of five Civil War ships that were decommissioned and burned on Cony Beach by the U.S. government between 1901 and 1920. Eastport's huge tides allowed the ships to be brought in and beached and then taken apart as the tide receded. Of note is that 14 Eastport men served on four of the ships.

Reversing Falls Park

There's plenty of room for adults to relax and kids to play at the 140-acre Reversing Falls Park in West Pembroke—plus shorefront ledges and a front-row seat overlooking a fascinating tidal phenomenon. It's connected via hiking trails to the Downeast Regional Land Trust's Reversing Falls Conservation Area (www.qrlt.org/ReversingFalls.htm), a nearly 200-acre property with 1.5 miles of shorefront and 70 acres of coastal wetlands. Pack a picnic and then check newspapers or information offices for the tide times, so you can watch the salt water surging through a 300-yard-wide passage at about 25 knots, creating a whirlpool and churning "falls." The park is at Mahar Point in West Pembroke, 7.2 miles south of Route 1. Coming from the south (Dennysville), leave Route 1 in West Pembroke when you see the Triangle Grocery Store. Turn right and go 0.3 mile to Leighton Point Road, where you'll see a sign saying, "Shore Access 5.5 miles." Turn right and go 3.8 miles, past gorgeous meadows, low shrubs, and views of Cobscook Bay. Turn right on Clarkside Road, at a very tiny Reversing Falls sign posted high on a telephone pole. Go about 1.5 miles to the end and then turn left onto a gravel road and continue two miles to the park.

Gleason Cove

This quiet park and boat launch is a delightful place to walk along the shorefront or to grab a table and spread out a picnic while drinking in the dreamy views over fishing weirs and islands in Passamaquoddy Bay. To get here, take Shore Road (opposite the New Friendly Restaurant) and then take a right on Gleason Cove Road.

ENTERTAINMENT

The **Eastport Arts Center** (36 Washington St., Eastport, 207/853-2358, www.eastportartscenter.com) is an umbrella organization for local arts groups, with headquarters and performing space in a former church. You can pick up a brochure with a complete schedule, which usually includes concerts, workshops, films, puppet shows, productions by local theater group **Stage East,** and other cultural events. Also based here is the **Penobscot Bay Symphony Orchestra,** formed in 2007 by conductor Trond Saeverud, who doubles as concertmaster of the Bangor Symphony Orchestra. Some years, the center provides a ferry to the free **SummerKeys** concerts, held Wednesday nights late June–early September in Lubec.

FESTIVALS AND EVENTS

For a small community, Eastport manages to pull together and put on plenty of successful events during the year.

Eastport's annual four-day **Fourth of July – Old Home Week** extravaganza includes a parade, pancake breakfasts, barbecues, a flea market, an auction, races, live entertainment, and fireworks. This is one of Maine's best Fourth of July celebrations and attracts a crowd of more than 10,000. Lodgings are booked months in advance, so plan ahead.

Indian Ceremonial Days, a three-day Native American celebration, includes children's games, canoe races, craft demos, talking circles, fireworks, and traditional food and dancing at Sipayik, the Pleasant Point Reservation, in Perry, the second weekend in August.

The **Eastport Salmon Festival** celebrates the area's aquaculture industry. If you like salmon, you'll *love* this event, which combines a salmon barbecue, craft booths, live entertainment, and boat trips at the Eastport breakwater the Sunday after Labor Day.

Also in September is the **Two Countries One Bay Art Studio Tour,** a weekend of open galleries and studios in communities edging Passamaquoddy Bay.

SHOPPING

Art, Crafts, and Antiques

Eastport has long been a magnet for artists and craftspeople yearning to work in a supportive environment, but the influx has increased in recent years. Proof of this is **The Eastport Gallery** (74 Water St., Eastport, 207/853-4166, www.eastportgallery.com, mid-June–Sept.), a cooperative whose works in varied media line the walls of a downtown building. The gallery also sponsors the annual **Paint Eastport Day,** usually held the second Saturday in September, when anyone is invited to paint a local scene; a reception and "wet paint" auction follow.

A gaggle of energetic women with local ties renovated a waterfront building, turning it into **The Commons** (51 Water St., Eastport, 207/853-4123), a fabulous gallery displaying works by nearly 100 area artists and artisans. The group has plans to renovate a nearby waterfront warehouse into more shops and a hotel.

Earth Forms (5 Dana St., Eastport, 207/853-2430, www.earthforms.biz) features potter Donald Sutherland's intriguing (and sometimes whimsical) wheel-thrown work—self-described as "functional, nonfunctional, and dysfunctional" pottery. You can often see him at work on his wheel. It's tough to walk out without buying one of these special pieces.

Woodworker Roland LaVallee's gallery **Crow Tracks** (11 Water St., Eastport, 207/853-2336, www.crowtracks.com) is filled with his intricate carvings of birds and local fauna. The tiny garden entryway just doubles the pleasure of a visit.

It's a delight to wander through the sculpted mermaids, angels, goddesses, flora, and fauna in the garden at **Ostrander** (83 Clark St., corner of Brewster St., Eastport, 207/853-4342). Inside are more sculptures, paintings, and garden art by Elizabeth Ostrander.

A number of very talented artists and artisans are tucked along the back roads of the area. You might get lucky and find them open, but it's wise to call before making a special trip. These include the **Salt Meadow Gallery and Studio** (Hersey Rd., Pembroke, 207/726-5153), in a log cabin chock-full of hand-painted floorcloths and woodcuts by Beverly Runyan; **Done Roving Farm and Carding Mill** (20 Charlotte Rd., Charlotte, 207/454-8148), a working farm where fiber artist Paula Farra creates and sells handspun yarns and felts in a variety of fibers and displays the works of other area artisans; **Wrenovations** (84 Mill Stream Rd., Robbinston, 207/454-2382), stained art creations by Mark Wren; and **Susan Designs** (behind Loring's Body Shop on Gin Cove Rd., Perry, 207/853-4315), where gifted quilt artist Susan Plachy sells her creations.

© HILARY NANGLE

It's possible to board a windjammer for a sail through Passamaquoddy Bay.

Gifts and a Whole Lot More

Describing **45th Parallel: The Store** (Rte. 1, Perry, 207/853-9500) is a tough assignment. You really have to *go there* and see for yourself. The aesthetic displays are worth the trip to this eclectic emporium. Housed in a one-story log building two miles (northeast, in the Calais direction) from the junction of Routes 190 and 1, the 45th Parallel is part antiques shop, part gift shop, part global marketplace—and entirely seductive.

Do stop in, if only for a few minutes, at **S. W. Wadsworth and Son** (42 Water St., Eastport, 207/853-4343), the oldest ship chandlery in

© TOM NANGLE

Downtown Eastport fronts on the harbor, and water lines in the granite breakwater are evidence of the giant tides.

the country and the oldest retail business in Maine. In addition to hardware and marine gear, you'll find nautical gifts and souvenirs.

RECREATION

Whale-Watching and Scenic Cruises

Eastporter Butch Harris gave the waterfront a shot in the arm when he bought the sleek *Sylvina Beal,* a historic 84-foot schooner built in 1911. His company, **Eastport Windjammers** (207/853-2500 or 207/853-4303, www.eastportwindjammers.com), offers a number of options to sail. The three-hour whale-watching cruise departs at 1:30 P.M. daily and heads out into the prime whale-feeding grounds of Passamaquoddy Bay—passing the Old Sow whirlpool (largest tidal whirlpool in the Northern Hemisphere), salmon aquaculture pens, and Campobello Island. En route, you'll see bald eagles, porpoises, possibly puffins and osprey, and more. Best months are July and August, when sightings are frequent, but Butch is a skilled spotter, so if they're there, he'll find them. The cost is $37 adults, $20 children under 12. A two-hour sunset cruise departs the Eastport Pier at 7 P.M. and costs $27 adults, $17 children.

Deep-Sea Fishing

Eastport Windjammers also offers a four-hour fishing trip on the *Quoddy Dam,* with all equipment provided. No license is required for recreational saltwater fishing. Bring a cooler or fish container if you want to keep your catch. The trip costs $30 adults and $20 children. It departs the Eastport Breakwater at 8 A.M.

Sea Kayaking, Canoeing, and Hiking

Explore the region by sea kayak with **Cobscook Hikes and Paddles** (13 Woodcock Way, Robbinston, 207/726-4776 summer, 207/454-2130 winter, www.cobscookhikesandpaddles.com), which services the area between Whiting and Calais. Registered Maine Guides Stephen and Tessa Ftorek lead three-hour ocean or lake paddles, designed to meet your interests and ability, for $50 per person. Two-hour sunrise or sunset paddles are $40. On Friday nights, you can watch luminescent organisms sparkle in the water on a two-hour Phosphorescent Paddle, for $45. The Ftoreks also offer guided full-day ($80) and half-day ($40) hikes and snowshoeing adventures in winter.

Star-Gazing

The Downeast Amateur Astronomers' **Downeast Observatory** (356 Old County Rd., Pembroke, 207/726-4621, www.downeastaa.com), with eight-inch DE8 reflector and three- and five-inch refractors, is open to the public for free by appointment, but donations are greatly appreciated. Contact Charlie Sawyer at the observatory for details.

ACCOMMODATIONS

Rates noted are for peak season.

Bed-and-Breakfasts

In 1833, renowned artist John James Audubon stayed at the elegant **Weston House** (26 Boynton St., Eastport, 207/853-2907 or 800/853-2907, www.westonhouse-maine.com, $85–95), so one of the three 2nd-floor guest rooms bears his name—and walls lined with Audubon bird prints. All rooms share two baths, but don't let that dissuade you from staying at this lovely home. Jett and John Peterson's family antiques and interesting art and crafts fill the beautifully decorated house on a quiet side street two blocks above the waterfront. Breakfast is outstanding (Jett is Eastport's favorite caterer), complete with candelabra and classical music. Outside are croquet and badminton facilities, plus lovely gardens with a gazebo, chairs, and table. Tea and sherry are available in the afternoon. With notice, Jett will prepare a private dinner and serve it in the formal dining room, a smart and delicious choice given Eastport's limited restaurants.

Pretty gardens surround the **Chadbourne House** (19 Shackford St., Eastport, 207/853-2727 or 888/853-2728, www.chadbournehouse.com, $130–170), Eastport's most elegant bed-and-breakfast. Jill and David Westphal's antiques-filled Federal-style home has four guest rooms, two with fireplaces and one that fills most of the 3rd floor. The double living room has two fireplaces. Guests gather each morning at the dining room table for David's breakfasts, and they can arrange in advance for a seafood dinner feast to be served in the garden. It's walking distance to downtown. One caveat: You'll have to remove your shoes in the entryway. Wi-Fi throughout.

The old-shoe-comfortable **Milliken House Bed and Breakfast** (29 Washington St., Eastport, 207/853-2955 or 888/507-9370, www.eastport-inn.com, $75–85) is a good choice for families, but be forewarned that it's more homestay than inn and you'll have to carry your luggage up at least one, and perhaps two, tall flights of stairs. Hosts Bill and Mary Williams welcome children and pets to their intown home that's an easy walk to shops and restaurants. Breakfasts are huge and served family-style in the very-Victorian dining room. There's a big TV in the double parlor downstairs, Wi-Fi throughout, and a phone is available. Call ahead in winter.

Motel

Guests at **The Motel East** (23A Water St., Eastport, 207/853-4747, $105–120) have front-row seats on Passamaquoddy Bay, overlooking Campobello Island. Get up early and catch the sunrise; later, watch boats unload their catches. Six good-size rooms and eight efficiency suites have Wi-Fi, phones, and cable TV, although all could use freshening. Request a balcony room; avoid those on the basement level. Free coffee in the lobby. It's open all year. The separate Friar Roads Cottage is available for $150 d a day.

Apartments

On the 2nd floor of **The Commons** (51 Water St., Eastport, 207/853-4123, www.thecommonseastport.com), a newly renovated downtown building on the waterfront, are two nicely appointed two-bedroom apartments with decks and spectacular harbor views. Tide Watcher has two baths and rents for $950 per week;

Water's Edge has one bath and rents for $900; either is $150 per night/three-night minimum, when available.

FOOD

Dining options have improved in Eastport in recent years, but as always in this region, ask locally about the current reputations. And always call before making a special trip, as hours and days of operation seem to change week to week, never mind season to season.

Local Flavors

Hilda and Sidney Lewis's **The Blue Iris** (31 Water St., Eastport, 207/853-2440, 6:30 A.M.–2 P.M. daily) shares space with a floral shop. Well-spaced indoor tables and outdoor ones on a bi-level deck all have water views. Breakfast is served all day; lunch is available beginning at 11 A.M. Service is cheerful but can be, um, leisurely.

Here's something a bit different. **Blueberry Point Chefs** (Rte. 1, P.O. Box 58, Perry 04667, 207/853-4629, www.blueberrypointchefs.com) is a cooking school held on a 150-acre blueberry farm with panoramic views over Passamaquoddy Bay. Chef Audrey Patterson's classes (usually held 5–8:30 P.M. Mon. late May–late Sept., $50 pp) conclude with a meal. Check the website for the specifics of each class. Also on the premises is the **Ice House Wine and Cheese Shop** (10 A.M.–5 P.M. Tues.–Sat.).

Family Favorites

Casual, friendly, and inexpensive is **The Happy Crab** (35 Water St., Eastport, 207/853-9400, www.happycrabeastport.com, 11 A.M.–8 P.M. daily), a grill and sports bar. Pizza and finger food are usually available after 8 P.M. until the bar closes. Play pool while you wait. If the weather's fine, grab a seat on the deck.

A popular roadside eatery with a well-deserved reputation, the aptly named **New Friendly Restaurant** (1014 Rte. 1, Perry, 207/853-6610, 11 A.M.–8 P.M. daily) lays on home-cooked offerings for "dinnah" (a Maine-ism meaning lunch), specializing in steak and seafood, including what many label the area's best lobster roll.

Time your meal right and you can watch the Deer Isle ferry arrive and depart or view the windjammer *Sylvina Beal* sail by from the bi-level **Eastport Chowder House** (167 Water St., Eastport, 207/853-4700, www.eastportchowderhouse.com, 11 A.M.–9 P.M. daily). Seafood, natch, is the specialty, with entrées in the $12–20 range. There's a bar downstairs and a harborfront deck, too.

Casual Dining

Breaking the norm of fried fish and lobster rolls for Eastport is **The Pickled Herring** (32 Water St., Eastport, 207/853-2323, www.thepickledherring.com, from 5 P.M. Thurs.–Sun.). Decent pizzas come from the wood-fired oven, and fancier fare is served, too. There's a nice wine list, and the bartender mixes a mean martini. Do make reservations.

Lobster

When the weather's clear, there's nothing finer than lobster at **Quoddy Bay Lobster** (7 Sea St., Eastport, 207/853-6640, 10 A.M.–6 P.M. Tues.–Sat. in season, plus 11 A.M.–4 P.M. Sun. in July–Aug.). Lobster is the headliner—watch boats unload their catch, it's that fresh—but there are other options. The only seating is at outside tables on the harbor's edge.

INFORMATION AND SERVICES

Information

Brochures are available at the **Quoddy Maritime Museum and Visitor Center** (70 Water St., Eastport, 10 A.M.–6 P.M. daily June–Sept.). In the museum section of the center is a huge model of the failed 1936 Passamaquoddy Tidal Power Project (an idea whose time hadn't come when it was proposed). A new tidal project is in the works, though.

Information also is available from the **Eastport Chamber of Commerce** (207/853-3633, www.eastport.net) and online at www.cobscookbay.com.

The handsome stone **Peavey Memorial Library** (26 Water St., Eastport, 207/853-4021), built in 1893, is named after the inventor of the Peavey grain elevator.

Public Restrooms

Restrooms are available at the library, and in summer there are portable toilets on Eastport's breakwater.

Calais and Vicinity

Calais (CAL-us, pop. 3,890) is as far as you'll get on the coast of Maine; from here on, you're headed inland.

Europeans showed up in this area as early as 1604, when French adventurers established an ill-fated colony on St. Croix Island in the St. Croix River—16 whole years before the Pilgrims even thought about Massachusetts. After a winter-long debacle, all became relatively quiet until 1779, when the first permanent settler arrived.

Southeast of Calais is tiny Robbinston, a booming shipbuilding community in the 19th century but today little more than a 500-person blip on the map.

SIGHTS

Downeast Heritage Center

In 2009, Maine's Passamaquoddy tribe was negotiating to purchase the former Downeast Heritage Center (39 Union St., Calais, 207/454-7878 or 877/454-2500, www.downeastheritage.org) and reopen it with displays on tribal heritage and culture.

Walking Tour

Pick up a copy of the *Walking Tour Guide to Calais Residential Historic District* at the Maine Tourism Information Center, on the waterfront. The guide, produced by the St. Croix Historical Society, briefly covers the town's history and maps and describes the architecture and early owners of 23 historic houses, four of which are listed on the National Register of Historic Places.

St. Croix Island

Unless you have your own boat, you can't get over to 6.5-acre St. Croix Island, an International Historic Site under joint U.S. and Canadian jurisdiction (Rte. 1, Red Beach Cove, eight miles south of Calais, www.nps.gov/maac, free).

The island is the site of the pioneering colony established by French explorers Samuel de Champlain and Pierre du Gua (Sieur de Monts) in 1604. Doomed by disease, mosquitoes, lack of food, and a grueling winter, 35 settlers died; in spring, the emaciated survivors abandoned their effort and moved on to Nova Scotia. In 1969, archaeologists found graves of 23 victims, but the only monument on the island is a commemorative plaque dating from 1904.

The current in the St. Croix River is strong, and tidal ranges can be as high as 28 feet, so neophyte boaters shouldn't even attempt a crossing, but local residents often picnic and swim off the island's sandy beach on the southern end. A the 16-acre roadside rest area on Route 1 at **Red Beach Cove,** a short heritage trail, with bronze statues depicting various key personae or cultures in the development of the colony, ends on the point with views of the island. Also here are picnic tables, restrooms, a gravel beach, and a boat launch.

Whitlock Mill Lighthouse

From the lovely Pikewoods Rest Area, beside Route 1, about four miles southeast of Calais, there's a prime view of 32-foot-high Whitlock Mill Lighthouse, on the southern shore of the St. Croix River. Built in 1892, the green flashing light is accessible only over private land, so check it out from this vantage point. You can also have a picnic break here.

© TOM NANGLE

It's hard to miss Katie's on the Cove, a delicious find just south of Calais.

Calais-Robbinston Milestones

A quirky little local feature, the Calais-Robbinston milestones are a dozen red-granite chunks marking each of the 12 miles between Robbinston and Calais. Presaging today's highway mileage markers, late-19th-century entrepreneur and journalist James S. Pike had the stones installed on the north side of Route 1 to keep track of the distance while training his pacing horses.

ENTERTAINMENT AND FESTIVALS

Music on the Green is a series of free concerts presented at 6:30 P.M. Wednesdays at Triangle Park in downtown Calais.

The **Brewer House** (590 Rte. 1, Robbinston, 12 miles south of Calais, 207/454-0333) sometimes hosts chamber music concerts featuring resident violinist Trond Saeverud.

Calais, Maine, and St. Stephen, New Brunswick, collaborate the first or second week of August for the nine-day **International Festival** of dinners, concerts, dances, a craft fair, ball games, and a cross-border parade and road race. Newspapers carry schedules (be sure to note which events are on eastern time and which are on Atlantic time).

SHOPPING

Downtown Calais has a few shops worthy of a look-see. **St. Croix Valley Antiques and Collectibles** (4 Monroe St., Calais, 866/420-1167) is a big shop with a wide range of furniture, quilts, baskets, and tableware. **The Dusty Rose** (22 North St., Calais, 207/454-7351) is chock-full of vintage finds for fans of old stuff. The **Urban Moose** (80 Main St., Calais, 207/454-8277) has an eclectic inventory that invites browsing. Perhaps most intriguing is Captain Craig Little's **Little Ships of the Maritimes,** tucked behind North Street downtown, which specializes in custom scale models. Nearly two dozen regional artists and artisans sell their works at **Cat's Eye Gallery** (272 North St., Calais, 207/454-

GRAND LAKE STREAM

For a tiny community of about 200 year-rounders, Grand Lake Stream has a well-deserved, larger-than-life reputation. It's the center of a vast area of rivers and lakes, ponds and streams – a recreational paradise, and more than 27,000 acres, including 62 miles of shore frontage, has been preserved by the **Downeast Lakes Land Trust** (www.downeastlakes.org). It's the town at the end of the world, remote in every sense of the word, yet just a half hour or so inland from Calais.

The famous stream is a narrow three-mile neck of prime scenic and sportfishing water connecting West Grand Lake and Big Lake. A dam spans the bottom of West Grand, and just downstream is a state-run salmon hatchery. Since the mid-19th century, the stream and its lakes have been drawing fishing fans to trout and landlocked-salmon spawning grounds, and fourth and fifth generations now return here each year.

Fly-fishing enthusiasts arrive in May and June for landlocked salmon and smallmouth bass (the stream itself is fly-fishing only); families show up in July and August for canoeing, bird-watching, swimming, fishing, and hiking; hunters arrive in late October for game birds and deer; and snowmobilers, snowshoers, and cross-country skiers descend as the snow piles up.

Canoe building has contributed to the area's mystique. The distinctive Grand Lake canoe (or "Grand Laker"), a lightweight, square-sterned, motorized 20-footer, was developed in the 1920s specifically for sportfishing in these waters. In the off-season, several villagers still hunker down in their workshops and turn out these stable cedar beauties. (Interested? Call Bill Shamel, 207/796-8199.)

ACTIVITIES

If you're in Grand Lake Stream only for the day, head for the **public landing** and bear right after the intersection with the Pine Tree Store, where you'll find a parking area, a dock, a portable toilet, and a boat launch. You can also walk the path on the eastern shore of the stream. Or, armed with a map from the Pine Tree Store, hike the 2.6-mile **Little Mayberry Cove Trail** edging the western shoreline of West Grand Lake.

Better yet, plan a day with a guide. The region has the greatest concentration of Registered Maine Guides in the state, which gives you an indication of the fishing, hunting, and canoeing opportunities here. Truly the best way to experience Grand Lake Stream is with a member of the **Grand Lake Stream Guides Association** (www.grandlakestreamguides.com). The website lists members and their specialties. You can arrange for one of these skilled guides to lead you on a fishing expedition, wildlife or photographic safari, or canoeing trip for a half day or longer.

FOLK ART FESTIVAL

A great time to visit the village is the last full weekend in July for the annual **Grand Lake Stream Folk Art Festival** (207/796-8199, www.glsfaf.com, 10 A.M.–5 P.M. Sat.–Sun., $5 one day, $8 both days), held on the town's grassy ballfield. Tents shelter approximately 50 top-notch juried artisans. Nonstop bluegrass and folk music is another attraction. An exhibit highlights the region's canoe-building tradition and another displays antique and contemporary quilts. Breakfast, lunch, and snacks are available. Complementing the festival are lakeside barbecues

2020). Books new, old, and rare are sold at the **Calais Book Shop** (405 Main St., Calais, 207/454-1110).

If you stop in at **Katie's on the Cove** (Rte. 1, Mill Cove, Robbinston, 207/454-3297 or 800/494-5283, 10 A.M.–5 P.M. Tues.–Sat. late May–mid-Oct.), do so at your own risk—chocoholics may need a restraining order. Joseph and Lea Sullivan's family operation, begun in 1982, has become a great success story. They now produce about four dozen varieties of homemade fudge, truffles, caramels, peanut brittle, even marzipan. The shop, 12 miles southeast of Calais and about 15 miles

© HILARY NANGLE

The annual Grand Lake Stream Folk Art Festival adds an artsy accent to the famed fishing community.

by the guides, usually lobster on Friday evening, chicken on Saturday evening, with tickets available at the Pine Tree Store, across from the festival grounds. A contra dance takes place Saturday night, and a music jam, open to anyone, occurs Sunday morning. Leashed pets are welcome on festival grounds.

PRACTICALITIES

Visit www.grandlakestream.com for more information.

The heart of Grand Lake Stream is Kurt and Kathy Cressey's Pine Tree Store (3 Water St., Grand Lake Stream, 207/796-5027, www.pinetreestore.com). People have been getting their gas and groceries here for more than 60 years. It's also a good source of local information (and gossip), and it sells pizza, sandwiches, and general-store merchandise. Be sure to check out their handmade pack baskets (sold at L. L. Bean).

To get to Grand Lake Stream, head north on Route 1 from Calais through Princeton. About two miles north of Princeton, turn left (west) onto Grand Lake Stream Road (also called Princeton Road). Continue about 10 miles to the village.

west of Eastport, is no place for unruly or demanding kids—space is limited and the candy is pricey.

RECREATION

Parks and Preserves

More than 50 miles of trails and gravel roads wind through the 17,257-acre Baring Unit of the **Moosehorn National Wildlife Refuge** (Charlotte Rd., Baring, 207/454-7161, http://moosehorn.fws.gov, sunrise–sunset daily, free), on the outskirts of Calais. Start with the 1.2-mile nature trail near the refuge headquarters, and get ready for major-league wildlife-watching: 35 mammal and 220 bird species have been spotted in the refuge's fields, forests, ponds, and marshes. Wear waterproof shoes and insect repellent. In August, help yourself to wild blueberries. During November deer-hunting season, either avoid the refuge Monday–Saturday or wear a hunter-orange hat and vest. Trails are accessible by snowshoes, snowmobile, or cross-country skis in winter. To reach refuge headquarters, take Route 1 north from downtown Calais about three miles. Turn left onto the Charlotte Road, and go 2.4 miles to the headquarters sign. The office is open 8 A.M.–4 P.M. Monday–Friday all year (except major national holidays); you can pick up free trail maps, bird checklists, and other informative brochures. If you want to help support the conservation of wildlife in eastern Maine and educational programs, you can join Friends of Moosehorn National Wildlife Refuge (R.R. 1, Box 202, Ste. 12, Baring, ME 04694). A check for a mere $15 will do the trick.

By the way, if you don't have time to walk the trails, watch for the elevated man-made nesting platforms—avian high-rises for bald eagles—outside of Calais alongside Route 1 North (near the junction with the Charlotte Road). Depending on the season, you may spot a nesting pair or even a fledgling. The chicks (usually twins but occasionally triplets) hatch around mid-May and try their wings by early August. A 400-square-foot observation deck across Route 1 is the best place for eagle-watching.

Continuing on the Charlotte Road past the Moosehorn Refuge headquarters, you'll come to **Round Lake** (locally called Round Pond), a lovely spot where you can picnic, swim, or put in a kayak or canoe. Across the road, with a great lake view, is the interesting old Round Pond Cemetery, dating from the early 19th century. (Why do graveyards always have the best views?) Just after the cemetery, a left turn puts you on Pennamaquam Lake Road (or Charlotte Road) toward Perry; a right turn takes you to Route 214, near Pembroke.

About six miles south of Calais, watch for signs pointing to **Devil's Head** and take the dirt road on the river side. The 315-acre site has a mile of frontage on the St. Croix River estuary and views to St. Croix Island. A road, with two parking areas, descends to the shoreline, and there are pit toilets and a marked hiking trail, approximately 1.5 miles looping from the road, leading to the highest point of coastal land north of Cadillac Mountain. According to locals, the headland was originally called d'Orville Head but it morphed into Devil's Head.

Calais has a lovely riverfront park at the foot of North Street. **Pike's Park** is the perfect place for a picnic. From here you have access to the **Calais Waterfront Walk,** which edges the river, running for 0.9 mile upriver and 0.6 downriver.

Golf

At the nine-hole **St. Croix Country Club** (River Rd./Rte. 1, Calais, 207/454-8875, late April–late Oct.), the toughest and most scenic hole is the seventh, one of five holes on the river side of Route 1.

ACCOMMODATIONS

Rates noted are for peak season.

Bed-and-Breakfasts

The classic Greek Revival–style ☾ **Brewer House** (590 Rte. 1, Robbinston, 207/454-0333, www.thebrewerhousebnb.com, $120–165 d) commands a knoll opposite the boat launch in Robbinston. Built by Captain John N. Marks in 1828, the house is distinguished by columns both in front and back, French nine-over-nine windows with carved Grecian moldings, Ionic pilasters, marble fireplaces, silver doorknobs, and an elliptical staircase—obviously the good captain was successful. The house also served as a stop on the Underground Railroad. The four guest rooms are furnished with antiques; some have ocean views, and some have shared baths. A full breakfast is served. The bed-and-breakfast has an artsy feel, as the J. B. Siem Gallery is on the property, and chamber concerts featuring violinist Trond Saeverud, concert master of the Bangor Symphony Orchestra, are presented here. The innkeepers speak English, German, Danish, Norwegian, Swedish, and a little Japanese.

Within easy walking distance of downtown is **Greystone Bed and Breakfast** (13 Calais Ave., Calais, 207/454-2848, www.greystonecalaisme.com, $80), Alan and Candace Dwelley's masterfully restored 1840 Greek Revival home. The property, listed on the National Historic Register, is an architectural gem within, with Corinthian columns and black marble fireplace mantels, and two guest rooms (one of which can be paired with a third, smaller room). The Dwelleys serve a more-than-full breakfast and are eager to share their recommendations for local sights and shopping.

Motel

The Gothic-styled, gingerbread-trimmed **Redclyffe Shore Motel and Dining Room** (Rte. 1, Robbinston, 207/454-3270, www.redclyffeshoremotorinn.com, $95) sits on a bluff jutting into the St. Croix River as it widens into Passamaquoddy Bay. The 16 motel units have cable TVs, phones, and sunset-facing river views. Redclyffe is locally popular for its greenhouse-style dining room (just ignore the plastic flowers), with ocean views, serving moderately priced fare. It's 12 miles south of Calais.

FOOD

Like the rest of Down East Maine, it's wise to call ahead as hours and days of operation change frequently. Hours noted are for peak season.

Local Flavors

If you're near downtown Calais, order picnic sandwiches to go at **Border Town Subz** (311 Main St., Calais, 207/454-8562, 10 A.M.–7 P.M. Mon.–Fri., 10 A.M.–3 P.M. Sat.), a reliable local favorite.

Another choice for picnic fixings, cottage staples, and other goodies is the **Sunrise County Farmers Market** (11 A.M.–3 P.M. Tues. late June–early Oct.). Look for it in the downtown park.

Casual Dining

White Christmas lights brighten the ceiling of **Bernardini's** (257 Main St., Calais, 207/454-2237, www.visitcalais.com, 11 A.M.–2 P.M. and 4–8 P.M. Mon.–Sat.), a popular downtown restaurant that has earned its repute with always-reliable Tuscany-inspired Italian cuisine; entrées are $11–20. The pleasant dining room is accented by woodwork salvaged from a local church. Save room for the tiramisu.

Fabulous soups, fresh and fat sandwiches, bright salads, and heartier choices, many with a Southwestern accent, make **Julianna's World Cafe** (North St., Calais, 207/454-2299, www.juliannasworldcafe.com, 11 A.M.–9 P.M. Mon.–Sat.) an especially appealing downtown spot, despite the lackluster interior decor. There's a full bar and free Wi-Fi.

Tucked behind McDonald's, **Solos Casual Fine Dining** (9 Chandler St., Calais, 207/454-0400, www.solosmaine.com, 4–9 P.M. Tues.–Sat., 4–8:30 P.M. Sun., $14–19) is a cozy restaurant in an older house. Since opening as a coffee house, it's evolved into a reliable dining choice with a wide-ranging menu. White tablecloths add a refined note. There's often live music. Lunch may be available, too.

INFORMATION AND SERVICES

Information

The **Maine Visitor Information Center** (39 Union St., Calais, 207/454-2211) has free Wi-Fi, clean restrooms, and scads of brochures, including those produced by the **St. Croix Valley Chamber of Commerce** (207/454-2308 or 888/422-3112, www.visitcalais.com). The information center is open 8 A.M.–6 P.M. daily mid-May–mid-October, 9 A.M.–5:30 P.M. daily the rest of the year.

Check out **Calais Free Library** (Union St., Calais, 207/454-2758, www.calais.lib.me.us).

Public Restrooms

Restrooms are available at the Maine Visitor Information Center (39 Union St., Calais) and the St. Croix International Heritage Site, in Red Beach.

Crossing into Canada

If you plan to cross into Canada, you'll have to pass customs checkpoints on both the Calais (U.S., 207/454-3621) and St. Stephen (Canada, 506/466-2363) ends of the bridges. Be sure to have the required identification (passport or passport card) and paperwork.

Pay attention to your watch, too—Calais is on eastern time, while St. Stephen (and the rest of Canada's Maritime Provinces) is on Atlantic time, one hour later.

BACKGROUND

The Land

Maine is an outdoor classroom for Geology 101, a living lesson in what the glaciers did and how they did it. Geologically, Maine is something of a youngster; the oldest rocks, found in the Chain of Ponds area in the western part of the state, are only 1.6 billion years old—more than two billion years younger than the world's oldest rocks.

But most significant is the great ice sheet that began to spread over Maine about 25,000 years ago, during the late Wisconsin Ice Age. As it moved southward from Canada, this continental glacier scraped, gouged, pulverized, and depressed the bedrock in its path. On it continued, charging up the north faces of mountains, clipping off their tops and moving southward, leaving behind jagged cliffs on the mountains' southern faces and odd deposits of stone and clay. By about 21,000 years ago, glacial ice extended well over the Gulf of Maine, perhaps as far as the Georges Bank fishing grounds.

But all that began to change with meltdown, beginning about 18,000 years ago. As the glacier melted and receded, ocean water moved in, covering much of the coastal plain and working its way inland up the rivers. By 11,000 years ago, glaciation had pulled back from all but a few minor corners at the top of Maine, revealing the south coast's beaches and the

ESTUARIES AND MUDFLATS

Maine's estuaries, where fresh- and salt water meet, are ecosystems of outstanding biological importance. South of Cape Elizabeth, where the Maine coast is low and sandy, estuaries harbor large salt marshes of spartina grasses that can tolerate the frequent variations in salinity as runoff and tides fluctuate. Producing an estimated four times more plant material than an equivalent area of wheat, these spartina marshes provide abundant nutrients and shelter for a host of marine organisms that ultimately account for as much as 60 percent of the value of the state's commercial fisheries.

The tidal range along the Maine coast varies 9-26 vertical feet, southwest to northeast. Where the tide inundates sheltered estuaries for more than a few hours at a time, spartina grasses cannot take hold, and mudflats dominate. Although it may look like a barren wasteland at low tide, a mudflat is also a highly productive environment and home to abundant marine life. Several species of tiny primitive worms called nematodes can inhabit the mud in densities of 2,000 or more per square inch. Larger worm species are also very common. One, the bloodworm, grows up to a foot long and is harvested in quantity for use as sportfishing bait.

More highly savored among the mudflat residents is the soft-shell clam, famous for its outstanding flavor and an essential ingredient of an authentic Maine lobster bake. But because clams are suspension feeders – filtering phytoplankton through their long siphon, or "neck" – they can accumulate pollutants that cause illness, including hepatitis. Many Maine mudflats are closed to clam harvesting because of leaking septic systems, so it's best to check with the state's Department of Marine Resources or the local municipal office before digging a mess of clams yourself.

For birds – and bird-watchers – salt marshes and mudflats are an unparalleled attraction. Long-legged wading birds such as glossy ibis, snowy egret, little blue heron, great blue heron, tricolored heron, green heron, and black-crowned night heron frequent the marshes in great numbers throughout the summer, hunting the shallow waters for mummichogs and other small salt-marsh fish, crustaceans, and invertebrates. Mid-May-early June, and then again mid-July-mid-September, migrating shorebirds pass through Maine to and from their subarctic breeding grounds. On a good day, a discerning bird-watcher can find 17 or more species of shorebirds probing the mudflats and marshes with pointed bills in search of their preferred foods. In turn, the large flocks of shorebirds don't escape the notice of their own predators – merlins and peregrine falcons dash in to catch a meal.

unusual geologic traits—eskers and erratics, kettleholes and moraines, even a fjord—that make the rest of the state such a fascinating natural laboratory.

Today's Landscape

Three distinct looks make up the contemporary Maine coastal landscape. (Inland are even more distinct biomes: serious woodlands and mountains as well as lakes and ponds and rolling fields.)

Along the **Southern Coast,** from Kittery to Portland, are fine-sand beaches, marshlands, and only the occasional rocky headland. The **Mid-Coast** and **Penobscot Bay,** from Portland to the Penobscot River, feature one finger of rocky land after another, all jutting into the Gulf of Maine and all incredibly scenic. **Acadia** and the **Down East Coast,** from the Penobscot River to Eastport and including fantastic Acadia National Park, have many similarities to the Mid-Coast (gorgeous rocky peninsulas, offshore islands, granite everywhere), but, except on Mount Desert Island, takes on a different look and feel by virtue of its slower pace, higher tides, and quieter villages.

Rare pitcher plants can be sighted in peat bogs in Down East Maine.

GEOGRAPHY

Bounded by the Gulf of Maine (Atlantic Ocean), the St. Croix River, New Brunswick Province, the St. John River, Québec Province, and the state of New Hampshire (and the only state in the Union bordered by only one other state), Maine is the largest of the six New England states, roughly equivalent in size to the five others combined—offering plenty of space to hike, bike, camp, sail, swim, or just hang out. The state—and the coastline—extends from 43° 05' to 47° 28' north latitude, and 66° 56' to 80° 50' west longitude. (Technically, Maine dips even farther southeast to take in five islands in the offshore Isles of Shoals archipelago.) It's all stitched together by 22,574 miles of highways and 3,561 bridges.

Maine's more than 5,000 rivers and streams provide nearly half of the watershed for the Gulf of Maine. The major rivers are the Penobscot (350 miles), the St. John (211 miles), the Androscoggin (175 miles), the Kennebec (150 miles), the Saco (104 miles), and the St. Croix (75 miles). The St. John and its tributaries flow northeast; all the others flow more or less south or southeast.

CLIMATE

Whoever invented the state's oldest cliché—"If you don't like the weather, wait a minute"—must have spent at least several minutes in Maine. The good news, though, is that if the weather is lousy, it's bound to change before too long. And when it does, it's intoxicating. Brilliant, cloud-free Maine weather has lured many a visitor to put down roots, buy a retirement home, or at least invest in a summer retreat.

The serendipity of it all necessitates two caveats: *Always pack warmer clothing than you think you'll need.* And *never arrive without a sweater or jacket—even at the height of summer.*

The National Weather Service assigns Maine's coastline a climatological category distinct from climatic types found in the interior.

The coastal category, which includes Portland, runs from Kittery northeast to Eastport and about 20 miles inland. Here, the ocean moderates the climate, making coastal winters warmer and summers cooler than in the interior (relatively speaking, of course). From early June through August, the Portland area—fairly typical of coastal weather—may have three to eight days of temperatures over 90°F, 25–40 days over 80°, 14–24 days of fog, and 5–10 inches of rain. Normal annual precipitation for the Portland area is 44 inches of rain and 71 inches of snow (the snow total is misleading, though, since intermittent thaws clear away much of the base).

The Seasons

Maine has four distinct seasons: summer, fall, winter, and mud. Lovers of spring need to look elsewhere in March, the lowest month on the popularity scale with its mud-caked vehicles, soggy everything, irritable temperaments, tank-trap roads, and often the worst snowstorm of the year.

Summer can be idyllic—with moderate temperatures, clear air, and wispy breezes—but it can also close in with fog, rain, and chills. Prevailing

© HILARY NANGLE

Look atop telephone poles and on rocky ledges for osprey nests.

winds are from the southwest. Officially, summer runs June 20 or 21–September 20 or 21, but June, July, and August is more like it, with temperatures in the Portland area averaging 70°F during the day and in the 50s at night. The normal growing season is 148 days.

A poll of Mainers might well show autumn as the favorite season—days are still warmish, nights are cool, winds are optimum for sailors, and the foliage is brilliant. Fall colors usually begin appearing far to the north about mid-September, reaching their peak in that region by the end of the month. The last of the color begins in late September in the southernmost part of the state and fades by mid-October. Early autumn, however, is also the height of hurricane season, the only potential flaw this time of year.

Winter, officially December 20 or 21–March 20 or 21, means deep snow and cold inland and an unpredictable potpourri along the coastline. When the cold and snow hit the coast, it's time for cross-country skiing, ice fishing, snowshoeing, ice-skating, ice climbing, and winter trekking and camping.

Spring, officially March 20 or 21–June 20 or 21, is the frequent butt of jokes. It's an ill-defined season that arrives much too late and departs all too quickly. Ice floes dot inland lakes and ponds until "ice-out" in early–mid-May; spring planting can't occur until well into May; lilacs explode in late May and disappear by mid-June. And just when you finally can enjoy being outside, blackflies stretch their wings and satisfy their hunger pangs. Along the coast, onshore breezes often keep the pesky creatures to a minimum.

Northeasters and Hurricanes

A northeaster is a counterclockwise, swirling storm that brings wild winds out of—you guessed it—the northeast. These storms can occur any time of year, whenever the conditions brew them up. Depending on the season, the winds are accompanied by rain, sleet, snow, or all of them together.

THE ROCKY SHORELINE AND THE MARINE ENVIRONMENT

On Maine's more exposed rocky shores – the dominant shoreline from Cape Elizabeth all the way Down East to Lubec – where currents and waves keep mud and sand from accumulating, the plant and animal communities are entirely different from those in the inland aquatic areas. The most important requirement for life in this impenetrable, rockbound environment is probably the ability to hang on tight. Barnacles, the calcium-armored crustaceans that attach themselves to the rocks immediately below the high-tide line, have developed a fascinating battery of adaptations to survive not only pounding waves but also prolonged exposure to air, solar heat, and extreme winter cold. Glued in place, however, they cannot escape being eaten by dog whelks, the predatory snails that also inhabit this intertidal zone. Whelks are larger and more elongate than the more numerous and ubiquitous periwinkle, accidentally transplanted from Europe in the mid-19th century.

Also hanging onto these rocks, but at a lower level, are the brown algae – seaweeds. Like a marine forest, the four species of rockweed provide shelter for a wide variety of life beneath their fronds. A world of discovery awaits those who make the effort to go out onto the rocks at low tide and look under the clumps of seaweed and into the tide pools they shelter. Venture into these chilly waters with mask, fins, and wet suit and still another world opens for natural-history exploration. Beds of blue mussels, sea urchins, sea stars, and sea cucumbers dot the bottom close to shore. In crevices between and beneath the rocks lurk rock crabs and lobsters. Now a symbol of the Maine coast and the delicious seafood it provides, the lobster was once considered "poor man's food" – so plentiful that it was spread on fields as fertilizer. Although lobsters are far less common than they once were, they are one of Maine's most closely monitored species, and their population continues to support a large and thriving commercial fishing industry.

The same cannot be said for most of Maine's other commercially harvested marine fish. When Europeans first came to these shores four centuries ago, cod, haddock, halibut, hake, flounder, herring, and tuna were abundant. No longer. Overharvested, their seabed habitat torn up by relentless dragging, these groundfish have all but disappeared. It will be decades before these species can recover – and then only if effective regulations can be put in place soon.

The familiar doglike face of the harbor seal, often seen peering alertly from the surface just offshore, provides a reminder that wildlife populations are resilient – if given a chance. A century ago, there was a bounty on harbor seals because it was thought they ate too many lobsters and fish. Needless to say, neither fish nor lobsters increased when the seals all but disappeared. With the bounty's repeal and the advent of legal protection, Maine's harbor seal population has bounced back to an estimated 15,000–20,000. Scores of them can regularly be seen basking on offshore ledges, drying their tan, brown, black, silver, or reddish coats in the sun. Though it's tempting to approach for a closer look, avoid bringing a boat too near these haul-out ledges, as it causes the seals to flush into the water and imposes an unnecessary stress on the pups, which already face a first-year mortality rate of 30 percent.

Positive changes in our relationships with wildlife are even more apparent with the return of birds to the Maine coast. Watching the numerous herring gulls and great black-backed gulls soaring on a fresh ocean breeze today, it's hard to imagine that a century ago egg collecting had so reduced their numbers that they were a rare sight. In 1903, there were just three pairs of common eiders left in Maine; today, 25,000 pairs nest along the coast. With creative help from dedicated researchers using sound recordings, decoys, and prepared burrows, Atlantic puffins are recolonizing historic offshore nesting islands. Osprey and bald eagles, almost free of the lingering vestiges of DDT and other pesticides, now range the length of the coast and up Maine's major rivers.

© HILARY NANGLE

Fog often shrouds the coast of Maine.

Hurricane season officially runs June–November but is most prevalent late August–September. Some years, the Maine coast remains out of harm's way; other years, head-on hurricanes and even glancing blows have eroded beaches, flooded roads, splintered boats, downed trees, knocked out power, and inflicted major residential and commercial damage.

Sea Smoke and Fog

Sea smoke and fog, two atmospheric phenomena resulting from opposing conditions, are only distantly related, but both can radically affect visibility and therefore be hazardous. In winter, when the ocean is at least 40°F warmer than the air, billowy sea smoke rises from the water, creating great photo ops for camera buffs but especially dangerous conditions for mariners.

In any season, when the ocean (or lake or land) is colder than the air, fog sets in, creating perilous conditions for drivers, mariners, and pilots. Romantics, however, see it otherwise, reveling in the womblike ambience and the muffled moans of foghorns. Between April and October, Portland averages about 31 days with heavy fog, when visibility may be a quarter mile or less.

Storm Warnings

The National Weather Service's official daytime signal system for wind velocity consists of a series of flags representing specific wind speeds and sea conditions. Beachgoers and anyone planning to venture out in a kayak, canoe, sailboat, or powerboat should heed these signals. The flags are posted on all public beaches, and warnings are announced on TV and radio weather broadcasts, as well as on cable TV's Weather Channel and the NOAA broadcast network.

History

Prehistoric Mainers: The Paleoindians

As the great continental glacier receded northwestward out of Maine about 11,000 years ago, some prehistoric grapevine must have alerted small bands of hunter-gatherers—fur-clad Paleoindians—to the scrub sprouting in the tundra, burgeoning mammal populations, and the ocean's bountiful food supply. Because come they did—at first seasonally and then year-round. Anyone who thinks tourism is a recent Maine phenomenon needs only to explore the shoreline in Damariscotta, Boothbay Harbor, and Bar Harbor, where heaps of cast-off oyster shells and clamshells document the migration of early Native Americans from woodlands to waterfront. "The shore" has been a summertime magnet for millennia.

Archaeological evidence from the Archaic period in Maine—roughly 8000–1000 B.C.—is fairly scant, but paleontologists have unearthed stone tools and weapons and small campsites attesting to a nomadic lifestyle supported by fishing and hunting (with fishing becoming more extensive as time went on). Toward the end of the tradition, during the late Archaic period, emerged a rather anomalous Indian culture known officially as the Moorehead phase but informally called the Red Paint People; the name is due to their curious trait of using a distinctive red ocher (pulverized hematite) in burials. Dark red puddles and stone artifacts have led excavators to burial pits as far north as the St. John River. Just as mysteriously as they had arrived, the Red Paint People disappeared abruptly and inexplicably around 1800 B.C.

Following them almost immediately—and almost as suddenly—hunter-gatherers of the Susquehanna Tradition arrived from well to the south, moved across Maine's interior as far as the St. John River, and remained until about 1600 B.C., when they, too, enigmatically vanished. Excavations have turned up relatively sophisticated stone tools and evidence that they cremated their dead. It was nearly 1,000 years before a major new cultural phase appeared.

The next great leap forward was marked by the advent of pottery making, introduced about 700 B.C. The Ceramic period stretched to the 16th century, and cone-shaped pots (initially stamped, later incised with coiled-rope motifs) survived until the introduction of metals from Europe. Houses of sorts—seasonal wigwam-style dwellings for fishermen and their families—appeared along the coast and on offshore islands.

The Europeans Arrive

The identity of the first Europeans to set foot in Maine is a matter of debate. Historians dispute the romantically popular notion that Norse explorers checked out this part of the New World as early as A.D. 1000. Even an 11th-century Norse coin found in 1961 in Brooklin (on the Blue Hill Peninsula) probably was carried there from farther north.

Not until the late 15th century, the onset of the great Age of Discovery, did credible reports of the New World (including what's now Maine) filter back to Europe's courts and universities. Thanks to innovations in naval architecture, shipbuilding, and navigation, astonishingly courageous fellows crossed the Atlantic in search of rumored treasure and new routes for reaching it.

John Cabot, sailing from England aboard the ship *Mathew,* may have been the first European to reach Maine, in 1498, but historians have never confirmed a landing site. No question remains, however, about the account of Giovanni da Verrazzano, an Italian explorer commanding *La Dauphine* under the French flag, who reached the Maine coast in May 1524, probably at the tip of the Phippsburg Peninsula. Encountering less-than-friendly Indians, Verrazzano did a minimum of business and sailed onward. His brother's map of the site labels it "The Land of Bad People." Esteban Gomez and John Rut followed in Verrazzano's wake, but nothing came of their exploits.

Nearly half a century passed before the Maine coast turned up again on European explorers' itineraries. This time, interest was fueled by reports of a Brigadoon-like area called Norumbega (or Oranbega, as one map had it), a myth that arose, gathered steam, and took on a life of its own in the decades after Verrazzano's voyage.

By the early 17th century, when Europeans began arriving in more than twos and threes and getting serious about colonization, Native American agriculture was already under way at the mouths of the Saco and Kennebec Rivers, the cod fishery was thriving on offshore islands, Indians far to the north were hot to trade furs for European goodies, and the birchbark canoe was the transport of choice on inland waterways.

In mid-May 1602, Bartholomew Gosnold, en route to a settlement off Cape Cod aboard the *Concord,* landed along Maine's southern coast. The following year, merchant trader Martin Pring and his boats *Speedwell* and *Discoverer* explored farther Down East, backtracked to Cape Cod, and returned to England with tales that inflamed curiosity and enough sassafras to satisfy royal appetites. Pring produced a detailed survey of the Maine coast from Kittery to Bucksport, including offshore islands.

On May 18, 1605, George Waymouth, skippering the *Archangel,* reached Monhegan Island, 11 miles off the Maine coast, and moored for the night in Monhegan Harbor (still treacherous even today, exposed to the weather from the southwest and northeast and subject to meteorological beatings and heaving swells; yachting guides urge sailors not to expect to anchor, moor, or tie up there). The next day, Waymouth crossed the bay and scouted the mainland. He took five Indians hostage and sailed up the St. George River, near present-day Thomaston. As maritime historian Roger Duncan has put it:

The Plimoth Pilgrims were little boys in short pants when George Waymouth was exploring this coastline.

Waymouth returned to England and awarded his hostages to officials Sir John Popham and Sir Ferdinando Gorges, who, their curiosity piqued, quickly agreed to subsidize the colonization effort. In 1607, the *Gift of God* and the *Mary and John* sailed for the New World carrying two of Waymouth's captives. After returning them to their native Pemaquid area, Captains George Popham and Raleigh Gilbert continued westward, establishing a colony (St. George or Fort George) at the tip of the Phippsburg Peninsula in mid-August 1607 and exploring the shoreline between Portland and Pemaquid. Frigid weather, untimely deaths (including Popham's), and a storehouse fire doomed what's called the Popham Colony, but not before the 100 or so settlers built the 30-ton pinnace *Virginia,* the New World's first such vessel. When Gilbert received word of an inheritance waiting in England, he and the remaining colonists returned to the Old World.

In 1614, swashbuckling Captain John Smith, exploring from the Penobscot River westward to Cape Cod, reached Monhegan Island nine years after Waymouth's visit. Smith's meticulous map of the region was the first to use the "New England" appellation, and the 1616 publication of his *Description of New-England* became the catalyst for permanent settlements.

The French and the English Square Off

English dominance of exploration west of the Penobscot River in the early 17th century coincided roughly with French activity east of the river.

In 1604, French nobleman Pierre du Gua, Sieur de Monts, set out with cartographer Samuel de Champlain to map the coastline, first reaching Nova Scotia's Bay of Fundy and then sailing up the St. Croix River. In midriver, just west of present-day Calais, a crew planted gardens and erected buildings on today's St. Croix Island while de Monts and Champlain went off exploring. The two men reached the island Champlain named l'Isle des Monts Deserts (Mount Desert Island) and present-day Bangor before returning to face the winter with their ill-fated compatriots. Scurvy, lack of fuel and water, and a ferocious winter wiped out nearly half of the 79 men. In spring 1605, de Monts, Champlain, and other survivors headed southwest, exploring the coastline all the way to Cape Cod before heading northeast again and settling permanently at Nova Scotia's Port Royal (now Annapolis Royal).

Eight years later, French Jesuit missionaries en route to the Kennebec River ended up on Mount Desert Island and, with a band of French laymen, set about establishing the St. Sauveur settlement. But leadership squabbles led to building delays, and English marauder Samuel Argall—assigned to reclaim English territory—arrived to find them easy prey. The colony was leveled, the settlers were set adrift in small boats, the priests were carted off to Virginia, and Argall moved on to destroy Port Royal.

By the 1620s, more than four dozen English fishing vessels were combing New England waters in search of cod, and year-round fishing depots had sprung up along the coast between Pemaquid and Portland. At the same time, English trappers and dealers began usurping the Indians' fur trade—a valuable income source.

The Massachusetts Bay Colony was established in 1630 and England's Council of New England, headed by Sir Ferdinando Gorges, began making vast land grants throughout Maine, giving rise to permanent coastal settlements, many dependent on agriculture. Among the earliest communities were Kittery, York, Wells, Saco, Scarborough, Falmouth, and Pemaquid—places where they tilled the acidic soil, fished the waters, eked out a barely-above-subsistence living, coped with predators and endless winters, bartered goods and services, and set up local governments and courts.

By the late 17th century, as these communities expanded, so did their requirements and responsibilities. Roads and bridges were built, preachers and teachers were hired, and militias were organized to deal with internecine and Indian skirmishes.

Even though England yearned to control the entire Maine coastline, her turf, realistically, was primarily south and west of the Penobscot River. The French had expanded from their Canadian colony of Acadia, for the most part north and east of the Penobscot. Unlike the absentee bosses who controlled the English territory, French merchants actually showed up, forming good relationships with the Indians and cornering the market in fishing, lumbering, and fur trading. And French Jesuit priests converted many a Native American to Catholicism. Intermittently, overlapping Anglo-French land claims sparked locally messy conflicts.

In the mid-17th century, the strategic heart of French administration and activity in Maine was Fort Pentagoet, a sturdy stone outpost built in 1635 in what is now Castine. From here, the French controlled coastal trade between the St. George River and Mount Desert Island and well up the Penobscot River. In 1654, England captured and occupied the fort and much of French Acadia, but, thanks to the 1667 Treaty of Breda, title returned to the French in 1670, and Pentagoet briefly became Acadia's capital.

A short but nasty Dutch foray against Acadia in 1674 resulted in Pentagoet's destruction ("levell'd with ye ground," by one account) and the raising of a third national flag over Castine.

The Indian Wars (1675-1760)

Caught in the middle of 17th- and 18th-century Anglo-French disputes throughout Maine were the Wabanaki (People of the Dawn), the collective name for the state's major Native American tribal groups, all of whom spoke Algonquian languages. Modern ethnographers label these groups the Micmacs, Maliseets, Passamaquoddies, and Penobscots.

In the early 17th century, exposure to European diseases took its toll, wiping out three-quarters of the Wabanaki in the years 1616–1619. Opportunistic English and French

© HILARY NANGLE

York is one of the best places to soak up Maine's pre-Revolutionary War–era history.

traders quickly moved into the breach, and the Indians struggled to survive and regroup.

But regroup they did. Less than three generations later, a series of six Indian wars began, lasting nearly a century and pitting the Wabanaki most often against the English but occasionally against other Wabanaki. The conflicts, largely provoked by Anglo-French tensions in Europe, were King Philip's War (1675–1678), King William's War (1688–1699), Queen Anne's War (1703–1713), Dummer's War (1721–1726), King George's War (1744–1748), and the French and Indian War (1754–1760). Not until a get-together in 1762 at Fort Pownall (now Stockton Springs) did peace effectively return to the region—just in time for the heating up of the revolutionary movement.

Comes the Revolution

Near the end of the last Indian War, just beyond Maine's eastern border, a watershed event led to more than a century of cultural and political fallout. During the so-called Acadian Dispersal, in 1755, the English expelled from Nova Scotia 10,000 French-speaking Acadians who refused to pledge allegiance to the British Crown. Scattered as far south as Louisiana and west toward New Brunswick and Québec, the Acadians lost farms, homes, and possessions in this *grand dérangement.* Not until 1785 was land allocated for resettlement of Acadians along both sides of the Upper St. John River, where thousands of their descendants remain today. Henry Wadsworth Longfellow's epic poem *Evangeline* dramatically relates the sorry Acadian saga.

In the District of Maine, on the other hand, with relative peace following a century of intermittent warfare, settlement again exploded, particularly in the southernmost counties. The 1764 census tallied Maine's population at just under 25,000; a decade later, the number had doubled. New towns emerged almost overnight, often heavily subsidized by wealthy investors from the parent Massachusetts Bay Colony. With almost 4,000 residents, the largest town in the district was Falmouth (later renamed Portland).

In 1770, 27 Maine towns became eligible, based on population, to send representatives to the Massachusetts General Court, the colony's legislative body. But only six coastal towns could actually afford to send anyone, sowing seeds of resentment among settlers who were thus saddled with taxes without representation. Sporadic mob action accompanied unrest in southern Maine, but the flashpoint occurred in the Boston area.

On April 18, 1775, Paul Revere set out on America's most famous horseback ride—from Lexington to Concord, Massachusetts—to announce the onset of what became the American Revolution. Most of the Revolution's action occurred south of Maine, but not all of it.

In June, the Down East outpost of Machias was the site of the war's first naval engagement. The well-armed but unsuspecting British vessel HMS *Margaretta* sailed into the bay and was besieged by local residents angry about a Machias merchant's sweetheart deal with the British. Before celebrating their David-and-Goliath victory, the rebels captured the *Margaretta,* killed her captain, and then captured two more British ships sent to the rescue.

In the fall of 1775, Colonel Benedict Arnold—better known to history as a notorious turncoat—assembled 1,100 sturdy men for a flawed and futile "March on Québec" to dislodge the English. From Newburyport, Massachusetts, they sailed to the mouth of the Kennebec River, near Bath, and then headed inland with the tide. In Pittston, six miles south of Augusta and close to the head of navigation, they transferred to a fleet of 220 locally made bateaux and laid over three nights at Fort Western in Augusta. Then they set off, poling, paddling, and portaging their way upriver. Skowhegan, Norridgewock, and Chain of Ponds were among the landmarks along the grueling route. The men endured cold, hunger, swamps, disease, dense underbrush, and the loss of nearly 600 of their comrades before reaching Québec in late 1775. In the Kennebec River Valley, Arnold Trail historical signposts today mark highlights (or, more aptly, lowlights) of the expedition.

Four years later, another futile attempt to dislodge the British, this time in the District of Maine, resulted in America's worst naval defeat until World War II—a little-publicized debacle called the Penobscot Expedition. On August 14, 1779, as more than 40 American warships and transports carrying more than 2,000 Massachusetts men blockaded Castine to flush out a relatively small enclave of leftover Brits, a seven-vessel Royal Navy fleet appeared. Despite their own greater numbers, about 30 of the American ships turned tail up the Penobscot River. The captains torched their vessels, exploding the ammunition and leaving the survivors to walk in disgrace to Augusta or even Boston. Each side took close to 100 casualties, three commanders—including Paul Revere—were court-martialed, and Massachusetts was about $7 million poorer.

The American Revolution officially came to a close on September 3, 1783, with the signing of the Treaty of Paris between the United States and Great Britain. The U.S.-Canada border was set at the St. Croix River, but, in a massive oversight, boundary lines were left unresolved for thousands of square miles in the northern District of Maine.

Trade Troubles and the War of 1812

In 1807, president Thomas Jefferson imposed the Embargo Act, banning trade with foreign entities—specifically, France and Britain. With thousands of miles of coastline and harbor villages dependent on trade for revenue and basic necessities, Maine reeled. By the time the act was repealed, under president James Madison in 1809, France and Britain were almost unscathed, but the bottom had dropped out of New England's economy.

An active smuggling operation based in Eastport kept Mainers from utter despair, but the economy still had continued its downslide. In 1812, the fledgling United States declared war on Great Britain, again disrupting coastal trade. In the fall of 1814, the situation reached its nadir when the British invaded the Maine coast and occupied all the shoreline between the St. Croix and Penobscot Rivers. Later that same year, the Treaty of Ghent finally halted the squabble, forced the British to withdraw from Maine, and allowed the locals to get on with economic recovery.

Statehood

In October 1819, Mainers held a constitutional convention at the First Parish Church on Congress Street in Portland. (Known affectionately as "Old Jerusalem," the church was later replaced by the present-day structure.) The convention crafted a constitution modeled on that of Massachusetts, with two notable differences: Maine would have no official church (Massachusetts had the Puritans' Congregational Church), and Maine would place no religious requirements or restrictions on its gubernatorial candidates. When votes came in from 241 Maine towns, only nine voted against ratification.

For Maine, March 15, 1820, was one of those good news/bad news days: After 35 years of separatist agitation, the District of Maine broke from Massachusetts (signing the separation allegedly, and disputedly, at the Jameson Tavern in Freeport) and became the 23rd state in the Union. However, the Missouri Compromise, enacted by Congress only 12 days earlier to balance admission of slave and free states, mandated that the slave state of Missouri be admitted on the same day. Maine had abolished slavery in 1788, and there was deep resentment over the linkage.

Portland became the new state's capital (albeit only briefly; it switched to Augusta in 1832), and William King, one of statehood's most outspoken advocates, became the first governor.

Trouble in the North Country

Without an official boundary established on Maine's far northern frontier, turf battles were always simmering just under the surface. Timber was the sticking point—everyone wanted the vast wooded acreage. Finally, in early 1839, militia reinforcements descended on the disputed area, heating up what has come to be known as the Aroostook War, a border confrontation with no battles and no casualties (except a farmer who was shot by friendly militia). It's a blip in the historical timeline, but remnants of fortifications in Houlton, Fort Fairfield, and Fort Kent keep the story alive today. By March 1839, a truce was negotiated, and the 1842 Webster-Ashburton Treaty established the border once and for all.

Maine in the Civil War

In the 1860s, with the state's population slightly more than 600,000, more than 70,000 Mainers suited up and went off to fight in the Civil War—the greatest per-capita show of force of any northern state. About 18,000 of them died in the conflict. Thirty-one Mainers were Union Army generals, the best known being Joshua L. Chamberlain, a Bowdoin College professor, who commanded the Twentieth Maine regiment and later became president of the college and governor of Maine.

During the war, young battlefield artist Winslow Homer, who later settled in Prouts Neck, south of Portland, created wartime sketches regularly for such publications as *Harper's Weekly*. In Washington, Maine senator Hannibal Hamlin was elected vice president under Abraham Lincoln in 1860 (he was removed from the ticket in favor of Andrew Johnson when Lincoln came up for reelection in 1864).

Maine Comes into Its Own

After the Civil War, Maine's influence in Republican-dominated Washington far outweighed the size of its population. In the late 1880s, Mainers held the federal offices of acting vice president, Speaker of the House, secretary of state, Senate majority leader, Supreme Court justice, and several important committee chairmanships. Best known of the notables were James G. Blaine (journalist, presidential aspirant, and secretary of state) and Portland native Thomas Brackett Reed, presidential aspirant and Speaker of the House.

In Maine itself, traditional industries fell into decline after the Civil War, dealing the economy a body blow. Steel ships began replacing Maine's wooden clippers, refrigeration techniques made the block-ice industry obsolete, concrete threatened the granite-quarrying trade, and the output from Southern textile mills began to supplant that from Maine's mills.

Despite Maine's economic difficulties, however, wealthy urbanites began turning their sights toward the state, accumulating land (including islands) and building enormous summer "cottages" for their families, servants, and hangers-on. Bar Harbor was a prime example of the elegant summer colonies that sprang up, but others include Grindstone Neck (Winter Harbor), Prouts Neck (Scarborough), and Dark Harbor (on Islesboro in Penobscot Bay). Vacationers who preferred fancy hotel-type digs reserved rooms for the summer at such sprawling complexes as Kineo House (on Moosehead Lake), Poland Spring House (west of Portland), or the Samoset Hotel (in Rockland). Built of wood and catering to long-term visitors, these and many others all eventually succumbed to altered vacation patterns and the ravages of fire.

As the 19th century spilled into the 20th, the state broadened its appeal beyond the well-to-do who had snared prime turf in the Victorian era. It launched an active promotion of Maine as "The Nation's Playground," successfully spurring an influx of visitors from all economic levels. By steamboat, train, and soon by car, people came to enjoy the ocean beaches, the woods, the mountains, the lakes, and the quaintness of it all. (Not that these features didn't really exist, but the state's aggressive public relations campaign at the turn of the 20th century stacks up against anything Madison Avenue puts out today.) The only major hiatus in the tourism explosion in the century's first two decades was 1914–1918, when 35,062 Mainers joined many thousands of other Americans in going off to the European front to fight in World War I. Two years after the war ended, in 1920 (the centennial of its statehood), Maine women were the first in the nation to troop to the polls after ratification of the 19th Amendment granted universal suffrage.

Maine was slow to feel the repercussions of the Great Depression, but eventually they came, with bank failures all over the state. Federally subsidized programs, such as the Civilian Conservation Corps (CCC) and the Works Progress Administration (WPA), left lasting legacies in Maine.

Politically, the state has contributed notables on both sides of the aisle. In 1954, Maine elected as its governor Edmund S. Muskie, only the fifth Democrat in the job since 1854. In 1958, Muskie ran for and won a seat in the Senate, and in 1980 he became secretary of state under president Jimmy Carter. Muskie died in 1996.

Elected in 1980, Waterville's George J. Mitchell made a respected name for himself as a Democratic senator and Senate majority leader before retiring in 1996, when Maine became only the second state in the union to have two women senators (Olympia Snowe and Susan Collins, both Republicans). After his 1996 reelection, president Bill Clinton appointed Mitchell's distinguished congressional colleague and three-term senator, Republican William Cohen of Bangor, as secretary of defense, a position he held through the rest of the Clinton administration. Mitchell spent considerable time during the Clinton years as the U.S. mediator for Northern Ireland's "troubles" and subsequently headed an international fact-finding team in the Middle East.

Government and Economy

STATE GOVERNMENT

Politics in Maine isn't quite as variable and unpredictable as the weather, but pundits are almost as wary as weather forecasters about making predictions. Despite a long tradition of Republicanism dating from the late 19th century, Maine's voters and politicians have a national reputation for being independent-minded—electing Democrats, Republicans, or independents more for their character than their political persuasions.

Four of the most notable recent examples are Margaret Chase Smith, Edmund S. Muskie, George J. Mitchell, and William Cohen—two Republicans and two Democrats, all Maine natives. Republican senator Margaret Chase Smith proved her flintiness when she spoke out against McCarthyism in the 1950s. Ed Muskie, the first prominent Democrat to come out of Maine, won every race he entered except an aborted bid for the presidency in 1972. George Mitchell, as mentioned, has gained a stellar reputation, as has William Cohen. In a manifestation of Maine's strong tradition of bipartisanship, Mitchell and Cohen worked together closely on many issues to benefit the state and the nation (they even wrote a book together).

In the 1970s, Maine elected an independent governor, James Longley, whose memory is still respected (Longley's son was later elected to Congress as a Republican, and his daughter to the state senate as a Democrat). In 1994, Maine voted in another independent, Angus King, a relatively young veteran of careers in business, broadcasting, and law. The governor serves a term of four years, limited to two terms.

The state's Supreme Judicial Court has a chief justice and six associate justices.

Maine is ruled by a bicameral, biennial citizen legislature comprising 151 members in the House of Representatives and 35 members in the state senate, including a relatively high percentage of women and a fairly high proportion of retirees. Members of both houses serve two-year terms. In 1993, voters passed a statewide term-limits referendum restricting legislators to four terms.

Whereas nearly two dozen Maine cities are ruled by city councils, about 450 smaller towns and plantations retain the traditional form of rule: annual town meetings. Town meetings generally are held in March, when newspaper pages bulge with reports containing classic quotes from citizens exercising their rights to vote and vent. A few examples: "I believe in the pursuit of happiness until that pursuit infringes on the happiness of others"; "I don't know of anyone's dog running loose except my own, and I've arrested her several times"; and "Don't listen to him; he's from New Jersey."

ECONOMY

When the subject of the economy comes up, you'll often hear reference to the "two Maines," as if an east–west line bisected the state in half. There's much truth to the image. Southern Maine is prosperous, with good jobs (although never enough), lots of small businesses, and a highly competitive real-estate market. Northern Maine struggles along, suffering from its immensity and lack of infrastructure as much as from its low population density.

The coast follows that same pattern. The Southern Coast reaps the benefit of its proximity to Boston. Not only is it a favorite weekend getaway for Boston-area residents, it's increasingly becoming part of Boston's suburbs as more and more people move there and commute to the city. Tourism thrives here seasonally. Retail is strong, thanks to Kittery. And traditional maritime-related businesses continue, although real-estate pressures have contributed to their weakening, as fishermen struggle to hold on to wharves and to live near where they work.

Portland is the state's largest city and has a strong economy, supported by tourism and maritime-related businesses. Years ago,

Portland made the wise decision to preserve its waterfront for maritime use, so it's still very much a working waterfront. Not surprisingly, Freeport's economy is retail based. Brunswick, Bath, and the surrounding towns are supported by the three Bs: Bowdoin College, Brunswick Naval Air Station, and Bath Iron Works.

Mid-Coast and Penobscot Bay and increasingly the Blue Hill Peninsula have strong maritime-related businesses, including lobstering, fishing, clamming, worm digging, and their support services. Also driving this region is a vital creative economy of artists and artisans, boatbuilders and cabinetmakers, and entrepreneurial professionals, such as architects and designers. Small businesses, technology-based companies, and telemarketing provide employment, as does tourism. These three regions are also extremely popular with retirees, who often take up second careers or are active in the local community as mentors and volunteers.

The farther Down East you travel, the harder it is to eke out a living. In Washington County, many folks cobble together some semblance of year-round employment in wreath making, fishing, clamming, guiding, logging, blueberry raking, and whatever else is available. Tribal officials in this region are hoping to bring a liquefied natural-gas port to Perry, increasing prospects for tribal members, but strong opposition exists. As one local official told me: "Everyone complains that there are no jobs, but whenever an opportunity comes along, no one wants to risk changing the lifestyle." And that's a conundrum that's bound to continue for at least the foreseeable future.

The People

Maine's population didn't top the one-million mark until 1970. Thirty years later, according to the 2000 census, the state had 1,274,923 residents. Along the coast, Cumberland County, comprising the Greater Portland area, has the highest head count.

Despite the longstanding presence of several substantial ethnic groups, plus four Native American tribes (about 1 percent of the population), diversity is a relatively recent phenomenon in Maine, and the population is about 95 percent Caucasian. A steady influx of refugees, beginning after the Vietnam War, forced the state to address diversity issues, and it continues to do so today.

Natives and "People from Away"

People who weren't born in Maine aren't natives. Even people who *were* born here may experience close scrutiny of their credentials. In Maine, there are natives and *natives.* Every day, the obituary pages describe Mainers who have barely left the houses in which they were born—even in which their grandparents were born. We're talking roots!

Along with this kind of heritage comes a whole vocabulary all its own—lingo distinctive to Maine, or at least New England. (For help in translation, see the Glossary.)

Part of the "native" picture is the matter of "native" produce. Hand-lettered signs sprout everywhere during the summer advertising native corn, native peas, even—believe it or not—native ice. In Maine, homegrown is well grown.

"People from away," on the other hand, are those whose families haven't lived here year-round for a generation or more. But people from away (also called flatlanders) exist all over Maine, and they have come to stay, putting down roots of their own and altering the way the state is run, looks, and *will* look. Senators Snowe and Collins are natives, but Governor King came from away, as did most of his cabinet members. You'll find other flatlanders as teachers, corporate executives, artists, retirees, writers, town selectmen, and even lobstermen.

In the 19th century, arriving flatlanders were mostly "rusticators" or "summer complaints"—summer residents who lived well, often in enclaves, and never set foot in the state off-season. They did, however, pay property taxes, contribute to causes, and provide employment for local residents. Another 19th-century wave of people from away came from the bottom of the economic ladder: Irish escaping the potato famine and French Canadians fleeing poverty in Québec. Both groups experienced subtle and overt anti-Catholicism but rather quickly assimilated into the mainstream, taking jobs in mills and factories and becoming staunch American patriots.

The late 1960s and early 1970s brought bunches of "back-to-the-landers," who scorned plumbing and electricity and adopted retro ways of life. Although a few pockets of diehards still exist, most have changed with the times and adopted contemporary mores (and conveniences).

Today, technocrats arrive from away with computers, faxes, cell phones, and other high-tech gear and "commute" via the Internet and modern electronics. Maine has played a national leadership role in telecommunications reform—thanks to the university system's early push for installation of state-of-the-art fiber optics.

Native Americans

In Maine, the *real* natives are the Wabanaki (People of the Dawn)—the Micmac, Maliseet, Penobscot, and Passamaquoddy tribes of the eastern woodlands. Many live in or near three reservations, near the headquarters for their tribal governors. The Passamaquoddies are at Pleasant Point, in Perry, near Eastport, and at Indian Township, in Princeton, near Calais. The Penobscots are based on Indian Island, in Old Town, near Bangor. Other Native American population clusters—known as "off-reservation Indians"—are the Aroostook Band of Micmacs, based in Presque Isle, and the Houlton Band of Maliseets, in Littleton, near Houlton.

In 1965, Maine became the first state to establish a Department of Indian Affairs, but just five years later the Passamaquoddy and Penobscot tribes initiated a 10-year-long land-claims case involving 12.5 million Maine acres (about two-thirds of the state) weaseled from the Indians by Massachusetts in 1794. In late 1980, a landmark agreement, signed by president Jimmy Carter, awarded the tribes $80.6 million in reparations. Despite this, the tribes still struggle to provide jobs on the reservations and to increase the overall standard of living. A 2003 referendum to allow the tribes to build a casino was defeated. The latest attempt to increase jobs and money is a controversial plan to bring a liquified natural gas port to tribal lands in Perry.

One of the true success stories of the tribes is the revival of traditional arts as businesses. The Maine Indian Basketmakers Association has an active apprenticeship program, and two renowned basket makers—Mary Gabriel and Clara Keezer—have achieved National Heritage Fellowships. Several well-attended annual summer festivals—in Bar Harbor, Grand Lake Stream, and Perry—highlight Indian traditions and heighten awareness of Native American culture. Basket making, canoe building, and traditional dancing are all parts of the scene. The splendid Abbe Museum in Bar Harbor features Indian artifacts, interactive displays, historic photographs, and special programs. Gift shops have begun adding Native American jewelry and baskets to their inventories.

Acadians and Franco-Americans

Within about three decades of their 1755 expulsion from Nova Scotia in *le grand dérangement,* Acadians had established new communities and new lives in northern Maine's St. John Valley. Gradually, they explored farther into central and southern coastal Maine and west into New Hampshire. The Acadian diaspora has profoundly influenced Maine and its culture, and it continues to do so today. Along the coast, French is spoken on the streets of Biddeford, where there's an annual Franco-American festival and an extensive Franco-American research collection.

African Americans

Although Maine's African-American population is small, the state has had an African-American community since the 17th century; by the 1764 census, there were 322 slaves and free blacks in the District of Maine. Segregation remained the rule, however, so in the 19th century, blacks established their own parish, the Abyssinian Church, in Portland. Efforts are under way to restore the long-closed church as an African-American cultural center and gathering place for Greater Portland's black community. For researchers delving into "Maine's black experience," the University of Southern Maine, in Portland, houses the African-American Archive of Maine, a significant collection of historic books, letters, and artifacts donated by Gerald Talbot, the first African American to serve in the Maine legislature.

Finns

Finns came to Maine in several 19th-century waves, primarily to work the granite quarries on the coast and on offshore islands and the slate quarries in Monson, near Greenville. Finnish families clustered near the quarries in St. George and on Vinalhaven and Hurricane Islands—all with landscapes similar to those of their homeland. Today, names such as Laukka, Lehtinen, Hamalainen, and Harjula are interspersed among the Yankee names in the Mid-Coast region.

Russians, Ukrainians, and Byelorussians

Arriving after World War II, Slavic immigrants established a unique community in Richmond, just inland from Bath. Only a tiny nucleus remains today, along with an onion-domed church, but a stroll through the local cemetery hints at the extent of the original colony.

The Newest Arrivals: Refugees from War

War has been the impetus for the more recent arrival of Asians, Africans, Central Americans, and Eastern Europeans. Most have settled in the Portland area, making that city the state's center of diversity. Vietnamese and Cambodians began settling in Maine in the mid-1970s. A handful of Afghanis who fled the Soviet-Afghan conflict also ended up in Portland. Somalis, Ethiopians, and Sudanese fled their war-torn countries in the early to mid-1990s, and Bosnians and Kosovars arrived in the last half of the 1990s. With every new conflict comes a new stream of immigrants—world citizens are becoming Mainers, and Mainers are becoming world citizens.

Culture

Mainers are an independent lot, many exhibiting the classic Yankee characteristics of dry humor, thrift, and ingenuity. Those who can trace their roots back at least a generation or two in the state and have lived here through the duration can call themselves natives; everyone else, no matter how long they've lived here, is "from away."

Mainers react to outsiders depending upon how those outsiders treat them. Treat a Mainer with a condescending attitude, and you'll receive a cold shoulder at best. Treat a Mainer with respect, and you'll be welcome, perhaps even invited in to share a mug of coffee. Mainers are wary of outsiders and often with good reason. Many outsiders move to Maine because they fall in love with its independence and rural simplicity, and then they demand that the farmer stop spreading that stinky manure on his farmlands, or they insist that the town initiate garbage pickup, or they build a glass-and-timber McMansion in the midst of white clapboard historical homes.

In most of Maine, money doesn't impress folks. The truth is, that lobsterman in the old truck and the well-worn work clothes might be sitting on a small fortune. Or living on it. Perhaps nothing has caused more troubles between natives and newcomers than the rapidly increasing value of land and the taxes that go with that. For many visitors, Maine real estate is a bargain they can't resist.

If you want real insight into Maine character, listen to a CD or watch a video by one Maine master humorist, Tim Sample. As he often says, "Wait a minute; it'll sneak up on you."

FINE ART

In 1850, in a watershed moment for Maine landscape painting, Hudson River School artist par excellence Frederic Edwin Church (1826–1900) vacationed on Mount Desert Island. Influenced by the luminist tradition of such contemporaries as Fitz Hugh Lane (1804–1865), who summered in nearby Castine, Church accurately but romantically depicted the dramatic tableaux of Maine's coast and woodlands that even today attract slews of admirers.

By the 1880s, however, impressionism had become the style du jour and was being practiced by a coterie of artists who collected around Charles Herbert Woodbury (1864–1940) in Ogunquit. His program made Ogunquit the best-known summer art school in New England. After Hamilton Easter Field established another art school in town, modernism soon asserted itself. Among the artists who took up summertime Ogunquit residence was Walt Kuhn (1877–1949), a key organizer of New York's 1913 landmark Armory Show of modern art.

Meanwhile, a bit farther south, impressionist Childe Hassam (1859–1935), part of writer Celia Thaxter's circle, produced several hundred works on Maine's remote Appledore Island, in the Isles of Shoals off Kittery, and illustrated Thaxter's *An Island Garden*.

Another artistic summer colony found its niche in 1903, when Robert Henri (born Robert Henry Cozad, 1865–1929), charismatic leader of the Ashcan School of realist/modernists, visited Monhegan Island, about 11 miles offshore. Artists who followed him there included Rockwell Kent (1882–1971), Edward Hopper (1882–1967), George Bellows (1882–1925), and Randall Davey (1887–1964). Among the many other artists associated with Monhegan images are William Kienbusch (1914–1980), Reuben Tam (1916–1991), and printmakers Leo Meissner (1895–1977) and Stow Wengenroth (1906–1978).

But colonies were of scant interest to other notables, who chose to derive their inspiration from Maine's stark natural beauty and work mostly in their own orbits. Among these are genre painter Eastman Johnson (1824–1906); romantic realist Winslow Homer (1836–1910), who lived in Maine for 27 years and whose studio in Prouts Neck (Scarborough) still overlooks the surf-tossed scenery he so often depicted; pointillist watercolorist Maurice Prendergast (1858–1924); John Marin (1870–1953), a cubist who painted Down East subjects, mostly around Deer Isle and Addison (Cape Split); Lewiston native Marsden Hartley (1877–1943), who first showed his abstractionist work in New York in 1909 and later worked in Berlin; Fairfield Porter (1907–1975), whose family summered on Great Spruce Head Island, in East Penobscot Bay; and Andrew Wyeth (1917–2009), whose reputation as a romantic realist in the late 20th century surpassed that of his illustrator father, N. C. Wyeth (1882–1945).

On a parallel track was sculptor Louise Nevelson (1899–1988), raised in a poor Russian-immigrant family in Rockland and far better known outside her home state for her monumental wood sculptures slathered in black or gold. Two other noted sculptors with Maine connections were William Zorach (1887–1966) and Gaston Lachaise (1882–1935), both of whom lived in Georgetown, near Bath.

Contemporary year-round or seasonal Maine residents with national (and international) reputations include Vinalhaven's Robert Indiana, Lincolnville's Alex Katz, North Haven's Eric Hopkins, Deer Isle's Karl Schrag, Tenants Harbor's Jamie Wyeth (third generation of the famous family), Kennebunk's Edward Betts, and Cushing's Lois Dodd and Alan Magee.

MAINE FOOD SPECIALTIES

Everyone knows Maine is *the* place for lobster, but there are quite a few other foods that you should sample before you leave.

For a few weeks in May, right around Mother's Day (the second Sunday in May), a wonderful delicacy starts sprouting along Maine woodland streams: **fiddleheads,** the still-furled tops of the ostrich fern *(Matteuccia struthiopteris).* Tasting vaguely like asparagus, fiddleheads have been on May menus ever since Native Americans taught the colonists to forage for the tasty vegetable. Don't go fiddleheading unless you're with a pro, though; the lookalikes are best left to the woods critters. If you find them on a restaurant menu, indulge.

As with fiddleheads, we owe thanks to Native Americans for introducing us to **maple syrup,** one of Maine's major agricultural exports. The annual crop averages 110,000 gallons. The syrup comes in four different colors/flavors (from light amber to extra dark amber), and inspectors strictly monitor syrup quality. The best syrup comes from the sugar or rock maple, *Acer saccharum.* On Maine Maple Sunday (usually the fourth Sunday in March), several dozen syrup producers open their rustic sugarhouses to the public for "sugaring-off" parties – to celebrate the sap harvest and share the final phase in the production process. Wood smoke billows from the sugarhouse chimney while everyone inside gathers around huge kettles used to boil down the watery sap. (A single gallon of syrup starts with 30-40 gallons of sap.) Finally, it's time to sample the syrup every which way – on pancakes and waffles, in tea, on ice cream, in puddings, in muffins, even just drizzled over snow. Most producers also have containers of syrup for sale.

The best place for Maine maple syrup is atop pancakes made with Maine **wild blueberries.** Packed with antioxidants and all kinds of good-for-you stuff, these flavorful berries are prized by bakers because they retain their form and flavor when cooked. Much smaller than the cultivated versions, wild blueberries are also raked, not picked. Although most of the Down East barren barons harvest their crops for the lucrative wholesale market, a few growers let you pick your own blueberries in mid-August. Contact the Wild Blueberry Commission (207/581-1475, www.wildblueberries.maine.edu) or the state Department of Agriculture (207/287-3491, www.getrealmaine.com) for locations, recipes, and other wild-blueberry information, or log on to the website of the Wild Blueberry Association of North America (207/570-3535, www.wildblueberries.com).

The best place to simply *appreciate* blueberries is Machias, site of the renowned annual Wild Blueberry Festival, held the third weekend in August. While harvesting is underway in the surrounding fields, you can stuff your face with blueberry everything – muffins, jam, pancakes, ice cream, pies. Plus you can collect blueberry-logo napkins, T-shirts, fridge magnets, pottery, and jewelry.

Another don't-miss while in Maine is Maine-made **ice cream.** Skip the overpriced Ben and Jerry's outlets. Locally made ice cream and gelato are fresher and better and often come in an astounding range of flavors. The big name in the state is Gifford's, with regional companies being Shain's and Round Top. All beat the out-of-state competition by a long shot. Even better are some of the one-of-a-kind dairy bars and farmstands. Good bets are John's, in Liberty; Morton's, in Ellsworth; and Mt. Desert Ice Cream and Ben and Bill's, both in Bar Harbor.

Finally, whenever you get a chance, shop at a **farmers market.** Their biggest asset is serendipity – you never know what you'll find. Everything is locally grown and often organic. Herbs, unusual vegetables, seedlings, baked goods, meat, free-range chicken, goat cheese, herb vinegars, berries, exotic condiments, smoked salmon, maple syrup, honey, and jams are just a few of the possibilities. The Maine Department of Agriculture (207/287-3491, www.getrealmaine.com) provides info on markets.

THE LOBSTER EXPERIENCE

No Maine visit can be considered complete without the "real Maine" experience of a "lobsta dinnah" at a lobster wharf/pound/shack. Keep an eye on the weather, pick a sunny day, and head out.

If you spot a lobster place with Restaurant in its name and no outside dining, keep going. What you're looking for is the genuine article. You want to eat outdoors, at a wooden picnic table, with a knockout view of boats and the sea. Whatever place you choose, the drill is much the same, and the "dinners" are served anytime from noonish on (some places close as early as 7 P.M.).

First of all, dress very casually so you can manhandle the lobster without messing up your good clothes. If you want beer or wine, call ahead and ask if the place serves it; you may need to bring your own, since many such operations don't have beer/wine licenses, much less liquor licenses. In the evening, carry some insect repellent, in case mosquitoes crash the party.

A basic one-pound lobster and go-withs (cole slaw or potato salad, potato chips, perhaps corn on the cob, and butter or fake butter for dipping) should run $15 or less, but of course that depends on the current market. Depending on your hunger, though, you may want to indulge in a shore dinner (lobster, steamed clams, potato chips, and maybe chowder, cole slaw, or corn), for which you may have to part with $18-24. Don't skip dessert; many lobster pounds are known for their homemade pies.

It's not unusual, either, to see lobster-wharf devotees carting picnic baskets with hors d'oeuvres, salads, and baguettes. I've even seen candles and champagne. Creativity abounds, but don't stray too far from the main attraction – the crustaceans.

Typically, you'll need to survey a chalkboard or whiteboard menu and step up to a window to order. You'll either give the person your name or get a number. A few places have staff to take your order or deliver your meal, but usually you head back to the window when your name or number is called. Don your plastic lobster bib and begin the attack. If you're a neophyte, watch a pro at a nearby table. Some pounds have "how-to" info on printed paper placemats. If you're really worried (you needn't be), contact the Maine Lobster Promotion Council (382 Harlow St., Bangor, www.mainelobsterpromotion.com). It publishes a brochure with detailed instructions. Don't worry about doing it "wrong"; you'll eventually get what you came for, and it'll be an experience to remember.

For the ultimate lobster feeding frenzy, plan to be in Rockland the first weekend in August, when volunteers at the annual Maine Lobster Festival stoke up the world's largest lobster cooker and serve thousands of pounds of lobsters nonstop to more than 50,000 enthusiastic diners.

The two best collections of Maine art are at the **Portland Museum of Art** (7 Congress Sq., Portland, 207/775-6148) and the **Farnsworth Art Museum** (16 Museum St., Rockland, 207/596-6457). The Farnsworth, in fact, focuses only on Maine art, primarily from the 20th century. The Farnsworth is the home of the Wyeth Center, featuring the works of three generations of Wyeths.

The **Ogunquit Museum of American Art,** appropriately, also has a very respectable Maine collection (in a spectacular setting), as does the Monhegan Museum. Other Maine paintings, not always on exhibit, are at the Bowdoin College Museum of Art in Brunswick.

CRAFTS

Any survey of Maine art, however brief, must include the significant role of crafts in the state's artistic tradition. As with painters, sculptors, and writers, craftspeople have gravitated to Maine—most notably since the establishment in 1950 of the Haystack Mountain School of Crafts. Started in the Belfast area, the school put down roots on Deer Isle in 1960. Craft

Here (by region) are great places to experience lobster. All are described in more detail in the destination chapters.

SOUTHERN COAST

Kittery Point: Chauncey Creek Lobster Pier, 207/439-1030
Ogunquit: Barnacle Billy's, 207/646-5575

GREATER PORTLAND

Cape Elizabeth (near Portland): The Lobster Shack, 207/799-1677
Portland: Portland Lobster Company, 207/775-2112
South Freeport: Harraseeket Lunch and Lobster Company, 207/865-3535

MID-COAST REGION

Boothbay Harbor: The Lobster Dock, 207/635-7120
Cundy's Harbor: Holbrook's Wharf and Grille, 207/729-0848
Damariscotta/Pemaquid Peninsula: Broad Cove Marine Services, Medomak, 207/529-5186; Shaw's Fish and Lobster Wharf, New Harbor, 207/677-2200; Pemaquid Fishermen's Co-op, Pemaquid Harbor, 207/677-2801; Muscongus Bay Lobster, Round Pond, 207/529-5528; Round Pond Lobster Co-Op, Round Pond, 207/529-5725; South Bristol Fishermen's Co-op, South Bristol, 207/644-8224
Georgetown: Five Islands Lobster Company, 207/371-2990
Small Point: The Lobster House, 207/389-1596

PENOBSCOT BAY

Belfast: Young's Lobster Pound, 207/338-1160
Lincolnville Beach: The Lobster Pound Restaurant, 207/789-5550
South Thomaston (near Rockland): Waterman's Beach Lobster, 207/596-7819
Spruce Head (near Rockland): Miller's Lobster Company, 207/594-7406

BLUE HILL PENINSULA AND DEER ISLE

Castine: Dennett's Wharf, 207/326-9045
Surry: Perry Long's Lobster Shack and Pier, 207/667-1955

ACADIA REGION

Bernard (Mount Desert Island): Thurston's Lobster Pound, 207/244-7600
Trenton: Trenton Bridge Lobster Pound, 207/667-2977

THE DOWN EAST COAST

Eastport: Eastport Chowder House, 207/853-4700; Quoddy Bay Lobster, 207/853-6640

studios are abundant in Maine, and many festivals include craft displays.

DOWN EAST LITERATURE

Maine's first big-name writer was probably the early 17th-century French explorer Samuel de Champlain (1570–1635), who scouted the Maine coast, established a colony in 1604 near present-day Calais, and lived to describe in detail his experiences. Several decades after Champlain's forays, English naturalist John Josselyn visited Scarborough and in the 1670s published the first two books accurately describing Maine's flora and fauna (aptly describing, for example, blackflies as "not only a pesterment but a plague to the country").

Today, Maine's best-known author lives not on the coast but just inland in Bangor—Stephen King (b. 1947), wizard of the weird.

Chroniclers of the Great Outdoors

John Josselyn was perhaps the first practitioner of Maine's strong naturalist tradition in American letters, but the Pine Tree State's rugged scenic beauty and largely unspoiled environment have given rise to many ecologically and environmentally concerned writers.

The 20th century saw the arrival in Maine of crusader Rachel Carson (1907–1964), whose 1962 wake-up call, *Silent Spring,* was based partly on Maine observations and research. The Rachel Carson National Wildlife Refuge, headquartered in Wells and comprising 10 chunks of environmentally sensitive coastal real estate, covers nearly 3,500 acres between Kittery Point and the Mid-Coast region.

The tiny town of Nobleboro, near Damariscotta, drew nature writer Henry Beston (1888–1968); his *Northern Farm* lyrically chronicles a year in Maine. Beston's wife, Elizabeth Coatsworth (1893–1986), wrote more than 90 books—including *Chimney Farm,* about their life in Nobleboro.

Fannie Hardy Eckstorm (1865–1946), born in Brewer to Maine's most prosperous fur trader, graduated from Smith College and became a noted expert on Maine (and specifically Native American) folklore. Among her extensive writings, *Indian Place-Names of the Penobscot Valley and the Maine Coast,* published in 1941, remains a sine qua non for researchers.

The out-of-doors and inner spirits shaped Cape Rosier adoptees Helen and Scott Nearing, whose 1954 *Living the Good Life* became the bible of Maine's back-to-the-landers.

Classic Writings on the State

Historical novels, such as *Arundel,* were the specialty of Kennebunk native Kenneth Roberts (1885–1957), but Roberts also wrote *Trending into Maine,* a potpourri of Maine observations and experiences (the original edition was illustrated by N. C. Wyeth). Kennebunkport's Booth Tarkington (1869–1946), author of the *Penrod* novels and *The Magnificent Ambersons,* described 1920s Kennebunkport in *Mary's Neck,* published in 1932.

A little subgenre of sociological literary classics comprises astute observations (mostly by women) of daily life in various parts of the state. Some are fiction, some nonfiction, some barely disguised romans à clef. Probably the best-known chronicler of such observations is Sarah Orne Jewett (1849–1909), author of *The Country of the Pointed Firs,* a fictional 1896 account of "Dunnet's Landing" (actually Tenants Harbor); her ties, however, were in the South Berwick area, where she spent most of her life. Also in South Berwick, Gladys Hasty Carroll (1904–1999) scrutinized everyday life in her hamlet, Dunnybrook, in *As the Earth Turns* (a title later "borrowed" and tweaked by a soap-opera producer). Lura Beam (1887–1978) focused on her childhood in the Washington County village of Marshfield in *A Maine Hamlet,* published in 1957, while Louise Dickinson Rich (1903–1972) entertainingly described her coastal Corea experiences in *The Peninsula,* after first having chronicled her rugged wilderness existence in *We Took to the Woods.* Ruth Moore (1903–1989), born on Gott's Island, near Acadia National Park, published her first book at the age of 40. Her tales, recently brought back into print, have earned her a whole new appreciative audience. Elisabeth Ogilvie (b. 1917) came to Maine in 1944 and lived for many years on remote Ragged Island, transformed into "Bennett's Island" in her fascinating "tide trilogy": *High Tide at Noon, Storm Tide,* and *The Ebbing Tide.* Ben Ames Williams (1887–1953), the token male in this roundup of perceptive observers, in 1940 produced *Come Spring,* an epic tale of hardy pioneers founding the town of Union, just inland from Rockland.

In the mid-19th century antislavery crusader Harriet Beecher Stowe (1811–1896), seldom recognized for her Maine connection, lived in Brunswick, where she wrote *The Pearl of Orr's Island,* a folkloric novel about a tiny nearby fishing community.

Mary Ellen Chase was a Maine native, born in Blue Hill in 1887. She became an English professor at Smith College in 1926 and wrote about 30 books, including some about the Bible as literature. She died in 1973.

Two books do a creditable job of excerpting literature from throughout Maine—something of a daunting task. The most comprehensive is *Maine Speaks: An Anthology of Maine*

Literature, published in 1989 by the Maine Writers and Publishers Alliance. *The Quotable Moose: A Contemporary Maine Reader,* edited by Wesley McNair and published in 1994 by the University Press of New England, focuses on 20th-century authors.

A World of Her Own

For Marguerite Yourcenar (1903–1987), Maine provided solitude and inspiration for subjects ranging far beyond the state's borders. Yourcenar was a longtime Northeast Harbor resident and the first woman elected to the prestigious Académie Française. Her house, now a shrine to her work, is open to the public by appointment in summer.

Essayists, Critics, and Humorists Native and Transplanted

Maine's best-known essayist is and was E. B. White (1899–1985), who bought a farm in tiny Brooklin in 1933 and continued writing for the *New Yorker. One Man's Meat,* published in 1944, is one of the best collections of his wry, perceptive writings. His legions of admirers also include two generations raised on his classic children's stories *Stuart Little, Charlotte's Web,* and *The Trumpet of the Swan.*

Writer and critic Doris Grumbach (b. 1918), who settled in Sargentville, not far from Brooklin but far from her New York ties, wrote two particularly wise works from the perspective of a Maine transplant: *Fifty Days of Solitude* and *Coming into the End Zone.*

Maine's best contemporary exemplar of humorous writing is the late John Gould (1908–2003), whose life in rural Friendship has provided grist for many a tale. Gould's hilarious columns in the *Christian Science Monitor* and his steady book output made him an icon of Maine humor.

Pine Tree Poets

Born in Portland, Henry Wadsworth Longfellow (1807–1882) is Maine's most famous poet; his marine themes clearly stem from his seashore childhood (in "My Lost Youth," he wistfully rhapsodized, "Often I think of the beautiful town/That is seated by the sea . . .").

Widely recognized in her own era, poet Celia Thaxter (1835–1894) held court on Appledore Island in the Isles of Shoals, welcoming artists, authors, and musicians to her summer salon. Today, she's best known for *An Island Garden,* published in 1894 and detailing her attempts at horticultural TLC in a hostile environment.

Edna St. Vincent Millay (1892–1950) had connections to Camden, Rockland, and Union and described a stunning Camden panorama in "Renascence."

Whitehead Island, near Rockland, was the birthplace of Wilbert Snow (1883–1977), who went on to become president of Connecticut's Wesleyan University. His 1968 memoir, *Codline's Child,* makes fascinating reading.

A longtime resident of York, May Sarton (1912–1995) approached cult status as a guru of feminist poetry and prose—and as an articulate analyst of death and dying during her terminal illness.

Among respected Maine poets today are William Carpenter (b. 1940), of Stockton Springs; and Appleton's Kate Barnes (b. 1932), named Maine's Poet Laureate from 1996 to 1999. Although she comes by her acclaim legitimately, Barnes is also genetically disposed, being the daughter of writers Henry Beston and Elizabeth Coatsworth.

Maine Lit for Little Ones

Besides E. B. White's children's classics, *Stuart Little, Charlotte's Web,* and *The Trumpet of the Swan,* America's kids were also weaned on books written and illustrated by Maine island summer resident Robert McCloskey (1914–2003)—notably *Time of Wonder, One Morning in Maine,* and *Blueberries for Sal.* Neck-and-neck in popularity is prolific Walpole illustrator-writer Barbara Cooney (1917–1999), whose award-winning titles included *Miss Rumphius, Island Boy,* and *Hattie and the Wild Waves.* Cooney produced more than 100 books, and it seems as if everyone has a different favorite.

ESSENTIALS

Getting There

Coastal Maine has two major airports, two major bus networks, a toll highway, limited Amtrak service, and some ad hoc local transportation systems that fill in the gaps.

BY AIR

Coastal Maine's major airline gateway is **Portland International Jetport** (PWM, 207/774-7301, www.portlandjetport.org), although visitors headed farther northeast sometimes prefer **Bangor International Airport** (BGR, 207/947-0384, www.flybangor.com). The "international" in their names is a bit misleading. Charter flights from Europe often stop at Bangor for refueling and customs clearance, and sometimes bad weather also diverts flights there. Portland has a few flights connecting to maritime Canada. But Boston's Logan Airport is the nearest airport with direct flights from Europe and other worldwide destinations.

Airlines serving Portland and/or Bangor are **AirTran** (800/433-7300), **Continental** (800/523-3273), **Delta** (800/221-1212), **Jet Blue** (800/538-2583), **United Express** (800/864-8331), and **US Airways** (800/428-4322). All increase their flight frequency during the summer to accommodate stepped-up demand.

Portland Jetport Facilities

Portland's airport is small and easy to navigate. Food options are few, but you won't starve. A business center in the gate area has Internet access. Visitor information is dispensed from a desk (not always staffed, unfortunately) between the gates and the baggage-claim area. Note: Since Portland is the terminus of most flights, baggage service isn't a priority; expect to hang around for a while. If you have an emergency, contact the airport manager (207/773-8462).

Ground Transportation: The Greater Portland Transportation District's **Metro** (207/774-0351, www.gpmetrobus.com) bus route #1 connects the airport with the Portland Transportation Center and intown Portland Monday through Saturday. **Taxis** are available outside baggage claim.

Mid-Coast Limousine (207/236-2424 or 800/937-2424) provides car service, by reservation, between Portland and Camden.

Car rentals at the airport include **Alamo** (207/775-0855 or 877/222-9075, www.alamo.com), **Avis** (207/874-7500 or 800/230-4898, www.avis.com), **Budget** (207/772-6789 or 800/527-0700, www.drivebudget.com), **Hertz** (207/774-4544 or 800/654-3131, www.hertz.com), and **National** (207/773-0036 or 877/222-9058, www.nationalcar.com).

Bangor Airport Facilities

Bangor's airport has scaled-down versions of Portland's facilities but all the necessary amenities. If you need help, contact the airport manager (207/947-0384).

Ground Transportation: Bangor Area Transportation (BAT, 207/882-4670, www.bgrme.org) buses connect the airport to downtown Bangor. Buses run Monday–Saturday. **West's Coastal Connection** (207/546-2823 or 800/596-2823, www.westbusservice.com) has scheduled service along Route 1 to Calais, with stops en route. **Taxis** are available outside baggage claim.

Car rentals at the airport include **Alamo** (207/947-0158 or 800/462-5266, www.goalamo.com), **Avis** (207/947-8383 or 800/230-4898, www.avis.com), **Budget** (207/945-9429 or 800/527-0700, www.drivebudget.com), **Hertz** (207/942-5519 or 800/654-3131, www.hertz.com), and **National** (207/947-0158 or 800/227-7368, www.nationalcar.com).

Regional Airports

Airports accessible via US Airways/Business Express from Boston are **Hancock County Airport** (BHB, 207/667-7329, www.bhbairport.com) near Bar Harbor and **Knox County Regional Airport** (RKD, 207/594-4131, www.knoxcounty.midcoast.com) at Owls Head, near Rockland and Camden. Hancock County Airport has rental-car offices for Budget and Hertz and is also serviced by the Island Explorer bus late June–Columbus Day. Knox County has a Budget car-rental desk (207/594-0822).

Boston Logan Airport

If you fly into Boston (BOS), you easily can get to Maine via rental car (all major rental companies at the airport, but it's not pleasant to navigate Logan in a rental car) and Concord Coachlines bus (easiest and least-expensive option). You'll need to connect to North Station to take Amtrak's Downeaster train.

BY CAR

The major highway access to Maine from the south is **I-95,** which roughly parallels the coast until Bangor, before shooting up to Houlton. Other busy access points are **Route 1,** also from New Hampshire, departing the coast in Calais at the New Brunswick province border; **Route 302,** from North Conway, New Hampshire, entering Maine at Fryeburg; **Route 2,** from Gorham, New Hampshire, to Bethel; **Route 201,** entering from Québec province, just north of Jackman, and a couple of crossing points from New Brunswick into Aroostook and Washington Counties in northeastern Maine.

BY BUS

Concord Coachlines (800/639-3317, www.concordcoachlines.com) departs downtown

Boston (South Station Transportation Center) and Logan Airport for Portland almost hourly from the wee hours of the morning until late at night, making pickups at all Logan airline terminals (lower level). Most of the buses continue directly to Bangor; three daily non-express buses continue along the coast to Searsport before turning inland to Bangor. The Portland bus terminal is the Portland Transportation Center, Thompson Point Road, just west of I-295. If you're headed for downtown Portland from the bus terminal, board the Metro city bus at the terminal and show your bus ticket to receive a free trip.

Also servicing Coastal Maine but with far less frequent service is **Greyhound** (www.greyhound.com).

BY RAIL

Amtrak's Downeaster (800/872-7245, www.thedowneaster.com) makes five daily round-trip runs between Boston's North Station and Portland Transportation Center, with stops in Wells, Saco, and seasonally in Old Orchard Beach (May 1 to October 31). From the Portland station, Portland's Metro municipal bus service will take you gratis to downtown Portland; just show your Amtrak ticket stub.

Getting Around

The Maine Department of Transportation (800/877-9171) operates the Explore Maine site (www.exploremaine.org), which has information on all forms of transportation in Maine.

BY BUS

Concord Coachlines (800/639-3317, www.concordcoachlines.com) has the most extensive bus network, with routes designed to assist students, island ferry passengers, and day-trippers. Buses from Boston's Logan Airport stop in downtown Portland and follow a mostly coastal route through Brunswick, Bath, Wiscasset, Damariscotta, Waldoboro, Rockland, Camden, Belfast, and Searsport, ending in Bangor, and then follow the same route in reverse.

Once-a-day buses to and from Calais coordinate with the Bangor bus schedules. The Calais line, stopping in Ellsworth, Gouldsboro, Machias, and Perry (near Eastport), is operated by **West's Coastal Connection** (207/546-2823 or 800/596-2823, www.westbusservice.com). Flag stops along the route are permitted.

Portland and South Portland have **city bus service,** with some wheelchair-accessible vehicles. A number of smaller communities have established **local shuttle vans** or **trolley-buses,** but most of the latter are seasonal. Trolley-buses operate (for a fee) in Ogunquit, Wells, the Kennebunks, Portland, Bath, and Boothbay. Mount Desert Island and the Schoodic Peninsula have the **Island Explorer,** an excellent free summer (from late June) bus service.

BY CAR

No matter how much time and resourcefulness you summon, you'll never really be able to appreciate Coastal Maine without a car. Down every little peninsula jutting into the Atlantic lies a picturesque village or park or ocean view.

Two lanes wide from Kittery in the south to Fort Kent at the top, U.S. Route 1 is the state's most congested road, particularly in July and August. Mileage distances can be extremely deceptive, since it will take you much longer than anticipated to get from point A to point B. If you ask anyone about distances, chances are good that you'll receive an answer in hours rather than miles. If you're trying to make time, it's best to take the Maine Turnpike or I-95; if you want to see Maine, take U.S. 1 and lots of little offshoots. That said, bear in mind that even I-95 becomes megacongested on summer weekends, and especially summer *holiday* weekends.

Note that the interstate can be a bit confusing to motorists. Between York and Augusta, I-95 is the same as the Maine Turnpike, regulated by the Maine Turnpike Authority (877/682-9433, 800/675-7453 travel conditions, www.maineturnpike.com). All exit numbers along I-95 reflect distance in miles from the New Hampshire border. I-295 splits from I-95 in Portland and follows the coast to Brunswick before veering inland and rejoining I-95 in Gardiner. Exits on I-295 reflect distance from where it splits from I-95 just south of Portland at exit 44.

If your destination is the Mid-Coast, take I-295 to Brunswick and then pick up Route 1 North. If it's Penobscot Bay, consider taking I-95 (you'll save time by splitting off and looping around on I-295) to Augusta and then taking Route 17 to Rockland or Route 3 to Belfast. If your destination is the Blue Hill Peninsula or above, stay on I-95 to Bangor and then take Route 1A to the coast. For Calais, stay on I-95 to Bangor and then take Route 9 to Route 1 South to Calais.

Road Conditions

For real-time information on road conditions, weather, construction, and major delays, dial 511 in Maine, 866/282-7578 from out of state, or visit www.511maine.gov. Information is available in both English and French.

Driving Regulations

Seat belts are mandatory in Maine. Unless posted otherwise, Maine allows right turns at red lights after you stop and check for oncoming traffic. *Never* pass a stopped school bus in either direction. Maine law also requires drivers to turn on their car's headlights any time the windshield wipers are operating.

Roadside Assistance

Since Maine is enslaved to the automobile, it's not a bad idea for vacationers to carry membership

© TOM NANGLE

Use the free Island Explorer bus to explore Acadia National Park.

PRONUNCIATION 101: HOW TO SAY IT LIKE A NATIVE

Countless names for Maine cities, towns, villages, rivers, lakes, and streams have Native American origins; some are variations on French; and a few have German derivations. Below are some pronunciations to give you a leg up when requesting directions along the Maine coast.

Arundel – Uh-RUN-d'l
Bangor – BANG-gore
Bremen – BREE-m'n
Calais – CAL-us
Castine – Kass-TEEN
Damariscotta – dam-uh-riss-COTT-uh
Harraseeket – Hare-uh-SEEK-it
Isle au Haut – i'll-a-HO, I'LL-a-ho (subject to plenty of dispute, depending on whether or not you live in the vicinity)
Katahdin – Kuh-TA-din
Lubec – Loo-BECK
Machias – Muh-CHIGH-us
Matinicus – Muh-TIN-i-cuss
Medomak – Muh-DOM-ick
Megunticook – Muh-GUN-tuh-cook
Monhegan – Mun-HE-gun
Mount Desert – Mount Duh-ZERT
Narraguagus – Nare-uh-GWAY-gus
Naskeag – NASS-keg
Passagassawakeag – Puh-sag-gus-uh-WAH-keg
Passamaquoddy – Pass-uh-muh-QUAD-dee
Pemaquid – PEM-a-kwid
Saco – SOCK-oh
Schoodic – SKOO-dick
Steuben – Stew-BEN
Topsham – TOPS-'m
Wiscasset – Wiss-CASS-it
Woolwich – WOOL-itch

in AAA in case of breakdowns, flat tires, and other car crises. Contact your nearest AAA office or AAA Northern New England (425 Marginal Way, Portland 04101, 207/780-6800 or 800/482-7497, www.aaanne.com). The emergency road service number is 800/222-4357.

HITCHHIKING

Even though Maine's public transportation network is woefully inadequate, and the crime rate is one of the lowest in the nation, it's still risky to hitchhike or pick up hitchhikers.

Tips for Travelers

VISAS AND OFFICIALDOM

Since 9/11, security has been excruciatingly tight for foreign visitors, with customs procedures in flux. For current rules, visit www.usa.gov/visitors/arriving.shtml. It's wise to make two sets of copies of all paperwork, one to carry separately on your trip and another left with a trusted friend or relative at home.

SMOKING

Maine now has laws banning smoking in restaurants, bars, and lounges as well as enclosed areas of public places, such as shopping malls. Only a handful of bed-and-breakfasts and country inns permit smoking, and increasingly motels, hotels, and resorts are limiting the number of rooms where smoking is permitted. Some accommodations ban smoking anywhere on the property, and many have instituted high fines for smoking in a nonsmoking room. If you're a smoker, motels with direct outdoor access make it easiest to satisfy a craving.

ACCOMMODATIONS, FOOD, AND ALCOHOL

Accommodations

For all accommodation listings, rates are quoted for peak season, which is usually July and August but may extend through foliage (mid-October). Rates drop, often dramatically, in the shoulder and off-season at accommodations that remain open. Especially during peak season, many accommodations require a two- or three-night minimum.

For the best rates, be sure to check Internet specials and to ask about packages. Many accommodations also provide discounts for members of travel clubs such as AAA, to seniors and the military, and other such groups.

Unless otherwise noted, accommodations listed have private baths.

Food

Days and hours of operation listed for places serving food are for peak season. These do change often, sometimes even within a season, and it's not uncommon for a restaurant to close early on a quiet night. To avoid disappointment, call before making a special trip.

Alcohol

As in the rest of the country, Maine's minimum drinking age is 21 years—and bar owners, bartenders, and serving staff can be held legally accountable for serving underage imbibers. If your blood alcohol level is 0.08 percent or higher, you are legally considered to be operating under the influence.

TIME ZONE

All of Maine is in the eastern time zone—the same as New York, Washington, D.C., Philadelphia, and Orlando. Eastern standard time (EST) runs from the last Sunday in October to the first Sunday in April; eastern daylight time (EDT), one hour later, prevails otherwise. Surprising to many first-time visitors is how early the sun rises in the morning and how early it sets at night.

If your itinerary also includes Canada, remember that the provinces of New Brunswick and Nova Scotia are on Atlantic time—one hour later than eastern—so if it's noon in Maine, it's 1 P.M. in these provinces.

ADVENTURES IN LEARNING

A surprising number of educational programs operate along the Maine coast. Whether you want to improve your foreign-language skills, learn to craft furniture, build a boat, sail, play a musical instrument, or even experience a family-oriented nature-based vacation, there's a course for you. Here's a sampling.

HOME, SWEET HOME

In 1974, enterprising entrepreneurs Pat and Patsy Hennin jumped on the do-it-yourself bandwagon and established the **Shelter Institute** (873 Rte. 1, Woolwich, 207/442-7938, www.shelterinstitute.com) to train neophytes in energy-efficient home design and construction techniques. Since then, thousands of students have taken courses here, and enthusiastic alumni (and their building projects) span the globe. Students range in age from late teens to early 80s. Courses take place on the school's 68-acre campus in Woolwich, five miles north of Bath. Visitors are welcome any time, and anyone who appreciates fine woodworking tools *has* to visit the institute's **Woodbutcher Tools** retail shop and bookstore, open 9 A.M.-4:30 P.M. Monday-Friday, 9 A.M.-3 P.M. Saturday.

CONTEMPLATIVE SKIFF BUILDING

Word of mouth seems to be the best marketing tool for **The Carpenter's Boatshop** (440 Old County Rd., Pemaquid, 207/677-3768, www.carpentersboatshop.org). Founded in 1979 by Bobby Ives, an engaging Congregational minister, and his late wife, Ruth, the boatshop accepts interested applicants of any denomination to join a community dedicated to both spirituality and boatbuilding. This is no laid-back, contemplative religious retreat; serious boatbuilding supports the community. Sessions run mid-September-mid-June, and there's no tuition. Room and board are provided. The diverse group of 6-8 students all become part of the boatbuilding crew, working at least 40 hours a week in the huge shingled barn/boatshop. Each student builds a 9.5-foot Monhegan skiff, contributes to the construction of three types of stock wooden boats, helps with all the daily chores, and spends Saturday morning doing valuable community service on the Pemaquid Peninsula. During daily prayer gatherings, students can participate or use the time for reading or other reflective pursuits. Marine author Peter Spectre, an admitted skeptic, admiringly describes this unique program: "Just consider what all these people have done for themselves and the community."

CREATING A SMALLER WORLD

Begun in 1986 to provide language classes for adults, **Penobscot School** (28 Gay St., Rockland, 207/594-1084, www.languagelearning.org) has become a multicultural clearinghouse with ties around the globe. In fall, winter, and spring, the school offers day and evening courses in nearly a dozen languages, sponsors ethnic dinners and festivals, organizes language-immersion weekends, and puts on international study programs in local schools. July-September, international students (ages 18-65) arrive at the school for intensive three-week English-language courses. On summer weekdays, visitors are often invited for lunch at the school to interact with students practicing their English.

SAILING, SAILING

The best way to explore Maine's coast is aboard a boat. **Bay Island Sailing School**

(207/596-7550 or 800/421-2492, www.baysailing.com), based in Rockland, is an American Sailing Association-approved summer program that has weekday, weekend, and live-aboard learn-to-sail classes – and special courses for teenagers and women. Contact the school for details.

FURNISH YOUR FUTURE

Alumni of the one-, two-, and 12-week workshops at the **Center for Furniture Craftsmanship** (25 Mill St., Rockport, 207/594-5611, www.woodschool.org), established in 1993, can't say enough about their experiences. One-week to nine-month courses are for various skill levels, from beginner to pro. The center can help arrange for lodging and meals. It's open all year.

MUSICAL INTERLUDE

You're never too old to learn how to play a musical instrument or to sing. **Summerkeys** (207/733-2316 June 15–Oct. 15, 973/316-6220 Oct. 15–June 15, www.summerkeys.com) is a music school without admission requirements. Its premise is inviting: "Come as you are to enjoy the study, the work and the beauty of the Maine Coast." The Lubec school offers instruction in a number of musical instruments, including piano, violin, flute, guitar, cello, and clarinet as well as in voice. Beginners are welcome.

WOODWISE BOAT WAYS

Build a boat, a canoe, a classic sea chest, or a remote-control pond yacht. Those are just a sampling from the dozens of boatbuilding and related craft courses offered each summer at the 60-acre waterfront campus of **The WoodenBoat School** (41 WoodenBoat Lane, Brooklin, 207/359-4651, www.thewoodenboatschool.com). There's even a popular family week program. Lodging and meals packages are available.

B.A. IN FAMILY FUN

Explore tide pools, learn about animal tracks, discover the diversity of bats, go whale-watching, and take a hike and learn about the natural world in the process at College of the Atlantic's **Family Nature Camp** (105 Eden St., Bar Harbor, 800/597-9500, www.coa.edu/summer). This hands-on, participatory naturalist-led program provides plenty of fodder for those "What I Did on My Summer Vacation" essays. The minimum age is five; extended family is welcome. Camp includes campus lodging, meals, field trips, and some boat tours.

TO EVERYTHING, TURN, TURN, TURN

Founded in 2004 by Ken Keoughan, the **Woodturning School** (10 Cappelletti Dr., Damariscotta, 207/380-8076, www.woodturningschool.org) introduces students to woodturning, a woodworking skill that produces hollow vessels. All tools are provided.

FIDDLING AROUND

Learn to play the fiddle by ear at the **Maine Fiddle Camp** (207/443-5411, www.mainefiddle.org), held on the grounds of Camp NEOFA in Montville. Campers stay in rustic cabins or tents and enjoy communal meals outdoors, and there's plenty of time to swim or hang out in the afternoon, before the evening concerts, dances, and jams. A weekend camp is usually held in June, with week-long sessions offered in August.

Health and Safety

There's too much to do in Maine, and too much to see, to spend even a few hours laid low by illness or mishap. Be sensible—be sure to get enough sleep, wear sunscreen and appropriate clothing, know your limits and don't take foolhardy risks, heed weather and warning signs, carry water and snacks while hiking, don't overindulge in food or alcohol, always tell someone where you're going, and watch your step. If you're traveling with children, you should quadruple your caution.

MEDICAL CARE

In the event of any emergency, dial 911.

Southern Coast

York Hospital (15 Hospital Dr., York, emergency 207/351-2157); **Wells Urgent Care** (109 Sanford Rd., Wells, 207/646-5211, 8 A.M.–7 P.M. daily); **Kennebunk Walk-In Clinic** (24 Portland Rd./Rte. 1, Kennebunk, 207/985-6027); **Southern Maine Medical Center** (Rte. 111, Biddeford, 207/283-7000, emergency 207/283-7100).

Greater Portland

Maine Medical Center (22 Bramhall St., Portland, emergency 207/871-2381); **Mercy Hospital** (144 State St., Portland, emergency 207/879-3265).

Mid-Coast

Mid-Coast Hospital (Bath Rd., Cooks Corner, Brunswick, 207/729-0181); **Parkview Hospital** (329 Maine St., a mile south of Bowdoin College, Brunswick, 207/373-2000); **St. Andrews Hospital and Healthcare Center** (3 St. Andrews La., Boothbay Harbor, 207/633-2121); **Miles Memorial Hospital** (Bristol Rd., Rte. 130, Damariscotta, 207/563-1234).

Penobscot Bay

Penobscot Bay Medical Center (Rte. 1, Rockport, 207/596-8000); **Waldo County General Hospital** (118 Northport Ave., Belfast, 207/338-2500 or 800/649-2536).

Blue Hill and Deer Isle

Blue Hill Memorial Hospital (57 Water St., Blue Hill, 207/374-3400, emergency 207/374-2836, www.bhmh.org).

Acadia Region

Maine Coast Memorial Hospital (50 Union St., Ellsworth, 207/664-5311 or 888/645-8829, emergency 207/664-5340, www.mainehospital.org); **Mount Desert Island Hospital** (10 Wayman La., Bar Harbor, 207/288-5081, www.mdihospital.org).

Down East

Down East Community Hospital (Upper Court St., Rte. 1A, Machias, 207/255-3356); **Regional Medical Center at Lubec** (43 S. Lubec Rd., Lubec, 207/733-5541); **Eastport Health Care** (Boynton St., Eastport, 207/853-6001); **Calais Regional Hospital** (50 Franklin St., Calais, 207/454-7521).

AFFLICTIONS

Lyme Disease

A bacterial infection that causes severe arthritis-like symptoms, Lyme disease is spread by bites from tiny deer ticks (not the larger dog ticks; they don't carry it). The best advice is to take precautions, especially when hiking: Wear a long-sleeved shirt and long pants, and tuck the pant legs into your socks. Light-colored clothing makes the ticks easier to spot. Buy tick repellent at a supermarket or convenience store and use it liberally. After any hike, check for ticks—especially behind the knees, and in the armpits, navel, and groin.

Rabies

If you're bitten by any animal, especially one acting suspiciously, head for the nearest hospital emergency room. For statewide information about rabies, contact the Maine Disease Control Administration in Augusta (207/287-3591).

Allergies

If your medical history includes extreme allergies to shellfish or bee sting, you know the risks of eating a lobster or wandering around a wildflower meadow. However, if you come from a landlocked area and are new to crustaceans, you might not be aware of the potential hazard. Statistics indicate that less than 2 percent of adults have a severe shellfish allergy, but for those victims, the reaction can set in quickly. Immediate treatment is needed to keep the airways open. If you have a history of severe allergic reactions to *anything,* be prepared when you come to the Maine coast dreaming of lobster feasts. Ask your doctor for a prescription for EpiPen (epinephrine), a preloaded, single-use syringe containing 0.3 mg of the drug—enough to tide you over until you can get to a hospital.

Seasickness

If you're planning to do any boating in Maine—particularly sailing—you'll want to be prepared. (Being prepared may in fact keep you from succumbing, since fear of seasickness just about guarantees you'll get it.) Talk to a pharmacist or doctor about your options.

Hypothermia and Frostbite

Wind and weather can shift dramatically in Maine, especially at higher elevations, creating prime conditions for contracting hypothermia and frostbite. At risk are hikers, swimmers, canoeists, kayakers, sailors, skiers, even cyclists.

To prevent hypothermia and frostbite, dress in layers and remove or add them as needed. Wool, waterproof nylon (such as Gore-Tex), and synthetic fleece (such as Polartec) are the best fabrics for repelling dampness. Polyester fleece lining wicks excess moisture away from your body. Especially in winter, always cover your head, since body heat escapes quickly through the head; a ski mask will protect ears and nose. Wear wool- or fleece-lined gloves and wool socks.

Special Considerations During Hunting Season

During Maine's fall hunting season (October–Thanksgiving weekend)—and especially during the November deer season—walk or hike only in wooded areas marked No Hunting, No Trespassing, or Posted. And even if an area *is* closed to hunters, don't decide to explore the woods during deer or moose season without wearing a "hunter orange" (read: eye-poppingly fluorescent) jacket or vest. If you take your dog along, be sure it, too, wears an orange vest. Hunting is illegal on Sundays.

Information and Services

MONEY

If you need to exchange foreign currency—other than Canadian dollars—do it at or near border crossings or in Portland. In small communities, such transactions are more complicated; you may end up spending more time and money than necessary.

Typical banking hours are 9 A.M.–3 P.M. weekdays, occasionally with later hours on Friday. Drive-up windows at many banks tend to open as much as an hour earlier and stay open an hour or so after lobbies close. Some banks also maintain Saturday-morning hours. Automated teller machines (ATMs) are abundant along coastal Maine.

Credit Cards/Travelers Checks

Bank credit cards have become so preferred and so prevalent that it's nearly impossible to rent a car or check into a hotel without one. MasterCard and Visa are most widely accepted in Maine, and Discover and American Express are next most popular; Carte Blanche, Diners Club, and EnRoute (Canadian) lag far behind. Be aware, however, that small restaurants (including lobster pounds), shops, and bed-and-breakfasts off the beaten track might not accept credit cards or nonlocal personal checks; you may need to settle your account with cash or travelers check.

Taxes

Maine charges a 5 percent sales tax on general purchases and services; 8.5 percent on prepared foods, candy, and lodging; 7 percent on camping; and 12.5 percent on auto-rentals.

Tipping

Tip 15–20 percent of the pre-tax bill in restaurants.

Taxi drivers expect a 15 percent tip; airport porters expect at least $1 per bag, depending on the difficulty of the job.

The usual tip for housekeeping services in accommodations is $1–4 per person, per night, depending upon the level of service. It's not necessary to tip at bed-and-breakfasts if the owners do the housekeeping.

Some accommodations add a 10- to 15-percent service fee to rates.

TOURISM INFORMATION AND MAPS

Maine Tourism Association

The Maine Tourism Association (207/623-0363, www.mainetourism.com) publishes the free annual magazine-style guidebook *Maine Invites You,* which details sights throughout the state and provides listings of chambers of commerce and other info helpful for travelers.

State Visitors Information Centers

The Maine Tourism Association operates state visitors information centers in Calais, Fryeburg (May–October), Hampden, Houlton, Kittery, and Yarmouth. These are excellent places to visit to stock up on brochures, pick up a map, ask advice, and use restrooms.

Maine Online

The Maine Office of Tourism has established an award-winning website: www.visitmaine.com. You'll find chamber of commerce addresses, articles, photos, information on lodgings, and access to a variety of Maine tourism businesses. But hundreds of other Maine pages are also up and running, so surf away. You can use the website to request a free state map and copy of *Maine Invites You.* The state's toll-free information hotline is 888/MAINE-45 (888/624-6345).

Maps

Peek in any Mainer's car, and you're likely to see a copy of *The Maine Atlas and Gazetteer,* published by DeLorme Mapping Company

TIPS FOR TIGHTWADS AND THE BUDGET CONSCIOUS

At first glance, Maine might seem pricey, but take another look. It is possible to keep a vacation within a reasonable budget; here are a few tips for doing so.

For starters, avoid the big-name towns and seek out accommodations in smaller, nearby ones instead. For example, instead of Damariscotta, consider Waldoboro; instead of Camden, try Belfast or Searsport; in place of Bar Harbor, check Trenton or Southwest Harbor. Or simply explore the Down East Coast, where rates are generally far lower than in other coastal regions.

Small, family-owned motels tend to have the lowest rates. Better yet, book a cabin or cottage for a week, rather than a room by the night. Not only can you find reasonable weekly rentals – especially if you plan well in advance – but you'll also have cooking facilities, allowing you to avoid eating all meals out.

Speaking of food, buy or bring a small cooler so you can stock up at supermarkets and farmers markets for picnic meals. Most Hannaford and Shaw's supermarkets have large selections of prepared foods and big salad bars and bakeries, and many local groceries have pizza and sandwich counters.

Do check local papers and bulletin boards for Public Supper notices. Most are very inexpensive, raise money for a good cause, and provide an opportunity not only for a good meal, but also to meet locals and gain a few insider tips.

Of course, sometimes you want to have a nice meal in a nice place. Consider going out for lunch, which is usually far less expensive than dinner, or take advantage of early-bird specials or of the Friday-night all-you-can-eat fish fries offered at quite a few home-cooking restaurants.

Take advantage of Maine's vast outdoor-recreation opportunities; many are free. Even Acadia, with its miles and miles of trails and carriage roads, and its Island Explorer bus service, is a bargain; buy a park pass and it's all yours to use and explore.

Take advantage of free events: concerts, lectures, farmers markets, art shows and openings, and family events. Most are usually listed in local papers.

Avoid parking hassles and fees and save gas by using local transportation services when available, such as the trolley network on the Southern Coast and the Island Explorer bus system on Mount Desert Island.

Finally, before making reservations for anything, check to see if there's a special Internet rate or ask about any discounts that might apply to you: AAA, senior, military, government, family rate, and so forth. If you don't ask, you won't get.

in Yarmouth. Despite an oversize format inconvenient for hiking and kayaking, this 96-page paperbound book just about guarantees that you won't get lost (and if you're good at map reading, it can get you out of a lot of traffic jams). Scaled at one-half inch to the mile, it's meticulously compiled from aerial photographs, satellite images, U.S. Geological Survey maps, GPS readings, and timber-company maps, and it is revised annually. It details back roads and dirt roads and shows elevation, boat ramps, public lands, campgrounds and picnic areas, and trailheads. DeLorme products are available nationwide in book and map stores, but you can also order direct (800/452-5931, www.delorme.com). The atlas is $19.95 and shipping is $4 (Maine residents need to add 5 percent sales tax).

The Maine Tourism Association also publishes a less detailed but free state map.

Area Code

Maine still has only one telephone area code,

207. To call long distance in state and out of state, dial 1 plus the area code before the number. For directory assistance, dial 411.

Toll-Free Calling

Any number with an area code of 800, 888, 877, 866, 855, 844, 833, or 822 is toll free.

Cell Phones

Transmission towers are now sprinkled everywhere in Maine; only a few pockets—mostly down peninsulas and in remote valleys and hollows—are out of cellular-phone range. That said, getting reception often requires doing the dance—moving left, right, up, and down to find the strongest signal.

Internet Access

Internet access is widely available at libraries and coffeehouses. Most hotels and many inns and bed-and-breakfasts also offer Internet access; many provide dataports or Wi-Fi.

RESOURCES

Glossary

To help you translate some of the lingo off the beaten track (e.g., country stores and county fairs, farmstands and flea markets), here's a sampling of local terms and expressions.

alewives herring

ayuh yes

barrens as in "blueberry barrens"; fields where wild blueberries grow

beamy wide (as in a boat or a person)

beans shorthand for the traditional Saturday-night meal, which always includes baked beans

blowdown a forest area leveled by wind

blowing a gale very windy

camp a vacation house (small or large), usually on freshwater and/or in the woods

chance serendipity or luck (as in "open by appointment or by chance")

chicken dressing chicken manure

chowder (pronounced "chowdah") soup made with lobster, clams, or fish, or a combination thereof; lobster version sometimes called lobster stew

chowderhead mischief- or troublemakers, usually interchangeable with idiot

coneheads tourists (because of their presumed penchant for ice cream)

cottage a vacation house (anything from a bungalow to a mansion), usually on salt water

culch (also cultch) "stuff"; the contents of attics, basements, and some flea markets

cull a discount lobster, usually minus a claw

cunnin' cute (usually describing a baby or small child)

dinner (pronounced "dinnah") the noon meal

dinner pail lunch box

dite a very small amount

dooryard the yard near a house's main entrance

Down East with the prevailing wind; the old coastal sailing route from Boston to Nova Scotia

downcellar in the basement

dry-ki driftwood, usually remnants from the logging industry

ell a residential structural section that links a house and a barn; formerly a popular location for the "summer kitchen," to spare the house from woodstove heat

exercised upset; angry

fiddleheads unopened ostrich-fern fronds, a spring delicacy

finest kind top quality; good news; an expression of general approval; also, a term of appreciation

flatlander a person not from Maine, often but not exclusively someone from the Midwest

floatplane a small plane equipped with pontoons for landing on water; the same aircraft often becomes a skiplane in winter

flowage a water body created by damming, usually beaver handiwork (also called "beaver flowage")

frappe a thick drink containing milk, ice cream, and flavored syrup, as opposed to a milkshake, which does not include ice cream (but beware: a frappe offered in other parts of the United States is an ice-cream sundae topped with whipped cream!)

from away not native to Maine

galamander a wheeled contraption formerly

used to transport quarry granite to building sites or to boats for onward shipment

gore a sliver of land left over from inaccurate boundary surveys. Maine has several gores; Hibberts Gore, for instance, has a population of one.

got done quit a job; was let go

harbormaster local official who monitors water traffic and assigns moorings; often a very political job

hardshell lobster that hasn't molted yet (more scarce, thus more pricey in summer)

hod wooden "basket" used for carrying clams

ice-out the departure of winter ice from ponds, lakes, rivers, and streams; many communities have ice-out contests, awarding prizes for guessing the exact time of ice-out, in April or May

Italian long soft bread roll sliced on top and filled with peppers, onions, tomatoes, sliced meat, black olives, and sprinkled with olive oil, salt, and pepper; veggie versions available

jimmies chocolate sprinkles, like those on an ice-cream cone

lobster car a large floating crate for storing lobsters

Maine Guide a member of the Maine Professional Guides Association, trained and tested for outdoor and survival skills; also called Registered Maine Guide

market price restaurant menu term for "the going rate," usually referring to the price of lobster or clams

molt what a lobster does when it sheds its shell for a larger one; the act of molting is called ecdysis (as a stripper is an ecdysiast)

money tree a collection device for a monetary gift

mud season mid-March to mid-April, when back roads and unpaved driveways become virtual tank traps

nasty neat extremely meticulous

near stingy

notional stubborn, determined

off island the mainland, to an islander

place another word for a house (as in "Herb Pendleton's place")

ployes Acadian buckwheat pancakes

pot trap, as in "lobster pot"

public landing see "town landing"

rake hand tool used for harvesting blueberries

roller-skiing cross-country skiing on wheels; popular among cross-country skiers, triathletes, and others as a training technique

rusticator a summer visitor, particularly in bygone days

scooch (or scootch) to squat; to move sideways

sea smoke heavy mist rising off the water when the air temperature suddenly becomes much colder than the ocean temperature

select a lobster with claws intact

Selectmen the elected men and women who handle local affairs in small communities; the First Selectman chairs meetings. In some towns, "people from away" have tried to propose substituting a gender-neutral term, but in most cases the effort has failed.

shedder a lobster with a new (soft) shell; generally occurs in July and August (more common then, thus less expensive than hardshells)

shire town county seat

shore dinner the works: chowder, clams, lobster, and sometimes corn on the cob, too; usually the most expensive item on a menu

short a small, illegal-size lobster

slumgullion tasteless food; a mess

slut a poor housekeeper

slut's wool dust balls found under beds, couches, and so on

snapper an undersize, illegal lobster

soda cola, root beer, and so on (referred to as "pop" in some other parts of the country)

softshell see "shedder"

some very (as in "some hot")

spleeny overly sensitive

steamers clams (before or after they are steamed)

sternman a lobsterman's helper (male or female)

summer complaint a tourist

supper (pronounced "suppah") evening meal, eaten by Mainers around 5 or 6 P.M. (as opposed to flatlanders and summer people, who eat dinner between 7 and 9 P.M.)

tad slightly; a little bit
thick-o'-fog zero-visibility fog
to home at home
tomalley a lobster's green insides; considered a delicacy by some
town landing shore access; often a park or a parking lot, next to a wharf or boat-launch ramp
upattic in the attic
Whoopie! Pie the trademarked name for a high-fat, calorie-laden, cakelike snack that only kids and dentists could love
wicked cold! frigid
wicked good! excellent
williwaws uncomfortable feeling

Suggested Reading

DESCRIPTION AND TRAVEL

Bumsted, L. *Hot Showers! Maine Coast Lodgings for Kayakers and Sailors.* 2nd ed. Brunswick, ME: Audenreed Press, 2000. Excellent, well-researched resource for anyone cruising the shoreline and yearning for alternatives to a sleeping bag. It offers some information on kayak access.

Dwelley, M. J. *Spring Wildflowers of New England.* 2nd ed. Camden, ME: Down East Books, 2000. Back in print after several years, this beautifully illustrated gem is an essential guide for exploring spring woodlands.

Dwelley, M. J. *Summer and Fall Wildflowers of New England.* 2nd ed. Camden, ME: Down East Books, 2004. Flowers are grouped by color; more than 700 lovely colored-pencil drawings simplify identification.

Karlin, L., and R. Sawyer-Fay. *Gardens Maine Style.* Camden, ME: Down East Books, 2001. A beautiful book depicting and describing private and some public gardens.

The Maine Atlas and Gazetteer. Yarmouth, ME: DeLorme, updated annually. You'll be hard put to get lost if you're carrying this essential volume; 70 full-page (oversize format) topographical maps with GPS grids.

Nangle, H. *Moon Maine.* 4th ed. Berkeley, CA: Avalon Travel, 2008. Explore the far reaches of Maine with a Maine resident and veteran travel writer.

Pierson, E. C., J. E. Pierson, and P. D. Vickery. *A Birder's Guide to Maine.* Camden, ME: Down East Books, 1981. An expanded version of *A Birder's Guide to the Coast of Maine.* No ornithologist, novice or expert, should explore Maine without this valuable guide.

Taft, H., J. Taft, and C. Rindlaub. *A Cruising Guide to the Maine Coast.* 5th ed. Peaks Island, ME: Diamond Pass Publishing, 2003. Don't even consider cruising the coast without this volume.

LITERATURE, ART, AND PHOTOGRAPHY

Curtis, J., W. Curtis, and F. Lieberman. *Monhegan: The Artists' Island.* Camden, ME: Down East Books, 1995. Fascinating island history interspersed with landscape and seascape paintings and drawings by more than 150 artists, including Bellows, Henri, Hopper, Kent, Porter, Tam, and Wyeth.

Maine Speaks: An Anthology of Maine Literature. Brunswick, ME: Maine Writers and Publishers Alliance, 1989.

McNair, W., ed. *The Maine Poets: An Anthology of Verse.* Camden, ME: Down East Books, 2003. McNair's selection of best works by Maine's finest poets.

Spectre, P. H. *Passage in Time.* New York: W. W. Norton, 1991. A noted marine writer cruises the coast aboard traditional windjammers; gorgeous photos complement the colorful text.

Van Riper, F. *Down East Maine: A World Apart.* Camden, ME: Down East Books, 1998. Maine's Washington County, captured with incredible insight and compassion by a master photographer and insightful wordsmith.

LOBSTER AND LIGHTHOUSES

Bachelder, Peter Dow, and P. M. Mason. *Maine Lighthouse Map and Guide.* Glendale, CO: Bella Terra Publishing, 2009. An illustrated map and guide providing directions on how to find all Maine beacons as well as brief histories.

Caldwell, W. *Lighthouses of Maine.* Camden, ME: Down East Books, 2002. A historical tour of Maine's lighthouses, with the emphasis on history, legends, and lore; reprint.

Corson, T. *The Secret Life of Lobsters.* New York: HarperCollins, 2004. Everything you wanted—or perhaps didn't want—to know about lobster.

Rezendes, P. *The Lighthouse Companion for Maine.* Windsor, CT: Tide-Mark Press, 2005. An easy-to-use directory of Maine lighthouses, arranged in alphabetical order and accompanied by photos, directions by land and sea, and contact information for arranging tours.

Woodward, C. *The Lobster Coast: Rebels, Rusticators, and the Struggle for a Forgotten Frontier.* New York: Viking, 2004. A veteran journalist's take on the history of the Maine Coast.

HISTORY

Duncan, R. F., E. G. Barlow, K. Bray, and C. Hanks. *Coastal Maine: A Maritime History.* Woodstock, VT: Countrymen Press, 2002. Updated version of the classic work.

Isaacson, D., ed. *Maine: A Guide "Down East."* 2nd ed. Maine League of Historical Societies and Museums, 1970. Revised version of the Depression-era WPA guidebook. Still interesting for background reading.

Judd, R. W., E. A. Churchill, and J. W. Eastman, eds. *Maine: The Pine Tree State from Prehistory to the Present.* Orono, ME: University of Maine Press, 1995. The best available Maine history, with excellent historical maps.

Paine, L. P. *Down East: A Maritime History of Maine.* Gardiner, ME: Tilbury House, 2000. A noted maritime historian provides an enlightening introduction to the state's seafaring tradition.

MEMOIRS

Dawson, L. B. *Saltwater Farm.* Westford, ME: Impatiens Press, 1993. Witty, charming stories of growing up on the Cushing peninsula.

Greenlaw, L. *The Lobster Chronicles: Life on a Very Small Island.* New York: Hyperion, 2002. Swordfishing boat captain Linda Greenlaw's account of returning to life on Isle au Haut after weathering *The Perfect Storm.*

Lunt, D. L. *Hauling by Hand: The Life and Times of a Maine Island.* Frenchboro, ME: Islandport Press, 1999. A sensitive history of Frenchboro (a.k.a. Long Island), eight miles offshore, written by an eighth-generation islander and journalist.

Wass, P. B. *Lighthouse in My Life: The Story of a Maine Lightkeeper's Family.* Camden, ME: Down East Books, 1987. Offshore adventures, growing up on Libby Island, near Machias.

NATURAL HISTORY

Bennett, D. *Maine's Natural Heritage: Rare Species and Unique Natural Features.* Camden, ME: Down East Books, 1988. A dated book that examines both the special ecology of the state and how it's threatened.

Conkling, P. W. *Islands in Time: A Natural and Cultural History of the Islands of the Gulf of Maine.* 2nd ed. Camden, ME: Down East Books, and Rockland, ME: Island Institute, 1999. A thoughtful overview by the president of Maine's Island Institute.

Kendall, D. L. *Glaciers and Granite: A Guide to Maine's Landscape and Geology.* Unity, ME: North Country Press, 1993. Explains why Maine looks the way it does.

Maine's Ice Age Trail Down East Map and Guide. Orono, ME: University of Maine Press, 2007. Also available online at http://iceagetrail.umaine.edu. Information on 46 glacial sites.

RECREATION

Hiking and Walking

AMC Maine Mountain Guide. 9th ed. Boston: Appalachian Mountain Club Books, 2005. The definitive statewide resource for going vertical. In a handy small format. (AMC has eliminated Acadia National Park and expanded its separate guide on Acadia's peaks.)

Cobscook Trails: A Guide to Walking Opportunities Around Cobscook Bay and the Bold Coast. 2nd ed. Whiting, ME: Quoddy Regional Land Trust, 2000. Essential handbook for exploring this part of the Down East Coast. Excellent maps.

Gibson, J. *50 Hikes in Coastal and Southern Maine.* 3rd ed. Woodstock, VT: Countryman Press/Backcountry Guides, 2001. Well-researched, detailed resource by a veteran hiker.

Roberts, P. *On the Trail in Lincoln County.* Newcastle/Damariscotta, ME: Lincoln County Publishing, 2003. A great guide to more than 60 walks in preserves from Wiscasset through Waldoboro, with detailed directions to trailheads.

Seymour, T. *Hiking Maine.* 2nd ed. Helena, MT: Falcon Press, 2002. Helpful—especially for less-well-known hikes in the Mid-Coast region. Not as comprehensive statewide as the Gibson hiking guide or the *AMC Maine Mountain Guide.*

Paddling

The Maine Island Trail: Stewardship Handbook and Guidebook. Rockland, ME: Maine Island Trail Association, updated annually. Available only with MITA membership (annual dues $45), providing access to dozens of islands along the watery trail.

Miller, D. *Kayaking the Maine Coast: A Paddler's Guide to Day Trips from Kittery to Cobscook.* 2nd ed. Woodstock, VT: Countryman Press/Backcountry Guides, 2006. A well-researched volume by a veteran kayaker. With her book and a copy of *Hot Showers!* (described earlier), you're all set.

Wilson, A., and J. Hayes. *Quiet Water Maine: Canoe Guides.* 2nd ed. Boston: Appalachian Mountain Club Books, 2005. Comprehensive handbook, with helpful maps, for inland paddling.

ACADIA NATIONAL PARK/ MOUNT DESERT ISLAND

Abrell, D. *A Pocket Guide to the Carriage Roads of Acadia National Park.* 2nd ed. Camden, ME: Down East Books, 1995.

Brechlin, E. D. *A Pocket Guide to Paddling the Waters of Mount Desert Island.* Camden, ME: Down East Books, 1996.

Gillmore, R. *Great Walks of Acadia National Park and Mount Desert Island.* Rev. ed. Goffstown, NH: Great Walks, 1994.

Helfrich, G. W., and G. O'Neil. *Lost Bar Harbor.* Camden, ME: Down East Books, 1982. Fascinating collection of historic photographs of classic turn-of-the-century "cottages," many obliterated by Bar Harbor's Great Fire of 1947.

Minutolo, A. *A Pocket Guide to Biking on Mount Desert Island.* Camden, ME: Down East Books, 1996.

Monkman, J., and M. Monkman. *Discover Acadia National Park: A Guide to the Best Hiking, Biking, and Paddling.* 2nd Ed. Boston: Appalachian Mountain Club Books, 2005. A comprehensive guide to well-chosen hikes, bike trips, and paddling routes, accompanied by an excellent pullout map.

Nangle, H. *Moon Acadia National Park.* 3rd ed. Berkeley, CA: Avalon Travel, 2009. A Mainer since childhood and veteran travel writer is the ideal escort for exploring this region in depth.

Roberts, A. R. *Mr. Rockefeller's Roads.* Camden, ME: Down East Books, 1990. The story behind Acadia's scenic carriage roads, written by the granddaughter of John D. Rockefeller (who created them).

St. Germain, T. A., Jr. *A Walk in the Park: Acadia's Hiking Guide.* 10th ed. Bar Harbor, ME: Parkman Publications, 2004. The best Acadia National Park hiking guide, in a handy Michelin-type vertical format. Part of the proceeds go to Friends of Acadia's Acadia Trails Forever campaign.

Internet Resources

GENERAL INFORMATION

State of Maine
www.maine.gov

Everything you wanted to know about Maine and then some, with links to all government departments and Maine-related sites. Buy a fishing license online, reserve a campsite at Lamoine State Park (near Acadia), or check the fall foliage conditions via the site's LeafCam. (You can also access foliage info at www.mainefoliage.com, where you can sign up for weekly email foliage reports in September and early October.) Also listed is information on accessible arts and recreation.

Maine Office of Tourism
www.visitmaine.com

The biggest and most useful of all Maine-related tourism sites, with sections for where to visit, where to stay, things to do, trip planning, packages, calendar of events, and search capabilities. Also lodging specials and a comprehensive calendar of events.

Maine Tourism Association
www.mainetourism.com

Find lodging, camping, restaurants, attractions, services, and more as well as links for weather, foliage, transportation planning, and chambers of commerce.

Maine Emergency Management Association
www.state.me.us/mema/weather/weather.htm

Five-day weather forecasts broken down by 32 zones.

Maine Campground Owners Association
www.campmaine.com
Find private campgrounds statewide.

Portland Papers
www.mainetoday.com
Home site for Maine's largest newspaper has current news as well as extensive information on travel, outdoor activities, entertainment, and sports.

TRANSPORTATION

Explore Maine
www.exploremaine.org
An invaluable site for trip planning, with information on and links to airports, rail service, bus service, automobile travel, and ferries, as well as links to other key travel-planning sites.

Maine Department of Transportation
www.511maine.gov
Provides real-time information about major delays, accidents, road construction, and weather conditions. You can get the same info and more by dialing 511 in-state.

PARKS AND RECREATION

Department of Conservation, Maine Bureau of Parks and Lands
www.parksandlands.com
Information on state parks, public reserved lands, and state historic sites, details on facilities such as campsites, picnic areas, and boat launches. Make state campground reservations online.

Acadia National Park
www.nps.gov/acad
Information on all sections of Acadia National Park. Make ANP campground reservations online.

Maine Audubon
www.maineaudubon.org
Information about Maine Audubon's eco-sensitive headquarters in Falmouth and all of the organization's environmental centers statewide. Activity and program schedules are included.

The Nature Conservancy
www.nature.org/wherewework/northamerica/states/maine
Information about Maine preserves, field trips, and events.

Maine Land Trust Network
www.mltn.org
Maine has dozens of land trusts statewide, managing lands that provide opportunities for hiking, walking, canoeing, kayaking, and other such activities.

Healthy Maine Walks
www.healthymainewalks.com
Lists places for walking statewide.

Bicycle Coalition of Maine
www.bikemaine.org
Tons of information for bicyclists, including routes, shops, events, organized rides, and much more.

Maine Birding
www.mainebirding.net
A must-visit site for anyone interested in learning more about bird-watching in Maine, including news, checklists, events, forums, trips, and more.

Maine Association of Sea Kayaking Guides & Instructors
www.maineseakayakguides.com
Information and links to about two dozen members who meet state requirements to lead commercial trips.

Maine Windjammer Association
www.sailmainecoast.com
Windjammer schooners homeported in Rockland, Camden, and Rockport belong to this umbrella organization; there are links to the websites of all the vessels for online and phone information and reservations.

ISLAND RESOURCES

Island Institute
www.islandinstitute.org

The institute serves as a clearinghouse/advocate for Maine's islands; the website provides links to the major year-round islands.

Maine Island Trail Association
www.mita.org

Information about the association and its activities along with membership details.

ARTS, ANTIQUES, AND MUSEUMS

Maine Archives and Museums
www.mainemuseums.org

Information on and links to museums, archives, historical societies, and historic sites in Maine.

Maine Art Museum Trail
www.maineartmuseums.org

Information on art museums with significant collections statewide, including Ogunquit Museum of Art (Ogunquit); Portland Museum of Art (Portland); Bowdoin College Museum of Art (Brunswick); and Farnsworth Art Museum (Rockland).

Maine Antiques Dealers Association
www.maineantiques.org

Lists member dealers statewide by location and specialty and provides information on upcoming antiques events.

FOOD AND DRINK

Maine Department of Agriculture
www.getrealmaine.com

Information on all things agricultural, including fairs, farmers markets, farm vacations, places to buy Maine foods, berry- and apple-picking sites, and more.

Portland Food Map
www.portlandfoodmap.com

A must for culinary travel in Maine's largest city. Information on anything and everything food- and drink-related, including openings and closings and links to reviews.

Index

A

Abbe Museum: 15, 19, 316
Abbott School: 271
Acadia Birding Festival: 320
Acadia National Park: 14, 15, 19; Isle au Haut 293-294; map 4-5; Mount Desert Island 307-314; Schoodic Peninsula 351-354
Acadia National Park Headquarters: 307-308
Acadians: 428
Acadia region: 297-365; map 299
Acadia Repertory Theatre: 338-339
accommodations: general discussion 441; *see also* camping; *specific place*
Adopt a Finback or Humpback Whale program: 317
aerial touring/flightseeing: 202, 303
African Americans: 429
air travel: 436-437
Alamo Theatre: 248
alcohol: 441
Aldermere Farm: 220
Alewife Run: 168
Allagash Brewing Company: 84
allergies: 445
All Fired Up!: 15, 320
Alna: 145
Ames, Ted: 282
Ames Pond: 287
amusement parks: 71
Anglers Restaurant: 22, 247
Annual Bluegrass Festival: 124
Annual Ogunquit Antiques Show: 45
Annual Strawberry Festival and Country Fair: 147
antiques: general discussion 23-24; *see also specific place*
Antiques on Nine: 23, 60
Aquaboggan Water Park: 71
Arey's Neck Woods: 212
Armbrust Hill Town Park: 212
Arrows: 20, 50
Arts in Rockland: 202
Arts in the Park (Belfast): 238
Arundel Barn Playhouse: 60
Asticou Azalea Garden: 19, 331-332
Atlantic Brewing Company: 328
Atlantic Salmon Museum: 249
auto travel: 437, 438-440
Avalon Antiques Market: 24, 148
Avena Botanicals Medicinal Herb Garden: 225

B

Back Bay Grill: 22, 103
Back Cove: 93-94
Backshore Beach: 273
Backwoods Mountain: 267
Bad Little Falls Park: 383
Bagaduce Ferry Landing: 267
Bagaduce Forge: 266
Bagaduce Music Lending Library: 256
Bailey Island: 87, 119
Bailey's Mistake: 381
Baker Island: 310
Bald Mountain: 225-226
Bar Harbor: 314-330; map 315
Bar Harbor Brewing Company & Soda Works: 328
Bar Harbor Historical Society: 317-318
Bar Harbor Music Festival: 319
Bar Harbor Town Band: 319
Bar Harbor Whale Museum: 15, 317
Bar Island: 321
Barred Island Preserve: 286-287
Barrett Park: 155
Barrett's Cove: 226
Bartlett Maine Estate Winery: 357
Bass Harbor: 337
Bass Harbor Light: 310
Bates-Morse Mountain Conservation Area: 136
Bath: 130-144; map 132-133
Bath Antiques Shows: 135
Bath Iron Works: 131
Bay Chamber Concerts (Rockland): 202
Bay Chamber Concerts (Rockport): 221
Bayside (Belfast area): 236
Bayside (Portland): 82
Beachcroft Trail: 311
beaches: Acadia region 311, 349, 359-360; Blue Hill Peninsula 267, 273; Deer Isle 287; Down East 381, 383-384, 395-396; Mid-Coast Region 125, 137-138, 154, 172-173; Penobscot Bay 188-189, 201, 203-205, 213, 226; Portland 86, 89, 93-95, 110; Southern Coast 46, 57-58, 72
Beach Olympics: 70
Beach to Beacon Race: 92
beanhole beans: 186
Bear Brook Trail: 311
Beatrix Farrand Garden: 317
Beech Mountain: 311
Beehive Trail: 311

beer/breweries: Acadia region 328; Mid-Coast Region 128; Portland 84, 91
Belfast: 235-242
Belfast Bay Festival: 238
Belfast City Park: 239
Belfast Co-op Store: 236
Belfast Curling Club: 240
Belfast Maskers: 238
Ben and Bill's Chocolate Emporium: 15, 23, 327
Bernard: 337
Bernard Langlais sculptures: 185
Berwick: 30-31
Berwick Academy: 30
Bicycle Coalition of Maine: 95
Biddeford: 69
Biddeford Art Walk: 70
Big Garden Island: 212
Big White Island: 212
biking: Acadia region 322, 340, 358; Blue Hill Peninsula 267; Deer Isle 287, 294; Down East 384-385, 391; Mid-Coast Region 136; Penobscot Bay 205, 213, 216, 225, 239, 246; Portland 88, 95, 110, 111; Southern Coast 38, 46, 58
Birch Harbor: 350
Birch Point Beach State Park: 203
Birdsacre: 302
birds/bird-watching: Acadia region 319, 358; Deer Isle 286, 287; Down East 370, 389, 410; Mid-Coast Region 136, 171, 173; Penobscot Bay 196-197, 213; Portland 94-95, 110, 111; Southern Coast 37
Biscay Pond: 173, 174
Blacksmith Shop (Castine): 271
Blackwoods Scenic Byway: 353
Blowing Cave: 55
Blue Goose Dance Hall: 236
Blue Hill: 20, 255-261
Blue Hill Concert Association: 257
Blue Hill Fair: 257
Blue Hill Heritage Trust: 257-258
Blue Hill Mountain: 257
Blue Hill Peninsula: 255-276; map 254
Blue Hill Town Park: 258
Blue Jacket Shipcrafters: 244-245
Blue Sky on York Beach: 21, 41
Boat Builders Festival: 154
boating excursions: general discussion 14, 15, 18, 19; Acadia region 322-324, 333, 340-341, 341; Blue Hill Peninsula 273-274; Deer Isle 287, 288-289; Down East 372, 376, 377, 378, 385, 396, 403; Mid-Coast Region 126, 138, 156, 157, 173-174; Penobscot Bay 189-190, 204, 205, 227, 239-240, 250; Portland 96-97, 111; Southern Coast 46-47, 58-59
Boothbay: 151
Boothbay Harbor: 151
Boothbay Peninsula: 151-164; map 153
Boothbay Playhouse: 154
Boothbay Railway Village: 152
Boothbay Region Land Trust: 154-155
Boot Head Preserve: 391
Booth Quarry: 212
botanical gardens: Acadia region 316, 331-333; Mid-Coast Region 155-156; Penobscot Bay 225
Bowdoin College: 119-121
Bowdoin College Museum of Art: 120-121
Bowdoin International Music Festival: 123
Bradbury Mountain State Park: 110-111
Brave Boat Harbor: 29
Breakwater Light: 201
Bresca: 21, 101
Brewer House: 407
Brick Store Museum: 55-56
Bristol: 164
Bristol Mills: 173
Broad Cove Church: 186
Brooklin: 262-269
Brooksville: 262-269
Brooksville Open Mic Nights: 265
Brown's Head Light: 211
Brunswick: 119-130
Brunswick Hydro: 122-123
Brunswick Literary Art Walk: 122
Brunswick-Topsham Land Trust: 125
Brunswick Women's History Trail: 121-122
Bucksport: 248-251
Bucksport Waterfront Walkway: 248
budget traveling: 447
Burnham Tavern: 380
Burning Tree: 23, 330
Burnt Island: 17, 152
Bush Estate (Walker's Point): 53, 55
bus travel: 437-438
Butler Preserve: 57

C

Cabot Mill Antiques: 23, 124
Cadillac Mountain: 14, 308
Calais: 406-412
Calais-Robbinston milestones: 407
Camden: 218-235; map 219
Camden Amphitheatre: 224

Camden Conference: 221
Camden Harbor Park: 224
Camden Hills State Park: 223-224
Camden Opera House: 221
Camden Snow Bowl: 225
Camp Ellis: 68
camping: Acadia region 305, 312, 343-344, 362; Deer Isle 290-291, 295; Down East 372, 378-379, 393; Mid-Coast Region 141, 162, 176-177; Penobscot Bay 184, 191, 241, 247, 251; Portland 110-111, 113; Southern Coast 40
Campobello Island: 394-398
canoeing: *see* kayaking/canoeing
Cape Jellison: 246
Cape Neddick: 33
Cape Porpoise: 53, 55
Cape Rosier: 264
Cape Rosier Artist Collective: 263
Capriccio: 45
Captain Alfred Skolfield Nature Preserve: 125
carriage roads: 308-310
car travel: 437, 438-440
Casco Bay Islands: 88-90
Castine: 20, 269-276
Castine Arts Association: 272
Castine Historical Society: 271-272
Castle Tucker: 24, 144, 146
Caterpillar Hill: 263
Causeway Beach: 287
Celebrate Castine: 272
Cellardoor Vineyard: 222
cell phones: 448
Center for Lifelong Learning: 382
Center for Maine Contemporary Art: 221
Center for the Arts at the Chocolate Church: 135
Chamberlain, Joshua L.: 122
Chamberlain Days: 122
Chapman-Hall House: 165-166
Charles Pond: 138
Charlotte Rhoades Park and Butterfly Garden: 338
Cherryfield Band: 371
Cherryfield-Narraguagus Historical Society: 370
Chester Pike's Galley: 23, 364
Chickawaukee Lake: 204
children, activities for: general discussion 15; *see also specific place*
Children's Museum of Maine: 84
Christmas by the Sea: 221
Christmas Cove: 173
Christmas Prelude: 60
churches/temples: Acadia region 316; Mid-Coast Region 121, 134, 145, 167-168; Penobscot Bay 186, 235-236; Southern Coast 55, 56-57
City Theater (Biddeford): 70
Clam Shack (Kennebunkport): 21, 67
Claremont Croquet Classic: 339
Cliff Path: 37
climate: 12, 415-416, 418
Coastal Maine Botanical Gardens: 155-156
Coastal Mountains Land Trust: 223
Cobscook: 19, 389
Coffin Pond: 125
Cohen, William: 425, 426
Cold River Vodka: 108
Coleman Pond: 226
College of the Atlantic: 317
Colonial Pemaquid: 166-167
Compass Harbor: 321
Concerts in the Park (Kennebunk): 59-60
Congress Street/Downtown Arts District (Portland): 81
Corea: 350
Corea Heath: 351, 358
costs and budgeting: 447
Country Roads Artists and Artisans Tour: 221
Country Store Museum: 338
Cox Pinnacle: 125
crafts: 432-433
Craig Brook National Fish Hatchery: 249
Cramer Park: 224
Cranberry Isles: 15, 346, 348-349
Cranberry Point Drive: 395
credit cards: 446
Crescent Beach (Wells): 46
Crescent Beach State Park: 86
Criterion Theatre and Arts Center: 319-320
Crockett Cove Woods Preserve: 285, 286
Cumberland and Oxford Canal: 82
Cundy's Harbor: 119
curling: 240
Curtis Island: 224
Cushing Peninsula: 185-187
Cutler: 380
Cutler Coast Public Preserve: 384
Cutler Road (Route 191): 381

D

Damariscotta: 164; map 165
Damariscove Island: 157
DaPonte String Quartet: 169

David Saul Smith Union: 120
Davistown Museum: 237
Day's Antiques: 23, 124
Deck House Restaurant and Cabaret Theater: 338
Decorator Show House: 36
Deering Oaks: 93
Deer Isle: 20, 276-296; map 277
Deer Isle Granite Museum: 280
DeLorme Mapping Co.: 108-109
demographics: 427-429
Desert of Maine: 108
Directions Craft Show: 320
distilleries: 108, 203
Diver Ed's Dive-In Theater Boat Cruise: 15, 322-323
Dock Square: 56
Dodge Point Preserve: 172
Donnell Pond Public Reserved Land: 358
Douglas N. Harding Rare Books: 23, 45
Down East: 366-412; map 368
Downeast Heritage Center: 406
Downeast Institute for Applied Marine Research and Education: 375
Downeast Observatory: 404
Downeast Scenic Railroad: 303
Down East Spring Birding Festival: 389
Down East Sunrise Trail: 384
Downtown Arts District (Portland): 81
Drakes Island Beach: 46
Dresden: 145
Dromore Burying Ground: 134
Duckfat: 22, 103
Duck Harbor Mountain: 294
Dyce's Head Lighthouse: 271

E

Eagle Hill Bog: 396
Eagle Island: 90
Eartha: 108-109
East Boothbay: 151
East End: 81-82
East End Beach: 93
East End Point: 89
Eastern Cemetery: 82
East Machias: 380, 381
Eastport: 398-406
Eastport Arts Center: 401
Eastport Salmon Festival: 401
East Quoddy Head Light: 396
Echo Lake: 311
economy: 426-427
educational programs: 442-443
Eggemoggin Reach Regatta: 265
Eighth Maine Regimental Memorial: 88
Eliot Mountain Trail: 333
Ellsworth: 301-306
Ellsworth Concert Band: 304
Emerson Hall: 271
Emmons Preserve: 57
estuaries: 414
Ethel H. Blum Gallery: 317
Evangeline: 22, 102
Evergreen Cemetery: 94
excursion boats: *see* boating excursions

F

Fall Festival Arts and Crafts Show: 221
fall foliage: 370
Farnsworth Art Museum: 17, 199-200
Farnsworth Homestead: 199
Fernald's Neck: 224-225
Ferry Beach State Park: 72
Fifth Maine Regiment Center: 88
fine arts: general discussion 430, 432; *see also specific place*
Fine Living Festival: 60
Fine Sand Beach: 349
First Church (Belfast): 235
First Friday (Stonington): 281
First Parish Church (Brunswick): 121
fish-chowder suppers: 147
Fisherman's Museum: 166
Fishermen's Festival: 154
fish/fishing: Acadia region 341, 358; Down East 375, 403, 408; Mid-Coast Region 122-123, 138, 156, 168; Penobscot Bay 249; Portland 111; Southern Coast 38, 46, 59
Five Fifty-Five: 21, 102
Five Rivers Arts Alliance: 123
Flash! In the Pans Community Steel Band: 20, 264-265
flightseeing/aerial touring: 202, 303
Flo's Steamed Dogs: 21, 40
food: general discussion 20-23, 431, 441; *see also specific place*
Footbridge Beach: 46
Fore River Sanctuary: 94
Fore Street: 21, 101
Fort Allen Park: 93
Fort Baldwin: 135
Fort Edgecomb: 147
Fort Foster: 29
Fort George State Park: 271

Fort Knox: 20, 243-244
Fort Madison: 272
Fort McClary Historic Site: 28-29
Fort O'Brien State Memorial: 381-382
Fort Point Light: 246
Fort Point State Park: 246
Fort Popham Historic Site: 132
Fort Pownall: 246
Fort William Henry: 166-167
Four Season Farm: 263
Fourth of July (Bar Harbor): 320
Fourth of July (Jonesport): 375
Fourth of July (Thomaston): 184
Fourth of July/Old Home Week (Eastport): 401
Fox Hill Drive: 395
Francine Bistro: 22, 233
Freeport: 107-115
Frenchboro: 347
Frenchboro Historical Society Museum: 347
Friday Gallery Walk (Belfast): 238
Fried Smelt Dinner: 375
Friends of Acadia (FOA): 309
frostbite and hypothermia: 445
Full Circle Fair: 257
Funtown/Splashtown USA: 71

G

galleries: Acadia region 354-355; Blue Hill Peninsula 258, 263, 265-266, 283-284; Deer Isle 283-284; Mid-Coast Region 166, 170; Penobscot Bay 195
Gates House: 381
Gazebo Concert Series: 135
Geary's Beach: 213
Geary's Brewing Company: 84
geography: 415
George B. Dorr Natural History Museum: 15, 317
Georges River Land Trust: 223, 237
Georges River Scenic Byway: 237
Georgetown Peninsula: 130
Giant Stairs: 124-125
Gilsland Farm: 95
Gleason Cove: 401
Goat Island Light: 55
Goldenrod, The: 21, 40
golf: Acadia region 322, 340, 360; Blue Hill Peninsula 273; Deer Isle 288; Down East 384, 396, 410; Mid-Coast Region 125, 136, 172; Penobscot Bay 205, 226-227, 239, 250; Portland 95-96; Southern Coast 37, 47, 58, 72
Good Life Center: 262-263
Googins Island: 110
Goose Rocks Beach: 53
Gorham Mountain: 311
Gouldsboro: 350
government: 426
Grand Auditorium (Ellsworth): 304
Grand Lake Stream: 408-409
Grand Lake Stream Folk Art Festival: 408-409
Grant Park: 321
gratuities: 446
Great Chebeague: 89-90
Greater Portland Landmarks: 86
Great Harbor Maritime Museum: 333
Great Head Trail: 310-311
Great Maine Lumberjack Show: 15, 304
Great Wass Island Preserve: 19, 376
Greek Heritage Festival (Portland): 92
Greek Heritage Festival (Saco): 70
Grimes Park: 212
Grindle Point Light: 220
Gritty McDuff's: 91
Gut, The: 168-169

H

Hackmatack Playhouse: 30
Hamilton Beach: 89
Hamilton Cove Preserve: 391
Hamilton House: 30
Hamilton Sanctuary: 137
Hancock: 351
Hancock County Friends of the Arts: 356
HarborArts: 221
Harbor Fest: 45
Harbor Park: 203
Harpswells: 119
Harrington House: 108
Harrington Meeting House: 167-168
Haystack Mountain School of Crafts: 279, 280
Head Beach: 137
Head Tide Church: 145
health and safety: 444-445; *see also specific place*
Hearse House: 271
Heath, The: 72
Hendricks Hill Museum: 153
Heritage Park (Belfast): 239
Herring Cove Provincial Park: 396
Higgins Mountain: 136
hiking: general discussion 15; Acadia region 310-311, 320-322, 333, 340, 358; Blue Hill

Peninsula 257-258, 273; Deer Isle 286-287, 294; Down East 370, 384, 391, 395-396, 403-404, 408; Mid-Coast Region 124-125, 136-137, 154-155, 171, 172; Penobscot Bay 195-196, 211-212, 225-226, 249; Portland 93, 94, 95, 110-111; Southern Coast 37, 44
Historical Society Museum (Islesboro): 220
hitchhiking: 440
Hockamock Head Light: 349
Hodgdon Pond: 311
Holbrook Island Sanctuary State Park: 267
Holt House: 256
Holt Mill Pond Preserve: 287
H.O.M.E. (Homeworkers Organized for More Employment): 248-249
Homer, Winslow: 94
horseback riding: 111
hospitals: 444
House and Garden Day (Penobscot Bay): 221
House and Garden Tour (Pemaquid region): 169
Hubbard Cottage: 394-395
Huber Preserve: 212
Hugo's: 21, 104
Hulls Cove Tool Barn and Sculpture Garden: 318
Hulls Cove Visitor Center: 307
Humboldt Field Research Institute: 371
hypothermia and frostbite: 445

I

Improv Acadia: 15, 319
Indian Ceremonial Days: 401
Indian Point/Blagden Preserve: 321-322
information and services: general discussion 446-448; *see also specific place*
Innstitute for the Arts and Sciences: 356
International Festival: 407
Internet access: 448
Isle au Haut: 20, 293-296
Isle au Haut Mountain: 212
Islesboro: 220
Islesford Historical Museum: 346, 348
Italian Street Festival: 92
itineraries: 13-24

J

Jackson Laboratory for Mammalian Research: 318
James P. White House: 235-236
Jasper Beach: 381, 383
Jewell Falls: 94
John Perkins House: 270
Johnson Memorial Park: 204
Jones Beach: 359
Jonesboro: 380
Jones Landing: 91
Jonesport/Beals area: 373-379
Jonesport Lobsterboat Races: 375
Jordan Pond House: 19, 312-314
Jordan Pond Nature Trail: 310
Josephine Newman Sanctuary: 137
Joshua L. Chamberlain Museum: 121
Just Barb's: 22, 247

K

kayaking/canoeing: Acadia region 322, 341, 358, 359; Blue Hill Peninsula 259, 273, 278; Deer Isle 287, 288; Down East 384-385, 391, 403-404, 408; Mid-Coast Region 126, 138, 158, 174; Penobscot Bay 189, 205, 213, 225, 249-250; Portland 94, 96, 111; Southern Coast 38, 46, 47, 59, 72
Kennebunk: 53
Kennebunkport: 13, 53
Kennebunks, The: 53-68; map 54
Kisma Preserve: 302-303
Kittery: 28-29, 32-33
Kittery Concerts in the Park: 29
Kittery Historical and Naval Museum: 28
Kneisel Hall Chamber Music School: 256-257
Knickercane Island: 155
Knight's Pond: 226
Kotzschmar Organ: 90

L

Lady Pepperrell House: 28
Laite Beach Park: 226
Lake Pemaquid: 174
La Kermesse: 70
Lake St. George State Park: 237
Lake Wood: 311
Landing at Pine Point: 70
Lane's Island Preserve: 212
Langlais, Bernard: 185
Laudholm Farm: 44
Laudholm Nature Crafts Festival: 45
Lawson's Quarry: 212
Le Domaine: 22, 360, 364
Legacy of the Arts: 320
Libby Island Light: 381
Liberty: 237
Liberty Point Drive: 395
Liberty Tool Company: 24, 237

lighthouses: general discussion 16-17; Acadia region 310, 349; Blue Hill Peninsula 271; Deer Isle 281; Down East 376, 381, 387, 388, 396, 406; Mid-Coast Region 152, 166; Penobscot Bay 187, 194-195, 200, 201, 203, 211, 220, 246; Portland 85, 86; Southern Coast 35, 46, 55, 69-70
Lighting of the Nubble: 36-37
Lily Pond: 288
Lincoln Arts Festival: 154
Lincoln County Community Theater: 169
Lincoln County Jail and Museum: 146
Lincoln Street Center for Arts and Education: 202
Lincolnville: 24, 218
Lincolnville Beach: 226
Linekin Preserve: 155
literature: 433-435
Little Chebeague: 89
L. L. Bean: 13, 16, 107-108
L. L. Bean Outdoor Discovery Schools: 111
L. L. Bean Summer Concert Series: 109
Lobster Festival (Frenchboro): 347
Lobster Festival (Winter Harbor): 354
lobstering cruise: 96
lobsters: general discussion 16-17, 432-433; *see also specific place*
Lobster Shack (Cape Elizabeth): 16, 22, 105
Lompoc Cafe: 328
Lubec: 18, 19, 387-394
Lubec Breakwater: 388
Lubec Historical Society: 388
Lucky Catch Lobster Tours: 16, 96
Lupine Festival: 281
Lyme disease: 444

M

Mache Bistro: 23, 329
Machias: 380
Machias Bay: 380-387
Machias Bay Chamber Concerts: 383
Machiasport: 380
Machias River: 385
Machias Seal Island (MSI): 19, 376, 385
Machias Wild Blueberry Festival: 383
Mackworth Island: 95
Main Beach (Ogunquit): 46
Maine Antique Toy and Art Museum: 169
Maine Brewers' Festival: 92
Maine Central Model Railroad: 19, 374-375
Maine Coastal Islands National Wildlife Refuge: 370
Maine Coast Sardine History Museum: 19, 375
Maine Discovery Center: 200
Maine Eastern Railroad: 124, 202
Maine Highland Games: 124
Maine History Gallery: 83
Maine Island Trail: 278
Maine Lighthouse Museum: 17, 200
Maine Lobster Festival: 202
Maine Lobster Museum and Hatchery: 316-317
Maine Maritime Academy: 271
Maine Maritime Museum: 13-14, 16, 24, 131-132
Maine Narrow Gauge Railroad and Museum: 83-84
Maine Sea Coast Mission: 332
Maine Sea Salt Company: 382
Maine State Ferry Service: 205
Maine State Music Theatre: 123
Maine Tourism Association: 446
Maine Wildlife Park: 109
Main Street Castine: 271
Main Street Historic District (Rockland): 201
Manana Island: 194
Manset: 337
Marginal Way: 43
Marie Reed Memorial Park: 201
marine life: 414, 417
Marine Park (Rockport): 224
Marine Resources Aquarium: 152-153
Marshall Point Lighthouse Museum: 17, 187
Marshfield: 380
Mary-Lea Park: 224
Mast Landing Sanctuary: 109-110
McCurdy Smokehouse: 388
MDI Garlic Festival: 339
Menigawum Preserve (Stratton Island): 174
MERI Center: 258-259
Merrill Auditorium: 90-91
Merryspring Park: 224
Mid-Coast Region: 116-179; map 118
Middle Mountain Park: 212
Milbridge: 369-373
Milbridge Anniversary Celebration: 371
Milbridge Historical Society Museum: 370
Miniature Village: 280-281
Mistake Island: 376
Mitchell, George J.: 425, 426
money: 446
Monhegan Island: 14, 17, 192-198
Monhegan Lighthouse: 194-195
Monhegan Museum: 194-195
Montpelier: 183
Montsweag Flea Market: 24, 136
Moody: 42

Moody Beach: 46
Moosehorn National Wildlife Refuge: 409-410
Moose Peak Light: 376
Moose Point State Park: 245
Morse Cove Public Launching Facility: 134
Mosman Park: 245
Mount Desert Festival of Chamber Music: 334
Mount Desert Garden Club Tour: 320
Mount Desert Island, Acadia National Park on: 307-314; map 4-5
Mount Desert Island Biological Laboratory: 318
Mount Desert Island Historical Society Museum: 337
Movies on the Lawn: 60
Mt. Agamenticus: 37
Mt. Battle: 14, 223-224
mudflats: 414
Mulholland Market: 388
Mulholland Point Lighthouse: 388
Munjoy Hill/East End: 81-82
Museum at Portland Head Light: 85
Museum in the Streets (Belfast): 236
Museum in the Streets (Thomaston): 183-184
Museum of African Culture: 84
Musical Wonder House: 24, 147
Music on the Green (Calais): 407
Music on the Mall (Brunswick): 124
Muskie, Edmund S.: 425, 426

N

Narrows Park: 212
Naskeag Point: 264
Natalie's at the Camden Harbour Inn: 22, 234
national parks: Acadia National Park 293-294, 307-314; Schoodic section of Acadia National Park 351-354
National Toboggan Championships: 221
Native American Festival: 316, 320
Native Americans: 428
Newbury Neck: 256
Newcastle: 164; map 165
New England Museum of Telephony: 303
New Harbor: 164
Nickels-Sortwell House: 24, 146
Nobleboro: 24, 174
Nobleboro Antique Exchange: 24, 169
Noonday Concerts: 91
North Atlantic Blues Festival: 202
North Berwick: 30-31
Northeast Harbor: 19, 331-336
North Haven: 215-217
Northport Music Theater: 238
Norton Pond: 226
Nott House: 56
Nubble Light/Sohier Park: 35

O

O'Brien Cemetery: 381
Oceanarium: 316-317
Ocean Park (Old Orchard): 68
Ocean Park Parade and Sandcastle Contest: 70
Odd Fellows Hall (Vinalhaven): 210
Ogunquit: 42-53
Ogunquit Arts Collaborative Gallery: 44
Ogunquit Beach: 13, 46
Ogunquit Heritage Museum: 45
Ogunquit Museum of American Art: 42-43
Ogunquit Performing Arts: 45
Ogunquit Playhouse: 45
Oktoberfest and Food Festival (Southwest Harbor): 339
Old Cemetery (Blue Hill): 256
Old Columbian Store: 388
Old Conway Homestead and Cramer Museum: 218
Olde Bristol Days: 169
Old German Church: 168
Old Orchard Beach: 68-74
Old Orchard free concerts: 70
Old Orchard Pier: 71
Old Port: 79, 81
Old Port Festival: 92
Old Walpole Meeting House: 167
Old York Historical Society: 33, 35
Olson House: 186-187, 199-200
1 Longfellow Square: 91
Open Garden Days (Belfast): 238
Opera House (Boothbay Harbor): 154
Opera House (Stonington): 281
Orland: 248
Orr's Island: 119
Ovens Mouth Preserve: 155
Owls Head Light State Park: 17, 203
Owls Head Transportation Museum: 200

P

packing: 12
Palace Playland: 71
Parker Point Road: 256
Park Loop Road: 14, 308
park ranger programs: 312
parks and gardens: Acadia region 321; Blue Hill Peninsula 258; Down East 383, 401, 410; Mid-Coast Region 171, 172; Penobscot

Bay 201, 203, 204-205, 211-212, 224, 239, 245-246; Portland 93-95
Parkside: 82
Parson Fisher House: 20, 255-256
Passamaquoddy Indian Reservation: 400
Pathfinders Walking Group: 391
Payson Park: 94
PCA Great Performances: 90
Peabody Memorial Library Summer Series: 375
Peaks Island: 88
Peary-MacMillan Arctic Museum: 120
Pejepscot Museum: 121
Pemaquid Art Gallery: 166
Pemaquid Beach Park: 172-173
Pemaquid Point: 164
Pemaquid Point Lighthouse: 17, 166
Pemaquid region: 164-179
Peninsula Potters Open Studios: 283
Penobscot Bay: 180-251; map 182
Penobscot Bay Symphony Orchestra: 401
Penobscot East Resource Center: 281
Penobscot Marine Museum: 24, 243
Penobscot Narrows Bridge and Observatory: 20, 244
Perkins Cove: 43-44
Perry Creek Preserve: 212
Petite Plaisance: 333
Petit Manan National Wildlife Refuge: 19, 370
Pettengill Farm: 108
Phippsburg: 136-137
Phippsburg Center: 134
Phippsburg Congregational Church: 134
Phippsburg Peninsula: 130, 132, 134-135
Picnic Rock: 57
Pierre Monteux School for Conductors and Orchestra Musicians: 356
Pie Sale: 339
Pike's Park: 410
Pineland Farms: 111
Pine Point: 69
Pitcher Pond: 226
Point of Maine: 381
politics: 426
Polly Cove Preserve: 212
Pooduck Beach: 267
Popham Beach: 137
PopTech: 221
Port Clyde: 187
Porter Preserve: 154-155
Porthole, The: 22, 100
Portland: 79-106; map 80
Portland, Greater: 75-114; map 78
Portland Freedom Trail: 85
Portland Harbor Museum: 16, 85
Portland Head Light: 13, 16, 85, 86
Portland Museum of Art (PMA): 13, 16, 82
Portland Observatory: 83
Portland Opera Repertory Theatre: 90-91
Portland Pirates (ice hockey): 97
Portland Red Claws (basketball): 97
Portland Sea Dogs (baseball): 97
Portland Stage Company: 91
Portland Symphony Orchestra: 90
Portland Trails: 95
Portland Women's History Trail: 85-86
potato vodka: 108
Pownalborough Court House: 145
Precipice Trail: 311
Primo: 22, 208
Project Puffin Visitor Center: 201
pronunciation guide: 440
Prospect Harbor: 350
Provence: 21, 49
puffins/puffin-watching: general discussion 377; Acadia region 323; Down East 376, 385; itinerary tips 14, 19; Mid-Coast Region 157, 173; Penobscot Bay 201; *see also* boating excursions
Pumpkin Island Light: 271
Pumpkin Patch: 24, 245

QR

Quarry Pond: 349
Quoddy Loop: 400
Quoddy Mist: 388
rabies: 444-445
Raccoon Beach: 395-396
Rachel Carson National Wildlife Refuge: 44
Rachel Carson Salt Pond/La Verna Preserve: 172
rail travel: 438
Raye's Mustard Mill Museum: 399
Red Beach Cove: 406
Redman's Beach: 359-360
Reid State Park: 137-138
Reverend Daniel Merrill House: 262
Reversing Falls Park: 401
Richmond Island: 86
Ridge Runners: 309
River Arts: 169
River Tree Arts (RTA): 60
R. Jorgensen Antiques: 23, 45
Robert P. Tristram Coffin Wildflower Sanctuary: 137

rock climbing: 311
Rockland: 198-208
Rockland Breakwater Light: 17, 201
Rockport: 218
rocky shorelines: 417
Roosevelt Campobello International Park: 394-396
Roosevelt Cottage/Visitor Center: 394
Roque Bluffs: 380
Roque Bluffs State Park: 383-384
Round Lake: 410
Round Pond: 311
Route 92 (Starboard Peninsula): 381
Route 191 (Cutler Road): 381
Ruggles House: 19, 374

S

Saco: 69
Saco Museum: 69
sailing: Blue Hill Peninsula 267; Deer Isle 287; Mid-Coast Region 157; Penobscot Bay 227; Portland 96-97; Southern Coast 58-59
Sailors' Memorial Museum: 220
Sail Power & Steam Museum: 201
Salad Days: 147-148
Salome Sellers House: 279-280
Salt Bay Chamberfest: 169
Salt Bay Farm: 171
Salt Bay Preserve Heritage Trail: 171
Saltwater Film Society: 202
Sand Beach (Acadia National Park): 311
Sandcastle-Building Contest: 45
Sarah Orne Jewett House: 30
Sardine History Museum: 19, 375
Savage Oakes: 203
Sayward-Wheeler House: 35-36
Scarborough Beach Park: 94
Scarborough Marsh: 94-95
Scarborough River Wildlife Sanctuary: 95
scenic drives: Acadia region 308, 352-354; Blue Hill Peninsula 256, 263-264; Down East 370, 381, 395; Penobscot Bay 237
Schoodic Arts Festival: 356
Schoodic Arts for All: 356
Schoodic Beach: 359-360
Schoodic Education and Research Center: 355-356
Schoodic Loop: 352-354
Schoodic National Scenic Byway: 353
Schoodic Peninsula: 350-365
Schoodic section of Acadia National Park: 14, 19, 351-354
Scott's Landing: 287
Sea Dog Brewery: 128
Seal Cove: 337
Seal Cove Auto Museum: 338
Seal Cove Pond: 311
Seamark Community Arts: 281
Sears Island: 245-246
Searsport: 242-247
Searsport Antique Mall: 24, 245
Seashore Trolley Museum: 53
seasickness: 445
Seaside Pavilion: 70
Seawall: 337
Second Friday Art Walks: 123-124
Sedgwick: 262-269
Sedgwick Historic District: 262
Settlement Quarry: 286
Shackford Head State Park: 400-401
Shalom Orchard Organic Winery and Bed and Breakfast: 357
Sheepscot: 145
Ship Harbor Nature Trail: 310
Shipyard Brewery: 84
Shipyard Cup: 154
Shirttail Point: 226
shopping: general discussion 23-24; *see also specific place*
Shore Acres Preserve: 286
Shore Path (Bar Harbor): 320-321
Sidewalk Arts Festival (Portland): 92
Sidewalk Art Show and Sale (Ogunquit Beach): 45
Sieur de Monts Spring: 308
skiing: Penobscot Bay 225; Portland 111
Skolfield-Whittier House: 121
Skoog Memorial Park: 212
Smith, Margaret Chase: 426
smoking: 441
Somes Sound: 19, 331
Somesville: 337
Sorrento: 351
South Berwick: 30-31
South Bristol: 164
Southern Coast: 25-74; map 27
Southern Maine Community College (SMCC): 86
Southport Island: 151, 153-154
Southport Memorial Library: 154
Southwest Harbor: 19, 337-345
Southworth Planetarium: 84
Sow's Ear Winery: 266
spectator sports: 97

Spouting Rock: 55
Spring Point Ledge Light: 16, 86
Spring Point Shoreline Walkway: 86
Spruce Head: 187
Stage East: 401
Stage Front: The Arts Downeast: 383
St. Andrew's Episcopal Church: 168
St. Andrew's Lawn Party and Auction: 169
St. Ann's Church: 55
St. Anthony's Monastery: 56-57
Stanwood Homestead Museum: 302
state parks: Blue Hill Peninsula 267, 271; Down East 383-384, 387-388, 400-401; Mid-Coast Region 137-138; Penobscot Bay 203, 223-224, 237, 245, 246; Portland 86, 110-111; Southern Coast 30, 72
St. Croix Island: 406
Steedman Woods: 37
St. George Peninsula: 187-192
Stockton Springs: 242
Stonington: 20, 276-292
Stonington Lobsterboat Races: 281
St. Patrick's Catholic Church: 168
Strand Theater: 202
Stroudwater: 82
St. Saviour's Episcopal Church: 316
Sullivan: 351
Summer in the Parks: 91
SummerKeys: 388-389, 401
Sunday in the Garden: 30
Sunset Rock Park: 212
surfing: 38, 46, 59, 72
Surfside: 22, 214
Swans Island: 349-350
Sweet Chariot Music Festival: 350
Sweetgrass Farm Winery and Distillery: 203
swimming: Acadia region 311, 349, 359-360; Blue Hill Peninsula 267, 273; Deer Isle 287, 288, 294; Down East 383-384; Mid-Coast Region 125, 137-138, 155, 172-173; Penobscot Bay 188-189, 203-205, 212-213, 226, 249; Southern Coast 37-38

T

Tate House: 84-85
taxes: 446
telephones: 447-448
Temple (Ocean Park): 70
Temple Heights Spiritualist Camp: 236
Tenants Harbor: 187
Third Friday Art Walks (Bath): 135
Thomas Point Beach: 125
Thomaston: 24, 183-185
Thompson Ice House: 168
Thompson Island Visitor Center: 307
Thorn Head Preserve: 136
Thuya Garden: 19, 332-333
Thuya Lodge: 332
Tidal Falls Preserve: 357-358
tides: 390
Tides Institute and Museum of Art: 399-400
time zone: 441
tipping: 446
Tip-Toe Mountain: 212
Topsham: 119
Topsham Fair: 124
tourism information: 446-448
Tours of Lubec and Cobscook: 19, 390
Tracy Shore Preserve: 172
train excursions: 124, 202
train travel: 438
transportation: general discussion 436-440; *see also specific mode of transportation; place*
Tremont: 337
Trescott: 381
trip planning: 10-12
Turrets, The: 317
Two Countries One Bay Art Studio Tour: 401
Two Lights State Park: 86

UV

Umbrella Cover Museum: 88
UMM Art Galleries: 382
University of Maine at Machias: 382-383
Vanderkay Summer Music Series: 257
Vaughan's Island Preserve: 57
Vaughan Woods State Park: 30
Verrazzano, Giovanni da: 419-420
Vesper Hill: 218, 220
Victoria Mansion: 82-83
Victorian Holiday: 92
Vinalhaven: 209-215; map 210
Vinalhaven Historical Society: 211
Vinalhaven Land Trust: 212
visas and officialdom: 441
vodka: 108

WXYZ

Wabanaki peoples: 428
Wadsworth-Longfellow House: 83
Waldoboro: 164
Waldoborough Historical Society Museum: 169
Waldo Theatre: 169

Walker Park (Rockport): 224, 226
Walker's Point (Kennebunkport): 53, 55
Walk-on Adventures: 16, 111
Waterfall Arts: 236
waterfalls: 94, 383
Waterman's Beach Lobster: 17, 22, 192
Waterman's Community Center: 215
weather: 12, 415-416, 418
Wedding Cake House: 55
Wells: 30-31, 42-53
Wells Auto Museum: 44-45
Wells Beach: 46
Wells Reserve at Laudholm Farm: 44
Wells Summer Concert Series: 45
Wendell Gilley Museum: 19, 337
WERU community radio: 256, 257
West End: 81
West Quoddy Head Light: 387
West Quoddy Head State Park: 14, 18, 387-388
Whaleback Park: 172
whale museum: 317
whale-watching: Acadia region 323; Down East 396, 403; itinerary tips 14, 15, 18, 19; Mid-Coast Region 157; Southern Coast 58; *see also* boating excursions
White, E. B.: 266
White Barn Inn: 20, 61-62, 67
White's Beach: 125
Whiting: 380
Whitlock Mill Lighthouse: 406
Whitneyville: 380
Wild Gardens of Acadia: 316
wildlife refuges: Acadia region 302-303, 321-322, 357-358; Blue Hill Peninsula 257-258, 267, 273; Deer Isle 285-287; Down East 370, 376, 391, 409-410; Mid-Coast Region 125, 136-137, 154-155, 172, 174; Penobscot Bay 212, 224-225, 249; Portland 94-95, 109-110; Southern Coast 29, 37, 44, 57, 70, 72
wildlife-watching: Deer Isle 287; Mid-Coast Region 154, 155; Penobscot Bay 213, 249, 250; *see also* birds/bird-watching; boating excursions; puffins/puffin-watching; whale-watching
Wild Salmon Research Center: 375
Wiley's Corner: 187
Willard Beach: 86
Wilson Museum: 270-271, 272
Windjammer Days (Boothbay Peninsula): 154
Windjammer Weekend (Camden Harbor): 221
windjamming: 204
wine/wineries: Acadia region 356-357; Blue Hill Peninsula 257, 266; Penobscot Bay 203, 222
Winnegance: 134
Winslow Memorial Park: 110
Winter Harbor: 15, 350
Wiscasset: 144-150
Wiscasset, Waterville, and Farmington Railway: 145
Witch Island Preserve: 174
Witherle Memorial Library: 271
Witherle Woods: 273
Wolfe's Neck Farm: 110
Wolfe's Neck Woods State Park: 110
Wonderland: 310
WoodenBoat publications: 262
Wood Island Lighthouse: 69-70
Woodlawn: 301-302
Wyeth Center: 199
Yoho Head: 381
York: 33
York Beach: 33
York Days: 36
York Harbor: 33
Yorks, The: 33-42; map 34
York's Wild Kingdom: 36
York Village: 33
York Village Annual Harvestfest: 36
zoo: 36

List of Maps

Front color maps
Maine: 2-3
Mount Desert Island/Acadia
National Park: 4-5

Discover Coastal Maine
chapter divisions map: 11
Icons of the Maine Coast: 13
Lighthouses, Lobster, and L. L. Bean: 17
14-Day Best of the Real Maine: 19

Southern Coast
Southern Coast: 27
The Yorks: 34
The Kennebunks: 54

Greater Portland
Greater Portland: 78
Downtown Portland: 80

Mid-Coast Region
Mid-Coast Region: 118
Bath Area: 132-133
Boothbay Peninsula: 153
Damariscotta/Newcastle: 165

Penobscot Bay
Penobscot Bay: 182
Vinalhaven: 210
Greater Camden: 219

Blue Hill Peninsula and Deer Isle
Blue Hill Peninsula Region: 254
Deer Isle: 277

Acadia Region
Acadia Region: 299
Bar Harbor: 315

The Down East Coast
The Down East Coast: 368

Acknowledgments

This book is dedicated to all the underappreciated tourism workers in Maine, the volunteers and lowly staffers, the waiters, waitresses, toll collectors, gate keepers, park rangers, traffic cops, ferry attendants, housekeepers, hostesses and front desk workers, tour guides, and everyone else who has contact with visitors. You make the state sing. We do appreciate you. You're the real face of Maine. Thank you.

Although I've lived in Maine since childhood (yes, I will always be a "from away"), and have traveled extensively in the state for both work and pleasure, every time I revisit a place, I find something new or changed, sometimes subtly, other times dramatically. Restaurants open and close. Outfitters change their offerings. Inns are sold. Motels open. New trails are cut. Museums expand. Hotels renovate. And on it goes. Which all goes to say, I couldn't have done this without the help of many people, who served as additional eyes and ears.

I'll start with Kathleen Brandes, who wrote the original editions of this book and whose friendship I valued and whose work and dedication I respected long before I took over with the last edition of this book. My appreciation for her meticulous research, her ability to capture a place or a person with a quick turn of phrase, and her dead-on accuracy has no bounds.

More thank-yous are due the folks at Avalon Travel who shepherded me through the process: Bill Newlin, Grace Fujimoto, Kevin McLain, and most especially my editor, Kathryn Ettinger. Also thank you to production and graphics coordinator Lucie Ericksen, cartography editor Brice W. Ticen, publicist Eva Zimmerman, and the many other behind-the-scenes Avalon staffers who worked on this book.

Special thank-yous, too, to those who sat down with me and shared local info, sheltered me along the way, fed me, helped with arrangements, verified information, called me with updates, or simply encouraged me: Bill and Cathy Shamel, Kathryn Rubeor, Bill Clarke, Maureen Hart, Abigail Oattes-Alley, Ben and Sonja Walter-Sundaram, Roy Kasindorf, Hélène Harton, Jeff and Teri Anderholm, Bill Haefele, Don Jalbert and Javier Montesinos, Jim Ash, Elizabeth Bertilozzi, Sarah Pebworth, Jack Burke, Julie Van de Graaf, Ed and Judy Hemminger, Lynn Karlin, Oscar Verest, Raymond Brunyanszki, Chip Gray, Gerard Kiladjian, Jim and Gillian Britt, Rauni Kew, Sara Masterson, Jonathan Cartwright, Stuart Barwise, Jean Ginn Marvin, Bill and Bonnie Alstrom, Barbara and Tim Rogers, Sarah Wills, Steve Viega, Traci Klepper, Marti Mayne, Abbe Levin, Barbara Whitten, Courtney McMennamin, and most especially Nancy Marshall, Charlene Williams, and Rose Whitehorse, of Nancy Marshall Communications. I couldn't have done this without all of your help and support.

More thanks are due to my email support team of sister freelance writers: Echo Garrett, Margie Goldsmith, Mickey Goodman, Irene S. Levine, and Judy Kirkwood.

I save my biggest thanks for my husband, Tom, who drove me everywhere and didn't complain (too much) when I made him backtrack two or three times along the same stretch of road while seeking an elusive address; who waited patiently while I visited practically every restaurant, inn, and bed-and-breakfast from Kittery to Calais; who let me order for him in restaurants; who tackled research projects; and who supported me in every way possible throughout the entire process, all while shooting photographs for the book. I couldn't have done it without him.

And to you, dear reader, thank you for using this book to plan your visit to Maine. Do me a favor, will you? Give me feedback to help make the next edition even better. Contact me at hilary@hilarynangle.com, and visit my blog at http://hilarynangle.wordpress.com for updates to this book.